S Effective Sentences 615

L Effective Language 661

P Punctuation 689

M Mechanics 741

A Advice for Multilingual Writers 785

SPECIAL TOPICS FOR MULTILINGUAL WRITERS

THE WRITER'S

HARBRACE HANDBOOK

CHERYL GLENN · LORETTA GRAY

6th Edition
MLA Update Edition

WADSWORTH
CENGAGE Learning™

The Writer's Harbrace Handbook, Sixth Edition
2016 MLA Update Edition
Cheryl Glenn and Loretta Gray

Product Director:
Monica Eckman

Product Team Manager:
Nicole Morinon

Product Manager: Laura Ross

Senior Content Developer:
Leslie Taggart

Content Developer:
Stephanie P. Carpenter

Associate Content
Developer: Erin Bosco

Product Assistant:
Claire Branman

Senior Managing Content
Developer: Cara Douglass-Graff

Marketing Director:
Stacey Purviance

Content Project Manager:
Rebecca Donahue

Senior Art Director:
Marissa Falco

Manufacturing Planner:
Betsy Donaghey

IP Analyst: Ann Hoffman

IP Project Manager:
Farah Fard

Production Service: Andrea
Archer, Angela Urquhart,
Thistle Hill Publishing Services

Compositor:
Cenveo® Publisher Services

Cover Designer:
Nifouler Moochhala,
nym DESIGN

Printed in the United States of America
Print Number: 01 Print Year: 2016

Library of Congress Control Number: 2015952423

Student Edition:
ISBN: 978-1-337-27963-5

Loose-leaf Edition:
ISBN: 978-1-337-27986-4

Cengage Learning
20 Channel Center Street
Boston, MA 02210
USA

Cengage Learning is a leading provider of customized learning solutions with employees residing in nearly 40 different countries and sales in more than 125 countries around the world. Find your local representative at **www.cengage.com**.

Cengage Learning products are represented in Canada by Nelson Education, Ltd.

To learn more about Cengage Learning Solutions, visit **www.cengage.com**.

Purchase any of our products at your local college store or at our preferred online store **www.cengagebrain.com**.

Contents

R | **PART 2** RESEARCH

D ‖ PART 3   DISCIPLINES AND DOCUMENTATION STYLES

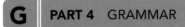

G PART 4 GRAMMAR

S PART 5 EFFECTIVE SENTENCES

M   **PART 8**   MECHANICS

A ┃ PART 9 ADVICE FOR MULTILINGUAL WRITERS

Preface

Welcome to *The Writer's Harbrace Handbook,* Sixth Edition. The book in your hands is part of a long tradition that started with *The Hodges Harbrace Handbook,* which is now celebrating its seventy-fifth birthday. Because each edition of *The Writer's Harbrace Handbook* changes in response to current studies in composition and linguistics, students can depend on the research-based guidance offered in this book. Each edition is also class-tested. In this book, just as in our classrooms, we strive to show, rather than just tell, students how to write. Our goal is to provide them with the advice they need in language they can understand. To that end, we use visuals, checklists, tip boxes, charts, examples, and annotated student papers that emphasize information discussed in the text.

The Sixth Edition continues to help students situate themselves rhetorically. Whether they are working on tablets or laptops, writing essays or composing in multiple media, students will find practical suggestions for successfully completing their assignments. We also continue to prepare students to write in a range of academic disciplines. Students will find not only guidelines for writing in the arts, humanities, sciences, and business but also fully annotated, full-length examples of many kinds of papers.

As in previous editions, early chapters support writing assignments that require limited or no use of secondary sources. These initial chapters are followed by a chapter on planning research and three chapters on finding, evaluating, and integrating source material. Because of our emphasis on cross-disciplinary writing, we include nine chapters devoted to the conventions and documentation guides that will help students write for a range of classes. The second half of the book comprises chapters on grammar, usage, sentence style, punctuation, and other mechanical concerns. Throughout, help is offered to multilingual writers who use English daily.

HOW DOES THIS EDITION ADDRESS THE "WPA OUTCOMES STATEMENT FOR FIRST-YEAR COMPOSITION (V3.0)"?

Since the last edition of this handbook was published, the Council of Writing Program Administrators (CWPA) has revised the "WPA Outcomes Statement for First-Year Composition." This document stresses the need to help students develop their (1) rhetorical knowledge, (2) critical thinking along with reading and composing practices, (3) understanding of composing processes, and (4) knowledge of conventions. We have revised this edition of *The Writer's Harbrace Handbook* to ensure that each of these areas is fully covered.

Rhetorical knowledge

- Chapter 1, "Reading, Writing, and the Rhetorical Situation," introduces students to the elements of the rhetorical situation and to the steps for reading and writing rhetorically. Additions to the chapter further consider the role of genre in writing, as well as that of a rhetorical audience.
- Chapter 6, "Multimodal Composing," presents rhetorical principles for interpreting and producing texts that integrate the written word with sound and/or images.
- Chapter 11, "Using Sources Critically and Responsibly," asks students to consider their rhetorical situation as they do research.
- In Part 3, "Disciplines and Documentation Styles," chapters 12, 14, 16, 18, and 20 cover the discipline-specific rhetorical knowledge that students need for informed research and successful writing.
- In Part 4, "Grammar," chapters 21 through 27 invite students to think rhetorically about grammar.
- *Situate Yourself* activities in each of the book's nine parts prompt students to apply what they learn in that section to real-world scenarios, making rhetorical choices as they do so.

Critical thinking, reading, and composing

- Chapter 1, "Reading, Writing, and the Rhetorical Situation," demonstrates how basic rhetorical principles enhance the analysis and production of texts.

- Chapter 4, "Managing Academic Writing," introduces strategies for developing ideas at various levels of intellectual complexity (according to Bloom's Taxonomy of Learning Domains), especially when writing under time constraints.
- Chapter 7, "Writing Arguments," demonstrates ways to analyze a text, reason logically, avoid rhetorical fallacies, incorporate evidence, and compose several types of arguments.
- Chapter 11, "Using Sources Critically and Responsibly," provides students with the strategies and language they need to demonstrate proficiency at the levels of intellectual complexity noted in Bloom's Taxonomy. Boxes provide students with sentence frames, or templates, that employ phraseology that is frequently used to summarize, synthesize, and respond to sources.

Processes

- Chapter 2, "Planning and Drafting Essays," helps students generate ideas for topics and organize their compositions.
- Chapter 3, "Revising and Editing Essays," introduces strategies for recursive writing, editing, and proofreading.
- Chapter 5, "Communicating Online," presents strategies for creating various types of online documents and helps students understand the linked and social nature of this context.
- Chapter 6, "Multimodal Composing," supports students in their interpretation and production of documents that use sound, visuals, and words.

Knowledge of conventions

- In Part 3, "Disciplines and Documentation Styles," chapters 13, 15, 17, and 19 present the most recent citation and documentation guidelines for various disciplines—MLA, APA, CMS, and CSE, respectively.
- In Part 7, "Punctuation," chapters 37–41 explain the conventions of punctuation.
- In Part 8, "Mechanics," chapters 42–45 include guidelines for other mechanical issues: spelling, capitalization, and the use of italics, abbreviations, acronyms, and numbers.

WHAT IS NEW TO THIS EDITION?

Based on our observations of the ever-changing student population, we have added new material to address current issues and challenges.

Stronger support for the research process

- A new chapter 8, "Planning Research," supports students through the early stages of a research project, as they generate a strong research question that both focuses their work and helps them develop a plan for completing their assignment on time.
- Chapter 9, "Finding Appropriate Sources," is reorganized to emphasize the use of databases in effective online searches and to help students more easily discover how to find images and keep track of sources (followed by new tips for creating an annotated bibliography in 11b).
- A new section, 10e, guides students in reading sources closely and critically.

More attention to specific audiences and genres

- The existing focus on elements writers consider in any communication situation now includes ways to zero in on a *rhetorical* audience (an audience who can help the writer achieve his or her goals) and strategies for taking *genre* into account.
- The new title of chapter 6, "Multimodal Composing," reflects the increased coverage of documents that incorporate sound, images, and words—features that students turn to more and more when communicating with rhetorical audiences.

At-a-glance and up-to-date documentation coverage

- New color-coded citation maps in the MLA, APA, Chicago, and CSE chapters demonstrate where in a source to find information that needs to be cited.
- Model citations are offered for a broader range of sources, including wiki entries, podcasts, and other online sources.
- This edition includes the updated documentation guidelines from the eighth edition of the MLA Handbook (2016). The style has been simplified to emphasize a common approach to a wide variety of source types. Chapter 13 introduces the new approach while continuing to offer numerous citation examples for students to use as models.
- Updated Chicago and CSE documentation chapters reflect the latest guidelines.

New activities and answers for Part 9 exercises

- New *Situate Yourself* activities prompt students to apply what they learn in a section to real-world scenarios. An activity opens each major section (part) of the handbook to show students why the concepts presented matter beyond the immediate context of the chapters in that section.
- Answers to exercises in Part 9, "Advice for Multilingual Writers," are now included at the back of the book so that students can check their progress on their own.

THE HISTORY

The Harbrace family of handbooks has the longest history of any set of handbooks in the United States. First published in 1941 by University of Tennessee English professor John C. Hodges, *The Harbrace Handbook of English* was a product of Hodges's classroom experience and his federally funded research, which comprised an analysis of twenty thousand student papers. Sixteen English professors from various regions of the United States marked those papers; they found a number of common mistakes, including (1) misplaced commas, (2) misspelling, (3) inexact language, (4) lack of subject-verb agreement, (5) superfluous commas, (6) shifts in tense, (7) misused apostrophes, (8) omission of words, (9) wordiness, and (10) lack of standard usage.

After collecting these data, Hodges worked with a cadre of graduate students to create a taxonomy of writing issues (from punctuation and grammar to style and usage) that would organize the first writing manual for American college students and teachers. This taxonomy still underpins the overall design and organization of nearly every handbook on the market today. Hodges's original handbook evolved into *The Writer's Harbrace Handbook*, Sixth Edition, which continues to respond to the needs of students and writing instructors alike.

HOW TO USE THIS HANDBOOK

The Writer's Harbrace Handbook routinely receives praise for its comprehensive treatment of a wide range of topics. Whether you have a question about drafting or revising a paper, using visuals, understanding the logic of arguments, identifying a complete sentence, capitalizing a word, punctuating a sentence (or any other question related to reading and writing rhetorically), the answer is at your fingertips.

Brief Table of Contents

If you have a topic in mind, such as writing a thesis statement or using commas correctly, check the contents list inside the front cover. With each topic is a number-and-letter combination (2c or 20d, for example) that corresponds to the number and letter at the top of the relevant right-hand page(s) in the book.

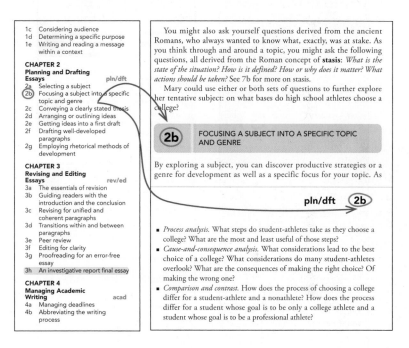

You might also ask yourself questions derived from the ancient Romans, who always wanted to know what, exactly, was at stake. As you think through and around a topic, you might ask the following questions, all derived from the Roman concept of **stasis**: *What is the state of the situation? How is it defined? How or why does it matter? What actions should be taken?* See 7b for more on stasis.

Mary could use either or both sets of questions to further explore her tentative subject: on what bases do high school athletes choose a college?

2b   FOCUSING A SUBJECT INTO A SPECIFIC TOPIC AND GENRE

By exploring a subject, you can discover productive strategies or a genre for development as well as a specific focus for your topic. As

pln/dft **2b**

- *Process analysis.* What steps do student-athletes take as they choose a college? What are the most and least useful of those steps?
- *Cause-and-consequence analysis.* What considerations lead to the best choice of a college? What considerations do many student-athletes overlook? What are the consequences of making the right choice? Of making the wrong one?
- *Comparison and contrast.* How does the process of choosing a college differ for a student-athlete and a nonathlete? How does the process differ for a student whose goal is to be only a college athlete and a student whose goal is to be a professional athlete?

Tabs

Colored tabs, which correspond to the distinctive colors of Parts 1 through 9 and the four documentation chapters, are staggered down the outside edges of the book's pages. These tabs help orient you to the section of the handbook you are in as you look up information.

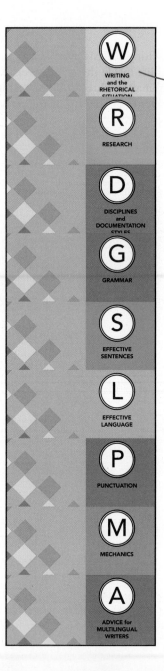

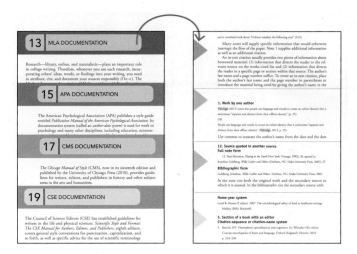

Index

You can also find information quickly by consulting the index at the back of the book, which provides chapter and section numbers as well as page numbers.

MLA, APA, CMS, and CSE Directories

To find the format to use for citing a source or listing a source in a bibliography, refer to one of these style-specific directories. If you use one of these directories often, put a sticky note on it so that you can locate it in an instant.

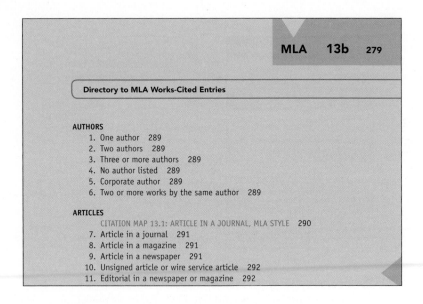

Revision Symbols

At the back of the book is a list of revision symbols. The symbols can be used to provide feedback on papers, and the list identifies chapters or sections where pertinent rules, guidelines, or strategies are discussed in more detail.

coh		Coherence	" "	38		Quotation marks
	24c–d	modifiers	**red**	34a(1)		Redundant
	4c	paragraphs	**ref**	25d		Reference
:	39d	Colon	**rep**	29b, 30d, 34b		Repetition
,	35	Comma	**rev**	4a–g		Revision
cs	23	Comma splice	**;**	36		Semicolon
con	34	Conciseness	**sg**			Singular
cst	15a	Consistency		39i		Slash
		verb tense	**/**			Slash
		point of view	**sp**	40a–e		Spelling
coor	28b–c	Coordination	**sub**	28a, 28c		Subordination
—	39e	Dash	**[ ]**	39g		Square brackets
⌣		Delete	**t**	26b		Tense
dev		Development	**trans**	3d		Transition
	3g	essays	∾			Transpose
	3f	paragraphs	**u**			Unity
. . .	39h	Ellipsis points		4c		paragraph
emp	30	Emphasis		27		sentence
ex	33	Exactness	⌀			Unnecessary
!	39c	Exclamation point				comma

Glossary of Usage

This glossary includes definitions of words that are commonly confused or misused (such as *accept* and *except*). Organized like a dictionary, it provides not only common meanings for the words but also example sentences demonstrating usage.

---

a lot of *A lot of* is conversational for *many, much,* or *a great deal of:* They do not have ~~a lot of~~ much time. *A lot* is sometimes misspelled as *alot.*

a while, awhile *A while* means "a period of time." It is often used with the prepositions *after, for,* and *in:* We rested for **a while.** *Awhile* means "a short time." It is not preceded by a preposition: We rested **awhile.**

accept, except The verb *accept* means "to receive": I **accept** your apology. The verb *except* means "to exclude": The policy was to have everyone wait in line, but parents with small children were **excepted.** The preposition *except* means "other than": Everyone **except** Joe will attend the conference.

advice, advise *Advice* is a noun: They asked their attorney for **advice.** *Advise* is a verb: The attorney **advised** us to save all relevant documents.

affect, effect *Affect* is a verb that means "to influence": The lobbyist's pleas did not **affect** the politician's decision. The noun *effect* means "a result": The **effect** of his decision on the staff's morale was positive and long lasting. When used as a verb, *effect* means "to produce" or "to cause": The activists believed that they could **effect** real political change.

agree on, agree to, agree with *Agree on* means "to be in accord with others about something": We **agreed on** a date for the conference. *Agree to* means "to

---

What to Know and Where to Find It: Twenty-Two Tips for Success

For a handy list of 22 key things to know about writing in college, work your way through the items on the back flap of the book.

TEACHING AND LEARNING RESOURCES

MindTap

MindTap® English for Glenn/Gray's *The Writer's Harbrace Handbook,* Sixth Edition, engages your students to become better thinkers, communicators, and writers by blending your course materials with content that supports every aspect of the writing process.

- Interactive activities on grammar and mechanics promote application in student writing.

- An easy-to-use paper management system helps prevent plagiarism and allows for electronic submission, grading, and peer review.
- A vast database of scholarly sources with video tutorials and examples supports every step of the research process.
- Professional tutoring guides students from rough drafts to polished writing.
- Visual analytics track student progress and engagement.
- Seamless integration into your campus learning management system keeps all your course materials in one place.

MindTap lets you compose your course, your way.

Online Instructor's Resource Manual

Available for easy download at cengagebrain.com, the password-protected Online Instructor's Resource Manual is designed to give instructors maximum flexibility in planning and customizing a course. The manual includes a variety of pedagogical questions (and possible solutions) relevant to those teaching a course with the handbook, sample syllabi with possible assignments for a semester-long course and for a quarter-long course, sample in-class collaborative learning activities, technology-oriented activities, and critical thinking and writing activities.

ACKNOWLEDGMENTS

The question was where to begin—so many people deserve thanks for their work on this book. We decided to start with our colleagues who reviewed previous editions and provided us with ideas for improving this edition. Their comments, questions, and occasional jokes made us see our work anew. We hope they will approve of the results of their feedback in these pages.

Rebecca Babcock, *University of Texas Permian Basin*
Ruby Blair, *Benedict College*
Lisa Carl, *North Carolina Central University*
Rebecca Cash, *SUNY-Adirondack*
Emily Cope, *University of Tennessee Knoxville*
Nancy Cox, *Arkansas Tech University*
Ellen Feig, *Bergen Community College*
Stefanie Frigo, *North Carolina Central University*

Frank Gruber, *Bergen Community College*
Jennifer Haber, *St. Petersburg College*
Amy Handy, *Austin Community College*
Kellye Manning, *University of Texas Permian Basin*
Robin Nicks, *University of Tennessee*
Coretta Pittman, *Baylor University*
India Marie Stewart, *Truett-McConnell College*
Kristen Weinzapfel, *North Central Texas College*
Cierra Winkler, *Truett-McConnell College*

As we drafted (and revised), we depended on the assistance of our colleagues and students. Penn State University PhD candidate Sarah Adams embodies grace, intelligence, and drive, making her the optimal traffic controller for large parts of this project; her tasks ranged from supervising the undergraduate contributions to composing the PowerPoint images. Professor Heather Brook Adams, University of Alaska Anchorage, provided a screenshot from her course blog, for which we are grateful. We are also indebted to Rick Hutchins and Joe Johnson, from Central Washington University, for their help with online materials that accompany this book. Finally, several undergraduate students provided samples of their written work and enriched our understanding of the writing process. To Sarah Cronin, Danielle Dezell, Kristin Ford, Heather Jensen, Alyssa Jergens, Mary LeNoir, Billy Lucas, Matthew Marusak, Cristian Núñez, Rachel Pinter, Carla Spohn, and Marianna Suslin, we give our heartfelt thanks. Without such students, where would we instructors be?

The successful completion of this project would have been impossible without the members of the Cengage Learning/Wadsworth staff, whose patience, good humor, and innovative ideas kept us moving in the right direction. Tops on our thank-you list are Monica Eckman, Product Director; Laura Ross, Product Manager; Leslie Taggart, Senior Content Developer; and Erin Bosco, Associate Content Developer. We are truly amazed by how they can make meetings so enjoyable and productive. For the scrupulous work that occurred after the project went into production, we are grateful to Rosemary Winfield, Senior Content Project Manager, and Angela Urquhart and Andrea Archer at Thistle Hill Publishing Services; for the striking interior design, we thank Anne Carter; and for helping us bring our work to you, we extend gratitude to Erin Parkins, Senior Marketing Manager.

Stephanie Carpenter, Content Developer extraordinaire, deserves a paragraph of thanks all her own. We are always thrilled when we get to work with Steph, whose insights, reliability, and energy are wonders to behold. She is our rock, particularly when we are desperately trying to balance our teaching with our research and writing. We can't imagine producing this handbook without her firm but gentle guidance, generosity of spirit, and editorial brilliance.

To all our friends and family members, we owe as much gratitude as a book could hold—at least a pageful for each day of our research and writing that they made possible. We know that they often changed their plans or sacrificed their own time so that we could complete this project. For their support, we are forever grateful.

Cheryl Glenn
Loretta Gray
June 2015

WRITING and the RHETORICAL SITUATION

Situate Yourself

Heartrending events often serve as opportunities for composing. The 2012 point-blank shooting of fifteen-year-old Malala Yousafzai drew worldwide attention to her family's fight for girls' education. Malala's story helped alert the rest of the world about the workings of the Taliban, the status of women and girls in the Middle East and South Asia, and education as a human right. The whole world watched—but also embraced the opportunity to advise, petition, report, and raise money for Malala's cause. The 2014 shooting of Michael Brown in Ferguson Township, Missouri, served as another rhetorical opportunity for change, prompting, as it did, protests, boycotts, essays, editorials, and news commentaries. These rhetorical acts illuminated and addressed such thorny issues as racially motivated homicide, the accountability of police departments, our militarized police force, the inconsistencies of witness testimony, and the grand jury system itself.

Make a list of the opportunities you've taken to make a difference with your words—whether the opportunity was dramatic or not, whether your influence was felt by a small number of people (perhaps only by you) or by an entire school, city, or community. Select one of these opportunities and describe the rhetorical situation:

- What compelled you to speak, write, or in some other way create a response?
- To whom were you directing your communication? What did you hope they would do in response?
- What elements of the larger context affected your message?

1 ‖ READING, WRITING, AND THE RHETORICAL SITUATION

You are a rhetorical being. Every single day, you use **rhetoric**; you use language purposefully to communicate intentionally, efficiently, and effectively. When you pick up a newspaper, glance over the front page, and then turn to the story that most intrigues you, you are reading rhetorically. You use rhetoric as you read course-related assignments, syllabi, Facebook updates, and Twitter feeds. You speak and listen rhetorically when you join a conversation, taking care to listen for the threads of what has already been said and by whom, and then respond appropriately to both the subject and the particular members of your audience. When you write rhetorically, you draft and revise a message aimed at a specific audience, an audience you consider capable of helping resolve a problem or create change. And you use rhetoric when you complete written course assignments as well as when you compose in-class essays, lecture or study notes, and text messages. Because you have been reading and writing, speaking and listening rhetorically—participating in rhetorical situations—for nearly all of your life, you already know a good deal about using rhetoric. You can build on your experience and knowledge.

In this chapter, you will see how reading and writing rhetorically are processes, each a series of sometimes overlapping steps. The chapter will help you

- understand the elements of any rhetorical situation (**1a**),
- recognize a rhetorical opportunity (**1b**),
- consider the intended audience (**1c**),
- establish a purpose for a message (**1d**), and
- think about the rhetorical effects of context (**1e**).

This chapter will also help you see exactly how reading and writing rhetorically can help you succeed with a variety of large and small class assignments, many of which are discussed in this handbook, including:

- an investigative report final essay (**3h**),
- a web presence for an organization (**5d, 5e**),

- an argument from personal experience and research (**7j**),
- an argument based on research (chapters **8–11**),
- an interpretation of a literary text (**12b**),
- a field report and a lab report (**18d**), and
- a business letter and a résumé (**20b, 20d**).

1a   UNDERSTANDING THE RHETORICAL SITUATION

When you hear the word *rhetoric,* you might think of language used to persuade. However, if you remember that rhetoric is the *purposeful* use of language, you will soon realize that persuading is not the only reason for using language. Other reasons include explaining concepts, describing experiences, and informing others about important ideas. The best way to establish a purpose for using language is to examine the **rhetorical situation** (figure 1.1), which is composed of the writer (or speaker), the audience, the opportunity, the message (purpose and genre), and the context in which you are communicating. Any assignment that asks you to read or write rhetorically will be easier and more enjoyable if you keep the rhetorical situation in mind.

Figure 1.1: The rhetorical situation.

Writers (or speakers) enter a rhetorical situation when they identify an **opportunity** to propose change through their language use. They may want to change other people's behaviors, opinions, or attitudes or just help them notice something new. Once writers have identified a rhetorical opportunity, they prepare a **message** (using words and sometimes images), often working within a particular **genre** (a purposeful form of communication distinguished by features and formatting, such as a report, proposal, case study, researched essay, and so on). The message is always prepared for a specific **audience**. The audience receives a writer's message within a specific **context** that includes the various perspectives on the issue that are already in circulation as well as how those perspectives were presented. Your primary role as a writer is to contribute to the rhetorical situation in a way that takes into account the elements of that situation.

In your role as a rhetorical (or critical) reader, you also follow a series of rhetorically based steps. Whether the text is an academic assignment, a job application, a college entrance exam, or a magazine article, you often begin by previewing the entire text to gauge the time and expertise necessary to read it. You might jump from the title to the table of contents (or headings) and then to a list of questions or a chapter, stopping to glance at any visuals and author information. Or you might skim the text **chronologically** (in order of occurrence) from beginning to end before you start reading for content and responding with comments and questions. When you finish your initial reading, you may begin rereading the text **recursively** (alternating between moving forward and looping back), maybe taking time to talk with peers or searching online to better understand the content. Any kind of preview of the text means staying alert for the author's major points, for transitional words that reveal sequence (**3d**), and for developmental structures (or other clues) that indicate summary, causation, repetition, exemplification, or intensification. You may want to respond to or question the author's important points, as though you were carrying on a conversation. To do so, you can use a pen, sticky notes, or an online annotation tool.

Thus, reading rhetorically helps you determine what you already know about a topic and what you are likely to learn from the text; it also helps you gauge the expertise and credibility of the writer and the rhetorical audience, purpose, and context of the text. In addition, learning to read rhetorically will help you distinguish between actual textual content and your personal response to that content and will prepare you to handle the heavy academic reading load you experience in college. The following checklist will help you read rhetorically.

✓ CHECKLIST for Reading Rhetorically

- What is your purpose for reading the text—pleasure, research, fulfillment of a course requirement, problem solving, inspiration?
- What is the author's purpose for writing? What do you know about this author's experience, credibility, use of reliable (or unreliable) sources, experience, and biases?
- How might you account for the author's choice of genre?
- What specific knowledge or experience does the reading demand? Does your knowledge or experience meet that demand? If not, how can you better prepare yourself?
- What are the key parts of the text? How do those parts relate to your purpose for reading? What specific information from this text will help you achieve your purpose?
- What is your strategy for previewing, reading, and rereading? Are you reading online or on paper? How will you respond to the text?
- With which passages do you agree or disagree, and why?
- As you read, what do you understand clearly? What do you want to know more about?
- What questions do you have for your instructor or peers? What questions—and answers—might they have for you?

Reading and writing rhetorically allow you to consider each of the elements of the rhetorical situation separately as well as in combination. In addition, when you read or write rhetorically, you consider how information is or should be delivered, including what genre and which medium or media are most appropriate for the situation. You evaluate the thesis statement (2c), the key points of the message, and the support provided for each point, as well as identify what must be said and what seems to be purposefully left unsaid. When you *read* rhetorically, you read more effectively and thus are able to speak or write knowledgeably about what you have read. When you *write* rhetorically, you generate ideas appropriate for your opportunity and situation and then communicate those ideas clearly to your audience in both a suitable genre and medium (chapters **2**, **3**, **5**, and **6**). Writing rhetorically also helps you improve your understanding of what you have read, researched, experienced, heard, and seen.

1b   RESPONDING TO A RHETORICAL OPPORTUNITY

A rhetorical situation offers you an opportunity to make change, often by solving a problem or addressing an issue together with a specific audience. A speeding ticket, a cancelled flight, an engagement, a repressive government—these are all circumstances that invite you to speak or write, opportunities for you to use words to address the problem of protesting a fine, rebooking your trip, planning a wedding, or protesting a regime. Once you engage the **rhetorical opportunity**—the issue compelling you to speak or write—you will be better able to gauge all the elements of your message (from word choice and organizational pattern to genre and medium of delivery) in terms of your rhetorical audience and your purpose.

As a rhetorical reader, you need to determine the author's reason for writing in the first place. Is the author writing to answer a question, solve a problem, address an issue, inform or entertain you? The title of the text, the summary, or the abstract may provide that information. The cover of *I Am Malala: The Girl Who Stood Up for Education and Was Shot by the Taliban* (shown in figure 1.2) reveals the book to be an autobiography of a young activist who champions the right for girls to be educated. For her stance, she was shot point-blank by anti-education Taliban soldiers. The unprovoked attack on Malala Yousafzai drew worldwide sympathy, of course, but very quickly the world watched with rapt attention as she recovered and continued to speak out. Thus, Malala's book has brought global attention to the status of and opportunities for young girls.

1c   CONSIDERING AUDIENCE

A clear understanding of the audience—their values, concerns, knowledge, and capabilities—helps writers formulate their purpose. Different audiences call for different purposes. Of course, the audience is

Figure 1.2: A student reads *I Am Malala: The Girl Who Stood Up for Education and Was Shot by the Taliban.*

anyone who reads a text, but the **rhetorical audience** consists of those specific people whom the author considers capable of being influenced by the words and of bringing about the proposed change in action, attitude, understanding, or policy. Thus, the writer's purpose will vary according to the rhetorical audience.

When you read rhetorically, you can become a member of the writer's rhetorical audience, someone who reads purposefully, often recording notes and questions, identifying important evidence within the text, forging connections among relevant passages, evaluating the quality of the supporting details and evidence. During the process, you calibrate how the text affects you, whether you will become part of a solution, decision, or change in attitude, practice, or policy. The better you understand the text, the better able you will be to synthesize the information it provides with what you already know.

As a writer, you need to think clearly about who exactly, in addition to your rhetorical audience, might read what you write. Therefore, you want to consider whether your word choices and examples are appropriate for both your intended and unintended audiences. As a reader, you want to use those same criteria to determine if an author has intentionally included you in or excluded you from the audience. The author's purpose, stance, assertions, examples, and word choices can help you make that determination.

Most generally, writers address one of three general audiences. A **specialized audience** demonstrates interest or expertise in the subject, often becomes a rhetorical audience, and thus helps resolve or address the issue (even if only by understanding the author's message). Someone who has an interest in gender, equality, opportunity, education, global issues, and current events is part of the specialized audience most likely to read *I Am Malala*. A **diverse audience** consists of readers with differing levels of expertise and varying interest in the subject at hand. For instance, when you are in a doctor's waiting room, browsing through *People* magazine, you might come across an excerpt from *I Am Malala*, entitled "My Second Life," which has been repurposed for a diverse audience. **Multiple audiences** are composed of a primary rhetorical audience and a secondary audience who have access to and may read the text, whether they have the potential to help address the issue or not. When you communicate online, be aware that you are likely writing for multiple audiences: although you have composed your message for your rhetorical audience (sometimes including confidential or sensitive information), your e-mail messages or Facebook posts can be forwarded to and easily accessed by others—not always with your permission, and not always with positive consequences.

(1) A specialized audience

A specialized and often rhetorical audience has a demonstrated interest in the subject. If your sister is a sociology major, she may be interested in the status of women in developing countries. She could be part of the audience for paragraph 1 that compares Pakistani life under the rule of founder Mohammad Ali Jinnah with that of General Zia ul-Haq. (For ease of reference, sample paragraphs in this chapter are numbered.)

1   Under Zia's regime life for women in Pakistan became much more restricted. Jinnah said, "No struggle can ever succeed without women participating side by side with men. There are two powers in the world; one is the sword and the other is the pen. There is a third power stronger than both, that of women." But General Zia brought in Islamic laws which

reduced a woman's evidence in court to count for only half that of a man's. Soon our prisons were full of cases like that of a thirteen-year-old girl who was raped and became pregnant and was then sent to prison for adultery because she couldn't produce four male witnesses to prove it was a crime. A woman couldn't even open a bank account without a man's permission. As a nation we have always been good at hockey, but Zia made our female hockey players wear baggy trousers instead of shorts, and stopped women playing some sports altogether.

—MALALA YOUSAFZAI with CHRISTINA LAMB, *I Am Malala*

Although you can probably read every word in the preceding excerpt, the specific incidents and historical leaders may not be familiar to you. A specialized, rhetorical audience has both interest in and knowledge of the topic under consideration. A rhetorical audience has, in addition, the ability to be influenced by the text, or to enact change based on it.

Many of the essays you will be assigned to write in college—in the sciences, history, economics, English, and psychology, for example—will be aimed at your instructor, who comprises a specialized audience, to be sure, as well as your rhetorical audience (the audience you want to influence with your knowledge and expertise). Your job as an academic writer, then, is to weigh what your instructor already knows with the specific additional information you need to supply so that she or he can help resolve the issue of just how well you are performing in class. Most of the materials you will be required to read in college are also aimed at a specialized audience, one with ever-developing expertise and interest in the topic. As part of such an audience, you will want to preview the text to assess what it demands of you in terms of time, effort, and knowledge. You will also want to review the directories within the text (table of contents, index, and bibliography) and the visual aids to orient yourself to the text and its context. You may also have to refer to a dictionary, an encyclopedia, or other resource as you read.

(2) A diverse audience

A diverse audience consists of readers with differing levels of expertise and varying interest in the subject at hand. Paragraph 2 is taken from physician Atul Gawande's essay on blushing, which explains this universal human behavior.

2   Why we have such a reflex is perplexing. One theory is that the blush exists to show embarrassment, just as the smile exists to show happiness. This would explain why the reaction appears only in the visible regions of the body (the face, the neck, and the upper chest). But then why do dark-skinned people blush? Surveys find that nearly everyone blushes, regardless of skin color, despite the fact that in many people it is nearly invisible. And you don't need to turn red in order for people to recognize that you're embarrassed. Studies show that people detect embarrassment *before* you blush. Apparently, blushing takes between fifteen and twenty seconds to reach its peak, yet most people need less than five seconds to recognize that someone is embarrassed—they pick it up from the almost immediate shift in gaze, usually down and to the left, or from the sheepish, self-conscious grin that follows a half second to a second later. So there's reason to doubt that the purpose of blushing is entirely expressive.

—ATUL GAWANDE, "Crimson Tide"

As a writer, you can easily imagine a diverse audience if you think of thoughtful, receptive, educated adults, with whom you may share some common ground. For instance, you may write a research essay for your anthropology instructor and send copies to your high school biology teacher as well as to your mom. As a reader, you may often find yourself a member of a diverse audience, one likely to include people with different beliefs, knowledge, and experience (7e(2)). If you go to concerts and theaters, you join a diverse audience, all of whom read the same program or playbill, regardless of their level of expertise. Rarely will you write for or read something by someone who is exactly like you (34c). This means that any connections established between writers and readers are made through language and involve the choice of words and technical terms (chapters 34–36), specific details, and examples (2f), all of which either invite readers into or exclude them from a text.

(3) Multiple audiences

Writers often need to consider multiple audiences, a task related to—yet different from—addressing a diverse audience. When you address a diverse audience, you try to reach everyone. When you consider multiple audiences, you gauge your choice of words and tone according to your primary audience, knowing that a secondary audience might have access to your text. For peer reviews, for example, your primary audience is the peer whose writing you are reviewing. Knowing that your instructor (the secondary audience) will also be reading your commentary, you may respond to your peer's writing with more thoughtfulness and tact than you would otherwise. When you know that your rhetorical situation includes multiple audiences, you can better adjust your words and edit your information. And when you consciously read as a member of either a primary or a secondary audience, you can better evaluate your responses.

When writing essays in college, you will regularly find yourself addressing multiple audiences. You may use research you have done in history class as the starting point for developing an essay for an economics class or compose an essay for a general (secondary) audience and submit it to an instructor who is a specialist in the subject (and therefore your primary audience).

The following checklist may help you assess an audience, whether you are doing so as the writer or the reader.

✔ CHECKLIST for Assessing Audience

- Who makes up the rhetorical audience for this writing? Who else might read it? How has the writer identified the primary audience and accommodated a secondary audience? What passages indicate that the writer has addressed the primary audience and also recognized the expectations of a secondary audience?

- What do you know about the backgrounds, values, and characteristics of the members of the rhetorical audience? What do the audience members have in common? How are they different?

- What background, values, and characteristics do you (as either the writer or a reader) share with the members of the rhetorical audience? How do you differ from them?

- How open are the members of this audience to views that are different from their own?

- What do you not know about this audience? In other words, what assumptions about its members might be risky to make?

- What kind of language, examples, and details are most appropriate (or inappropriate) for the members of this audience?

- What does this audience already know about the topic under consideration?

- What level of expertise will this audience expect from the writer?

Exercise 1

In both an introductory textbook and an advanced textbook in a discipline of your choice, locate a passage devoted to the same issue or concept and photocopy these passages. Prepare a class presentation in which you explain how each passage addresses the needs and expectations of a specific audience.

1d DETERMINING A SPECIFIC PURPOSE

When you calibrate your specific purpose to your rhetorical audience (1c), your words can stimulate change, modify a situation, address a need, or resolve a problem. Thus, successful writers make careful decisions about the words they choose, the tone they take, and the quality and quantity of details and examples they include so that they can easily orient and possibly influence their intended audience. Writers always align their overall purpose in terms of that rhetorical audience, whether they want to evoke emotions or challenge beliefs about a topic, amuse or entertain, report information, explain or evaluate the significance of information, analyze a situation, clarify a point, invite the audience to consider alternative points of view, or argue for or against a course of action. They also become familiar with the various methods of development (narration, description, and cause-and-consequence analysis; see 2g) for shaping that message. As a writer, then, your goal should be to compose a purposeful message that responds to an opportunity to make a change, striving to provide your audience with a clear plan for effecting that change.

Readers need to identify the writer's purpose as well, so they can determine just what response the writer expects from them. As a reader, you need to identify specific words or passages that convey the writer's purpose, whether the writer wants you to be entertained, informed, or persuaded. For example, the purpose of Malala Yousafzai's book is clear from the title (to inform and explain), but the inside front cover is even more specific: "*I Am Malala* will make you believe in the power of one person's voice to inspire change in the world." Malala is explaining, that is for sure, but she may also be inspiring her readers to make a change, take a stand, and speak out. The afterword Malala has written also makes her purpose clear:

> My goal in writing this book was to raise my voice on behalf of the millions of girls around the world who are being denied the right to go to school and realize their potential. I hope my story will inspire girls to raise their voices. . . . . My mission, our mission, demands that we act decisively to educate girls and empower them to change their lives and communities.

Often, visuals, such as the map in figure 1.3, help direct you to a writer's purpose, as do the chronological photographs throughout Malala's book,

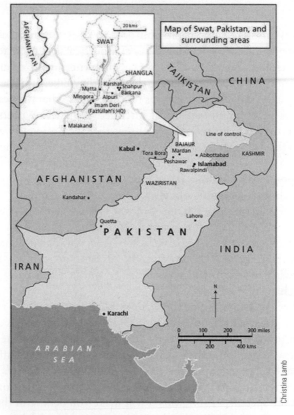

Figure 1.3: The opening visual of Malala's book helps orient her Western readers to the geography of Pakistan.

photographs spanning from her babyhood in Swat, Pakistan, to her recovery in Birmingham, England.

You can also look at a book's table of contents, index, appendixes, glossary, or other divisions to help orient yourself to the content and the writer's purpose. Malala, for instance, does not include the traditional index; instead, she includes a glossary that serves as a reference for her Western readers, many of whom will not immediately understand the terms and concepts of Pakistani culture, such as "FATA," "Hadith," and "imam." Thus, you might be able to tell from the glossary whether the book contains the information you need to conduct research or satisfy your curiosity about Pakistani politics, the Taliban, girls' educational opportunities, or another related topic that interests you.

Readers also need to establish their purpose for reading: to summarize what they are learning, apply this information to solve a problem, analyze the constituent parts of the text, make a decision, support a position, or combine the information in an original way. In figure 1.4, you can see how one reader responded to a passage in the text of Malala's book, particularly on learning that life for girls was even harder in Afghanistan than in Pakistan.

definition

We have a custom called <u>swara</u> by which a girl can be given to another tribe to resolve a feud. It is officially banned but still continues. In our village there was a widow called Soraya who married *example* a widower from another clan which had a feud with her family. Nobody can marry a widow without the permission of her family. *The widow had no power.* When Soraya's family found out about the union they were furious. They threatened the widower's family until a *jirga* of village *Do jirgas include any women?* elders was called to resolve the dispute. The *jirga* decided that the widower's family should be punished by handing over their most beautiful girl to be married to the least eligible man of the rival *Women and* clan. The boy was a good-for-nothing, so poor that the girl's father *girls are* had to pay all their expenses. Why should a girl's life be ruined to *traded* settle a dispute she had nothing to do with?

Figure 1.4: Annotated excerpt from *I Am Malala: The Girl Who Stood Up for Education and Was Shot by the Taliban*.

Your challenge as a reader is to grasp the meaning the author wants to convey to you within the particular rhetorical situation, just as your challenge as a writer is to make the purpose of your writing clear to your intended readers.

In order to succeed in college, academic readers and writers find the time to talk with their instructor (and check the assignment sheet) to review the rhetorical opportunity, purpose, audience, context, and message of each reading and writing assignment (4a). They also talk about their reading and writing with their peers, to make sure they are on the right track. So, ask questions, listen to the answers, and try to answer the questions of your peers as you all work together to establish what is most significant, maybe even memorable, about the writing and reading you are assigned.

✔ CHECKLIST for Assessing Purpose

- How is the rhetorical purpose of the text linked to its rhetorical audience? How might that audience help the writer fulfill the purpose of addressing an issue or resolving a problem?

- What purpose does the writer want the message to fulfill: to evoke emotion, to entertain or inspire, to convey information, or to argue for or against a course of action or an attitude? Does the writer have more than one purpose?

- What method or methods of development (narration, description, definition, comparison and contrast, process analysis, cause-and-consequence analysis, exemplification, classification and division, argument) does the author use to achieve that purpose?

- How well do the topic and the audience connect to the rhetorical purpose? What examples or choice of words help fulfill that purpose?

Depending on the writer's overall purpose, writing can be classified as expressive, expository, or argumentative. Any of these types of writing can help a writer fulfill an overall purpose.

(1) Expressive writing

Expressive writing emphasizes the writer's feelings and reactions to people, objects, events, or ideas. Personal letters and journals are often expressive, as are many essays and short stories. As you read paragraph 3, which comes from a memoir, notice how philosopher Kathleen Dean Moore conveys her thoughts about what it takes to be happy.

3   So many people are telling me what should make me happy. Buy a cute car. Be thin. Get promoted or honored or given a raise. Travel: Baja! Belize! Finish the laundry. The voices may or may not be my own; they are so insistent that I can't distinguish them from the ringing in my ears. Maybe they are the voices of my mother and father, long dead and well intended, wanting only that I would be happy. Or my husband Frank, fully alive but ditto in all other respects. My colleagues. Maybe they're the voices of advertisers, popular songwriters, even the president. Most of the time, I don't even think about making choices, plowing through my life as if I were pulled by a mule.

—KATHLEEN DEAN MOORE, "The Happy Basket"

(2) Expository writing

Much of the academic material you read—textbooks, news accounts, reports, books (such as the one by Malala Yousafzai featured in this chapter), and journal articles—is expository, as are most of the essays you will be asked to write in college. Expository writing focuses more on objects, events, or ideas than on the writer's feelings about them. Anytime you report, explain, analyze, or assess, you are practicing exposition. Paragraph 4, an excerpt from Nina Jablonski's book, *Skin*, explains why the covering on our bodies varies.

4   [A] distinctive attribute of human skin is that it comes naturally in a wide range of colors, from the darkest brown, nearly black, to the palest ivory, nearly white. This exquisite sepia rainbow shades from darkest near the equator to lightest near the poles. This range forms a natural cline, or gradient, that is related primarily to the intensity of the ultraviolet radiation (UVR) that falls on the different latitudes of the earth's surface. Skin color is one of the ways in which evolution has fine-tuned our bodies to the environment, uniting humanity through a palette of adaptation. Unfortunately, skin color has also divided humanity because of its

damaging association with concepts of race. The spurious connections made between skin color and social position have riven peoples and countries for centuries.

—NINA G. JABLONSKI, *Skin: A Natural History*

(3) Argumentative writing

Argumentative writing is intended to influence the reader's attitudes and actions. Most writing is to some extent an argument. Even something as apparently straightforward as a résumé can be seen as an argument for a job interview. However, writing is usually called argumentative if it clearly supports a specific position (chapter 7). As you read paragraph 5, note how Malala Yousafzai argues for education as a basic right, ending with a moving personal detail.

5   Today we all know education is our basic right. Not just in the West; Islam too has given us this right. Islam says every girl and every boy should go to school. In the Quran it is written, God wants us to have knowledge. He wants us to know why the sky is blue and about oceans and stars. I know it's a big struggle—around the world there are fifty-seven million children who are not in primary school, thirty-two million of them girls. Sadly, my own country, Pakistan, is one of the worst places: 5.1 million children don't even go to primary school even though in our constitution it says every child has that right. We have almost fifty million illiterate adults, two thirds of whom are women, like my mother.

—MALALA YOUSAFZAI, *I Am Malala*

Exercise 2

Write two paragraphs that begin to develop an expressive, expository, or argumentative essay on one of the following subjects.

1. your physical health
2. paying for college
3. your career goals
4. volunteer work
5. academic pressures
6. the key(s) to happiness
7. a good teacher
8. your cooking skills
9. your living situation
10. an admirable friend or relative

1e   WRITING AND READING A MESSAGE WITHIN A CONTEXT

Context includes the time and place in which a message is read or written, the writer and the intended audience, and the medium of delivery (print, digital, spoken, or visual); in other words, context comprises the set of circumstances under which the writer and reader (or speaker and listener) communicate. Social, political, religious, geographic, and other cultural factors, as well as attitudes and beliefs, influence context by helping or hindering successful communication. (Just think of the background information Malala needed to bring to her story in order to be understood by Westerners.) All of these factors serve as resources (positive influences) and constraints (obstacles) in any rhetorical situation.

Whatever you read, write, or speak is always influenced (positively or negatively) by the context in which it is written or spoken, read or heard. Writers who attend to the factors negatively or positively influencing the context in which they are writing more successfully convey their ideas to their audience and improve their chances of achieving their purpose. Readers who consider the overall context of a text constitute a more insightful and attuned rhetorical audience.

The medium of delivery is also part of the context. Composing a web page, for example, requires you to consider your words, of course, but also those additional features of organization, design, and style related to onscreen presentation of material. Reading online also requires an adjustment to visual and audio elements that can enhance (or distract from) your experience. Any digital method of delivery, then, requires you to make different kinds of rhetorical decisions than you make for a text in a wholly static print medium (chapter 5).

When you read the work of other writers, you will sometimes find the context for the work explicitly stated in a preface or an introduction, whether the context is geographic, political, or religious. Often, however, the context must be inferred. In either case, writers and readers must both identify and consider it.

✓ CHECKLIST for Assessing Context

- What factors influence the context in which you are writing: the time and place, the intended audience, and the medium of delivery (print, digital, spoken, or visual)?

- What other events (personal, local, or global) influence the context for writing?

- What are the expectations concerning the length of this written message? If a length has not been specified, what seems appropriate in terms of purpose and audience?

- What document design (Chapter 6) is appropriate, given the context?

- Under what circumstances will this piece of writing be read? How can you help the intended audience quickly see the purpose of the text within these circumstances?

2 | PLANNING AND DRAFTING ESSAYS

As an experienced writer, you already understand that writing is a process, one that includes responding to a rhetorical opportunity, aligning your purpose to your rhetorical audience, and choosing a medium of delivery. Even when you compose an e-mail message, you think through those decisions at the same time that you quickly draft your response, revising as you go. Often, you even cut and paste or delete material in order to clarify your meaning, adjust your tone, and achieve your purpose. The steps you follow when composing a quick e-mail are the same steps you use when you are writing more slowly to fulfill a formal academic assignment. Whether you are writing in or out of school, you revise and edit in light of your rhetorical opportunity, audience, purpose, and context (**1b–e**).

This chapter will help you understand your writing process by showing you how to

- recognize suitable subjects (**2a**),
- focus your ideas (**2b**),
- draft a purposeful thesis statement (**2c**),
- organize your ideas by method of development and/or genre (**2d**),
- express your ideas in multiple drafts (**2e**), and
- select and use various methods to develop effective paragraphs (**2f**) and essays (**2g**).

Most experienced writers break down their writing process into a series of (sometimes overlapping and even repetitive) steps that include generating, researching, organizing, developing, and clarifying ideas, often polishing their prose along the way. Because the writing process is **recursive**, you may find yourself returning to a specific activity (generating ideas, researching, or editing, for instance) several times as you plan and draft a piece of writing. During drafting, you may realize that you need to go back and generate more supporting ideas, modify your thesis, or even start over with a new thesis. As you become more conscious of your individual writing process, you will quickly recognize the importance of revisiting passages that merit revision. Each recursive sweep yields new ideas.

Despite the infinite variations of the writing process, it usually involves four basic, recursive stages, described in the following box.

STAGES OF THE WRITING PROCESS

- **Prewriting** is the initial stage of the writing process. As you begin thinking about a specific writing task, you consider the rhetorical opportunity (what interests you about it and how you can use words to respond to it), the rhetorical audience and purpose (genre), the context (resources and constraints, including the instructor's expectations for this piece of writing), and the medium of delivery. Then you start exploring your topic by talking with others working on the same assignment, keeping a journal, freewriting, asking questions, or conducting preliminary research. By now, you may already know the best ways to energize your thinking and jump-start your writing.

- **Drafting** involves writing down your ideas quickly, writing as much as you can, without worrying about being perfect or staying on topic. Some writers like to cluster their ideas and supporting material, creating a preliminary arrangement for a piece; others just write, write, write. After all, the more ideas you get down on paper (whether they are organized or not), the more options you will have as you begin to clarify your thesis, compose your first draft, and revise. Progress is your goal at this stage, not perfection.

- **Revising** offers you the opportunity to focus your purpose in terms of your audience, establish a clear thesis statement that conveys your main idea (2c), and organize your ideas toward those ends (2d). Now is the time to stabilize the overall arrangement of your piece, develop the individual paragraphs (2f and 3c), and reconsider your introduction and conclusion (3b). Revising is not the end, though; revising produces yet another draft meriting further revision and editing.

- **Editing** focuses on surface features: punctuation, spelling, word choice, grammar, sentence structure, and all the rest of the details of Standardized English (3f). As you prepare your work for final submission, you may want to read it aloud to discover which sentence structures and word choices could be improved. You may even catch a few spelling errors in the process.

2a | SELECTING A SUBJECT

If you are not assigned a subject and are free to choose your own, you can start by identifying a problem or issue that your words can address or resolve in cooperation with a rhetorical audience. You can think about what you already know—or would like to learn—about the problem as well as what is likely to interest your intended audience (**1d**). Your most successful writing will often emerge from your knowledge of or interest in politics, cultural groups, entertainment, leisure activities, sports, fashion, professions, or places, especially when you write for a rhetorical audience with a clear purpose and use well-chosen details and examples (**1c, 1d,** and **2f**). While traveling in Italy, for instance, you might keep a travelogue for your parents, recounting the details of your daily life, including the sights, foods, museums, and fashions you enjoy, so that they, too, can enjoy your trip, if only vicariously.

In college, on the other hand, you will most often write about subjects directly related to your academic coursework. In an adolescent psychology course, you may be assigned to write a research essay on a facet of adolescent psychology, one that you do not understand fully and that relates directly to the course. To locate a suitable topic that meets both those criteria, you might start by looking through your textbook (particularly in the section on suggestions for further reading and the marginal annotations you have made) and your lecture notes. Ask yourself whether anything you have learned so far has surprised, annoyed, or intrigued you. Maybe you have read something in your textbook that simply does not ring true to you. Any issue that unsettles you provides an opportunity for you to enter the scholarly conversation by explaining or arguing a point, supplying additional information, or overturning a traditional belief. When you discover a subject you want to explore further—adolescent depression, for instance—you can combine your need to know more with the opportunity to deliver that new information to your audience, in this case, to your instructor and the rest of the class.

(1) Keeping a journal to explore subjects

One tried-and-true way to explore a subject—or a range of issues—is by keeping a journal. Whether private or public, digital or handwritten, journals offer a convenient place to record your thoughts and explore topics that interest you. Some twenty-first-century journals are referred to as blogs. In a **personal journal,** you can write for your own benefit, reflecting on your experiences and inner life (a trip to Italy, an emotional disaster, a professional hope) or focusing on external events (such as political campaigns, natural disasters, sporting events, new books and films). Some writers prefer to keep a **reading journal,** where they record quotations, observations about a narrative or author, and any other reading-related material that they might then use in their own writing. Whatever type of journal you keep, allow yourself to write in it quickly, recording, reflecting, and exploring without worrying about spelling or grammar.

(2) Freewriting as a risk-free way to explore a subject

When **freewriting,** writers record whatever comes to mind about a subject, writing without stopping for a limited period of time—often no more than ten minutes. When they repeat themselves or get off track, writers keep going in order to generate ideas, make connections, and bring information and memories to the surface. Some writers use colored markers (or change the font or color in their word-processing program) to identify different subjects and make connections as well as to generate a tentative organization.

When Mary LeNoir's English instructor asked her to write for five minutes about how she chose a college, Mary produced the following freewriting as the first step toward her final essay (which appears in chapter 3).

I'm an athlete. I've always been an athlete, a competitive, team-sports athlete. But being an athlete won't be my job or pay my bills when I graduate from college. So when I was thinking about which school to attend, I tried hard not to let high school athletics and the college recruiting process cloud my decision making. I also tried not to listen to all the people who seem to think that "money" is how we student-athletes make our decision. That's not true. In fact, instead of scholarship money, school prestige, or possible major, many athletes place potential playing time over academics when they make their decision. It's as though they are announcing, "I'm going to X school to play Y sport, and I will have to take classes while I'm there." Still, playing time is not the only factor that takes over the decision-making process. Some athletes commit to a school for reasons they haven't really thought through, don't really understand. Some athletes make their decision based on their emotions, on how much they "like" the school (the Creamery, the quad, the student union, the dorms, or whatever) or like the coach or like the other players. They can end up in a school located halfway across the country from home, a school with rigorous academics that competes with a huge party scene. Sometimes, they don't find out until too late that they cannot balance the academics with the athletics, not to mention the parties and big classes. And they're too far from home to get the support they need. If they're not partiers (or if they party too much) or if they need a small class and don't have that, then, they're out of luck. I'm also aware of athletes choosing a school based on potential for a professional athletic career, even though the vast majority of them never make the grade. Instead, they will move on from their sport, unless they venture into coaching or play it with friends. I know I'm throwing out a lot of things here and will need to narrow it down to one focus and come up with a purpose, a thesis, and some kind of outline or plan.

Mary's freewriting generated a number of possibilities for developing an essay about why she chose the college she did: she cites academics, emotional responses, and athletics as strong reasons. She was responding to the opportunity to explain the selection process, especially to people who believe that student-athletes think only of how much scholarship money they will receive if they attend a particular college. Notice, however, that her freewriting leads her to describe other athletes, not herself, and that she realizes she needs to think about what comes next in her writing process.

(3) Questioning to push the boundaries of a subject

You can also explore a subject by asking yourself some questions. The simplest questioning strategy for exploring a subject comes from journalism. **Journalists' questions**—*Who? What? When? Where? Why?* and *How?*—are easy to use and can help you generate ideas about any subject. Using journalists' questions to explore how a student-athlete chooses a college could lead you to the following: *Who* qualifies as a student-athlete? *What* criteria do and should student-athletes use in choosing a college? *When* should student-athletes expect to give up their sports? *Where* can student-athletes best succeed? *Why* is financial aid not the only, or even the most important, selection criterion?

How might a student-athlete make the best decision, given his or her characteristics and circumstances?

You might also ask yourself questions derived from the ancient Romans, who always wanted to know what, exactly, was at stake. As you think through and around a topic, you might ask the following questions, all derived from the Roman concept of **stasis**: *What is the state of the situation? How is it defined? How or why does it matter? What actions should be taken?* See **7b** for more on stasis.

Mary could use either or both sets of questions to further explore her tentative subject: on what bases do high school athletes choose a college?

2b	FOCUSING A SUBJECT INTO A SPECIFIC TOPIC AND GENRE

By exploring a subject, you can discover productive strategies or a genre for development as well as a specific focus for your topic. As you prewrite, you will decide that some ideas seem worth pursuing while others seem inappropriate for the rhetorical opportunity you have identified, your rhetorical audience, your purpose, or the context in which you are writing. Thus, during the process of exploring, some ideas will fall away as new ones arise and your topic comes into sharper focus.

After generating ideas through strategies such as freewriting and questioning, you can use various rhetorical methods for developing the ideas (**2g**). In responding to a rhetorical opportunity to explain how student-athletes choose (or should choose) a college, Mary LeNoir needed to focus this fairly broad subject into a more narrow (and manageable) topic. Therefore, she considered how she might use each of the rhetorical methods of development to sharpen her focus:

- *Narration.* What is a typical story about a student-athlete deciding on a college?
- *Description.* How do colleges distinguish themselves in terms of size, course offerings, location, and cost? How do student-athletes differ? What distinctive characteristics of college and student produce the best matches?

- *Process analysis.* What steps do student-athletes take as they choose a college? What are the most and least useful of those steps?
- *Cause-and-consequence analysis.* What considerations lead to the best choice of a college? What considerations do many student-athletes overlook? What are the consequences of making the right choice? Of making the wrong one?
- *Comparison and contrast.* How does the process of choosing a college differ for a student-athlete and a nonathlete? How does the process differ for a student whose goal is to be only a college athlete and a student whose goal is to be a professional athlete?
- *Classification and division.* How might student-athletes' college-related needs and expectations be classified? How might colleges be categorized based on what they offer student-athletes?
- *Definition.* How can the "best" college be defined? What are the best reasons for choosing a college? Are these reasons defined by immediate or long-term benefits?

Mary also had to think of her topic in terms of various traditional academic genres. She could deliver her essay in one of the following forms.

- *Memoir.* What process did Mary herself go through as she made her decision? Over what time span? Who were the other characters in her decision-making process? What did they say? What was the setting of the decision making?
- *Profile.* What student-athlete made the biggest impression on Mary? Was the impression positive or negative? What are the key features of that person's personality, character, and values? What personal examples bring that athlete's decision making to life?
- *Investigative report.* What generalization about student-athletes' decision making merits deeper research? What information did library, questionnaire, and interview research reveal about the decision making of student-athletes? What details and facts help readers better understand the decision-making process?
- *Position argument.* What might be the most responsible decision-making process for high school athletes to use when choosing a college? What good reasons support this assertion? What examples, details, facts, and figures support the argument?

- *Proposal.* What problem do high school student-athletes have when choosing a college? What specific, research-based advice might Mary offer these athletes? What specific details about costs and benefits can she offer?
- *Evaluation.* On what basis should high school athletes choose a college? What are the best criteria for choosing a college? What evidence and examples can Mary offer that illustrate the ways athletes' individual decisions do or do not meet those criteria? What athlete has made the best decision? What criteria did that athlete use?
- *Critical analysis.* How might Mary explain the specific cultural, economic, political, and/or social forces that shape a high school athlete's choice of college? What are the obvious causes and consequences of the situation? What are the more subtle, yet still powerful, influences? How might a student-athlete respond to or resist those forces?

A combination of developmental strategies soon led Mary to a tentative focus on what was becoming an evaluation:

> After interviewing five student-athletes about their personal goals and circumstances and considering my own situation, I discovered that despite our differences, we all used three basic criteria in choosing our college: the overall atmosphere of the school, the potential for our athletic development, and the material conditions associated with attending the college (costs and geographic location).

Because some of Mary's friends believed that student-athletes chose a college solely on the basis of the financial aid offered, she wanted to explain how she and her fellow athletes actually made their decisions.

Whatever rhetorical method you use to bring a topic into focus, your final topic should be determined not only by the opportunity that is engaging you but also by your rhetorical audience, the way that audience connects with your purpose, and the context in which you are writing (the constraints and resources of time, place, and medium of delivery). Because writing is a form of thinking and discovering, your focus might not emerge until after you have written a draft or two.

The following checklist may help you assess your topic.

✓ **CHECKLIST** for Assessing a Topic

- What unresolved problem or issue related to this topic captures your interest? How can you use words to address this rhetorical opportunity for change?

- What audience might be interested in this topic? How might they help you address or resolve the issue you have identified?

- What is your purpose in writing about this topic for this audience? In other words, do you want to inform, entertain, or persuade them?

- Can you address the topic in the time and space (page length) available? Or should you narrow or expand the topic to accommodate a time constraint or length expectations?

- Do you have the information you need to address this topic? If not, how will you acquire additional information?

- What methods of development will best help you achieve your purpose? Is there a specific genre you should follow (proposal, evaluation, critical analysis, and so on)?

- Are you willing to take the time to learn more about the topic in order to engage the rhetorical opportunity? Are you willing to abide by the expectations of a specific genre?

Exercise 1

Use the journalists' questions (page 25) to generate more ideas about a subject that interests you (for instance, how you decided to enroll at your college). Then identify a rhetorical opportunity that emerges from your answers to those questions. How does that opportunity connect with your subject to create a specific topic that is appropriate for an essay?

2c | CONVEYING A CLEARLY STATED THESIS

Once you have identified an opportunity for change, determined a rhetorical audience receptive to that change, decided on a purpose for writing (to entertain, explain, teach, analyze, persuade, or compare), and focused your thoughts on a compelling topic, you have drawn close to settling on your controlling idea, or **thesis**. In the first draft or two, your thesis may still be tentative. By your final draft, however, you will have developed a clear thesis statement.

Many pieces of academic writing have a **thesis statement,** an explicit declaration (usually in one sentence) of the main idea, which identifies your topic and your stance on that topic. As such, your thesis statement conveys a single idea, clearly focused and specifically stated. A thesis can be thought of as a central idea stated in the form of an assertion, or **claim** (7d), which indicates what you believe to be true, interesting, or valuable about your topic. Every thesis must be supported by good reasons, evidence, and details.

An explicitly formulated thesis statement helps keep your writing on target and your rhetorical audience in mind. It identifies the topic, the purpose, and, in some cases, the plan of development and genre. Notice how the following thesis statements fulfill their purpose. The first is from a descriptive essay.

> If Lynne Truss were Catholic, I'd nominate her for sainthood.
>
> —**FRANK McCOURT,** Foreword, *Eats, Shoots & Leaves*

With this simple statement, McCourt establishes that the topic is Lynne Truss and indicates that he will propose all the reasons she should be a saint. He conveys enthusiasm and admiration for Truss's work.

The following thesis statement for a cause-and-consequence critical analysis sets the stage for the series of incidents that unfolded after surgeon and writer Richard Selzer was granted refuge in an Italian monastery when he had no hotel reservations:

> Wanderers know it—beggars, runaways, exiles, fugitives, the homeless, all of the dispossessed—that if you knock at the door of a monastery seeking shelter you will be taken in.
>
> —**RICHARD SELZER,** "Diary of an Infidel: Notes from a Monastery"

A profile illuminates a person by way of careful description and narration, as in the following thesis statement:

> Writing taught my father to pay attention; my father in turn taught other people to pay attention and then to write down their thoughts and observations.
>
> —**ANNE LAMOTT,** *Bird by Bird: Some Instructions on Writing and Life*

The main idea in an argumentative essay usually conveys a strong point of view, as in the following, which unmistakably argues for a specific course of action:

> Amnesty International opposes the death penalty in all cases without exception.
>
> —AMNESTY INTERNATIONAL, "The Death Penalty: Questions and Answers"

The following are possible thesis statements that Mary LeNoir might have written based on two of the rhetorical methods of development (**2g**). The first sentence suggests a proposal that is helping her find her way to an evaluation:

> Student-athletes who want to play only college sports and those who want to go pro should employ different criteria for selecting a college.

The following sentence focuses on cause-and-consequence evaluation:

> By establishing my criteria for a successful college experience, I was able to choose the best college for me.

It is just as important to allow your thesis statement to remain tentative in the early stages of writing as it is to allow your essay to remain flexible through the initial drafts, responsive to your ongoing research findings and insights. Rather than sticking with your original thesis, which you might have to struggle to support because it was not well conceived, you want to let your final thesis statement evolve as you think, explore, draft, and revise. The following tips might help you develop a thesis statement that is neither too obvious nor too general.

TIPS FOR DEVELOPING A THESIS STATEMENT

- Decide which feature of the topic opens up a rhetorical opportunity—a problem your words might resolve or a change they might bring about.
- Write down your point of view or assertion about it.

(continued on page 32)

(continued from page 31)

- Draft a thesis statement that includes the topic and your assertion about it.

- Mark the passages in your rough draft that support your position to see how well this thesis fits with ideas you've been developing.

- Ask yourself whether your thesis is too broad or too narrow to be sufficiently developed given the constraints of your project.

- After completing a draft, ask yourself whether the scope of your thesis should be adjusted to reflect the direction your essay has taken. Qualify your thesis if necessary, acknowledging any conditions where your assertion may not hold up.

- If you are still unhappy with your thesis, start again with the first tip and be even more specific.

A clear, precise thesis statement helps unify your message so that it is appropriate for your audience and your rhetorical purpose, accurately reflects the material you generate, and directs your readers through the writing that follows. Therefore, as you continue to write and revise, check your thesis statement frequently to make sure that all your supporting material (your assertions, good reasons, examples, and details) remain anchored to that thesis. Your thesis should influence your decisions about which details to keep and which to eliminate as well as guide your search for appropriate additional information to support your assertions.

A thesis statement is usually a declarative sentence (a topic and a comment about that topic) with a single main clause—that is, either a simple or a complex sentence (22c). If your thesis statement presents two or more related ideas, as a compound sentence does (22c), be sure that it allows for a single direction and focus. For example, the following thesis statement, composed of two sentences, coordinates two ideas, indicating a discussion that will contrast the human brain with those of other animals:

> There is something unusual about primates in general, and humans in particular. Compared with other animals, they have strikingly large brains relative to their bodies.
>
> —TOM STANDAGE, *Writing on the Wall: Social Media—The First Two Thousand Years*

If you wish to sharpen a thesis statement by adding information that qualifies or supports it, subordinate such material to the main idea:

> In elementary school, I had noticed the mean-spiritedness of some kids, part of it directed at me and my siblings.
>
> —MARY PIPHER, "Growing Our Souls"

As you develop your thesis statement, resist using such vague qualifiers as *interesting, important,* and *unusual,* which can signal that the topic lacks focus. For example, in the thesis statement "My education has been very unusual," the word *unusual* conveys very little. It might indicate that the writer's topic is weak and unfocused—or it might be masking a wonderfully wild, interesting idea that would appeal to an audience: "After my parents decided to teach me at home, I pursued educational avenues I didn't know existed." If you feel you need to soften your thesis or claim, then turn to such qualifiers as *frequently, often, generally, rarely,* or *sometimes.*

The following examples show how vague thesis statements can be improved:

Vague thesis	It is important to balance work with school.
Better thesis	Hardworking students who balance a part-time job with academic success often gain maturity and self-confidence.
Vague thesis	The concept of stem-cell research is interesting.
Better thesis	If controlled successfully in a laboratory setting, human stem cells could become the basis of transplantation-based therapies.
Vague thesis	Student-athletes choose a college for a number of reasons.
Better thesis	No matter what their sport or their professional aspirations, student-athletes generally use the same criteria in choosing a college: opportunity to play the sport, geographic location, financial aid, and emotional connection with the school.

The thesis statement most often appears in the first paragraph of an essay, although you can put yours wherever it best furthers your overall purpose (perhaps somewhere later in the introduction, or even in the conclusion). The advantage of putting the thesis statement in the first paragraph is that readers know from the beginning what your essay is about, to whom you are writing, your purpose for writing, and how the essay is likely to take shape. This thesis-first technique has proved to be especially effective in academic writing. If the thesis statement begins the opening paragraph, the rest of the sentences in the paragraph support or clarify it, as is the case in paragraph 1. (For ease of reference, each of the sample paragraphs in this chapter is numbered.)

1   *Right from the start I was a fearful child, and I quickly learned which fears I could admit to my parents.* Photographs reveal that I was terrified of Duke, the family bulldog, whose exuberance threatened to knock me over every time he stood up with his paws on my shoulders, covering my face with sloppy saliva kisses. Family legends reiterate that on weekend drives, long or short, I worried that we would run out of gas—a fear that persists to this day. Before I began first grade, I feared I would be booted out if I misspelled a word; my mother sent me off on the first day of school armed with the talismanic "a-n-t-i-c-i-p-a-t-e."

    —LYNN Z. BLOOM, *The Seven Deadly Virtues and Other Lively Essays*

If the thesis statement is the last sentence of the opening paragraph, the preceding sentences build toward it, as in paragraph 2.

2   The story of zero is an ancient one. Its roots stretch back to the dawn of mathematics, in the time thousands of years before the first civilization, long before humans could read and write. But as natural as zero seems to us today, for ancient peoples zero was a foreign—and frightening—idea. An Eastern concept, born in the Fertile Crescent a few centuries before the birth of Christ, zero not only evoked images of a primal void, it also had dangerous mathematical properties. *Within zero there is the power to shatter the framework of logic.*

    —CHARLES SEIFE, *Zero: The Biography of a Dangerous Idea*

Keep in mind that most academic writing features an easy-to-locate thesis statement. The following checklist may help you assess a thesis.

✔ **CHECKLIST** for Assessing a Thesis

- Does your thesis respond to an opportunity to create a change (in action, thinking, perception, or opinion) or to address a problem?
- Does your thesis accurately reflect your point of view about your topic?
- How does your thesis relate to the interests of your rhetorical audience? To your purpose? To the context in which you are writing?
- Where is your thesis located? How does it guide your readers? Would your readers benefit from having it stated earlier or later?
- Does your thesis reflect your overall purpose? Does it clarify your focus and indicate your coverage of the topic?
- What are the two strongest assertions you can make to support your thesis?
- What specific examples, details, or experiences support your assertions?

2d   ARRANGING OR OUTLINING IDEAS

Most writers benefit from a provisional organizational plan that helps them order their ideas and manage their writing. Other writers compose informal lists of ideas and then examine them for overlap, pertinence, and potential. While some ideas will be discarded, others might lead to a thesis statement, a provocative introduction, a reasonable conclusion, or an overall organizational plan. Some writers rely on more formal outlines, in which main points form the major headings and supporting ideas form the subheadings. Whatever method you choose for arranging your ideas, remember that you can always alter your plan to accommodate any changes your thinking undergoes as you proceed.

An outline of Mary LeNoir's essay might look something like the following:

TENTATIVE THESIS STATEMENT: No matter what their sport, student-athletes tend to choose a college using three criteria: (1) how much playing time they will have; (2) material considerations, mainly geographic location and financial aid; and (3) emotional connection with the school.

I. Many high school athletes fantasize about going pro after college, even though only a very few will.

    A. They also strive to predict how much playing time they will have on the college field.

    B. They consider schools with the most winning teams.

II. Then, they consider the material reasons for attending a particular school.

    A. They consider the geographic location of the school.

    B. They try to negotiate the best financial aid package available to a student-athlete of their caliber.

III. Many student-athletes ultimately base their decision on an emotional connection with the school.

    A. They always dreamed about playing their sport at a particular college.

    B. They fell in love with the campus or the city—or really liked the coach or the other players.

IV. How I worked through these criteria toward my decision

V. The consequences (positive and negative) of my decision

Notice that the last main points of Mary's outline are less well developed than the others. However, she is already beginning to organize her ideas from her freewriting, and she is developing her topic within the boundaries stated in her tentative thesis. Still, as she begins to draft, she may discover that her essay does not follow her outline exactly. She may find herself moving ideas around, deleting some, or adding others. An outline is a tool to help you get started—it is not an inflexible framework.

2e   GETTING IDEAS INTO A FIRST DRAFT

When writing a first draft, get your ideas down quickly. Spelling, punctuation, and correct usage are not important in the first draft—ideas are. Experienced writers like John Ciardi know that the most important thing about a first draft is to have done it, for it is something to work on—and against. Referring to a writer's frame of mind, Ciardi advises, "Write hot, edit cold." If you are not sure how to begin, look over some of the journal writing, listing, or outlining you have already done, and try to identify an issue or problem you can resolve or address by writing to a rhetorical audience. Your tentative thesis serves as your initial response to that opportunity to write. Then write down some main points you might like to develop, along with some supporting information for that development. Keep your overall plan in mind as you draft—or prop it up beside your computer screen. If you find yourself losing track of where you want to go, stop writing, reread what you have just written, and look again at your notes, however scrappy they seem. You might even talk with someone working on the same assignment, write in your journal, or imagine talking directly (rather than writing) to your intended audience. Most experienced writers revise their plans and rethink their topics as they write and revise. They anticipate—even welcome—such changes.

If you become stalled while attempting to write an early section of your essay, simply move to a later section, which might allow you to "restart your engine" by writing (rather than worrying about being stalled). Or work on something that seems easier to write, such as sentences that develop another supporting idea, an introduction, or a conclusion. Just keep writing, pursuing whatever path of thought interests you, always saving your drafts. You may well want to refer to that one "beautiful sentence" or brilliant detail in an earlier draft as you revise (chapter 3). Later in the revising process, you can experiment with ways of polishing, integrating, or deleting these passages (3f). What is important at this stage is to begin, remembering that writing is a form of discovering and understanding.

| **2f** | DRAFTING WELL-DEVELOPED PARAGRAPHS |

You compose a draft by developing paragraphs. If you are working from an informal list (2d), you will have a sense of where you want to take your ideas but may be uncertain about the number and nature of the paragraphs you will need. If you are working from an outline (2d), you can anticipate the number of paragraphs you will probably write and what you hope to accomplish in each paragraph. In the first case, you enjoy the freedom to pursue new ideas that occur as you draft. In the second, you enjoy the security of starting off with a clear direction. In both cases, however, your goal is to develop each paragraph fully and then ask yourself what additional paragraphs (or additional supporting information within any single paragraph) would further support your thesis statement and enhance your overall message in terms of your rhetorical opportunity, intended audience, and purpose.

Paragraphs have no set length. Typically, they range from 50 to 250 words, and paragraphs in books are usually longer than those in newspapers and magazines. There are certainly times when a long paragraph provides rich reading, as well as times when a long paragraph exhausts a single minor point, combines too many points, or becomes repetitive. On the other hand, short, one-sentence paragraphs can be used effectively to add emphasis (chapter 32) or to establish transition (3d). But short paragraphs can also indicate inadequate development. In that case, you can sometimes combine two or more short paragraphs (chapter 3) or expand a single one into a well-developed, well-supported, longer paragraph. Think of revising and developing your paragraphs as a luxury, an opportunity to articulate exactly what you want to say without anyone interrupting you—or changing the subject.

(1) Developing a paragraph with details

A good paragraph developed with details brings an idea to life. Consider the following well-developed paragraph by Brenda Jo Brueggemann:

3   *This reminds me of how I learned to drive growing up in western Kansas: my parents and grandparents turned me loose behind the wheel of grandpa's old blue Ford pickup in the big, open cow pasture behind their farm house, gave me some basic instructions on gears, clutches, brakes, accelerator—and then let me go.* It was exhilarating to get the feel of the thing, bumping along over gopher holes with dried cow patties flying behind me, creating a little dust cloud to mark the path I had taken, and not worrying about which way I should turn or go next. And I learned well the basics of the machine and its movement by driving this way. But soon I wanted more: a road to travel, a radio that actually worked, a destination and goal, a more finely tuned knowledge of navigation involving blinkers, lights, different driving conditions, and—most of all—the ability to travel and negotiate with others also on the road.

                —BRENDA JO BRUEGGEMANN, "American Sign Language and the Academy"

Notice how the series of details in paragraph 3 supports the main idea, or topic sentence (**3c**), which has been italicized to highlight it. Readers can easily see how one sentence leads into the next, creating a clear picture of the experience being described.

(2) Developing a paragraph with examples

Like details, examples contribute to paragraph development by making specific what otherwise might seem general and hard to grasp. **Details** describe a person, place, or thing; **examples** illustrate an idea with information that can come from different times and places. Both details and examples support the main idea of a paragraph.

The author of paragraph 4 uses several closely related examples (as well as details) to expand the idea of fourth-grade pressure with which she begins.

4   *I was in fourth grade and in trouble.* The students of Wildwood Elementary School in Burlington, Massachusetts, shifted in their uncomfortable metal seats as they waited for me to say my next line. A dog rested in my arms and an entire musical rested on my shoulders. I was playing Dorothy in *The Wizard of Oz*, and it was my turn to speak. Dorothy is *Hamlet* for girls. Next to Annie in *Annie* and Sandy in *Grease*, it is the dream role of every ten-year-old. Annie taught me that orphanages were a blast and being rich is the only thing that matters. *Grease* taught me being in a gang is nonstop fun and you need to dress sexier to have any chance of keeping a guy interested. But *The Wizard of Oz* was the ultimate. It dealt with friendship and fear and death and rainbows and sparkly red shoes.

—AMY POEHLER, *Yes Please*

Exercise 2

Examine some of your own writing—such as a recent draft of an essay, e-mail messages still on file, or entries in your journal—and select one paragraph that holds potential interest. Write out (by hand) the original paragraph. Then rewrite it, enriching and expanding it with additional details or examples.

2g EMPLOYING RHETORICAL METHODS OF DEVELOPMENT

When drafting an essay, you can develop a variety of paragraphs using **rhetorical methods**, approaches to writing that help you address and resolve various types of rhetorical opportunities. Using rhetorical methods can help you establish boundaries (definition); investigate similarities or differences (comparison or contrast); make sense of a person, place, or event (description and narration); organize concepts (classification and division), think critically about a process (process analysis or cause-and-consequence analysis); or convince someone (argumentation—see chapter 7). The strategies used for generating ideas, focusing a topic (2b), developing paragraphs and essays, and arranging ideas are already second nature to you. Every day, you use one or more of them to define a concept, narrate a significant incident, supply examples for an assertion, classify or divide information, compare two or more things, analyze a process, or identify a cause or consequence. As you draft, you may realize that you need to define a term or explain a process before you can take your readers further into your topic. Writers have the option of employing one, two, or several rhetorical methods to fulfill their overall purpose, which might be to explain, entertain, argue, or evaluate.

(1) Narration

A **narrative** discusses a sequence of events, normally in **chronological order** (the order in which they occur), to develop a particular point or set a mood. It often includes a setting, characters, dialogue, and description and usually makes use of transition words or phrases such as *first, then, later, that evening, the following week,* and so forth to guide readers from one incident to the next. Whatever its length, a narrative must remain focused on the main idea. The narrative in paragraph 5 traces Amy Poehler's role as Dorothy in the tornado scene:

5   In the second and final performance of *The Wizard of Oz*, I decided to take control during the tornado scene. I paused, put the blinking dog down on the stage, and walked a few feet away from it. "Toto, Toto! Where are you?" I said, pretending to look for my lost dog in the fearsome storm. The dog froze and played it perfectly. I got laughter

and some light applause for my efforts. I had improvised and it had worked. One could argue that it worked because of the dog. A good straight dog can really help sell a joke. Whatever. I have been chasing that high ever since.

—AMY POEHLER, *Yes Please*

(2) Description

By describing a person, place, object, or sensation, you can make your writing come alive. Often descriptions are predominantly visual, but even visual descriptions can include the details of what you hear, smell, taste, or touch; that is, descriptions appeal to the senses. The candy ad in Figure 2.1, for example, depends on the visual description of a smooth dark chocolate as well as the verbal description of a "delicious chocolate shell" and an "irresistibly smooth filling."

Description should align with your rhetorical opportunity as well as with your purpose and audience. In paragraph 6, Supreme Court Justice Sonia Sotomayor employs vivid descriptive details to convey how her working-poor Puerto Rican immigrant mother strived to comfort her children:

6   One memory of my mother's comforting sneaks up on me in the night sometimes. The bedroom I shared with Junior on Watson Avenue, with its one little window, was not just tiny but unbearably hot in summer. We had a little electric fan propped up on a chair, but it didn't help much. Sometimes I would wake up miserable in the middle of the night, with the pillow and sheets drenched in sweat, my hair dripping wet. Mami would come change the bed, whispering to me quietly in the dark so as not to wake Junior. Then she'd sit beside me with a pot of cold water and a washcloth and sponge me down until I fell asleep. The cool damp was so delicious, and her hands so firmly gentle—expert nurse's hands, I thought—that a part of me always tried to stay awake, to prolong this blissful taken-care-of feeling just a bit longer.

—SONIA SOTOMAYOR, *My Beloved World*

(3) Process analysis

Process paragraphs, in explaining how something is done or made, often use both description and narration. You might describe the items used in a process and then narrate the steps of the process

Image Courtesy of The Advertising Archives

Figure 2.1: The description of the candy and the appetizing image appeal to the reader's senses of taste and sight.

chronologically. By adding an explanation of a process to a draft, you could illustrate a concept that might otherwise be hard for your audience to grasp. In paragraph 7, Sam Swope explains the process by which an elementary school assistant principal tried (unsuccessfully) to intimidate students into identifying a fellow student who stole report cards.

7   Later that day, a frowning assistant principal appeared in the doorway, and the room went hush. Everyone knew why he was there. I'd known Mr. Ziegler only as a friendly, mild-mannered fellow with a comb-over, so I was shocked to see him play the heavy. His performance began calmly, reasonably, solemnly. He told the class that the administration was deeply disappointed, that this theft betrayed the trust of family, teachers, school, and country. Then he told the children it was their duty to report anything they'd seen or heard. When

Nito/Shutterstock.com

no one responded, he added a touch of anger to his voice, told the kids no stone would go unturned, the truth would out; he vowed he'd find the culprit—it was only a question of time! When this brought no one forward, he pumped up the volume. His face turned red, the veins on his neck bulged, and he wagged a finger in the air and shouted, "I'm not through with this investigation, not by a long shot! And if any of you know anything, you better come tell me, privately, in private, because they're going to be in a lot of trouble, *a lot of trouble!*"

—SAM SWOPE, "The Case of the Missing Report Cards"

(4) Cause-and-consequence analysis

Writers who analyze cause and consequence raise the question *Why?* and must answer it to the satisfaction of their audience, often differentiating the **primary cause** (the most important one) from **contributory causes** (which add to but do not directly cause an event or situation) and the **primary consequence** (the most important result) from **secondary consequences** (which are less important than the primary consequence). Writers who analyze cause and consequence usually link a sequence of events along a timeline. Always keep in mind, though, that just because one event occurs before—or after—another event does not necessarily make it a cause—or a consequence—of that event. In paragraph 8, journalist Christopher Hitchens analyzes the consequences of his chemotherapy.

8 It's quite something, this chemo-poison. It has caused me to lose about 14 pounds, though without making me feel any lighter. It has cleared up a vicious rash on my shins that no doctor could ever name, let alone cure. . . . Let it please be this mean and ruthless with the alien and its spreading dead-zone colonies. But as against that, the death-dealing stuff and life-preserving stuff have also made me strangely neuter. I was fairly reconciled to the loss of my hair, which began to come out in the shower in the first two weeks of treatment, and which I saved in a plastic bag so that it could help fill a floating dam in the Gulf of Mexico. But I wasn't quite prepared for the way that my razorblade would suddenly go slipping pointlessly down my face, meeting no stubble. Or for the way that my newly smooth upper lip would begin to look as if it had undergone electrolysis, causing me to look a bit too much like somebody's maiden auntie. (The chest hair that was once the toast of two continents hasn't yet wilted, but so much of it was shaved off for various hospital incisions that it's a rather

patchy affair.) I feel upsettingly de-natured. If Penélope Cruz were one of my nurses, I wouldn't even notice. In the war against Thanatos, if we must term it a war, the immediate loss of Eros is a huge initial sacrifice.

—CHRISTOPHER HITCHENS, "Topic of Cancer"

Writers also catalogue both causes and consequences, as Jordynn Jack does in paragraph 9, listing the possible contributions to and therapies for the condition known as autism.

9   [Activist mothers] argue against the dominant understanding of autism as a genetic neurological condition. [Jenny] McCarthy, and other mothers who agree with her position, argue instead that autism stems from a range of physiological conditions such as gastrointestinal dysfunction, vitamin deficiency, and chronic infections, which they attribute to a range of causes including vaccines, environmental toxins, processed foods, and allergies to gluten or casein. On the basis of this model, which they call the biomedical theory of autism, they focus their efforts on alternative health treatments, from dietary interventions to heavy metal chelation to hyperbaric oxygen therapy, all of which, they say, can help children recover from autism.

—JORDYNN JACK, *Autism and Gender: From Refrigerator Mothers to Computer Geeks*

(5) Comparison and contrast

A **comparison** points out similarities, and a **contrast** points out differences. When drafting, consider whether a comparison might help your readers see a relationship they might otherwise miss or whether a contrast might help them establish useful distinctions in order to better understand an issue or make a decision. Thus, paragraphs—or essays—that compare or contrast establish a relationship between two things (rather than simply listing all the points of comparison or contrast for one followed by all of them for the other). In paragraph 10, the Silicon Valley GOP (Republican) organization uses details to compare and contrast the positions the Republican and Democratic political parties take toward immigration and, thus, help potential voters make their decision at the polls. The poster in Figure 2.2 is a reminder to voters to act on that decision.

10   **Republicans** recognize that our nation is enriched by immigrants seeking a better life. In many cases immigrants have fled violence and oppression searching for peace and freedom. All suffered and sacrificed but hope for a better future for their children in America. Republicans agree that

Figure 2.2: This image creates a contrast using traditional symbols for the Republican and Democratic parties.

the lack of security along our borders has contributed to the flow of narco-trafficking, gang violence, and the yearly forced servitude and slavery of over 50,000 women and children from foreign countries by human smugglers. While our nation has been enriched by the determination, energy, and diversity of immigrants, Republicans believe that in this nation of laws, immigration policies should be followed and that securing our borders is vital to ensuring the safety of our citizens. **Democrats** believe that as the world superpower, it is a fundamental right for the United States to provide unconditional aid and comfort to the citizens of other nations. Democrats believe in open borders, unconditional amnesty, and that the laws of this nation be curtailed to provide non-emergency assistance and legal forms of identification to foreign nationals.

—SILICON VALLEY GOP

(6) Classification and division

To classify is to place things into groups based on shared characteristics. **Classification** is a way to understand or explain something by establishing how it fits within a category or group. For example, a book reviewer might classify a new novel as a mystery—leading readers to expect a plot based on suspense. **Division,** in contrast, separates something into component parts and examines the relationships among them. A novel can be discussed in terms of its components, such as plot, setting, and theme (chapter 12).

Classification and division represent two different perspectives: ideas can be put into groups (classification) or split into subclasses (division). As strategies for organizing (or developing) an idea, classification and division often work together. In paragraph 11, for example, both classification and division are used to differentiate among the range of human skin pigmentations (figure 2.3). Like many paragraphs, this one mixes rhetorical methods: the writer uses description, comparison and contrast, and cause-and-consequence analysis to support her major point of classification. Notice that the classification itself has a medical purpose: to evaluate the risk of skin cancer.

11　　In medicine, the classification of skin color has stemmed primarily from the need to quickly and reliably evaluate the risk of skin cancer in light-skinned patients, in the setting of a doctor's office. Because lightly pigmented people differ in their ability to tan and are not equally susceptible to sunburn and skin cancer risk, the method of skin phototyping, developed in 1975, helps physicians accurately predict a person's reaction

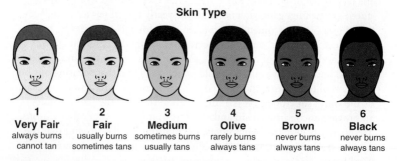

Skin Type

1	2	3	4	5	6
Very Fair	**Fair**	**Medium**	**Olive**	**Brown**	**Black**
always burns cannot tan	usually burns sometimes tans	sometimes burns usually tans	rarely burns always tans	never burns always tans	never burns always tans

Figure 2.3: The Fitzpatrick Scale (also Fitzpatrick skin typing or Fitzpatrick phototyping scale) is a numerical classification schema for the color of skin.

to moderate sun exposure. According to this classification system, there are six skin phototypes: three are referred to as "melanocompromised" (phototypes I–III) and three are considered "melanocompetent" (phototypes IV–VI). The definition of sun exposure in this system is thirty minutes of unprotected exposure without sunscreen at peak (summer) UVR levels.

—NINA G. JABLONSKI, *Skin: A Natural History*

(7) Definition

By defining a concept or a term, you efficiently clarify your meaning and so develop an idea. By defining a word for your readers, you immediately connect with them; they know what you are and are not talking about. Definitions are usually constructed in a two-step process: the first step locates a term by placing it in a class; the second step differentiates this particular term from other terms in the same class. For instance, "A concerto [the term] is a symphonic piece [the class] consisting of three movements performed by one or more solo instruments accompanied at times by an orchestra [the difference]." A symphony belongs to the same basic class as a concerto; it too is a symphonic piece. However, a symphony can be differentiated from a concerto in two specific ways: a symphony consists of four movements, and its performance involves the entire orchestra.

Paragraph 12 defines volcanoes by putting them into a class ("landforms") and by distinguishing them ("built of molten material") from other members of that class. The definition is then clarified by examples.

12 Volcanoes are landforms built of molten material that has spewed out onto the earth's surface. Such molten rock is called lava. Volcanoes may be no larger than small hills, or thousands of feet high. All have a characteristic cone shape. Some well-known mountains are actually volcanoes. Examples are Mt. Fuji (Japan), Mt. Lassen (California), Mt. Hood (Oregon), Mt. Etna and Mt. Vesuvius (Italy), and Paricutín (Mexico). The Hawaiian Islands are all immense volcanoes whose summits rise above the ocean, and these volcanoes are still quite active.

—JOEL AREM, *Rocks and Minerals*

Using definition and the other rhetorical methods just described will make your writing more understandable to your audience, because all of us—writers and readers, speakers and listeners—employ these rhetorical methods to help us make sense of the world around us. Even though these methods are familiar, however, you need to make sure that you use the one(s) best suited to your rhetorical situation, to supporting your thesis and making your purpose clear to your intended audience. As you draft and revise, you can easily check to see whether the rhetorical method employed in each paragraph keeps your essay anchored to its thesis statement and helps you address your rhetorical opportunity. You may need to expand, condense, or delete paragraphs accordingly (3c and 3f).

3 || REVISING AND EDITING ESSAYS

Revising, which literally means "seeing again," lies at the heart of all successful writing. When you are revising your writing, you resee it in the role of reader rather than writer. Revising involves considering a number of global issues: how successfully you have responded to the opportunity, how successfully you have conveyed your purpose to your rhetorical audience, how clearly you have stated your thesis, how effectively you have arranged your information, and how thoroughly you have developed your assertions with good reasons. **Editing**, on the other hand, focuses on local issues, which are smaller in scale. When you are editing, you polish your writing: you choose words more precisely (chapter **35**), shape prose more distinctly (chapter **36**), and structure sentences more effectively (chapters **28–33**). While you are editing, you are also **proofreading**, focusing even more sharply to eliminate surface errors in grammar, punctuation, and mechanics. Revising and editing often overlap (just as drafting and revising do), and peer review can be helpful throughout these stages of the writing process. Usually, revising occurs before editing, but not always. Edited passages may be redrafted, rearranged, and even cut as you revise further.

As you revise and edit your essays, this chapter will help you

- consider your work as a whole (**3a(1)** and **3a(2)**),
- evaluate your tone (**3a(3)**),
- compose an effective introduction and conclusion (**3b**),
- strengthen the unity and coherence of paragraphs (**3c**),
- improve transitions (**3d**),
- benefit from a reviewer's comments (**3e**),
- edit to improve style (**3f**),
- proofread to eliminate surface errors (**3g**), and
- submit a final draft (**3h**).

3a | THE ESSENTIALS OF REVISION

As you already know, you are revising throughout all the planning and drafting stages of your writing process, whether at the concept, word, phrase, sentence, or paragraph level. Even so, you will still do most of your revising after you have completed your initial draft. At that point, you read through the entire draft, reconsidering it as a whole at the same time that you rewrite specific sentences and paragraphs. A few writers prefer to start revising immediately after drafting, while their minds are still fully engaged by their topic. But most writers like to let a draft "cool off," so that when they return to it, they can assess it more objectively, with fresh eyes. Even an overnight cooling-off period will give you more objectivity as a reader and will reveal more options to you as a writer. You will be surprised at the good ideas that come to you as you sleep.

⊙ TECH SAVVY

Most word-processing programs enable you to track your revisions easily using a feature like Microsoft Word's Track Changes. Tracking changes is especially useful if your instructor requires you to submit all your drafts or if one or more peers are reviewing your drafts.

(1) Revising purposefully

As you reread a draft, you need to keep in mind your rhetorical audience, your purpose, and your thesis. Do you reach, maybe even please, your audience in every paragraph? Do you maintain your purpose throughout every single paragraph? Which paragraphs extend and support your thesis? Which ones repeat, contradict, or productively contradict what has come before? Which of your paragraphs simply digress (3c)?

Revision should enhance the development of your thesis while strengthening the connection between your rhetorical audience (1c) and purpose (1d). In order to meet the needs, the expectations, and even the resistance of those in your rhetorical audience, try to anticipate their point of view, their values, and their interests. By taking seriously the values of your audience, you can better anticipate their response (understanding, acceptance, or opposition) to your thesis statement, to each of your assertions, to the supporting examples and details you employ, and to the language you choose. In other words, revising successfully requires that you reread your work as both a writer and a reader. As a writer, ask yourself whether your words accurately reflect your purpose, meaning, and respect for your rhetorical audience. As a reader, ask yourself whether what seems clear and logical to you will also be clear to others.

(2) Adding essential information

Writers are always aware of what they have put on the page—but they seldom spend enough time considering what they may have left out. In order to ensure that you have provided all the information necessary for a reader to consider your thesis and supporting assertions, review the following questions: How might your rhetorical audience address or resolve the rhetorical opportunity for change? What does your audience already believe about this topic or issue? What information might your audience be expecting, pleased with, or surprised by? What specific information might strengthen your thesis in terms of purpose and audience?

Keep in mind that your best ideas will not always surface in your first draft; you will sometimes come up with an important idea only after you have finished that draft, let it cool off, and then looked at it again. No matter how complete a draft seems, you can use questioning strategies to check whether anything is missing (2a(3)) and whether an additional explanation, description, or example would strengthen your message and your connection with your audience. You might also share your draft with a peer who is working on the same assignment, asking that person to mark confusing, unclear, or provocative passages (3e).

(3) Creating the right tone

Tone reflects a writer's attitude toward the topic (1a). An appropriate tone is essential for engaging your rhetorical audience and achieving your purpose. As you read through your draft, then, compare the tone with your intended tone. Academic, workplace, and personal writing all call for an appropriate tone, one that accurately reflects your intention, as well as your confidence, your preparation, your fair-mindedness, and, perhaps most of all, your willingness to cooperate with your audience. You want all your words as well as your sentence structures to convey your intended tone. If any of the passages in your draft sound defensive, self-centered, uninformed, or undeveloped to you or to a peer reviewer, revise them. You want to ensure that your tone helps elicit from your readers the desired response—to you as well as to the information you are presenting.

Consider the tone in paragraph 1, in which Dorothy Allison describes some of the positive and negative things she remembers about growing up in South Carolina. (For ease of reference, each of the sample paragraphs in this chapter is numbered.)

1   Where I was born—Greenville, South Carolina—smelled like nowhere else I've ever been. Cut wet grass, split green apples, baby shit and beer bottles, cheap makeup and motor oil. Everything was ripe, everything was rotting. Hound dogs butted my calves. People shouted in the distance; crickets boomed in my ears. That country was beautiful, I swear to you, the most beautiful place I've ever been. Beautiful and terrible. It is the country of my dreams and the country of my nightmares: a pure pink and blue sky, red dirt, white clay, and all that endless green—willows and dogwood and firs going on for miles.

—**DOROTHY ALLISON,** *Two or Three Things I Know for Sure*

Exercise 1

Establishing a distinctive tone, create a paragraph about the place (city, town, building, or neighborhood) where you grew up. Identify specific words and phrases from paragraph 1 that helped you with your version. Be prepared to share your list of words and phrases with the class.

When Mary LeNoir revised the first draft reprinted later in this chapter (pages 85–94), she decided to adjust her tone because she thought it seemed too dry and academic. Of course, Mary wanted to sound like she had a lot of knowledge and insight about her topic. But she also wanted to connect immediately with her audience, helping them recognize that her essay could help clear up the question of how high school student-athletes actually choose a college. To meet her goals, she revised her introduction, striking a more natural and inviting tone that better aligned with her rhetorical opportunity (**1a**).

▣ TECH SAVVY ▬▬▬▬▬▬

The thesaurus in your word-processing program may give you advice that can affect the tone of your writing. This tool is easy to use; however, only you can make the word choices that will achieve the appropriate tone. For example, a thesaurus may suggest a synonym for a word that you have been intentionally repeating in order to establish a rhythm. Carefully consider the suggestions a thesaurus makes, weighing those suggestions in terms of your rhetorical opportunity as you revise.

3b   GUIDING READERS WITH THE INTRODUCTION AND THE CONCLUSION

Your introduction and conclusion orient your readers to the purpose of your essay as a whole. In fact, readers intentionally read these two sections for guidance and clarification.

(1) An effective introduction

Experienced writers know that the opening paragraph is their best chance to arouse the reader's interest with provocative information; identify rhetorical opportunity, topic, purpose, and writer as worthy of consideration; and set the overall tone. An effective introduction makes the intended audience want to read on. In paragraph 2, herpetologist Rick Roth introduces himself to a diverse audience, readers of *Sierra* magazine.

> 2   A lot of people know me as "Snake Man" now and don't know my real name. I've always been a critter person. My mother was never afraid of anything, and I used to actually get to keep snakes in the house. I'm 58, so this was a long time ago, when *nobody* got to keep snakes in the house. I've got 75 or so now at home—and a really cool landlord.
>
>   **—RICK ROTH, "Snake Charmer"**

Roth's friendly introduction immediately grabs readers' attention with his down-home language and unusual partiality for snakes. He then moves quickly to his childhood fascination with butterflies and dragonflies (thereby establishing common ground with those of his readers who are agitated by snakes) and goes on to explain his current occupation as the executive director of the Cape Ann Vernal Pond Team.

Introductions have no set length; they can be as brief as a couple of sentences or as long as two or more paragraphs, sometimes even longer. Although introductions always appear first, they are often drafted and revised after other parts of an essay. Just like the thesis statements they often include, introductions evolve during the drafting and revising stages, as the material is shaped, focused, and developed toward fulfilling the writer's overall purpose. Most writers experiment with several different introductions to determine which one is most effective.

You can awaken the interest of your audience by writing introductions in a number of ways.

(a) Opening with an unusual fact or statistic

3   Americans aren't just reading fewer books, but are reading less and less of everything, in any medium. That's the doleful conclusion of "To Read or Not to Read," a report released last week by the National Endowment for the Arts.

—JENNIFER HOWARD, "Americans Are Closing the Book on Reading, Study Finds"

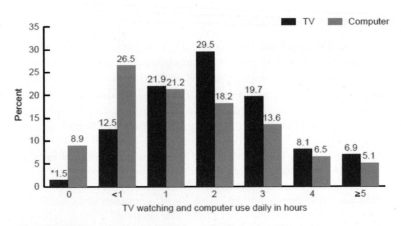

Figure 3.1: This bar graph from the Centers for Disease Control gives some clues about what Americans might be doing instead of reading.
Source: CDC/NCHS, National Health and Nutrition Examination Survey (NHANES) and NHANES National Youth Fitness Survey, 2012

(b) Opening with an intriguing statement

4   I belong to a Clan of One-Breasted Women. My mother, my grand-
mothers, and six aunts have all had mastectomies. Seven are dead. The
two who survive have just completed rounds of chemotherapy and
radiation.

—TERRY TEMPEST WILLIAMS, "The Clan of One-Breasted Women"

(c) Opening with an anecdote or example

5   I chuckled in amusement . . . as President Obama regaled the audience with his humor in what has to be one of the most enjoyable roles for
the commander-in-chief: standup comedian at the annual dinner for the
White House Correspondents Association. Obama's pace and timing were
a lot better than those of the professional comics charged with bringing
down the house that night. . . . Obama . . . was smooth and effortless,
confident that his zingers would find their mark. His swag quotient was
also pretty high that night. He let it be known that his musical prowess
consisted of more than a melodically accurate one-off rendition of a line
from Al Green's R&B classic "Let's Stay Together," which he had delivered
at an Apollo Theater fundraiser three months earlier. Obama's version of
the soul legend's tune went viral in Black communities as a sign of the
president's effortless embrace of Black Culture despite the criticism that
he keeps Blackness at bay. . . . At the Correspondents' dinner, Obama
showed his appreciation for Hip Hop and proved his Rap bona fides, and
not just by citing the easy or apparent fare. To truly strut his stuff, he'd
have to display an aficionado's grasp of Rap Culture's rage and appeal and
flash a little insider savvy.

—MICHAEL ERIC DYSON, "Orator in Chief"

(d) Opening with a question

6   A vast question loomed over all of my learning with the youth of
South Vista [California]: what is the purpose of schooling in a pluralist
society? The history of schooling in the United States, a country home
to epic linguistic, racial, and cultural diversity, has traditionally defined
this purpose rather clearly. The purpose of schooling has been to transition or mainstream the ways of knowing and being of those whose
cultures and languages fall outside the dominant stream into White,
DAE [dominant American English], middle-class norms. Yet volumes of
research and theorizing in the past three decades have profoundly challenged these narrow assimilatory goals. This work has critiqued both
the unsatisfactory academic results for young people of color and the

perpetuation of racial and cultural bias through assimilatory models of education.

—DJANGO PARIS, *Language across Difference*

(e) Opening with an appropriate quotation

7   "My wife and I like the kind of trouble you've been stirring, Miss Williams," he said, with a smile and a challenge. He had an avuncular, wizardy twinkle, very Albus Dumbledore. It made me feel feisty and smart, like Hermione Granger. They *liked* my kind of trouble. But let this be a lesson: When a woman of my great dignity and years loses her sanity and starts imagining she's one of Harry Potter's magical little friends, you can be sure that the cosmic gyroscope is wobbling off its center. . . .

—PATRICIA J. WILLIAMS, *Open House: Of Family, Friends, Food, Piano Lessons, and the Search for a Room of My Own*

(f) Opening with general information or background about the topic

8   Scientists have long touted the benefits of the Mediterranean diet for heart health. But now researchers are finding more and more evidence that the diet can keep you healthy in other ways, too, including lowering the risk of certain cancers and easing the pain and stiffness of arthritis.

—MELISSA GOTTHARDT, "The Miracle Diet"

(g) Opening with a thesis statement

9   Thinking is an action. For all aspiring intellectuals, thoughts are the laboratory where one goes to pose questions and find answers, and the place where visions of theory and praxis come together. The heartbeat of critical thinking is the longing to know—to understand how life works. Children are organically predisposed to be critical thinkers. Across the boundaries of race, class, gender, and circumstance, children come into the world of wonder and language consumed with a desire for knowledge. Sometimes they are so eager for knowledge that they become relentless interrogators—demanding to know the who, what, when, where, and why of life. Searching for answers, they learn almost instinctively how to think.

—BELL HOOKS, *Teaching Critical Thinking: Practical Wisdom*

However you open your essay, use your introduction to specify your topic, engage your readers' attention, initiate an appropriate tone aligned with your purpose, and establish your credibility (7f(1)).

(2) An effective conclusion

Just as a good introduction tantalizes readers, a good conclusion satisfies them. It helps readers recognize the important points of your essay and the significance of those points while, at the same time, wrapping up the essay in a meaningful, thought-provoking way. As you draft and revise, you may want to keep a list of ideas for your conclusion. Some suggestions for writing effective conclusions follow, beginning with the reliable method of simply restating the thesis and main points. This kind of conclusion can be effective for a long essay that includes several important points that you want the reader to recall.

(a) Rephrasing the thesis and summarizing the main points

10   The Endangered Species Act should not take into account economic considerations. Economics doesn't know how to value a species or a forest. Its logic drives people to exploit resources to the point of extinction. The Endangered Species Act tells us that extinction is morally unacceptable. It was enacted by a Congress and president in a wise mood, to express a higher value than a bottom line.

—DONELLA MEADOWS, "Not Seeing the Forest for the Dollar Bills"

(b) Calling attention to larger issues

11   While a [maple syrup] boil can have you hanging around the evaporator for twelve hours at a time and doing something to adjust the fire or draw off syrup every twenty or thirty minutes, you're generally just hanging out. There's no time to grade papers, and not even much time to read. But it's perfect for talking, for dreaming, and for listening to Caleb lift the occasional swirling fiddle tune up into the stream. As when I worked with Matthew putting up the roof, this has proved a great time with both boys. At Middlebury College I can count on extended conversations with students in my office. But our own college-age children, not surprisingly, rarely want to settle down for a long talk with Rita and me in the living room. At the sugarhouse, though, we can all have a never-ending sequence of five-minute conversations—about family members near and far, about movies or books, about the sounds and animals and boulders and brooks of the surrounding woods. These bursts of talk add up. They are the real sugaring off from the seasons that have brought us here.

—JOHN ELDER, *The Frog Run: Words & Wildness in the Vermont Woods*

(c) Calling for a change in action or attitude

12   Although [Anna Julia] Cooper published *A Voice* in 1892, its political implications remain relevant to twenty-first-century scholars and activists. As our society grows increasingly multicultural, and the borders between colors and countries grow ever more porous, the strategies for organizing communities of resistance must necessarily follow suit. Academics and activists engaged in efforts to transform inequitable social relations benefit from thinking not only about what separates but also what unites humanity.

—KATHY L. GLASS, "Tending to the Roots"

(d) Concluding with a vivid image

13   The more I wrote about [my jealousy] and the more I thought of the [AIDS] movie, the angrier I got at how often this writer friend mentioned her money to me, because that summer Sam and I had almost none, and she knew this. I kept writing about my childhood, about how often I had longed for what other girls had and for what other families seemed to be about. I taped Hillel's line to the wall by my desk: "I get up. I walk. I fall down. Meanwhile, I keep dancing." The way I dance is by writing. So I wrote about trying to pay closer attention to the world, about taking things less seriously, moving more slowly, stepping outside more often. Eventually what I was writing got funnier and compassion broke through, for me and also for my writer friend. And at this point I told her, as kindly as possible, that I needed a sabbatical from our friendship. Life really is so short. And finally I felt that my jealousy and I were strangely beautiful, like the men in the AIDS movie, doing the dance of the transformed self, dancing like an old long-legged bird.

—ANNE LAMOTT, "Jealousy"

(e) Connecting with the introduction

The introduction

14   The future of digital culture—yours, mine, and ours—depends on how well we learn to use the media that have infiltrated, amplified, distracted, enriched, and complicated our lives. How you employ a search engine, stream video from your phonecam, or update your Facebook status matters to you and everyone, because the ways people use new media in the first years of an emerging communication regime

can influence the way those media end up being used and misused for decades to come. Instead of confining my exploration to whether or not Google is making us stupid, Facebook is commoditizing our privacy, or Twitter is chopping our attention into microslices (all good questions), I've been asking myself and others how to use social media intelligently, humanely, and above all mindfully. This book is about what I've learned.

—HOWARD RHEINGOLD, *Net Smart: How to Thrive Online*

Throughout his book-length study, Howard Rheingold provides an insightful examination of the ways these new media are shaping our lives at the same time that we are shaping their use, all the while stressing the importance of keeping alert to the powers and limits of any new technology.

The conclusion

15   As laptop-carrying, smart-phone-using members of the digitally connected infosphere, we need to start by learning a new discipline: the literacy of attention. As citizens and cocreators of the cultures that shape us, we need participatory media skills. As collaborators in the collective intelligence that faces massive problems from global warming to water-sharing conflicts, we need to learn literacies of cooperation, mass collaboration, and collective action. As dwellers in the network society, we must understand and master the nature along with use of social networks, technical and human—and grasp the way both mediated and face-to-face social practices can increase or drain social capital. And in a world where nobody can trust the authority of any text they find online, the ability to quickly evaluate the validity or bogosity of information is no longer an intellectual nicety. Critical thinking about media practices has become an essential, learnable mental skill.

— HOWARD RHEINGOLD, *Net Smart: How to Thrive Online*

Whatever technique you choose for your conclusion, provide readers with a sense of closure. Bear in mind that they may be wondering, "So what? Why have you told me all this?" Your conclusion gives you an opportunity to address that concern. If there is any chance that readers may not understand your purpose, use your conclusion to clarify why you think they needed to read what they have just read.

Exercise 2

Thumb through a magazine you enjoy, skimming the introductions of all the articles. Select two introductions that catch your attention. Consider the reasons *why* they interest you. What specific techniques for an introduction did the authors use? Next, look through the same or another magazine for two effective conclusions. Analyze their effectiveness as well. Be prepared to share your findings with the rest of the class.

3c   REVISING FOR UNIFIED AND COHERENT PARAGRAPHS

When revising the body of an essay, writers are likely to find opportunities for further development within each paragraph (2f and 2g) and to discover ways to make each paragraph more unified by relating every sentence within the paragraph to a single main idea (3c(2)), which might appear in a topic sentence. After weeding out unrelated sentences, writers concentrate on coherence, ordering the sentences so that ideas progress logically and smoothly from one sentence to the next. A successful paragraph is well developed, unified, and coherent.

(1) Expressing the main idea in a topic sentence

Much like the thesis statement of an essay, a **topic sentence** states the main idea of a paragraph and comments on that main idea. Although the topic sentence is usually the first sentence in a paragraph, it can appear in any position within the paragraph, even as the closing sentence. Sometimes, paragraphs build up to the final, topic sentence; other times, all the sentences together imply an unstated topic sentence. If you want to ensure that your paragraphs are unified and coherent, you might want to place the topic sentence at the beginning of each paragraph. A topic sentence in that location will both remind you of your focus and be obvious to your readers, who will recognize and then follow your main idea immediately. More experienced writers often add interest to their writing by varying the placement of their topic sentences within different paragraphs.

When you announce your general topic in a topic sentence and then provide specific support for it, you are writing **deductively**. Your topic sentence appears first, like the one in italics in paragraph 16, which indicates that the author will offer evidence as to why we are suspicious of rapid cognition.

16   *I think we are innately suspicious of . . . rapid cognition.* We live in a world that assumes that the quality of a decision is directly related to the time and effort that went into making it. When doctors are faced with a difficult diagnosis, they order more tests, and when we are uncertain about what we hear, we ask for a second opinion. And what do we tell our children? Haste makes waste. Look before you leap. Stop and *think.* Don't judge a book by its cover. We believe that we are always better off gathering as much information as possible and spending as much time as possible in deliberation. We really only trust conscious decision making. But there are moments, particularly in times of stress, when haste does not make waste, when our snap judgments and first impressions can offer a much better means of making sense of the world.

—MALCOLM GLADWELL, *Blink*

If you want to emphasize the main idea of a paragraph or give its organization some extra support, you can begin and conclude the paragraph with two versions of the same idea. This strategy is particularly useful for long paragraphs because it gives readers whose attention may have wandered a second chance to grasp the main idea. In paragraph 17, both the first sentence and the last convey the idea that the English language has become a global language.

17   *English is the most widely spoken language in the history of our planet, used in some way by at least one out of every seven human beings around the globe.* Half of the world's books are written in English, and the majority of international telephone calls are made in English. English is the language of over sixty percent of the world's radio programs, many of them beamed, ironically, by the Russians, who know that to win friends and influence nations, they're best off using English. More than seventy percent of international mail is written and addressed in English, and eighty percent of all computer text is stored in English. *English has acquired the largest vocabulary of all the world's languages, perhaps as many as two million words, and has generated one of the noblest bodies of literature in the annals of the human race.*

—RICHARD LEDERER, "English Is a Crazy Language"

As you prepare to revise a draft, try underlining the topic sentences you can identify. If you cannot find a topic sentence in one of your paragraphs, add a sentence stating the main idea of that paragraph. If you find that you open every paragraph with a topic sentence, you might try experimenting with another pattern, revising a paragraph so that the topic sentence appears at the end, as in paragraph 18.

18   In 1982 my parents moved from Fargo, North Dakota, to Paxton [Nebraska] after a sudden job loss, simply because they weren't sure where else to go, and my brother and I had to be enrolled in school. My grandma told her son, my dad, "Come home for now." When we got to town, it was as if everyone was waiting. Mom took us to school, where the principal said, "You're Jack's kids? You'll do well, then." Down at Hehnke's grocery store, Henry welcomed us, embraced my dad. To me it wasn't a homecoming, despite how excited I was to be near my grandma and aunt. This wasn't our first move. In the past few years, I had lived in Minnesota and both of the Dakotas—I was tired of moving. Yet here it was different. Everything around me was both familiar and unfamiliar. *I carried with me the legacy of four generations of Osborns and Hoggs. In this town I was both insider and outsider.*

—**CHARLOTTE HOGG**, *From the Garden Club: Rural Women Writing Community*

Placing the topic sentence at the end of the paragraph works well when you are moving from specific supporting details to a generalization about those ideas—that is, when you are writing **inductively**. Effective writers try to meet the expectations of their readers, which often include the anticipation that the first sentence will be the topic sentence; however, writers and readers alike enjoy an occasional departure from the expected. And writers need to adjust paragraph structure to reflect the rhetorical purpose of each paragraph.

(2) Creating unified paragraphs

Paragraphs are **unified** when every sentence relates to the main idea; unity is violated when something unrelated to the rest of the material appears. Consider the obvious violation in paragraph 19.

19   The first time I visited Ohio State, I was stunned by the sheer size of it all. Nearly 50,000 students mobbed the main campus: undergrad, grad, dental, law, and medical students, people from all over the world. Hundreds of buildings, even more streets, alleys, dead ends, cubbyholes, and tucked-away coffee shops comprise an academic city, somehow separate from Columbus, Ohio, with which it shares a main street. High Street

neatly bisects Columbus from north to south, and the shot through campus is lined with head shops, pizza joints, and chains of restaurants, cell-phone companies, and running-shoe stores. *Yet that campus became so very familiar to me.* The thousands of Ohio State students live on and off campus, spreading out across both sides of High Street and stretching from North High, right smack in Worthington, to South High, in the Short North neighborhood. They live in dorm rooms, suites, old houses chopped up into apartments, high-rises, condos, and rented rooms. Yet despite the broad swathe of student housing, both on and off campus, despite the fact that students constantly bring the gritty and glassy parts of "Columbus" onto campus and the intellectual facets of campus into the city, the campus itself continues to feel like its own city, a city of museums, parks, lakes, libraries, galleries, arenas, parking decks, auditoriums, halls, and, of course, classrooms. A separate city. A big city. Little wonder that campus administrators have made "town-gown" relations a top priority.

Easy to delete, the italicized sentence about the campus becoming familiar violates the unity of a paragraph devoted to the description of a city within a city. But if the purpose of the essay had been to demonstrate how the biggest of cities could become smaller with each exploration, then the writer could develop that sentence into a separate paragraph.

As you revise your paragraphs for unity, the following tips may help you.

TIPS FOR IMPROVING PARAGRAPH UNITY

- **Identify.** Identify the topic sentence for each paragraph. Where is each located? Why is each one located where it is?

- **Relate.** Read each sentence in a paragraph and determine how (and if) it relates directly to or develops the topic sentence.

- **Eliminate.** Any sentence that does not relate to the topic sentence violates the unity of the paragraph—cut it, revise it, or save it to use elsewhere.

- **Clarify.** If a sentence "almost" relates to the topic sentence, either revise it or delete it. As you revise, you might clarify details or add information or a transitional word or phrase to make the relationship clear.

- **Rewrite.** If more than one idea is being conveyed in a single paragraph, either rewrite the topic sentence so that it includes both ideas and establishes a relationship between them or split the single paragraph into two paragraphs, dividing up the information accordingly.

(3) Arranging ideas into coherent paragraphs

Some paragraphs are unified (3c(2)) but not coherent. In a unified paragraph, every sentence relates to the main idea of the paragraph. In a **coherent** paragraph, the relationship among the ideas is clear and meaningful, and the progression from one sentence to the next is easy for readers to follow. Paragraph 20 has unity but lacks coherence.

Lacks coherence

20   The land was beautiful, gently rolling hills, an old orchard with fruit-bearing potential, a small clear stream—over eleven acres. But the house itself was another story. It had sat empty for years. Perhaps not empty, though that's what the realtor told us. There were macaroni and cheese boxes, how-to-play the mandolin books and videos, extra countertops, a kitchen sink, single socks looking for their mates, a ten-year-old pan of refried beans, and all sorts of random stuff strewn all through the house. Had the owner stayed there until he gave up on remodeling it? Had homeless people squatted there? Or had it been a hangout for teenagers—until the hole in the roof got too big for comfort? Who had been living there, and what kind of damage had they brought to the house? *We looked at the house with an eye toward buying it.* The price was right: very low, just what we could afford. And the location and acreage were perfect, too. But the house itself was a wreck. It needed a new roof, but it also needed a kitchen, flooring, drywall, updated plumbing and electricity—and a great big dumpster. We didn't know if we had the energy, let alone the know-how, to fix it up. Plus it wasn't like it was just the two of us we had to think about. We had three children to consider. If we bought it, where would we start working to make it inhabitable?

Although every sentence in this paragraph has to do with the writer's reaction to a house offered for sale, the sentences themselves are not arranged coherently; they are not in any logical order. First, the italicized topic sentence could be moved to the beginning of the paragraph, where it could control the meaningful flow of ideas. Then, the other sentences could be clustered according to subtopic: the land, the condition of the house, and the potential advantages and disadvantages of the purchase.

Revised for coherence

21   *We looked at the house with an eye toward buying it.* The land was beautiful, gently rolling hills, an old orchard with fruit-bearing potential, a small

clear stream—over eleven acres. But the house itself was another story. It had sat empty for years. Perhaps not empty, though that's what the realtor told us. There were macaroni and cheese boxes, how-to-play the mandolin books and videos, extra countertops, a kitchen sink, single socks looking for their mates, a ten-year-old pan of refried beans, and all sorts of random stuff strewn all through the house. Had the owner stayed there until he gave up on remodeling it? Had homeless people squatted there? Or had it been a hangout for teenagers—until the hole in the roof got too big for comfort? By now, the house needed a new roof as well as a kitchen, flooring, drywall, updated plumbing and electricity—and a great big dumpster. We didn't know if we had the energy, let alone the know-how, to fix it up. Plus it wasn't like it was just the two of us we had to think about. We had three children to consider. Still, the price was right: very low, just what we could afford. And the location and acreage were perfect, too.

Paragraph 21 is coherent as well as unified.

To achieve coherence as well as unity in your paragraphs, study the following patterns of organization (chronological, spatial, emphatic, and logical), and consider which ones you might use in your own writing.

(a) Using chronological order

When you use **chronological order**, you arrange ideas according to the order in which things happened. This organizational pattern is particularly useful for narration.

22   The story of blues, black rock, and funk has yet to be told without the intrusion of white rock as a reference point, yet the continuity is as fluid as a Hendrix guitar solo. Despite the efforts of the great black rock and rollers Chuck Berry, Little Richard, Bo Diddley, and Fats Domino, by the time of the rise of Elvis Presley in the early 1960s, rock music had become a white form. The mid-sixties' so-called "British Invasion" of the rock bands from Europe, led by the Beatles, the Rolling Stones, and the Animals, reinforced this myth, despite the fact that the groups were all profoundly influenced by the blues and black R&B of the 1950s. The musical dominance of Sly Stone and Jimi Hendrix in the latter part of the 1960s finally served to uproot the myth of rock as a white phenomenon. But in only a few short years rock music was resegregated by a shrewd music industry. It was not until the phenomenal crossover success of Prince in 1984 that the popular white image of rock and roll came under scrutiny once again.

—**RICKEY VINCENT**, *Funk: The Music, the People, and the Rhythm of the One*

(b) Using spatial order

When you arrange ideas according to **spatial order**, you orient the reader's focus from right to left, near to far, top to bottom, and so on. This organizational pattern is particularly effective in descriptions. Often the organization is so obvious that the writer can forgo a topic sentence, as in paragraph 23.

23   I went to see a prospective student, Steve, up on the North Branch Road. His mother, Tammi, told me to look for the blue trailer with cars in the yard. There were *lots* of junk cars—rusted, hoods up, and wheels off, a Toyota truck filled with bags of trash. The yard was littered with transmission parts, hubcaps, empty soda bottles, Tonka trucks, deflated soccer balls, retired chain saws and piles of seasoned firewood hidden in the overgrowth of jewelweed. A pen held an assortment of bedraggled, rain-soaked chickens and a belligerent, menacing turkey. A small garden of red and yellow snapdragons marked the way to the door.

    —TAL BIRDSEY, *A Room for Learning: The Making of a School in Vermont*

(c) Using emphatic order

When you use **emphatic order**, you arrange information in order of importance, usually from least to most important. Emphatic order is especially useful in expository and persuasive writing, both of which involve helping readers understand logical relationships (such as what caused something to happen or what kinds of priorities should be established). The information in paragraph 24 leads up to the writer's conclusion—that forgiveness can be liberating.

24   In talking to people about forgiveness, I've been surprised at the resistance that some smart, sensitive people feel to this subject. They believe that to forgive is to condone somehow the harmful things people have done; that it's not only a pardon for past crimes but a virtual license to commit them again; that to forgive is to lack the guts to call a spade a spade and to condemn what deserves condemnation. They feel that the admonition to forgive is a kind of coercion that takes no account of the offense, the presence, absence, or degree of contrition in the offender, or the emotional readiness of the victim to let go. I have a friend who told me point-blank, and with some passion, "I don't believe in forgiveness," largely for these reasons. But she admitted, "Once I understand, I can't hold a grudge any more. That's a big thing for me. Understanding."

    —ROBERT KAREN, *The Forgiving Self: The Road from Resentment to Connection*

(d) Using logical order

Sometimes the movement within a paragraph follows a **logical order**, from specific to general or from general to specific. A paragraph may begin with a series of details and conclude with a summarizing statement, as paragraphs 18 and 25 do, or it may begin with a general statement or idea, which is then supported by particular details, as in paragraphs 21 and 26.

25   Whether one reads for work or for pleasure, comprehension is the goal. Comprehension is an active process; readers must interact and be engaged with a text. To accomplish this, proficient readers use strategies or conscious plans of action. Less proficient readers often lack awareness of comprehension strategies, however, and cannot develop them on their own. For adult literacy learners in particular, integrating and synthesizing information from any but the simplest texts can pose difficulties.

—MARY E. CURTIS AND JOHN R. KRUIDENIER, *"Teaching Adults to Read"*

26   Regardless of the factors that make us more or less able to handle difficult experiences, it's important when taking up mindfulness practice to be aware of your capacities and limits. Some practices, such as sitting with the breath for long periods or participating in a silent meditation retreat, tend to bring up difficult thoughts and feelings. Freud discovered that if he simply asked a patient to lie on a couch and say whatever came to mind, eventually all sorts of unwanted thoughts and feelings would emerge. Similarly, sitting in silent meditation for long periods will sooner or later bring up all sorts of pleasant and unpleasant thoughts and feelings. Some of these will inevitably be hard to handle.

—RONALD SIEGAL, *The Mindfulness Solution*

Exercise 3

Working with a classmate, skim through your personal reading materials (things you are reading for courses or for pleasure) and together, select a paragraph that lacks coherence and unity. Each of you should revise that paragraph and then compare your revisions. Next, collaborate on an improved joint revision that you can share with the rest of the class. As you revise (alone and together), consider the paragraph's topic sentence and the other sentences as well, adding and deleting supporting information as you see fit. If you reorder the sentences within the paragraph, make a conscious decision to use chronological, spatial, emphatic, or logical order. Explain your choice of order to the rest of the class.

3d | TRANSITIONS WITHIN AND BETWEEN PARAGRAPHS

Even if its sentences are arranged in a seemingly clear sequence, a single paragraph may lack internal coherence, and a series of paragraphs may lack overall coherence if transitions are abrupt or nonexistent. When revising, you can improve coherence by using pronouns, repetition, or conjunctions and transitional words or phrases (24c(5)).

(1) Using pronouns to establish links between sentences

In paragraph 27, the writer enumerates the similarities of identical twins raised separately. She mentions their names only once, but uses the pronouns *both*, *their*, and *they* to keep the references to the twins always clear.

27   Jim Springer and Jim Lewis were adopted as infants into working-class Ohio families. **Both** liked math and did not like spelling in school. **Both** had law enforcement training and worked part-time as deputy sheriffs. **Both** vacationed in Florida, **both** drove Chevrolets. Much has been made of the fact that **their** lives are marked by a trail of similar names. **Both** married and divorced women named Linda and had second marriages with women named Betty. **They** named **their** sons James Allan and James Alan, respectively. **Both** like mechanical drawing and carpentry. **They** have almost identical drinking and smoking patterns. **Both** chew **their** fingernails down to the nubs.

—CONSTANCE HOLDEN, "Identical Twins Reared Apart"

(2) Repeating words, phrases, structures, or ideas to link a sentence to those that precede it

In paragraph 28, the repetition of the shortened forms of *No Child Left Behind* links sentences to preceding sentences, as does the repeated use of the pronoun *they*.

28   I recently encountered a mother who told me that her school "had some of those **Nickleby** kids" . . . in reference to **No Child Left Behind** kids. **NCLB**. It was said in a derogatory way, like the school was being dragged down because of these children. So who are these "**Nickleby**" kids? The voiceless ones who slipped through the system because **they** were someone else's problem. **They** were in someone else's school. But you know

what? **They** weren't. And aren't. **They** are in almost every school. Your child's school. My daughters' schools. And **they** are gifted young people with much to offer our communities, our country and our world.

—MARGARET SPELLINGS, "Spellings Addresses PTA Convention"

Secretary of Education Spellings also uses parallelism (another kind of repetition) in the sentences beginning with *they.* Parallelism is a key tool for writing coherent sentences and paragraphs (chapter 31).

(3) Using conjunctions and other transitional words or phrases to indicate how ideas are related

Conjunctions and other transitional words or phrases indicate the logical relationship between ideas. In the following sentences, in which two clauses are linked by different conjunctions, notice the subtle changes in the relationship between the two ideas:

The athlete stretched, **and** he studied her carefully.

The athlete raced **while** he filmed her with his iPhone.

The athlete frowned **because** he was making her nervous.

The athlete shouted out, **so** he walked away.

The athlete won the next race; **later** he was glad he had left the track.

The following list of frequently used transitional connections, arranged according to the kinds of relationships they establish, can help you with your reading as well as your writing.

TYPES OF TRANSITIONAL CONNECTIONS

Addition	and, and then, further, furthermore, also, too, again, in addition, besides
Alternative	or, nor, either, neither, on the other hand, conversely, otherwise
Comparison	similarly, likewise, in like manner
Concession	although this may be true, even so, still, nevertheless, at the same time, notwithstanding, nonetheless, in any event, that said
Contrast	but, yet, or, and yet, however, on the contrary, in contrast

(continued on page 70)

(continued from page 69)

Exemplification	for example, for instance, in the case of
Intensification	in fact, indeed, moreover, even more important, to be sure
Place	here, beyond, nearby, opposite to, adjacent to, on the opposite side
Purpose	to this end, for this purpose, with this objective, in order to, so that
Repetition	as I have said, in other words, that is, as has been noted, as previously stated
Result or cause	so, for, therefore, accordingly, consequently, thus, thereby, as a result, then, because, hence
Sequence	next, first, second, third, in the first place, in the second place, finally, last, then, afterward, later
Summary	to sum up, in brief, on the whole, in sum, in short
Time	meanwhile, soon, after a few days, in the meantime, now, in the past, while, during, since

When revising an essay, you must consider the effectiveness of the individual paragraphs at the same time as you consider how well those paragraphs work together to achieve the overall purpose, which your thesis statement declares. Some writers like to revise at the paragraph level before addressing larger concerns; other writers cannot work on individual paragraphs until they have grappled with larger issues related to the rhetorical situation (the opportunity, overall purpose, rhetorical audience, and context; **1b–e**) or have finalized their thesis statement (**2c**).

The following checklist can guide you in revising your paragraphs.

✓ **CHECKLIST** for Revising Paragraphs

- Identify the clear (or clearly implied) topic sentence (**3c(1)**).
- Explain how all the ideas in the paragraph relate to the topic sentence (**3c(2)**). How does each sentence link to previous and later ones? Are the sentences arranged in chronological, spatial, emphatic, or logical order, or are they arranged in some other pattern (**3c(3)**)?

- What transitions are effective? (**3d**)?
- What rhetorical method or methods have been used to develop the paragraph (**2g**)?
- What evidence do you have that the paragraph is adequately developed (**2f**)? What idea or detail might be missing (**3a(2)**)?
- How does the paragraph itself link to the preceding and following ones (**3d**)?

Since there is no predetermined order to the writing process, you can do whatever works best for you each time you revise. Be guided by the principles and strategies discussed in this chapter, but trust also in your own good sense.

3e | PEER REVIEW

Because writing is a medium of communication, good writers check to see whether they have successfully conveyed their ideas to their readers. Your instructor is one reader, to be sure, but your instructor may not be your rhetorical audience. Besides, your instructor may be the last person to read your finished writing. Before you submit your work to your instructor, take advantage of other opportunities for getting responses to it. Consult with readers—at the writing center, in your classes, or in online writing groups—asking them to help you with the specific questions you have about your writing.

(1) Establishing specific evaluation standards

Although you will always write within a rhetorical situation (**1a**), you will often do so in the context of a class assignment that is explicit about opportunity, rhetorical audience, purpose, and format. If you are fortunate, you will be responding to a clearly stated assignment and working with specific evaluation standards (addressing everything from thesis statement and topic sentences to correctness and format) that your instructor has provided. Such standards serve as a starting point when discussing your draft with your writing group, a classmate, or a writing center tutor. For example, if your instructor indicates that your essay will be evaluated primarily in terms of whether you have a clear thesis statement (**2c**) and adequate support for it (**2f** and **2g**), then those features should be your primary focus. Your secondary concerns may be the overall effectiveness of the introduction (**3b(1)**), sentence length and variety (chapter **33**), or mechanical correctness (chapters **42–45**).

Although evaluation standards cannot guarantee useful feedback, they can help you describe the type of feedback you want in a writer's memo (**3e(2)**). They can also help your reviewers focus on specific kinds of advice to give as they respond to your draft.

A peer reviewer's comments should be based on the evaluation criteria, pointing out what the writer has done well and suggesting how to improve particular passages, being both honest and helpful. A reviewer may frame a recommendation in terms of personal engagement with the text: "This is an interesting point. However, it's not clear if this is your thesis." If a reviewer spots a problem that the writer did not identify, the reviewer should ask the writer about discussing it and abide by the writer's decision. Ultimately, the success of the essay is the responsibility of the writer, who weighs the reviewer's advice, rejecting comments that might take the essay in a different direction and applying any suggestions that help fulfill the rhetorical purpose (**1d**).

If you are developing your own criteria for evaluation, the following checklist can help you get started. Based on the elements of the rhetorical situation, this checklist can be easily adjusted to meet your specific needs for a particular assignment.

✔ CHECKLIST for Evaluating a Draft of an Essay

- How does the essay fulfill all the requirements of the assignment?
- What opportunity does the essay address (**1b**)?
- What is the rhetorical audience for the essay (**1c**)? Is that audience appropriate for the assignment? Who might comprise a secondary audience?
- What is the tone of the essay (**3a(3)**)? How does the tone align with the overall purpose, the intended audience, and the context for the essay (**1c–e**)?

- How has the larger subject been focused into a topic (2b)? What is the thesis statement (2c)?

- What assertions support the thesis statement? What specific evidence (examples or details) supports these assertions?

- What pattern of organization is used to arrange the paragraphs (3c(3))? What makes this pattern effective for the essay? What other pattern(s) might prove to be more effective?

- How is each paragraph developed (2f and 2g)?

- What specifically makes the introduction effective (3b(1))? How does it address the rhetorical opportunity and engage the reader?

- How is the conclusion appropriate for the essay's purpose (3b(2))? How exactly does it draw the essay together?

(2) Informing reviewers about your purpose and your concerns

When submitting a draft for review, introduce your work and list your concerns to increase your chances of receiving the kind of help you want. You can orally orient your writing group, tutor, or peer reviewer in just a few minutes. Or, when you are submitting a draft electronically, you might attach a cover letter consisting of a paragraph or two—sometimes called a **writer's memo**. In either case, adopting the following model can help ensure that reviewers will give you useful responses.

SUBMITTING A DRAFT FOR REVIEW

Topic and Purpose

State your topic and the opportunity for your writing (1b). Identify your thesis statement (2c), purpose (1d), and rhetorical audience (1c). Such information gives reviewers useful direction.

Strengths

Mark the passages of your draft you are confident about. Doing so directs attention away from areas you do not want to discuss and saves everyone time.

(continued on page 74)

(continued from page 73)

Concerns

Put question marks by the passages you find troublesome and ask for specific advice wherever possible. For example, if you are worried about your conclusion, say so. Or if you suspect that one of your paragraphs may not fit the overall purpose, direct attention to that paragraph. You are most likely to get the kind of help you want and need when you ask for it specifically.

Mary LeNoir's writer's memo follows.

Topic, Rhetorical Opportunity, Audience, and Purpose: I'm focusing on the way high school student-athletes actually choose a college. Because I've gone through the decision-making process, I know that many people—adults and students alike—think we student-athletes make our choice on the basis of "how good a deal" we're getting from our chosen school, a deal in terms of scholarship money and playing time. I want to address this opportunity to change their thinking. Yes, many high school student-athletes hope or secretly hope that they will go to college, play well, get noticed, and turn pro—no matter what kind of school they attend. But most of us know that we're playing college sports because we love to play, not because of the money we're offered or even the dream of going pro. I want to inform people of how we student-athletes actually make our college choice, a decision not always based on what the most logical reason (a monetary one) might be.

Concerns: I'm concerned about being able to spell out the three kinds of thinking that go into our decision making. I'm also concerned about how to provide the kinds of support for those three kinds of thinking that will ring true to my audience. Even though I've interviewed some of my friends at other schools, I'm not sure the interviews work well. I'm also not confident about whether my current conclusion actually shows the importance of my topic and my thinking.

Mary submitted the draft on pages 76–80 for peer review in a first-year writing course. She worked with two classmates, giving them a set of criteria she had prepared. Because the reviewers were learning how to conduct peer evaluations, their comments are representative of responses you might receive in a similar situation. As members of writing groups gain experience and learn to employ the strategies outlined in this section, their advice usually becomes more helpful.

⬤ TECH SAVVY

Some instructors require students to do peer reviewing online, rather than during class time, and usually provide specific peer-review guidelines and procedures for doing so. What follows are some general suggestions for on-line reviewing.

- If you are responding to a classmate's draft via e-mail, reread your comments before sending them to be sure that your tone is appropriate and that you have avoided the kinds of misunderstandings that can occur with e-mail messages (**5b** and **5c**).
- Always save a copy of your comments in case your e-mail message is lost or inadvertently deleted.
- If you are responding to a classmate's draft using an online course-management program, such as WebCT, ANGEL, or Blackboard, remember that your comments may be read by other classmates, too.
- Follow the advice in **3e(1)**, just as you would if you were commenting on a paper copy of your classmate's draft.

As you read the following assignment and then Mary's draft, remember that a first draft will not be a model of perfect writing—and also that this is the first time peer reviewers Ernie Lujan and Andrew Chama responded to it. Mary sent Ernie and Andrew her essay electronically, and they added their comments at the end of the essay.

The assignment: Draft a three- to four-page, double-spaced essay in which you analyze the causes or consequences of a choice you have had to make in the last year or two. Whatever choice you analyze, make sure that it concerns a topic you can develop with confidence and without violating your sense of privacy. Also, consider the expectations of your audience and whether the topic you have chosen will allow you to communicate something meaningful to readers. As you draft, establish a rhetorical audience for your essay, a group that might act on or be persuaded by any recommendation or new knowledge that grows out of your analysis.

1

First Draft

The Search: High School Student-Athletes Choose a College

Mary LeNoir

According to a recent National Collegiate Athletic Association (NCAA) advertising campaign, I am one of over 380,000 NCAA student-athletes. Most of us will enter a profession other than sports. An academically weighted decision, then, holds a higher probability for future success than a decision based on sports. Many high school student-athletes strive to play their sport at the collegiate level; they're tempted by the idea of turning an average college volleyball team into champs, reviving the football glory of the school, or, most of all, of continuing to experience the physical and emotional highs of playing sports.

It all begins in the hearts of little leaguers and peewee soccer players. Though we begin our athletic careers hitting off a tee or paddling in the pool on a kickboard, many of us grow to hone our athletic abilities and practice our skills to be the best and play against the best. We play sports year round; for our schools, club teams, all-star teams, AAU teams. We attend camps, separate workouts, and practices. Our love of picking grass during peewee soccer games evolves into the love of the competition and triumph over our opponents. Aspirations of great collegiate careers and even dreams of playing professional athletics consume our minds' thoughts, driving the discipline behind our work ethic. College prospects come knocking on our doors, prepared to enable our dreams and paint before us the golden vision of our future athletic careers wearing blue and white or orange and maroon. Tempting is the sound of turning an average

2

volleyball team into champs or reviving the football glory of the school. Yes, we see our futures, we've prepared for our futures, and our futures will last us maybe four to five years if we are so lucky; perhaps seven to ten years for those more fortunate. And those favorites of the heavens, they will make lasting careers. Our young hearts are ignorant of the cruel reality of this "love of the game," for who would ever think it could end?

These dreams become reality for about 16 percent of collegiate athletes; a percent that feeds all professional men's sports (basketball, baseball, football, ice hockey, and soccer) and one professional women's sport (basketball). In addition, if one is able to make the pros, a professional athletic career, on average, lasts around five years. This 16 percent fails to include the many other sports offered at competitive college levels. Most collegiate athletes do not even have the option of professional careers, for the extent of their sport lies in playing at the collegiate level, coaching after college, or the Olympics. Furthermore, injuries keep numbers of great athletes from reaching their athletic peak; either cutting their college career short or ruining any professional chances.

High school athletes recruited for highly competitive collegiate athletics approach their decision with a heavy emphasis on both athletics and academics. Though the recruiting process for the athlete's sport may appear to cloud the academic reputation of the school, the athlete is first and foremost enrolling for the academics offered. A thorough examination of the college as a whole may afford the athlete the best of both worlds.

3

Having spoken to numbers of collegiate student-athletes, three major factors played a huge role in their decision and none of them had to do with athletics or academics: tuition, location, and atmosphere of the school. Could they see themselves happy farther from home or closer to home? Would they prefer an urban or rural location, the size of a huge state school or the more intimate setting of a small liberal arts college?

Finally, is the school affordable? Then, the next step included the academics and athletics. How important was the athletic and academic reputation for their decision? Future playing time may affect the decision—would the athletes have a chance to play or would they ride the bench for four years? With that said, could the students handle both the academics and athletics of the school? Most of these collegiate athletes admitted to not examining these questions to their full extent. Many relied on the first three factors with some emphasis on academics and the majority on their future athletic careers.

However, three athletes stood out as examples of performing thorough college searches and finally deciding on three schools that fit their academic, athletic, and personal needs: Johns Hopkins University, Penn State University, and The University of Richmond. The athlete who chose Johns Hopkins grew up about a half hour from the university. She desired to play lacrosse at an institution that offered stellar academics and a solid lacrosse program and, preferably, one closer to home. Johns Hopkins was of particular interest for her due to the nursing program. She was prepared for the rigorous academics along with the commitment to a division one lacrosse program and, therefore, was not caught off guard by either demand.

4

    The second athlete, also a lacrosse player, chose Penn State University. She is from Ohio and desired a school a bit farther from home. She wanted a big school with a great academic reputation that offered a variety of majors from which to choose. A contrast to the first athlete, she was not set on a particular profession such as nursing, rather, she wanted the flexibility to explore her academic endeavors as an underclassman. Penn State's academic appeal was the school's broad range of academics offered and the academic support extending to career services. The second athlete, too, desired a competitive lacrosse program; however, she also aimed to play and contribute, whereas the first was content with being a member of the team, focusing more on her nursing major. Penn State's lacrosse program had been building and gaining a considerable reputation. This second athlete desired to help take the team to a higher level and help grow Penn State's lacrosse reputation.

    The third athlete was a baseball player for the University of Richmond. He desired good academics, however, his main focus was baseball and he wanted a potential professional career in baseball. Tuition did play a major role in that he needed to earn a scholarship if he were to attend a college out of state, which he did. Location and size also became relevant factors after he examined the school's baseball program. A baseball scholarship offer and good academics paved the way for him to visit the school and then decide if he loved it or if the baseball scholarship was enough for him to accept the other aspects of the school. Unlike the first two athletes, he chose primarily based on his sport and his potential chance of a professional baseball career.

Dear Mary,

Until I read your draft, I hadn't thought at all about how student-athletes make their college choice. I guess I just thought that they went wherever they got the most scholarship money. Or, if they weren't all that good, they attended a smaller, less competitive school where they'd get some playing time. So I think you have a rhetorical opportunity to address. Lots of your readers won't have a clue.

What I'm unsure about is your organization. I'm torn between thinking you should organize according to student-athlete or by the reason for choosing a college. (I'm also wondering if you need to use the term "student-athlete," when "athlete" would work.) Mostly, I think that the second organizational pattern would be more effective, because you'd have a basis for arranging the material. You could move from least to most important reason, whatever that is.

So I think that your thesis, purpose, and audience are primary concerns in this draft. And the surface errors, lack of citations, and need for quotations (from the interviews) are secondary concerns. I also think that you need to strengthen the list of criteria or reasons student-athletes choose their college. Maybe you can talk to these people again and see if you can come up with some reasons they all share.

Great first draft! Thanks for letting me read it and respond.

Ernie

Dear Mary,

    This is an interesting topic—one that I think you have strong feelings about, judging from your very descriptive second paragraph. It seems that you have a lot you want to say about student-athletes and the college search, and I think with more drafting you'll be better able to pinpoint your exact purpose for writing.

    I love your idea of doing research by talking to actual students about their enrollment decisions. What a great idea! Because you are interviewing several students, your essay has the potential to contrast the experiences of the students, which might be instructive to some readers. On one hand, the essay might work as a how-to guide for athletes who have a college decision ahead of them. On the other hand, the essay might counter some misinformation held by college students who don't play sports.

    As a next step, I'd try to identify the specific audience you want to address and clarify what you want that audience to know. If you compare and/or contrast what you hear from the athletes you interview, you might want points of similarity and difference to serve as your main points. Maybe the three factors you mention in the essay could be these points.

    I'd love to read another draft of this essay. Great work so far!

                                        Andrew

Before revising, Mary considered the comments she received from Ernie and Andrew. Since she had asked them to respond to her introduction, conclusion, and organization, she had to weigh all of their comments—relevant and irrelevant—and address the ones that seemed most useful as she prepared her next draft.

Exercise 4

Reread Mary's first draft and the peer reviewers' responses. Identify the comments you think are the most useful, and explain why. Which comments seem to be less useful? Explain why. What additional comments would you make if Mary had asked you to review her draft?

After Mary had time to reconsider her first draft and to think about the responses she received from Ernie and Andrew, she made a number of large-scale changes, especially with regard to organization. She also strengthened her thesis statement and cleaned up the surface errors. After these and other revisions, more peer review, and some careful editing and proofreading, Mary was ready to submit her essay to her instructor. Her final draft is on pages 85–94.

3f   EDITING FOR CLARITY

If you are satisfied with the revised structure of your essay and the content of your paragraphs, you can begin editing individual sentences for clarity, effectiveness, and variety (chapters 28–33). The following checklist for editing contains cross-references to chapters or sections where you can find more specific information.

✔ **CHECKLIST** for Editing

1 Sentences

- What is the unifying idea of each sentence (28)?
- How have you varied the lengths of your sentences? How many words are in your longest and shortest sentences?
- How have you varied the structure of your sentences? How many are simple? How many use subordination or coordination? If you overuse any one sentence structure, revise for variation (33).
- Does each verb agree with its subject (25e)? Does every pronoun agree with its antecedent (26c)?
- Which sentences have or should have parallel structure (31)?
- Do any sentences contain misplaced or dangling modifiers (27d and 27e)?
- Do any of your sentences shift in verb tense or tone (25b)? Is the shift intentional?

2 Diction

- Have you repeated any words (32)? Is your repetition intentional?
- Are your word choices exact, or are some words vague or too general (35)?
- Have you used any language that is too informal (34b)?
- Is the vocabulary you have chosen appropriate for your audience, purpose, and context (1c–e and 34)?
- Have you defined any technical or unfamiliar words for your audience (34b(4))?

3g PROOFREADING FOR AN ERROR-FREE ESSAY

Once you have revised and edited your essay, it is your responsibility to format it properly and proofread it. Proofreading means making a special search to ensure that the final product you submit is free from error, or nearly so. An error-free essay allows your reader to read for meaning, without being distracted by incorrect spelling or punctuation that can interfere with meaning. Even though proofreading is usually the last step in the writing process, proofreading occasionally uncovers problems that call for further revision or editing.

Because the eye tends to see what it expects to see, many writers miss errors—especially minor ones, such as a missing comma or apostrophe—even when they think they have proofread carefully. To proofread well, then, you need to read your work more than once, read it aloud, and read it backwards. Some people find it useful to read through a paper several times, checking for a different set of items on each pass. Other writers rely on peer editors to help with proofreading.

The proofreading checklist that follows refers to chapters and sections in this handbook where you will find detailed information to help you. Keeping a dictionary (**34d**) at hand makes it easy to look up any words whose meaning or spelling you are unsure about.

✔ CHECKLIST for Proofreading

1 Spelling (42)

- Have you double-checked the words you frequently misspell and any the spell checker may have missed (for example, misspellings that still form words, such as *form* for *from*)?
- If you used a spell checker, did it overlook homophones (such as *there/their, who's/whose,* and *it's/its*) (**42c**)?
- Have you double-checked the spelling of all foreign words and all proper names?

2 Punctuation (36–40) and Capitalization (43)

- Does each sentence have appropriate closing punctuation, and have you used only one space after each end punctuation mark (**41**)?
- Is all punctuation within sentences—commas (**37**), semicolons (**38a**), apostrophes (**39**), dashes (**41d**), and hyphens (**42f**)—used appropriately and placed correctly?
- Are direct quotations carefully and correctly punctuated (**40a**)? Where have you placed end punctuation with a quotation (**40d**)? Are quotations capitalized properly (**40a** and **43c(1)**)?
- Are all proper names, people's titles, and titles of published works correctly capitalized (**43a** and **43b**)?
- Are titles of works identified with quotation marks (**40b**) or italics (**44a**)?

3h AN INVESTIGATIVE REPORT FINAL ESSAY

After her intensive revision, Mary edited and proofread her essay. The version that she ultimately submitted to her instructor follows.

LeNoir 1

Mary LeNoir

Professor Glenn

English 15

1 November 2014

How High School Athletes Really Choose a College

It all begins in the hearts of little leaguers, peewee soccer players, and little swimmers with their kickboards—that yearning to play and win. These small athletes grow, improve, and hone their athletic abilities in order to be the best and play against the best. They play sports year round—for their schools, club teams, all-star teams, Amateur Athletic Union (AAU) teams, and for themselves. They attend camps, workouts, and practices, lots of practices. Aspirations of great collegiate careers and even dreams of playing professional sports begin to consume them, driving their self-discipline and work ethic. Eventually, college prospects come knocking on their doors in the form of recruiters wearing college colors (blue and white or orange and maroon) and talking about how dreams might come true. In those college recruiters, high school athletes see their future. The smart ones know that their future as a competitive athlete might last through the college years, if they're lucky. They already accept the fact that only a very select few ever reach professional status.

The urge to win is a familiar feeling; mentioning it in the first sentence is a good way to hook readers.

LeNoir 2

To answer this question, the author interviewed student-athletes and thereby built her thesis statement.

So against all odds of professional success, why do high school athletes agree to the heavy commitment of playing college sports, knowing full well that college sports will take them only as far as . . . well, college?

Most people think high school athletes base their choice of college on scholarship money and promised playing time. To find out how high school athletes actually make their choice of college, I interviewed five college athletes who play various sports at five different kinds of colleges.

The author explains how she went about answering the question posed in the previous paragraph.

My goal was to uncover the personal reasons or evaluative criteria they used as they made their choices. To answer my question, I selected male and female athletes who play major sports, as well as sports that are popular regionally rather than nationally. These athletes attend big state universities, state-system schools, and smaller liberal arts colleges. Paige Wright represents lacrosse at Johns Hopkins University; Nick Huang, football at Capitol University; Bobby Dorsey, baseball at the University of Richmond; Marye Taranto, lacrosse at the University of Virginia; and Theresa Morales, lacrosse at Penn State University.

I asked these athletes why they wanted to play college sports and how they moved through their college search process. I soon discovered that, despite their diverse goals and circumstances, all these athletes used the same three criteria for choosing their college: (1) how the school could further the athlete's career as either a player or a coach (including playing time), (2) the material conditions associated with attending the school (mainly financial aid and geographic location), and (3) the emotional connection the athlete had with the school.

LeNoir 3

College coaches recruit high school athletes who will contribute to their athletic programs. Neither the coach nor recruiter can guarantee the student's collegiate athletic career, nor promise that the athlete will start, play a specific number of games each season, or play all four years. However, the coach and recruiter can offer the athlete tentative ideas about what they think the athlete could contribute to the team and when the athlete might be able to play in competitive games. These ideas help an athlete visualize himself or herself on that team at that particular school.

A strong topic sentence begins this paragraph.

Knowing that his chances were good but far from guaranteed, Bobby held to the idea of playing professional baseball after college. Therefore, the rising success of the University of Richmond baseball program had a major influence on Bobby's choice. "In high school, I was not set on playing professional baseball, but I knew it could potentially be what I wanted. That meant I needed to be seen playing" (personal interview). He went on to explain that professional baseball teams do not recruit players based on the status of the college they attend. He continued:

An effective topic sentence moves the essay forward.

> Well, yes, obviously if you play at a big-time baseball program your odds are pretty great of getting drafted. But what's more important than winning college championships is building your reputation as a player, and that means you need to play. You're more likely to get talked about [having] played and done well at a less well-known school than if you sat on the bench for four years at some top-ten program. Richmond needed my position [shortstop] and made me feel like I had a good chance of playing, if not my freshman year, most definitely my sophomore year. (Dorsey)

Interview material is used effectively here.

LeNoir 4

Nick described similar circumstances that affected his choice: the opportunity to be noticed by a pro football team was just as important to him. Fortunately for Nick, football is akin to baseball in that, if the player is good enough, professional recruiters will find him, even at a Division III program like Capitol University. For Nick, Capitol offered the small-school atmosphere he desired along with a real chance to play football regularly, boosting his chances at having a professional football career. Bobby and Nick both wanted a chance to play the kind of college ball that could keep alive their dream of playing professional sports. Their two sports happen to be two of the most popular professional sports.

That said, what were high school athletes thinking when they signed on to play a college sport that held no opportunity to play professionally afterward? Theresa admitted her athletic career would be over after four years of college:

> Even though there is no professional lacrosse league for women, I could always coach or help start a program at a school. But I wanted to do something else—that's one of the reasons Penn State appealed to me. The school offered so many majors and amazing academic support. I felt I needed that freedom to explore and figure out what I wanted to do with my life. (Morales)

Theresa went on to explain that her professional goals in no way diminished her competitive nature or desire to excel on the lacrosse field during her college years:

> Sports have been so much a part of my life that I could not imagine not playing in college. And because I'm competitive, there

This paragraph opens with a question that the writer goes on to answer.

was no way I was going to commit to some school that was not serious about winning, that did not have a real chance, or where I would not have a chance to play.

Besides, college athletics is a good way to prepare for any profession: I am competitive. I love to win, and in order to win I train, work hard, practice discipline, and budget my time—all qualities vital to success in life. Job recruiters are well aware of an athlete's commitments, and it looks great on a résumé to have played a varsity sport in college while having kept up a good GPA. (Morales)

Marye and Paige, who also play lacrosse, also mentioned their competitiveness and the importance of getting to play. They, too, felt that being able to add varsity athletics to their résumés was important. However, Marye and Paige went on to present criteria other than "playing time" that had a strong influence on their final decision about a college.

The second cluster of criteria that athletes use when making their decision includes the material conditions associated with a college, things that are the same for students and student-athletes alike. Costs and the geographical location of the school—these are logistics that do not disappear just because you are an athlete. Being recruited and given a scholarship does not imply the athlete will say yes, despite problems with the material conditions. For instance, Marye's athletic scholarship was the key to attending her dream school, the University of Virginia (UVA). Marye had long loved UVA and its lacrosse team and had been accepted academically. But because she had not received an academic scholarship, her family would be expected to pay the full tuition, which she and her

Use of supporting details and explanation strengthens this paragraph.

LeNoir 6

parents simply could not afford. Fortunately, Marye was also a highly recruited lacrosse player, one UVA became even more interested in after she had been admitted on academic grounds. The athletic scholarship offered to Marye made UVA affordable for her, giving her the opportunity to receive an education from one of the best academic institutions in the country and to live her dream of playing college lacrosse, neither of which would have been possible without her athletic scholarship. (See fig. 1.)

Fig. 1. Playing lacrosse for a top college team is a dream of many high school players. Paul A. Souders/Corbis. *Two Lacrosse Players.* 1988. *Corbis Images.*

This is a strong paragraph, with good transitions.

Paige's situation presented an insurmountable obstacle: geographic location. Because her parents could not afford traveling expenses (neither for themselves nor for her), Paige simply had to attend a school close to home. Thus, Paige could not consider, let alone commit to, a school across the country. Johns Hopkins University was particularly appealing because it was about a forty-minute car ride from her home. Bobby's choice of college spoke to circumstances and criteria that combined both Marye's and Paige's. Bobby did not want to attend an in-state school; he wanted to move away and experience another region of the country. However, he and his parents could not afford constant traveling expenses, let alone out-of-state tuition. Bobby's parents told him that he would either have to attend a school in the state of Delaware or earn some kind of scholarship in order to go out of state. His baseball scholarship at University of Richmond not only afforded him an opportunity to play college ball and attend college far away from home—but he was also drafted.

All five athletes emphasized the importance of the "right" atmosphere in their college search, which actually meant an atmosphere that they connected with on an emotional level. When I asked each athlete to explain what she or he meant by "atmosphere," why it ranked higher than the other factors, and what exactly was the "right atmosphere" for each of them, they responded fully to all three aspects of the question.

This transitional paragraph leads into the following ones.

For all of these athletes, the school's atmosphere included athletic, academic, and social factors, the physical look and geographic location of the school, and the way all these features came together to enhance the student's emotional connection with the school.

Paige emphasized the size and social reputation of Johns Hopkins, the familiar weather, and the look and layout of the campus. She claimed that visiting the school was crucial to her decision because the atmosphere is "felt," not described or quantified in statistics:

A good couple days was what I needed to really test the feel [of the school]. What I had heard about the athletics and academics was the thing that kind of attracted me to look at the school and prompted me to visit in the first place. But, how I felt walking on campus, observing the students . . . this would be my home for the next four years! I wanted to fall in love. (Wright)

Nick and Theresa offered similar comments about the size and social features of their schools. Theresa knew she wanted a beautiful college town with a large student body, a place like Penn State. She wanted social options and a general camaraderie of school spirit among the faculty and students. In contrast, Nick desired a more intimate, college-like setting with a less intense social scene, which Capitol offered.

Having an idea of what "atmosphere" meant, I then asked them to touch on the academic and athletic elements, explaining how those contributed to the emotional connection. Bobby wanted a smaller school with a solid academic reputation and the chance to play baseball. For him, it was important to play baseball at a school with a competitive reputation in the sport. Academically, Bobby had no specific career goal in mind other than baseball. Still, he did not disregard the academics; a university with a good academic reputation but a manageable coursework load was what he wanted. Paige, however, did have a specific career as a nurse in mind. This factor attracted her to Johns Hopkins, which is known for its medical program. Unlike Bobby, Paige emphasized the academic aspect of her college experience and desired a top-notch nursing program; thus, she knew she would be embarking on a rigorous academic schedule and was fully prepared for that commitment.

Marye offered me a slightly different definition of "atmosphere." Still including what the others mentioned, Marye simply named the atmosphere she already had in mind: her dream school, the University of Virginia. She had grown up loving UVA; she had a long history of an emotional connection. Playing lacrosse as a young girl, Marye imagined wearing the UVA uniform, which she thought "was the coolest-looking uniform ever," and winning national championships in the blue and orange. She had visited the school numerous times in high school to see games and visit her sister. For Marye, "atmosphere" meant attending her dream school and playing lacrosse there. The reputation of UVA lacrosse ranks among the highest in the country; UVA teams are always in the top ten of polls and compete for ACC (Atlantic Coast Conference) championships. As for academics, Marye said,

> Yes, my love of the school was primarily based on this childhood dream of playing lacrosse there. UVA happens to have a stellar academic reputation too, which is a bonus for me. Not to say I would have thrown away my academics and gone to any old school if it had great lacrosse. It's just, to be honest, I saw my future through this kind of tunnel-vision dream . . . I didn't think about what I wanted to do after college. Now, having graduated, I feel a bit ashamed about my ignorance of UVA's academics. [We are] among the best in the country! I don't know how many kids dreamt of a UVA education, which I now can't describe how much I appreciate. But back in high school, I wanted to go to UVA to play lacrosse. (Taranto)

LeNoir 10

All these athletes described complex reasons for choosing their college, reasons as complex as my own. My love for lacrosse propelled my decision to take my sport only as far as the college level, where I would pursue my professional goals, which would no longer include lacrosse. All my decisions were based on my wanting to achieve my goals of playing my sport in college and pursuing my career after college. And just like all of these other athletes, I thought about other factors than the sport I would play. In some ways, whether we hope to play sports after college or not, we all made an emotional connection with the college of our choice.

The essay ends with a reasonable and thoughtful conclusion

LeNoir 11

Works Cited

Dorsey, Robert. Personal interview. 20 Oct. 2014.

Huang, Nick. Personal interview. 14 Oct. 2014.

Morales, Theresa. Personal interview. 22 Oct. 2014.

"NCAA Launches Latest Public Service Announcements, Introduces New

Student-Focused Website." *National Collegiate Athletic Association,*

13 Mar. 2007, fs.ncaa.org/Docs/PressArchive/2007/Announcements/

NCAA%2bLaunches%2bLatest%2bPublic%2bService%2bAnnouncements

%2bIntroduces%2bNew%2bStudent-Focused%2bWebsite.html.

Taranto, Marye. Personal interview. 18 Oct. 2014.

Wright, Paige. Personal interview. 26 Oct. 2014.

Exercise 5

Compare the two versions of "How High School Athletes Really Choose a College" that appear in this chapter and write a two-paragraph summary describing how Mary revised and edited her work. If she had shown her final draft to you, asking for your advice before submitting it for a grade, what would you have advised? Write a one-paragraph response to her draft.

4 ‖ MANAGING ACADEMIC WRITING

As you realize by now, the writing you do in college differs from the writing you did in high school or any you have done on the job in terms of schedule, genre, intellectual challenge, evaluation—and consequences. In college, you have to write for every course (not just English or history) and often within tight time frames. Current events sometimes prompt unscheduled writing assignments that must take the form of specific genres (report, evaluation, proposal, memo, argument, research essay, or analysis) that meet the expectations of readers across academic fields. Furthermore, your writing is often evaluated cumulatively, over the course of a semester, rather than as individual assignments. In addition, instead of asking you to demonstrate what you know, many of your college writing assignments require you to conduct research, synthesize information, make decisions, support views, and propose solutions to problems.

At this point, you are focusing on such issues as opportunity, purpose, and rhetorical audience, regardless of your format or genre. As your writing becomes more complex, your critical thinking will become more sophisticated as well. Thus, college writing brings with it new challenges to your creativity, speed, and adaptability.

Planning, drafting, revising, getting feedback on, and editing a piece of writing over a stretch of days or weeks may often be a luxury, one available only if you prepare a portfolio of your best writing. This chapter will help you

- manage deadlines (**4a**),
- abbreviate the writing process (**4b**),
- plan for essay examinations (**4c**), and
- prepare a portfolio of your writing (**4d**).

4a MANAGING DEADLINES

The only way you can expand your writing abilities at the same time that you meet the demands of your ever-increasing number of writing assignments is to learn how to manage deadlines. You will almost always be working under deadlines—whether for academic essays, job application packages, grant proposals, or other time-sensitive documents. Preparing ahead of time always helps, and there are a number of ways you can do that. For instance, in-class essay exams are often scheduled around midterm, and you can start preparing for such an exam on the first day of class. As you read your assignments, listen to lectures, and participate in class discussions, make an effort to determine what your instructor considers most important about the material you are learning. If you are paying careful attention but cannot tell exactly what the instructor deems most important, ask. And whenever an instructor gives you instructions on a writing assignment, ask questions about the criteria of evaluation until you know exactly what is expected of you.

The best way to approach a writing assignment with a longer deadline, such as a research paper, is to start early. If you are choosing your own topic, begin as soon as you can to record your ideas on paper or an electronic notepad and then narrow these down (**2b**). The sooner you identify a subject, the sooner you can conduct preliminary research in preparation for a discussion with your instructor. You want to ensure that your topic is worthy of the assignment as well as one you can complete within the timeline. Timelines work best for you if you work from the due date backward. To use your timeline to your advantage (figure 4.1), be sure to include intermediate deadlines for writing an introduction with a thesis statement, composing a first draft, meeting with your instructor, reviewing drafts with a classmate, revising your draft, and editing. Do your best to stick to your timeline.

4b ABBREVIATING THE WRITING PROCESS

Students and employees, who are often expected to write well with little notice, can successfully abbreviate the writing process the same way experienced writers do. When faced with a short deadline, you can

"Thank goodness you're here—I can't accomplish anything unless I have a deadline."

David Sipress/The New Yorker Collection/The Cartoon Bank

Figure 4.1: Deadlines have their uses.

try to narrow the topic as quickly as possible, and connect the assignment to what you already know well and what you can easily research. A topic with a sharp focus can be handled more thoughtfully and thoroughly in a short time than a broad topic; for instance, rather than writing about fracking in general, you might consider writing about the consequences of fracking on your family's farm and finances. Once you have a focused topic, quickly organize your ideas by using a rough outline or a rough grouping of ideas.

The following tips will help you abbreviate the writing process.

TIPS FOR ABBREVIATING THE WRITING PROCESS

- Generate ideas about the assignment or topic with a friend or colleague who is facing or has faced the same kind of deadline. That person can help you clarify your line of reasoning and develop counterarguments. Take notes.

- Draft an introductory paragraph that frames your position or approach and includes a clear thesis statement. If appropriate, e-mail your paragraph to your instructor, a classmate, or a colleague to get assurance that you are on the right track.

- If your thesis statement and basic approach are on track, write down your main points. Then, flesh out those points with examples and supporting text until you have a first draft.

- Read your draft aloud, slowly. Make sure that your topic sentences are clear. Reading aloud will help you locate passages that need transitional words or phrases to help your reader along.

- Write a conclusion that reiterates your main points and suggests their implications.

- Read over your text to make sure that it fulfills the assignment. Reread your introduction and conclusion to see how they frame your piece. Examine your topic sentences and supporting details to make sure that they help you fulfill your purpose in terms of your rhetorical audience.

- Proofread one last time. Submit your work on time.

◉ TECH SAVVY

You can use your computer to help you manage writing tasks efficiently.

- If you do not have much time for revising and editing, you can use the grammar checker and spell checker of your word-processing program to help you proofread, even while you are drafting.

- Many on-campus writing centers can receive drafts of student writing via e-mail or through a website; tutors at these centers can usually schedule appointments electronically. Writing tutors will often respond to a draft or an appointment request within twenty-four hours. If the writing center on your campus offers these services, you can use the center as a source of helpful advice on short notice when you have a tight deadline.

4c TAKING ESSAY EXAMINATIONS

If your instructor has posed a clear question, one that includes an operative term (such as "describe" or "compare") to initiate your thinking (see the list of terms on pages 100–101), and has provided explicit instructions, you are (almost) home free if you have studied well and planned for the essay exam all semester. Write out your answer, framing it with a thesis statement and developing your main points in line with the meaning of the operative term. As you develop those points, weave in supporting arguments, details, and examples. If a question does not clearly convey what is expected of you, ask your instructor for clarification. The steps described in the following sections will help you improve your ability to take essay examinations and write effectively under pressure.

(1) Allocating time

If the exam has more than one question, determine how much time to allot to each one. If you are faced with two questions that are worth the same number of points, give half the time to one and half to the other. When certain questions are weighted more heavily than others, however, you need to divide your time accordingly. However you allocate your time, allow ten minutes for final revising and proofreading.

Stick to the time allotment for each question. If you do not finish, leave room to complete your answer later and move on to the next question. Partial answers to *all* questions usually gain you more points than complete answers to only *some* questions. Besides, you can use the ten minutes you saved to add to any incomplete answers, even if you have to draw arrows to the margins or to the back of the page or supply rough notes (**4c(3)**). Your instructor will probably appreciate the extra effort.

(2) Reading instructions and questions carefully

Students who take time to read instructions and questions carefully do better than those who do not. So invest a few minutes in studying each question, identifying its operative terms, putting the question in your own words, and then jotting down a few notes in the margin next to it. If you have been given a choice of questions to answer, choose those that best suit your knowledge yet do not overlap.

Most exam questions contain specific instructions about how, as well as what, to answer. Be alert for operative terms such as those in the list below, which identify the writing task and provide specific cues for organizing your response. When you are given more general directions, look for such words as *similar* or *different*, *identify*, and *why*. You will also need to determine whether you are being asked to call up course-related information from memory or to respond more creatively with your own interpretations, hypotheses, or solutions. Words such as *think, defend,* and *argue* signal that you are to frame a thesis and support it rather than recite course-specific information.

Most essay exam questions begin with or contain one of the operative terms in the following list and end with a reference to the information you are to work with. Understanding these terms and framing your answers in response to them will help you focus on what is being asked.

TERMS USED IN ESSAY EXAM QUESTIONS

Compare   Examine the points of similarity (compare) or difference (contrast) between two ideas or things (**2g(5)**), drawing upon your clear understanding of information.

Define   State the class to which the item to be defined belongs, and clarify what distinguishes it from the others of that class (**2g(6)**), tapping into your remembered knowledge.

Describe   Use details in a clearly defined order to give the reader a clear mental picture of what you are being asked to describe (**2g(2)**), again calling on information that you remember and understand.

Discuss   Examine, analyze, evaluate, apply information, or state pros and cons. This term gives you wide latitude in addressing the topic and thus can be more difficult to work with than some of the others in this list, since you must decide on a focus. *Discuss* can be interpreted in various ways and is, unfortunately, the term that appears most frequently on exam questions, so choose your own focus for the term.

Evaluate   Appraise the advantages and disadvantages of the idea or thing specified. This term draws on your comprehension as well as on your ability to analyze—to take something apart, to examine it, and perhaps categorize it. Often an evaluation question requires you to recommend a course of action.

Explain   Clarify and interpret (**2g(3)**), reconcile differences, or state causes (**2g(4)**). When you *explain*, you draw upon your remembered knowledge as well as your ability to analyze and apply information.

(continued on page 102)

(continued from page 101)

Illustrate	Offer concrete examples, or, if possible, create figures, charts, or tables that provide information about the topic, summoning up the concrete knowledge that you can apply as support for your assertions.
Summarize	State the main points in a condensed form, omitting details and curtailing examples. Fully comprehended knowledge must be boiled down into easy-to-understand terms.
Trace	Narrate a sequence of events that show progress toward a goal or comprise a process (**2g(1)** and **2g(3)**). Both creativity and analysis are in play in a narration of this sort.

(3) Organizing your answer

Even under time constraints, you should be able to draft a rough outline or jot down a few phrases for an informal list (**2d**) within the time allotted for each question. Focus your thesis immediately. Then list the most important points you plan to cover. You might decide to rearrange ideas later, but the first step is to get some down on paper. Before you begin to compose your answer, quickly review your list, deleting any irrelevant or unimportant points and adding any better ones that come to mind. Number the points in a logical sequence determined by chronology (reporting events in the order in which they occurred), by causation (showing how one event led to another), or by order of importance (given the possibility that you might run out of time, move from the most important to the least important point). As an example, consider figure 4.2, which shows the thesis statement and list of supporting points that biology major Trish Parsons quickly composed and edited during the first few minutes of an essay exam. Trish was responding to the following question: "Discuss whether the term 'junk DNA' is an appropriate name for the nucleic DNA that does not code for proteins."

Sometimes, the language of the question will tell you how you should organize your answer. Consider this example:

> Describe the ways the two political parties influenced President Obama's immigration plan.

At first glance, this exam question might seem to state the topic without indicating how to organize a description of it. *To influence*, however, is to be responsible for certain consequences. In this case, the two-party

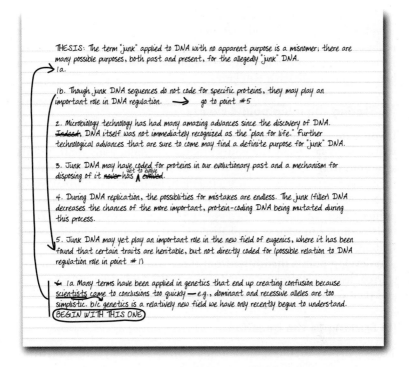

THESIS: The term "junk" applied to DNA with no apparent purpose is a misnomer; there are many possible purposes, both past and present, for the allegedly "junk" DNA.

1a.

1b. Though junk DNA sequences do not code for specific proteins, they may play an important role in DNA regulation. ⟶ go to point #5

2. Microbiology technology has had many amazing advances since the discovery of DNA. ~~Indeed,~~ DNA itself was not immediately recognized as the "plan for life." Further technological advances that are sure to come may find a definite purpose for "junk" DNA.

3. Junk DNA may have coded for proteins in our evolutionary past and a mechanism for disposing of it ~~never~~ has ∧ evolved.
   (yet to evolve)

4. During DNA replication, the possibilities for mistakes are endless. The junk (filler) DNA decreases the chances of the more important, protein-coding DNA being mutated during this process.

5. Junk DNA may yet play an important role in the new field of eugenics, where it has been found that certain traits are heritable, but not directly coded for (possible relation to DNA regulation role in point #1)

6. 1a Many terms have been applied in genetics that end up creating confusion because scientists came to conclusions too quickly — e.g., dominant and recessive alleles are too simplistic. b/c genetics is a relatively new field we have only recently begun to understand. (BEGIN WITH THIS ONE)

Figure 4.2: A writer's quick outline for an essay exam response.

political system is being viewed as a cause, and you are being asked to identify its consequences (**2g(4)**). Once you have recognized the meaning of *influence*, you might decide to discuss the consequences you identify in different paragraphs.

Here is another example:

> Consider Picasso's treatment of the human body early and late in his career. How did his concept of bodily form persist throughout his career? How did it change?

The reference to two different points in the artist's career, along with the words *persist* and *change*, indicates that your task is to compare and contrast. You could organize your response to this question by discussing Picasso's concept of the body's form when his paintings were realistic and when they were cubist—preferably covering the same points in the same order in each part of the response. Or you could begin by establishing similarities and then move on to discuss differences. There is almost always more than one way to organize a thoughtful response. Devoting at least a few minutes to organizing your answer can help you better demonstrate what you know.

(4) Stating the main points clearly

If you state your main points clearly, your instructor will see how well you have understood the course material. Make your main points stand out from the rest of the answer to an exam question by making them the first sentence of each paragraph; by using transitional words such as *first, second,* and *third*; or by creating headings to separate your points. Once you have outlined your essay exam answer, you will know which points you want to emphasize, even if they change slightly as you write. Use your conclusion to summarize your main points. Just in case you develop points that differ from those you had in mind when you started, leave space for an introduction at the beginning of the answer and then write it after you have written the rest.

(5) Sticking to the question

Always answer each essay exam question as precisely and directly as you can, perhaps using some of the instructor's language in your thesis statement. If your thesis statement implies an organizational plan, follow that plan as closely as possible. If you move away from your original thesis because better ideas occur to you as you write, simply go back and revise your thesis statement (2c). If you find yourself drifting into irrelevance, stop and draw a line through that material.

If you face a vague or truly confusing question and your instructor does not clarify it, go ahead and construct a clear(er) question and then answer it. Rewriting the instructor's question can seem like a risky thing to do, but figuring out a reasonable question that is related to what the instructor has written is actually a responsible move, if you can answer the question you have posed.

(6) Revising and proofreading each answer

Save a few minutes to reread each answer, making whatever deletions, corrections, and marginal notes you think are necessary. If you see that something is missing (maybe something in your notes), ask yourself if you can still manage to include it quickly (even if you have to write in the margins or on the back of the page). Unless you are certain that your instructor values neatness more than knowledge, do not hesitate to make additions and corrections. Simply draw a caret (∧), marking the exact place in the text where you want an addition or correction to be placed. Making corrections will allow you to focus on improving what you have already written, whereas recopying your answer just to make it look neat is an inefficient use of time (and you may have recopied only half your essay when the time is up). Finally, check spelling, punctuation, and sentence structure.

4d PREPARING A WRITING PORTFOLIO

College writing brings with it new demands: unfamiliar genres and purposes, time-management issues, and more writing overall. Though challenging, these demands are often balanced by opportunities for you to submit your best writing for final evaluation. You probably already know that artists, architects, designers, photographers, musicians, and even teachers often assemble a representative selection of their work for the consideration of gallery owners, schools, potential employers, or potential clients. Just as those professionals revise and reflect on the work they submit, so will you, as you go through the process of preparing a writing portfolio for your instructor's evaluation.

The purpose of a writing portfolio is to display your accomplishments—their range, depth, and quality—for another person, usually your instructor but sometimes a potential employer. Sometimes, you will be given free rein to decide what to include, but most often, your instructor will specify how many pieces and kinds of writing should make up the portfolio. For instance, if your semester-long writing course includes six writing assignments, you might be asked to submit your four best pieces, each representing a different genre, purpose, or stage of revision. Or your instructor might indicate that you can include five pieces of writing, as long as one of them is based on library research and contains correctly formatted citations and documentation of sources. In addition to the finished pieces of writing, you might also be expected to include organizing tools (such as notes or outlines), a rationale for your choices, and a letter of reflection on your progress. Some writing portfolios also include examples of group work, peer reviews, or discs or portable hard drives that showcase work delivered electronically. Whatever you ultimately decide to include in your portfolio, it should be writing that you feel good about. Keep in mind that your grade will be based on a summative evaluation of the portfolio, not on the individual examples.

As you select, revise, and assemble pieces of writing for your portfolio, then, you are evaluating your writing, just as your instructor will do as he or she deliberates on the writing portfolio as a whole. Given the evaluative nature of portfolios, you will want to present the most persuasive and informative selection of your writing that you can. To that end, consider including the following elements in your portfolio:

- **Cover sheet.** Includes your name, your instructor's name, the course title and number, and the date.
- **Table of contents.** Directs the reader to the types, lengths, and titles of the various pieces; compels you to label and consciously sequence your writing.
- **Page numbers.** Makes locating pieces easier.
- **Reflective essay.** Usually the opening essay, describing the contents of the portfolio, providing a rationale for the selections, and reflecting on your development (strengths and weaknesses) as a college writer, summarizing where you started, where you are, and where you are heading.

After assembling a portfolio, many college writers request a peer review, taking full advantage of their writing group's expertise and help to evaluate the portfolio's effectiveness. Peer evaluation can alert you to strengths and weaknesses in everything pertaining to your portfolio, from arguments in your reflective essay and surface errors to issues of sequencing and selection.

5 ‖ COMMUNICATING ONLINE

Whether you are at home, work, or school, you can easily communicate with others through online forums, various social media, and linked documents, thereby dramatically expanding your contacts as well as your work's audience and context. Composing and delivering your work online differs somewhat from writing essays or research papers delivered in hard copy. This chapter will help you

- assess the rhetorical situation for online writing (**5a**),
- participate in online discussions (**5b**),
- understand conventions for online communication (**5c**),
- compose effective documents in an online environment (**5d**), and
- manage the visual elements of a website (**5e**).

5a   ASSESSING THE ONLINE RHETORICAL SITUATION

Whenever you compose an e-mail message, create a web page or job application package, engage in an online discussion, or post a Facebook or blog update, you are using rhetoric, or purposeful language, to influence the outcome of an interaction (**1a**). Some online communication is so spontaneous you may forget that you are responding to a rhetorical situation, one in which your message can carry an impact just as powerful (negative or positive) as any created by a static print document. For that reason, online communication, like print and oral communication, merits attention to rhetorical audience, purpose, context, and tone.

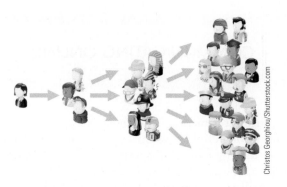

Christos Georghiou/Shutterstock.com

The key distinction of online communication is its instant access to a wide range of audiences, including secondary audiences (**1c(3)**) whose interests and values can be far different from those of your intended rhetorical audience. Most online communicators have learned the hard way how easily a confidential e-mail can reach an unintended audience. Thus, online communication offers enormous challenges in terms of audience, which are evident whether you are composing within an online learning platform (or course management program) like Blackboard, ANGEL, or WebCT; contributing to a campus club's listserv or website; or updating your status on Facebook or Twitter. For example, if your political science instructor asks you to contribute regularly to a class-related blog on contemporary and often controversial issues, the instructor and your classmates comprise your primary audience. Unless the course blog has specific privacy settings, anything you post will immediately be available to a variety of secondary audiences via the Internet, audiences who may not understand the context within which you are exploring a topic. Therefore, as you compose online, you will want to consider the responses of multiple audiences.

Like those for print and oral communication, online audiences are just as varied, whether they are primary or secondary, specialized, diverse, or multiple (**1c**). When writing a personalized e-mail, for instance, you address your rhetorical audience, a small primary audience, and adjust your purpose, message, and tone accordingly. In contrast, your posts to your political science course blog address a rhetorical audience that is broader, yet specialized, and your purpose, message, and tone will be appropriate within the context of an ongoing full-class discussion.

If you decide to create a web page or blog about a current issue or controversy, such as gun control or the debate over genetically modified food, you will be composing for a diverse audience whose members have varying levels of knowledge, understanding of specialized terms, and interest in your subject matter. Therefore, factual accuracy, appropriate tone, and informative examples should be major concerns.

Purpose must always align with audience, whether the rhetorical context is in print, in person, or online. Thus, whether you wish to express your point of view, create a mood, or amuse or motivate, your purpose must be readily recognizable to your rhetorical audience. In an e-mail message, you can state your purpose in the subject line; in your posts to a course-related blog, you can immediately announce the subject, so that your audience understands how your purpose and comments connect to that subject. And on a web page, your mission statement serves as your purpose. For instance, the website for English 414, Research Writing (figure 5.1), a course designed for students in various disciplines, states that one of the site's primary purposes is to "provide users with a variety of resources" in order to "help students improve their critical information literacy competencies as they work toward becoming more savvy, practiced, and independent researchers. The home page of this site also defines the term information literacy for readers. Regardless of how your audience encounters your online composition (receiving your email message, locating your webpage through a search engine, or by participating in a class's online course-management system), those readers expect to pinpoint your purpose quickly as easily. Therefore, you need to take extra care to clarify your purpose and make it readily apparent to any audience.

In an online context, the boundary between writer and audience becomes blurred as both writer and audience nearly simultaneously shape and reshape the message, context, and purpose (as figure 5.1 illustrates). The accessibility and speed of such online discussions (5b) encourages people to comment on or extend what has already been posted. This flow of new material contributes to an always evolving rhetorical context, requiring you to be familiar with the preceding discussion and to understand the conventions of the forum (including the values of your audience) in order to communicate productively.

Courtesy Cheryl Glenn, Anna Bjartmarsdottir, and Heather Adams

Figure 5.1: Announcing its purpose, this web page for a research writing course offers options for the final assignment.

Timeliness is another important feature of an online rhetorical situation. Internet users expect online compositions to be up-to-date, given the ease of revising (correcting and updating) electronic documents. Just as social network accounts, such as Twitter, Tumblr, and Facebook, are constantly being updated, personal, professional, and academic websites must be as well. The only useful online sources are up-to-date online sources. As you know, it is frustrating to access a web page only to discover that it is months or even years out of date. For example, a web page about TSA screening procedures that appeared before 9/11 will be markedly different from one produced after that date. In order for such a document to be current, it would have to include continuous updates on various new passenger-screening procedures, imaging technologies for screening, and the TSA's 3-1-1 policy for liquids, gels, and aerosols (see figure 5.2). Whether you are reading or composing online material, you want the information to be current, detailed, and correct.

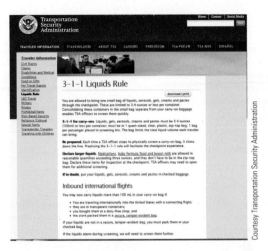

Courtesy Transportation Security Administration

Figure 5.2: Recent TSA screening procedures include rules for personal hygiene products.

5b PARTICIPATING IN ONLINE DISCUSSION COMMUNITIES

Participating in online discussion communities offers you several benefits: you can learn more about a topic that interests you; network with friends, classmates, and online acquaintances; and strengthen your writing skills. Communicating via blogs, listservs, chat rooms, and other online forums also helps you improve your ability to evaluate online information and advice in many of the ways you already evaluate print sources (chapter **10**).

Whenever—and however—you participate in an online forum, take care to present yourself as a trustworthy, credible writer and person. To do so, start by reading over what has already been said about the topic before adding your comments to an existing thread or starting a new one. Keep in mind both the specific information and the overall tone of the messages posted by others, and monitor your own messages for tone and clarity. For instance, in the exchange in figure 5.3, the instructor draws inferences from the student's previous post and poses several pointed questions to spark further reflection by the student.

Because tone is difficult to convey in online postings, take care when responding to others: intention and consequence do not always align.

Heather Brook Adams | 8:12 PM | Reply

Your points are well taken. I am most interested in your feeling like there is a level of political engagement you "should" embrace. Where does that sense of responsibility and obligation come from? Do you really feel that you "should" follow politics and current events? Or do you think that these are the sorts of things that we are supposed to feel? After all, you articulate some level of hopelessness in light of an "underlying power struggle."

Do public speakers hold themselves to a higher standard of this obligation? If so, where and when does that obligation break down?

These are just questions for thinking. Of course, anyone is welcome to respond!

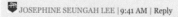
JOSEPHINE SEUNGAH LEE | 9:41 AM | Reply

Well, being a college student who is thinking about making some kind of difference in this world or in someone's life, I know that there really is not much I can do to help anyone as I would like to if I don't know what their problems are. I am a sociology major, and we learn that people are influenced not only by one another directly but also by larger groups or powers indirectly. Even if I want to help people on a more personal level, often times, the source of their problems stem from what is happening around them, and this includes political issues. Part of me wants to just keep my head in the sand, but I feel as though I am missing out on something big if I continue to do that.

Perhaps I do see politics as an endless power struggle, but as I said, I do not really know much about it. Debate is just so complex to me. It is an exchange that does not work if someone does not listen. Without listening, it is just an exchanging of words. I am more concerned about action to back up words. Without a following action, I don't know what the purpose of debate was.

I think everyone is equal in their obligation to speak. Some people actually speak in public, others speak out visually or in other ways. Some people can not speak, but they are there crying out silently. It all depends on who listens and responds with actions.

Courtesy Cheryl Glenn

Figure 5.3: A thread from a course blog, *Rhetoric and Civic Life*, featuring messages between an instructor (Adams) and her student (Lee).

Jokes, criticism, suddenly changing the topic, asserting what has already been said or argued—these are missteps that many online users make. So either stay on topic or indicate that you are changing the topic, gently stating your reason for making the change. Your purpose is to enrich the conversation, not to joke around, let alone criticize the posts of others. If you have a question about a previous post, raise it respectfully. If you detect a factual error, diplomatically present what you believe to be the correct information. And if someone criticizes you online (an attack referred to as **flaming**), try to remember how difficult tone is to convey and give that person the benefit of the doubt. Except in the most informal of e-mail correspondence, stay alert to all the conventions of correct English. If you use all lowercase letters, misspell words, or make usage errors, readers of your online writing may come away with a negative impression of you, especially if the correspondence is within a business, academic, or professional context. Finally, given that friends, teachers, and professional colleagues can easily access your online writing, take care to establish a professional relationship with the multiple audiences in your online groups and always monitor your privacy settings.

Exercise 1

Locate a blog devoted to a subject you are interested in or conduct a Twitter or Tumblr search for terms related to that subject. Read through the recent and archived posts to get a clear idea of the rhetorical situation before introducing yourself to others in the group. Then, ask a question or post a comment related to the subject under discussion. After reading responses to your post, write a paragraph describing the experience.

5c | NETIQUETTE AND ONLINE WRITING

Netiquette (from the phrase *Internet etiquette*) is a set of social practices developed by Internet users in order to promote respectful online interactions.

TIPS FOR USING NETIQUETTE IN ONLINE INTERACTIONS

Audience

- Keep in mind the potential audience(s) for your message: those for whom it is intended and others who may read it. If privacy is important, do not use online communication.
- Make the subject line of your message as descriptive as possible so that your reader(s) will immediately recognize the topic.

(continued on page 114)

(continued from page 113)

- Keep your message focused and limit it to one screen, if possible. If you want to attach a text or graphic file, keep its size under 1 MB. Readers' time or bandwidth may be limited, or their mobile device may be subject to an expensive usage plan.

- Before uploading a large file, consider reducing the resolution (and file size) of an image, which rarely affects quality.

- Avoid using fancy fonts and multiple colors unless you are certain that they will appear on your audience's screen.

- Give people adequate time to respond, remembering that they may be away from their computers or may be contemplating what to say.

- Consider the content of your message, making sure that it pertains to the interests and needs of your audience.

- Respect copyright. Never post something written by someone else without their permission or pass it off as your own.

Style and Presentation

- Maintain a respectful tone, whether your message is formal or informal.

- Be sure of your facts, especially when you are offering a clarification or a correction.

- Present ideas clearly and logically, using bullets or numbers if doing so will help.

- Pay attention to spelling and grammar. If your message is formal, you will certainly want to proofread it (perhaps even in hard copy) and make corrections before sending it out.

- Use emoticons (such as ☺) and abbreviations (such as IMHO for "in my humble opinion" or LOL for "laughing out loud") *only* when you are sure your audience will understand them and find them appropriate.

- Use all capital letters only when you want to be perceived as SHOUTING.

- Use boldface only if you wish the reader to be able to quickly locate a key item in your message, such as the due date for a report or the name of someone to contact.

- Abusive, critical, or profane language is never appropriate.

Context

- Observe what others say and how they say it before you engage in an online discussion; note what kind of information participants find appropriate to exchange.

- If someone is abusive, ignore that person or change the subject. Do not respond to flaming.
- Tone is difficult to convey online, and thus gentle sarcasm and irony may inadvertently come across as personal attacks.
- Do not use your school's or employer's network for personal business.

Credibility

- Use either your real name or an appropriate online pseudonym to identify yourself to readers. Avoid suggestive or inflammatory pseudonyms.
- Be respectful of others even when you disagree, and be welcoming to new members of an online community.

5d | COMPOSING EFFECTIVE ONLINE DOCUMENTS

As you know, websites are sets of electronic pages, anchored to a home page. Websites do not use the traditional linear arrangement of print texts (in which arguments, passages, and paragraphs unfold sequentially, from start to finish). Rather, websites are created and delivered with text, graphics, and animations integrated into their content. As such, they rely on **hypertext** (electronic text that includes **hyperlinks**, or **links**, to other online text, graphics, and animations) to emphasize arrangement and showcase content.

You are probably accustomed to navigating websites by clicking on hyperlinks. The home page of the American Museum of Natural History (figure 5.4) illustrates both the integration of text and graphics on a web page and the use of hyperlinks for navigation within a website.

Another important online tool is the navigation bar that stretches across the top of a web page. The home page of the American Museum's website (figure 5.4) features a well-organized navigation bar that includes tabs for planning a visit, exhibitions, research, the calendar, and joining the museum that run across the top of the page. Each of these tabs redirects users to other web pages with more information. On the top right are two windows: one for searching keywords or topics and another for selecting a language. Including these windows for subjects and languages indicates a respect for the varying interests and languages of the museum's patrons.

Figure 5.4: The navigation bar on the home page of the Museum of Natural History provides coherence as well as awareness of audience.

The **arrangement** (the pattern of organization of the ideas, text, and visual elements in a composition) of the site is clear because information is grouped meaningfully. The site is thus easy to use. Under the "Plan Your Visit" tab (figure 5.5), for instance, you can find pertinent information: the museum hours, directions and parking, dining, coat check, and popular tours. Arrangement also involves the balance of visual

Figure 5.5: Each tab of the horizontal menu offers the reader pertinent information.

elements and text. The American Museum's home page (figure 5.4) is unified by the use of a blue banner across the top and in the planetarium itself as well as the shades of beige across the navigation bar, in some of the planetarium lights, and at the bottom framing the featured exhibits. The entire website is given coherence by the blue banner and navigation bar, which appear on every page. Finally, the American Museum's logo, prominent in the upper left corner of the blue banner, serves as a visual reminder of the official nature of this site. Visual links—such as the current images that are presented as a slide show on the home page and that link to in-depth blog posts, videos, and other exhibits—combine arrangement and **delivery** (the presentation and interaction of visual elements with content).

Your web documents will likely be less elaborate than those of the American Museum of Natural History website. Nevertheless, remember that websites (and other online compositions) are available to diverse audiences, and so their context, purpose, tone, and message should be given as much forethought as possible (**1a**). Because of the flexible nature of electronic composition, you can be creative when planning, drafting, and revising web documents.

(1) Planning a website

As you develop any web document, including a website, you need to keep all the elements of the rhetorical situation in mind: rhetorical audience, purpose, message, and context. With your audience and purpose in mind, you must decide which ideas or information you should emphasize and then how best to arrange your web document to achieve that emphasis. And you also need to consider the overall impression you want the document to make. Do you want it to be motivational, informative, entertaining, or analytical? Do you want it to look snazzy, soothing, fun, or serious? In addition, while you are generating the content (with your overall purpose in mind), you also need to consider the supplementary links and information that will help you achieve your overall purpose. Fortunately, you do not have to do everything at once. Fine-tuning the visual design can wait until the content is in place.

When you are planning a website, you may find it helpful to create a storyboard or other visual representation of the site's organization.

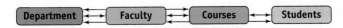

Figure 5.6: Linear pattern for organizing a website.

You can sketch a plan on paper or in a word-processing file if your site is fairly simple, or you can use index cards tacked to a bulletin board if it is more complex. If you have some time to devote to the planning process, you may want to learn how to use a program such as Dreamweaver, wix.com, weebly.com, or Wordpress to help you map out your site (such website design software is often available on computers in school labs).

The possibilities for organizing a website are endless. As starting points, you can consider three basic arrangement patterns—linear, hierarchical, and radial. A linear site (figure 5.6) is easy to set up, as it is presented with a narrative structure, running from beginning to end. Hierarchical arrangements and radial arrangements are more complex to develop and may be better suited to group projects. The hierarchical arrangement (figure 5.7) branches out at each level, and the radial arrangement (figure 5.8) features individual pages that can be linked and viewed in a variety of sequences.

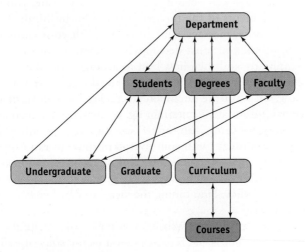

Figure 5.7: Hierarchical pattern for organizing a website.

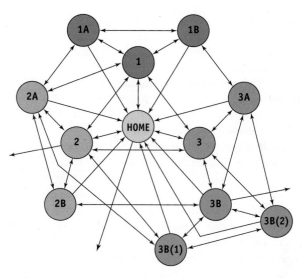

Figure 5.8: Radial pattern for organizing a website.

Whatever arrangement you choose, keep in mind how your arrangement will affect a user's experience in navigating the website. However you decide to organize your site, be sure to represent each main element in your plan. A good plan will be invaluable to you as you draft text, incorporate visual and multimedia elements, and refine your arrangement.

(2) Developing online documents

When you plan and compose a web page or website, you will rely on hypertext. You will also rely on design or visual elements (such as background and color) and links (to the home page as well as to all other pages of the website) to establish consistency and orienting guideposts for your readers. Those design and visual elements and links create important associations among the concepts and ideas in your web document and serve as valuable tools for its development. Your inclusion of links allows the website user (your audience) to read the information in whatever sequence is most productive for that user. Thus, a hypertext document (one created with online capabilities in mind) offers unlimited options for ordering the content, as users click on the various links in any order they choose. Because the individual interests and personalities of those who read your web document will lead them to navigate it in different ways, you will want to consider how users' different approaches may affect the intended purpose of your document and try to arrange your material accordingly.

Some basic principles can help you use hyperlinks effectively in your web documents.

(a) Enhancing coherence with hyperlinks

The choice and placement of hyperlinks should be a vital part of your organizational plan. A site map, located on the home page, is essential for a large site and helpful for a compact one, as it provides a snapshot of the site's content and arrangement as well as direct access to its various pages. Hyperlinks to the individual pages of a website not only indicate logical divisions of the document but also provide transitions based on key words or ideas. As navigational signposts, hyperlinks serve as powerful rhetorical tools that provide coherence and reflect an effective arrangement.

(b) Taking advantage of the flexibility of hyperlinks

You can use individual words, phrases, or even sentences as textual hyperlinks. Hyperlinks can also be icons or other graphical elements, such as pictures or logos that reflect the information contained in each link (see figure 5.9). If you do use graphical links, be sure that their appearance is appropriate for the transitions you are indicating. In addition, you must get permission to use text, graphics, or multimedia elements taken from other sources. Even though such material is often free, its source must be acknowledged (**11g**).

Internal hyperlinks are those that take the user between pages or sections of the website in which they appear. When creating links to content *external* to your website (such as a hyperlink in a web page about hurricanes that links to a meteorologist's website), be sure to select sites containing relevant, accurate, up-to-date, and well-presented information. You should use any contact information provided on a site to request permission to link to it, and you should check your links periodically to be sure that they are still active.

(c) Evaluating the rhetorical impact of hyperlinks

Textual and graphical links establish persuasive rhetorical associations for users. Compare the rhetorical impact of linking an image of One

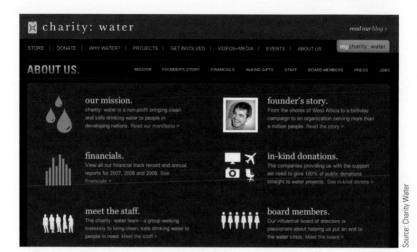

Source: Charity Water

Figure 5.9: The hyperlinks on this charity's "About Us" web page parallel the labels on the navigation bar and are accompanied by icons that reflect the information accessed through the links.

World Trade Center (or "Freedom Tower") to a page about public memorials with that of linking the same image to a page about global terrorism. Because hyperlinks serve various rhetorical purposes, be sure to evaluate the impact of any hyperlinks you include in your web document as you plan, compose, and revise it. You will also want to evaluate the rhetorical impact of the hyperlinks on web documents you are reading or using.

◘ TECH SAVVY

To create a web page, you do not have to understand the computer code (HTML) that allows a browser to display text. Programs such as Moveable Type (a blogging platform) and iWeb, referred to generally as WYSIWYG (What You See Is What You Get) HTML editors, will do such coding for you automatically. But some writers find that knowledge of the basic HTML commands can be useful for troubleshooting and editing a web page. A number of tutorials on the use of HTML are available on the Internet.

(3) Drafting web documents

When drafting a web document, you will undoubtedly consider various ways to organize your material. You may draft text for a linear arrangement and then later break the text into separate sections for different pages, which you link in sequence. At times, however, the arrangement and means of delivery required for an online document will force you to draft in unfamiliar ways. For example, you may find that you need to write the text for a website in chunks, drafting the text for a single page, including hyperlinks, and then moving on to the next page. Or you might wait until you revise your site to add hyperlinks or to replace some of your initial text links with graphical ones.

Once you have drafted and revised your site, get feedback from your classmates or colleagues, just as you would for an essay or a report. Since a website can include many pages with multiple links and images, you may want to ask for feedback not only about the content of your site but also about layout, graphics, and navigation (5e).

Professional web developers often put a site that is still in a draft stage on the Internet and solicit reactions from users, a process called **usability testing**. The developers then refine the site based on those reactions. Because websites are more interactive than printed texts, it is a good idea to seek input from users throughout site development. To solicit feedback, specify on your home page how users can contact you, taking care to consider your online security. To that end, you may want to open a separate, free e-mail account, rather than making your personal e-mail address available.

Usability testing is particularly important given the wide variety of potential audiences for online documents. Your web document should be accessible to users who do not have a fast Internet connection as well as to those who have physical limitations affecting seeing, hearing, or keyboarding. Consider simplifying the design by using a restricted number of graphic elements, facilitating the downloading of materials by using low-resolution images (which have smaller file sizes), and avoiding animated graphics. To accommodate users with physical disabilities or different means of accessing web documents (for example, visually impaired users who employ talking computer programs that read web pages), incorporate basic accessibility features such as **alt tags** (descriptive lines of text for each visual image that can be read by screen-reading software). Such accommodations will make your online writing accessible to the greatest number of users.

The following checklist will help you plan a website and develop ideas for each page.

✓ **CHECKLIST** for Planning and Developing a Website

- What information, ideas, or perspective should a user take away from your site?

- How does the arrangement of your site reflect your overall purpose? How does it assist your intended users in understanding your purpose?

- Ideally, how would a user navigate your website? What are the other options for navigating within your site?

- Should you devote each page to a single main idea or combine several ideas on one page?

- How will you help users return to the home page and find key information quickly?

- What key connections between ideas or pieces of information might be emphasized through the use of hyperlinks?

- Will a user who follows external links be able to get back to your site?

- To ensure that your website has more impact than a paper document, have you used web-specific resources—such as hyperlinks, sound and video clips, and animations—in creating it? How do those multimedia elements help you achieve your purpose?

- Do you need graphics—charts, photos, cartoons, clip art, logos, and so on—to enhance the site so that it will accomplish your purpose? Where should key visual elements be placed to be most effective?

- How often will you update your site?

- How will you solicit feedback for revisions to your site?

- Will your site be accessible to users with slow Internet access and those with physical limitations?

Exercise 2

Plan and compile information for a web page that supports a paper you are writing for one of your classes. If you have access to software that converts documents to web pages, start by converting your document. Make adjustments to it based on the criteria in the preceding checklist. Finally, critique your web page.

5e VISUAL ELEMENTS AND RHETORICAL PURPOSE

Visual design sends messages to users: an effective design not only invites them to explore a website but also conveys the designer's rhetorical purpose (chapter 6). All the design elements of an online document, like the tone and style of a printed one, are rhetorical tools that help you achieve your purpose and reach your intended audience. For instance, if a user has a negative reaction to a website photograph of a natural disaster that affected humans (natural disasters being one of the featured exhibits at the American Museum of Natural History), that reaction is likely to affect the user's view of the site in general. When you choose visual elements such as photographs, try to anticipate how various members of your audience may react.

(1) Basic design principles for easy navigation

A number of basic principles apply to the visual design of web documents.

- **Balance** involves the way in which the design elements used in a document are related to one another spatially. Web pages with a symmetrical arrangement of elements convey a formal, static impression, whereas asymmetrical arrangements are informal and dynamic.
- **Proportion** has to do with the relative sizes of design elements. Large elements attract more attention than small ones and will be perceived as more important.

- **Movement** concerns the way in which our eyes scan a page for information. Most of us look at the upper-left corner of a page first (where the American Museum of Natural History has placed its logo) and the lower-right corner last. Therefore, the most important information on a web page should appear in those locations. Vertical or horizontal arrangement of elements on a page implies stability; diagonal and zigzagging arrangements suggest movement.

- **Contrast** between elements can be achieved by varying their focus or size. For instance, a web page about the Siberian Husky might show a photo of one of these dogs in sharp focus against a blurred background; the image of the dog might also be large relative to other elements on the page to enhance contrast. In text, you can emphasize an idea by presenting it in a contrasting font—for example, a playful display font such as **Marker Felt Thin** or an elegant script font such as *Edwardian Script*. An easy-to-read (sans serif) font such as Arial or Helvetica, however, should be used for most of the text on a web page.

- **Unity** refers to the way all the elements (and pages) of a site combine to give the impression that they are parts of a complete whole. For instance, choose a few colors and fonts to reflect the tone you want to convey, and use them consistently throughout your site. Creating a new design for each page of a website makes the site seem chaotic and therefore ineffective.

(2) Using color and background in online composition

Like the other elements of a web document, color and background are rhetorical tools that can be used to achieve various visual effects (figure 5.10). Current web standards allow the display of a wide array of colors for backgrounds, text, and frames. You can find thousands of background graphics on the Internet or create them with software.

To avoid confusion, designers recommend using no more than three main colors for a document, although you may use varying intensities, or shades, of a color (for example, light blue, dark blue, and medium blue) to connect related materials. Besides helping to organize your site, color can have other specific effects. Bright colors, such as red and yellow, are more noticeable and can be used on a web page to emphasize a point or idea. In addition, some colors have associations you may

Figure 5.10: The use of a consistent color palette on this web page enhances the purpose of the website. The Organic World Foundation promotes organic farming; the visual composition suggests simplicity and purity.

wish to consider. For instance, reds can indicate danger or an emergency, whereas brown shades such as beige and tan suggest a formal atmosphere. Textual hyperlinks usually appear in a color different from that of the surrounding text on a web page so that they are more visible to users. Select colors for textual hyperlinks that fit in with the overall color scheme of your document and help readers navigate between pages on your site.

Background, too, contributes to a successful website. Although a dark background or one with a pattern can create a dramatic appearance, it often makes text difficult to read and hyperlinks difficult to see. If you do use a dark or patterned background, be sure that the color of the text offers enough contrast to be readable onscreen and that you provide a version that will print clearly if your rhetorical audience is likely to want to print it.

✓ **CHECKLIST** for Designing an Online Document

- Have you used no more than three colors, perhaps varying the intensity of one or more of them?

- Does a background color or pattern on your page make the text difficult or easy to read? If your audience will want to print the page, will it be readable?

- Have you chosen a single, easy-to-read font such as Arial or Helvetica for most of your text? Are the type styles (bold, italic, and so on) used consistently throughout the document?

- Have you used visual elements sparingly? Are any image files larger than 4 or 5 MB, making it likely that they will take a long time to transfer? If so, can you reduce their size using a lower resolution or by cropping?

- Have you indicated important points graphically by using bullets or numbers, or visually by dividing the text into short blocks?

- Is any page or section crowded? Can users scan the information on a single screen quickly?

- Does each page include adequate white space for easy reading?

- Have you made sure that all the links work?

- Have you identified yourself as the author and noted when the site was created or last revised?

- Have you run a spell check and proofread the site yourself?

6 ‖ MULTIMODAL COMPOSING

Every day, we experience **multimodal** communication (a mashup of "multiple" and "modes"). We successfully interpret cascades of spoken and written words, music, photos, graphics, and design features, quickly making sense of visual and **sonic** (sound) messages. Just as important as our ability to see, hear, and experience those messages is our ability to compose **multimodal documents**—documents that use sound, visuals, and words, both separately and in combination, to communicate with a rhetorical audience.

In this chapter, you will learn the rhetorical principles of combining visual and sonic elements with text, the genres of visual documents, and the conventions of layout and delivery—all of which will help you achieve your rhetorical purpose. More specifically, this chapter will help you

- understand multimodal documents in terms of the rhetorical situation (**6a**),
- employ the design principles of visual and sonic rhetoric (**6b**),
- combine visual, verbal, and sonic elements effectively (**6c**), and
- identify the common genres and effective design features of multimodal documents (**6d**).

6a ‖ MULTIMODAL DOCUMENTS AND THE RHETORICAL SITUATION

Opportunity, audience, purpose, message, and context—the same rhetorical elements underlying the interpretation and composition of verbal texts—apply to visual documents as well. A **visual document** uses such elements as still photographs and images, video, film, animation, pictures, drawings, and **graphics** (diagrams and tables) and follows purposeful design elements and layout. Often, visual documents combine visual elements and verbal text to respond to an opportunity, express meaning, and deliver a message to a rhetorical audience. For example, the Twitter profile (figure 6.1) uses both words and images to convey

Figure 6.1: Your multimodal Twitter profile page conveys a purposeful image to your audience.

the author's portrayal of herself as an adventurer, adding maps and graphs to illustrate her proficiency in biking and hiking. With a backdrop of majestic mountains and rugged vehicles in the fore, her Twitter page suggests the frontier, pioneering, and exploration, informing and entertaining the author's Twitter audience.

Consider the brochure in figure 6.2, which features "winning solutions" to the problem of global warming. With the color green synonymous with "eco-friendly," this brochure serves a distinct informative purpose, that of refocusing "individual, state, national and global efforts" toward undoing global warming. The rhetorical audience consists of readers with a vested interest in the topic of global warning who are already predisposed to the message. Therefore, the brochure only needs to respond to (rather than elicit) the audience's already established interest in the topic. The creator of the brochure has no need to argue the importance of paying attention to global warming and can concentrate instead on outlining various strategies for slowing the progress of the problem. In other words, the purpose of the brochure is not to persuade so much as to deliver new information that a rhetorical audience will want to consider putting to use. Thus, the audience and purpose of the brochure are linked by the seven winning solutions, all bulleted. Whether a Twitter page, magazine advertisement, brochure, poster, billboard, newsletter, or website, every visual document—regardless of its purpose (**1d**)—must take into account the relationship between purpose and audience.

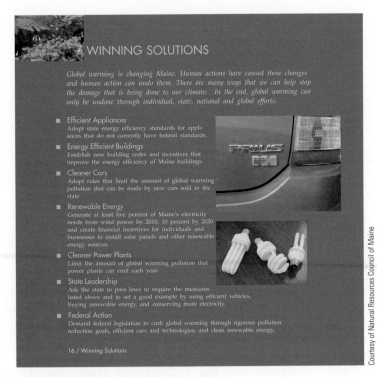

Figure 6.2: An effective brochure that is aimed at a specific audience.

The rhetorical situation also influences the choice of genre: Twitter and web pages, posters and billboards, videos and still images, proposals and reports—these genres offer different methods of delivery and serve different purposes. Posters and billboards, for instance, include a small amount of text, allowing the audience to absorb the message visually and instantly. Such ease of access helps these predominantly visual documents reach a large, diverse audience. The Target billboard (figure 6.3) includes very little text and the red-and-white Target logo. The **white space** (blank areas around text, graphics, or images) keeps the drive-by audience's focus on the three short commands, "Sit. Stay. Shop."

By contrast, the creator of the global warming brochure (figure 6.2) assumes that the rhetorical audience will take the time to read the more extensive text, probably while sitting. Thus, the volume of specialized

Figure 6.3: The Target billboard optimizes the effects of minimal text and maximum white space.

information in a brochure makes this genre particularly appropriate for an educated, already interested audience.

Exercise 1

Select a visual document that has caught your attention. Write for five to ten minutes in response to that document. Then, working with one or two classmates, analyze the document in terms of the opportunity and rhetorical audience it addresses, the components of the rhetorical situation, and the relationship between words and images. Explain how a sonic element could enhance the visual. Be prepared to share your document and analysis with the rest of the class.

6b   VISUAL DESIGN PRINCIPLES

After considerations of purpose, audience, context, and genre, the designer of a visual document must analyze just how the various elements can best articulate a message. Just as writers organize words into sentences and paragraphs, designers structure the visual elements of their documents in order to establish coherence, develop ideas, and achieve their purpose. Experienced designers always stand back several feet from a visual document in order to see which visual, textual, and special elements draw their attention. If the elements compete, no part of the document gets sufficient attention. (The abundant white space of the Target billboard, figure 6.3, draws attention to the three main words.) Therefore, the visual delivery of complicated information requires strategies different from those used in the delivery of traditional verbal texts. Rather than relying on paragraph breaks, transitions, and topic sentences, designers of visual documents call on four important principles to organize, condense, and develop ideas: alignment, proximity, contrast, and repetition. These four design principles will help you organize complex information, making it both visually appealing and easily accessible to your audience.

(1) The principle of alignment

The principle of alignment involves the use of an invisible grid system, running vertically and horizontally, to place and connect elements on a page. The fewer the invisible lines, the stronger the document design. For instance, the poster in figure 6.4 has two obvious sets of primary lines: one set that moves from left to right over the top half of the poster and a strong line down the center of the bottom half. These lines organize and unify the poster and give it a sharp, clean look, directing the viewer's eye to the smiling young people leaning on the fence. The words along the bottom of the poster, "RURAL ELECTRIFICATION ADMINISTRATION," reveal that the happy expressions are related to the expectation of electrification. The broad red-and-white and blue-and-white stripes affirm the patriotism of the federal program for rural electrification. Overall, the poster communicates that rural Americans can look forward to a better future because of electricity.

(2) The principle of proximity

The principle of **proximity** requires the grouping of related textual or visual elements, such as the horizontal stripes and the fence rails in the poster in figure 6.4. Dissimilar elements are separated by white space (**6a**). The audience perceives each grouping (or chunk) of elements in a well-designed visual document as a single unit and interprets it as a whole before moving on to the next group. In the Target billboard (figure 6.3), the three single commands comprise such a chunk. In

Digital Image The Museum of Modern Art/Licensed by Scala/Art Resource, NY

Figure 6.4: This Rural Electrification Administration poster by Lester Beall (1934) was purposefully designed to herald progress.

other words, the chunks serve a function similar to sections in a written document, organizing the page and reducing clutter. In the poster in figure 6.4, the proximity of the text to the image of the young people links the textual and visual elements and allows them to be interpreted together.

(3) The principle of contrast

The principle of **contrast** establishes a visual hierarchy, providing clear clues as to which elements are most important and which are less so.

The most salient textual or visual elements (such as the three red words in figure 6.3 and the red, white, and blue stripes in the poster in figure 6.4) stand out from the rest of the document, while other elements (the logos or a line of text, for instance) are not as noticeable. The most significant elements of a document are generally contrasted with other elements by differences in size, color, or typeface. Academic and professional documents, for example, usually have their headings in bold or italic type or capital letters to distinguish them from the rest of the text. The brochure in figure 6.2 (on page 129) features a large title in capital letters, "WINNING SOLUTIONS," which dominates the page; the identical size and typeface of all the headings indicate that they are of equal importance but subordinate to the title. Just a brief glance at this brochure allows the viewer to determine the hierarchy of information and the basic structure.

(4) The principle of repetition

The principle of **repetition** has to do with the replication throughout a document of specific textual or visual elements, such as the geographic locations in the Twitter profile (figure 6.1), the headings in the brochure (figure 6.2), the three one-word commands in the billboard (figure 6.3), and the stripes in the poster (figure 6.4). As you already know, nearly all academic and professional papers use a consistent typeface for large blocks of text, thereby creating a unified look throughout these documents. Visual documents follow a similar strategy, purposefully limiting the number of typefaces, colors, and graphics in order to enhance coherence with repetition. The repeated bullets and the repeated typefaces in the headings and text of the brochure on global warming, the consistent typeface of the commands in the Target ad, and the stripes in the poster for rural electrification help structure these visual documents and reinforce their unity.

6c   COMBINING VISUAL, VERBAL, AND SONIC ELEMENTS

Although words or images alone can have a tremendous impact on an audience, the combination of the two, together with sonic elements, can become necessary when no element alone can successfully respond to a rhetorical opportunity or reach a rhetorical audience, let alone fulfill the designer's purpose. Newspapers and magazines have long included powerful images to heighten the emotional impact of a text. Diagrams usually accompany a set of product-assembly instructions to reinforce the process analysis of the assembler.

Sound, too, contributes to the overall effectiveness of a multimodal message, whether the sound includes spoken dialogue or voice-over (in a video, advertisement, or PowerPoint presentation), music, or sound effects (sizzling, whooshing, sighing, laughter, running, breathlessness, and so on). YouTube videos offer compelling multimodal (visual, textual, and sonic) compositions, whether featuring cute kitties, job applicants, Baltic Sea excursions, cooking lessons, or tennis instruction. Thus, when used in combination—words and images, images and sound, words and sound, or all three together—these modes can work to reinforce the message, or they can play together ironically, contradicting each other.

(1) Advertisements

The words and image in the advertisement in figure 6.5 work together to argue that the viewer should consider buying a particular car. The central image depicts a fast-moving Aston Martin, with a crack of almost audible lightning in the background. "Don't worry, Daniel Craig was scared too" alludes to the actor who plays the intrepid James Bond. If he's scared, chances are you will be, too! Considering only the image, a viewer focuses on the car itself, prominently placed at the center of the frame, its sleek shiny body a strong contrast to the rugged bluff and streak of lightning. The storm, the curvy road, the fast car—all convey a dangerous ride, with the storm and speed invoking sonic elements. The textual elements ironically and prominently assure the viewer not to worry, for braver men have been scared, too. At the bottom left is the logo of the car itself.

Without the accompanying text, the image in figure 6.5 might convey the message that the Aston Martin is simply fast, with no mention of safety, luxury, or comfort. But combined with the textual and sonic elements, the image's message is clarified: the car provides an elegant getaway during a crisis; little wonder, then, that 007 drove one just like it.

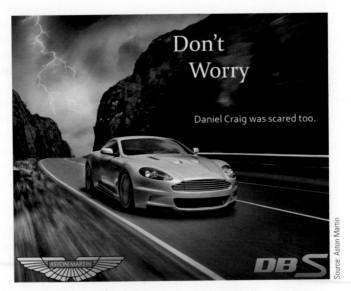

Figure 6.5: Words, images, and implied sounds are necessary to convey the purpose of this advertisement.

(2) Graphics

Many academic and professional documents that are composed primarily of text also include visual displays, or **graphics**, to clarify written material (and provide white space). Graphics can illustrate a concept, present data, provide visual relief, or simply attract readers' attention. Different types of graphics—tables, charts or graphs, and pictures—serve different purposes, even multiple purposes in a given document, but all graphics enable readers to absorb information relatively quickly. If it is possible that readers might not receive the intended message through visuals alone, graphics can always be supplemented with textual discussion.

(a) Tables
Tables use a row-and-column arrangement to organize data (numbers or words) spatially; they are especially useful for presenting great amounts of numerical information in a small space, enabling the reader to draw direct comparisons among pieces of data or even to locate specific

Average Time Spent per Day with Major Media by
US Adults, 2010–2013
hrs:mins

	2010	2011	2012	2013
Digital	**3:14**	**3:50**	**4:31**	**5:09**
• Online*	2:22	2:23	2:27	2:19
• Mobile (nonvoice)	0:24	0:49	1:33	2:21
• Other	0:26	0:28	0:31	0:36
TV	**4:24**	**4:34**	**4:38**	**4:31**
Radio	**1:36**	**1:34**	**1:32**	**1:26**
Print**	**0:50**	**0:44**	**0:38**	**0:32**
• Newspapers	0:30	0:26	0:22	0:18
• Magazines	0:20	0:18	0:16	0:14
Other	**0:42**	**0:36**	**0:20**	**0:14**
Total	10:46	11:18	11:39	11:52

Note: ages 18+; time spent with each medium includes all time spent with that
medium, regardless of multitasking; for example, 1 hour of multitasking online
while watching TV is counted as 1 hour for TV and 1 hour for online; *includes
all internet activities on desktop and laptop computers; **offline reading only
Source: eMarketer, July 2013

Source: eMarket.com

**Figure 6.6: This table makes it easy to see the increasing amount of
time Americans spend each day using various media.**

items. When you design a table, be sure to label all of the columns and
rows accurately and to provide both a title and a number for the table.
In the table shown in figure 6.6, you can see that the columns, labeled
"2010," "2011," "2012," and "2013," contain information important
for people interested in the amount of time Americans spend with
major media, whether digital (online and mobile), television, radio,
print (newspapers and magazines), and "other." The table number and
title traditionally appear above the table body, and any notes or source
information are placed below it.

Most word-processing programs have settings that let you insert a
table wherever you need one. You can determine how many rows and
columns the table will have, and you can also size each row and each
column appropriately for the information it will hold.

(b) Charts and graphs

Like tables, charts and graphs also display relationships among statistical data in visual form; unlike tables, they do so using lines, bars,

or other visual elements rather than just letters and numbers. Data can be displayed in several different graphic forms: pie charts, line graphs, and bar charts are the most common examples. These forms, like photos and other images, are referred to as figures. The figure number and title traditionally appear below the image, as all the figures in this chapter demonstrate, along with captions and source information (see **11c**).

Pie charts are especially useful for showing the relationship of parts to a whole (see figure 6.7), but these graphics can only be used to display sets of data that add up to 100 percent. (In the chart in figure 6.7, the percentage of time the average smartphone owner spends on various phone-related tasks represents 100 percent.)

Breakdown of the Average Smartphone Owner's Daily Time-Spend
On average, U.S. smartphone owners spend 58 minutes daily on their phones

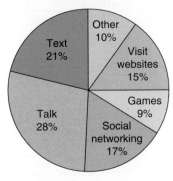

Figure 6.7: The colors and labels distinguish among the purposes of smartphone use.

Line graphs show the change in the relationship between one variable (indicated as a value on the vertical axis, or *y* axis) and another variable (indicated as a value on the horizontal axis, or *x* axis). The most common *x*-axis variable is time. Line graphs are very good at showing how a variable changes over time. A line graph might be used, for example, to illustrate the progression of sleep stages during one night, trends in financial markets over a number of years, or grade distribution over the course of decades (see figure 6.8).

Bar charts show correlations between two variables that do not involve smooth changes over time. For instance, a bar chart might illustrate gross national product for several nations, the relative speeds of various computer processors, or statistics about the composition of the U.S. workforce (see figure 6.9).

(c) Pictures and Videos
Pictures include photos, sketches, technical illustrations, paintings, icons, and other visual representations that remain still. **Videos**, including visual representations of all kinds and genres, move:

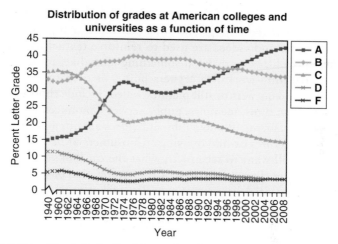

Figure 6.8: The red line indicates the rising number of college students receiving As.

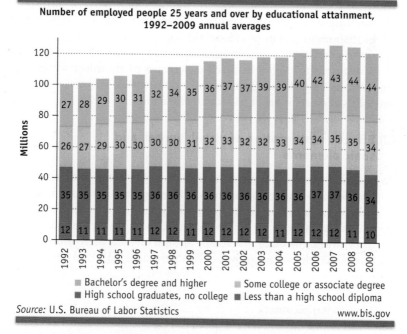

Figure 6.9: This bar chart illustrates the composition of the U.S. workforce with respect to level of education.

sometimes, the images themselves move; other times, the videographer splices together clips and stills that indicate movement. Both photographs and videos are used to reinforce textual descriptions, to show a reader exactly what something looks like, to demonstrate how something works, to argue a point, or even to persuade. In addition to sequences of still pictures, videos include short documentaries, fiction films, memoirs, public service announcements (PSAs), and advertisements. Photographs and videos are often more effective than still pictures or line drawings. Consumers of used-car ads, for instance, will want to see exactly what the car looks like in photographs or film clips, not in an artistic interpretation of its appearance. Likewise, potential visitors to Costa Rica will want to experience full-color photos of dazzling beaches, verdant forests, and azure water—or embedded film clips, perhaps with music and other sounds, showing Costa Rican sites.

However, despite the specific (and often tantalizing) information that photographs and videos can deliver, they are not always the most effective type of image. If you are assembling a new piece of furniture or installing a new printer, you may prefer following line drawings, rather than photographs or videos: although both the photograph and video provide a more realistic image, line drawings enable the designer of a document to highlight specific elements of an object while de-emphasizing or eliminating unnecessary information. Arrows, pointers, and labels add useful detail to such an illustration.

(3) Effective integration of visual, verbal, and sonic elements

To integrate visual and sonic elements into written text, position them purposefully; you might place images close together in a document or embed an image or clip at the beginning or end of a document so as not to disrupt the text. Or you might launch oral instructions, descriptions, or music (or other enhancing sounds) with a mere mouseover (that is, when the cursor moves over a particular point on the document or site).

(a) Considering proximity

Proximity—placing an image as close as possible to the text that refers to it—is one way of establishing a connection between the verbal and visual elements. Think of how helpful it can be to have images accompanying printed instructions for assembling a piece of furniture, setting up a new computer, or following a complicated recipe. When an image aligns with verbal instructions, the document is effective and instructive.

Wrapping the text around an image also serves to integrate visual and verbal elements (see figure 6.10); such text wrapping places an image and its corresponding text in very close proximity. In addition, cropping unnecessary elements from an image strengthens connections between it and the textual components of a document, highlighting what is most important while preserving what is authentic. When a visual element (a graph or table) is too large to fit on the same page as the related text, it is placed on a separate page or moved to an appendix. Thus, proximity must occasionally be forfeited for the sake of in-depth explanation or detailed support.

Figure 6.10: Wrapping the text around this image integrates multimodal elements.

Photos 12/Alamy

(b) Including captions and labels

Captions and labels are also crucial to the integration of visual and verbal components of a document. In academic texts, tables and figures are labeled by being numbered consecutively and separately, with captions for tables appearing above the table, captions for figures appearing below the figure, and source information about both tables and figures appearing below both. Moreover, the body of an academic text includes **anchors**, specific references to each image or graphic used, such as "see Figure 5" and "as shown in Table 2" (see the research paper in **15c**). In popular magazines and newspapers, on the other hand, images and graphics are rarely labeled and anchored in this way. More often, these text-enhancing visuals are integrated into the text through the use of captions and layout. Although the conventions of academic and professional documents vary, no figure or table should be inserted into a text document without either a caption or a label (or both) to explain its relevance in the larger context of the work.

(c) Working with sound

Online technologies offer plentiful opportunities for you to incorporate audio content into your works. Writers who create podcasts, soundtracks, voice-overs, video-audio clips, and other sounds use downloads and streaming media (which can be played without downloading). Whether they search for sounds (and images) distributed under a Creative Commons license (which offers them at no charge), seek permission from the copyright holder, or create their own, twenty-first-century writers are finding that sounds of all kinds are easily accessible and applicable.

6d COMMON GENRES AND EFFECTIVE FEATURES OF MULTIMODAL DOCUMENTS

Although all multimodal documents adhere to the same rhetorical principles, each of the common genres is distinguished by its effective features. In addition to the documents already mentioned in this chapter, posters, flyers, brochures, and newsletters are among the most common genres of multimodal documents. Publishing software, such as PagePlus or Microsoft Publisher, offers standard templates for designing these documents.

(1) Posters and flyers

Posters and **flyers**, colorful sheets that paper walls, utility poles, and bulletin boards around most college and university campuses, are used to advertise organizations, events, issues, and services. Although posters and flyers often fulfill the same purpose, they are not always aimed at the same rhetorical audiences. Therefore, their effectiveness depends on how and where they appear. Posters, for instance, usually appear on large walls and are seen from afar. For those reasons, a poster usually employs much more visual than verbal (or textual) information so that its audience can absorb the message at a glance (like billboards; see figure 6.3). By contrast, the smaller, usually more text-heavy, single-sheet flyer is intended for mass distribution and is often handed out to passersby. Yet, despite these differences, both posters and flyers are meant to be seen by as many people as possible—with text and images that readily appeal to a target group (the rhetorical audience).

Because the purpose of posters and flyers is to reach as many people as possible—and as quickly as possible—it is vitally important that the audience be able to locate the important information immediately. Both posters and flyers need a focal point that captures attention and highlights the basic information: who? what? where? when? and maybe even why? Thus, artfully minimalistic posters and flyers are more effective than those that overwhelm viewers with too many images or typefaces and too much text.

The poster in figure 6.11 relies heavily on color, repetition, and contrast to convey its message: "Live Heart Smart." Sponsored by the Centers for Disease Control and Prevention and circulated just before and during February (American Heart Month), the poster shows an ageless

Figure 6.11: This poster combines text and images effectively. It was designed to be scanned by viewers in the backward *S* pattern, as shown on the right.

and generic woman wearing Valentine's Day red, with hearts forming her hair and serving as her words. Red and hearts are repeated throughout the poster, both in images and in words. The text of the poster is aligned in two blocks at the top and bottom, and the lines of text within each block are in close proximity. The white space works to focus the viewer's attention on the figure of the woman. Her graceful hands encircling her heart further emphasize the poster's serious message.

Most people "read" posters and flyers by scanning them in a backward S pattern, beginning at the top left and ending at the bottom right. The poster in figure 6.11 was designed to take advantage of that scanning strategy. The large lines of type at the top, centering on the red boldfaced word "Heart," provide a natural starting point. The eye is drawn downward over the curve of the hearts in the woman's hair, then across her hands and heart as a turning point, and, finally, to the words "wear red" in all capital letters just below the waist of her red dress.

Online documents that share the characteristics of posters and flyers often receive wide distribution: political advertisements (or critiques), public service documents, meme arguments (see p. 149), and entertainment documents are just a few examples. Created for online distribution, these posterlike documents may include visual, textual, and sound elements, often with the text superimposed on a visual supplied by another party. The public service announcement in figure 6.12 leverages the best qualities of an effective visual: the visual of the snow-capped

Figure 6.12: This public service announcement exemplifies the posterlike attributes of some documents distributed via social media.

dog with the warm eyes (contrast), the grouping of the dog's needs (proximity), the alignment of the parallel texts, and the repetition of the concepts of warmth, shelter, and inside.

TIPS FOR DESIGNING EFFECTIVE POSTERS AND FLYERS

- Identify your rhetorical audience.
- Determine your purpose.
- Consider where your poster will appear or how your flyer will be distributed.
- Provide a clear focal point.
- Aim for visual simplicity.
- Strive for coherence.
- Chunk information.
- Remember the backward *S* scanning pattern.

---

(2) Brochures

Like posters and flyers, **brochures** (see figures 6.2 and 6.13) or pamphlets rely on the integration of engaging text, visual elements, and effective design to convey information. Because the rhetorical audience has usually already indicated interest by requesting or picking up the brochure, the designer must maintain that interest with striking photographs and bold colors that contrast with the text color. Like all successful communicators, designers of brochures are guided by several basic rhetorical principles: layout, repetition, and chunking.

Brochure designers realize that their documents will be read quickly, so they choose a layout that allows for easy scanning. Therefore, a brochure incorporates design features that serve as signposts for readers, helping them navigate the document. Headings and subheadings allow a reader to gain an overview of the document's contents and pinpoint specific information. Bullets are often used to organize information and make it quickly accessible. The principle of repetition is applied to the document's overall structure. Each page may have the same basic layout, with variations in content and color, or a simple image or symbol may appear throughout the document to unify it. In the brochure for cancer patients in figure 6.13, each left-hand page contains an image of a survivor; the facing page has the same layout throughout the document,

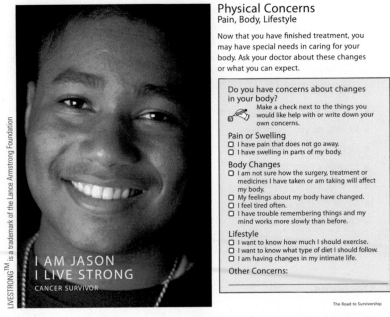

Physical Concerns
Pain, Body, Lifestyle

Now that you have finished treatment, you may have special needs in caring for your body. Ask your doctor about these changes or what you can expect.

Do you have concerns about changes in your body?
Make a check next to the things you would like help with or write down your own concerns.

Pain or Swelling
☐ I have pain that does not go away.
☐ I have swelling in parts of my body.

Body Changes
☐ I am not sure how the surgery, treatment or medicines I have taken or am taking will affect my body.
☐ My feelings about my body have changed.
☐ I feel tired often.
☐ I have trouble remembering things and my mind works more slowly than before.

Lifestyle
☐ I want to know how much I should exercise.
☐ I want to know what type of diet I should follow.
☐ I am having changes in my intimate life.

Other Concerns:

I AM JASON
I LIVE STRONG
CANCER SURVIVOR

LIVESTRONG™ is a trademark of the Lance Armstrong Foundation

The Road to Survivorship   3

Figure 6.13: This brochure's repeated design features provide the reader with signposts.

with variations in the checklist content. The statement "ɪ ʟɪᴠᴇ sᴛʀᴏɴɢ" is repeated beneath each picture.

Brochures break text into blocks or chunks. In a typical brochure, the folds differentiate the blocks of text. In addition, the brochure in figure 6.13 uses a box with a background color to distinguish the checklist from the introductory paragraph at the top of the page.

Exercise 2

Choose a document containing one or more images that you composed for another class or for an extracurricular activity. Bring the document (or a color photocopy of it) to class. Have your classmates look at the document from several feet away and ask them to report what their eyes are drawn to. As you lead a discussion about the document, be prepared to explain how you created it and chose the image(s). Be receptive to suggestions from your classmates for improving your document—especially if they suggest ways you can add sonic elements. Your classmates can tell you if the elements are competing for, directing, or in need of additional attention.

TIPS FOR DESIGNING EFFECTIVE BROCHURES

- Identify your rhetorical audience.
- Design each page of the brochure for ease of scanning (remember the backward S pattern).
- Provide verbal and visual signposts for your readers: headings, subheadings, shading, and bullets.
- Chunk the text to emphasize main points.
- Employ striking photographs and bold colors to contrast with black type.

7 ‖ COMPOSING ARGUMENTS

Every day, you argue; you make claims that you support with good reasons, supportive details, and examples. You argue to address an issue or resolve a problem, bridge misunderstandings, amplify understanding, or influence opinions and actions. When you explain a lab experiment to your roommate, send a reminder to a client who needs to sign a contract, petition your academic advisor for a late drop, or request a refund from an airline, you are composing an argument in response to a rhetorical opportunity. You are expressing a point of view, establishing yourself as credible, using logical reasoning, and connecting your claim with the interests of your rhetorical audience.

Argument and *persuasion* are often used interchangeably, but they differ in two basic ways. **Argument** uses good, often logical reasons to convince a rhetorical audience that a claim is true or reasonable or that an attitude or action is desirable, maybe even the best one. **Persuasion**, on the other hand, has traditionally referred to winning or conquering with the use of emotional reasoning, moving an audience to action. But because all arguments so often involve some measure of "winning" (even if that means just gaining the ear of a rhetorical audience) and the use of reasoning (ethical, logical, and emotional), this book uses *argument* to cover the meanings of both terms.

A respectful acknowledgment of the beliefs, values, and expertise of your rhetorical audience is crucial for coming close to achieving the purpose of an argument, which always goes beyond mere victory over an opponent. After all, argument is an important way to invite exchange, understanding, cooperation, consideration, joint decision making, agreement, or negotiation of differences. Thus, argument serves three basic and sometimes overlapping purposes: to analyze a complicated issue or question an established belief, to express or defend a point of view, and to invite or convince an audience to change a position or adopt a course of action (in order to address or resolve a problem).

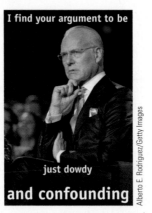

I find your argument to be

just dowdy

and confounding

Alberto E. Rodriguez/Getty Images

Figure 7.1: Multimodal argument memes are popular on social media sites, where they spread and evolve quickly—or die out. Graduate students Sarah Summers and Bill Riley launched a meme featuring *Project Runway*'s Tim Gunn.

This chapter will help you

- determine the purpose and the rhetorical audience of an argument (**7a**),
- consider different viewpoints (**7b**),
- distinguish fact from opinion (**7c**),
- take a position or make a claim (**7d**),
- provide evidence to support a claim (**7e**),
- use the rhetorical appeals to ground an argument (**7f**),
- select an appropriate type of argument (**7g**),
- reason effectively and ethically (**7h**),
- avoid rhetorical fallacies (**7i**), and
- analyze an argument (**7j**).

7a | DETERMINING THE PURPOSE OF AN ARGUMENT

What opportunity for change calls to you? Why have you decided to respond to that opportunity? What topic is under discussion? What is at stake? What is likely to happen as a result of making this argument? How important are those consequences? Who is in a position to act, react, or collaborate in response to your argument?

When composing an argument, take care to establish the relationships among your topic, purpose, and rhetorical audience, especially given the fact that the audience often shapes the purpose.

- If there is little likelihood that you can convince members of your rhetorical audience to change a strongly held value or belief, you might achieve a great deal more by inviting that same audience to understand your position and offering to understand theirs.
- If the members of your rhetorical audience are not firmly committed to a position, you might be able to convince them to agree with or at least consider the opinion you are expressing or defending.
- If the members of your rhetorical audience agree with you in principle, you might invite them to undertake a specific action—such as voting for a proposed school tax levy or attending a committee meeting.

No matter how you imagine those in your rhetorical audience responding to your argument, you must establish **common ground** with them, a belief or value you share with your audience that provides a basis of agreement. Often common ground takes the form of a goal toward which you both want to work (our schools need to be updated) or an assumption you both share (all our nation's children deserve a good education). Establishing common ground is crucial to your ability to move your purpose forward.

7b   CONSIDERING ARGUABLE STATEMENTS

Because people invariably hold different points of view, not everyone will always agree with you, nor you with them. Thus, a good deal of the writing you will do in school or at work will require you to take an arguable position on a topic. The first step toward finding a topic for argumentation is to consider issues that inspire different opinions and opportunities for change.

Behind any effective argument is a question that can generate more than one reasonable answer. If you ask "Are America's schools in trouble?" almost everyone will say "yes." But if you ask, "In what ways can America's schools be improved?" you will hear different answers. Answers differ because people approach questions with various backgrounds, experiences, and assumptions. As a consequence, writers and speakers are often tempted to use reasoning that supports what they already believe, have experienced, or observed. Therefore, you will need to research your topic and demonstrate that you are well informed about it, that you are knowledgeable about the various viewpoints toward your topic and the general points of agreement. (For help addressing differing viewpoints within an argument, see 7e(2).)

You compose an argument with or for a rhetorical audience. Rarely will you be in a position to plow ahead with your decision; most often, you will need to consult with others. Therefore, when you choose a topic for argumentation, you are responding to an opportunity to write, one that allows you to take a stance, research, question, and confer. First, you focus on a topic, on the part of some general subject that you will address (2b), and then you pose a question about it (taking care not to pose a yes-or-no question). In the student example at the end of this chapter, Billy Lucas focused on all-contact youth football, posing a question about the dangers of tackling for young children.

As you formulate your question, consider (1) your values and beliefs with respect to the topic, (2) how your assumptions might differ from those of your rhetorical audience, (3) what your purpose is for writing to this audience, and (4) how you might establish common ground with them while respecting any differences between your opinion and theirs. The initial question you raise will evolve into an arguable statement, your **thesis**.

Stasis theory, a four-question process developed by the ancients, helped Billy analyze the issue of all-contact youth football as he developed his thesis. Stasis theory asks:

- What are the facts?
- What is the problem?
- How serious is the problem?
- What can be done (what is a plan of action)?

In response to "What are the facts?" Billy recognized that all-contact youth football is a popular sport, with fans who believe it is the best preparation for high school and college play. In response to "What is the problem?" he knew that full-contact youth football leads to brain trauma and permanent damage in young players. "How serious is the problem?" allowed Billy to provide facts, figures, and examples of tackle-related brain damage that is exclusive to young players. Finally, when facing the question of a "plan of action," Billy could offer alternatives to the tackle.

As Billy continued to develop his thesis, he also established common ground with his rhetorical audience, agreeing with them about the fun, training, and popularity of the sport. His purpose was to inform his rhetorical audience about the dangers of all-contact youth football and provide alternatives to the tackle itself. His initial critical question for himself ("What are the drawbacks of all-contact youth football?") led to his arguable thesis statement about the ban on tackling at the youth level.

To determine whether a topic might be suitable, make a statement about the topic once you've worked through the questions of stasis theory ("I believe strongly that . . . " or "My view is that . . . ") and then check to see if that statement can be argued. Answering the questions in the following box will also help you begin to develop your thesis.

TIPS FOR ASSESSING AN ARGUABLE STATEMENT ABOUT A TOPIC

- What reasons can you state that support your belief (or point of view) about the topic? List those reasons. How did your belief develop? Experience, research, social media, television, Internet, family values? What else do you need to know? What additional research should you conduct?

- Who or what groups might disagree with your statement? Why? List those groups.

- What are other viewpoints on the topic and reasons supporting those viewpoints? List them. What else do you need to know about?

- On what detail do all viewpoints agree?

- What is your purpose in writing about this topic? In other words, what will your rhetorical audience take from your message: information, analysis, evaluation, pleasure, opinion?

- How does your purpose connect with your rhetorical audience? Describe that audience in terms of background, status, education, values, beliefs, and practices.

- What do you want your audience to do in response to your argument? In other words, what do you expect from your audience? Write out your expectation.

As you move further into the writing process, researching and exploring your topic at home, in the library, and online (chapters **8** and **9**), you will clarify your purpose and refine your thesis statement.

7c   DISTINGUISHING BETWEEN FACT AND OPINION

As you develop your thesis statement into an argument, you use both facts and opinions. You must distinguish between these two kinds of information so that you can use both to your advantage as you establish your credibility (**7f(1)**), an essential feature of successful argumentation. **Facts** are reliable pieces of information that can be verified through independent sources or procedures, and they are often based on online or library research. **Opinions** are assertions or inferences that may or may not be based on facts, no matter how widely accepted the opinion might be. Moreover, even verifiable facts cannot speak for themselves, especially when taken out of the original context. Neither facts nor opinions are preferable. Their power depends on how responsibly and thoughtfully you employ them in your argument.

To determine whether a statement you have read is fact or opinion, ask yourself questions like these: Can it be proved? Can it be challenged? How often is the same result achieved? If a statement can consistently be proved true, then it is a fact. If it can be disputed, then it is an opinion, no matter how significant or reasonable it may seem.

Fact   Milk contains calcium.

Opinion   Americans should drink more milk.

To say that milk contains calcium is to state a well-established fact: it can be verified by consulting published studies or by conducting laboratory tests. Whether or not this fact is significant depends on how a writer chooses to use it. To say that Americans need to drink more milk is to express an opinion that may or may not be supported by facts. When considering the statement "Americans should drink more milk," a thoughtful reader might ask, "How much calcium does a human need? Why do humans need calcium? Is cow's milk good for humans? Might leafy green vegetables provide a richer source of calcium?" Anticipating questions such as these can help you develop an argument as well as help you recognize the evidence that will best support that argument, where you can obtain such evidence, and what to do if you discover conflicting evidence.

Because the line between fact and opinion is not always clear, writers and readers of arguments must be prepared to assess the reliability of the information before them, whether they obtain the information at the library, online, or during an interview. They also need to evaluate the beliefs supporting the argument, the kinds and quality of sources used, and any objections that could be made.

Exercise 1

Determine which of the following statements are facts and which are opinions. In each case, what kind of verification would you require in order to accept the statement as reliable?

1. Malala Yousafzai is the youngest recipient of the Nobel Peace Prize.
2. A college degree guarantees a higher income over the course of a lifetime.
3. Women who are overweight or who have a family history of diabetes have a higher risk of gestational diabetes.
4. *The Phantom of the Opera* is the longest running show on Broadway.
5. Every American student can and should learn to write well in college.
6. Santa Fe is the oldest state capital in the United States.
7. Kettle bell exercises benefit everyone.
8. The United States waged war against Iraq because Iraq was harboring weapons of mass destruction.
9. When combined, ammonia and chlorine bleach produce a poisonous gas.
10. New York will never fully recover from the 9/11 terror attacks.

7d TAKING A POSITION OR MAKING A CLAIM

When making an argument, a writer takes a position on a particular topic. Whether the argument analyzes, questions, expresses, defends, invites, or convinces, the writer's position needs to be clear. That position, which is called the **claim** (or **proposition**), clearly states what the writer wants the audience to do with the information being provided. The claim is the thesis of the argument and usually appears in the introduction and sometimes again in the conclusion.

(1) Extent of a claim

Claims vary in extent; they can be absolute or moderate, large or limited. Absolute claims assert that something is always true or false, completely good or bad. Moderate claims make less sweeping assertions. Absolute claims often include such words as *all*, *none*, *every*, *always*, and *never*, whereas moderate claims use the terms *many*, *some*, *often*, *usually*, *seldom*, and *few*.

Absolute claim	All full-contact football is dangerous and should be banned.
Moderate claim	Because full-contact youth football is dangerous, players should play flag or touch football until they get older.
Absolute claim	Harry Truman was the best president the United States has ever had.
Moderate claim	One of our best presidents, Harry Truman, established domestic policies that advanced civil rights.

Moderate claims are not necessarily superior to absolute claims. After all, writers frequently need to take a strong position for or against something, such as "no one should drink and drive" or "racism is everyone's problem." But the stronger the claim, the stronger the evidence needed to support it. Be sure to consider the quality and the significance of the evidence you use—not just its quantity.

Researched facts, figures, data, and examples enhance the quality of evidence.

(2) Types of claims

(a) Substantiation claims

Without making a value judgment, a **substantiation claim** asserts that something exists or is evident. This kind of point can be supported by evidence.

> The job market for those with only a high school diploma is limited. [One only has to read the headlines or talk with an employment counselor to learn that this is the case.]

> The post office is raising rates and losing money again. [News media remind us of this fact nearly every year.]

(b) Evaluation claims

According to an **evaluation claim**, something has a specific quality: it is good or bad, effective or ineffective, successful or unsuccessful.

> The high graduation rate for athletes at Penn State is a direct result of the school's supportive academic environment. [Penn State football players have the highest graduation rate in the Big Ten, according to NCAA reports.]

> The public transportation system in Washington, DC, is reliable and safe. [Police, district, and travel reports offer the same assertion.]

Sometimes, writers use an evaluation claim as a way to invite their audience to consider an issue.

> It is important for us to consider the graduation rate of all Big Ten athletes, regardless of the sport they play.

(c) Policy claims

When making **policy claims,** writers call for specific action.

> We must establish the funding necessary to hire the best qualified high school teachers.

> We need to build a light-rail system linking downtown with the western suburbs.

Much writing involves substantiation, evaluation, and policy claims. When writing about the job market for engineers with recent degrees, you might tap your ability to substantiate a claim; when writing about literature (chapter 12), you might need to evaluate a character. Policy claims are commonly found in arguments about social or political issues such as health care, social security, affirmative action, or defense spending. These claims often grow out of substantiation or evaluation claims: first, you demonstrate that a problem exists; then, you establish the best solution for that problem, often bolstering your proposed solution with researched evidence, facts, and examples.

Figure 7.2: Policy claims, such as the one made by this 1961 British political poster, call for specific action. In this case, the requested action is to vote for Conservative candidates.

TIPS FOR MAKING A CLAIM ARGUABLE

- Write down your opinion.
- Describe the situation and experiences that produced your opinion.
- Decide who constitutes the rhetorical audience for your opinion and what you want that audience to do about or with your opinion.
- Write down the verifiable and reliable (researched) facts that support your opinion.
- Transform your initial opinion into a thoughtful claim that reflects those facts and considers at least two sides of the issue.
- Ask yourself, "So what?" If the answer to this question shows that your claim leads nowhere, start over, beginning with the first tip.

Exercise 2

The following argument is an excerpt from a book analyzing racial strife in the United States and written by Cornel West, a scholar specializing in race relations. Evaluate the claims it presents. Are they absolute or moderate? Can you identify a substantiation or evaluation claim? What policy claim is implicit in this passage? (The sentences are numbered for ease of reference.)

> [1]To engage in a serious discussion of race in America, we must begin not with the problems of black people but with the flaws of American society—flaws rooted in historic inequalities and longstanding cultural stereotypes. [2]How we set up the terms for discussing racial issues shapes our perception and response to these issues. [3]As long as black people are viewed as a "them," the burden falls on blacks to do all the "cultural" and "moral" work necessary for healthy race relations. [4]The implication is that only certain Americans can define what it means to be American—and the rest must simply "fit in."

> —**Cornel West,** *Race Matters*

7e	PROVIDING EVIDENCE FOR AN EFFECTIVE ARGUMENT

Effective arguments are well developed and responsibly supported. You should explore your topic in enough depth that you have the evidence to support your position intelligently and ethically, whether that evidence is based on personal experience or on research (chapters 2 and 8). You want to establish the reasons your rhetorical audience may already agree with you, the specific reasons they may have to disagree with you, and the most productive ways you can respond to those reasons.

(1) Establishing the claim

If you want readers to take your ideas seriously, you must establish the reasons that have led to your claim and the opinions, values, and assumptions that underlie your thinking. As you explore your topic, make a list of the reasons that have led to your belief (**2d** and **2f**). When Billy was working on his argumentative essay (at the end of this chapter; see pages 181–186), he listed the following reasons for his belief that full-contact football should be banned for pre-high school players:

1. Professional and college leagues admit the dangers of full-contact football, based on medical research findings.
2. Both leagues have already set regulations in place to protect "defenseless" players.
3. Young players, whose brains and spines are particularly vulnerable, regularly sustain hard, damaging hits.
4. Scientific research continues to reveal the progressive brain damage caused by full-contact football, particularly for young players.

Whether you have one reason or several, be sure to provide sufficient evidence from credible sources to support your claim. Whether derived from responsible research, personal experience, or professional expertise, your evidence should include

- facts,
- statistics,
- examples,
- observation, and/or
- testimony.

This evidence must be accurate, representative, and sufficient. Accurate information should be verifiable by others (**7c**). Recognize, however, that even if the information a writer provides is accurate, it may not be representative or sufficient if it was drawn from an exceptional case, a biased sample, or a one-time occurrence. If, for example, you are writing an argument about the advantages of using Standardized English but you draw all of your supporting evidence from a proponent of the English-Only movement, your evidence represents only the views of that movement. Such evidence is neither representative of all the support for the use of Standardized English nor sufficient to support a thoughtful argument. In order to better represent your viewpoint, you should consult more than a single source (chapter **9**).

When gathering evidence, be sure to think critically about the information you find. If you are using the results of polls or other statistics or statements by authorities, you must evaluate your evidence according to how recent and representative the information is, as well as how it was gathered. Consider, too, whether the authority you plan to quote is actually qualified to address the topic under consideration and is likely to be respected by your readers.

Whatever form of evidence you use—facts, statistics, examples, or testimony—you need to make clear to your audience exactly *why* and *how* the evidence supports your claim. After all, even accurate information has to be interpreted by the writer and the reader. As soon as the relationship between your claim and your evidence is clear to you, make that connection explicit to your readers, helping them understand your thinking and appreciate the quality of your evidence.

(2) Responding to diverse views

Issues are controversial because good arguments can be made on all sides. Therefore, effective arguments consider and respond to other points of view. Fairness, respect, and acknowledgment of other points of view are crucial for connecting with your audience. So when you introduce diverse views and then respectfully demonstrate why you disagree with each of them you are using **refutation**, the most common strategy for addressing opposing points of view. But perhaps a more productive approach is that of **counterargument**, a process of taking seriously and responding to opposing viewpoints, sometimes agreeing with an opposing viewpoint for good reasons, a move called a **concession**. By openly admitting that you agree with opponents on one or more specific points, you demonstrate that you are fair-minded and credible (7f(1)). Your concessions also increase the likelihood that your opponents will find merit in parts of your argument.

Whether you agree or disagree with other positions, you must recognize and assess them. It is hard to persuade people to agree with you if you insist that they are entirely wrong. If you admit that they are partially right, they are more likely to admit that you could be partially right as well. In this sense, argument involves working with an audience as much as getting them to work with you.

In his essay (pages 181–186), Billy examines the opposing viewpoints his rhetorical audience holds about youth football, enumerating and responding to them one by one. Sometimes, Billy agrees at the same time that he moves the viewpoint further. In other words, he makes a concession. Other times, Billy does not agree, but he offers a middle ground, where both viewpoints might come together. Thus, Billy's argument contains a section of productive counterargument, in which he reflects upon the three main reasons his audience believes that all-contact youth football is good.

Exercise 3

The following paragraph is the conclusion of an argument written by Tucson writer Debra Hughes shortly after the January 2011 shooting of Representative Gabrielle Giffords and eighteen other people at a local political rally. Hughes's piece connects inflammatory rhetoric with such acts of violence. Write a short analysis of this paragraph in which you note (a) an opposing viewpoint to which she is responding, (b) a refutation she offers to this viewpoint, (c) a concession she makes, and (d) any questions this excerpt raises for you.

[1]Habits are hard to break. [2]Only days after the shooting, Arizona passed laws prohibiting picketing within three hundred feet of any home, cemetery, funeral home, or house of worship before, during, or after a ceremony or burial. [3]As the shooting victims were being laid to rest, a group called Angel Action donned white wings and stood with hundreds of others dressed in white, to shield mourners from potential protests by fanatics, such as the Westboro Baptist Church congregants, who have been disrupting services for US soldiers slain in Iraq and Afghanistan. [4]The Westboro group is emblematic of the flashpoints of opinion and controversy across the land. [5]In the weeks and months ahead, only determined national leadership and conscientious, principled activity and restraint on the part of major media, and on the part of each citizen, can restore humanity and civility to American discourse.

—Debra Hughes, "The Tucson Shootings: Words and Deeds"

7f	USING THE RHETORICAL APPEALS TO GROUND AN ARGUMENT

Human beings do not form their beliefs or act on the basis of facts or logic alone; if we did, we would all agree and would act accordingly. Scientific findings would stop us from indulging in unhealthy eating, drinking, and smoking; we would never speed or use a cell phone while driving. Our actions and attitudes would change as soon as we learned the facts. But logical reasoning alone is never enough to get anybody to change. If you want your argument to be heard, understood, and even acted on, you need to follow the necessary steps for gaining a fair hearing.

You can shape effective arguments through a combination of persuasive strategies, which include the **rhetorical appeals** of ethos, logos, and pathos. **Ethos** (an ethical appeal) establishes the speaker's or writer's credibility and trustworthiness. An ethical appeal demonstrates goodwill toward the audience, good sense or knowledge of the subject at hand, and good character. Establishing common ground with the audience is another feature of ethos. However, ethos can rarely carry an argument by itself; therefore, you also need to use **logos** (a logical appeal). Logos demonstrates an effective use of reason and judicious use of evidence, whether that evidence consists of facts, statistics, comparisons, anecdotes, expert opinions, or observations. You employ logos when you are supporting claims, drawing reasonable conclusions, and avoiding rhetorical fallacies (7i). But logic may not be sufficient to persuade an audience, unless the audience feels emotionally stirred by the topic under discussion. Therefore, **pathos** (an emotional appeal) involves using language that will connect with the beliefs and feelings of the audience. If you misuse pathos in an attempt to manipulate your audience (as sentimental movies and manipulative speakers often do), your attempt can easily backfire. Still, pathos can be used successfully when it establishes empathy, authentic understanding, and a human connection. The most effective arguments are those that combine these three persuasive appeals—ethos, logos, and pathos—responsibly and knowledgeably.

In the next three subsections, additional passages from Debra Hughes's "Tucson Shootings: Words and Deeds" illustrate how a writer can use all three of the rhetorical appeals.

(1) Ethical appeals

In her introductory paragraphs, Debra Hughes captures the atmosphere of downtown Tucson on the evening of the shootings and demonstrates her knowledge of the day's events, her credibility as a local Tucsonan, and her goodwill toward her readers, who have "their own heavy feelings."

> The night of the mass shootings in Tucson, a downtown art gallery hosted an already scheduled [exhibition of images] from François Robert's photography series *Stop the Violence* . . . of human bones arranged in the shapes of a handgun, grenade, knife, Kalashnikov, fighter jet, and other symbols of violence, all starkly set on black backgrounds. Those images confronted viewers with their own heavy feelings. That morning six people had been killed and thirteen wounded in the shooting rampage at Gabrielle Giffords's political rally at a local Safeway. Jared Lee Loughner had tried to assassinate the Arizona congresswoman, using a Glock 19 semiautomatic pistol and firing thirty-one rounds into the crowd in about fifteen seconds.
>
> The shooting took place at a small shopping center in my neighborhood. . . . Our bank is there, along with the stores where we mail our packages, buy pastries, toothpaste, and paper towels, and where we regularly run errands. That morning people had gathered to hear what their state representative had to say. She called the event "Congress at Your Corner."
>
> In the afternoon, . . . Pima County Sheriff Clarence Dupnik, a seventy-five-year-old with the sagging cheeks and drooping eyes of a bulldog, spoke his mind. "People tend to pooh-pooh this business about all the vitriol that we hear inflaming the American public . . . ." He was alluding to talk-show hosts and politicians who use inflammatory rhetoric, and he added that the effect of their words should not be discounted. "That may be free speech, but it's not without consequences." Almost immediately a heated public debate began over whether or not political rhetoric had spurred Jared Lee Loughner to kill.

(2) Logical appeals

Logos, the logical appeal, is considered to be especially trustworthy, as it is rooted in a writer's reliance on reason and supporting evidence (facts, statistics, observations, interviews with authorities, survey results, and so on) to build an argument. Logical appeals, however, need to be examined closely to determine whether facts are accurate, testimony has been considered within its context, and sources are reliable. To help her audience appreciate the connection she's trying to make, Hughes builds on the sheriff's testimony, constructing her logos with facts, expert opinions, observations, and vivid examples, while recognizing all sides of the controversy. She ends the following excerpt by quoting an obvious (and ironic) logical fallacy:

> Tucson forensic psychologist Dr. Gary Perrin, a professional familiar with violent crime, was asked if a mentally disturbed person might distort strong messages into a belief that violent acts are noble. Perrin replied, "In . . . the past few years, rhetoric has increased. Words are powerful, and certainly words can make a [mentally unstable] person act in a certain way." But he emphasized that violent acts are "situational, and many things contribute. Words can be one of the factors."
>
>   . . . Within a week of the shooting a Google search produced 55 million results about the event, including myriad bloggers arguing over free speech. Steven Colbert, on his Comedy Central TV show, aired a segment entitled "The Word: Life, Liberty, and the Pursuit of Angriness," in which he deadpanned, "If incendiary rhetoric isn't connected to the Arizona tragedy, it logically follows that it must be good."

(3) Emotional appeals

Emotional appeals, pathos, stir feelings and help a writer connect with the audience. Although emotional appeals can be manipulative (like unethical appeals to faulty logic or to false authority), they can be used ethically and logically to move the audience to a new way of thinking or acting.

In the following passage, which moves toward her conclusion, Hughes continues to use logos while alluding to moderation and personal responsibility, thus evoking feelings that people on all sides of the issue can share.

> The night before Gabrielle Giffords was shot, she sent an email offering congratulations to Kentucky Secretary of State Trey Grayson, . . . [newly] named director of Harvard University's Institute of Politics. . . . "After you get settled, I would love to talk about what we can do to promote centrism and moderation. I am one of twelve Democrats in a GOP district (the only woman) and we need to figure out how to tone our rhetoric and partisanship down." . . .
>
>   The Tucson shooting and its aftermath are being followed around the world, especially in places where violence is a problem. Venezuelan magazine editor Sergio Dahbar wrote, "The Giffords shooting is being followed very closely in Latin America because we also have this illness. We have the

illness of intolerance." A well-known maxim from Victor Hugo commenting on unrest in France in the 1830s runs, "The guilty one is not he who commits the sin, but the one who causes the darkness."

—DEBRA HUGHES, "The Tucson Shootings: Words and Deeds"

Although ethos is often developed in the introduction to an argument, logos in the body, and pathos in the conclusion, these classical rhetorical appeals can overlap and appear throughout an argument.

7g TYPES OF ARGUMENTS

All arguments are not alike. Arguments differ in the use of rhetorical appeals, the reliance on various kinds of reasoning, and the arrangement of the components, with arrangement being the most distinguishing feature.

Unless your instructor asks you to demonstrate a particular type of argument, the decisions you make about developing your argument should be based on your topic, your audience, and your purpose. You can develop a good plan by simply listing the major points you want to make (**2d**), deciding what order to put them in, and then determining where to include refutation or counterargument with concession (**7e(2)**). You must also decide whether to place your thesis statement (or claim) at the beginning or the end of your argument. Once you sort out the reasons supporting your claim, you need to develop each reason with a separate paragraph (unless, of course, you are summarizing the reasons in the conclusion).

Your conclusion should move beyond a repetition of what has already been stated and instead emphasize your connection with your audience, a connection that reinforces your rhetorical purpose: getting readers to take a particular course of action, to further their understanding, or to accept the implications of your claim (**7d**). Billy's essay (pages 181–186) ends with a conclusion that not only reinforces his informative purpose but also links it with the issue of safety.

(1) Classical argument

If your audience has not yet taken a position on your issue, you may want to use a classical argument, which assumes that an audience is prepared to follow a well-reasoned argument. A classical argument takes advantage of the power of the rhetorical appeals in its opening, or introduction, by establishing the writer's ethos; at the same time, it establishes common ground with the audience and introduces the issue. The body of the classical argument relies on the power of logos: it provides background information, introduces the claim, offers reasons supporting the claim, and presents productive counterargument (or refutation) and concession. In this section, you will first establish common ground and then acknowledge and respond to opposing viewpoints. Finally, classical argument typically closes with a strong appeal to pathos, making an emotional connection with the audience.

FEATURES OF THE CLASSICAL ARRANGEMENT

- **Introduction.** Introduce the issue and capture the attention of the audience. Try using a short narrative or a strong example (**2f(2)** and **2g**). Begin establishing your credibility (using the rhetorical appeal of ethos) and common ground with the rhetorical audience.

- **Background information.** Provide your audience with a history of the situation and state how things currently stand. Define any key terms. Draw the attention of your audience to those points that are especially important and explain why they are meaningful.

- **Proposition.** Introduce the position you are taking and outline the basic reasons that support it. Frame your position as a thesis statement or a claim (**2c** and **7d**).

- **Proof or confirmation.** Discuss the reasons that have led you to take your position. Each reason must be clear, relevant, and representative. Provide facts, expert testimony, and any other research-based evidence that supports your claim and demonstrates logos.

- **Counterargument or refutation.** Recognize, discuss, and disprove the arguments of people who hold a different position and with whom you continue to disagree.

- **Concession.** Concede any point with which you agree or that has merit; show why this concession does not damage your case but rather enriches it.

- **Conclusion.** Summarize your most important points and appeal to your audience's feelings, making a personal connection. Describe the consequences of your argument in a final attempt to connect with your audience (using the emotional appeal of pathos) and encourage your audience to consider (if not commit to) a particular course of action.

(2) Rogerian argument

When you are addressing an audience strongly opposed to your position, you can demonstrate your understanding of their view by using a Rogerian argument, derived from the work of psychologist Carl R. Rogers. Rogers claimed that people often fail to understand each other because of their predisposition to judge, evaluate, agree, or disagree, before they even listen to, let alone understand, what is being said. Rogers's model for an argument calls for the suspension of judgment (positive or negative) until each side is able to restate fairly and accurately what others believe—thereby demonstrating mutual understanding. When each person in a conflict demonstrates this ability, the likelihood of misunderstanding is reduced and that of moving forward together is increased.

Skills such as paraphrasing and summarizing (**11e**) are essential to a Rogerian argument. Although this model can be used to achieve a number of goals, it is especially useful for identifying common ground and building consensus. To demonstrate that you have given fair consideration to the views of others, you begin a Rogerian argument not by refuting those views but by paraphrasing them, demonstrating that you understand the thinking and values behind those views. Only then do you introduce your own position, weaving in as much agreed-on information as possible, and explaining why you believe your position has merit. Because the Rogerian model relies on consensus, you conclude your argument by describing how everyone concerned about the issue could benefit from adopting your position (the way Billy does in his argument on pages 181–186). This emphasis on being fair-minded, nonconfrontational, and inclusive gives ethos (**7f(1)**) an essential place in a Rogerian argument.

The summary of benefits with which a Rogerian argument concludes gives you the opportunity to draw together the threads of your argument and appeal to the audience to accept your position. In the following conclusion to an argument for using writing to change the world, notice how the author cites benefits for the natural world and for all people, including terrorists:

> As writers, we can extend the circle of caring to plants and animals, to rivers and oceans and coral reefs. And we can form a caring circle of human beings that includes young and old, rich and poor, gay and straight, the immigrant, the homeless, the emotionally sturdy and the mentally ill, and those in prison, no matter what their religion. I would even include "terrorists" in the circle. They too are human, and can only be properly dealt

with if we see them as people with needs, desires, and ideals like ourselves. Ultimately, placing them outside the circle will only hurt all of us. When any humans are dehumanized, we all lose some of our humanity.

—MARY PIPHER, *Writing to Change the World*

To write an argument based on the Rogerian models, use the following plan as your guide.

FEATURES OF THE ROGERIAN ARRANGEMENT

- **Introduction.** Establish that you have paid attention to views different from your own, which helps you establish your ethos. Build trust by stating these views clearly and fairly.

- **Concessions.** Reassure the people you hope will adopt your position by showing that you agree with them to some extent, can employ some of their ideas, and thus do not think that they are completely wrong.

- **Thesis.** Having earned the confidence of your audience, state your claim, or proposition.

- **Support.** Explain why you have taken this position and provide support for it, employing logos, the appeal to logic and reason.

- **Conclusion.** Conclude by describing how you, your audience, and other people can benefit from adopting your position; employ pathos to make an emotional connection with the audience. Indicate the extent to which adopting this position will resolve the problem you are addressing. If you are offering a partial solution to a complex problem, concede that further work may be necessary.

---

(3) Toulmin argument

The Toulmin model, devised by philosopher Stephen Toulmin, defines an *argument* as a logical progression from **reasons** (accepted evidence or **data** that support a claim) to the **claim** (an arguable statement of fact, opinion, or belief; a **thesis**), based on **assumptions** (the underlying, often unstated, **warrants** that connect the claim and the reasons for the claim). If the assumption is controversial, it requires **evidence** (the independent support or justification that Toulmin refers to as **backing**). Writers who draw evidence from what they view

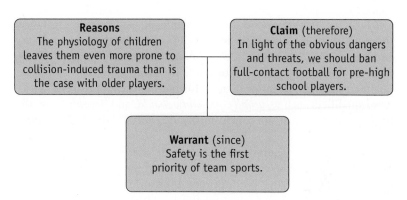

Figure 7.3: An assumption linking reasons and a claim.

as reliable authorities (scientists, researchers, government agencies, and other researched sources) should be able to cite the credentials of those authorities. Writers who base an argument on the law or another written code that has been widely accepted (a university's mission statement, NFL guidelines, or a surgical procedure, for instance) should be able to cite the exact statute, code, precedent, or regulation in question or even quote it verbatim.

Thus, a Toulmin argument establishes a reasonable relationship among reasons, the claim, and the evidence (see figure 7.3). The following argument demonstrates such a relationship:

> Given that nearly one hundred American high school football players received catastrophic head injuries over a thirteen-year period, with 71 percent of them suffering a previous concussion during the same season, and 39 percent of them playing with residual symptoms, younger players, with even more vulnerable brains, should not play full-contact football.

Reasons	Older, stronger players are regularly hurt, but the physiology of children leaves them even more prone to collision-induced trauma than is the case with older players.
Claim	In light of the obvious dangers and threats, we should ban full-contact football for pre-high school players.
Assumption	Safety is the first priority of team sports.

Of course, few arguments are as simple as this example. For instance, some youth teams may consider developing talent their first priority and see tackling as a means of developing talent on the gridiron. Thus, writers often need to make allowances for exceptions. The writer has qualified his claim in terms of age: "for pre-high school players." One-word qualifiers such as *usually, probably, should,* and *possibly* show the degree of certainty of the conclusion, and rebuttal terms such as *unless* indicate exceptions.

When using the Toulmin model to shape your arguments, you may be able to identify the claim, the reasons, and the qualifiers more easily than the underlying assumptions. Like an unstated premise in a syllogism (**7h(2)**), the evidence for the assumption is rarely presented explicitly. In the example above, the evidence is the popularity of youth football and the value that parents, coaches, and players place on youth football, as demonstrated by their attendance, participation, and financial backing (all of which can be researched and stated). To determine the evidence for an assumption in an argument you are writing, trace your thinking back to your initial assumption. As you do so, remember that evidence (or backing) for that assumption can take different forms—it may be a law or regulation, a belief that your reasons came from a reliable source or that what is true of a sample is true of a larger group, or a widely accepted value.

Exercise 4

Read the editorial pages of several consecutive issues of your school newspaper. Look for editorials that analyze or question an established belief, express or defend an opinion, invite consideration, or try to convince. Choose an editorial that strikes you as well argued, well developed, and well organized—even if it does not change your belief or your action (but perhaps your understanding). Bring several copies of the editorial to class, and be prepared to discuss its purpose, audience, use of rhetorical appeals, and conclusion.

7h | REASONING EFFECTIVELY AND ETHICALLY

Although many people believe that successful arguments are always only logical, such so-called logical arguments rely on a considered combination of ethical, emotional, and logical components. However, logos (logical reasoning) underpins all ethical and compelling arguments. Logic is a means through which you can develop your ideas, realize new ones, and determine whether your thinking is clear enough to convince readers to agree with you. Thus, the quality of the reasoning either enhances or detracts from your overall argument.

(1) Inductive reasoning

You use inductive reasoning every day when you draw on a number of specific facts or observations to reach a logical conclusion. For example, if you get a stomachache within fifteen minutes of eating ice cream, you might conclude that there is a connection. Perhaps you are lactose intolerant. If you clear out the brush by the side of your house and end up with an angry, itchy rash, you might conclude that you have been exposed to poison ivy. This use of evidence to form a generalization is called an **inductive leap,** and the extent of such a leap should be in proportion to the amount of evidence gathered.

Inductive reasoning involves moving (or leaping) from discovering evidence to interpreting it, and it can help you arrive at probable, believable conclusions (but not absolute, enduring truth). Making a small leap from evidence (a stomachache or a rash) to a probable conclusion (lactose intolerance or exposure to poison ivy) is more effective and ethical than using the same evidence to make a sweeping claim that could easily be challenged (ice cream is bad for everyone or no one should clear brush) (7d(1)). Generally, the greater the weight of the evidence, the more reliable the conclusion.

When used in argument, inductive reasoning often employs facts (7c) and examples (2f(2)). When writers cannot cite all the information that supports their conclusions, they choose the evidence that is most reliable and most closely related to the point they are making.

(2) Deductive reasoning

You also use deductive reasoning daily, whenever you apply a generalization (or generalized belief) to series of specific cases. For instance, if you believe that you are lactose intolerant, you will decline offers of milk, ice cream, cheese, and any other food that contains lactose. At the heart of a deductive argument is a **major premise** (a generalized belief that is assumed to be true), which the writer applies to a specific case (the **minor premise**), thereby yielding a conclusion, or claim. For example, if you know that all doctors must complete a residency and that Imogen is in medical school, then you can conclude that Imogen must complete a residency. This argument can be expressed in a three-part structure called a **syllogism**.

Major premise	All doctors must complete a residency. [generalized belief]
Minor premise	Imogen is studying to become a doctor. [specific case]
Conclusion	Imogen must complete a residency. [claim]

Sometimes the premise is not stated, for the simple reason that the writer assumes that an audience shares the belief.

Imogen has graduated from medical school, so she must complete a residency.

In this sentence, the unstated premise is that all doctors must complete a residency. A syllogism with an unstated premise—or even an unstated conclusion—is called an **enthymeme**. Frequently found in written arguments, enthymemes can be very effective because they presume shared beliefs or knowledge. For example, the argument "The college needs to build a new dormitory because the present overcrowded dorms are unsafe" contains the unstated premise that the college has a responsibility to reduce unsafe conditions.

Figure 7.4: Mrs. Lockhorn has worked out a deductive argument relating her husband's alleged ignorance to his not-yet-realized state of bliss, but her reasoning is flawed.

7i | AVOIDING RHETORICAL FALLACIES

Logical reasoning fortifies the overall effectiveness of an argument as well as builds the ethos of the speaker or writer. Constructing an argument effectively means avoiding errors in logic known as **rhetorical fallacies**, which weaken an argument as well as the writer's ethos. These fallacies signal to your audience that your thinking is not entirely trustworthy and that your argument is not well reasoned or researched. Flaws in logical reasoning are often used to humorous effect (figures 7.4, 7.5, 7.6, 7.7, 7.8, 7.9).

Therefore, you need to recognize and avoid several kinds of rhetorical fallacies. As you read the arguments of others (**10a**) and revise the arguments you draft (chapter **3**), keep the following common fallacies in mind.

(1) Non sequitur

A *non sequitur,* the basis for most of the other rhetorical fallacies, attempts to make a connection where none actually exists (the phrase is Latin for "it does not follow"). Just because the first part of a statement is true does not mean that the second part is true, will become true, or will necessarily happen.

Faulty   Heather is married and will start a family soon.

This assertion is based on the faulty premise that *all* women have children soon after marrying (**7h(2)**).

(2) Ad hominem

The *ad hominem* fallacy refers to a personal attack that draws attention away from the issue under consideration (the Latin phrase translates to "toward the man himself").

Faulty   With his penchant for expensive haircuts, that candidate cannot relate to the common people.

The fact that a candidate pays a lot for a haircut may say something about his vanity but says nothing about his political appeal.

(3) Appeal to tradition

The appeal to tradition argues that because things have always been done a certain way, they should continue that way (figure 7.5).

Faulty   Because they are a memorable part of the pledge process, fraternity hazings are part of a respected tradition.

Times change; what was considered good practice in the past is not necessarily considered acceptable now.

Figure 7.5: Maiming and pillaging have a long history, but that does not mean they should continue.

(4) Bandwagon

The bandwagon fallacy argues that everyone is doing, saying, or thinking something, so you should, too. It makes an irrelevant and disguised appeal to the human desire to be part of a group.

Faulty Everyone texts while driving, so I do, too.

Even if the majority of people text while driving, doing so has proved to be dangerous. The majority is not automatically right.

(5) Begging the question

The begging-the-question fallacy presents the conclusion as though it were a major premise. What is assumed to be fact actually needs to be proved.

Faulty If we replace the current football coach, our team will play better.

Any connection between the current coach and the team's skill has not been established.

Figure 7.6: The major premise about penguins is true, but it does not relate to the minor premise about old television shows, let alone lead to the conclusion.

(6) Equivocation

The rhetorical fallacy of equivocation falsely relies on the use of one word or concept in two different ways.

> **Faulty**   Today's students are illiterate; they do not know the characters in Shakespeare's plays.

Traditionally, *literacy* has meant knowing how to read and write, how to function in a print-based culture. Knowing about Shakespeare's characters is not the equivalent of literacy; someone lacking this special kind of knowledge might be characterized as uneducated or uninformed but not as illiterate.

(7) False analogy

A false analogy assumes that because two things are alike in some ways, they are alike in others as well.

> **Faulty**   The United States lost credibility with other nations during the war in Vietnam, so we should not get involved in Syria, or we will lose credibility again.

The differences between the war in Southeast Asia in the 1960s and 1970s and the current conflict in Syria may well be greater than their similarities.

(8) False authority (or appeal to authority)

The fallacy of false authority assumes that an expert in one field is credible in another. Every time you see a celebrity selling perfume, a sports figure selling undershirts, or a talk-show host selling financial advice, you are the target of an appeal to authority.

> **Faulty**   We should buy Electrolux appliances because they make entertaining easier and more pleasurable for Kelly Ripa.

Kelly Ripa's role as a talk-show host does not qualify her as an expert in electrical appliances. (Her experience as a wife and mother might, though.)

Figure 7.7: This sign exemplifies a false dilemma, as though only two alternatives exist when, in reality, there are more than two.

(9) False cause

Sometimes called *post hoc, ergo propter hoc* (meaning "after this, so because of this"), the fallacy of false cause is the assumption that because one event follows another, the first is the cause of the second.

> **Faulty**   If police officers wear cameras, there will be no more occasions of police misconduct.

The assumption is that if police officers wear cameras, they will not engage in, let alone be accused of, misconduct. Making such a connection is like announcing that people who are being watched will always behave responsibly (which is certainly not the case).

(10) False dilemma

Sometimes called the *either/or fallacy*, a false dilemma is a statement that only two alternatives exist, when in fact there are more than two.

> **Faulty**   We must either frack across the entire state of Pennsylvania or be completely dependent on foreign oil.

Other possibilities for generating energy without using foreign oil exist.

Figure 7.8: Without careful thinking, we often make hasty judgments about other people, especially about those who are not like us.

(11) Guilt by association

The fallacy of guilt by association is an unfair attempt to besmirch a person's credibility by linking that person with untrustworthy people or suspicious actions.

Faulty   You should not vote for her for class treasurer because her mother was arrested for shoplifting last year.

The mother's behavior should not be held against the daughter.

(12) Hasty generalization

A hasty generalization is a conclusion based on too little evidence or on exceptional or biased evidence.

Faulty   Ellen is a poor student because she failed her first history test.

Ellen's performance may improve in the weeks ahead. Furthermore, she may be doing well in her other subjects.

(13) Oversimplification

A statement or argument that implies a single cause or solution for a complex problem, leaving out relevant considerations and complications, relies on the oversimplification fallacy.

Faulty   We can eliminate unwanted pregnancies by teaching birth control and abstinence.

Teaching people about birth control and abstinence does not guarantee the elimination of unwanted pregnancies.

(14) Red herring

Sometimes called *ignoring the question*, the red herring fallacy dodges the real issue by drawing attention to a seemingly related but irrelevant one.

Faulty   Why worry about violence in schools when we ought to be worrying about international terrorism?

International terrorism has no direct relationship with school violence.

(15) Slippery slope

The slippery slope fallacy assumes that one thing will inevitably lead to another—that if one thing is allowed, it will be the first step in a downward spiral.

Faulty   Handgun controls guarantee that only criminals will have guns.

Handgun control has not led to more criminals with guns in other countries (England, for example).

"It started out with lactose, but now he's intolerant of everything."

Sidney Harris The New Yorker Collection/The Cartoon Bank

Figure 7.9: Applying a slippery slope argument, this cartoon suggests that lactose intolerance leads to general intolerance.

Be alert for rhetorical fallacies in your writing. When you find such a fallacy, be sure to moderate your claim, clarify your thinking, or, if necessary, eliminate the fallacious statement. Even if your argument as a whole is convincing, rhetorical fallacies can damage your credibility (**10a**).

Exercise 5

For each of the following statements, write one or two sentences in which you identify and explain the faulty reasoning. Next, rewrite each statement so that it avoids rhetorical fallacies.

1. The university must either build more classrooms or admit fewer new students.
2. If we join the "Black Lives Matter" movement, we will overcome racism.
3. If more women had advanced degrees, they would break through the glass ceiling.
4. If the government cuts food stamps, recipients will get jobs.
5. Our nation's children would not be fighting obesity if they watched less television.

7j   SAMPLE ARGUMENT

The following argumentative essay is Billy's response to an assignment asking him to identify a specific problem on campus, in his hometown, or in the world at large and then recommend a solution for that problem. As you read Billy's essay (which he formatted according to MLA guidelines; see chapter **13**), consider how he argued his case and whether he argued effectively. Note his use of the rhetorical appeals (ethos, logos, and pathos), the classical arrangement, and deductive reasoning. Also, identify the kinds of evidence he uses (facts, examples, testimony, and authority).

Billy Lucas

Professor Pisani-Babich

English 138T

14 April 2015

Friday Night Fright: Banning Kids' Tackle Football

Eleven-year-old Donte Goss lies in a hospital bed, electrodes attached, eyes dazed. Donte's teary mother tells the *Friday Night Tykes* cameraman that Donte had said to her, "I don't know you; leave me alone" ("Now They're Playing Scared"). So begins the third episode of this season's new reality show, *Friday Night Tykes*, a glorification of kids' football in the "Friday Night Lights" country of Texas. Donte, tackled and knocked unconscious the day before, has suffered a severe concussion. Visibly shaken, Donte's parents assure the television viewing audience (nearly half of whom support tackle football, see fig. 1) that Donte will return to the

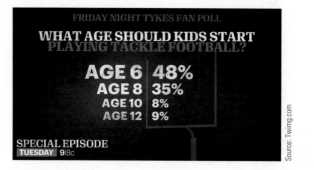

Fig. 1. A majority of *Friday Night Tykes* viewers support tackle football. Friday Night Tykes. "NFL players and health experts talk young kids and tackle football on a special #FridayNightTykes TUE 9/8c on @ESQTV." *Twitter*, 30 Mar. 2014, 10:15 a.m., storify.com/srubin1392/positives-of-friday-night-tykes.

Sidebar notes:

The writer's last name and the page number appear as the running head on each page of the paper.

Billy opens his essay with a concrete example to "hook" his readers and set up his argument against youth football tackling.

Billy includes a visual that recognizes the opposing argument.

Lucas 2

field again—when the doctors clear him. Still, these parents have limits: after Donte's third concussion, he will no longer be allowed to play football.

Billy's second paragraph provides an historical overview of the situation.

In the Texas Youth Football Association (TYFA), what with its rivalries, aggressive parents, and wildly competitive coaches, Donte's parents shine as reasonable beings. In their world, tackle football begins at age six, on-field head injuries are ignored, and game-time medical

Billy uses medical research findings to support the idea that will become his thesis.

assistance goes unprovided ("TYFA Football Programs"). Physical peril and extreme competitiveness are celebrated while the medical profession as well as the public speak of the long-term dangers of repetitive concussions. According to medical researchers David Xavier Cifu and Craig C. Young, American high school football players demonstrated "94 catastrophic head injuries (significant intracranial bleeding or edema) over a 13-year period" and "seventy-one percent of high school players suffering such injuries had a previous concussion in the same

Billy ends his second paragraph with his arguable thesis statement.

season, with 39% playing with residual symptoms." With still so much to learn about brain injuries, why do we continue to expose ever-younger children to the risks of tackle football? In light of the obvious dangers and threats, we should ban full-contact football for pre-high school players.

Billy uses this paragraph, too, to demonstrate the care he has taken to research and build an ethical, logical argument.

The national debate over the danger of concussions and brain injuries in football began in earnest fifteen years ago, when the National Football League (NFL) acknowledged those dangers by enacting changes to rules and equipment and by sponsoring studies of players' health and sports concussions. Following suit, the National Collegiate Athletic Association (NCAA) has also enacted rules to

Lucas 3

better protect its players from helmet-to-helmet injuries leading to concussions (Roling).

Regardless of the strides the NFL and NCAA have taken to protect our nation's best professional and college players, no such safeguards have been taken for youth football. Unlike the pro and collegiate teams, no single governing body regulates high school football, let alone youth football in the United States. Yet, even if there were a governing body, that body—either through laws or equipment—could not undo the high risk of concussion on the youth level, risks much higher than those for older players. No regulation short of prohibition could adequately protect the millions of young players involved in full-contact football.

The dangers of concussions and brain injuries are significant for NFL, college, and high school football players, but the risks for younger players are even greater due to their stage of physical development. Simply put, the physiology of children leaves them more prone to collision-induced trauma. As Dr. Mark Hyman explains, a child's head is similar in size to that of an adult, but the neck "[is] much weaker than an adult's neck. The combination creates a danger. When a child takes a hard blow . . . it is more difficult to keep the head steady. The result is greater force to the brain from being jerked inside the skull." And neurologist Larry Robbins refers to younger children as "bobbleheads," whose brains take the entire shock of an impact. He argues that even minor impacts, even single hits, are major head traumas for those immature developing brains, creating an extremely risky and dangerous situation for those players.

Billy sticks to his guns, conceding that football—at all levels—is a truly popular sport but invoking the dangers to the youth, thereby establishing common ground: we all agree that young players should be kept safe.

In this paragraph, especially, Billy establishes common ground: we must keep our youth players safe.

Lucas 4

In the following paragraphs, Billy lays out specific opposing arguments, carefully considering them without losing his focus on his own argument or alienating his readers.

When we now know so much about the risks and dangers involved—and know that there is still much we do not understand—why do we continue to allow children to play full-contact football? Proponents of youth football offer a number of arguments for full-contact football, the single most popular sport in the United States.

The first argument is that young players need to play full contact to learn the sport. Supporters argue that kids must be pushed, that they themselves wish they had played full-contact football at an early age, that life is tough. While it is true that learning to play early can be an advantage, youth footballers can learn all the fundamental skills of the game without engaging in full contact. Younger football players can learn the basic skills of running, passing, defending, and game strategies through flag football. Even Hall of Fame quarterback Tom Brady waited until high school to play organized tackle football because his parents found full-contact football too dangerous.

Billy's refutation of opposing arguments is always fair-minded, and he constantly makes the concession that football is, indeed, a popular sport.

The second reason proponents give for continuing full-contact youth football is that other sports with even greater risk of injury face no bans. Indeed, concussions are a danger in other youth sports, like soccer and hockey, and no reforms have been laid down for those sports. But just because they haven't made changes doesn't mean they shouldn't. To prevent concussions and brain injuries, young soccer players should not be permitted to "head" the ball, nor should youth hockey players be permitted to engage in full contact. Concussions in soccer and other sports are caused primarily by single-impact incidents, not by the continual head hits of football. And as journalist Gregg Easterbrook

Lucas 5

points out, the medical profession is only just learning of the long-term
dangers of continual and numerous hits over a football season, especially
for young players (162). Football—like no other sport—carries the
greatest risks.

The third argument supporters use is that improved equipment
decreases the risks of tackle football. But not even helmet technology
and other protective measures can prevent concussions, especially among
youth footballers, according to Brian L. Mahaffey, a physician and
sports medicine specialist (436). Concussions do not result from external
contact from a head hit but rather result from the movement of the brain
inside the skull that happens on contact. Therefore, there is no indication
that the new technology will help reduce the risks of concussions at the
youth level.

Football is the most popular sport in the United States. Its stars
are venerated, its toughest plays admired by youths and their parents
alike. Little wonder, then, that support for full-contact football for all
ages is strong. But given our increasing understanding of the serious
risks of football-related brain injuries, maybe it is time to consider viable
alternatives, modified versions of the game (like flag football) that will
allow our youth to play and compete without significant health risks.
When they have matured physically and mentally, then they will be
better prepared to engage in full-contact tackle football. The NFL, the
NCAA, and other sports-related organizations should support this critical
decision, overriding the opinions of parents, youth coaches, and fans of
Friday Night Tykes.

> Billy again concedes the popularity and value of football. He artfully offers replacements for the "tackle" in the youth league.

> Billy takes his readers further than a mere summary of all his arguments; rather, he prepares them for the football these youth will play when they get older.

Lucas 6

Works Cited

Cifu, David Xavier, and Craig C. Young. "Repetitive Head Injury Syndrome."
    Medscape, WebMD, 27 Mar. 2014, emedicine.medscape.com/article/92189.

Easterbrook, Gregg. *The King of Sports: Football's Impact on America.* St. Martin's
    Press, 2013.

Hyman, Mark. "Why Kids Under 14 Should Not Play Tackle Football." *Time,*
    6 Nov. 2012, ideas.time.com/2012/11/06/why-kids-under-14-should-not-
    play-tackle-football/.

Mahaffey, Brian L. "Concussions in High School Sports: Are They Worth the
    Risk? Should School Football Be Banned?" *Missouri Medicine,* vol. 109,
    no. 6, 2012, pp. 445-49.

"Now They're Playing Scared." *Friday Night Tykes,* Esquire Network, 21 Jan. 2014.

Robbins, Larry. "Let's Ban Tackle Football Under Age 18." *Real Clear Sports,*
    6 Dec. 2012, www.realclearsports.com/articles/2012/12/06/lets_ban_
    tackle_football_until_age_18_97818.html.

Roling, Chris. "College Football Rule Changes 2013: Breaking Down Most
    Important New Rules." *Bleacher Report,* 29 Aug. 2013, bleacherreport.
    com/articles/1754276- college-football-rule-changes-2013-breaking-
    down-most-important-new-rules.

"TYFA Football Programs." *Texas Youth Football and Cheer Association,* 29
    Mar. 2015, www.tyfa.com/tyfa-football-programs..

Exercise 6

Reread Billy Lucas's essay and identify what you consider to be his
values. Which ones does he reveal as he argues against tackle football in the youth leagues? What personal experiences might have
shaped those values?

Situate Yourself

You have an internship with a state senator who would like you to do some research on cyberbullying. He is particularly interested in the question of whether anonymity gives people the license to harass others. Read the following set of quotations and write a brief in which you summarize, synthesize, and respond to these views (which have been invented for the purposes of this exercise).

1. **Diane Lee, law professor ("Free and Distasteful Speech," page 10)**

   Freedom of expression is protected under the First Amendment, so anonymous trolls may use words and images to provoke others, even when these words and images are distasteful. Determining what is provocative and what is harassment is a matter of interpretation.

2. **Jason Howard, college counselor ("The Right to Be Sued," page 127)**

   When comments are interpreted as defaming someone or intentionally inflicting emotional distress, the people who made them can be sued. Websites where comments have been posted can revoke the privilege of anonymity.

3. **Ed Parsons, journalist for the magazine *Yes* ("Mixing Up the Problem," page 21)**

   Anonymity and incivility must be separated. If we protect anonymity but discourage incivility, we would promote democratic discourse while avoiding the loss of free speech.

4. **Julia Leonard, activist ("Protecting a Vulnerable Population," page B1)**

   Some anonymous interactions are justified, especially those on sensitive issues. Others target vulnerable populations. There should be a way to protect those who are not doing harm while punishing those who are.

8 | PLANNING RESEARCH

Research is much more than the act of searching for information. It consists of posing intriguing, challenging questions. Seeking information is a response to these questions. In fact, thinking of research as **inquiry**, as asking questions and finding answers, will help you craft a research question, or a set of related questions, as well as create a plan that focuses your attention and makes your work efficient.

This chapter will help you

- use the rhetorical situation to guide your research (**8a**),
- formulate an effective research question (**8b–c**), and
- create a research plan to help you stay on schedule (**8d**).

8a | RESEARCH AND THE RHETORICAL SITUATION

To make the most of the time you spend doing research, think carefully about your rhetorical situation early in the research process. Establishing your purpose and anticipating your audience's questions will allow you to work efficiently. When you receive an assignment that requires you to do some research, begin by asking yourself what the purpose of your research will be and who will benefit from your findings. Common purposes for doing research include the following:

- **To inform an audience.** The researcher reports current thinking on a specific topic, including opposing views, factual information, and credible evidence.

  Example   To inform an audience about current nutritional guidelines for children

- **To analyze and synthesize information and then offer possible solutions.** The researcher analyzes a topic and synthesizes the available information about it, looking for points of agreement and disagreement and for gaps in coverage. Sometimes the researcher offers possible ways to address any problems found.

Example   To analyze and synthesize various proposals for alternative energy sources

- **To convince an audience with facts and arguments.** The researcher states a position and backs it up with data, statistics, testimony, corroborating texts or events, or supporting arguments. The researcher's purpose is to persuade readers to take the same position.

Example   To persuade an audience to support a political candidate

- **To invite readers to debate.** Instead of trying to convince others of a particular point of view or persuade them to take action, the researcher asks readers to discuss an issue and search for common ground.

Example   To invite an audience to discuss proposals for preventing the spread of the Ebola virus

Sometimes a researcher has to consider more than one purpose. For example, in the introduction of a lab report, a researcher analyzes and synthesizes previous work on a topic and locates a research niche—an area in need of further study. The researcher then attempts to convince readers that his or her current study will address this need. The body of the report is informative: it describes the materials used, explains the procedures followed, and presents the results. In the conclusion, the researcher may try, based on the results of the experiment or study, to persuade the audience to take some action (such as giving up smoking, eating fewer carbohydrates, or funding future research).

Next, consider your audience. Who are your readers, and what do they most need to know? What kinds of sources and evidence will they find reliable? Also important is consideration of your stance (or attitude). Will you be able to keep an open mind as you do your research? Will you be able to take into account multiple points of view?

Before you start to write, be sure you understand your instructor's expectations for length, format, due date, and other practical matters. Creating a research plan will help you meet these expectations and complete your work on time (**8d**).

8b | FORMULATING RESEARCH QUESTIONS

The starting point for any writing project is the rhetorical opportunity—the issue or problem that has prompted you to write. For research assignments, it is helpful to turn the issue or problem into a question that can guide your work. Research questions often arise when you try to relate what you are studying to your own experience. For instance, you may start wondering about voting regulations while reading about past elections for a history class and, at the same time, noticing news stories about the role technology plays in current elections or the unfair practices reported in some states. Each of these observations may give rise to a different question. Focusing on the influence of technology may prompt you to inquire, "What are the possible consequences of having only electronic ballots?" However, if you focus on unfair voting practices, you may ask, "How do voting procedures differ from state to state?" Because you can ask a variety of research questions about any topic, choose the one that interests you the most and allows you to fulfill your assignment.

To generate useful research questions, you may find it helpful to ask yourself about causes, consequences, processes, definitions, or values, as shown in the following list:

- **Cause:** Does smoking cannabis cause cancer?
- **Consequence:** What are the consequences of taking selective serotonin reuptake inhibitors (SSRIs) for more than five years?
- **Process:** How are standardized tests used to predict college-level academic success?
- **Definition:** Do psychiatrists currently agree on a definition for Internet addiction?
- **Value:** Should the federal minimum wage be raised?

Although choosing just one question will make your research efficient, you may find it beneficial to answer more than one question when you write your paper. For example, if you explain the debate over the minimum wage, you may also decide to define *federal minimum wage*. Regardless of how many questions you ask, the best research questions are challenging, focused, and connected to current facts or events.

Another way to generate and situate a research question is to find a claim (or an assertion) made in a text you are currently reading and pose a question related to that claim:

In "School Should Be about Learning, Not Sports," journalist Amanda Ripley states that the allure of high school competitive sports is "a fantasy with a short shelf life." She worries that when students believe in this fantasy, they do not take their academic courses seriously and may inadvertently sabotage their future in a culture and economy that values highly educated workers. However, while Ripley points out problems caused by competitive sports, she fails to acknowledge any benefits that students might gain from competitive sports. *Are there any advantages to having competitive sports teams in high school? If there are, do they offset the drawbacks Ripley mentions?*

When you start by addressing a claim, you acknowledge that research is an ongoing conversation. As a participant in this conversation, you recognize the contributions of others before you ask questions or offer comments and suggestions.

TIPS FOR FINDING A CHALLENGING RESEARCH QUESTION

First find a topic.

- What problem or issue from one of your classes would you like to address?
- What have you read or observed recently that piqued your curiosity?
- What local or school problem would you like to explore or help solve?
- Is there anything (lifestyles, political views, global events) that you find unusual or intriguing enough to investigate?

Once you have a topic, jot down all the questions you have about that topic. (Think about causes, consequences, processes, definitions, and values.) Choose the most specific question that will interest both you and your audience and that will help you address your assignment. Be sure the question cannot be easily answered with a *yes* or *no*.

8c | TESTING RESEARCH QUESTIONS

You can test your research question to see whether it is effective by first making sure you and others are sincerely interested in answering this question. At the same time, double-check your assignment for length restrictions and decide whether your research question is specific enough to be addressed in the space available. Finally, because any assignment comes with deadlines, determine whether you have the time and resources available to answer the question by the due date.

TIPS FOR TESTING YOUR RESEARCH QUESTION

To test your research question, start a conversation about it by having a friend or classmate interview you about its potential. If no one is available, sharpen your ideas by *writing* your answers.

- Why is it important for you to answer this research question?
- Are there more than two ways of answering this question?
- Why is it important for your audience to know the answer to the question?
- Why does the answer to your question require research?
- What type of research might help you answer your question?
- Will you be able to carry out the necessary research in the amount of time and space allowed?

After you have a strong research question, you are ready to start gathering information and exploring sources.

Exercise 1

Each of the following subjects would need to be narrowed down for a research paper. To experiment with framing a research question, compose two questions about each subject that could be answered in a ten-page paper (refer to the list on page 191 for examples of questions).

1. college education
2. divorce
3. standardized tests
4. extreme sports
5. body image
6. social networking

8d	CREATING A RESEARCH PLAN

As you craft your research question, you may find it helpful to draft a plan for your research project as well.

1. Create a research question.   *Due:* _____

It is easy to rush to answer your question, even before you have done any research. Try to keep an open mind until you have consulted some of your sources.

2. Note the assignment's requirements.   *Due:* _____

Clarify your instructor's expectations. *What is the due date? What is the approximate length of the research project? What style manual should you use (MLA, APA, CMS, CSE)? What point of view is appropriate (first person, third person, a combination)? What is the medium of delivery? Are you expected to print out a document? Post a document online? Prepare an oral presentation? Incorporate visuals?* If you have not already received sufficient information about your assignment, ask your instructor these questions as soon as possible.

3. Establish your audience and purpose.   *Due:* _____

Knowing who your readers are and what your purpose is will help you not only to decide what types of sources to use but also to establish an appropriate tone. Your instructor will be one of your readers. *Does your assignment expect you to consider other readers as well?*

4. Decide which types of sources to use.   *Due:* _____

Assignments differ. *Will your research require the use of a wide range of sources—books, articles, and websites? Or does your assignment call for the use of historical archives?* If you are having trouble determining which sources to use, ask your instructor or a reference librarian for help.

5. Find, review, and evaluate sources.   *Due:* _____

Chapters **9** and **10** provide guidance in finding and evaluating sources. Be sure to give yourself plenty of time to locate your sources, read them, and take notes.

6. **Prepare an outline or description of the overall structure of your paper. Start with your research question or formulate a thesis statement.**

   Due: _____

Some research papers begin with a research question in the introductory paragraph. Others include a thesis statement instead of a research question. If you are required to begin with a thesis statement, this statement will form the governing idea of your essay (2c). Remember that thesis statements are related to your purpose. *Are you providing your audience with general information? Are you reporting on your analysis of information? Are you proposing a solution to a problem? Are you persuading your audience to change their opinion or take action?*

7. **Write a first draft.** *Due:* _____

As you write, keep your research question or thesis statement in mind, revising it if you need to. Be willing to do additional research if necessary.

8. **Get the response of readers.** *Due:* _____

Allow time before you turn in your final draft to get feedback from other readers—students in your class or tutors at a writing center.

9. **Revise.** *Due:* _____

Use reader feedback to revise your work (3e).

10. **Edit, proofread, and polish (3f–g).** *Due:* _____

9 ‖ FINDING APPROPRIATE SOURCES

Whenever you do research, you can choose from a wide variety of sources—books, articles, online material, even your own fieldwork. Choosing appropriate sources depends on your assignment and research question. If you are unsure of what types of sources to use, ask a reference librarian or review the assignment with your instructor.

This chapter will help you

- determine which sources best address the assignment (**9a**),
- use online search tools to find sources (**9b**),
- locate reference works, articles, books, online sources, and images (**9c–g**),
- organize your sources (**9h**), and
- conduct field research (**9i**).

9a ‖ CONSIDERING KINDS OF SOURCES

As you consider which sources might be the most useful for your project, remember that there are significant differences among kinds of sources.

(1) Primary and secondary sources

Primary sources provide firsthand information. In the humanities, primary sources may include documents such as archived letters, historical records, and papers, as well as literary, autobiographical, and philosophical texts. Primary sources do not have to be in written form. Artwork, photographs, and audio and video recordings are also considered primary sources. In the social sciences, primary sources can be field observations, case histories, survey data, and interviews. In the natural sciences, primary sources are generally empirical and include field observations and experimental results. **Secondary sources** are commentaries on or descriptions of primary sources. They may offer summary or interpretation and appear as reviews, reports, scholarly biographies, and surveys of the work done on a specific topic.

Compare the following excerpts. The first is from a primary source, a book published in 1789. The second, which comments on that book, is from a secondary source, a book published in 2010. (The superscript numbers in the second excerpt direct readers to bibliographic information at the end of the book.)

Primary source

Now private ethics has happiness for its end: and legislation can have no other. Private ethics concerns every member, that is, the happiness and the actions of every member, of any community that can be proposed; and legislation can concern no more.

—**JEREMY BENTHAM,** *The Principles of Morals and Legislation*

Secondary source

One writer, Jeremy Bentham, gained enduring fame through his pronouncement that the overriding aim of government should be to secure the greatest happiness of the greatest number of people by maximizing pleasures and minimizing pain.[10] In his more optimistic passages, he wrote about a science of happiness, a "felicific calculus" by which governments could measure the expected pleasures and pains resulting from policy proposals and choose the one that would produce the greatest net happiness.[11]

—**DEREK BOK,** *The Politics of Happiness*

If you were writing about Bentham and decided to quote him, using a quotation you found in Bok's book, you would have to cite Bok's book as an indirect source. For examples, see the style guidelines for citing and documenting indirect sources in chapter **13** (Modern Language Association), chapter **15** (American Psychological Association), or chapter **17** (*Chicago Manual of Style*).

(2) Scholarly and popular sources

Scholarly books and journals contain reports of original research written by experts for an academic audience. Professional or trade books and magazines feature articles written by staff writers or industry specialists. Popular books, magazines, and newspapers are generally written by staff writers, though scholars are frequently invited to contribute articles written for a lay audience.

(3) Current and older material

When writing about current issues, you will need to use up-to-date sources. However, to place an issue in a historical context, search for older sources and documents from the appropriate historical period.

(4) Biased or impartial sources

You will find the best support for your assertions by using sources that are impartial, that is, sources that treat all points of view fairly (chapter **10**). Nonetheless, including a clearly biased source can be useful to bring in other viewpoints or to demonstrate that certain ways of discussing an issue are faulty in some way (**7b, 7i**).

9b   SEARCHING ELECTRONICALLY

Whenever you are searching for sources—either electronic or print material—you will need to know how to use online search tools. Your library's website will likely have a search tool for its catalog of print sources and various search tools connected to the library's **databases**. The better you are at using these tools, the more efficient your research will be. If you go to the library, a reference librarian will be able to help you learn to use these tools.

Whether you are using a popular **search engine** (such as Bing, Google, or Yahoo!), a **subject directory** designed for academic research (such as Internet Public Library or The WWW Virtual Library), or a search tool on your library's website, you will be able to narrow your findings by conducting an **advanced search**.

Searches generally start with **keywords**, so choosing just the right word or phrase is important. If you start with a keyword search and find that you are not locating useful sources, you could first try a related term or a synonym, for example, using *wind energy* for *wind power*. You could also try using terms that are more specific or more general. If you were interested in sources of wind energy, a search for *wind farms* would be more specific than *wind energy* and more general than *wind turbines*. Most online search tools allow you to filter your results by searching for sources that match (1) the exact phrase, (2) some words but not others, (3) words related in form, or (4) alternative spellings of a word. When you know the name of an

TIPS FOR REFINING KEYWORD SEARCHES

The options for refining your search will vary depending on the database or search engine you choose, but most will include the following methods.

- Use **quotation marks** around terms to search for exact phrases. If you find that many search results are irrelevant when you do a general search, enclose a phrase in quotation marks to narrow results.

- Combine words or phrases using the connectors AND, OR, or NOT (sometimes called **Boolean operators**) to limit or widen a search. For example, you could try *Marion AND Ohio* for results that include both keywords, *Buckeye OR Ohio* for results that contain information about either keyword, or *Marion NOT Ohio* for results that exclude mention of Ohio.

- Use **truncation** to broaden a search so that results will include various forms of a word (for example, *manage, management, manager*). Use the root of the words you are searching for and place an asterisk after it (*manag**).

- Use **wildcards** (such as a question mark: *industriali?ation*) to broaden a search so that the results will include various spellings (for example, *industrialization* and *industrialisation*).

- Use **parentheses** around terms to further customize and group one term with keywords: *obesity AND (childhood OR preschoolers)*.

author or the title of a work, you will be able to search for the author or title directly.

Most search tools have features that allow you to perform advanced searches and thus limit the results in a number of ways. *ProQuest*, the database shown in figure 9.1, for example, shows a few ways one user has limited a search by source type and date, among other options.

9c   LOCATING REFERENCE WORKS

To begin a research project, you may find it useful to consult general or specialized reference works, including the encyclopedias, dictionaries, bibliographies, atlases, almanacs, and other resources available at your library. These works—many available online—will help you find background information about people, events, and concepts related to your topic. Especially helpful are specialized reference works—such as the

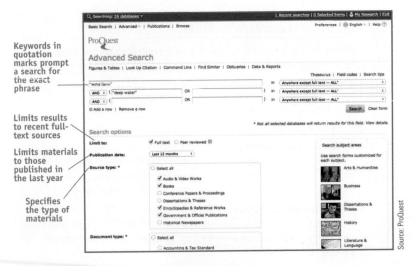

Keywords in quotation marks prompt a search for the exact phrase

Limits results to recent full-text sources

Limits materials to those published in the last year

Specifies the type of materials

Source: ProQuest

Figure 9.1: Advanced search using keywords in a database.

Encyclopedia of Psychology or the *Dictionary of American History*—which not only provide in-depth information on a topic but also offer extensive lists of other sources to consult. *Wikipedia* is a popular source for information, but it is sometimes considered unreliable because contributors are not always experts in a field and because facts are not always verified before they are published.

9d   LOCATING ARTICLES

Articles in **periodicals** (publications that appear at regular intervals) offer information that is often more recent than that found in books. Periodicals include journals, magazines, and newspapers and can be published in print, online, or both. **Scholarly journals** contain reports of original research written by experts for an academic audience. **Professional** (or **trade**) **magazines** feature articles written by staff writers or industry specialists who address on-the-job concerns. **Popular magazines** and **newspapers**, generally written by staff writers, carry a combination of news stories that attempt to be objective and essays that reflect the opinions of editors or guest contributors. The following are examples of the various types of periodicals:

Scholarly journals: *Journal of Developmental Psychology, Journal of Business Communication*

Trade magazines: *Farm Journal, Automotive Weekly*

Magazines (news): *Time, Newsweek*

Magazines (public affairs): *The New Yorker, National Review*

Magazines (special interest): *National Geographic, Discover*

Newspapers: *The New York Times, USA Today*

To find articles, you may search the web, but such a general search will most likely yield unreliable sources as well as others that charge a fee for you to access an article. A better way to locate articles is to access your library's **databases**, which are collections of articles indexed according to author, title, date, keywords, and other features (9b). The databases you may access include general databases covering a wide range of subject areas and specialized databases and indexes that offer material specific to one subject or discipline. For older articles that are not online, consult a print index at your library.

GENERAL DATABASES

Academic Search Complete: Multidisciplinary database of journals and magazines, many full-text versions, via EBSCOhost

Expanded Academic ASAP: Database of journals and periodicals covering a wide variety of disciplines

Google Scholar: Search tool for articles, books, and other documents from academic sources and other sites, though it may be necessary to access the full text via your library

InfoTrac: Database of articles on a wide variety of subjects from journals and magazines

JSTOR: Database for digital library books, primary sources, and articles from journals in the arts, humanities, sciences, and social sciences

LexisNexis Academic: Database strong in coverage of legal as well as local, national, and world news sources

ProQuest: Large database of news and academic sources, in areas ranging from arts, literature, and social sciences to business, technology, medicine, and natural sciences

SUBJECT-SPECIFIC DATABASES

ERIC: Database for information on education

MLA International Bibliography: Database of research in literature, language, and film

PsycINFO: Database for psychology research

ScienceDirect: Database for research in the physical, life, health, and social sciences

To search a database, you will usually begin with a keyword search for terms related to your research question. If your list of results is too large, use the tips for refining keyword searches (**9b**).

A database search will generally yield an **abstract**, a short summary of an article. By scanning the abstract, you can determine whether to locate the complete text of the article, which can often be downloaded and printed. You can access your library's databases by using its computers or, if you have a password, by linking from a remote computer.

Exercise 1

With your research question in mind, locate a scholarly article, a magazine article, and a newspaper article. Explain how these articles will help you answer your research question.

9e   LOCATING BOOKS

Three types of books are commonly used in the research process. **Scholarly books** are written by experts to advance knowledge of a certain subject. Most include original research. Before being published, these books are reviewed by scholars in the same field as the author(s), a process known as peer review. **Trade books** are also written by experts or scholars, and often by journalists or freelance writers as well. Authors of trade books write to inform a general audience of research that has been done by others. **Reference books** such as encyclopedias and dictionaries provide factual information in short articles or entries written and reviewed by experts in the field. The audience for these books includes both veteran scholars and those new to a field of study.

You can find books related to your research question by using your library's online catalog and conducting searches using a keyword, author, or title. Experiment with keywords, choosing a word or phrase you think might be found in the title of a book or in notes in the catalog's records (see figure 9.2). You can also try a subject search by entering words related to your topic; if the search does not yield any results, ask a reference librarian for a subject-heading guide. (A source's detailed record in your library catalog will feature subject headings that you may also use to expand your search.) Once you find the online catalog record for a book you would like to use, write down its **call number**, which indicates where the book is shelved. Some library catalogs will also allow you to send yourself a text message that includes the call number. Take time when you reach the shelves to scan for related books nearby that may offer additional information.

If a particular book is not available at your school's library, you have several options. Frequently, library websites have links to the catalogs of other libraries. By using such links, you can determine whether another library has the book you want and order it directly from that library or through the interlibrary loan service. In addition, your library may offer access to the database *WorldCat*, which locates books as well as images, sound recordings, and other materials.

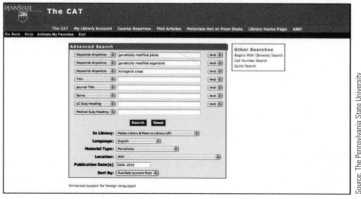

Source: The Pennsylvania State University

Figure 9.2: By specifying three sets of keywords, the researcher narrows her search.

Exercise 2

With your research question in mind, find the titles of a scholarly book, a trade book, and a reference book. Search online for information about these books, and explain how they will help you address your research question.

9f LOCATING ONLINE SOURCES

Material on the web varies greatly in its reliability. Although the facts provided on some websites have been carefully checked, facts on other websites have not undergone close examination.

Colleges, universities, and individual scholars may have reliable websites, blogs, or other information related to your topics. But quality can vary, so carefully evaluate any online source you are thinking of using (**10c**).

By sifting through your search results, you will be able to find a great deal of useful information, for example, current news events, maps, historical documents, and government reports, statistics, and legislative materials. Here is a list of types of websites to consider as you do your research:

- **Government sites.** Federal, state, and local governments provide an abundance of information. USA.gov directs you to sources on topics ranging from art to zoos.
- **News sites.** Newspapers, magazines, radio, and television stations sponsor websites that provide frequently updated news reports. Archived news stories are also sometimes available (though your library may offer easier access via a database).
- **Discussion lists and forums.** You may be able to find experts on topics by joining newsgroups, discussion groups, forums, or online mailing lists. To find such groups or access archived discussions, use a search engine or specialized service such as Google Groups.
- **Digital archives.** Archives are of particular interest if you need artifacts from the past—maps, speeches, drawings, documents, and recordings. The National Archives and the Library of Congress are good places to start.

- **Blogs and wikis.** As starting points, blogs and wikis can provide overviews of topics or issues as well as links to primary sources. However, because they are not generally reviewed by experts, they are often not considered reliable academic sources. Avoid using information from these sources without your instructor's approval.

Exercise 3

Search online for sources related to your research question. Explain how you could use each source.

9g | LOCATING IMAGES

If your rhetorical situation calls for the use of images, the Internet offers you billions from which to choose. However, if an image you choose is copyrighted, you will need to contact the author, artist, or designer for permission to use it, and you may even need to purchase it. Figure 9.3 is an example of an image with a caption and a credit line, which signifies that the image is used with permission. You do not need to obtain permission to use images in the public domain or those cleared for reuse.

Many search engines allow you to search for images. Collections of specific images are also available at the following Web sites:

Figure 9.3: Genetically modified foods look like naturally produced foods. (Photo © Tom Grill/ Getty Images)

Advertisements

Ad*Access	library.duke.edu/digitalcollections/adaccess/
Adflip	www.adflip.com

Art

National Gallery of Art	images.nga.gov/en/page/show_home_page.html
Metropolitan Museum of Art	www.metmuseum.org/about-the-museum /press-room/news/2014/oasc-access

Photography

National Geographic	www.natgeocreative.com/ngs/photography
Smithsonian Images	siarchives.si.edu/collections

9h KEEPING TRACK OF SOURCES

As you start gathering sources, be sure to keep them organized. For online and other nonprint sources, it is a good idea to keep a separate record of the **access date** (the date on which you visited the source) and the **publication date** (the date on which the source was published or last modified). The publication date generally appears on the bottom of the website's home page.

- **Bookmarks.** Bookmark any sources you find on the web, using the most stable URL you can find, which in the case of online journals, magazines, and newspapers is a home page.
- **Database and library accounts.** Your library site may allow you to use your personal account to collect and organize sources using book-marking tools. Some databases also offer this service, which will allow you to save and retrieve your search history.
- **Downloads.** If you decide to download PDFs or other materials, be sure they have recognizable titles or names and save them in folders clearly labeled for your project.

- **Photocopies and printouts.** Keep printouts together by stapling them and placing them in clearly labeled file folders.
- **Reference management systems.** To organize your bibliographic entries, consider using a reference management system such as End-Note, RefWorks, or Zotero. Check to see which system your library supports.

9i	DOING FIELD RESEARCH

Interviews, observations, and surveys are the most common methods of **field research**, a study done in a natural setting, rather than in a laboratory. Any study you design may have to be approved by the ethics board or institutional review board (IRB) at your college or university. The board's approval indicates that a study protects the privacy and welfare of human participants.

(1) Interviews

You may find that your research question can be answered, in part, by someone with firsthand experience in the area you are researching. Interviews can take place in person, over the phone, or via e-mail or videoconference.

1. **Arrange the interview.** E-mail or call to request an interview. Be sure to introduce yourself, briefly describe your project, and explain your reasons for requesting the interview. Try to accommodate the person you hope to interview by asking him or her to suggest an interview date. If you intend to record your interview, ask for permission.

2. **Prepare for the interview.** Consult sources on your topic, especially any written by the person you will be interviewing. Start preparing your list of questions before the day of the interview, using a blend of open (or broad) questions and focused (or narrow) questions. Here are a few examples:

   Open questions

   What do you think about _____?

   What are your views on _____?

   Why do you believe _____?

Focused questions

How long have you worked as a/an _____?

When did you start _____?

3. **Conduct the interview.** Before the interview begins, remind the person you are interviewing that you will be recording the conversation or taking notes. Although you will have prepared questions, do not feel that you must ask all your questions in order. Listen closely to responses and follow up with related questions, perhaps even ones you had not thought of beforehand. If responses are elaborate, you may find that you do not have to ask each of your questions.

4. **Reflect on the interview.** Review and expand your notes or transcribe the relevant parts of the recording. Write extensively about the interview, asking yourself what you found most important, most surprising, and most puzzling. Send your thanks via a written note or an e-mail message. If you have follow-up questions, it is better to include them in an e-mail message.

(2) Surveys

Whereas an interview elicits information from one person whose name you know, a survey provides information from a number of anonymous people.

1. **Compile a list of questions.** To be effective, a survey questionnaire should be short and focused. If the list of questions is too long, people may not be willing to take the time to answer them all. If the questions are not focused on your research topic, you will find it difficult to integrate the results into your project. Following are some examples of types of survey questions:

Questions that require a simple yes-or-no answer:

Do you commute to work in a car? (Circle one.)

Yes   No

Multiple-choice questions:

How many people do you commute with? (Circle one.)

0   1   2   3   4

Questions with answers on a checklist:

How long does it take you to commute to work? (Check one.)

___ 0–30 minutes   ___ 30–60 minutes

___ 60–90 minutes   ___ 90–120 minutes

Questions with a ranking scale:

If the car you drive or ride in is not working, which of the following types of transportation do you rely on? (Rank the choices from 1 for most frequently used to 4 for least frequently used.)

___ bus   ___ shuttle van   ___ subway   ___ taxi

Open questions:

What feature of commuting do you find most irritating?

2. **Decide who you would like to participate and how you will contact them.** Some surveys are done in person or by phone. Others are sent to participants via regular mail or e-mail. Surveys conducted through e-mail often include a link to a Web service such as SurveyMonkey.

3. **Design the survey to introduce your purpose and review your distribution method.** Begin your survey questionnaire with an introduction stating the purpose of the questionnaire, how the results will be used, and how many questions it contains or approximately how long it should take to complete. In the introduction, assure participants that their answers will remain confidential. Before you distribute your questionnaire, check with your instructor or the institutional review board on your campus to make certain that you have followed appropriate guidelines. It is often helpful to ask a few friends to "test-drive" your questionnaire to see whether all the questions are clear and neutral (rather than calling for a particular response).

4. **Analyze your results.** Once the questionnaires have been completed and returned, tally the results for all but the open questions. Read through the open questions and look for patterns in the responses. Create categories for the responses that will help you tally the answers.

(3) Observations

If your research question focuses on human or animal behavior in a natural setting, conducting an observation will be key to the success of your study.

1. **Establish the goals of your observation.** With a clear purpose in mind, you will be able to focus your attention.

2. **Set up an appointment, if necessary.** In some settings, such as in a school, hospital, or zoo, you will need to obtain permission for your observation.

3. **Take detailed notes.** A helpful method for note-taking during observations is to divide each page in half vertically. Keep your notes on the left side of the page and leave space on the right side of the page for later commentary.

4. **Analyze your observation.** Review your notes, looking for both patterns and behaviors or events that veer from the ordinary. On the right side of your notes, write down your comments; whenever possible, explain the patterns and deviations you have found.

Exercise 4

Of all the types of sources discussed in this chapter, which will you use to address your research question? If you created a research plan (**8d**), return to that plan and set dates for deciding which types of sources to use and how much time each of them will require.

10 EVALUATING PRINT AND ONLINE SOURCES

As you gather sources that may address your research question, review each one closely and decide how, or even whether, you can use it in your paper. Start by determining whether the information the source contains is credible. This chapter will help you

- assess an author's credibility (**10a**),
- assess a publisher's credibility (**10b**),
- evaluate online sources (**10c**), and
- read sources closely and critically (**10d**).

10a CREDIBILITY OF AUTHORS

Credible (or trustworthy) authors present facts accurately, support their opinions with compelling evidence, connect their ideas reasonably, and demonstrate respect for any opposing views. To evaluate the credibility of authors whose work you might like to use, consider their credentials, examine their values and beliefs, and note the response they receive from other readers. Credentials include academic or professional training, publications, and experience. The author's credentials may be found on the jacket or in the preface of a book, in a note in an article, or on a page in the journal or on the website devoted to providing background on contributors. Some search tools will allow you to see the influence of the author's work by including a link to other sources that cite articles or books written by the author.

An author's values and beliefs underpin his or her research and publications. To determine what these values and beliefs are, consider the author's purpose and intended audience. For example, on the subject of malpractice suits, a lawyer may write an article to convince patients to sue health providers, a doctor may write an essay for other doctors to highlight the frivolous nature of malpractice claims, and a linguist might prepare a conference paper that reveals miscommunication to be

---

✓ CHECKLIST for Assessing an Author's Credentials

- Does the author's education or profession relate to the subject of the work?
- With what institutions, organizations, or companies has the author been affiliated?
- What awards has the author won?
- What other works has the author produced?
- Do other experts speak of the author as an authority or link to the author's work?

---

at the core of malpractice suits. By identifying the underlying values and beliefs, you can responsibly discuss information in your sources.

Published reviews often include information for determining whether an author is credible. Though a work by any credible author may get some negative responses, use carefully the work of a writer whom more than one reviewer characterizes as biased, ill-informed, or careless with facts.

Finding flaws in a source does not mean that you should not use it. On the contrary, if you found, for example, material that included economic, political, religious, or social biases, you could point out such flaws, as Natalie Angier does when she questions the views of certain evolutionary psychologists.

> Now, it makes sense to be curious about the evolutionary roots of human behavior. It's reasonable to attempt to understand our impulses and actions by applying Darwinian logic to the problem. We're animals. We're not above the rude little prods and jests of natural selection. But evolutionary psychology as it has been disseminated across mainstream consciousness is a cranky and despotic Cyclops, its single eye glaring through an over-whelmingly masculinist lens. I say masculinist rather than male because the view of male behavior promulgated by hardcore evolutionary psychologists is as narrow and inflexible as their view of womanhood is.
>
> —**NATALIE ANGIER,** *Woman: An Intimate Geography*

10b CREDIBILITY OF PUBLISHERS

When doing research, consider not only the credibility of authors but also the credibility of the media through which their work is made available to you. The facts in some types of publications are checked more carefully than those in others.

When evaluating books and articles, you can usually assume that publishers associated with universities demand a high standard of scholarship, including review of the work by other scholars in the field. Work published in popular magazines and newspapers is generally reliable and may provide useful overviews of a topic, but such publications do not require scholarly review and may not include bibliographies or citation of sources for other researchers to consult. Because magazines and newspapers often report research results that were initially published elsewhere, try to find the original source to ensure the accuracy of their reports.

The following excerpt from a magazine article about overconfidence in business professionals includes direct quotations and identifies the author of those statements but provides no article title, publication date, or page numbers:

> "In conflicts involving mutual assessment, an exaggerated assessment of the probability of winning increases the probability of winning," Richard Wrangham, a biological anthropologist at Harvard, writes. "Selection therefore favors this form of overconfidence." Winners know how to bluff. And who bluffs the best? The person who, instead of pretending to be stronger than he is, actually believes himself to be stronger than he is. According to Wrangham, self-deception reduces the chances of "behavioral leakage"; that is, of "inadvertently revealing the truth through an inappropriate behavior."
>
> —MALCOLM GLADWELL, "Cocksure"

If readers want to know more about Wrangham's thoughts on overconfidence, they will have to do extra work because the writer of this magazine article includes no bibliographic information.

Compare the excerpt from Gladwell's article to the following excerpt from Richard Wrangham's journal article, published in *Evolution and Human Behavior*:

> According to Hinde (1993: 33), for example, in-group bias is associated with increased cohesiveness and cooperation and, thus, more effective social action. Among individuals in competition, self-deception may enhance performance by deflecting attention from anxiety, pain, and fatigue (Starek and Keating 1991).
>
> —RICHARD WRANGHAM, "Is Military Incompetence Adaptive?"

In this article on overconfidence, Wrangham also refers to the work of others, but because he is writing for an academic audience, he is expected to include dates with the names of those whose work he mentions and corresponding bibliographic entries at the end of the article, as well as page numbers for any direct quotations. Readers are thus able to consult the original sources mentioned. By checking the references that the author of a source uses, you can find out how reliable and valid the author's claims are.

10c EVALUATION OF ONLINE SOURCES

If you are evaluating an online source that also appears in print, you can follow the guidelines for print-based sources. But if you are evaluating a web or other online source, you need to consider additional features of the medium. For help locating important information, see figures 10.1 and 10.2, which show the top and bottom of the same web source (the blue numbers refer to tips on page 215).

Figure 10.1: Top of a web page from Global Journalist.
Source: Global Journalist

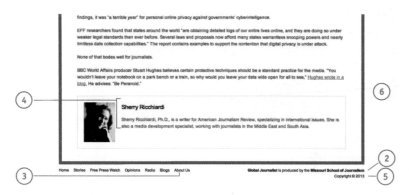

Figure 10.2: Bottom of a web page from Global Journalist.
Source: Global Journalist

1. Check the URL for information about the sponsoring organization. Colleges and universities are indicated by the suffix *.edu*, government departments and agencies by *.gov*, professional and nonprofit organizations by *.org*, and businesses by *.com*. As you access the various types of sites to evaluate their content, keep in mind that every site is shaped to achieve a specific purpose and to address a specific audience.

2. Locate the name of the sponsor. This information is generally found at the bottom of the page.

3. Determine the organization's or company's stance on your research question. You will be able to find out more information on an "About Us" or "Our Vision" page. Links may be found at the top of the page, at the bottom of the page, or both.

4. Examine the author's credentials. If the author's name is not given near the title, look at the bottom of the page. Information about the author's credentials can often also be found at the bottom of the page. Because this information is provided by the author, sponsor, or publisher, it is always a good idea to search elsewhere for additional information about the author (10a).

5. Identify the date of publication. Some articles place the publication date (or date of most recent update) near the title, but often it is at the bottom of the page. Determine whether the date is sufficiently current.

6. Check links and cited sources. By examining the sources the author uses, you will be able to gauge the reliability of the information provided. Consider unreliable any web source that does not provide a link or enough bibliographic details for you to track down the original source for information presented as factual.

✓ CHECKLIST for Evaluating Online Sources

- Who is the author? Is this author credible? (**10a**)

- Who is the sponsor? A government agency? An institution of higher education? A business? An individual? Is the sponsor credible? (**10b**)

- To what extent has the source's information been reviewed by others?

- Is there a list of original sources available so that you can consult them to check facts?

- When was the source last updated? Is the information up to date? How current are the source's links? If it includes dead links, the source may not be recent enough to be useful.

Exercise 1

Find online sources that have three different kinds of sponsors but contain material relevant to your research question or to a specific subject, such as global warming, saving energy, or disaster relief efforts. Explain the differences and similarities among the three sites you have chosen.

10d RELEVANCE AND TIMELINESS

A source is useful only when it is relevant to your research question. Given the ever-growing amount of information available on most topics, you should be prepared to put aside a source that will not help you answer your research question or achieve your purpose. Some writers veer off track when they cannot bring themselves to abandon a source they like, even if it is no longer relevant—as often happens when their focus has changed during the process of conducting research, drafting the paper, and revising it. It is better to abandon an irrelevant source than to write a poorly focused paper.

Seldom will an entire book, article, or website be useful for a specific research paper. A book's table of contents can lead you to relevant chapters or sections, and its index can lead you to relevant pages. Websites have links that you can click on to locate relevant information. Once you find potentially useful material, read it closely and critically (10e).

Useful sources are also up to date. A common research error is to do a simple search on the Web or on a library database and use the first sources listed. These sources, however, may not be the most recent. Take the time to do an advanced search, which allows you to select the dates of articles you would like to review (9b). If you are writing about a specific era in the past, you should also consult contemporary sources—sources written during that period.

To determine when a source was published, look for the date of publication. In books, it appears with other copyright information on the page following the title page. (See the example on page 290.) Dates of periodicals appear on their covers and frequently on the top or bottom of pages throughout each issue (see page 287). The publication date on a website (the date when the site was published or last modified) frequently appears at the bottom of each screen on the site.

✓ CHECKLIST for Establishing Relevancy and Timeliness ▬▬▬

- Does the table of contents, index, or directory of the work include key words related to your research question?
- Does the abstract of a journal article contain information on your topic?
- If an abstract is not available, are any of the article's topic sentences relevant to your research question?
- Do the section heads of the source include words connected to your topic?
- On a website, are there links that lead to relevant information?
- Is the work recent enough to provide useful information?
- If you need a source from another time period, is the work from the right period?

Exercise 2

Using the questions in the Checklist for Establishing Relevancy and Timeliness, make sure the sources you found for Exercise 1 are useful.

10e   READING CLOSELY AND CRITICALLY

Once you have determined that the sources you have collected might be useful, allow yourself time to read them closely. Not only will you educate yourself about your topic, but you will also be able to discuss the strengths and weaknesses of what you have read, and you will find it easier to write about it later on. Approach each source with an open mind, but at the same time be prepared to question your sources. By reading critically, you will pay attention to both the claims an author makes and the support for those claims.

CRITERIA FOR EVALUATING SOURCES

TYPE OF SOURCE	PURPOSE	AUTHORS/PUBLISHERS
Scholarly books	To advance knowledge among experts	Experts/University presses
Trade (or commercial) books	To provide information of interest to the general public	Experts, journalists, professional writers/ Commercial presses
Reference books	To provide factual information	Experts/Commercial and university presses
Articles from scholarly journals	To advance knowledge among experts	Experts/Publishers associated with professions or universities
Articles from magazines or newspapers	To report current events or provide general information about current research	Journalists and professional writers (sometimes experts)/ Commercial presses
Editorials from newspapers	To state a position on an issue	Journalists/Commercial presses
Sponsored websites	To report information	Often a group author
Interviews with experts	To report views of an expert	Professional or student writer reporting views of expert

SOURCES DOCUMENTED?	PRIMARY AUDIENCE	CHIEF ADVANTAGE
Yes	Other experts	Reliable because they are written and reviewed by experts
Sometimes	Educated public	Accessible because the language is not overly technical
Yes	Other experts and educated public	Reliable because the entries are written by experts
Yes	Other experts	Reliable because the entries are written and reviewed by experts
No	General public	Accessible because the language is not overly technical
No	General public	Current because they are published daily
No	General public	Accessible by computer
No	General public	Reliable because the interviewee is an expert

✔ CHECKLIST for Reading Closely and Critically

To show that you have read each article closely and with an open mind, you should be able to answer questions such as these:

- What is the author's argument? (chapter 7)
- What is the purpose of the argument? Who is its audience?
- What specific claims does the author make? What evidence does the author use to support these claims?
- What are the author's assumptions? Do you share these assumptions?
- Does the author represent diverse points of view? Does the author respond to divergent points of view?
- After reading the article, do you find yourself agreeing with the author? Disagreeing with the author? Agreeing with some points and disagreeing with others?
- What questions would you like to ask the author?

11 USING SOURCES CRITICALLY AND RESPONSIBLY

For your research project, you will have to discuss what others have discovered, joining a conversation in which you play an essential role: you will decide how the different ideas in your sources connect to each other and to your own views. To make a smooth transition between the words you read and the words you write, you will need to develop a system for managing all the information you have found and for acknowledging the sources you will integrate into your paper. This chapter will help you to

- take notes and organize them effectively (**11a**);
- compile a working bibliography or an annotated bibliography (**11b**);
- acknowledge sources (**11c**);
- quote, paraphrase, and summarize sources (**11d–e**);
- analyze and respond to sources (**11f**);
- synthesize sources (**11g**); and
- avoid plagiarism (**11h**).

11a TAKING AND ORGANIZING NOTES

Managing information is critical for a research project in which you will have to attribute specific words and ideas to others while adding your own ideas. Most research projects start with note-taking. Choose the method that best meets the requirements of your project and your own working style:

- take notes in a notebook or on index cards
- type notes using a web-based research tool, such as Zotero
- write notes directly on pages you have photocopied or printed out from an online source

TIPS FOR TAKING AND ORGANIZING NOTES

- **Subject heading.** Use a short descriptive phrase to summarize the content of the note. This phrase will help you retrieve information later.

- **Type of note.** Indicate whether the note is a quotation (**11d**), a paraphrase (**11e**), a summary (**11e**), or your own thoughts. Place quotations between quotation marks (**40**). Indicate any changes to quotations with square brackets (**41f**) or ellipsis points (**41g**). If you are using a computer to take notes, you can change font color to indicate your own thoughts.

- **Bibliographic information.** Provide complete bibliographic information in a working bibliography (**11b**). Jot down the author's name and/or the title of the source. If the source has page numbers, indicate which pages your notes refer to.

- **Computer folders.** Create a master folder (or directory) for the project. Within that folder, create separate folders for your notes, drafts, and bibliography. In your notes folder, create a separate file for each source.

Remember that your notes will be most useful to you when it comes time to begin your draft if they are comprehensive and accurate.

Figure 11.1 shows one of the notes Marianna Suslin took before drafting her paper on genetically modified food (**13c**).

Another way to take notes is to use photocopies of articles and excerpts from books or printouts of sources from the Internet. On a printout or photocopy, you can mark quotable material while also jotting down your own ideas in the margins. The example in figure 11.2 also comes from the work Marianna Suslin did for her research paper (**13c**). Make sure to record bibliographic information if it is not shown on the photocopy or printout. If you have downloaded an article from a database as a PDF file, consider using the Comment feature of Adobe Acrobat or Adobe Reader to make notes.

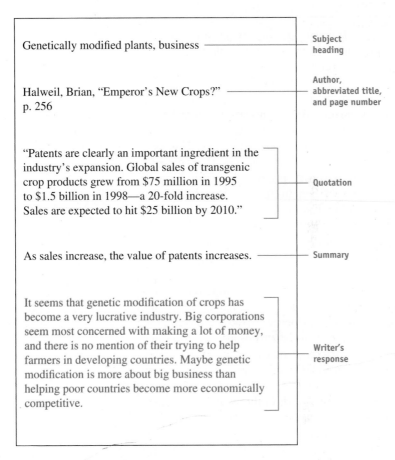

Genetically modified plants, business —————— Subject heading

Halweil, Brian, "Emperor's New Crops?" —————— Author, abbreviated title, and page number
p. 256

"Patents are clearly an important ingredient in the industry's expansion. Global sales of transgenic crop products grew from $75 million in 1995 to $1.5 billion in 1998—a 20-fold increase. Sales are expected to hit $25 billion by 2010." —————— Quotation

As sales increase, the value of patents increases. —————— Summary

It seems that genetic modification of crops has become a very lucrative industry. Big corporations seem most concerned with making a lot of money, and there is no mention of their trying to help farmers in developing countries. Maybe genetic modification is more about big business than helping poor countries become more economically competitive. —————— Writer's response

Figure 11.1: Contents of a useful note.

11b CREATING A WORKING BIBLIOGRAPHY

Effective research depends in part on meticulous record keeping. By creating a **working bibliography**, you will have a record of the sources you might use in your final project. A working bibliography contains all the information you might need in your final bibliography. For each work it should include title, authors' names, and publication date, along with other

Genetic tinkering is the process of adding a gene or genes (the transgene) to plant or animal DNA (the recipient genome) to confer a desirable trait, for example, inserting the genes of an arctic flounder into a tomato to give antifreeze properties, or inserting human genes into fish to increase growth rates.

Author defines "genetic engineering"; his use of the word "tinkering" reveals how he feels about the technology.

examples of genetic modification

But, as we are about to discover, this is a technology that no one wants, that no one asked for, and that no one but the biotech companies will benefit from. This is why the biotech lobby has such a vast, ruthless, and well-funded propaganda machine. If they can reinvent our food and slap a patent on it all, they have just created an unimaginably vast new market for themselves.

Author believes no one but big corporations will benefit from this technology.

And to try to convince a suspicious public, they have given us dozens of laudable reasons why the world will benefit from this tinkering. The companies who so enthusiastically produce millions of tons of pesticides every year are now telling us that GMOs will help reduce pesticide use. The companies who have so expertly polluted the world with millions of tons of toxic chemicals are now telling us that GM will help the environment. The companies who have so nonchalantly used child labor in developing countries, and exported dangerous pesticides that are banned in the developed countries to the developing countries, are now telling us that they really do care about people and that we must have GM to feed the world.

Author seeks to discredit biotech companies.

Rees, Andy. *Genetically Modified Food: A Short Guide for the Confused.* Pluto Press, 2006, p. 8.

Figure 11.2: Photocopied source with notes.

information needed to locate the source. Note that not all documentation styles require you to include the URLs for online sources in your final bibliography, but you will do well to record them for quick access later.

Creating a working bibliography can also help you evaluate the quality of your research. If you find that your most recent source is ten years old, for example, or that you have relied exclusively on information from magazines or websites, you may need to find some other sources.

Right from the start, entries should follow the bibliographic format you have been instructed to use. This book covers the most common formats: MLA (chapter **13**), APA (chapter **15**), CMS (chapter **17**), and CSE (chapter **19**).

If you are asked to prepare an **annotated bibliography** (also called an **annotated list of works cited**), provide a bibliographic entry for and a summary of each of your sources. You may also wish to include comments or personal responses on how information in the source is related to your research question or to that in other sources. These comments will be helpful when you are drafting. Check with your instructor to find out whether your annotated bibliography should include both summaries and commentaries.

A working bibliography is equivalent to a rough draft. In final form, you will have to make sure that you have placed each element of the bibliographic entry in conventional order (author, title, date, and so on).

TIPS FOR CREATING AN ANNOTATED BIBLIOGRAPHY

- Find out which documentation style you should use: MLA, APA, CMS, or CSE.
- Provide a complete bibliographic entry for each of your sources in the required documentation style.
- Summarize the content of each source in two or three sentences. Refer to the main point of the source (*What is it about?*). If relevant, describe the intended audience or the scope of the source (*What is the range of subtopics included? What historical period does the source cover?*).
- In writing your summaries, use your own words instead of inserting quotations. That way, when you consult your annotations, you will not inadvertently use quotations as your own words (**11e**).
- Comment on the sources by connecting the information you find to your research question and to the information you find in other sources.

The following sample annotated bibliography entry was written for a research project (following MLA style) on the question of whether the minimum wage should be raised for restaurant servers.

Provides a complete bibliographic entry — Alderman, Liz. "Minimum Wage in Europe Offers Ammunition in U.S. Debate." *The New York Times,* 13 Feb. 2013, nyti.ms/17XQaWY. In this newspaper article, written in response to the debate over President Obama's proposal to increase the federal minimum wage, Liz Alderman reports that European countries are having a similar debate. Alderman focuses on countries with advanced economies such as France, which has a minimum wage, and Germany, which does not. Although Alderman does not state her opinion, she does quote Simon Tilford, an economist at the Centre for European Reform, who believes that a balance has to be found. A minimum wage that is too low increases poverty levels; a minimum wage that is too high increases production costs so companies find it difficult to be competitive.   — *Summarizes the source*

Additional comments focus on information related to the research question — With regard to restaurant servers, Alderman mentions that in Germany some people working in food service commonly earn €6 an hour, approximately $8.00, an amount considered low in Europe but high in the United States. According to the United States Department of Labor, the national minimum cash wage for workers who receive tips, which applies to most restaurant servers, is $2.13. It is important to remember, though, that tipping customs differ from country to country.   — *Connects information in this source to information found elsewhere*

For some assignments, this entry would have to be condensed for the final draft of the annotated bibliography:

> In response to the debate over President Obama's proposal to increase the federal minimum wage, Liz Alderman describes similar debates taking place in a few European countries. Part of the debate focuses on providing an adequate wage without adversely affecting businesses.

11c   ACKNOWLEDGING YOUR SOURCES

You can integrate sources into your own writing in a number of ways: quoting exact words, paraphrasing sentences, and summarizing longer pieces of text or even entire texts. Whenever you use ideas from a source, you must give credit to that source. The way in which you introduce your source will depend on which documentation style you follow. Most style manuals offer two options: In MLA style, you may

(1) put the author's name in parentheses at the end of the sentence or (2) introduce the author's name within a sentence. In either case, place a page number, if one is available, in parentheses (**13a**). The author's name refers the reader to the full bibliographic citation at the end of your essay.

Use the first method (author's name in parentheses) when you are using statistics or statements to support a major idea in your paragraph.

> Displaying body art, especially tattoos, is gaining in popularity (Grief, Hewitt, and Armstrong 371). However, little is known about the reasons college-age students obtain tattoos. Some students use body art to identify themselves with a specific group (Craig 37). Others see body art as self-expression (Armstrong 230), perhaps suggesting their adventurous nature (Duke 243). Still others use body art, especially tattoos, to remember a significant event (Reams 72). The purpose of this study is to explore whether these are typical reasons for students at this university to have tattoos and whether other reasons exist as well.

Cite the author's name in the text if you are going to discuss the source's statistics or ideas in more detail. It is common to first introduce the author's full name and include any important information about the author. For example, in an essay on the development of literacy, the following statement becomes more credible with information about Catherine Snow's background:

> *professor of education at Harvard University,*
> ➤ According to Catherine Snow, college-level literacy is based on "the ability to read in ways adjusted to one's purpose" (12).

In subsequent references to the author, use just the last name. Other style guides such as APA require use of just the last names of authors for first and subsequent references.

> ➤ According to Snow (2012), college-level literacy is based on "the ability to read in ways adjusted to one's purpose" (p. 12).

Phrases such as *According to Catherine Snow,* and *from the author's perspective* are called **attributive tags** because they attribute, or ascribe, information to a source. In academic writing, most attributive tags consist of the name of an author (or a related noun or pronoun) and a verb such as *states*, *reports*, or *argues*.

ATTRIBUTIVE TAGS FOR QUOTING, PARAPHRASING, AND SUMMARIZING

Attributive tags indicate which source you are using and alert readers that the words or ideas that follow are from a source and are not your own.

- In "Cybersecurity Today" Chris Allen states that _____.
- According to Allen, _____.
- In Allen's view, _____.
- The writer points out that _____. She also stresses that _____.

The following is a list of verbs commonly found in attributive tags.

admit	conclude	find	reject
advise	deny	imply	reply
argue	disagree	indicate	state
believe	discuss	insist	suggest
claim	emphasize	note	think
concede	explain	observe	

Most often attributive tags begin a sentence, but they can also appear in the middle or at the end of a sentence.

➤ **According to Jim Cullen,** "The American Dream would have no drama or mystique if it were a self-evident falsehood or a scientifically demonstrable principle" (7).

➤ "The American Dream," **claims Jim Cullen,** "would have no drama or mystique if it were a self-evident falsehood or a scientifically demonstrable principle" (7).

➤ "The American Dream would have no drama or mystique if it were a self-evident falsehood or a scientifically demonstrable principle," **asserts Jim Cullen in his book *The American Dream: A Short History of an Idea That Shaped a Nation*** (7).

The placement of the attributive tags will depend on what part of the sentence you would like to emphasize and on how the sentence connects to surrounding sentences.

Attributive tags include neutral, objective verbs (*Cullen stated*) or verbs that are more descriptive and subjective (*Cullen insists*). If your assignment allows the insertion of your opinion, you can use descriptive verbs or add an adverb to the verb in the attributive tags: *persuasively* argues, *inaccurately* represents. The appropriate verb tense for the attributive tag—simple present tense (*the author states*), the simple past tense (*the author stated*), or the present perfect (*the author has stated*)—will depend on the context of the sentence (25a–b) and on the guidelines for your discipline (chapters 13, 15, 17, 19).

If you include visuals or graphics as sources, you must introduce and label them as figures and assign them Arabic numbers (9g). You can then refer to them within the text in a parenthetical comment, as in this example (following APA style): "The Maori of New Zealand are also well-known for their hand-carved facial tattoos, known as *Moko* (see Figure 1)." Include a title or caption with the figure number.

11d USING DIRECT QUOTATIONS

Direct quotations draw attention to key passages. Include a direct quotation only if

- you want to retain the beauty or clarity of someone's words
- you need to reveal how the reasoning in a specific passage is flawed or insightful
- you plan to discuss the implications of the quoted material

Keep quotations as short as possible and make them an integral part of your text.

Place any quotation of another person's words in quotation marks. However, if you set off the material as an indented **block quotation**, leave the quotation marks out. The length of a passage determines whether it should be set off as a block quotation. According to MLA style, a quotation four lines or longer should be set off (chapter 13). If you are following APA style, quotations are set off when they include forty or more words (chapter 15). The general rule for CMS is to use block quotations for passages of one hundred words or more (chapter 17). CSE does not specify a word or line limit.

If you need to clarify a quotation by changing it in any way, place square brackets around the added or changed words (41f).

➤ The critic notes that in this role, "he [Brad Pitt] successfully conveys a diverse range of emotion" (23).

If you want to omit part of a quotation, replace the deleted words with ellipsis points (41g).

➤ When asked about the future of the industry, Owens responded, "Overseas markets ₌ ₌ ₌ are critical to the financial success of Hollywood films" (54).

When modifying a quotation, be sure not to alter its essential meaning.

Each quotation you use should also have an attributive tag to help readers understand why the quotation is important. A sentence that consists of only a quotation is called a **dropped quotation**. Notice how the attributive tag improves the dropped quotation below:

Joel Achenbach recognizes that compromises
➤ ~~Compromises~~ must be made to promote safer sources of energy.: "To accommodate green energy, the grid needs not only more storage but more high-voltage power lines" ~~(Achenbach~~ 137).

Readers want to know how a quotation is related to your point, so whenever possible provide a sentence or two before or after the quotation explaining its relevance.

➤ Joel Achenbach recognizes that compromises must be made to promote safer sources of energy: "To accommodate green energy, the grid needs not only more storage but more high-voltage power lines" (137). If we are going to use green energy to avoid depending on types of energy that cause air pollution, we may have to tolerate visual pollution in the form of power lines strung between huge towers.

CHECKLIST FOR USING DIRECT QUOTATIONS

- Have you copied all the words and punctuation accurately?
- Have you attributed the quotation to a specific source?
- Have you used square brackets around anything you added or changed in a direct quotation? (41f)
- Have you used ellipsis points to indicate anything you omitted? (41g)
- Have you included an attributive tag with the quotation?
- Have you included a sentence or two before or after a quotation to indicate its relevance? Have you made it an integral part of the text?
- Have you used quotations sparingly? Rather than using too many quotations, consider paraphrasing or summarizing the information instead.

11e PARAPHRASING AND SUMMARIZING

A **paraphrase** is a restatement of someone else's ideas in approximately the same number of words. Paraphrasing allows you to demonstrate that you have understood what you have read; it also enables you to help your audience understand it. Paraphrase when you want to

- clarify difficult material by using simpler language
- use another writer's idea but not his or her exact words
- create a consistent tone for your work
- interact with a point that your source has made

Your paraphrase should be entirely in your own words and should accurately convey the content of the original passage. As you compare the source below with the paraphrases that follow, note the similarities and differences in both sentence structure and word choice.

Source

Zimmer, Carl. *Soul Made Flesh: The Discovery of the Brain—and How It Changed the World.* Free Press, 2004, p. 7.

> The maps that neuroscientists make today are like the early charts of the New World with grotesque coastlines and blank interiors. And what little we do know about how the brain works raises disturbing questions about the nature of our selves.

Inadequate paraphrase

> The maps used by neuroscientists today resemble the rough maps of the New World. Because we know so little about how the brain works, we must ask questions about the nature of our selves (Zimmer 7).

If you simply change a few words in a passage, you have not adequately restated it. You may be accused of plagiarism (**11h**) if the wording of your version follows the original too closely, even if you provide a page reference for the source.

Adequate paraphrase

> Carl Zimmer compares today's maps of the brain to the rough maps made of the New World. He believes that the lack of knowledge about the workings of the brain raises serious questions about our nature (7).

In the second paraphrase, both vocabulary and sentence structure differ from those in the original. This paraphrase also includes an attributive tag (*Carl Zimmer compares*).

Any paraphrase must accurately maintain the sense of the original. If you unintentionally misrepresent the original because you did not understand it, you are being *inaccurate*. If you deliberately change the gist of what a source says, you are being *unethical*. Compare the original statement below with the paraphrases.

Source

Hanlon, Michael. "Climate Apocalypse When?" *New Scientist,* Nov.
    2007, p. 20.

> Disastrous images of climate change are everywhere. An alarming graphic recently appeared in the UK media showing the British Isles reduced to a scattered archipelago by a 60-metre rise in sea level. Evocative scenes of melting glaciers, all-at-sea polar bears and forest fires are routinely attributed to global warming. And of course Al Gore has just won a Nobel prize for his doomsday flick *An Inconvenient Truth*, starring hurricane Katrina. . . .
>
> There is a big problem here, though it isn't with the science. The evidence that human activities are dramatically modifying the planet's climate is now overwhelming—even to a former paid-up sceptic like me. The consensus is established, the fear real and justified. The problem is that the effects of climate change mostly haven't happened yet, and for journalists and their editors that presents a dilemma. Talking about what the weather may be like in the 2100s, never mind the 3100s, doesn't sell.

Inaccurate or unethical paraphrase

> Evocative scenes of melting glaciers, landless polar bears, and forest fires are attributed to global warming in Al Gore's *An Inconvenient Truth*. The trouble is that Gore cannot predict what will happen (Hanlon 20).

Accurate paraphrase

> According to Michael Hanlon, the disastrous images of climate change that permeate the media are distorting our understanding of what is actually happening globally and what might happen in the future (20).

Although both paraphrases include a reference to an author and a page number, the first focuses misleadingly on Al Gore, whereas the second paraphrase notes the much broader problem, which can be blamed on the media's focus on selling a story.

Instead of paraphrasing source material, especially when it is long, you could summarize it instead. When you summarize, you condense the main point(s) of your source. Although a summary omits much of the detail used by the writer of the original source, it accurately reflects the essence of that work. In most cases, then, a **summary** reports a writer's main idea and the most important support given for it.

Whereas the length of a paraphrase is usually close to that of the original material, a summary is shorter than the material it reports. When you paraphrase, you restate an author's ideas to present or examine them in detail. When you summarize, you present the gist of the author's ideas, without including background information and details. Summaries can include short quotations of key words or phrases, but you must always enclose another writer's exact words in quotation marks when you blend them with your own.

Source

Marshall, Joseph M., III. "Tasunke Witko (His Crazy Horse)." *Native Peoples,* Jan.-Feb. 2007, pp. 76–79.

> The world knows him as Crazy Horse, which is not a precise translation of his name from Lakota to English. *Tasunke Witko* means "his crazy horse," or "his horse is crazy." This slight mistranslation of his name seems to reflect the fact that Crazy Horse the man is obscured by Crazy Horse the legendary warrior. He was both, but the fascination with the legendary warrior hides the reality of the man. And it was as the man, shaped by his family, community and culture—as well as the events in his life—that he became legend.

Summary

> The Lakota warrior English speakers refer to as "Crazy Horse" was actually called "his crazy horse." That mistranslation may distort impressions of what Crazy Horse was like as a man.

This example reduces five sentences to two, retaining the key idea but eliminating the source author's analysis and speculation. A writer who believes that the audience needs to understand the analysis might decide to paraphrase rather than summarize the passage.

Exercise 1

Find a well-developed paragraph in one of your recent reading assignments. Rewrite it in your own words, varying the sentence structure of the original. Make your paraphrase approximately the same length as the original. Next, write a one-sentence summary of the same paragraph.

11f ANALYZING AND RESPONDING TO SOURCES

Though quotations, paraphrases, and summaries are key to academic writing, thinking critically involves more than referring to someone else's work. Quotations, paraphrases, and summaries call for responses. Your readers will want to know what you think about an article, a book, or another source. They will expect you to indicate its strengths and weaknesses and to mention the impact it has had on your own ideas.

Your response to a source will be based on your analysis of it. You can analyze a source according to its rhetorical situation (**1a**), its use of rhetorical appeals (**7f**), or its reasoning (**7h**). You can also evaluate a source by using some common criteria: currency, coverage, and reliability.

(1) Considering the currency of sources

Depending on the nature of your research, the currency of sources may be an important consideration. Using up-to-date sources is crucial when researching most topics. Historical research may also call for sources from a specific period in the past. When you consider the currency of a source, start by looking for the date of its publication. Then, examine any data reported. Even a source published in the same year that you are doing research may include data that are several years old and thus possibly irrelevant. In the following example, the writer questions the usefulness of an out-of-date statistic mentioned in a source:

According to Jenkins, only 50 percent of all public schools have web pages (23); however, this statistic is taken from a report published in 1997. A more recent count would likely yield a much higher percentage.

(2) Noting the thoroughness of research

Coverage refers to the comprehensiveness of research. The more comprehensive a study is, the more convincing are its findings. Similarly, the more examples an author provides, the more compelling are his or her conclusions. Claims or opinions that are based on only one instance are often criticized for being merely anecdotal or otherwise unsubstantiated. The writer of the following response suggests that the author of the source in question may have based his conclusion on too little information:

> Johnson concludes that middle-school students are expected to complete an inordinate amount of homework given their age, but he bases his conclusion on research conducted in only three schools (90). To be more convincing, Johnson needs to conduct research in more schools, preferably located in different parts of the country.

(3) Checking the reliability of findings

Reliability is a requirement for reported data. Researchers are expected to report their findings accurately and honestly, not distort them to support their own beliefs or claim others' ideas as their own. To ensure the reliability of their work, researchers must also report all relevant information and refrain from excluding any that weakens their conclusions. When studies of the same phenomenon give rise to disputes, researchers should discuss conflicting results or interpretations. The writer of the following response focuses on the problematic nature of her source's methodology:

> Jamieson concludes from her experiment that a low-carbohydrate diet can be dangerous for athletes (73), but her methodology suffers from lack of detail. No one would be able to confirm her experimental findings without knowing exactly what and how much the athletes consumed.

Researchers use common phrases when responding to sources. The following list includes a few examples. See **26e** for help deciding when to use the first-person pronoun *I*.

COMMON PHRASES FOR RESPONDING TO SOURCES

Responding, in agreement

- Recent research confirms that <u>Baron</u> is correct in asserting that _____.
- <u>Moore</u> aptly notes that _____.
- I agree with <u>Gyasi</u> that _____.

Responding, in disagreement

- Several of <u>Bender's</u> statements are contradictory. He asserts that _____, but he also states that _____.
- In stating that _____, <u>Porter</u> fails to account for _____.
- I disagree with <u>Lurie</u> on this point. I believe that _____.

Responding, in agreement and in disagreement

- Although I agree with <u>Blake</u> that _____ and that _____, I disagree with his conclusion that _____.
- In a way, the author is correct: _____. However, from a different perspective, _____.
- Though <u>Day</u> may be right that _____, I must point out that _____.

11g   SYNTHESIZING SOURCES

While *thesis* is typically defined as a claim, an informed opinion, or a point of view, *synthesis* refers to combinations of claims, opinions, or points of view. When you synthesize sources, you combine them, looking for similarities, differences, strengths, weaknesses, and so on.

In the following excerpt, the writer reports two similar views on the topic of ecotourism.

> The claim that ecotourism can benefit local economies is supported by the observations of Ellen Bradley, tour leader in Cancun, Mexico, and Rachel Collins, county commissioner in Shasta County, California. Bradley insists that ecotourism is responsible for creating jobs and improved standards of living in Mexico (10). Likewise, Collins believes that ecotourism has provided work for people in her county who had formerly been employed by the timber industry (83).

Notice that the writer uses the transition *likewise* (**3d**) to indicate a comparison. In the next excerpt, on the topic of voting fraud, the writer contrasts two different views, using the transition *although*.

> Although Ted Kruger believes voting fraud is not systematic (45), that does not mean there is no fraud at all. Kendra Berg points out that voter rolls are not updated often enough (18), which leaves the door open for cheaters.

In both examples, the writers not only summarize and respond to sources but synthesize them as well. Below, you will find common phrases for synthesizing sources.

COMMON PHRASES FOR SYNTHESIZING SOURCES

- The claim that _____ is supported by the observations of <u>Blair</u> and <u>Jones</u>. <u>Blair</u> insists that _____. Likewise, <u>Jones</u> believes that _____.
- <u>Perez</u> asserts that _____. <u>Mehan</u> supports this position by _____.
- Although <u>Miller</u> believes that _____, this interpretation is not held universally. For example, <u>Klein</u> notes that _____.
- <u>Kim</u> asserts that _____; however, she fails to explain _____. <u>Lee</u> points out that _____.

11h AVOIDING PLAGIARISM

When you do research, your work depends on research that was done previously, and the research you are working on has the potential to influence future research. An essential part of this scholarly tradition is the acknowledgment of earlier work—not just prior scientific research but artistic, political, philosophical, religious, and other work as well. In fact, acknowledging the contributions of others is so highly valued that copyright and patent laws exist to protect intellectual property. Before you start drafting your project, be sure you understand what to acknowledge, how to acknowledge it, and how to avoid **plagiarism**—the presentation of someone else's ideas as your own.

(1) Determining what to acknowledge

Although you will need to acknowledge the great majority of your sources, it is not necessary to credit information that is **common knowledge**—well-known facts, noncontroversial information, or information that is available in a variety of sources. For example, writing *The* Titanic *hit an iceberg and sank on its maiden voyage* is not problematic: this event has been the subject of many books and movies, so the general outline of the event is considered common knowledge. However, if you are preparing a research project about the *Titanic* and wish to include new information about its sinking, such as the role of the tides, you will be providing information or ideas that must be documented. By carefully recording your own thoughts as you take notes, you should have little difficulty distinguishing between what you knew to begin with and what you have learned through research.

Here are two questions you can ask yourself to decide whether information is considered common knowledge:

- Can the information be found in a number of sources? Check several to find out. These sources should not refer to other sources.
- Is the information commonly known among other students taking the course?

If you have any doubts about whether information is common knowledge, err on the side of caution and acknowledge your source. Taking even part of someone else's work and presenting it as your own can result in charges of plagiarism.

Plagiarism is illegal, and penalties range from receiving a failing grade on an essay or in a course to being expelled from school. Never compromise your integrity or risk your future by submitting someone else's work as your own.

Rules for **fair use**—the section of U.S. copyright law that permits material to be used without permission—covers most of the writing you will do in your courses. You are required to cite and document your source material, but you do not have to seek written permission from authors. If, however, you decide to post your research online, you will have to seek permission for images or extensive portions of text. In such situations, ask your instructor for guidance.

❶ CAUTION

Although it is fairly easy to copy material from a source or even to purchase a paper online, it is just as easy for a teacher or employer to locate that same material and determine that it has been plagiarized. Your instructors routinely use search engines such as Google or special services such as Turnitin when they see abrupt changes in writing or shifts within an essay that lead them to suspect that a student has submitted work that was plagiarized, downloaded, or written by others. Take extra care to avoid such deceptive, deliberate plagiarism.

MATERIALS THAT SHOULD BE ACKNOWLEDGED

- Written works, both published and unpublished
- Opinions and judgments that are not your own
- Statistics and other facts that are not widely known
- Images and graphics, such as works of art, drawings, charts, graphs, tables, photographs, maps, and advertisements
- Personal communications, such as interviews, letters, and e-mail messages
- Electronic communications, including television and radio broadcasts, motion pictures and videos, sound recordings, websites, blogs, wikis, and online discussion groups

(2) Citing quoted or paraphrased material

To draw responsibly on the words and ideas of others, consider the following examples (in MLA style).

Source

We propose that while social network use does make people feel better about themselves, these increased feelings of self-worth can have a detrimental effect on behavior.

Wilcox, Keith, and Andrew T. Stephen. "Are Close Friends the Enemy? Online Social Networks, Self-Esteem, and Self Control." *Journal of Consumer Research*, vol. 40, no. 1, 2013, pp. 90–103. (page 90).

Quotation with documentation

> Keith Wilcox and Andrew T. Stephen, both professors of business, claim that "while social network use does make people feel better about themselves, these increased feelings of self-worth can have a detrimental effect on behavior" (90).

Quotation marks show where the copied words begin and end; the number in parentheses indicates the exact page on which those words appear (**11d**). The authors' names are identified in the sentence, although their names could have been omitted at the beginning of the sentence and noted within the parenthetical reference instead:

> Although users of social networks may experience an increase in self-esteem, "these increased feelings of self-worth can have a detrimental effect on behavior" (Wilcox and Stephen 90).

Paraphrase with documentation

> Keith Wilcox and Andrew T. Stephen, both professors of business, claim that using social networks may increase self-esteem but that such increased positive feelings can adversely affect behavior (90).

This example, in MLA style, includes both authors' names and a parenthetical citation, which marks the end of the paraphrase and provides the page number where the information can be found. Remember that your paraphrases must be both accurate and ethical (**11e**).

Be sure to review any paraphrase closely to make sure that both the words and the ordering of words differ significantly from those of the source material. Just as you cannot falsely represent someone else's ideas as your own, you cannot pass off someone else's writing style as your own. **Patchwriting** refers to paraphrases that are too close to the wording of the source. If you have trouble thinking of new ways to express the original information, step away from your desk for an hour or more. When you return, write down what you remember without looking at the source. You may find it easier to use your own words and style without the original material in front of you. If you are still having trouble, spend some time rereading your source so that you thoroughly understand it.

(3) Understanding citation and documentation

Citation and documentation go hand in hand. When you mention someone else's work by quoting, paraphrasing, or summarizing it, you are *citing* that work. Documentation refers to the information you include in parentheses, footnotes, or bibliographies that allows readers to find the material you used.

Systems for documentation vary according to discipline. Each system provides two main sets of guidelines. First are guidelines for citing each instance of quotation, paraphrase, or summary of a source *in* the text. These are generally referred to as in-text citation or in-text documentation guidelines. They are usually shortened forms, including just the author's name and page number, for example.

Second is a system of documentation that requires complete bibliographic information about sources. In most cases, the bibliographic information is included in a list at the end of a work. This book covers four documentation systems: MLA (chapter **13**), APA (chapter **15**), CMS (chapter **17**), and CSE (chapter **19**).

Exercise 2

After reading the source material, decide which of the quotations and paraphrases that follow it are written correctly and which are problematic. Be prepared to explain your answers.

Source

Finegan, Edward. *Language: Its Structure and Use.* Wadsworth, 2012. (page 403)

> Language is a central factor in a person's identity. Asking people to change their customary language patterns is not like asking them to wear different styles or colors of sweaters. It is asking them to assume a new identity and to espouse the values associated with that identity, that is the identity of speakers of a different dialect. One reason nonstandard varieties successfully resist the urgings of education is that vernacular language varieties are deeply entwined with the social identities and values of their speakers.

1. Asking people to use another language is akin to asking them to acquire new identities.

2. Edward Finegan believes that asking people to use another language is akin to asking them to acquire new identities (403).

(continued on page 242)

(continued from page 241)

3. According to Edward Finegan, speakers of any nonstandard variety of English are uneducated (403).

4. Edward Finegan states that language is a central part of a person's identity (403).

5. Language choices, social identities, and values are intertwined (Finegan 403).

6. "One reason nonstandard varieties successfully resist the urgings of education is that vernacular language varieties are deeply entwined with the social identities and values of their speakers" (Finegan 403).

DISCIPLINES
and
DOCUMENTATION
STYLES

Situate Yourself

You have been assigned papers in four different courses this term. For each of the following assignments, locate two chapters that will help you write these papers. One of the chapters should focus on an academic area (for example, Writing in the Social Sciences) and the other chapter should focus on a specific documentation style (for example, APA Documentation). Then list three features that distinguish each assignment from those in other academic areas.

1. In a succinct and well-reasoned essay, identify and evaluate the historical significance of three excerpts: one from the Pennsylvania Charter of Privileges, one from The Declaration of Independence, and one from the Articles of Federation.

2. Using empirical evidence from five articles, critically examine the claims made about context-dependent memory and mood-dependent memory.

3. Select a character from a novel who responds in a significant way to parental expectations. Then write a well-developed essay in which you analyze the character's attempts to break away from those expectations, the degree to which the character's attempts are successful, and the significance of these attempts for the novel as a whole.

4. Choose an earthquake or volcanic eruption that has occurred within the last ten years and discuss the causes and impacts of this natural disaster.

12 | WRITING ABOUT LITERATURE

If You Give a Mouse a Cookie. The Phantom Tollbooth. The Diary of Anne Frank. Ever since that first book report, you have been writing about—and interpreting—literature. When you write about literature in college—whether the work is fiction, drama, poetry, an essay, or a memoir—you do many of the same things you did as a child: you discuss plot, characters, dialogue, and setting. But you also may discuss theme, imagery, and symbolism, using various critical approaches to anchor your interpretation.

When you write about literature, you tap many of the same strategies you use when writing about other topics: you establish an opportunity for writing, explore and focus your subject, formulate a purposeful thesis statement that is supported by reference to the literary work itself, address a rhetorical audience, and arrange your thoughts in the most effective way. In short, when you write about literature, you respond to the rhetorical situation. This chapter will help you

- recognize the various genres of literature (**12a**),
- realize the value of careful reading (**12b**),
- use the specialized vocabulary for discussing literature (**12c**),
- employ various critical approaches for interpreting literature (**12d**), and
- apply the conventions for writing about literature (**12e** and **12f**).

12a | LITERATURE AND ITS GENRES

Works of literature can be divided into categories, or **genres.** A genre can be identified by its particular features and conventions (**1a, 2b**). Some of the most widely studied literary genres are fiction, drama, and poetry, though many forms of nonfiction (including personal essays and memoirs, literacy narratives, and manifestos) are also studied in college courses on literature.

All literature is imaginative literature, and most imaginative literature appears on a page or screen and is meant to be read, especially **fiction**, a term applied specifically to novels and short stories. **Drama** differs from other imaginative literature in one specific way: it is meant to be performed—whether on stage, screen, or television. Fiction and drama share the same elements (setting, characters, plot, dialogue) and are distinguished by their method of presentation. Novels usually include extensive descriptions of characters and setting as well as passages revealing what characters are thinking. In drama, however, characters reveal what they are thinking through either spoken dialogue with other characters or a **dramatic soliloquy** (a speech delivered to the audience by an actor alone on the stage). Poetry shares the components of both fiction and drama. But poetry distinguishes itself from the other literary genres with its extensive use of connotative language, imagery, allusions, figures of speech, symbols, sound, meter, and rhythm.

12b	RHETORICAL READING AND LITERARY INTERPRETATION

Once you have established a basic understanding of the literary text itself—plot, characters, setting—you can read rhetorically (or actively), building your interpretation and planning your writing (see the "Checklist for Reading Rhetorically" in chapter 1). As you read rhetorically, examine your own reactions, using sticky notes, a highlighter, or a pen to record them (1a). Are you amused, moved, or confused? Which characters interest you? What interactions between characters are the most compelling? Does the literary text remind you of any experience of your own or of other works you have read? Are you being transported to a different historical or geographical setting, or are you encountering a familiar setting and cast of characters? These first impressions provide the seeds from which your interpretation, analysis, and strong essays will grow.

(1) Your personal response to reading literature

Because what you bring to the page is so important, consider how your reading might be shaped by the very factors that define you. If you respond positively or negatively to a character, a plot twist, or the setting in a novel or play, ask yourself whether this response has anything to do with your home life, childhood, psychological makeup, political beliefs, gender or sexual orientation, cultural or ethnic group, social class, religion, geographic location, or educational experiences and interests.

Your personal and academic experiences can influence what you identify as an opportunity for writing as well as the theoretical approach on which you base your interpretation (**12d**). Keep in mind, though, that just as your experiences and values can enhance your understanding of a literary work, they can also blind you to other points of view—yet another way your identity can shape your response.

(2) Developing your topic using evidence in the text

If you are choosing your own topic, your first step is to reflect on your personal response as you formulate a tentative thesis statement (**2c**). Next, consider what specific evidence from the text will best explain and support your interpretation and thesis statement.

Most readers (including your instructor) will be interested in what *you* think, so you need to discover a way to demonstrate your originality by focusing on a topic you can develop adequately and then applying one or more rhetorical methods (**1d, 2g**). You might explain why you consider the main character flawed yet heroic, classify a poem as a political protest, or describe a setting that anchors the meaning of a literary work. Perhaps you can compare and contrast two poems on a similar subject or explore cause-and-consequence relationships in a novel. What circumstances, for instance, lead to an otherwise intelligent character's monumentally bad decision? You might point out how features of a family's house in a novel illustrate the underlying conflicts of that family. Or you might trace the repeated appearance of an object (hands, dark skies, or a cat, for example) throughout a story and explain how that repetition serves to remind the reader of some particular idea or theme.

(3) Researching what other readers have said about a literary work

You will undoubtedly anchor your essay in your own interpretation, but you enrich that interpretation with the sometimes conflicting responses of others, from literary experts to classmates. Whether your research begins at the library (chapter **9**), with an online discussion group (**5b**), with class discussions, or in a book club, you are engaging in literary-based dialogue with others. Although it is tempting to lean heavily on the interpretations of the scholarly experts you encounter in library research (chapter **9**), use their analyses in ways that enrich your own interpretation and support your own points. No matter what outside sources you tap, be sure to use them responsibly, by crediting and citing them (chapter **11**).

To locate scholarly material on a specific writer, work, or literary theory, you can start by consulting your library's resources. Your library's catalog (**9b**) and certain reference books are the best starting points. For instance, *The MLA International Bibliography*, an index of books and articles about literature, is an essential resource for literary studies and is available in print and online. Works such as *Contemporary Authors, The Oxford Companion to English Literature*, and *The New Princeton Handbook of Poetic Terms* can be useful when you are beginning your research or when you have encountered terms you need to clarify. Any librarian can introduce you to even more resources.

(4) Types of literary interpretation

Writing about a literary work requires you to focus on the work itself and to demonstrate that you have read it carefully—a process known as **close reading.** (Compare close reading with reading rhetorically, discussed in **1a** and **12b**.) Close reading allows you to offer an **interpretation,** an explanation of what you see in a work. When your interpretation explains the work's overall meaning in terms of one of its features (the setting, the main character, or a recurring image, for instance), it is an **analysis.** Most common is the **character analysis,** in which a writer interprets the significance of a major or minor character in the text. But analyses can also focus on a pivotal scene, a recurring image, the use of dialect, or a certain interaction.

Explication, generally used only with poetry, is an interpretation that attempts to explain every element in a literary work. When explicating William Wordsworth's "A Slumber Did My Spirit Seal," a writer might note that the *s* sound reinforces the hushed feeling of sleep and death in the poem. But it would also be necessary to consider the meanings of *slumber, spirit,* and *seal.*

An **evaluation** of a literary work gauges how successfully the author communicates meaning to readers or how successfully one part of the work contributes to the meaning conveyed by the other parts. Common types of evaluation are book, theater, and film reviews (16e). Like any other interpretation, an evaluation is a type of argument in which a writer cites both positive and negative textual evidence to convince readers to accept a clearly formulated thesis. (See chapters 2 and 7.)

Summarizing a literary work can be a useful way to make sure that you understand it, that you have read it closely. But do not confuse summary with analysis, explication, or evaluation. Those who have read the work do not need to read a summary of it; there is no need to provide a summary unless your instructor has specifically asked for one.

12c | VOCABULARY FOR DISCUSSING LITERATURE

Like all specialized fields, literature has its own vocabulary, which describes the various features of literary texts, the concepts of literary analysis, and the language of understanding, interpreting, and writing about literature.

(1) Characters

The **characters** are the humans or humanlike personalities (aliens, robots, animals, and other creatures) who carry the plot forward; they usually include the **protagonist**, the main character who is in external or internal conflict (or maybe both). However the conflict manifests, it usually reveals the central idea, or **theme** of the work (12c(7)).

Because you need to understand the characters in any work you read, pay close attention to their appearance, language, actions, and interactions. Also pay attention to what the narrator or other characters say about them and how the other characters treat and react to them.

(2) Imagery

The imagery in a piece of literature is conveyed by **descriptive language,** or words that describe a sensory experience. Notice the images in the following excerpt from an essay by Susan Kates that focuses on the birth—and anticipated adoption—of her son, pictured with Kates in figure 12.1:

Courtesy of Susan Kates

Figure 12.1: Author Susan Kates with baby Carson.

I have seen babies born on television but never in real life. At last Carson emerges, screaming and wriggling, a red, angry infant. Violet holds him first, tears running down her cheeks, then hands him to the nurse who hands him to me for a moment and then to Frank. He weighs five pounds. Dusty, who has massaged Violet's legs and coached her throughout the birth, is visibly upset. Although there has been some question from the beginning about who the biological father might be, Dusty has always believed he's the one. He looks at Frank and pulls a ball cap awkwardly toward his face to hide the fact he is crying. "Send that boy to college," he says softly. Then he walks out of the room.

—SUSAN KATES, "Adoption Story"

The emerging "red, angry infant," the screaming, the wriggling, the tears—preceded by massages and followed by tears and handoffs—all of these images convey the emotional power of the moment: two sets of parents, a birth, and an adoption.

(3) Narrator

The **narrator** of a literary work tells the story, just as author Susan Kates does in the preceding example. The voice doing the telling can *seem* to be that of the actual author, but such a voice might actually be that of the author's **persona**, a fictionalized construction of the author. The narrator's voice could also be that of a specific character (or one of several characters who are taking turns telling the story). The story of "The Yellow Wallpaper," for example, is told strictly in first-person narration, from the protagonist's point of view, as she recounts her problems with her powerful physician husband, being confined against her will, and her eventual descent into insanity. Sometimes, the narrative voice is that of an all-knowing presence (referred to as an **omniscient narrator**) that transcends characters and author alike. Once you determine whose point of view the narrator represents, you can begin to understand the narrator's attitude toward events, characters, and readers. By determining the narrator's tone and the impact it has on you as a reader, you can gain insight into the author's purpose **(3a(3))**.

(4) Plot

The plot is what happens in the story, the sequence of events (the narrative)—and more. The plot establishes how events are patterned or related in terms of conflict and resolution. Narrative answers "What comes next?" and plot answers "Why?" Consider this example from *The Yellow Wallpaper,* written by Charlotte Perkins Gilman and first published in 1892 (figure 12.2):

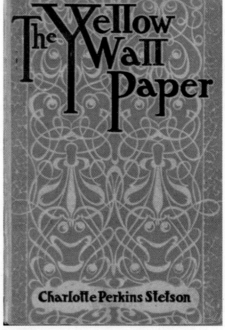

Narrative

A physician diagnoses his wife and confines her to a room with yellow wallpaper.

Plot

The physician husband of a highly imaginative woman diagnoses her as temporarily nervous and moves her into a room with yellow wallpaper, where she is restricted to silence, idleness, without any mental stimulation (other than the journal she has hidden).

A plot usually begins with a conflict, an unstable situation that sets events in motion (for instance, the

Figure 12.2: In "The Yellow Wallpaper," a doctor confines his wife to an upstairs bedroom in an attempt to restore her mental health. The cover of the 1899 publication displays the pattern of the wallpaper and uses Gilman's married name at the time of the story's initial publication.

Source: Charlotte Perkins Gilman

state of tension or animosity between the powerful, patronizing husband and his confined wife, yearning to write in her journal). In what is called the **exposition,** the author introduces the characters (husband and wife, with a new baby implied), setting (a rented nineteenth-century summer mansion), and background (the doctor's social power in terms of his wife's best interests, the growing women's rights movement)—the elements that not only constitute the unstable situation but also relate to the events that follow. The subsequent series of events leads to the **climax,** the most intense event in the narrative, when the narrator completely identifies with the woman she believes is trapped behind the yellow wallpaper. The climax is also referred to as the **turning point** because what follows is **falling action** (or **dénouement**) that leads to a resolution of the conflict and a more stable situation, though not necessarily a happy ending. For instance, in "The Yellow Wallpaper," the narrator has a complete breakdown.

(5) Setting

Setting involves place—not just the physical setting, but also the social setting (the morals, manners, and customs of the characters). Setting also involves time—not only historical time, but also the length of time covered by the narrative. Setting includes **atmosphere,** or the emotional

Courtesy of Cory Maylett

Figure 12.3: An example of a nineteenth-century colonial mansion in California, known as the Carson Mansion.

response to the situation, often shared by the reader with the characters. For example, nineteenth-century California, the setting of "The Yellow Wallpaper," is a markedly different setting from any twenty-first-century possibilities (figure 12.3). The narrator tells us that her husband has rented "ancestral halls," a "colonial mansion" for the summer, where he has immediately confined her to an upstairs room that seems to have been a nursery. The room has barred windows, torn wallpaper, and a scratched floor. The physical appearance of the impressive summer rental with its shabby upstairs room helps the reader to better understand the social setting and cultural values of the time period, and thus the story itself.

(6) Symbols

Frequently used by writers of literature, a **symbol** is usually a physical object that stands for something else, usually something abstract. For example, at the beginning of "The Yellow Wallpaper," the narrator recounts the barred windows and strangely printed wallpaper. Soon, the bars symbolize her incarceration just as the wallpaper seems to have trapped a woman within its pattern. The wallpaper also symbolizes a means of mental stimulation, as the narrator reads it as both "flamboyant" and "dull" but mostly as a shape shifter, in which she detects a female prisoner. During the scenes throughout the short story, the narrator frequently refers to that trapped woman behind the wallpaper, who must surely be tearing at the paper and scraping the floor. Anyone reading this story carefully would note that the wallpaper serves as a symbol of women's subordination—and the narrator's courage in facing that harsh truth.

When you write about a particular symbol, first note where it appears in the literary work. To determine what the symbol might mean, consider why it appears in those places and to what effect. Once you have an idea about the meaning, trace the incidents in the literary work that reinforce your interpretation.

(7) Theme

The main idea of a literary work is its **theme**. Depending on how they interpret a work, different readers may identify different themes. To test whether an idea is central to the work in question, check to see if the idea is supported by the setting, plot, characters, and symbols. If you can relate these components to the idea you are considering, then it can be interpreted as the work's theme. The most prominent literary themes arise out of external or internal conflict: character versus character, character versus herself or himself, character versus nature, or character versus society. "The Yellow Wallpaper" offers the theme of character versus society, as the narrator struggles to regain her social standing, her artistic endeavors, and access to her child—despite her doctor-husband's legal power over her.

When you believe you have identified the theme of a literary work, state it as a sentence—and be precise. A theme conveys a specific idea; it should not be confused with a topic.

Topic	a physician's care of his ill wife
Vague theme	the subordination of nineteenth-century married women
Specific theme	"The Yellow Wallpaper" deals with a conflict between an imaginative woman and a society that insists that she abandon her artistic endeavors.

✓ CHECKLIST for Interpreting a Literary Work

- From whose point of view is the story told?
- Who is the protagonist? How is his or her character developed?
- With whom or what is the protagonist in conflict?
- How are the other characters depicted and distinguished through dialogue?
- What symbols, imagery, or figures of speech (**35a(3)**) does the author use? To what effect?
- What is the theme of the work? How does the author use setting, plot, characters, and symbols to establish that theme?

12d   APPROACHES TO INTERPRETING LITERATURE

An interpretation of a literary work can be shaped by your personal response to what you have read, by the views of other readers whom you wish to support or challenge, or by a specific type of literary theory.

Literary theory, the scholarly discussion of how the nature and function of literature can be determined, ranges from approaches that focus almost exclusively on the text itself (its language and structure) to approaches that show how the text relates to author, reader, language, society, culture, economics, or history. Familiarity with literary theory enriches your reading of literature as well as your understanding of the books and essays about literature that you will discover when you do research (chapter **9**). Literary theory can also help you decide how you want to focus your writing about literature.

Although the most popular theoretical approaches to literature overlap somewhat, each has a different primary focus: the reader, some feature of the social or cultural context, the text itself, or the author or characters. Interpreting literature involves a responsible reliance on one or more of these approaches—*whatever your interpretation, the text should support it.*

(1) Reader-response theory

According to **reader-response theory,** readers construct meaning as they read and interact with the elements within a text (**1a, 12b(4)**). Thus, meaning is not fixed *on* the page but rather depends on what each reader brings *to* the page. Furthermore, the same reader can have different responses to the same literary work when rereading it later: a young mother, for instance, might find "The Yellow Wallpaper" much more unsettling now than when she first read it in high school. Although a reader-response approach to literature encourages diverse interpretations, you cannot simply say, "Well, that's what this work means to me," or "That's my interpretation." You must demonstrate to your audience how the elements of the work support your interpretation.

(2) Feminist and gender-based literary theories

The significance of sex, gender, or sexual orientation within a particular social context is the interpretive focus of **feminist** and **gender-based literary theories.** These theories enable a reader to analyze the ways in which a work (through its characters, theme, or plot) promotes or challenges the prevailing intellectual or cultural assumptions of its day regarding issues related to gender and sexuality, such as patriarchy and compulsory heterosexuality. As you can already tell, "The Yellow Wallpaper" provides a rich text for a feminist analysis, particularly in terms of the social pressures and cultural expectations that supported the solitary confinement of an artistic woman. Using a gender-based approach, you might read Henry James's *The Bostonians* and focus on the positive features of the domestic relationship between the financially independent Olive Chancellor and Verena Tarrant, the women's-rights activist she supports. In addition, you might use gender theory to explain why Jake Barnes in Ernest Hemingway's *The Sun Also Rises* bonds with some men and is contemptuous of others.

(3) Race-based literary theory

A useful form of race-based literary criticism, **critical race theory,** focuses on the significance of race relations within a specific historical and social setting in order to explain the experience and literary production of any people whose history is characterized by political, social, or psychological oppression. Previously neglected works such as Zora Neale Hurston's *Their Eyes Were Watching God* (figure 12.4), Rudolfo Anáya's *Bless Me, Ultima,* and Frederick Douglass's *Narrative,* which demonstrate how racism affects the characters' lives, have taken on considerable cultural value in the last twenty-five years. **African American literary criticism,** for example, has been particularly successful in invigorating the study of great African American writers, whose works can be more fully appreciated when readers consider how literary elements of the works have been informed by the social forces that helped produce them. Closely associated with critical race theory is **postcolonial theory,** which takes into account the relationship of the colonized with the colonizer

Figure 12.4: In *Their Eyes Were Watching God*, a mature and complex black woman recounts her life in three "acts," based on her relationships with three very different men.

and the challenge a text can direct at the dominant powers at a particular time and place, asserting a drive toward the liberation of oppressed social groups. Joseph Conrad's *Heart of Darkness,* Jean Rhys's *Wide Sargasso Sea,* Sherman Alexie's *The Absolutely True Diary of a Part-Time Indian,* and Jimmy Santiago Baca's *A Place to Stand* can all be read productively through the lens of postcolonial theory. Many of these same books can be read through critical race, gender, and feminist theory as well. Louise Erdrich's *The Round House* could be read through all three—as well as through class-based theory.

(4) Class-based literary theory

Class-based literary theory draws on the work of Karl Marx, Terry Eagleton, and others who have addressed the implications of social hierarchies and the accompanying economic tensions, which divide people in profoundly significant ways. Thus, a class-based approach can be used to explain why Emma Bovary is unhappy, despite her "good" (that is, financially advantageous) marriage, in Gustave Flaubert's *Madame Bovary,* why Bigger Thomas gets thrown into such a confused mental state in Richard Wright's *Native Son,* or why a family loses its land in John Steinbeck's *The Grapes of Wrath.*

(5) Context-based literary theory

Context-based literary theory considers the historical period during which a work was written and the cultural and economic patterns that prevailed during that period. For example, recognizing that Willa Cather published *My Ántonia* during World War I can help account for the darker side of that novel about European immigrants' harsh life in the American West. Critics who use a context-based and class-based approach known as **cultural studies** consider how a literary work interacts with economic conditions, socioeconomic classes, and other cultural artifacts (such as songs or fashion) of the period in which it was written.

(6) Psychoanalytic theories

Psychoanalytic theories, as applied to literature, focus on the psychological states of the author and the characters as well as the reader. The theories help readers discern the motivations of characters, envision the psychological state of the author as implied by the text, and evaluate the psychological reasons for their own interpretations. Readers may apply a psychoanalytic approach to explain why Hamlet is deeply disturbed by his mother's remarriage, for example.

Theorists who use the work of psychiatrist Carl Jung to explore **archetypes** (meaningful images that arise from the human unconscious and that appear as recurring figures or patterns in literature) are also using a psychoanalytic approach to interpret literature. Archetypal figures include the hero, the earth mother, the warrior, the outcast, and the cruel stepmother. Archetypal patterns include the quest, the initiation, the test, and the return.

Exercise 1

Attend a film, a play, or a poetry reading at your school or in your community—or watch one online or on television. Write a two- to three-page essay analyzing the work, using one of the theoretical approaches discussed in this section.

12e CONVENTIONS FOR WRITING ABOUT LITERATURE

Writing about literature involves adhering to several conventions.

(1) Using first person

When writing an analysis of a piece of literature, you may use the first-person singular pronoun, *I*.

Although some critics believe Rudolfo Anáya's novel to be about witchcraft, I think it is about the power of belief.

By using *I*, you indicate that you are presenting your opinion about a work. When you propose or argue for a particular belief or interpretation or offer an opinion, you must support it with specific evidence from the text itself.

(2) Using present tense

Use the present tense when discussing a literary work, since the author of the work is communicating to the reader at the present time (**25b(1)**).

In "A Good Man Is Hard to Find," the grandmother reaches out to touch her killer just before he pulls the trigger.

Similarly, use the present tense when reporting how other writers have interpreted the work you are discussing.

As Toni Morrison demonstrates in her analysis of the American literary tradition, black Americans continue to play a vital role.

(3) Documenting sources

When writing about a work assigned by your instructor, you may not need to give the source and publication information. However, if you are using an edition or translation that may be different from the one your reader(s) will use, you should indicate this. You can document the version of the work you are discussing by using the MLA format for listing works cited (**13b**), although your bibliography in this case will consist of only a single entry.

An alternative way of providing documentation for a single source is by acknowledging the first quotation from or reference to the work using a superscript number and then providing an explanatory note on a separate page at the end of your paper.

In-text citation

. . . as Toni Morrison states (127).[1]

OR

. . . tendency to misread texts by African American writers (Morrison 127).[1]

Note

1. Toni Morrison, *Playing in the Dark: Whiteness and the Literary Imagination*. Vintage Books, 1992. All subsequent references to this work will be identified with page numbers in parentheses within the text.

If you use this note form, you do not need to repeat the bibliographical information in a separate entry or include the author's name in subsequent parenthetical references to page numbers. Check with your instructor about the format he or she prefers.

When you use a bibliography to provide publication data, you must indicate specific references whenever you quote a line or passage. According to MLA style, such bibliographic information should be placed in the text in parentheses directly after the quotation. A period, a semicolon, or a comma should follow the parentheses (**13a(1)** and **40d(1)**). Quotations from short stories and novels are identified by the author's name and page number:

"A man planning to spend money on me was an experience rare enough to feel odd" (Gordon 19).

Quotations from poems are referred to by line number:

"O Rose, thou art sick!" (Blake 1).

Quotations from Shakespeare's plays are identified using abbreviations of the titles; the following line is from act I, scene I, line 28 of Shakespeare's play *Much Ado about Nothing*:

"How much better it is to weep at joy than to joy at weeping" (*Ado* 1.1.28).

(4) Quoting poetry

When quoting from poems and verse plays, type quotations involving three or fewer lines in the text and insert a slash (see **41h**) with a space on each side to separate the lines.

"Does the road wind uphill all the way? / Yes, to the very end" (Rossetti 1-2). Christina Rossetti opens her poem "Uphill" with this two-line question and answer.

Quotations of more than three lines should be indented a half inch from the left-hand margin and use the same spacing as rest of the text. Do not add slashes at the ends of lines, and make sure to follow the original text for line breaks, special indenting, or spacing. For this type of block quotation, place your citation after the final punctuation mark.

(5) Referring to authors' names

Use the full name of the author of a work in your first reference and only the last name in all subsequent references. For instance, write

"Junot Díaz" or "Dorothy Allison" the first time and use "Díaz" or "Allison" after that. Never refer to a female author differently than you do a male author. For example, use "Robert Browning and Elizabeth Barrett Browning" or "Browning and Barrett Browning" (not "Browning and Mrs. Browning" or "Browning and Elizabeth").

12f	LITERARY INTERPRETATION OF A SHORT STORY

In the following literary interpretation, English major Kristin Ford focuses on (**2b**) the political and personal implications of a woman's mental illness as portrayed in Charlotte Perkins Gilman's short story "The Yellow Wallpaper."

Ford 1

Kristin Ford

Professor Glenn

English 232

19 November 2014

The Role of Storytelling in Fighting Nineteenth-Century Chauvinism

> The writer provides a critical overview of the story, demonstrating her understanding of it.

Widely considered to be one of the most influential pieces of early feminist literature, "The Yellow Wallpaper," published in 1892 by Charlotte Perkins Gilman, illustrates nineteenth-century men's patronizing treatment of and abusive power over women, exploring the smudged line between sanity and insanity, men's alleged ability to distinguish between the two, and women's inability to pull themselves out of depression or any form of mental illness without seeming to further demonstrate their insanity. The protagonist of Gilman's story descends into madness, a mental state unnecessarily exacerbated, if not caused, by her husband's prescribed "rest cure," which entailed total inactivity and isolation. Such

> The writer defines *double bind,* which is the operative term for her thesis.

was her double bind: the stronger the constraints of the cure, the worse her mental illness. She had no way to resolve her problem.

> The writer includes historical background for the story. She uses past tense to refer to these actions and beliefs.

During Gilman's time, women were understood largely in relation to the "Cult of True Womanhood," which prescribed women's "proper" place in society, especially within the middle and upper classes. Piety, purity, submissiveness, and domesticity were not merely encouraged but demanded in order for a woman to avoid breaking this strict social code (Lavender). Such virtues meant that a "true woman" of that time was a wife, housewife, and mother—always yielding to the demands of her husband and her family. Any woman who went against these norms risked

Ford 2

being cast out or labeled insane (Mellor 156). Men dominated medicine, and mental illness remained largely unexplored and thus misunderstood. Many doctors still feared it and thus ignorantly tried to pass off serious psychological disorders as cases of "nervousness" or "hysteria" or "fragile constitutions" (Tierny 1456). One of the most influential doctors at that time, Silas Weir Mitchell, made popular his "rest cure," which was thought to be especially effective for such disorders.

These societal views are reflected in "The Yellow Wallpaper." The physician husband of the main character imposes the "rest cure" on her. She is forced to obey her husband and has no choice in her treatment. Furthermore, her husband does not listen when she tries to tell him more about her condition, her fears, and her aspirations. This feature of the story—men not listening to their wives—accurately reflects the social climate of the late nineteenth century, when husbands could impose their rules on their wives with little (if any) thought given to what the women knew, felt, or wanted.

> The writer uses the literary present tense to describe the action in the story itself.

Such a male-centered ideology fostered the development of the "rest cure," initiated by Weir Mitchell in the late 1880s. He describes his "Rest Treatment for Nervous Disorders" as well as the temperament of women in his book *Fat and Blood: And How to Make Them*:

> The writer uses information from a physician's writings to support her interpretation and bolster her historical connection.

> The American woman is, to speak plainly, too often physically unfit for her duties as woman, and is perhaps of all civilized females the least qualified to undertake those weightier tasks which tax so heavily the nervous system of man. She is not fairly up to what nature asks from her as wife and mother. How will she sustain

Ford 3

herself under the pressure of those yet more exacting duties which nowadays she is eager to share with the man? (13)

Because of this general belief about American women's fragility (or weakness), Weir Mitchell often diagnosed patients as having neurasthenia, a catch-all term for any nervous disorder that affected mainly women. Many cases, like the one depicted in "The Yellow Wallpaper," were what would now be considered postpartum depression, a legitimate psychological disorder requiring medication and therapy.

Conversely, Weir Mitchell's theory was that neurasthenia was all in a woman's head. His rest treatment, prescribed only for women, involved complete rest, little mental stimulation, and overfeeding. A woman was not allowed to leave her bed for months at a time, and she was certainly never allowed to read or write (Weir Mitchell 39). This tendency to diagnose women as "hysterical," coupled with the era's chauvinism, made it easy for doctors like Weir Mitchell to simply, almost flippantly, dismiss the protesting pleas of mentally ill women.

Gilman herself was prescribed this treatment. In "Why I Wrote 'The Yellow Wallpaper,'" Gilman describes how she tried the "rest cure" for three months and "came so near the border of mental ruin that I could see over" (820). In the end, in order to save herself from insanity, Gilman had to ignore what society told her. She could not lead a domestic, sedentary life without falling into insanity. However, according to Weir Mitchell, such a life was considered sane for a woman, a prime indicator of her mental stability. The resulting conflict between Gilman's personal experience and Weir Mitchell's impersonal theory begs the question

The writer presents relevant biographical information about the author of the story.

Ford 4

"What is true sanity?" For Gilman, the only way to cure herself of her madness was the very thing she was told she could not do: write and engage in mental stimulation. This is the double bind that women of the day faced. What Gilman was prescribed to do caused her to fall further into mental illness, but doing what she needed to do to get over the illness was considered a symptom of insanity. This is the same double bind trapping Gilman's protagonist throughout the story.

The rest cure is a tool to suppress all mental activity in women (Tierny 1457). At the beginning of the story, the struggle is among competing factors: what the protagonist is told, what she knows is right, and what she feels she should do. She wants to listen to her husband, but she senses that her illness will not be cured by his proposed remedy. All the while her husband assures her that she only needs the "rest cure" and she will be the wife and mother she should be. Throughout "The Yellow Wallpaper," the wife repeatedly says that although she may be getting physically better, mentally she is not. Her husband repeatedly replies, "Never for one instant let that idea enter your mind! There is nothing so dangerous, so fascinating to a temperament like yours" (Gilman, "Yellow Wallpaper" 814). In addition, he often admonishes her to get well. Gilman juxtaposes what men believed at this time with the actual implications of this cure for the female mind. Although her husband remarks that she seems to be getting better and better, the woman slowly descends further into her madness, showing just how oblivious men, even renowned physicians, were to the struggles of women.

Ford 5

Gilman's goal in this story is to expose this "rest cure" for what it truly is and make clear the struggle women have in a society in which they are expected to be entirely domestic and submissive to men. Gilman makes a particular yet subtle argument when she demonstrates the "domesticated" woman's double bind: If she uses her imagination in an "unsuitable" way, she is exhibiting mental illness. The cure for that illness is constraint, a prohibition on imagination and activity, which only worsens her mental condition. Gilman experienced another double bind as a female author functioning within a realm of male control and expectations. Any woman who published, particularly if her stories dealt with mentally ill women, was revealing her own mental instability. Of course, if an author was not able to write and publish, she would feel even worse.

Gilman portrays the feminist challenge to society's standards through character development and the interactions between the physician husband and his wife. When developing the character of the husband, Gilman illustrates his dominance over his wife through much of their dialogue. The physician speaks to his wife much like an adult speaking to a child. Gilman juxtaposes the husband's view of the woman's improving health against what the reader actually sees happening: the woman creeps around the room becoming completely involved in the pattern of the wallpaper, clearly a sign that she is becoming increasingly ill. This disconnect between what the husband wants to believe and the reality of his wife's condition exemplifies the disconnect in their marital life. It demonstrates the lack of understanding men had toward women and the lack of concern with which they reacted to women's problems.

In "The Yellow Wallpaper," Gilman produced an insightful work using the symbolism of a room turned jail cell to express her views on the way women were treated in her society. Gilman masterfully crafted a story that describes a woman's descent into madness, using that descent as an allegory for the oppression of women of the late nineteenth century. Beyond its importance as a powerful piece of feminist literature, "The Yellow Wallpaper" made a profound impact on society. After the publication of "Why I Wrote 'The Yellow Wallpaper,' " Weir Mitchell quietly changed his "rest cure." For a respected physician in the late nineteenth century to change his practice based on the literary work of a woman is powerful testimony to the impact of "The Yellow Wallpaper."

Ford 7

Works Cited

Gilman, Charlotte P. "Why I Wrote 'The Yellow Wallpaper.'" *The Norton Anthology of American Literature,* 8th ed., vol. C, W. W. Norton, 2011.

---. "The Yellow Wallpaper." *The Norton Anthology of American Literature,* 8th ed., vol. C, W. W. Norton, 2011, pp. 792-803.

Lavender, Catherine. "Notes on the Cult of Domesticity and True Womanhood." *Women in New York City, 1890-1940*, College of Staten Island, CUNY, Fall 1998, csivc.csi.cuny.edu/history/files/lavender/386/truewoman.pdf.

Mellor, Ann K. *Romanticism and Feminism.* Indiana UP, 1988.

Tierny, Helen. *Women's Studies Encyclopedia.* Greenwood, 1997.

Weir Mitchell, Silas. *Fat and Blood: And How to Make Them.* J. B. Lippincott, 1882.

Exercise 2

Based on your reading of Kristin Ford's essay on "The Yellow Wallpaper," what personal or political values do you think she brought to her interpretation of that text? Which of the theoretical approaches to literature did she use as the basis for her interpretation (**12d**)? Write a one- or two-page paper analyzing her interpretation of the story.

13 | MLA DOCUMENTATION

Research—library, online, and naturalistic—plays an important role in college writing. Therefore, whenever you use such research, incorporating others' ideas, words, or findings into your writing, you need to attribute, cite, and document your sources responsibly (11c–e). The Modern Language Association (MLA) provides guidelines for citing and documenting research in literature, languages, linguistics, history, philosophy, and composition studies. The *MLA Handbook*, 8th edition, details these guidelines for writers. Referring to the handbook, this chapter presents

- guidelines for citing sources within the text of a paper (13a),
- guidelines for documenting sources in a works-cited list (13b), and
- a sample student paper (13c).

13a | MLA-STYLE IN-TEXT CITATIONS

(1) Citing material from other sources

The citations you use within the text of a research project refer readers to the list of works cited at the end of the paper, tell them where to find the borrowed material in the original source, and indicate the boundaries between your ideas and those you have borrowed. In the following example, the parenthetical citation guides the reader to page 38 of the book by Carter in the works-cited list.

In-text (or parenthetical) citation

Whereas the last execution in Canada took place in 1962, in 2011 there were 598 murders in Canada and 14,610 in the United States (Carter 38).

Works-cited entry

Carter, Jimmy. *A Call to Action: Women, Religion, Violence, and Power*. Simon and

Schuster, 2014, p. 15.

When you need to add supplementary comments to your writing—for example, when you wish to explain a point further with tangential information or when you need to provide background information or context—consider using sequentially numbered notes. Superscript numbers are inserted in the appropriate places in the text to indicate an annotated end note. These optional notes themselves are gathered at the end of the paper on a separate page titled "Notes." Each note begins with an indent.

In-text note number

Many death-penalties proponents argue that it deters murder and violent crimes.[1]

Notes entry

1. Researchers Roy D. Adler and Michael Summers argue that "each execution carried out is correlated with about 74 fewer murders the following year" (A13).

Many notes will supply specific information that would otherwise interrupt the flow of the paper. Note 1 supplies additional information as well as an additional citation. MLA style does not provide specific guidance for formatting notes; however, your instructor may have formatting preferences.

The MLA does provide detailed guidance for creating in-text citations, which usually provide two pieces of information about borrowed material: (1) information that directs the reader to the relevant source on the works-cited list and (2) information that directs the reader to a specific page or section within that source. The author's last name and a page number suffice. To create an in-text citation, place both the author's last name and the page number in parentheses or introduce the material being cited by giving the author's name in the sentence and supply only the page number in parentheses. Any sentence punctuation, such as a period, appears outside of the parentheses.

One of the arguments against the death penalty is that the United States remains the only NATO or North American country that "still executes its citizens" (Carter 37).

Former President Jimmy Carter, an anti-death-penalty activist, writes that he and Rosalyn regularly "intercede with U.S. governors . . . who may be able to commute the ultimate punishment to life imprisonment" (37).

When referring to information from a range of pages, separate the first and last pages with a hyphen: (34-42). If the page numbers have the same hundreds or thousands digit, do not repeat it when listing the final page in the range: (234-42) or (1350-55) but (290-301) or (1395-1402).

If you refer to an entire work or a work with only one page, no page numbers are necessary.

The following examples are representative of the types of in-text citations you might be expected to use.

1. Work by one author named in an attributive tag
Signal the material being cited by mentioning the author's name in your sentence.

Roxanne Mountford lists the nineteenth-century denominations often led by women: "the Society of Friends, the Methodist Church, the Holiness tradition" (51).

2. Work by one author named in parentheses
If your sentence does not name the author, include the author's name before the page reference in parentheses.

By the mid-nineteenth century, "hundreds of American women preachers" were leading churches in such denominations as the "Society of Friends, the Methodist Church, and the Holiness tradition" (Mountford 51).

3. More than one work by the same author

Provide a shortened title in an attributive tag or in parentheses that identifies the relevant work. Use a comma to separate the author's name (or names) from the shortened title (usually the first word or phrase) when both are in parentheses.

Many sociolinguists agree that the U.S. carries language prejudice, especially against African American children, "especially if their dialects are nonstandard" (Holloway, *Codes* 93).

OR

Karla F. C. Holloway argues that language prejudice is especially strong toward African American children, "especially if their dialects are nonstandard" (*Codes* 93).

4. Work by two authors

Textbooks provide a historical evidence of classroom practice, but not a complete picture of teaching or learning (Eldred and Mortensen 35).

5. Work by three or more authors

Use only the first author's last name followed by the abbreviation *et al.* (Latin meaning "and others").

In one important study, women graduates complained more frequently about "excessive control than about lack of structure" (Belenky et al. 205).

6. Works by different authors with the same last name

When your works-cited list includes works by different authors with the same last name, provide a first initial and last name in parenthetical citations, or use the author's first and last name in the text.

Pre-Aristotelian rhetoric still has an impact today (S. Miller 331-43).

If two authors have the same last name and first initial, spell out each author's first name in the parenthetical citation.

7. Work by a corporate author

A work has a corporate author when individual members of the group that created it are not identified.

Strawbale constructions are now popular across the nation (National Ecobuilders 2).

8. Two or more works in the same citation

When two sources provide similar information or when you combine information from two sources in the same sentence, cite both sources, separating them with a semicolon.

Agricultural scientists believe that crop productivity will be adversely affected by solar dimming (Beck and Watts 90; Harris-Green 153-54).

9. Multivolume work

When you cite material from more than one volume of a multivolume work, include the volume number (followed by a colon and a space) before the page number.

Katherine Raine claims that "true poetry begins where human personality ends" (2: 247).

You do not need to include the volume number in a parenthetical citation if your list of works cited includes only one volume of a multivolume work.

10. Anonymous work

The Tehuelche people left their handprints on the walls of a cave, now called Cave of the Hands ("Hands of Time" 124).

Use the title of an anonymous work in place of an author's name. If that title is long, provide a shortened version. For example, the shortened title for "Chasing Down the Phrasal Verb in the Discourse of Adolescents" is "Chasing Down."

11. Indirect source

If you need to include material that one of your sources quoted from another work because you cannot obtain the original source, use the following format (*qtd.* is the abbreviation for "quoted").

The critic Susan Hardy Aikens has argued on behalf of what she calls "canonical multiplicity" (qtd. in Mayers 677).

A reader turning to the list of works cited should find an entry for Mayers, the source consulted, but not for Aikens.

12. Poetry, drama, and sacred texts

When you refer to poetry, drama, or sacred texts, give the numbers of lines, acts, and scenes or of chapters and verses, rather than page numbers. This enables readers to consult any edition, rather than just the one you have used. Act, scene, and line numbers (all Arabic numerals) are separated by periods with no space before or after them.

The following example illustrates a citation referring to lines of poetry.

Emily Dickinson alludes to her dislike of public appearance in "I'm Nobody! Who Are You?" (5-8).

The following citation shows that the famous "To be, or not to be" soliloquy appears in act 3, scene 1, lines 56-89 of *Hamlet*.

In *Hamlet*, Shakespeare presents the most famous soliloquy in the history of the English theater: "To be, or not to be . . ." (3.1.56-89).

MLA guidelines recommend treating biblical chapters and verses similarly; the progression is from larger to smaller units. Citations of biblical material identify the book of the Bible, the chapter, and the pertinent verses. In the following example, the writer refers to the creation story in Genesis, which begins in chapter 1 with verse 1 and ends in chapter 2 with verse 22.

The Old Testament creation story, told with remarkable economy, culminates in the arrival of Eve (*New American Standard Bible*, Gen. 1.1-2.22).

Mention in your first citation which version of the Bible you are using. List only book, chapter, and verse in subsequent citations. Note that the names of biblical books are neither italicized nor enclosed in quotation marks.

13. Constitution

When referring to the US Constitution, use the document title, and do not italicize or enclose it in quotation marks. The following are common abbreviations for in-text citations:

UNITED STATES CONSTITUTION	US Const.
ARTICLE	art.
SECTION	sec.

The testimony of two witnesses is needed to convict someone of treason
(US Const., art. 3, sec. 3).

14. Works with numbered paragraphs or sections (online sources)

If paragraphs in an electronic source (or online publication) are numbered, cite the number(s) of the paragraph(s) after the abbreviation *par.* (for one paragraph) or *pars.* (for more than one). If a section number is provided, cite that number after the abbreviation *sec.* (or *secs.* for more than one). Do not cite page numbers unless the source is a PDF, which has stable numbering.

Alston describes three types of rubrics for evaluating customer service (pars. 2-15).

Hilton and Merrill provide examples of effective hyperlinks (sec. 1).

If a source includes no numbers distinguishing one part from another, you should cite the entire source. In this case, to establish that you have not accidentally omitted a number, avoid using a parenthetical citation by providing what information you have within the sentence that introduces the material.

Raymond Lucero's *Shopping Online* offers useful advice for consumers who are concerned about transmitting credit card information over the Internet.

15. Works in time-based media

In a video or audio recording, you may wish to cite material from a specific time or range of times, as measured by your media player. Cite the hour(s), minute(s), and second(s), placing colons between each unit.

Pierre is shown of earshot, skating with Helene, when Prince Kuragin says, "I may have to force the issue" ("Episode 2" 00:13:40-45).

(2) Guidelines for in-text citations and quotations

Placement of in-text citations

When you acknowledge your use of a source by placing the author's name and a relevant page number in parentheses, insert this parenthetical citation directly after the information you used, generally at the end of a sentence but *before* the final punctuation mark.

Oceans store almost half the carbon dioxide released by humans into the atmosphere (Wall 28).

However, you may need to place a parenthetical citation earlier in a sentence to indicate that only the first part of the sentence contains borrowed material. Place the citation after the clause containing the material but before a punctuation mark (a comma, semicolon, or colon).

Oceans store almost half the carbon dioxide that humans release into the atmosphere (Wall 28), a fact that provides hope for scientists studying global warming but alarms scientists studying organisms living in the oceans.

If you cite the same source more than once in a paragraph, with no intervening citations of another source, you can place one parenthetical citation at the end of the last sentence in which the source is used: (Wall 28, 32).

Lengthy quotations

When a quotation is four or more lines long, set it off from the surrounding text by indenting it a half inch from the left margin, keeping it double-spaced. The right-hand margin is not indented, nor does the passage appear in quotation marks.

In *The Sense of Style*, Steven Pinker describes writing to an audience as more difficult than the natural social interaction of speaking to someone:

> We enjoy none of this give-and-take [of speaking to someone] when we cast our bread upon the waters by sending a written missive out into the world. The recipients are invisible and inscrutable, and we have to get through to them without knowing much about them or seeing their reactions. At the time that we write, the reader exists only in our imaginations. . . . We have to visualize ourselves in some kind of conversation . . . and put words into the mouth of the little avatar who represents us in this simulated world. (28)

For these reasons, picturing and then addressing a rhetorical audience is essential.

Note that the period precedes the parenthetical citation at the end of an indented (block) quotation. Note, too, how the writer introduces and then comments on the block quotation from Pinker, explaining the significance of the block quotation to the writer's larger essay.

Punctuation within citations and quotations

Punctuation marks clarify meaning in quotations and citations. The following list summarizes their common uses.

: A colon separates volume numbers from page numbers in a parenthetical citation.

(Raine 2: 247)

, A comma separates the author's name from the title when it is necessary to list both in a parenthetical citation.

(Pipher, *Writing to Change the World*)

A comma also indicates that page or line numbers are not sequential.

(44, 47)

... Ellipsis points indicate an omission within a quotation.

"They lived in an age of increasing complexity and great hope; we in an age of . . . growing despair" (Krutch 2).

- A hyphen indicates a continuous sequence of pages or lines.

(44-47)

. A period separates acts, scenes, and lines of dramatic works.

(3.1.56)

? A question mark placed inside the final quotation marks indicates that the quotation is a question. Notice that the period after the parenthetical citation marks the end of the sentence.

Peter Elbow asks, "What could be more wonderful than the pleasure of creating or appreciating forms that are different, amazing, outlandish, useless—the opposite of ordinary, everyday, pragmatic?" (542).

When placed outside the final quotation marks, a question mark indicates that the quotation has been incorporated into a question posed by the writer of the research project.

What does Kabat-Zinn mean when he advises people to practice mindfulness "as if their lives depended on it" (305)?

[ ] Square brackets enclose words that have been added to the quotation as clarification and are not part of the original material.

"The publication of this novel [*Beloved*] establishes Morrison as one of the most important writers of our time" (Boyle 17).

13b MLA LIST OF WORKS CITED

All of the works you cite should be listed at the end of your paper, beginning on a separate page with the heading *Works Cited*. For sample lists of works cited, see pages 95, 186, 268, 321-322.

TIPS FOR PREPARING A LIST OF WORKS CITED

- Center the heading *Works Cited* (not italicized) one inch from the top of the page.
- Arrange the list of works alphabetically by the author's last name.
- If a source has more than one author, alphabetize the entry according to the last name of the first author.
- If you use more than one work by the same author, alphabetize the works by the first major word in each title. For the first entry, provide the author's complete name (last name given first), but substitute three hyphens (---) for the author's name in subsequent entries. However, if that author is also the first author in a collaboration, write out the author's name in full and then the names of the other author(s).
- For a work without an author or editor, alphabetize the entry according to the first important word in the title.
- Type the first line of each entry flush with the left margin and indent subsequent lines one-half inch (a hanging indent).
- If your list includes entries with URLs, omit the *http://* prefix but include *www.* if part of the address. If the URLs are long enough to run onto a second line, try to break them only at a punctuation mark, ideally a slash.
- For entries including a publisher's name, omit articles and corporate terms (Co., Inc.). To cite something from a university press, include abbreviations as in U of Missouri P. Otherwise, spell out publishers' names, including words like Books and Press.
- Double-space equally throughout—between lines of an entry and between entries.

Directory to MLA Works-Cited Entries

An effective works-cited entry helps readers locate your source, primarily by citing traits (like author, title, and location) shared across most source types—from podcasts to print books.

These traits are referred to as the nine *core elements*, and every source contains some combination (but not necessarily all) of them:

1. Author
2. Title of Source
3. Title of Container
4. Other Contributors
5. Version
6. Number
7. Publisher
8. Publication Date
9. Location

Here is an overview of these elements, with general information about what they do and how they should be formatted. The sections that follow will show how the elements work together to form citations for various source types.

THE CORE ELEMENTS

1. Author

The person or people who wrote or otherwise created the source—or whose work on the source you are choosing to emphasize. This could mean an author, an editor (for a work with no author), a director, a composer, a director, a performer, or a narrator.

One author. Place the last name before the first, separating them with a comma. Add any middle name or initial after the first name. Use another comma before any abbreviation (*Jr.*) or number that follows the name.	Halberstam, David. Johnston, Mary K. King, Martin Luther, Jr.

(continued on page 282)

(continued from page 281)

Omit titles, affiliations, and degrees. Indicate the end of this unit of the entry with a period. For electronic sources, pseudonyms and social media handles may be used.	@pronounced_ng.
Two authors. List names in the same order used in the original source. The first person's name is inverted (that is, the last name appears first); the second is not. Separate the names with a comma before *and*.	West, Nigel, and Oleg Tsarev.
Three or more authors. Provide just the first person's name (inverted) and the abbreviation *et al.* (for *et alii*, meaning "and others").	Quirk, Randolph, et al.
Corporate or group author. Omit any initial article (*a, an,* or *the*) from the name.	Department of Natural Resources.
Editor, Producer, Writer, etc. If the central contributor is not an author but another role, follow the name(s) with a descriptor of that role.	Gibb, Susan, and Karen Enochs, editors.

Judd Apatow, producer. |

2. Title of Source

The title of the specific source you are citing. This could be a whole book or a short poem within it, if your focus is on that poem. Always conclude this element with a period.

Longer works. Italicize the titles of books, films, plays, websites, and other stand-alone, full works. Capitalize all major words (nouns, pronouns, verbs, adjectives, adverbs, and subordinating conjunctions).	*The Good Thief.*

The Lives of Others. |

Shorter works. Use quotation marks to enclose the titles of shorter works, such as periodical articles, short stories, poems, songs, and television episodes. Short works like these are almost always found within a larger source, or container (see core element 3).

"Three Days to See."

"Selling the Super Bowl."

"Generations."

Untitled sections of works. When you are citing a specific section of a larger work, such as the introduction of a text, name this section without additional formatting in place of a title.

Introduction.

Preface.

Afterword.

Subtitles. Always include a subtitle if the work has one. Use a colon to separate a main title and a subtitle. However, if the main title ends in a question or exclamation mark, no colon is used.

Lost in Translation: Life in a New Language.

"Silence: Learning to Listen."

Titles within titles. When an italicized title includes the title of another work normally italicized, do not italicize the embedded title.

Essays on Death of a Salesman.

If the embedded title normally requires quotation marks it should be italicized as well as enclosed in quotation marks.

Understanding "The Philosophy of Composition" and the Aesthetic of Edgar Allan Poe.

When a title in quotation marks includes the title of another work normally italicized, retain the italics.

"A Salesman's Reading of *Death of a Salesman*."

If the embedded title is normally enclosed in quotation marks, use single quotation marks.

"The European Roots of 'The Philosophy of Composition.'"

3. Title of Container

A larger source containing the source you are citing. When citing a full, stand-alone source, element 3 is the same as element 2. However, when citing an essay within a periodical or an episode of a television show, the container is the periodical or show.

(continued on page 284)

(continued from page 283)

Containers. Italicize most containers, and follow them with commas.	*The Washington Post,* *Orphan Black,*

4. Other Contributors

Additional noteworthy contributors to the work not listed in element 1. These may include editors, translators, performers, etc. Introduce each name (or set of names) with a description of the role played. Format all names as first name followed by last name. Conclude with a comma.

After a stand-alone source (no container). In this case, the contributor role will follow a period and should be capitalized.	Winter, Enrique. *Sign Tongue.* Translated by David McLoughlin,
After a source within a source (container). In this case, the contributor role will follow a comma and should be lowercase.	Adele, performer. "Hello." *25,* written by Adele and Greg Kurstin,
With more than one contributor. Place commas between them.	Smith, Gordon. "Gloves Off." *Better Call Saul,* directed by Adam Bernstein, performance by Bob Odenkirk,

5. Version

Description of a source that appears in more than one version. This element appears most frequently for books that appear in multiple editions, whether these are numbered or indicated merely as "revised" or similar. It may also apply to the "director's cut" or a film, a version of software, or similar.

Edition. Use the abbreviation *ed.* for edition and *rev.* for revised, but spell out almost any other word in this context, including *version.* Also write out descriptions like *expanded* or *revised,* but use numerals for numbered editions.	expanded ed., 15th ed., rev. ed.,

Formatting. Capitalize descriptions if they follow a stand-alone source + period. Conclude with a comma.

. Version 2.1,

, updated ed.,

6. Number

Number indicating source's place in a sequence. This could refer to volume and/or issue numbers for journals, to volume numbers for books that appear in multiple volumes, or to season and episode numbers for shows.

Volumes and issues. Use the abbreviations *vol.* for volume and *no.* for issue across all source types.

vol. 122, no. 1,

Other uses. Spell out other serialized text types.

season 3, episode 9,

Formatting. Capitalize descriptions if they follow a stand-alone source + period. Always conclude with a comma.

. No. 17,

, vol. 14, no. 2,

7. Publisher

Organization that delivers source to the public. Publishers should be listed for books, films, television shows, and similar, but *not* for periodicals, works published directly by authors or editors, Web sites for which the publisher's name is the same as the title, or Web sites that do not produce the works they house (examples: *YouTube, WordPress*).

Publishers' names. In all cases excepting university presses, spell names out in full. Omit only initial articles (*The, A*) and corporate words and abbreviations (*Corporation, Inc.*). Follow with a comma.

Vintage Books,

Melville House,

Simon and Schuster,

NOTE: Do not include the city of publication.

(continued on page 286)

(continued from page 285)

University presses. Use the abbreviation *U* for *University* and *P* for *Press.*

Temple UP, U of Iowa P,

More than one publisher or sponsoring organization. Separate the names with a forward slash.

Whitney Museum / Columbia University,

Divisions and Imprints. Today, larger publishing companies may house divisions that, in turn, house several very specific imprints. When there are three levels listed on a title page, list the division—the middle one. When there are two, list the imprint.

Grove Press (not Grove Atlantic)

Vintage Books (not Random House or Vintage International)

8. Publication Date

When the source was made available to the public. This could mean when a work was published or republished in print, most recently updated online, released in theaters or on iTunes, broadcast on television, or performed live. It might be a year, a month, a specific date, or even a specific time.

Date. Provide what is available. Begin with the day, then an abbreviation of the month (except for May, June, and July), and then the year, with no punctuation between them, followed by a comma. Sources like books only provide a copyright year, while Twitter posts will provide a time stamp. Times should follow dates, with a comma between.

2015,

Jan. 2016,

Apr.-May 2009,

8 Feb. 2016,

15 Mar. 2016, 10:36 a.m.,

Access Information. If the source you are citing is likely to change or no longer be accessible at the link you provide, include access information – the day, month, and year you referenced it—after the location (element 9). Only use an access date if necessary.

date updated
6 Jan. 2016, gameofthrones.
wikia.com/wiki/Aegor_Rivers.
date accessed
Accessed 23 Mar. 2016.

9. Location

Where to find the specific source. This could be a page number or range for print sources; a direct URL or DOI for online sources; or another type of identifier for specific source types. This is also the place to record the location of a lecture, live performance, or similar.

Punctuation. Always end the location with a period.

Sources with page numbers. When page numbers are available, provide them. Prefix with the abbreviation *p.* or *pp.* If page numbers have the same hundreds or thousands digit, do not repeat it when listing the final page in the rage.

p. 98.　　pp. 55–59.

pp. 300–315.

pp. 190–95.　pp. 1680–99.

Online sources. If a digital object identifier (DOI) is given, provide this, placing *doi:* before the number. Otherwise, provide the URL, ideally a permalink, in full, so readers can access your source directly. Do not include *http://* prefixes. End with a period.

doi:10.1109/MS.2005.151.

money.cnn.com/2015/11/18/news/gender-pay-gap/.

www.pinterest.com/diy.

Remember that not all sources contain all of the nine core elements, and some of them contain additional or optional elements, which you'll learn about in the sections that follow.

CONTAINERS WITHIN CONTAINERS

Some sources are housed in containers within larger containers. For instance, if you cite an article (source) from a journal (container #1) that you accessed through a service like *ProQuest* (container #2), then you will need to include information about that larger container, too. This will help readers retrace your steps.

To create a works-cited entry for a source found in a container within a container, do the following:

- List core elements 1 (author) and 2 (title of source).

(continued from page 287)

- List core elements 3-9 that provide information about the first container (ending with a period).
- List core elements 3-9 that provide information about the second container.

In the following example, a writer has identified and ordered source information for a television episode using the core elements. She used this process to create the works-cited entry that follows.

SOURCE

1. Author.   Dan Nowak.

2. Title of Source.   "Unraveling."

CONTAINER 1

3. Title of Container,   *The Killing,*

4. Other Contributors,   directed by Lodge Kerrigan,

5. Version,

6. Number,   season 4, episode 2,

7. Publisher,   AMC,

8. Publication date,   1 Aug. 2014.

9. Location.

CONTAINER 2

3. Title of Container,   *Netflix,*

4. Other Contributors,

5. Version,

6. Number,

7. Publisher,

8. Publication date,

9 Location.   www.netflix.com/watch/70306003.

Work Cited

Dan Nowak. "Unraveling." *The Killing,* directed by Lodge Kerrigan, season 4, episode 2, AMC, 1 Aug. 2014. *Netflix,* www.netflix.com/watch/70306003.

AUTHORS IN WORKS-CITED ENTRIES

1. One author

Pinker, Steven. *The Sense of Style: The Thinking Person's Guide to Writing in the 21st Century.* Viking Press, 2014.

2. Two authors

Altick, Richard D., and Andrea A. Lunsford. *Preface to Critical Reading.* 6th ed., Henry Holt, 1984.

3. Three or more authors

Bullock, Jane A., et al. *Introduction to Homeland Security.* Elsevier, 2005.

4. No author listed

Primary Colors: A Novel of Politics. Warner Books, 1996.

5. Corporate author

Institute of Medicine. *Blood Banking and Regulation: Procedures, Problems, and Alternatives.* National Academy Press, 1996.

6. Two or more works by the same author

Joy, Camden. *Boy Island: A Novel.* Quill Publishing, 2000.

---. *Lost Joy.* TNI Books, 2002.

List entries alphabetically by title, giving the author name in the first entry. For subsequent entries, type three hyphens in place of the author's name followed by a period.

ARTICLES

A **journal** is a publication written for a specific discipline or profession. **Magazines** and **newspapers** are written for the general public. Some are published in print, some online, and some in both formats. Additionally, many articles can be accessed through online databases. You can find most of the information required for a works-cited entry for a print

CITATION MAP 13.1: ARTICLE IN A JOURNAL, MLA STYLE

To cite an article from a journal, include the following core elements.

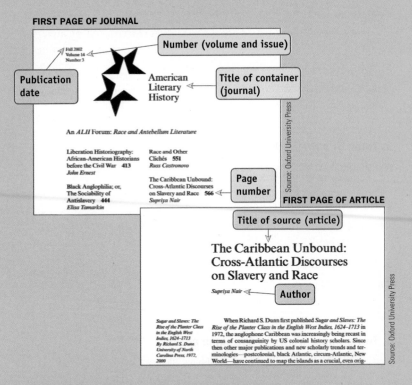

FIRST PAGE OF JOURNAL

Number (volume and issue)

Publication date

Title of container (journal)

American Literary History

Page number

FIRST PAGE OF ARTICLE

Title of source (article)

The Caribbean Unbound: Cross-Atlantic Discourses on Slavery and Race

Supriya Nair

Author

Source: Oxford University Press

WORKS-CITED ENTRY FOR AN ARTICLE IN A JOURNAL

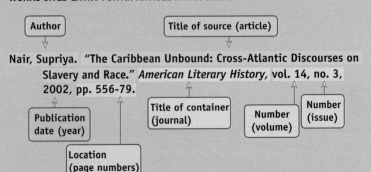

Author

Title of source (article)

Nair, Supriya. "The Caribbean Unbound: Cross-Atlantic Discourses on Slavery and Race." *American Literary History*, vol. 14, no. 3, 2002, pp. 556-79.

Publication date (year)

Location (page numbers)

Title of container (journal)

Number (volume)

Number (issue)

journal article on the first page of the journal (citation map 13.1) or at the bottom of the first page of the article you are citing. For help finding information required to cite articles found via databases, see citation map 13.2.

Magazine and newspaper articles are often interrupted by advertisements or other articles. If the first part of an article appears on pages 45 through 47 and the rest on pages 92 through 94, give only the first page number followed by a plus sign: pp. 45+.

7. Article in a journal

PRINT

Caillouet, Ruth R. "Everything I Need to Know About Teaching I Learned from *Beowulf*."

English Journal, vol. 98, no. 1, 2008, pp. 42-46.

ONLINE

Johnson, Fred. "Perspicuous Objects: Reading Comics and Writing Instruction." *Kairos: A*

Journal of Rhetoric, Technology, and Pedagogy, vol. 9, no. 1, 2014, kairos.technorhetoric.

net/19.1/topoi/johnson/.

8. Article in a magazine

PRINT

Chown, Marcus. "Into the Void." *New Scientist,* 24 Nov. 2007, pp. 34-37.

ONLINE

Associated Press. "N. Korea Proposes Joint Probe over Sony Hacking." *Mashable,* 20 Dec. 2014,

mashable.com/2014/12/20/north-korea-joint-probe-sony-hack/#qqgEHOEbwqqC.

For monthly or bimonthly magazines, include the month or range of months. For weekly magazines, also include the date.

9. Article in a newspaper

PRINT

Moberg, David. "The Accidental Environmentalist." *Chicago Tribune,* 24 Sept. 2002, sec. 2,

pp. 1+.

ONLINE

Krasnow, Bruce. "Making Cerrillos a Capital Town Again." *Santa Fe New Mexican*, 26 Mar.

2016, www.santafenewmexican.com/life/features/making-cerrillos-a-capital-town-

again/article_fc639074-8280-5951-a05b-4dc8b0c2fd59.html.

When the name of the city is not part of a locally published newspaper's name, it should be given in brackets after the title: *Star Telegram* [Fort Worth]. Specify the section by inserting the letter and/or number as it appears in the newspaper (A7 or 7A, for example); for numbered sections, use the prefix *sec.* followed by the number, as in the PRINT example on the previous page.

10. Unsigned article

"View from the Top." *National Geographic*, July 2001, p. 140.

11. Editorial

PRINT

Beefs, Anne. "Ending Bias in the Human Rights System." Editorial. *The New York Times,*

22 May 2002, p. A27.

ONLINE

"A Bump in the Road for Tesla." Editorial. *The Washington Post*, 13 June 2013,

www.washingtonpost.com/opinions/a-bump-in-the-road-for-tesla/2013/06/

13/03cb3988-d3a3-11e2-b05f-3ea3f0e7bb5a_story.html.

12. Review

PRINT

Denby, David. "Horse Power." Review of *Seabiscuit,* directed by Gary Ross. *The New Yorker,*

4 Aug. 2003, pp. 84-85.

Graham, Catherine. Review of *Questionable Activities: The Best*, by Judith Rudakoff.

Canadian Theatre Review, no. 113, 2003, pp. 74-76.

ONLINE

Dombal, Ryan. Review of *Yeezus,* by Kanye West. *Pitchfork*, 18 June 2013, pitchfork.com/

reviews/albums/18172-kanye-west-yeezus/.

Begin with the name of the reviewer. Then list the title of the review (if any), the phrase *Review of* and the title of the work being reviewed, and the name of the author, editor, or director.

CITATION MAP 13.2: ARTICLE IN A DATABASE, MLA STYLE

Include the following core elements when citing an article in a database.

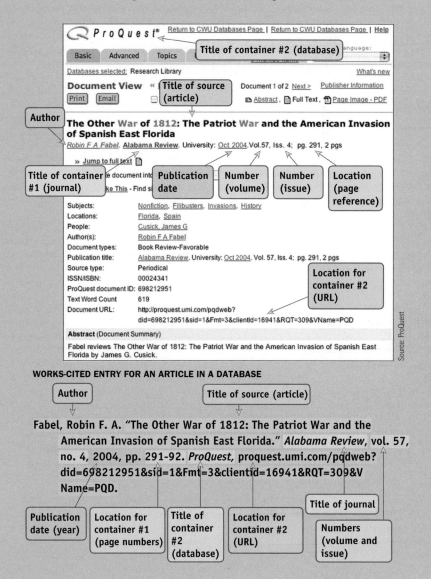

WORKS-CITED ENTRY FOR AN ARTICLE IN A DATABASE

Author

Title of source (article)

Fabel, Robin F. A. "The Other War of 1812: The Patriot War and the American Invasion of Spanish East Florida." *Alabama Review*, vol. 57, no. 4, 2004, pp. 291-92. *ProQuest*, proquest.umi.com/pqdweb?did=698212951&sid=1&Fmt=3&clientid=16941&RQT=309&VName=PQD.

Publication date (year)

Location for container #1 (page numbers)

Title of container #2 (database)

Location for container #2 (URL)

Title of journal

Numbers (volume and issue)

13. Article accessed through a database

Taylor, Steven J. "Caught in the Continuum: A Critical Analysis of the Principle of the Least
Restrictive Environment." *Research and Practice for Persons with Severe Disabilities*, vol.
29, no. 4, 2004, pp. 218-30. *ERIC,* doi:10.2511/rpsd.29.4.218.

Folks, Jeffrey J. "Crowd and Self: William Faulkner's Sources of Agency in The Sound and
the Fury." *Southern Literary Journal*, vol. 34, no. 2, 2002, pp. 30+. *Project MUSE,* doi:
10.1353/slj.2002.0003.

Many print materials are also available through online (usually
subscription-based) databases (*JSTOR, Project MUSE, PsycINFO,
LexisNexis, ProQuest,* etc.). You will likely have access to these databases
through your school's library, or with your student ID or email login.
Ask a librarian if you have any questions about how to gain access. See
p. 287 to review information about citing sources in containers within
containers. In this case, the article is your source, the periodical is container #1, and the database is container #2.

14. Abstract from a database

Landers, Susan J. "FDA Panel Findings Intensify Struggles with Prescribing of Antidepressants."
Abstract. *American Medical News*, vol. 47, no. 37, 2004, pp. 1-2. *Gale Resources,* cuny-lb.
hosted.exlibrisgroup.com/hc:everything: TN_gale_hrca166593067.

This sample abstract does not have an assigned DOI, so a permalink
URL is used.

BOOKS

When preparing a print book's entry for the list of works cited, be sure
to copy the bibliographic information directly from the title page and
copyright page of the book (see citation map 13.3). When citing books
accessed online, you may have to scroll to the top or bottom of the page
or click around to locate information.

15. Basic format for a book

PRINT

Min, Anchee. *The Cooked Seed: A Memoir.* Bloomsbury, 2013.

ONLINE (FREE ACCESS)

Whitman, Walt. *Leaves of Grass.* 1900. *Bartleby.com,* 1999, bartleby.com/142/.

DATABASE

Ames, James Barr, et al. *A Selection of Cases on the Law of Torts.* Harvard Law Review
  Publishing, 1893. *HathiTrust,* cuny-lb.hosted.exlibrisgroup.com/hc:everything:TN_
  hathi_trustnyp.33433008576310.

ON AN E-READER

Mankell, Henning. *Treacherous Paradise.* Kindle ed., Alfred A. Knopf, 2013.

16. Edition after the first

Martin, Carol Lynn, and Richard Fabes. *Discovering Child Development.* 2nd ed., Wadsworth,
  2008.

17. Republished book

Alcott, Louisa May. *Work: A Story of Experience.* 1873. Penguin Press, 1995.

After the title of the book, provide the original publication date, followed by a period.

18. Translated book

Garrigues, Eduardo. *West of Babylon.* Translated by Nasario Garcia, U of New Mexico P, 2002.

19. Book with an author and an editor

Stoker, Bram. *Dracula.* Edited by Glennis Byron, Broadview Press, 1998.

20. Book with an editor instead of an author

Kachuba, John B., editor. *How to Write Funny.* Writer's Digest Books, 2000.

21. Graphic novel or illustrated book

Bechdel, Alison. *Fun Home: A Family Tragicomedy.* Houghton Mifflin, 2006.

Helfer, Andrew. *Malcolm X: A Graphic Biography.* Illustrated by Randy DuBurke, Hill and
  Wang, 2006.

You can choose to emphasize the writer, artist, or illustrator in the
author position, but identify any role that is not the writer. If the writer
and illustrator are the same, cite just as you would a book.

22. Multivolume work - entire

Young, Ralph F., editor. *Dissent in America.* 2 vols, Longman Publishing, 2005.

CITATION MAP 13.3: BOOK, MLA STYLE

Include the following core elements when citing a book.

TITLE PAGE

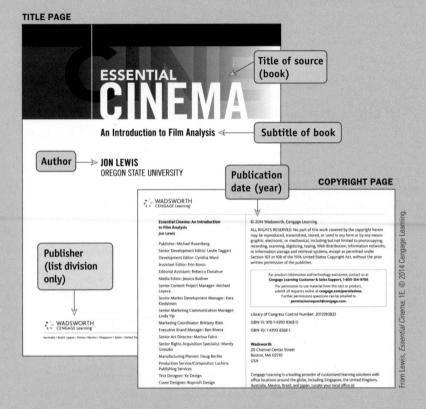

Title of source (book)

Subtitle of book

Author

Publication date (year)

COPYRIGHT PAGE

Publisher (list division only)

WORKS-CITED ENTRY FOR A BOOK

Author

Title

Lewis, Jon. *Essential Cinema: An Introduction to Film Analysis.*
     Wadsworth, 2014.

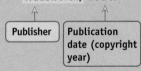

Publisher

Publication date (copyright year)

Cite the total number of volumes in a work when you have used material from more than one volume.

23. Multivolume work - single volume

Young, Ralph F., editor. *Dissent in America*. Vol. 1, Longman, 2005.

If you have used only one volume, include that volume's number instead. It is optional to include the total number of volumes when citing just one; if you do wish to include this information, place it at the end of the entry.

24. Book in a series

Sumner, Colin, editor. *Blackwell Companion to Criminology*. Blackwell, 2004. Blackwell
Companions to Sociology 8.

When citing a book that is part of a series (another type of container), add the name of the series (without italics) to the end of the entry. If a number is listed, close with this information.

25. Anthology or textbook with readings

Buranen, Lisa, and Alice M. Roy, editors. *Perspectives on Plagiarism and Intellectual Property
in a Postmodern World*. State U of New York P, 1999.

Cite an anthology (a collection of works by different authors) or textbook as you would an edited book (see example 20).

SECTIONS OF BOOKS

26. Selection from an anthology or textbook

Rowe, David. "No Gain, No Game? Media and Sport." *Mass Media and Society*, edited by
James Curran and Michael Gurevitch, 3rd ed, Oxford UP, 2000, pp. 346-61.

Cite the author(s) of the selection; place the title of the article, essay, story, or poem in quotation marks (put plays in italics); and italicize the title of the anthology in which the selection was published for the first time. Then note the anthology's editors (with *edited by*) and note the edition if it is not the first. List the publication data for the anthology and then the range of pages on which the individual selection appears. (Citation map 39.4 demonstrates how to locate this information.)

27. Two or more selections from the same anthology or textbook

Clark, Irene L. "Writing Centers and Plagiarism." Buranen and Roy, pp. 155-67.

Howard, Rebecca Moore. "The New Abolitionism Comes to Plagiarism." Buranen and Roy, pp. 87-95.

Include an entry for the entire anthology (as in example 25). This anthology entry will include all publication data; therefore, individual citations need include only the name(s) of the author(s) of the selection, the title of the work, the name(s) of the editor(s), and the inclusive page numbers of the work.

28. Introduction, preface, foreword, or afterword to a book

Olmos, Edward James. Foreword. *Vietnam Veteranos: Chicanos Recall the War*, by Lea Ybarra, U of Texas P, 2004, pp. ix-x.

29. Selection from a multivolume work

Baxby, Derrick. "Jenner, Edward." *Oxford Dictionary of National Biography*, edited by H. C. G. Matthew and Brian Harrison, vol. 30, Oxford UP, 2004, pp. 4-8.

If required by your instructor, include the total number of volumes after the location (page range), like so: pp. 4-8. 60 vols.

30. Part of an online book

Strunk, William, Jr. "Elementary Rules of Usage." *The Elements of Style*, 1918. *Bartleby.com*, 1999, www.bartleby.com/141/strunk.html.

31. Entry in a reference work

When citing a specific dictionary definition, indicate which one you used if the entry has two or more.

PRINT

"Reactive." Definition 2a. *Merriam-Webster's Collegiate Dictionary*, 10th ed, 2001.

ONLINE

"Iran." *Encyclopaedia Britannica Online*, 2002. Accessed 6 Mar. 2014.

32. Sacred text

PRINT

New American Standard Bible. Anaheim Foundation, 1997.

The Qur'an. Translated by Muhammad A. S. Abdel Haleem, Oxford UP, 2004.

ONLINE

Hymns of the Samaveda. Translated by Ralph T. H. Griffith, 1895. *Internet Sacred Texts*
    Archive, edited by John B. Hare, 2008, www.sacred-texts.com/hin/sv.htm.

Begin with the title of the work, rather than information about editors
or translators.

ONLINE SOURCES

33. Entire Web site

McGann, Jerome J., editor. *The Complete Writings and Pictures of Dante Gabriel Rossetti.*
    IATH / NINES Consortium, www.rossettiarchive.org/. Accessed 20 Mar. 2016.

American Cancer Society. 2016, www.cancer.org/. Accessed 24 Mar. 2016.

If a Web site does not provide all the information usually included in
a works-cited entry, list as much as is available. When the author, title,
and/or publisher of a site share similar or identical names, you only
need to list it once; in these cases, prefer to list the title. If there is no
specific date of publication or if the site may change without indication, include a date of access.

34. Page on or section of a Web site

"Do We Know What Causes Bone Cancer?" *American Cancer Society,* 21 Jan. 2016,
    www.cancer.org/cancer/bonecancer/detailedguide/bone-cancer-what-causes.

35. Posting to a discussion forum

Currency22. "Re: Satellite Imaging." *SERIAL,* Reddit, 19 Mar. 2016, www.reddit.com/r/
    serialpodcast/comments/4azd62/satellite_imaging/. Accessed 25 Mar. 2016.

If the posting has no title, use *Online posting* (or similar) in its place.

36. Social networking post or comment

Horta, Jasmine. "If we want our country to grow, then we need to make necessary changes, and our school should be on the top of that list... ." *Facebook*, 26 Mar. 2016, www.facebook.com/Jasmine.horta. Accessed 26 Mar. 2016.

@astamesh. "Unbreak My Heart of Darkness #90sABook." *Twitter*, 24 Mar. 2016, 5:15 p.m., twitter.com/astamesh/status/713120329833562113.

The content of the post should appear in full, in quotation marks. If the post is long, consider using only the first part of it and ending with ellipses (...).

37. Entire blog

Sullivan, Andrew. *The Dish*. dish.andrewsullivan.com/. Accessed 1 July 2015.

38. Blog entry

Silver, Nate. "As More Attend College, Majors Become More Career-Focused." *FiveThirtyEight: Nate Silver's Political Calculus*, New York Times, 25 June 2013, nyti.ms/19wZXDH.

39. Wiki entry

"Ghiscari Religion." *Game of Thrones Wiki,* Wikia, 28 Jul. 2015, gameofthrones.wikia.com/wiki/Ghiscari_religion. Accessed 25 Mar. 2016.

40. Online video clip

SciShow. "Is Sharknado Possible?" *YouTube,* 31 July 2013, www.youtube.com/watch?v=w2Qk-jz_tWc.

"Billie Holiday-Strange fruit-HD." *YouTube*, uploaded by prokoman1, 22 Dec. 2011, www.youtube.com/watch?v=Web007rzSOI.

If the video is the original work of its poster, list the poster in the author position. If the user just posted the video but did not create it, place this information after the Web site, introduced by the words *uploaded by.*

AUDIO AND VISUAL SOURCES

41. Map or chart

PRINT

Cincinnati and Vicinity. Map. Rand McNally, 2008.

(continued on p. 302)

CITATION MAP 13.4: SELECTION FROM AN ANTHOLOGY, MLA STYLE

Include the following core elements when citing a book.

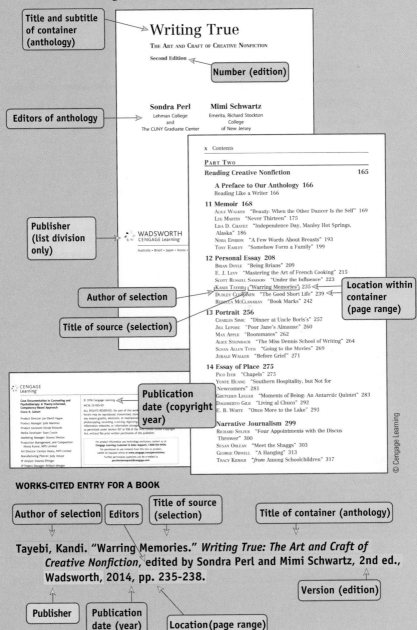

Title and subtitle of container (anthology) → Writing True
THE ART AND CRAFT OF CREATIVE NONFICTION
Second Edition ← **Number (edition)**

Editors of anthology → Sondra Perl
Lehman College
and
The CUNY Graduate Center

Mimi Schwartz
Emerita, Richard Stockton College
of New Jersey

Publisher (list division only) → WADSWORTH
CENGAGE Learning·
Australia · Brazil · Japan · Korea ·

x Contents

Location within container (page range)

Author of selection

Title of source (selection)

CENGAGE Learning

Case Documentation in Counseling and Psychotherapy: A Theory-Informed, Competency-Based Approach
Diane R. Gehart

Product Director: Jon-David Hague
Product Manager: Julie Martinez
Product Assistant: Nicole Richards
Media Developer: Sean Cronin
Marketing Manager: Shanna Shelton
Production Management, and Composition: Manoj Kumar, MPS Limited
Art Director: Carolyn Deacy, MPS Limited
Manufacturing Planner: Judy Inouye
IP Analyst: Deanna Ettinger
IP Project Manager: Brittani Morgan

© 2016 Cengage Learning
WCN: 01-100-101

ALL RIGHTS RESERVED. No part of this work covered by the copyright herein may be reproduced, transmitted, stored, or used in any form or by any means graphic, electronic, or mechanical, including but not limited to photocopying, recording, scanning, digitizing, taping, Web distribution, information networks, or information storage and retrieval systems, except as permitted under Section 107 or 108 of the 1976 United States Copyright Act, without the prior written permission of the publisher.

For product information and technology assistance, contact us at Cengage Learning Customer & Sales Support, 1-800-354-9706.
For permission to use material from this text or product, submit all requests online at www.cengage.com/permissions.
Further permissions questions can be e-mailed to permissionrequest@cengage.com.

Publication date (copyright year)

WORKS-CITED ENTRY FOR A BOOK

Author of selection **Editors** **Title of source (selection)** **Title of container (anthology)**

Tayebi, Kandi. "Warring Memories." *Writing True: The Art and Craft of Creative Nonfiction*, edited by Sondra Perl and Mimi Schwartz, 2nd ed., Wadsworth, 2014, pp. 235-238.

Version (edition)

Publisher **Publication date (year)** **Location (page range)**

(Map or Chart, continued from p. 300)

ONLINE

Smith, John, and William Hole. *Virginia.* Map. 1624. *Library of Congress,* www.loc.gov/
item/99446115.

United States, Department of Health and Human Services, "30 Day Prevalence of Daily Use
of Cigarettes, by Grade, 1976-2014." Chart. Office of Adolescent Health, 6 Mar. 2016,
www.hhs.gov/ash/oah/adolescent-health-topics/substance-abuse/tobacco/trends.html.

42. Advertisement

PRINT

Nu by Yves Saint Laurent. Advertisement. *Allure,* June 2003, p. 40.

ONLINE

"Joan Rivers—Got Milk?" Advertisement. 1995. *Vintage Ad Browser,*
www.vintageadbrowser.com/got-milk-ads#adp6no8puhjsjxv4. Accessed 25 Mar. 2016.

43. Cartoon or comic strip

PRINT

Cheney, Tom. Cartoon. *The New Yorker,* 9 June 2003, p. 93.

Trudeau, Garry. "Doonesbury." *The Daily Record* [Ellensburg], 21 Apr. 2005, p. A4.

ONLINE

Wilkinson, Signe. "Early Olympic Uniform Design." *Slate,* 28 July 2012, 9:00 a.m.,
www.slate.com/articles/news_and_politics/cartoons/2012/07/cartoonists_take_on_
the_olympics.html.

44. Work of art or photograph

ORIGINAL

Gauguin, Paul. *Ancestors of Tehamana.* 1893, Art Institute of Chicago.

Marmon, Lee. *White Man's Moccasins.* 1954, Native American Cultural Center, Albuquerque.

After the date the work was created, list the location of the organization or individual holding it and the city in which the work is located
(unless that city is listed as part of the name of a museum or similar).

REPRODUCTION OR ONLINE

Vermeer, Johannes. *Young Woman with a Water Pitcher*. 1662. *The Metropolitan Museum of Art*, 2000-2016, www.metmuseum.org/toah/works-of-art/89.15.21/.

Marmon, Lee. *Engine Rock*. 1985. *Lee Marmon Gallery*, www.leemarmongallery.com/enginerock.html.

For a reproduction of a work of art (such as an image of it online), provide publication information for the source.

45. Podcast

STREAMING

Marc Maron, host. "David Sedaris." *WTF with Marc Maron*, episode 402, 1 July 2013, www.wtfpod.com/podcast/episodes/episode_402_-_david_sedaris.

DOWNLOADED, VIA APP

Whitehurst, Annie Sage, performer. "Napoleon." *Limetown,* written by Dan Moyer, episode 3, Two-Up Productions, 12 Oct. 2015. *Podcasts,* iTunes.

To highlight a specific contributor, begin the entry with that name.

46. Television or radio program

BROADCAST

"'Barbarian' Forces." *Ancient Warriors,* narrated by Colgate Salsbury, directed by Phil Grabsky, Learning Channel, 1 Jan. 1996.

Abumrad, Jad, and Robert Kulwich, narrators. "Choice." *Radiolab*, New York Public Radio, 14 Nov. 2008.

Streep, Meryl. Interview by Terry Gross. *Fresh Air*, National Public Radio, 6 Feb. 2012.

STREAMED ONLINE

Sirota, Nadia, host. "Saarhiaho, Kaija: Ears Open." *Meet the Composer*, episode 7, New York Public Radio, 30 July 2015, www.wqxr.org/#!/story/kaija-saariaho-mtc-ears-open/.

STREAMED THROUGH A SUBSCRIPTION SERVICE

Louis C.K. "Pamela Part 1." *Louie*, performance by Pamela Adlon, season 4, episode 10, FX,
2 June 2014. *Netflix*, www.netflix.com/watch/80041317.

47. Film

IN THE THEATER

The Great Beauty. Directed by Paulo Sorrentino, Indigo Films, 2013.

Servillo, Toni, performer. *The Great Beauty*. Written and directed by Paulo Sorrentino, Indigo
Films, 2013.

Treat a film watched through a streaming service much as you would a
television show. See the examples in 46.

48. Movie or show on DVD or Blu-ray

Redford, Robert, director. *A River Runs Through It*. Screenplay by Richard Friedenberg,
1992. Columbia Pictures, 1999.

Note the release date for the recording and include the original release
date of the film when relevant.

49. Clip or section from a DVD

Abbate, Allison, producer. "From Script to Screen." *Fantastic Mr. Fox*, directed by Wes
Anderson, Twentieth Century Fox, 2009, disc 1.

Include disc numbers at the end of the entry.

50. Music or sound recording

ALBUM

Franklin, Aretha, performer. *Amazing Grace: The Complete Recordings*. Atlantic, 1999.

Horne, Lena, performer. "The Man I Love." *Stormy Weather,* composed by George Gershwin
and Ira Gershwin, recorded 15 Dec. 1941. BMG, 1990.

ONLINE

Miranda, Lin-Manuel. "Cabinet Battle #1." *Hamilton*. Atlantic Records, 25 Sept. 2015. *First
Listen,* National Public Radio, 21 Sept. 2015, www.npr.org/2015/09/21/440925873/
first-listen-cast-recording-hamilton. Accessed 22 Sept. 2015.

If the performance is a reissue from an earlier recording, provide the original date of recording (preceded by *recorded*).

OTHER SOURCES

51. Work on a CD-ROM

"About Richard III." *Cinemania 96*, Microsoft, 1996.

Jordan, June. "Moving towards Home." *Database of Twentieth-Century African American Poetry on CD-ROM*, Chadwyck, 1999.

52. Digital file (PDF, JPEG) or application (app)

National Center for Emerging and Zoonotic Infectious Diseases. "CDC and the Food Safety Modernization Act." *CDC Division of Foodborne, Waterborne, and Environmental Diseases*, May 2011, www.cdc.gov/ncezid/dfwed/pdfs/fsma-fact-sheet-508c.pdf.

Podcasts. Version 2.2, Apple, 17 Sept. 2014, iTunes.

These are PDFs, JPEGs, MP3s, and other documents, images, or recordings that be downloaded and used without online access.

53. Live performance

Auburn, David, playwright. *Proof*. Directed by Daniel Sullivan, performance by Mary-Louise Parker, Walter Kerr Theater, New York, 8 Oct. 2002.

Cite the date of the performance you attended.

54. Lecture, speech, or presentation
LIVE

Melissa Harris-Perry. Address. Barbara Jordan Lecture Series, Nittany Lion Inn, Pennsylvania State U, University Park, 9 Apr. 2015.

Scharnhorst, Gary. Guest lecture. English 296.003, Dane Smith Hall, U of New Mexico, Albuquerque, 30 Apr. 2013.

ONLINE

Malcolm X. "The Ballot or the Bullet." Detroit, 12 Apr. 1964. *American Rhetoric:*
Top 100 Speeches, edited by Michael E. Eidenmuller, 2016, www.edchange.org/
multicultural/speeches/malcolm_x_ballot.html.

Identify the site and the date of the lecture or presentation. Use the title
if available; otherwise, provide a descriptive label.

55. Conference paper in published proceedings

Crosetto, Alice. "Food in Children's Literature: An Exploration of Use and Meaning."
Proceedings of the 54th Annual Midwest Modern Language Association, November 8-11,
2012, MMLA, 2012.

56. Published dissertation

Fukuda, Kay Louise. *Differing Perceptions and Constructions of the Meaning of Assessment in*
Education. Dissertation. Ohio State U, 2001. UMI, 2002.

Include the name of the university granting the degree, the date of
completion, and the publication information. In the example, UMI
stands for "University Microfilms International," which publishes many
dissertations.

57. Published letter

Jackson, Helen Hunt. "To Thomas Bailey Aldrich." 4 May 1883. *The Indian Reform Letters*
of Helen Hunt Jackson, 1879-1885, edited by Valerie Sherer Mathes, U of Oklahoma P,
1998, pp. 258-59.

In general, treat a published letter like a work in an anthology, adding
the date of the letter and the number (if the editor assigned one).

58. Personal letter or e-mail

Lethem, Jonathan. Letter to the author. 30 June 2013.

Socarides, Alexandra. "Re: Scholarships for Women." Received by Lai Young, 15 Feb. 2015.

59. Personal interview

Stein, Sherry. Personal interview. 20 Feb. 2015.

60. Pamphlet, bulletin, or report

Stucco in Residential Construction. Lath and Plaster Bureau, 2000.

If the pamphlet has an author, begin with the author's name.

61. Government publication

PRINT

United States, Office of Management and Budget. *A Citizen's Guide to the Federal Budget.*
   Government Printing Office, 1999.

ONLINE

United States, Congress, Senate, Special Committee on Aging. *Global Aging: Opportunity or*
   Threat for the U.S. Economy? Government Printing Office, 2003. 108th Congress, 1st
   session, Senate Report 108-30. *HathiTrust,* babel.hathitrust.org/cgi/pt?id=purl.
   32754076955941;view=1up;seq=1.

United States, Department of State, Bureau of Democracy, Human Rights, and Labor.
   "Algeria." *2014 Country Reports on Human Rights Practices,* www.state.gov/j/drl/rls/
   hrrpt/humanrightsreport/index.htm?year=2014&dlid=236592.

If there is no named author, begin with the name of the government,
followed by the agency. Italicize the title of a book or pamphlet. Indicate the city of publication. Federal publications are usually (but not
always) printed by the Government Printing Office. When the name
of an author, editor, or compiler appears, begin the entry with that
name, followed by *editor* or *compiler* if the person is not the author.
Alternatively, insert that name after the publication's title and introduce
it with the word *By* or *Edited by* or *Compiled by*. For congressional documents, provide the number and session of Congress and the type and
number of publication. (Spell out all words, even if the documents do
not. Note that S stands for "Senate"; H or HR stands for "House of
Representatives.")

CITATION MAP 13.5: WORK FROM A WEB SITE, MLA STYLE

Include the following elements when citing a document you find online.

Location (URL)

Title of container (site) and Publisher (sponsor)

Title of source (short work/page)

Publication date (last update)

Title of source (short work/page)

Title of container (site) and Publisher (sponor)

"Climate Change Impacts. "United States Environmental Protection Agency, 23 Feb. 2016, www3.epa.gov/climatechange/impacts/.

Publication date (last update)

Location (URL)

62. Historical document

Eisenhower, Dwight D. Farewell Address. 1961. *Our Documents: 100 Milestone Documents from the National Archives,* foreword by Michael Beschloss, Oxford UP, 2003, pp. 217-19.

63. Legal source

PRINT

Chavez v. Martinez. 538 US 760. Supreme Court of the United States. 2003. *United States Reports,* Government Printing Office, 2004.

ONLINE

Tennessee v. Lane. 541 US 509. Supreme Court of the United States. 2004. *Supreme Court Collection,* Legal Information Institute, Cornell U Law School, 28 Jan. 2014, www.law.cornell.edu/supct/html/02-1667.ZS.html.

Include the last name of the first plaintiff, the abbreviation v. for "versus," the last name of the first defendant, data on the law report (volume, abbreviated name, and page or reference number), the name of the deciding court, and the year of the decision. Although law cases are italicized in the text of a paper, they are not italicized in works-cited entries.

64. Public law

PRINT

No Child Left Behind Act of 2001. Pub. L. 107-10. 115 Stat. 1425-2094. 8 Jan. 2002.

ONLINE

Individuals with Disabilities Education Act. Pub. L. 105-17. 104 Stat. 587-698. Library of Congress, 4 June 1997, thomas.loc.gov/cgi-bin/query/z?j108:I06264:j108IGNACE.html.

Do not italicize laws. Include the name of the act, its public law number, its Statutes at Large cataloging number and page numbers, and the date it was enacted. Note the use of abbreviations, which are encouraged in legal citations (though MLA does not provide these guidelines).

13c | SAMPLE MLA-STYLE PAPER

(1) Submit a title page if your instructor requires one

The MLA recommends omitting a title page and instead providing identifying information on the first page of the essay, including your name, the instructor's name, the name of the course with its section number, and the date. If your instructor requires a separate title page, follow his or her specific directions for doing so.

(2) Sample MLA-style paper

Interested in the controversy surrounding genetically modified foods, Marianna Suslin explores both sides of the debate as she comes to her conclusion.

TIPS FOR PREPARING AN MLA-STYLE ESSAY

- Double-space throughout.
- Number all pages (including the first one) with an Arabic numeral in the upper right-hand corner, one-half inch from the top. Put your last name before the page number.
- On the left side of the first page, one inch from the top, type a double-spaced heading that includes your name, the name of your instructor, the course number, and the date of submission.
- Double-space between the heading and the title of your essay and the line(s) of your title. Center your title.
- Double-space between your title and the first line of the text.
- Indent the first paragraph and every subsequent paragraph one-half inch.

One inch

Suslin 1

The writer's last name and the page number appear as the running head on each page.

Marianna Suslin

Professor Squier

Sociology 299, Section 1

27 November 2014

A header consisting of writer's name, instructor's name, course title, and date is aligned at the left side.

Genetically Modified Foods and Developing Countries

Genetic engineering first appeared in the 1960s. Since then,

Center the title.

thousands of genetically modified plants, also referred to as

"genetically modified organisms" (GMOs) and "transgenic crops,"

Double-space throughout.

have been introduced to global markets. Those who argue for continued

support of genetic modification claim that the crops have higher yield,

Use one-inch margins on all sides of the page.

grow in harsher conditions, and benefit the ecology. The Monsanto

Corporation, perhaps the biggest producer of GMOs, boasts that

they "think holistically about how our food is grown so farmers

have the tools they need to have better harvest—to make a plate of

meats, grains, fruits, and vegetables within the reach of every family"

("Discover Us"). Scientific experts, too, argue that genetic engineering

can benefit poor farmers in developing countries, given that genetically

modified plants increase the production of food, thereby alleviating

world hunger. Despite such altruistic claims, the practice of genetic

The last sentence in the first paragraph is the thesis statement.

engineering—of inserting genetic material into the DNA of a plant—

offers no clear answers as to whether genetically engineered foods

can and should be the solution for the problem of ongoing hunger in

developing countries.

One of the most important benefits of the technology to both

The second paragraph provides background information.

proponents and opponents of genetic engineering is its potential to

One-inch bottom margin

Suslin 2

improve the economies of developing countries and the lives of their

inhabitants (see fig. 1). According to Sakiko Fukuda-Parr, "Investing in

agricultural technology . . . [is one the most] practical actions the rich

world could take to contribute to reducing global poverty" (3). Agriculture

is the source of income for the world's poorest—70% of those living on

less than a dollar a day support themselves through agriculture. These

farmers could benefit greatly from higher yielding crops that could grow

in nutrient-poor soil. Genetic modification shows how "high-yielding

Direct quotations are used as evidence. varieties" can "dramatically increase yields and farm incomes" (Fukuda-

Parr 3). However, as others assert, investing in agricultural technology is

not the same as investing in GMO technology.

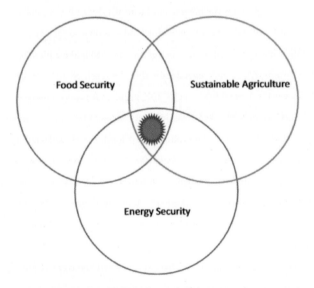

Fig. 1. At the nexus—meeting the demands for a growing population (Songstad et al. 6).

Suslin 3

Theoretically, genetic engineering can increase farm productivity, thereby giving people in developing countries a leg up in the global market, especially since such countries are often resource poor, "rich" only in terms of human labor. Farming on nutrient-poor land tends to be only at the subsistence level. Hence, GMO proponents argue that the higher yield of genetically modified, pest-resistant crops that can thrive in nutrient-poor soil enables farmers to produce and export crops not needed for subsistence and thereby improve the local economy (Fukuda-Parr 1). Genetic modification also delays the ripening process, which allows poor farmers to store the crops longer, giving them a longer period during which to sell those crops without fear of spoilage. Too often, small-scale farmers "suffer heavy losses" due to "uncontrolled ripening and spoiling of fruits and vegetables" (Royal Society et al. 238).

Today, 18% of people living in developing countries do not have enough food to meet their needs (Royal Society et al. 235). "Malnutrition plays a significant role in half of the nearly 12 million deaths each year of children under five in developing countries" (UNICEF, qtd. in Royal Society et al. 235). Genetically modified foods that produce large yields even in nutrient-poor soils could potentially help to feed the world's increasing population. Moreover, scientists are working on ways to make the genetically modified foods more nutritious than unmodified crops, which would not only feed larger numbers of people with less food but also combat malnutrition. The genetic modification of food crops has already been achieved in some species to increase the amount of protein, starch, fats, or vitamins. For example, a genetically modified rice "exhibits

Indent each paragraph one-half inch.

The writer describes some advantages of growing genetically modified crops.

A work by an organization is cited.

Suslin 4

an increased production of beta-carotene," which is a precursor to vitamin A (Royal Society et al. 240). Because vitamin A deficiencies are common in developing countries and contribute to half a million children becoming partially or totally blind each year, advances in genetic engineering offer hope for millions (Royal Society et al. 239).

Proponents also argue that genetically modified crops can decrease the damage modern farming technologies inflict on the ecology of developing nations. For example, pest-resistant plants, such as the new cotton, require much less insecticide, which is a great move from an ecological perspective[1] (Royal Society et al. 238).

Despite the potential benefits of genetic engineering for farmers throughout the world, many scientific and lay people remain skeptical about this new technology. Detractors argue that GMOs are likely to cause "irreversible loss to the biodiversity," "incurable diseases to the human mass," and "unfair trade and structural inequalities," leaving undeveloped countries even more vulnerable (Laxman and Ansari 299). Considering the health, ecological, and financial risks of genetically modified foods, many people in developing countries also feel that the risks outweigh the benefits. As Lekha Laxman and Abdul Haseeb Ansari remind us,

> [t]he developing and least developed nations are . . . not only caught in the crossfire in the agricultural trade battle at the WTO between the USA and the EU involving GMOs . . . , they are also under increasing pressure to safeguard the natural endowment of biodiversity and natural resources whilst simultaneously working towards development. (297)

A superscript number indicates an endnote.

Long quotations are indented one half inch.

Suslin 5

No matter how many potential benefits genetically modified crops may
bring, if they are not safe for consumption or the environment, they will
hurt the economies of developing countries.

The writer
describes the
disadvantages
of eating
genetically
modified
foods.

In "Genetically Modified Food Threatens Human Health," Jeffrey
Smith argues that inserting foreign genetic material into food is extremely
dangerous because it may create unknown toxins or allergens. Smith argues
that soy allergies increased significantly after genetically modified soybean
plants were introduced in the United Kingdom (103). Smith also points to
the fact that gene insertion could damage a plant's DNA in unpredictable
ways. For example, when scientists were working with the soybean plant,
the process of inserting the foreign gene damaged a section of the plant's
own DNA, "scrambling its genetic code" (105). The sequence of the gene
that was inserted had inexplicably rearranged itself over time, creating
a new protein that has not been evaluated for safety (105). In a recent
interview, former GMO researcher and genetic scientist Vrain extends
Smith's argument, describing the genetic pollution of GMO plants,
especially the terminator plants, as highly dangerous: "Imagine if you had
a field of corn with a gene for infertility and the gene spread around to the
whole agricultural area and was picked up from other crops."

A direct
quotation of
a phrase from
a cited work
is integrated
into the text.

In *Genetically Modified Food: A Short Guide for the Confused,*
Andy Rees argues a similar point: genetically modified foods carry
unpredictable health and ecological risks. He cites the 1989 incident in
which bacteria genetically modified to produce large amounts of the
food supplement L-tryptophan "yielded impressively toxic contaminants
that killed 37 people, partially paralyzed 1,500 and temporarily disabled

Suslin 6

5,000 in the US" (75). Rees also argues that genetically modified foods

can have possible carcinogenic effects. He states that "given the huge

complexity of genetic coding, even in very simple organisms such as

bacteria, no one can possibly predict the overall, long-term effects of GM

[genetically modified] foods on the health of those who eat them" (78).

Rees cites a 1999 study on male rats fed genetically modified potatoes

to illustrate the possible carcinogenic effect. The study found that the

genetically modified potatoes had "a powerful effect on the lining of the

gut (stomach, small bowel, and colon)" leading to a proliferation of cells.

According to histopathologist Stanley Ewen, this proliferation of cells

caused by genetically modified foods is then likely to "act on any polyp

Three ellipsis present in the colon . . . and drastically accelerate the development of
points mark
an omission cancer in susceptible persons" (qtd. in Rees 78). Scientific researchers are
in quoted
material. not the only ones to decry the problems of GMOs: Tad Inoue weighs in

on Facebook about the dangers of genetically modified food products

"that the food industry is trying to push on us," describing these foods as

"unhealthy and destructive to our health." He ends his post with the plea

for us to "buy organic if possible and lobby to have GM products clearly

and accurately labeled."

   In addition to the health risks involved in consuming genetically

modified foods, some also argue that such foods will aid big US

corporations—not benefit farmers in developing countries. In "The
The writer
cites statistical Emperor's New Crops," Brian Halweil brings up the fact that global sales
evidence.
for genetically modified crops grew from seventy-five million dollars in

1995 to one and a half billion dollars in 1998, which is a twenty-fold

Suslin 7

increase. Genetically modified crops are obviously lucrative for large

companies. In addition, of the fifty-six transgenic products approved for

commercial planting in 1998, thirty-three belong to just four corporations

(Halweil 256).

The spread of genetic engineering can change power relations

between nations (Cook 3), giving powerful nations even more control

over developing ones. For example, all transgenic seeds are patented and

terminators. Because the seeds are patented, it is illegal for farmers to

practice "seed saving"—reserving a certain amount of seeds from the

harvest to plant in the next growing season. (Besides, most GMO seeds are

for terminator plants, anyway.) Farmers thus have to depend entirely on

the big corporations for their seeds every single season.

The writer focuses on social issues related to genetically modified crops.

Since these corporations have a monopoly on genetically modified

seeds, the prices for these seeds are likely to remain high, and poor farmers

are unlikely to be able to afford them. Genetically altered seeds, then,

become just one more way that rich countries and their corporations

exploit the people of developing countries. Genetic engineering could

easily become one more way of hindering the development of poor

countries—not the opportunity for economic improvement and increased

social equality that its proponents claim it is. Unscrupulous companies

could use the economic vulnerability of developing countries to develop

and test genetically modified products that have been rejected in the

United States or Europe (Newell 68). Thus, people in developing countries

will be the ones who suffer when genetically modified products turn out to

be hazardous in any way.

Suslin 8

The writer continues to explore both sides of the controversy.

With many concerned about the health risks associated with GMOs, there has been a push to institute the practice of labeling genetically modified foods. International organizations such as Greenpeace and Friends of the Earth have advocated food labeling for GMOs because they believe that consumers should have the right to choose whether or not to buy genetically modified foods (Huffman 3). The FDA, however, contends that scientific studies "detect no substantial difference between food from traditional crops and GM crops" (*Federal Register*) and regards genetic modification as not altering the product enough to require labeling. Interestingly, one of the reasons for not labeling genetically modified food is the concern that consumers will shun the products with the GMO label, and thus the industry producing genetic modifications will suffer (Weirich 17). The interests of corporate giants, therefore, appear to be able to influence decision making in the United States, where the government and economy are comparatively strong. The impact of corporations on the governments of poorer countries, then, is likely to be much more pronounced, and poorer countries are likely to be victimized by big corporations.

Some evidence suggests that genetically modified foods do not live up to their promise and, therefore, cannot necessarily benefit farmers, especially those in poor countries. Rees, for example, argues that genetically modified crops will not be able to ameliorate world hunger. He believes that there is already more than enough food being produced to feed everyone in the world without these crops and that people go hungry

Suslin 9

because that food is not distributed equitably or priced fairly (49). Rees is among the researchers who argue that genetically modified crops have not increased farmers' incomes, regardless of what proponents of genetic engineering may claim. He points to a 2003 research study by Caroline Saunders at Lincoln University, New Zealand, which determined that "GM food releases have not benefited producers anywhere in the world" and that "the soil association's 2002 'Seeds of Doubt' report, created with feedback from farmers and data from six years of commercial farming in North America, shows that GM soy and maize crops deliver less income to farmers (on average) than non-GM crops" (50-51). The potential financial benefit of genetically modified crops thus remains uncertain.

While proponents of genetic engineering insist that genetically modified crops can increase yield and help feed the hungry, opponents point to health risks and challenge whether genetically modified foods are beneficial or bountiful. However, even if these foods do prove to be as beneficial as proponents claim, there is nothing to ensure that this technology will benefit poor farmers in developing countries. Since large corporations create, hold patents on, and distribute all genetically modified seeds, poor farmers may not have access to or money for these seeds and their countries continue to be at a disadvantage. Therefore, it is far from certain whether this new technology will benefit developing nations in the dramatic way its proponents assert.

The writer's conclusion is based on her own insights as well as on research reported on the previous pages.

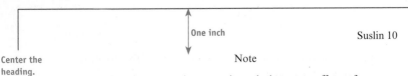

One inch

Suslin 10

Center the
heading.

Note

1. There is concern, however, about the long-term effects of crops

The number
on the note
matches the
superscript
number in
the body of
the paper.

genetically engineered for pest resistance. Since these plants continually

produce the pesticide, insects are constantly exposed to the chemical. Such

exposure increases the likelihood that the insects will develop a tolerance

for the pesticide.

Suslin 11

One inch

Works Cited

Cook, Guy. *Genetically Modified Language: The Discourse of Arguments for GM Crops and Food.* Routledge, 2005.

"Discover Us." *Discover Monsanto,* 2016, discover.monsanto.com/discover-us/.

Easton, Thomas A., editor. *Taking Sides: Clashing Views on Controversial Environmental Issues.* 11th ed., McGraw-Hill, 2005.

Federal Register. Vol. 54, no. 104, 1992, FR22991.

Fukuda-Parr, Sakiko, editor. *The Gene Revolution: GM Crops and Unequal Development.* Earthscan, 2007.

Halweil, Brian. "The Emperor's New Crops." Easton, pp. 249-59.

Huffman, W. E. "Production, Identity Preservation, and Labeling in a Marketplace with Genetically Modified and Non-Genetically Modified Foods." *Plant Physiology,* vol. 134, 2004, pp. 3-10. *PubMed Central,* doi:10.1104/pp.103.033423.

Inoue, Tad. "GM (Genetically Modified) Food Industry." *Facebook*, 18 Mar. 2014, www.facebook.com/tad.inoue.

Laxman, Lekha, and Abdul Haseeb Ansari. "GMOs, Safety Concerns, and International Trade: Developing Countries' Perspective." *Journal of International Trade Law and Policy*, vol. 10, no. 3, 2011, pp. 281-307.

Newell, Peter. "Corporate Power and 'Bounded Autonomy' in the Global Politics of Biotechnology." *The International Politics of Genetically Modified Food: Diplomacy, Trade, and Law*, edited by Robert Falkner, Palgrave, 2007, pp. 67-84.

Rees, Andy. *Genetically Modified Food: A Short Guide for the Confused.* Pluto Press, 2006.

Center the heading.

Alphabetize the entries according to the authors' last names.

Indent the second and subsequent lines of each entry one-half inch.

Royal Society et al. "Transgenic Plants and World Agriculture." Easton,
pp. 234-45.

Smith, Jeffrey M. "Genetically Modified Food Threatens Human Health
Health." *Humanity's Future*, edited by Louise I. Gerdes, Gale, 2006,
pp. 103-08.

Songstad, David D., et al, editors. "Convergence of Food Security, Energy
Security, and Sustainable Agriculture." *Food Security*, vol. 7, no. 4, 2014,
pp. 929-30. *SpringerLink*, doi:10.1007/s12571-015-0468-3.

Vrain, Thierry. "GMO Spokesman Turned GMO Whistleblower Followed the
Science." Interview by Tsiporah Grignon, *Common Ground*, 1 Oct. 2013,
commonground.ca/2013/10/dr-thierry-vrain-gmo-whistleblower/.

Weirich, Paul, editor. *Labeling Genetically Modified Food: The Philosophical
and Legal Debate*. Oxford UP, 2007.

14 || WRITING IN THE SOCIAL SCIENCES

The **social sciences** include such disciplines as psychology, anthropology, sociology, political science, and economics. Researchers in these disciplines study how humans behave as members of groups—families, peer groups, ethnic communities, political parties, and many others. The goal of research in the social sciences is to examine and explain behavior occurring under a particular set of circumstances. For example, Danielle Dezell, the student whose report is featured later in this chapter (**14e**), investigated whether students depend on gender stereotypes to assign status to certain occupations. Typical assignments in the social sciences are library research papers, case studies, and laboratory or field reports.

This chapter will help you

- determine the rhetorical audience, purpose, and research question for a paper in the social sciences (**14a**);
- decide which types of evidence, sources, and reasoning to use in such a paper (**14b**);
- use appropriate language, style, and formatting when writing the paper (**14c**);
- understand the types of writing assignments you might receive in social sciences courses (**14d**); and
- learn the conventions for writing a laboratory report (**14e**).

14a || AUDIENCE, PURPOSE, AND THE RESEARCH QUESTION

The first step toward completing a writing assignment for a course in the social sciences is to determine your rhetorical audience and purpose. Your audience will always include your instructor, but it could include students in your class and sometimes people outside your class. For example, you may have the opportunity to present your work at a student research conference. Identifying your rhetorical audience will help you decide how much background information to present, how much technical language to include, and what types of reasoning and sources to use.

Most researchers in the social sciences write either to inform or to persuade. If they are simply reporting the results of a study, their purpose is informative. However, if they urge their audience to take some action, their purpose is persuasive. Once you know what your purpose is and to whom you are writing, you can craft a research question that will help you find sources, evaluate them, and use them responsibly (chapters **8–11**). Here are some examples of types of research questions that could be posed about the topic of community service performed by students:

Questions about causes or purposes
What reasons do students give for performing community service?

Questions about consequences
What do students believe they have learned through their community service?

Questions about process
How do instructors help students get involved in community service?

Questions about definitions or categories
What does community service entail?

Questions about values
What values do instructors hope to cultivate by encouraging students to perform community service?

All of the writers of the student papers in this book started with a research question. For example, Rachel Pinter and Sarah Cronin, whose paper appears at the end of chapter **15**, asked a question about process:

How have trends in tattooing changed over the years?

14b   EVIDENCE, SOURCES, AND REASONING

Researchers in the social sciences study the behavior of humans and other animals. To make accurate observations of their subjects' activities, these researchers either design controlled laboratory experiments or conduct field research. Interviews and surveys are the two most common techniques for gathering data in the field, although observations are also widely used. Both laboratory experiments and field research yield data that social-science researchers can use as evidence to make statements (or claims) about the behavior of humans and other animals.

Researchers in the social sciences distinguish between quantitative studies and qualitative studies. **Quantitative studies**, such as laboratory experiments and surveys, yield data that can be presented in numerical form as statistics. Using statistical data and formulas, researchers show how likely it is for a behavior to occur or to have certain consequences. If you decide to undertake a quantitative study, you should turn your research question into a **hypothesis**, a prediction of what the results of your experiment or survey will be. The study you design will be based on this hypothesis, which should be as objective as possible. Obviously, you cannot entirely eliminate the influence of your own preconceptions, but you can strive to be impartial by avoiding value judgments. The results of your study will either prove or disprove your hypothesis. Be prepared to provide possible explanations for either result.

Hypotheses are best formed after a sustained period of observation and preliminary research. When presenting her hypothesis about gender stereotypes and occupational status, Danielle Dezell states her prediction in the context of existing research.

Although studies have not correlated participant gender and occupational status (Parker et al., 1989), Teig and Susskind (2008) found that occupational gender did correlate with occupational status. The current study expects to find that people's ranking of occupational status correlates with the stereotyped gender of the occupation.

Researchers who perform **qualitative studies**, such as observations and interviews, are interested in interpreting behavior by first watching, listening to, or interacting with individuals or a group. If you decide to conduct a qualitative study, you will not reason *from* a hypothesis but will reason *to* a hypothesis. You will observe a phenomenon and note what you see or hear. Then, instead of reporting numbers as evidence, you will provide detailed descriptions and discuss their significance. Although you may not be able to demonstrate the degree of impartiality prescribed for quantitative research, you should be as objective as possible.

Researchers in the social sciences recognize that some studies have both quantitative and qualitative features. They also expect to use both primary and secondary sources (see 9a) in many of their research projects. Primary sources consist of data derived from experiments, observations, surveys, or interviews. Secondary sources are articles or case studies written about a research topic. Be sure to cite any sources you use and to provide a corresponding bibliographic entry in the reference list at the end of your paper.

14c   CONVENTIONS OF LANGUAGE AND ORGANIZATION

(1) Style guidelines

The words and grammatical structures you use in a paper in the social sciences will depend on the style manual prescribed by the discipline in which you are writing. Most of the social sciences follow the guidelines presented in the *Publication Manual of the American Psychological Association* (see chapter 15). This manual stresses the importance of writing prose that is clear, concise, unbiased, and well organized. The following specific tips can help you write in the style recommended by the manual.

TIPS FOR PREPARING A PAPER IN THE SOCIAL SCIENCES

- Use the active voice as often as possible, although the passive voice may be acceptable for describing methodology. (See 25c(2).)

- Choose verb tenses carefully. Use the present tense to discuss results and report conclusions (as in "The findings suggest . . ."). Reserve the past tense for referring to specific events in the past and for describing your procedures (as in "Each participant signed a consent form . . .").

- Use a first-person pronoun rather than referring to yourself or to any coauthor(s) and yourself in the third person.

  I
  ˄The experimenter described the procedure to each participant.

  We
  ˄The experimenters retested each participant after a rest period.

- Clarify noun strings by placing the main noun first.

   the method for testing literacy NOT the literacy testing method

(2) Organization

Assignments in the social sciences will generally require you to (1) state a research question, thesis, or hypothesis; (2) discuss research that has already been published about your topic; (3) describe your methodology; and (4) present your conclusions or results. Specific types of assignments are discussed in **14d**.

To organize the information they are presenting, writers in the social sciences use tables and graphs as well as headings, which are designed to signal levels of importance (**15c**). Danielle Dezell includes a table to display her results (see page 338). If you decide to use a table in your paper, be sure to refer to the table by number (for example, Table 1) and explain the significance of the information it provides. Without a brief discussion of the table, your readers may have difficulty understanding why you included it.

Graphs provide a visual representation of data. Danielle uses line graphs to highlight her comparison of gender stereotypes and perceptions of occupational status (see page 339). Graphs are labeled as numbered figures. Like tables, they should be discussed in the text.

● TECH SAVVY

Table
To insert a table into a document, choose Table on the main menu bar of your word processor and click on Insert and then on Table in the pulldown menu. You will see a dialogue box that allows you to choose the number of rows and columns for your table.

Graph
To insert a graph into a document, choose Insert on the main menu bar and select Object from the pulldown menu. From the list of object types, choose Microsoft Graph Chart. You can then enter your data into the spreadsheet provided.

(3) Reference list

At the end of any paper you write for a course in the social sciences, you should include a list of all the sources you used. By doing so, you provide your readers with the details they need to consult these sources on their own. You can find guidelines for creating a reference list in **15b** and sample lists of references on pages 342–343 and 385–386.

14d	EXAMPLES OF WRITING IN THE SOCIAL SCIENCES

(1) Literature review

Literature reviews are written by both students and professionals. They may be parts of larger assignments, or they may be stand-alone assignments. The purpose of literature reviews, sometimes called library reports, is to bring together several related sources on a specific topic in order to examine that topic closely. Writing a literature review will require you to read a number of sources and then summarize, critique, and synthesize those sources (see chapter **11**). Literature reviews generally include the following elements:

- Statement of the research question or thesis
- Presentation of background information, using sources
- Discussion of major findings presented in the sources
- Application or connection of those findings to the specific research question
- Conclusions
- References

An excerpt from a literature review is shown in figure 14.1. In the report's introduction, authors Matthew Gervais and David Sloan Wilson present background information for their study. Notice that the authors maintain a neutral stance that conveys an impression of impartiality, although they clearly and strongly state their point of view. A student-written example of a library research report is Rachel Pinter and Sarah Cronin's paper on tattooing (see **15c**).

The first paragraph presents past studies on the topic.

INTRODUCTION

L AUGHTER AND HUMOR were accorded high evolutionary significance by Darwin (1872) and have received increasing attention from biologists and psychologists during the last 30 years. This attention has resulted in myriad empirical advances and has left laughter and humor well characterized on multiple proximate levels (see Provine 2000; Vaid 2002; Bachorowski and Owren 2003; van Hooff and Preuschoft 2003; Wild, Rodden et al. 2003). Laudably, this research has spawned a number of hypotheses attempting to explain the ultimate evolutionary origins of laughter and humor (e.g., Eibl-Eibesfeldt 1989; Weisfeld 1994; Pinker 1997; Ramachandran 1998; Harris 1999; Miller 2000; Provine 2000; Owren and Bachorowski 2001; Caron 2002; Howe 2002; Jung 2003; Storey 2003). Nevertheless, the scientific study of laughter and humor is still in its infancy relative to other comparable subjects in emotions and communication research.

Many empirical questions about laughter and humor remain unanswered or neglected. For example, most researchers (e.g., Provine 2000; Owren and Bachorowski 2003; Vettin and Todt 2004) have failed to make the important distinction between Duchenne (stimulus-driven and emotionally valenced) and non-Duchenne (self-generated and emotionless) laughter (Keltner and Bonanno 1997; see also Wild, Rodden et al. 2003). While laughter has recently been found to occur most frequently during casual conversation and not following deliberate humor (Provine 1993; LaGreca et al. 1996; Vettin and Todt 2004), researchers have yet to question whether such conversational laughter is different in kind from that following humor. This oversight might well be the root cause of the widespread confusion concerning the diversity of forms and functions that characterizes laughter today (Keltner and Bonanno 1997).

As regards theory, the results of empirical findings of laughter and humor research remain disjointed and only partially accounted for by any one framework. In most cases, such hypotheses are not mutually exclusive but potentially complementary, yet a synthesis remains unrealized. As a result, theoretical limitations abound.

The next two paragraphs discuss gaps in the research.

Figure 14.1: An excerpt from the introduction of a literature review. (Note: If the parenthetical citations were in APA style, a comma would be used between authors and dates, and multiple citations would be arranged alphabetically.)

(2) Case study

A case study is a qualitative project that requires a researcher to describe a particular participant or group of participants. The researcher refrains from making generalizations about the participant(s) in the study and

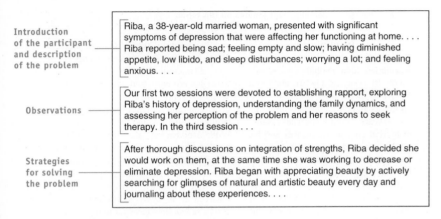

Introduction of the participant and description of the problem — Riba, a 38-year-old married woman, presented with significant symptoms of depression that were affecting her functioning at home. . . . Riba reported being sad; feeling empty and slow; having diminished appetite, low libido, and sleep disturbances; worrying a lot; and feeling anxious. . . .

Observations — Our first two sessions were devoted to establishing rapport, exploring Riba's history of depression, understanding the family dynamics, and assessing her perception of the problem and her reasons to seek therapy. In the third session . . .

Strategies for solving the problem — After thorough discussions on integration of strengths, Riba decided she would work on them, at the same time she was working to decrease or eliminate depression. Riba began with appreciating beauty by actively searching for glimpses of natural and artistic beauty every day and journaling about these experiences. . . .

Figure 14.2: An excerpt from a case study.

instead focuses on the behavior of the participant(s). After describing the behavior, the researcher usually suggests a solution to the problem faced by the participant(s). Most case studies include the following information:

- An introduction to the participant(s)
- A description of the problem
- Observations
- A presentation of strategies to solve the problem

Figure 14.2 is a collection of excerpts from a case study, from the seventh edition of *Case Studies in Psychotherapy*.

(3) Laboratory or field (observation) report

Social science students and professionals often conduct research in a laboratory or in the field (that is, in a natural setting). Reports based on this type of research contain standard sections: introduction, method, results, and discussion. An example of a laboratory report is Danielle Dezell's paper on gender stereotypes and occupations (14e).

| **14e** | LABORATORY REPORT ON A GENDER-STEREOTYPING EXPERIMENT |

Written according to the style guidelines of the American Psychological Association (APA), which are discussed in Chapter 15, the following laboratory report by Danielle Dezell includes the standard sections mentioned in 14d(3). Danielle's report also includes several appendices: a copy of the prompt she used, a script for the study, and a participant consent form. Because Danielle asked fellow students to participate in her study, she was required to submit a proposal for her study and the consent form to the institutional review board at her university for approval (9i). Although Danielle collaborated with Cameron Dooley and Elaine Acosta on the experiment described in the report, she wrote the report on her own.

Running head: GENDER STEREOTYPES AND PERCEPTIONS   1

Gender Stereotypes and Perceptions of Occupational Status

Among University Students

Danielle Dezell

Central Washington University

GENDER STEREOTYPES AND PERCEPTIONS   2

Abstract

The writer introduces the purpose of the study.

This study investigated whether the gender of participants affected their view of certain occupations and whether the gender typically associated with an occupation affected participants' ranking of the status of that occupation. Participants were asked (1) to write a response to a prompt designed to elicit gender-specific pronouns and (2) to rate the status of one of three occupations typically associated with a gender. The results were compared to see whether the interaction between participant gender and stereotypical occupational gender influenced the perception of the status of the occupation and to discover whether participant gender influenced the perception of occupational gender.

GENDER STEREOTYPES AND PERCEPTIONS   3

Gender Stereotypes and Perceptions of Occupational Status

Among University Students

Occupational gender stereotypes are important to examine for their

possible influence not only on a person's occupational choice but also on

perceptions of status associated with occupations. When university-age

students consider possible careers, they often choose one based on their

own gender and on the stereotypical gender assigned to an occupation

(Evans & Diekman, 2009). They may also choose an occupation

according to the status they believe it to have. An investigation into

gender stereotypes about occupations is a first step in limiting their

influence on students' career choices.

Gender stereotypes begin in early childhood, when children see how

society views certain professions. These societal influences can have long-

term effects on how children may stereotype various occupations

(Firestone, Harris, & Lambert, 1999). Several studies using school-age

children as participants have examined the strength of these early

stereotypes. Miller and Hayward (2006) showed that participants often

preferred occupations that were stereotyped to their own gender (i.e.,

boys preferred stereotypically male jobs, and girls preferred stereotypically

female jobs). Another study conducted by Teig and Susskind (2008)

looked at both status and stereotypes. When participants were asked to

rate the status of jobs, the researchers found that out of the 18 highest

ranked jobs, only 3 were classified as feminine. Of all the occupations,

27.8% of masculine occupations had a high status ranking, while 15.4% of

female occupations had a high status ranking. Participants in this study

The writer establishes the importance of her report.

By discussing the work of other researchers, the writer not only provides readers with necessary information but also demonstrates her credibility.

GENDER STEREOTYPES AND PERCEPTIONS   4

classified both *librarian* and *elementary school teacher* as stereotypically

feminine occupations. The researchers found that there was a significant

correlation between the gender of the participant and how he or she

ranked the status of an occupation. However, the researchers pointed

out that as girls grew older, their tendency to stereotype lessened. Boys,

though, continued to carry gender stereotypes into adulthood. Miller and

Hayward (2006) noted that men generally prefer occupations traditionally

performed by men.

The writer refers to previous studies and synthesizes their findings.

In a study whose participants were college-age students, Shinar

(1975) looked at how the participants rated the masculinity and

femininity of various occupations on a 1-to-7 Likert scale (1 being

masculine and 7 being *feminine*). The study showed that both men

and women held gender stereotypes about certain occupations. The

participants rated *miner* as a fully masculine job (mean rating of 1.000)

and *manicurist* as a mostly feminine job (mean rating of 6.667). Shinar

also reported that *head librarian* had a mean rating of 5.583, *high school

teacher* a mean rating of 4.000, and *carpenter* a mean rating of 1.667.

What is interesting is that Shinar showed that both women and men

demonstrated gender stereotyping, whereas, over 30 years later, Seguino

(2007) and Miller and Hayward (2006) found that men had much stronger

stereotypes than women. Miller and Hayward also suggested that women

grow out of a stereotyping mindset by age 18.

Although certain occupations clearly seem to be gender stereotyped,

occupational status is not always related to gender. Parker, Chan, and Saper

(1989) found that there was no significant correlation between participant

gender and occupational status ratings. It might be tempting to believe

GENDER STEREOTYPES AND PERCEPTIONS 5

that jobs associated with masculinity would be ranked as having higher social status, but these researchers showed that the status of many traditionally masculine jobs (e.g., *heavy equipment operator*) was considered low. This finding is especially interesting because it suggests that when people choose an occupation, they might rely more on the perception of the gender associated with an occupation than on the perception of status.

> The writer adds her own voice to the discussion of gender stereotypes.

One way to test how people stereotype a job according to gender is to ask them to assign a pronoun to a certain occupation. This simple test provides insight into how gender stereotypes of occupations work and whether males or females are more likely to hold such stereotypes. A study looking at the gender people attributed to different gender-neutral characters introduced in a dialogue script found that both men and women were more likely to assume that a character was male. The same study also found that men and women had equal biases toward gender assumptions (Merritt & Kok, 1995). In a similar study, participants were asked to attribute a gender to various stuffed animals. Both children and adults used the male pronoun to describe stuffed animals that were gender-neutral (Lambdin, Greer, Jibotian, Wood, & Hamilton, 2003).

This study aims to discover both whether participants stereotype certain occupations as being either male or female and whether participants rate the status of an occupation based on whether the occupation has historically been a masculine, feminine, or gender-neutral occupation. The findings of previous studies suggest that both males and females do stereotype certain occupations. Although studies have not correlated participant gender and occupational status (Parker et al., 1989),

> After reporting the work of other researchers in previous paragraphs, the writer now introduces her hypothesis.

GENDER STEREOTYPES AND PERCEPTIONS   6

Teig and Susskind (2008) found that occupational gender did correlate with occupational status. The current study expects to find that people's ranking of occupational status correlates with the stereotyped gender of the occupation.

Method

Participants

A total of eight groups participated in the study. Numbers of participants in each group varied. Overall, there were 40 participants, 11 males and 29 females. All participants were students at Central Washington University and were 19 years old or older. The participants were all volunteers and were randomly assigned to one of three experimental conditions.

Materials

The materials for each experimental condition were a sheet of paper that presented one of three different writing prompts and asked for four pieces of demographic information (Appendix A). A script from which the researcher read (Appendix B) was also used. Each writing prompt was a scenario about an employee of a school who had a problem; however, the employee's occupation in each prompt differed. The occupations and their associated gender stereotypes were as follows: *librarian* (female), *woodshop teacher* (male), and *high school teacher* (gender neutral). The occupations were chosen based on the percentage of females employed in each occupation, according to statistics from the Bureau of Labor Statistics (2010). The statistics showed that *high school teacher* was the most gender-neutral occupation (54.9% female).

Information on methodology helps readers decide whether the researcher's findings are reliable and valid.

GENDER STEREOTYPES AND PERCEPTIONS   7

The occupation *librarian* was found to be gender segregated toward females (81.8% female). There were no statistics for *woodshop teacher*, though there were statistics for *carpenter* (1.6% female). Because most carpenters are male, it is quite likely that most people would stereotype the occupation of woodshop teacher as male. A focus on jobs that were all in a school environment prevented the creation of confounds based on the status of a work environment.

The writing prompts excluded any language that might allow the participant to infer the gender of the person in the prompt (e.g., no pronouns were used). A 5-point Likert scale was used to measure how participants rated the status of an occupation. Each of the three prompt sheets used identical wording in the directions, prompts, Likert scale, and demographic items (i.e., gender, age, class standing, and major); the only difference among the prompts was the occupation used.

Procedure

Each group of participants had two administrators. The study took approximately 15 minutes. One administrator passed out consent forms (Appendix C), collected them, and then distributed the prompts, while the other administrator read the appropriate directions from the script (Appendix B). Once the participants had the prompt, they were given 10 minutes to complete the story. After the administrators collected the stories, participants were debriefed and provided with the opportunity to ask questions.

Results

The descriptive statistics can be found in Table 1. A two-way between-subjects ANOVA with $\alpha = .05$ showed that the interaction

Statistics are used to report results.

GENDER STEREOTYPES AND PERCEPTIONS   8

Table 1

Descriptive Statistics

Gender of Participant	Occupation in Prompt	Mean	Std. Deviation	*N*
F	High School Librarian	2.75	.452	12
	High School Teacher	2.75	.463	8
	High School Woodshop Teacher	2.56	.527	9
	Total	2.69	.471	29
M	High School Librarian	5.00	.545	1
	High School Teacher	3.20	1.304	5
	High School Woodshop Teacher	3.20	.837	5
	Total	3.36	1.120	11
Total	High School Librarian	2.92	.760	13
	High School Teacher	2.92	.862	13
	High School Woodshop Teacher	2.79	.699	14
	Total	2.88	.757	40

between participant gender and occupation in the prompts was not significant, $F(2, 34) = .88$, $p > .05$. Of the two main effects, only gender was significant, $F(1, 34) = .001$, $p < .05$. However, occupation had a nonsignificant main effect, $F(2, 34) = .052$, $p > .05$. The averages of means are graphed in Figure 1. The homogeneity of variance test was significant, $F(5, 34) = .003$, $p < .05$. The first chi-square test, which was run on the interaction between participant gender and type of pronoun used by the participant in responding to the prompt, had a Pearson's correlation of .267, which is not significant. The second chi-square test between occupation in the prompt and pronoun type had a highly significant Pearson's correlation of .000.

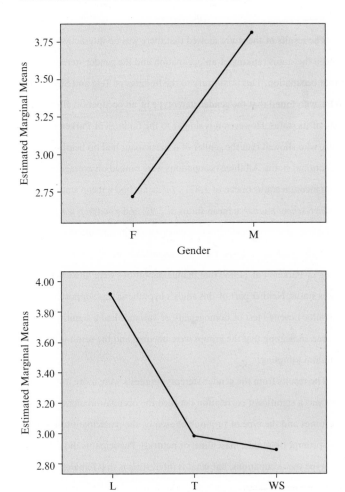

GENDER STEREOTYPES AND PERCEPTIONS 9

Figure 1. Means for main effects.

Discussion

The statistics reported in the previous section are explained in this section.

The results of the study showed that there was no interaction between the status ranking of an occupation and the gender stereotyping of that occupation. This is contrary to the findings of Teig and Susskind (2008), who found that the gender stereotype of an occupation affects the rating of its status. However, it is similar to the findings of Parker et al. (1989), who showed that the gender of a participant had no bearing on occupational status. All three occupations were ranked on average as having medium status (mean of 2.875). *Librarian* had a mean status of 2.92; *high school teacher*, a mean status of 2.92; and *woodshop teacher*, a mean status of 2.79. While there may not be a significant difference, the mean status ranking is lowest for *woodshop teacher*, which agrees with the finding of Parker et al. (1989) that manual labor jobs were rated as having a lower status. Neither part of this study's hypothesis was supported by the results. Levene's test of homogeneity of variance had a significant outcome, indicating that the groups were unequal and the result is not due to random sampling.

The results from the gender-stereotyping tests were more intriguing. There was a significant correlation between the occupation mentioned in the prompt and the type of pronoun chosen by the participant to respond to the prompt (feminine, masculine, or neutral). Participants did stereotype the occupations, but what is interesting is that females used gender-specific pronouns much more than males did. When writing their stories about the various occupations, male participants used gender-neutral pronouns 72% of the time, whereas female participants used

GENDER STEREOTYPES AND PERCEPTIONS   11

gender-neutral pronouns only 41% of the time. These findings are

The writer compares her results with those of other researchers.

contrary to those of Merritt and Kok (1995), who found that when

participants are presented with unspecified characters, they generally

designate the gender as male. The findings of this study also contradict

the occupational stereotype findings of Shinar (1975), who stated that

men use stereotypes more than women, and of Miller and Hayward

(2006), who reported that females tend to use fewer stereotypes once they

are enrolled in college.

One of the biggest limitations of the study was that there were so

The writer acknowledges some limitations of the study.

few participants, especially men. Data elicited from a larger number of

male participants would have provided a more accurate picture of how

men view occupational stereotypes. The prompts could also have been

worded better. Because of the awkward wording of the prompts,

participants had a good idea of what the study was looking for and so

may have adjusted their responses. Another limitation is that there were

only three occupations. Including a greater number of occupations would

have made it possible to state conclusions about gender stereotypes more

firmly. Future studies should include not only more occupations but also

occupations that obviously have different statuses. This study chose

occupations that were all in the same environment in order to avoid

confounds; however, if there were many different types of occupations

from a variety of environments, participants might not be able to

determine as easily the researcher's intent. Despite these limitations, this

study suggests that people are starting to have fewer assumptions about

the relation between gender and occupation.

GENDER STEREOTYPES AND PERCEPTIONS   12

References

Bureau of Labor Statistics. (2010). *Household data: Annual averages* [Data file]. Retrieved from http://www.bls.gov/cps/cpsa2010.pdf

Evans, C., & Diekman, A. (2009). On motivated role selection: Gender beliefs, distant goals, and career interest. *Psychology of Women Quarterly, 33*(2), 235–249. doi:10.1111/j.1471-6402.2009.01493.x

Firestone, J., Harris, R., & Lambert, L. (1999). Gender role ideology and the gender based differences in earnings. *Journal of Family and Economic Issues, 20*(2), 191–215. doi:10.1023/A:1022158811154

Lambdin, J. R., Greer, K. M., Jibotian, K. S., Wood, K. R., & Hamilton, M. C. (2003). The animal = male hypothesis: Children's and adult's beliefs about the sex of non-sex-specific stuffed animals. *Sex Roles, 48*(11/12), 471–482. doi:10.1023/A:1023567010708

Merritt, R. D., & Kok, C. J. (1995). Attribution of gender to a gender-unspecified individual: An evaluation of the people = male hypothesis. *Sex Roles, 33*(3/4), 145–157. doi:10.1007/BF01544608

Miller, L., & Hayward, R. (2006). New jobs, old occupational stereotypes: Gender and jobs in the new economy. *Journal of Education & Work, 19*(1), 67–93. doi:10.1080/13639080500523000

Parker, H., Chan, F., & Saper, B. (1989). Occupational representativeness and prestige rating: Some observations. *Journal of Employment Counseling, 26*(3), 117–131. Retrieved from http://www.employmentcounseling.org

Seguino, S. (2007). Plus ça change? Evidence on global trends in gender norms and stereotypes. *Feminist Economics, 13*(2), 1–28. doi:10.1080/13545700601184880

GENDER STEREOTYPES AND PERCEPTIONS 13

Shinar, E. (1975). Sexual stereotypes of occupations. *Journal of Vocational Behavior, 7*(1), 99–111. Retrieved from http://www.sciencedirect.com/science/journal/00018791

Teig, S., & Susskind, J. (2008). Truck driver or nurse? The impact of gender roles and occupational status on children's occupational preferences. *Sex Roles, 58*(11/12), 848–863. doi:10.1007/s11199-008-9410-x

Appendix A
Sample Prompts

DO NOT WRITE YOUR NAME ANYWHERE ON THIS PAGE.
THANK YOU.

Instructions: Please read the following scenario; then write one or two
paragraphs describing what the person would do in response to this
situation. If you run out of room, you may use the back of the page. Then
go to the bottom of the page to rate the occupational status of the
profession and fill out the demographic information.

*The high school woodshop teacher arrives late to school. Upon arriving at
the classroom with no keys, the woodshop teacher realizes the door is locked.
There is a group of students waiting to go to class. What does the woodshop
teacher do?*

*The high school librarian arrives late to school. Upon arriving at the library
with no keys, the librarian realizes the door is locked. There is a group of
students waiting to go in. What does the librarian do?*

*The high school teacher arrives late to school. Upon arriving at the
classroom with no keys, the teacher realizes the door is locked. There is a
group of students waiting to go to class. What does the teacher do?*

On a scale of 1 to 5, where 1 is a low-status occupation and 5 is a high-
status occupation, how would you rate the occupation of the person in the
story? Please circle your choice.

        Lowest Status   1   2   3   4   5   Highest Status

Your gender: _____Age: ____ Class standing: _____ Major: _____

GENDER STEREOTYPES AND PERCEPTIONS   15

Appendix B

Script for the Study

(As participants enter room, Administrator 2 gives each a consent form and a pencil and asks each one to take a seat anywhere. When all are seated, Administrator 1 says the following:)

Thank you for volunteering to participate in this study. You have been given a consent form. When you have read and signed the consent form, we will collect them and begin. I'm going to highlight some main points while you are reading through it. The total testing time is 15 minutes. You do not have to participate in the study; refusal to participate will not affect your grade in any class or any of your privileges at CWU. You can agree to this study now and then leave at any time if you change your mind. If you wish to stop at any time, please tell us right away. The data collected from you in this study are completely anonymous.

(Administrator 2 collects consent forms. Administrator 1 says the following:)

You will now be given a pencil and the writing prompt. When you receive the paper, please leave it face down until instructed. Once you have turned over the story, you will have 10 minutes to read the prompt and write a response. When you have completed writing, please remain seated and quiet until the 10 minutes have passed. The administrator will then collect your papers. Please ask any questions you have now. You will be able to ask more questions once the stories have been collected.

Please turn over your paper and read the instructions. Please do not write your name on the paper.

GENDER STEREOTYPES AND PERCEPTIONS   16

(After 10 minutes have gone by, Administrator 1 continues:)

Please stop writing. Be sure you have filled in the bottom of the page.

Debrief: *This study was designed to discover whether students associate the type and status of an occupation with a particular gender. Your prompt did not give any indication of the gender of the occupation. We will analyze your pronoun choice to see what gender you assumed the occupation to be.*

Are there any questions? Thank you for your participation. You are free to leave. This is a week-long study, so please do not discuss it.

Appendix C
Consent Form

**CENTRAL WASHINGTON UNIVERSITY
RESEARCH PARTICIPANT CONSENT FORM**

Study Title:	Gender Stereotypes and Occupational Status
Principal Investigator(s):	Danielle Dezell, Cameron Dooley, and Elaine Acosta. Dept. of Psychology, Central Washington University. (509) 555-1234, student321@university.edu
Faculty Sponsor:	Dr. Sally Lifland. Dept. of Psychology, Central Washington University. (509) 555-4321, ProfessorSL@university.edu

1. **What you should know about this study:**
   - You are being asked to take part in a research study.
   - This consent form explains the research study and your part in the study.
   - Please read it carefully and take as much time as you need.
   - Ask questions about anything you do not understand, now or later.
   - You are a volunteer. If you change your mind about participating, you may quit at any time without fear of penalty.
   - While you are in this study, the study team will keep you informed of any new information that could affect whether you want to stay in the study.
2. **Why is this research being done?**
   This research is to show how college students perceive occupational status in order to better understand occupational stereotypes.
3. **Who can take part in this study?**
   Any CWU student over the age of 18 is able to participate in this study.
4. **What will happen if you join this study?**
   If you agree to be in this study, you will be asked to write a short response to a prompt. The prompt consists of three sentences. It

GENDER STEREOTYPES AND PERCEPTIONS   18

describes a situation in which the subject is a professional. Your
response will consist of one or two paragraphs describing what the
subject should do in this situation.

[Some of the consent form items have been omitted.]

13. What does your signature on this consent form mean?
By signing this consent form, you are not giving up any legal rights.
Your signature means that you understand the study plan, have been
able to ask questions about the information given to you in this form,
and agree to take part in the study.

Participant's Name (print): _____

Participant's Signature: _____ Date: _____

Phone Number: _____ E-mail: _____

Signature of Investigator: _____ Date: _____

GENDER STEREOTYPES AND PERCEPTIONS   19

Appendix D
Raw Data

Subject	Gender	Occupation	Pronoun	Status
1	F	L	F	3
2	F	L	F	3
3	F	L	N	3
4	F	L	F	3
5	F	L	F	3
6	F	L	F	3
7	F	L	F	2
8	F	L	N	3
9	F	L	F	3
10	F	L	F	2
11	F	L	N	2
12	F	L	F	3
13	F	WS	M	3
14	F	WS	M	3
15	F	WS	M	3
16	F	WS	M	2
17	F	WS	M	2
18	F	WS	N	2
19	F	WS	N	3
20	F	WS	M	2

(continued)

GENDER STEREOTYPES AND PERCEPTIONS   20

Subject	Gender	Occupation	Pronoun	Status
21	F	WS	M	3
22	F	T	N	3
23	F	T	N	3
24	F	T	N	3
25	F	T	M	2
26	F	T	N	3
27	F	T	N	2
28	F	T	N	3
29	F	T	N	3
30	M	L	N	5
31	M	WS	M	4
32	M	WS	N	3
33	M	WS	N	3
34	M	WS	M	2
35	M	WS	N	4
36	M	T	N	5
37	M	T	F	4
38	M	T	N	2
39	M	T	N	3
40	M	T	N	2

15 ‖ APA DOCUMENTATION

The American Psychological Association (APA) publishes a style guide entitled *Publication Manual of the American Psychological Association.* Its documentation system (called an *author-date system*) is used for work in psychology and many other disciplines, including education, economics, sociology, and business management. Updates to the style guide are provided at www.apastyle.org. This chapter presents

- guidelines for citing sources within the text of a paper (**15a**),
- guidelines for documenting sources in a reference list (**15b**), and
- a sample student paper (**15c**).

15a ‖ APA-STYLE IN-TEXT CITATIONS

APA-style in-text citations usually include just the last name(s) of the author(s) of the work and the year of publication. If you do not know the author's name, use a shortened version of the source's title instead.

Be sure to specify the page number(s) for any quotations you use in your paper. The abbreviation *p.* (for "page") or *pp.* (for "pages") should precede the number(s). If visible paragraph numbers are provided instead of page numbers, use the abbreviation *para.* For documents that have neither page nor paragraph numbers, include the name of the section or an abbreviated heading. Then determine the number of the paragraph and include that number.

The following examples are representative of the types of in-text citations you can expect to use.

1. Work by one author

Paltridge (2012) states that people use language and visuals to create an online identity that is sometimes "separate and distinct from their offline identity" (p. 25).

OR

People use language and visuals to create an online identity that is sometimes "separate and distinct from their offline identity" (Paltridge, 2012, p. 25).

Use commas to separate the author's name from the date and the date from the page number. Include page numbers only when quoting from the source.

2. Work by two authors

According to Goodie and Fortune (2013), "impaired control . . . is a gambler's belief that he or she cannot control his or her own problematic gambling behaviors" (p. 2).

OR

Many compulsive gamblers believe they have no control over their behaviors (Goodie & Fortune, 2013).

When the authors' names are in parentheses, use an ampersand (&) to separate them.

3. Work by more than two authors

Interference between conversation and driving occurs because both are "complex, multimodal, attention-demanding tasks" (Bergen, Medeiros-Ward, Wheeler, Drews, & Strayer, 2013, Introduction section, para. 2).

For works with three to five authors, cite all the authors the first time the work is referred to, but in subsequent references give only the last name of the first author followed by *et al.* (meaning "and others").

The research of Bergen et al. (2013) confirms previous studies "demonstrating that language use, even without a handheld device, interferes with successful control of a vehicle" (Discussion section, para. 2).

For works with six or more authors, provide only the last name of the first author followed by *et al.* in both the first and subsequent citations.

4. Anonymous work
Use a shortened version of the title to identify an anonymous work.

Chronic insomnia often requires medical intervention ("Sleep," 2009).

This citation refers to an article identified in the bibliography as "Sleep disorders: Standard methods of treatment."

If the word *Anonymous* is used in the source itself to designate the author, it appears in place of an author's name.

The documents could damage the governor's reputation (Anonymous, 2013).

5. Two or more works by different authors in the same parenthetical citation

Smokers frequently underestimate the long-term effects of smoking (O'Conner, 2010; Polson & Truss, 2012).

Arrange the citations in alphabetical order, using a semicolon to separate them.

6. Two or more works by the same author in the same parenthetical citation

Emerging variations of Mandarin Chinese have been discussed in terms of the prestige their use bestows (Zhang, 2008, 2012).

Jameson (2007a, 2007b) has proposed an anxiety index for use by counselors.

Order the publication dates of works by the same author from earliest to most recent; however, if the works have the same publication date, distinguish the dates with lowercase letters (*a, b, c,* and so on) assigned according to the order in which the entries for the works are listed in your bibliography.

7. Personal communication

State educational outcomes are often interpreted differently by teachers in the same school

(J. K. Jurgensen, personal communication, May 4, 2014).

Letters, memos, e-mail messages, interviews, and telephone conversations are cited in the text only, not in the reference list.

8. Indirect source

Bakewell (2010) points out how essential Montaigne believed "relaxation and affability" to be for one's well-being (p. 171).

OR

Montaigne (as cited in Bakewell, 2010) believed "relaxation and affability" to be essential for one's wellbeing (p. 171).

In the reference list, include a bibliographic entry for the source read, not for the original source. Use an indirect source only when you are unable to obtain the original.

9. Web source

Cite a web source such as an online newspaper or a website according to the guidelines already mentioned. If there is no date, use the abbreviation *n.d.* If no page numbers are provided in a source, give the number of the paragraph containing the words you are quoting, preceded by the abbreviation *para.*

Researchers believe that athletes should warm up before exercising, but according to Kolata (2010), "what's missing is evidence showing actual effects on performance" (para. 18).

If the source is divided into sections, use the section heading and the number of the paragraph following that heading: (Methods, para. 2).

(continued from page 361)
Publication Data

City and state. Identify the city in which the publisher of the work is located, including the two-letter U.S. Postal Service abbreviation for the state. If two or more cities are given on the title page, use the first one listed. If the publisher is a university press whose name mentions a state, do not include the state abbreviation. When a work has been published in a city outside the United States, include the name of the country.

Boston, MA:

Lancaster, PA:

University Park: Pennsylvania State University Press.

Oxford, England:

Publisher's name. Provide only enough of the publisher's name so that it can be identified clearly. Omit words such as *Publishers* and abbreviations such as *Inc.* However, include *Books* and *Press* when they are part of the publisher's name. The publisher's name follows the city and state or country, after a colon. A period ends this unit of information.

New Haven, CT: Yale University Press.

New York, NY: Harcourt.

Cambridge, England: Cambridge University Press.

AUTHORS IN REFERENCE ENTRIES

Citations begin with the authors' last names, followed by initials for first and middle names. Consult this section when deciding how to list different numbers of authors.

1. One author

Read, A. (2013, May). Rural sustainability: Factors and resources for communities to

consider. *Public Management 95*(4), 14–17. Retrieved from http://icma.org/en/press/

pm_magazine/about_pm

2. Two to seven authors

Zenz, G., Tahmasebi, N., & Risse, T. (2013). Towards mobile language evolution

exploitation. *Multimedia Tools and Applications 66*(1), 147–159. doi:10.1007/s11042-

011-0973-0

Articles and chapters. Do not italicize or place in quotation marks the titles of short works such as journal articles or book chapters. The title of an article or chapter appears before the book title or the name of the journal, magazine, or newspaper. Capitalize only the first word of the title and any proper nouns.

Treating posttraumatic stress disorder.

Subtitles. Always include any subtitle provided for a source. Use a colon to separate a main title and a subtitle. Capitalize only the first word of the subtitle and any proper nouns.

Reading images: The grammar of visual design.

Living in Baghdad: Realities and restrictions.

Volume, Issue, Chapter, and Page Numbers

Journal volume and issue numbers. A journal paginated *continuously* designates only the first page of the first issue in a volume as page 1. The first page of a subsequent issue in the same volume is given the page number that follows the last page number of the previous issue. In contrast, each issue of a journal paginated *separately* begins with page 1. When you use an article from a journal paginated continuously, provide only the volume number (italicized). When you use an article from a journal paginated separately, provide the issue number (placed in parentheses) directly after the volume number. Do not insert a space between the volume and issue numbers. Italicize only the volume number. Place a comma after this unit of information.

Journal of Applied Social Psychology, 32,

Behavior Therapy, 33(2),

Book chapters. Provide the numbers of the first and last pages of the relevant chapter preceded by the abbreviation pp. (for "pages"). Place this information in parentheses. Use an en dash (a short dash; see **41d** and **45g(2)**) between the page numbers.

New communitarian thinking (pp. 126–140).

(continued on page 362)

TIPS FOR IN-TEXT CITATIONS AND QUOTATIONS

When you cite a source, you may focus either on the researcher or on the researcher's findings:

- If you focus on the researcher, include that person's name in the sentence and place the publication date of the specific source (article, book, etc.) in parentheses directly after the name: *Diaz (2011) reported that all-night cram sessions do not improve performance*. When making subsequent references to the researcher within the same paragraph, you do not need to provide the date.

- If you focus on the researcher's findings, place the researcher's name and the date (separated by a comma) in parentheses at the end of the sentence: *All-night cram sessions do not improve performance (Diaz, 2011)*.

Punctuation of quotations depends on whether the quotation is forty or more words long or less than forty words long.

- If the quotation has forty or more words, set it off from the rest of the text as a block quotation without quotation marks. The parenthetical citation is placed at the end of the quotation *after* the end punctuation (in this case, a period):

Sulloway and Zweigenhaft (2010) report the effect of birth order on individuals' decisions to take more risks in sports:

> Data on 700 brothers whose major league careers ended by 2008, and who collectively played in more than 300,000 baseball games, reveal significantly heterogeneous results for birth order and its relationship to specific abilities in baseball, including skill, power, self-restraint, and risk taking. As predicted, younger brothers were more likely to engage in the risky business of stealing bases; they attempted more steals per game, and they were more likely to succeed in doing so. (p. 412)

- If the quotation has fewer than forty words, enclose it in double quotation marks and incorporate it into the text. Place the source and page number in parentheses (*p.* for "page" and *pp.* for "pages"). Use a period after the last parenthesis.

According to recent research on the effects of birth order, "laterborns are 1.5 times more likely than first-borns to engage in activities such as football, soccer, rugby, bobsledding, and skydiving" (Sulloway & Zweigenhaft, 2010, p. 412).

OR

Sulloway and Zweigenhaft (2010) report that "laterborns are 1.5 times more likely than first-borns to engage in activities such as football, soccer, rugby, bobsledding, and skydiving" (p. 412).

15b APA-STYLE REFERENCE LIST

All of the works you cite should be listed at the end of your paper, beginning on a separate page with the heading "References." The following tips will help you prepare your list.

TIPS FOR PREPARING A REFERENCE LIST

- Center the heading "References" one inch from the top of the page.

- Include entries for only those sources you explicitly cite in your paper but not for personal communications or original works cited in indirect sources.

- Arrange the list of works alphabetically by the author's last name or by the last name of the first author. For a work without an author, alphabetize the entry according to the first important word in the title.

- If you use more than one work by the same author(s), arrange the entries according to the date of publication, placing the entry with the earliest date first. (See item 6.) If two or more works by the same author(s) have the same publication date, the entries are arranged so that the titles of the works are in alphabetical order, according to the first important word in each title; lowercase letters are then added to the date (2015a, 2015b) to distinguish the works. (See item 7.)

- When an author's name appears both in a single-author entry and as the first name in a multiple-author entry, place the single-author entry first.

- Type the first line of each entry flush with the left margin and indent subsequent lines one-half inch or five spaces (a hanging indent).

- Double-space between lines of each entry and between entries.

ONLINE SOURCES

OTHER SOURCES

The following guidelines are for books, articles, and most electronic sources. For additional guidelines for documenting electronic sources, see pages 371–374.

GENERAL DOCUMENTATION GUIDELINES FOR PRINT-BASED SOURCES

Author or Editor

One author. Use the author's first initial and middle initial (if given) and his or her last name. Invert the initials and the last name; place a comma after the last name. Include a space between the first and middle initials. Any abbreviation or number that is part of a name, such as *Jr.* or *II*, is placed after a comma following the initials. Indicate the end of this information unit with a single period.	Walters, D. M. Thayer-Smith, M. S. Villa, R. P., Jr.
Two to seven authors. Invert the last names and initials of all authors. Use commas to separate last names from initials. Use an ampersand (&) (in addition to the comma) before the last name of the last author.	Vifian, I. R., & Kikuchi, K. Kempf, A. R., Cusack, R., & Evans, T. G.
Eight or more authors. List the first six names, add three ellipsis points, and include the last author's name.	Bauer, S. E., Berry, L., Hacket, N. P., Bach, R., Price, T., Brown, J. B., . . . Green, J.
Corporate or group author. Provide the author's full name.	Hutton Arts Foundation. Center for Neuroscience.
Editor. If a work has an editor or editors instead of an author or authors, include the abbreviation *Ed.* for "editor" or *Eds.* for "editors" in parentheses after the name(s).	Harris, B. E. (Ed.). Stroud, D. F., & Holst, L. F. (Eds.).

(continued on page 360)

(continued from page 359)
Publication Date

Books and journals. Provide the year of publication in parentheses, placing a period after the closing parenthesis. For books, this date can be found on the copyright page, which is the page following the title page (see citation map 15.2, on page 367). The publication date of a journal article can be found at the bottom of the first page of the article (see citation map 15.1, on page 365). For a work that has been accepted for publication but has not yet been published, place *in press* in parentheses. For a work without a date of publication, use *n.d.* in parentheses.

(2011).

(in press).

(n.d.).

Magazines and newspapers. For monthly publications, provide both the year and the month, separated by a comma. For daily publications, provide the year, month, and day. Use a comma between the year and the month.

(2015, January).

(2008, June 22).

Conferences and meetings. If a paper presented at a conference, symposium, or professional meeting is published, the publication date is given as the year only, in parentheses. For unpublished papers, provide the year and the month in which the gathering occurred, separated by a comma.

(2008)

(2014, September).

Title

Books. Capitalize only the first word and any proper nouns in a book title. Italicize the entire title and place a period at the end of this information unit.

An introduction to Vygotsky.

Avoiding work-related stress.

Journals, magazines, or newspapers. In the name of a journal, magazine, or newspaper, capitalize all major words, as well as any other words consisting of four or more letters. Italicize the entire name and place a comma after it.

Journal of Child Psychology,

Psychology Today,

Los Angeles Times,

3. Eight or more authors

Kawakami, K., Phills, C. E., Greenwald, A. G., Simard, D., Pontiero, J., Brnjas, A., . . .
Dovidio, J. F. (2012). In perfect harmony: Synchronizing the self to activated social
categories. *Journal of Personality and Social Psychology, 102*(3), 562–575.

4. No author listed

Atlas of the world (19th ed.). (2012). New York, NY: Oxford University Press.

Start the entry with the title.

5. Corporate author

American Psychiatric Association. (2013). *Diagnostic and statistical manual of mental disorders*
(5th ed.). Washington, DC: Author.

When the author and the publisher are the same, use the word *Author*
as the publisher at the end of the entry.

6. Two or more works by the same author
The book published first is listed first.

Eagleman, D. (2009). *Sum: Tales from the afterlives.* Edinburgh, Scotland: Canongate Books.

Eagleman, D. (2011). *Incognito: The secret lives of the brain.* New York, NY: Pantheon Books.

7. Two or more works by the same author published in the same year
If works appear in the same year, list them alphabetically by title and
add letters (*a*, *b*, and so on) to the year.

Wheelen, C. (2013a). *The centrist manifesto.* New York, NY: Norton.

Wheelen, C. (2013b). *Naked statistics: Stripping the dread from the data.* New York, NY: Norton.

ARTICLES (PRINT)

8. Article in a journal paginated by volume

North, M. S., & Fiske, S. T. (2013). Act your (old) age: Prescriptive, ageist biases over
succession, consumption, and identity. *Personality and Social Psychology Bulletin, 39,*
720–734. doi:10.1177/0146167213480043

Some journals include a DOI (digital object identifier) on the first page
of an article, in both print and electronic versions. Include the DOI at
the end of the entry.

9. Article in a journal paginated by issue

Hall-Lew, L., & Stephens, N. (2013). Country talk. *Journal of English Linguistics, 40*(3), 256–280.

Provide the issue number (placed in parentheses) directly after the volume number (italicized). (See citation map 15.1 for an example.)

10. Abstract of a journal article

Huang, H. D., & Hung, S. A. (2013). Comparing the effects of test anxiety on independent and integrated speaking test performance [Abstract]. *TESOL Quarterly, 47*(2), 244–269.

11. Article in a monthly, biweekly, or weekly magazine

Finkel, M. (2013, June). First Australians. *National Geographic, 223*(6), 66–83.

For monthly publications, provide both the year and the month. For magazines published weekly or biweekly, add the day of the issue: (2015, May 8).

12. Article in a newspaper

Das, A. (2014, October 24). Benefit puts the wind in his sails. *The Wall Street Journal*, pp. C1-C2.

Include both the section letter and the page numbers.

13. Letter to the editor

Budington, N. (2010, July 20). Social class and college admissions [Letter to the editor]. *The New York Times*, p. A26.

14. Editorial

Editorial: Print is dead! Or is it? [Editorial]. (2012). *New Oxford Review, 79*(10), 4–7.

15. Book review

Weissinger, J. (2012). Retromania: Pop culture's addiction to its own past [Review of the book *Retromania: Pop culture's addiction to its own past,* by S. Reynolds]. *Journal of Popular Music Studies, 24*(2), 247–254.

If the review does not have its own title, use the title of the book, but do not italicize it.

CITATION MAP 15.1: ARTICLE IN A JOURNAL, APA STYLE

To cite an article from a journal, include the following elements. If an issue number is provided, include that as well.

FIRST PAGE OF ARTICLE

Tricksters and the Marketing of Breakfast Cereals ← **Title of article**

THOMAS GREEN ← **Author**

BREAKFAST CEREALS ARE SOLD BY TRICKSTERS. FROM LUCKY THE Leprechaun to the Cookie Crook to the mischievous live-action squirrels who vend General Mills Honey Nut Clusters, an astounding number of Saturday morning television commercials feature 30-second dramatizations of trickster tales that are designed to promote breakfast cereals. True, breakfast cereals are not the only products sold by tricksters, and not all cereals are sold by tricksters—especially in the last decade. But the association is common enough to persist as an unexamined assumption that seems obvious to most Americans once it is pointed out. Naturally, breakfast cereals are often sold by animated tricksterish mascot characters, and naturally such commercials feature motifs and narrative patterns that are common in trickster tales. But the perception of an inherent internal logic in this scheme overlooks a couple of key questions. Why, for example, are tricksters considered a particularly appropriate or effective means of marketing breakfast cereals? And why breakfast cereals in particular (and a few other breakfast products), almost to the exclusion of tricksters in other types of marketing campaigns? The answers to these questions, it turns out, may lie back in the semi-mystical, pseudoreligious origins of prepared breakfast foods and the mating of the mythology of those foods with the imperatives of the competitive, prepared-foods marketplace.

Title of journal | **Volume number** | **Issue number** | **Year of publication**

The Journal of Popular Culture, Vol. 40, No. 1, 2007 ←
© 2007, Copyright the Authors
Journal compilation © 2007, Blackwell Publishing, Inc.

REFERENCE LIST ENTRY FOR AN ARTICLE FROM A JOURNAL

Author | **Year of publication** | **Title of article**

Green, T. (2007). Tricksters and the marketing of breakfast cereals. *The Journal of Popular Culture, 40*(1), 49–68.

Title of journal | **Volume number** | **Issue number** | **Page numbers**

BOOKS (PRINT)

When preparing an entry for the reference list, be sure to copy the bibliographic information directly from the title page of the book (see citation map 15.2).

16. Book with author(s) listed

Pollan, M. (2013). *Cooked: A history of transformation.* New York, NY: Penguin.

Skov, V., & Robbins, A. (2015). *Integrative art therapy and depression: A transformative approach.* London, England: Jessica Kingsley.

Capitalize only the first word and any proper nouns in the title and subtitle. Italicize both title and subtitle. Include the city of publication and the United States Postal Service two-letter state abbreviation. For books published outside the United States, include the country.

17. Book with editor(s)

Reich, J. W., Zautra, A. J., & Hall, J. S. (Eds.). (2012). *Handbook of adult resilience.* New York, NY: Guilford Press.

Provide only enough of the publisher's name so that it can be identified clearly. Omit *Publishers, Inc.,* and *Co.,* but retain *Books* and *Press.*

18. Edition after the first

Radvansky, G. A., & Ashcraft, M. H. (2013). *Cognition* (6th ed.). Boston, MA: Pearson.

19. Translation

Gombrowicz, W. (2014). *Trans-Atlantyk* (D. Borchardt, Trans.). New Haven, CT: Yale University Press. (Original work published 1953)

20. Multivolume work

Hawthorne, N. (1962–1997). *The centenary edition of the works of Nathaniel Hawthorne* (Vols. 1–23). Columbus: Ohio State University Press.

If the multivolume work was published over a period of more than one year, use the range of years for the publication date. If the publisher is a university press whose name mentions a state, do not include the state abbreviation.

CITATION MAP 15.2: BOOK, APA STYLE

Include the following elements when citing a book.

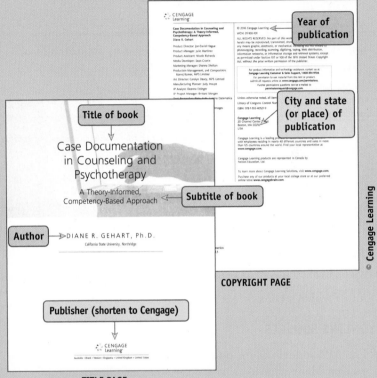

Year of publication

City and state (or place) of publication

COPYRIGHT PAGE

Title of book

Case Documentation in Counseling and Psychotherapy

A Theory-Informed, Competency-Based Approach ← Subtitle of book

Author ▷DIANE R. GEHART, Ph.D.
California State University, Northridge

Publisher (shorten to Cengage)

CENGAGE Learning

TITLE PAGE

REFERENCE LIST ENTRY FOR A BOOK

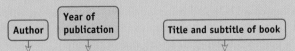

Author | Year of publication | Title and subtitle of book

Gehart, D. R. (2016). *Case documentation in counseling and psychotherapy: A theory-informed, competency-based approach.* Stamford, CT: Cengage.

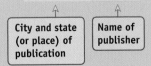

City and state (or place) of publication | Name of publisher

© Cengage Learning

21. Government report

Executive Office of the President. (2003). *Economic report of the President, 2003* (GPO Publication No. 040-000-0760-1). Washington, DC: Government Printing Office.

22. Chapter or article from an edited book

Empson, R. (2007). Enlivened memories: Recalling absence and loss in Mongolia. In J. Carsten (Ed.), *Ghosts of memory: Essays on remembrance and relatedness* (pp. 58–82). Malden, MA: Blackwell.

23. Selection from a reference work

Miceli, G. (2010). Agrammatism. In H. A. Whitaker (Ed.), *Concise encyclopedia of brain and language* (pp. 14–17). Amsterdam, Netherlands: Elsevier.

24. Republished book

Petersen, J. (2009). *Our street* (B. Rensen, Trans.). London, England: Faber. (Original work published 1938)

25. Book with a title within its title

Wheen, F. (2007). *Marx's* Das Kapital: *A biography*. New York, NY: Atlantic Monthly Press.

A title within a book title is not italicized.

ONLINE SOURCES

The APA guidelines for online sources are similar to those for print sources. Many scholarly journals use a Digital Object Identifier (DOI) to simplify searching for an article. The DOI is listed on the first page of the article, which usually contains the abstract. Citation map 15.3 shows the location of a DOI and other pertinent bibliographic information on the first page of an online journal. If available, insert the DOI (without a period following it) at the end of the entry.

To cite an article without a DOI, use the URL for the periodical's home page. If the URL has to continue on a new line, break it before a punctuation mark or other special character. Do not add a period after the URL. Citation map 15.4 shows a citation that includes a URL.

CITATION MAP 15.3: ARTICLE IN A DATABASE, APA STYLE

Include the following elements when citing an article in a database. If there is no Digital Object Identifier (DOI), use the URL for the journal's home page instead of the URL of the article.

DATABASE RECORD FOR AN ARTICLE

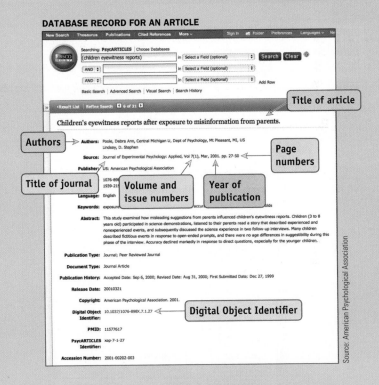

Source: American Psychological Association

REFERENCE LIST ENTRY FOR AN ARTICLE IN A DATABASE

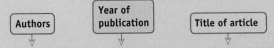

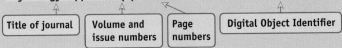

Poole, D. A., & Lindsay, D. S. (2001). Children's eyewitness reports after exposure to misinformation from parents. *Journal of Experimental Psychology: Applied, 7*(1), 27–50. doi:10.1037//1076-898X.7.1.27

CITATION MAP 15.4: SECTION IN A WEB DOCUMENT, APA STYLE

Include the following elements when citing a section in a document you find on the web.

TITLE PAGE OF A WORK FROM A WEBSITE

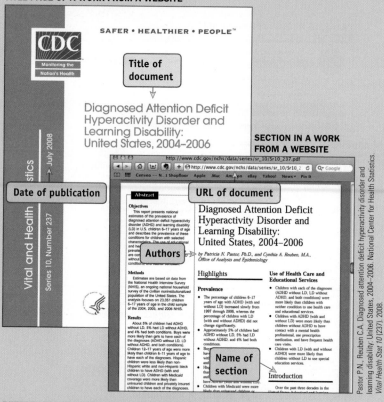

SECTION IN A WORK FROM A WEBSITE

REFERENCE LIST ENTRY FOR A DOCUMENT FROM THE WEB

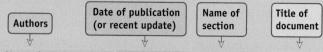

Authors	Date of publication (or recent update)	Name of section	Title of document

Pastor, P. N., and Reuben, C. A. (2008, July). Introduction. In *Diagnosed Attention Deficit Hyperactivity Disorder and Learning Disability: United States, 2004–2006*. Retrieved from http://www.cdc.gov /nchs/data/series/sr_10/sr10_237.pdf

URL of document

26. Article from a database

Hill, E. J., Erickson, J. J., Holmes, E. K., & Ferris, M. (2010). Workplace flexibility, work hours, and work-life conflict: Finding an extra day or two. *Journal of Family Psychology, 24*(3), 349–358. doi:10.1037 /a0019282

Marantz, A. (2015, January 5). The virologist. *The New Yorker, 91*(1), 20–26. Retrieved from http://www.newyorker.com

27. Article from an online journal

Buhrmester, M. D., Blanton, H., & Swann, W. B., Jr. (2011). Implicit self-esteem: Nature, measurement, and a new way forward. *Journal of Personality and Social Psychology, 100*(2), 365–385. doi:10.1037 /a0021341

Stewart, J. (2014). Violence and nonviolence in Buddhist animal ethics. *Journal of Buddhist Ethics, 21*, 623–655. Retrieved from http://blogs.dickinson.edu/buddhistethics/

28. Article from an online magazine

Saletan, W. (2008, August 27). Unfinished race: Race, genes, and the future of medicine. *Slate.* Retrieved from http://www.slate.com

29. Article from an online newspaper

Shellenbarger, S. (2010, July 21). Kids quit the team for more family time. *The Wall Street Journal.* Retrieved from http://online.wsj.com /home-page

30. Online book

Pine, R. C. (2004). *Science and the human prospect.* Retrieved from http://home.honolulu .hawaii.edu/~pine/book1-2.html

If access to the book is not free, use "Available from" instead of "Retrieved from." If you are reading a book on a Kindle or similar device, you may use either the DOI or place of download instead of the publication data.

31. Online book chapter

Brady, V. (2006). A flaw in the nation-building process: Negotiating the sacred in our multicultural society. In E. B. Coleman & K. White (Eds.), *Negotiating the sacred: Blasphemy and sacrilege in a multicultural society* (pp. 43–49). Retrieved from http://epress.anu.edu.au/nts _citation.html

32. Blog post

Myers, P. Z. (2015, January 6). The genetic load problem [Web log post]. Retrieved from

http://scienceblogs.com/pharyngula/2015/01/06/the-genetic-load-problem/

If you are quoting a comment instead of the original post, place in square brackets *Web log comment.*

33. Lecture notes posted online

Gabaix , X. (2004). *Lecture 14: Happiness* [Lecture notes]. Retrieved from http://ocw.mit

.edu/courses/economics/14-13-economics-and -psychology-spring-2004/lecture-notes/

34. Short work from a website

Ennis, R. H. (2002, July 20). *An outline of goals for a critical thinking curriculum and its*

assessment. Retrieved from http://faculty.ed.uiuc .edu/rhennis/outlinegoalsctcurassess3

.html

When the work is from a large website, such as one sponsored by a university or governmental body, provide the name of the host organization before the URL. Do not include a date with the retrieval information unless the work is likely to change or be updated, as in a wiki for example.

Mollett, A., Moran, D., & Dunleavy, P. (2011). *Using Twitter in university research, teaching*

and impact activities: A guide for academics and researchers. Retrieved January 10, 2015,

from London School of Economics website: http://blogs.lse.ac.uk/impactofsocialsciences

/files/2011/11/Published-Twitter_Guide_Sept_2011.pdf

American School Counselor Association. (2006). *Position statement: Equity for all students.*

Retrieved from http://asca2.timberlakepublishing.com /content.asp?contentid=503

When no author is listed, use the name of the organization hosting the website as the author of the document.

35. E-mail messages and other personal communication

Personal communications such as e-mail messages, letters, interviews, and telephone conversations are not included in the reference list but should be cited in the text as follows: (S. L. Johnson, personal communication, September 3, 2013).

36. Online encyclopedia

Dowe, P. (2007). Causal processes. In E. N. Zalta (Ed.), *The Stanford encyclopedia of philosophy* (Fall 2008 ed.). Retrieved from http://plato .stanford.edu/archives/sum2007 /entries/cognitive-science/

37. Wiki entry

Déjà vu. (n.d.). In *Wikipedia.* Retrieved May 20, 2013, from http://en.wikipedia.org/wiki /Deja_vu

If no date is provided, use the abbreviation *n.d.*

38. Article in a newsletter

Brady, B. Essential strategies for teaching large classes. (2013, August). *TESOL Connections.* Retrieved from http://www.tesol.org/read-and -publish/newsletters-other-publications/ tesol-connections

39. Report online

Yones, M. (n.d.). *Psychology of happiness and unhappiness.* Retrieved from International Institute of Management website: http://www.iim-edu .org/executivejournal/index.htm

If the report has a number, mention the number in parentheses after the title: *Title* (Report No. XX).

40. Online government document

Pashler, H., Bain, P., Bottge, B., Graesser, A., Koedinger, K., McDaniel, M., & Metcalfe, J. (2007). *Organizing instruction and study to improve student learning* (NCER 2007–2004). Washington, DC: National Center for Education Research, Institute of Education Sciences, U.S. Department of Education. Retrieved from Institute of Education Sciences website: http://ncer.ed.gov

If no authors had been listed, this entry would have been written as follows:

National Center for Education Research, Institute of Education Sciences. (2007). *Organizing instruction and study to improve student learning* (NCER 2007–2004). Retrieved from http://ncer.ed.gov

41. Online audio and video

Davies, D. (Host). (2010, July 13). A psychiatrist's prescription for his profession [Audio file].

In T. Gross & D. Miller (Executive producers), *Fresh air.* Retrieved from http://www.npr.org
/templates/story/story.php?storyId=13

For podcasts, place the main contributor at the beginning of the entry; place in parentheses the contributor's role (producer, director, writer, host, presenter). Place between square brackets the medium (audio file, video file, podcast, webcast).

Gopnik, A. (Presenter). (2009, July 28). Moments of absolute absorption [Video file]. In

D. McGee & P. W. Kunhardt (Executive producers), *This emotional life.* Retrieved from

http://www.pbs.org/thisemotionallife /perspective/meaning-happiness

OTHER SOURCES

42. Film, video, or DVD

Seidler, D. (Writer), & Hooper, T. (Director). (2011). *The king's speech* [Motion picture].
England: Momentum Pictures.

43. Television series episode

Weiner, M. (Writer), & Hornbacher, S. (Director). (2013). The doorway [Television series
episode]. In M. Weiner (Executive producer), *Mad men.* New York, NY: AMC.

If referring to the series as a whole, write *Television series* in the square brackets.

44. Advertisement

RosettaStone [Advertisement]. (2010, July). *National Geographic, 218*(1), 27.

45. Dissertation from a database

Aakre, J. M. (2010). Attributional style in schizophrenia: Associations with suspiciousness
and depressed mood (Doctoral dissertation). Retrieved from http://www.ohiolink.edu

46. Published interview

Bell, G. (2012). Why people really love technology: An interview with Genevieve Bell
[Interview by A. C. Madrigal]. Retrieved from http://www.theatlantic.com/

An interview you conducted personally is considered a personal communication. See item 35.

47. Map or chart

Central Intelligence Agency (Cartographer). (2011). China physiography [Map]. Retrieved from https://www.cia.gov/library/publications /cia-maps-publications/

48. Work of art

Bates, D. (1995). *Male head IV* [Sculpture]. Fort Worth, TX: Modern Art Museum of Fort Worth.

Condo, G. (2009). *The fallen butler* [Painting]. New York, NY: Museum of Modern Art.

49. Photograph

[Photograph of Louise Bieriot]. (1909). Bain Collection. Library of Congress, Washington, DC.

If you are using a photograph you have taken yourself, you do not need to include an entry on your references page.

50. Lecture, speech, or address

The White House, Office of the Press Secretary. (2013, April 23). *Remarks by the president at teacher of the year event.* Retrieved from http://www.whitehouse.gov/the-press-office /2013/04/23/remarks-president-teacher-year-event

15c SAMPLE APA-STYLE PAPER

The APA recognizes that a paper may have to be modified so that it adheres to an instructor's requirements. The following boxes offer tips for preparing a title page, an abstract page, and the body of a typical student paper. For tips on preparing a reference list, see **15b**.

TIPS FOR PREPARING THE TITLE PAGE OF AN APA-STYLE PAPER

- The title page includes both the full title of the paper and a shortened version of it. The shortened version, along with a page number, is placed in the header. On the left side of the header, include the words "Running head:" (note the colon) and a version of your title that consists of no more than fifty characters. Use all uppercase letters for this title. On the right side of the header, insert the page number. The title page is page 1 of your paper.

- Place the full title in the upper half of the page, with your name below it. You may include your affiliation or a course name or number if your instructor requests one. Double-space these lines.

TIPS FOR PREPARING THE ABSTRACT AND THE BODY OF AN APA-STYLE PAPER

- The header for the remaining parts of the paper (including the abstract page, which is page 2) is similar to the header on the title page. It should have the shortened title on the left and the page number on the right. The body of the paper begins on page 3.
- Center the word "Abstract" one inch from the top of the page.
- Unless your instructor provides a word limit, be sure that your abstract is no more than 250 words. For advice on summarizing, see **11e**.
- Double-space throughout the body of the abstract. Do not indent the first line of the abstract.
- Provide the title again on page 3. Center it one inch from the top of the page.
- Use one-inch margins on both the left and right sides of all pages.
- Double-space throughout the body of the paper, indenting each paragraph one-half inch or five to seven spaces.
- Use headings to set off sections and subsections. The APA specifies five levels of headings, but most papers that students write require only the first two or three levels (see the student example in **14e**):

Level 1 headings are centered and boldfaced, with each major word capitalized:

Methodology for Data Analysis

Level 2 headings are flush with the left margin and boldfaced, with each major word capitalized:

Materials and Procedures

Level 3 headings are boldfaced and indented. They begin with a capital letter and end with a period:

>   **Sampling procedures.**

Level 4 headings are boldfaced, italicized, and indented. They begin with a capital letter and end with a period:

>   ***Use of a random generator.***

Level 5 headings are italicized and indented. They begin with a capital letter and end with a period:

>   *Problems with general data points.*

Running head: SOCIAL STATUS OF AN ART   1

The running head should consist of no more than 50 characters

Use one-inch margins on both sides of the page

The Social Status of an Art:

Historical and Current Trends in Tattooing

Rachel L. Pinter and Sarah M. Cronin

Central Washington University

If required by the instructor, the course name and number replace the institutional affiliation

SOCIAL STATUS OF AN ART

2

Abstract

Current research demonstrates that the social practice of tattooing has changed greatly over the years. Not only have the images chosen for tattoos and the demographic of people getting tattoos changed, but the ideology behind tattooing itself has evolved. This paper first briefly describes the cross-cultural history of the practice. It then examines current social trends in the United States and related ideological issues.

Center the heading

An abstract generally contains between 150 and 250 words

The Social Status of an Art: Historical and
Current Trends in Tattooing

Center the title

Tattoos, defined as marks made by inserting pigment into the skin, have existed throughout history in countless cultures. Currently, tattoos are considered popular art forms. They can be seen on men and women from all walks of life in the United States, ranging from a trainer at the local gym to a character on a television show or even a sociology professor. Due to an increase in the popularity of tattooing, studies of tattooing behavior have proliferated as researchers attempt to identify trends. This paper seeks to explore both the history of tattooing and its current practice in the United States.

Use one-inch margins on both sides of the page

The writers' thesis statement forecasts the content of the essay

Artifacts such as 7,000-year-old engravings attest to the long history of tattooing (Krcmarik, 2003). Tattoos have been identified on a number of Egyptian and Nubian mummies (Krcmarik, 2003), as well as on Ötzi, the 5,300-year-old Iceman mummy found in the Alps (Owen, 2013). However, unlike the tattoos displayed today, early tattoos may have had purposes other than adornment. Ötzi's tattoos, for example, are thought to mark acupuncture points (Owen, 2013).

The writers provide historical and cultural information about tattooing

The practice of tattooing is not only old but widespread as well. In Asia, tattooing has existed for thousands of years in Chinese, Japanese, Middle Eastern, and Indian cultures (Krcmarik, 2003). In the British Isles, the pre-Roman Picts living in present-day Scotland practiced tattooing, but the type of tattooing recognized today did not flourish until the 19th century (Perzanowski, 2013). Many of the sailors traveling with Captain James Cook returned to England with tales of exotic tattooing practices and sometimes with actual tattoos.

SOCIAL STATUS OF AN ART   4

The Samoans in the South Pacific, whom Cook and his crew would have seen, are famous for their centuries-old tattooing practice, known as *tatau*—the word from which *tattoo* is said to have originated. The Maori of New Zealand are also well known for their hand-carved facial tattoos, known as *Moko* (see Figure 1).

In the western hemisphere, tattooing has been noted in the written accounts of European explorers and colonists who encountered tattooed members of indigenous tribes such as the Mayans in Central America and the Natchez who lived in present-day Mississippi (Perzanowski, 2013). Tattooing became popular in the United States during the 1900s and has experienced advances and retreats in social acceptance since then. Starting in the 1960s, (Krcmarik, 2003).

Clearly, the history of tattooing spans generations and cultures. The practice has gained and lost popularity, often as a result of rather extreme changes in the ideologies supporting or discouraging it. This roller-coaster pattern of acceptance is well demonstrated in the United States. Since the

Tim Graham/Getty Images

Figure 1. A Maori man with a facial tattoo. From Tim Graham (Photographer). (n.d.). Traditional Tattoos on Face of Maori Warrior [Photograph]. Retrieved from http://www.gettyimages.com/detail/photo /maori-warrior-uk-high-res-stock-photography/sb10066698pt-002

SOCIAL STATUS OF AN ART 5

19th century, the wearing of tattoos has allowed for subculture identification by such persons as sailors, bikers, circus "freak" performers, and prison inmates (DeMello, 1995). As a collective group behavior indicating deviant subculture membership, tattooing flourished during this time but remained plagued by negative stereotypes and associations. In the last 15 years, however, the practice has represented a more individualistic yet mainstream means of body adornment. As Figure 2 illustrates, it is not unusual to see a white-collar worker sporting a tattoo.

The writers discuss changing perspectives on the appropriateness of tattoos

Tattooing is now common among both teenagers and older adults, men and women, urbanites and suburbanites, the college-educated and the uneducated, and the rich as well as the poor (Kosut, 2006). Today, according to The Harris Poll (2012), 21% of adults in the United States have one or more tattoos. Table 1 indicates the wide range of Americans wearing tattoos in 2003, 2008, and 2012.

Citation of a work by one author

The trend toward acceptance of tattoos may be a result of how American society views the people who wear them. Earlier, tattoos were

Eric Anthony Johnson/Photolibrary/Getty Images

Figure 2. Tattoos are becoming more common among middle-class professionals. From Eric Anthony Johnson (Photographer). (n.d.). Father with Tattooed Arm Holding Baby Daughter [Photograph]. Retrieved from http://www.gettyimages.com/detail/photo/father-with-tattooed-arm -holding-baby-high-res-stock-photography/128263816

SOCIAL STATUS OF AN ART 6

Table 1

Percentages of American Adults With One or More Tatoos

Category	Year		
	2003	2008	2012
All adults	16	14	21
Region			
East	14	12	21
Midwest	14	10	21
South	15	13	18
West	20	20	26
Age range			
18–24	13	9	22
25–29	36	32	30
30–39	28	25	38
40–49	14	12	27
50–64	10	8	11
65+	7	9	5
Sex			
Male	16	15	19
Female	15	13	23

Note. Adapted from "One in Five U.S. Adults Now Has a Tattoo," by S. Braverman, 2012, *Harris Interactive.*"

depicted in mainstream print and visual media as worn by people with low socioeconomic or marginal status; now, they are considered to be an artful expression among celebrities as well as educated middle- and upper-class individuals (Kosut, 2006). This shift in the symbolic status of tattoos— to a form of self-expression among the social elite rather than deviant expression among the lower classes—has allowed tattoos to be obtained in greater numbers, owing in great part to the importance placed on self-expression in the United States. Even in the workplace, where employees had often been forbidden to display tattoos, employers now "take advantage of the open-mindedness and innovation that younger [tattooed] employees bring into the workplace" (Org, 2003, p. D1).

SOCIAL STATUS OF AN ART   7

As the popularity and acceptability of tattoos has increased, tattooing has become part of the greater consumer culture and has thus undergone the process of commercialization that frequently occurs in the United States (Perzanowski, 2013). Tattoos are now acquired as status symbols, and their prevalence helps to sell tattoo maintenance products, clothing, and skateboards (Kosut, 2006). This introduction into the consumer culture allows tattoos to gain even more popularity; they are now intertwined with mainstream culture.

Statistics on the frequency of tattooing among specific age groups generally show increases (Armstrong, Owen, Roberts, & Koch, 2002; Mayers, Judelson, Moriarty, & Rundell, 2002), although one study (Corso, 2008) showed a slight decrease. The Harris Poll has been tracking the popularity of tattoos since 2003. Between 2003 and 2012, popularity among adults increased by 5%. The most likely to have tattoos are between the ages of 30 and 39, and the least likely to have tattoos are those 65 and older. Women are currently 4% more likely to have tattoos than men, though before 2012 men were more likely to have tattoos.

Significantly, the increase in acquisition of tattoos has resulted in trends concerning the images and locations of tattoos, which appear to be divided along lines of gender. Many of the tattoo images commonly found on men include, but are not limited to, death themes, various wildlife, military insignia, tribal armbands, and family crests or last names. During the 1980s, cartoon images such as Bugs Bunny and the Tasmanian Devil were also popular for males. Males choose various locations for tattoos, but the most popular male sites are the upper body, especially the chest and arms, according to tattoo artist Mike Powell (personal communication, March 20, 2015). Conversely, females often obtain tattoos that symbolize traditional femininity. A noticeable trend for females in the 1980s was the rose tattoo, which was often located on the breast or ankle. Stars, hearts, butterflies, and other flowers now rival the rose in popularity.

Two citations of articles, both written by four authors, are separated by a semicolon

The writers list statistics to support a claim

SOCIAL STATUS OF AN ART 8

The writers include a photograph to support a point

The ankle continues to be a popular location for females today. Other popular spots for tattoos include the hip, foot (see Figure 3), and back. Regardless of their site, tattoos on women are now larger than they used to be (M. Powell, personal communication, July 12, 2015).

The art of tattooing has existed in many culturally determined forms throughout human history, and its current manifestations are as varied as the cultures themselves. However, based on the current literature, the social behavior of tattooing is still quite common in the United States. In fact, Kosut (2006) argues, "New generations of American children are growing up in a cultural landscape that is more tattoo-friendly and tattoo-flooded than any other time in history" (p. 1037). Because today's children

Last paragraph is the conclusion

see tattoos and tattoo-related products everywhere, usually in neutral or positive situations, they will likely be more accepting of tattoos than earlier generations were. Certainly, the tattooing trend shows no signs of decreasing significantly.

ColorBlind Images/Blend Images/Corbis

Figure 3. Many females who get a tattoo choose to have it on the foot. From ColorBlind Images (Photographer). (n.d.). Tattoo on a Young Woman's Foot [Photograph]. Retrieved from https://secure.corbisimages.com /stock-photo/royalty-free/42-15416265/tattoo-on-a-young-womans-foot

References

Armstrong, M. L., Owen, D. C., Roberts, A. E., & Koch, J. R. (2002).

College students and tattoos: Influence of image, identity, and

family. *Journal of Psychosocial Nursing, 40*(10), 20–29.

Braverman, S. (2012, February 23). *One in five U.S. adults now has a

tattoo.* Retrieved from http://www.harrisinteractive.com/NewsRoom

/HarrisPolls/tabid/447/mid/1508/articleId/970/ctl

/ReadCustom%20Default/Default.aspx

Corso, R. A. (2008, February 12). *Three in ten Americans with a tattoo say

having one makes them feel sexier.* Retrieved from http://www

.harrisinteractive.com/Insights/HarrisVault.aspx

DeMello, M. (1995). Not just for bikers anymore: Popular representations

of American tattooing. *Journal of Popular Culture, 29*(3), 37–53.

Retrieved from http://www.wiley.com/WileyCDA/WileyTitle

/productCd-JPCU.html

Kosut, M. (2006). An ironic fad: The commodification and consumption of

tattoos. *Journal of Popular Culture, 39*(6), 1035–1049. Retrieved from

http://www.wiley.com/WileyCDA/WileyTitle/productCd-JPCU.html

Krcmarik, K. L. (2003). *History of tattooing.* Retrieved from Michigan

State University website: http://www.msu.edu/~krcmari1

/individual/history.html

Mayers, L. B., Judelson, D. A., Moriarity, B. W., & Rundell, K. W. (2002).

Prevalence of body art (body piercing and tattooing) in university

undergraduates and incidence of medical complications. *Mayo

Clinic Proceedings, 77*, 20–34.

Center the
heading

Alphabetize
the entries
according to
the author's
(or first
author's)
last name

Indent second
and subsequent
lines of each
entry one-half
inch or five
spaces

No period
follows a
URL at the
end of an
entry

SOCIAL STATUS OF AN ART 10

Org, M. (2003, August 28). The tattooed executive. *The Wall Street Journal*. Retrieved from http://online.wsj.com/public/us

Owen, J. (2013, October 16). *5 surprising facts about Ötzi the Iceman*. Retrieved from http://news.nationalgeographic.com/news/2013 /10/131016-otzi-ice-man-mummy-five-facts

Perzanowski, A. (2013). Tattoos & IP norms. *Minnesota Law Review*, *98*(2), 511–591. Retrieved from http://www.minnesotalawreview.org

An entry for an article from a database without a Digital Object Identifier (DOI) includes the URL for the journal's home page.

16 | WRITING IN THE HUMANITIES

The humanities include disciplines such as art and art history, history, film, music, dance, philosophy, religion, cultural studies, rhetoric, foreign languages and literatures, and English studies. (For information on writing about literature, see chapter **12**.) Scholars in the humanities analyze the artifacts of human culture to better record, reconstruct, and explain the wide variety of human experience, both past and present. Common writing assignments in the humanities include the informal reflection or response, explanation, analysis, interpretation, evaluation or review, and synthesis projects.

In courses in the humanities, you will write in a number of ways and for various purposes; it is therefore important to analyze your rhetorical situation and identify a rhetorical opportunity before you begin drafting. This chapter will help you

- determine the audience, purpose, and research question for a paper in the humanities (**16a**);
- decide which types of evidence, sources, and reasoning to use (**16b**);
- follow appropriate style, formatting, and documentation conventions (**16c**);
- understand the types of writing assignments you are likely to receive in humanities courses (**16d**); and
- analyze a sample critical review (**16e**) and a sample critical analysis (**16f**).

16a | AUDIENCE, PURPOSE, AND THE RESEARCH QUESTION

Before writing a paper for a humanities course, you need to determine your rhetorical opportunity (**1b**), your audience (**1c**), and your purpose (**1d**). Establishing your rhetorical opportunity (what you are writing in response to—and why) will not only help you shape your research question, it will also help you align your purpose with your audience.

Figure 16.1: A critical review of an undergraduate art exhibition could be assigned in a humanities course.

Usually, your audience includes your instructor, but it can also include other readers, such as your classmates, members of the campus community, townspeople, and alumni. If you are writing a review of an exhibition installed by the visual arts department, your audience might include all those types of readers. Knowing who comprises your audience helps you determine how much background information to provide, how technical your language should be, and what kinds of evidence will be most persuasive.

Most researchers in the humanities write to convey an interpretation, evaluation, or history of a specific event, social movement, or cultural artifact (written words, artworks, and other creations). Once you have determined your purpose for writing, you can develop a specific research question that will help you find and evaluate sources and use those sources responsibly (see chapters **8–11**). The following are some research questions that scholars in the humanities might pose about the experience of African Americans during the civil rights movement:

Questions about causes or purposes (analysis)
What events stimulated the Montgomery bus boycott during the civil rights movement?

Questions about consequences (interpretation)
How did jazz musician John Coltrane contribute to the success of the civil rights movement?

Questions about process (explanation)
What did civil rights workers do to gain national attention for their cause?

Questions about definitions or categories
What kinds of protest tactics did different African American leaders, such as Martin Luther King and Malcolm X, advocate for during the civil rights movement?

Questions about values (evaluation)
What does the struggle for equal rights for African Americans reveal about the values of white Americans during the 1960s?

Response and synthesis projects would engage different questions:

Questions of response
How do you feel about the progress of civil rights in the United States?

Questions of synthesis
How has social inequality remained constant throughout U.S. history?

16b   EVIDENCE, SOURCES, AND REASONING

Because writers in the humanities observe and interpret cultural artifacts in order to understand and explain human experience, they rarely make statements of absolute fact. Instead they develop their interpretations in several steps: first, they develop a **summary** for each text or artifact, recording the main points of each (**11e**); second, they conduct detailed analyses of texts or other cultural artifacts, relying on textual evidence, logical reasoning, the historical record, and the work of other scholars in order to present a compelling argument. Analyzing and combining multiple sources into a reasonable claim is referred to as **synthesis** (**11g**). Then, after considering and synthesizing the available evidence, researchers advance a moderate claim (**7d(1)**), or **thesis**, that expresses their interpretation of a work of art, performance, movement, or experience (**2c**).

(1) Using primary sources

Most researchers in the humanities begin their studies by working directly with a **primary source**, which can be a person, an object, or a text. For art historians, this primary source might be a drawing, a painting, or a sculpture. Art historians evaluate their primary sources by paying attention to the formal qualities of the work (line, color, shape, texture, composition, and so forth) and to images or themes that might have symbolic importance. Often, they summarize the artifact's distinctive qualities and themes. They then write an explanation of how these features work together to create meaning in the work. For instance, in a classic analysis of Jan van Eyck's *Arnolfini Portrait* (figure 16.2) in his book *Early Netherlandish Painting*, art historian Erwin Panofsky argues that the elaborate details of the scene, such as the dog (representing fidelity), the two additional figures reflected in a mirror on the wall who may have served as witnesses, and van Eyck's signature on the wall indicate that the scene documents a wedding. More recently, art historians have challenged this

interpretation: in her article "In the Name of God and Profit: Jan van Eyck's *Arnolfini Portrait*," Margaret Carroll argues that the painting does not portray a wedding but is an important document that gives the wife power of attorney; in "The Arnolfini Double Portrait: A Simple Solution," Margaret Koster suggests instead that the painting is a memorial for Arnolfini's wife, painted after her death. Each of these different interpretations synthesizes formal and stylistic evidence from the painting itself, previous scholarship, and expert knowledge of the cultural context in which it was created.

Figure 16.2: Jan van Eyck's *Arnolfini Portrait*, from the fifteenth century, has been the subject of many analyses by art historians.

For historians, **primary sources** include letters, diaries, government documents, newspapers, pamphlets, maps, photographs, cookbooks, medical guides, and other materials produced during a particular time period about some person, group, or event. For example, when writing her biography of nineteenth-century Paiute activist Sarah Winnemucca, Sally Zanjani used letters written by Winnemucca, transcriptions of her public speeches, newspaper accounts of her activities, photographs, diaries, and other firsthand accounts to reconstruct Winnemucca's personal life and motivations. Like other historians, Zanjani analyzed these sources by comparing what they say, evaluating the reliability of their creators, and then generating her own interpretation of the information they present.

(2) Using secondary sources

Researchers in the humanities also use **secondary sources**, or works written by later historians or scholars about the event or person or about the primary sources, to understand what these scholars think about the topic and to help establish the social and historical context for the topic. For instance, Zanjani referred to earlier scholarly biographies of Winnemucca and then demonstrated how her work offers new evidence about Winnemucca's life. Zanjani also relied on historians for historical context that was not explicitly discussed in her primary sources, such as information about nineteenth-century American Indian reservations, government military policies regarding Indians, and so forth.

(3) Using logic and observation

In addition to using primary and secondary sources, some researchers in the humanities (philosophers, theologians, and so on) rely on evidence that is grounded in the rules of formal logic and individual observation. A theory or interpretation is considered valid if it adequately explains a particular phenomenon of human experience and if the reasons used to support the conclusion are logically sound (7h). Consider, for example, the following passage:

> Free will in the sense that matters, in the sense that makes you responsible for your actions and that gives meaning to both your strivings and your regrets, is determined by *how* your brain deals with the reasons it

finds for acting. Philosophers have established that you can still have free will and moral responsibility when the decisions your brain arrives at are *your* decisions, based on your very own reasoning and experience, not on any brainwashing or manipulation by others. If your brain is normal, it enables you to consider and reconsider your options and values indefinitely, and to reflect on what kind of a person you want to be, and since these reflections can lead to decisions and the decisions can lead to actions, you can be the author of your deeds and hence have free will in a very important sense.

—Daniel C. Dennett, "Some Observations on the Psychology
of Thinking about Free Will"

Here, Dennett concludes that humans with normally functioning brains have free will, based on the following logical premises:

The ability to act consciously constitutes free will. [major premise]

A normally functioning brain allows humans to act consciously. [minor premise]

Humans with normally functioning brains have free will. [conclusion]

16c   CONVENTIONS OF LANGUAGE AND ORGANIZATION

(1) Following conventions of style

When writing a paper for a course in the humanities, you will use language and apply formatting as prescribed by the style manual of the particular discipline. Some writers in the humanities, particularly those writing about languages and literature, use MLA style (chapter 13). Other writers in the humanities, including historians and art historians, follow the conventions outlined in *The Chicago Manual of Style* (CMS) or in Kate Turabian's *A Manual for Writers of Term Papers, Theses, and Dissertations*, which is based on CMS style (chapter 17).

Unlike writers in the sciences, whose processes are meant to ensure objectivity in their writing, most writers in the humanities strive for objectivity but recognize that an interpretation is colored by the perspective of the person expressing it. Thus, writers in the humanities often acknowledge their own position on a topic, especially if it has a clear effect on their interpretation. In particular, many writers in the humanities use the first-person pronoun *I* when describing the results of their research. Writers in the humanities also use the active voice, which focuses readers' attention on the agent performing the action (**25c**).

(2) Organizing information in particular ways

Papers in the humanities follow no specific format, but nearly all humanities papers are organized by an introductory thesis statement that indicates the author's position on the topic (**2c**), assertions and evidence that support and develop the thesis statement, and a conclusion that elaborates on the major claim and provides convincing conclusions, reasonable inferences, and promising implications, all of which demonstrate why the topic is important. (Specific formats for organizing papers in the humanities are discussed in **16d**.)

Headings can help you organize your writing. Most short humanities papers do not require headings, but for longer papers, Turabian's style manual suggests the following levels of headings:

- First-level headings are centered and boldfaced (or italicized), with major words capitalized.

A First-Level Heading

- Second-level headings are centered and not boldfaced (or italicized), with major words capitalized.

A Second-Level Heading

- Third-level headings are flush with the left margin and boldfaced (or italicized), with major words capitalized.

A Third-Level Heading

(3) Including a bibliography

Include any sources you have used in your paper in a bibliography at the end of the paper. A bibliography not only demonstrates that you have done sufficient research but also allows your readers to consult any of the sources they are interested in. You can find information on putting together a bibliography according to CMS style in **17a** and a sample bibliography in **17b**.

16d   EXAMPLES OF WRITING IN THE HUMANITIES

(1) Reflection or response papers

Your humanities instructors may require you to write **reflection papers** (also known as *response papers*): short, informal pieces that express your thoughts on a reading, a performance, or a work of art studied in a course. Often, your instructor will want to know how well you understood the text, performance, or artwork and what you thought of the concepts it presented. Sometimes, your instructor will ask you to reflect on how a book, an art exhibit, or a performance relates to the course content, what you thought about it before you encountered it, and how your experience of it affected your thinking. An informal reflection or response paper may also be assigned to encourage you to start thinking about a topic for a research paper and to help you identify a rhetorical opportunity for that paper.

To write a reflection paper, start by summarizing your best understanding of the text, event, or cultural artifact, enumerating the main points. (Keep in mind that even if others have read or experienced the text or performance, they may have understood it differently.) Explain how you respond to the event or work and then discuss how the event or work relates to other material you have read or discussed in class. Instructors often want evidence that you are making connections among various topics covered in a course; that is, they would like to see that you are synthesizing information. As you write, refer to specific elements of the event or work as support for your summary, response, synthesis, and interpretation. Finally, follow any specific instructions you may have been given.

In the following excerpt from a reflection paper, student Matthew Marusak makes a connection between his response to a film about sexual harassment and an article on the role of silence in sexual harassment that he read in a class assignment. He begins by summarizing his understanding of the reading and his response to the film and then offers his own interpretation of their message, synthesizing what he has read, watched, and experienced.

In "Witnessing Silence," Cheryl Glenn discusses the critical role silence plays in cases of sexual harassment, specifically in Anita Hill's famous testimony against Clarence Thomas. Glenn places particular emphasis on the double bind in which Hill found herself: she could continue to remain silent about the incident, or she could speak up and face public humiliation, with the added risk that no one would take her seriously. I would like to discuss the elements of Hill's initial decision to remain silent in connection with the 2005 film *North Country*, a fictionalized account of the first landmark sexual harassment class action lawsuit. The film stars Charlize Theron as Josey Aimes, a single mother who takes a job in an iron mine in Minnesota, despite protests from her father, who insists the mine is no place for a woman. Unfortunately, Josey's male coworkers feel the same, and she and her few female coworkers are harassed daily. Josey, however, is the only one to speak out; the other women, fearing for their jobs, remain silent and turn on Josey, demanding that she keep silent. Ultimately, Josey quits and brings a lawsuit against the company. Like Anita Hill, the character of Josey Aimes is treated with scorn and experiences public humiliation for speaking out against male tyranny. She feels the same emotions as Hill did, including disbelief and a loss of self-worth. Where Hill and Aimes differ is in their class positions; yet Glenn suggests that both working-class and professional women often put up with sexual harassment for the same reason: they need their jobs.

I can imagine I would go through a similar response to sexual harassment: trying to cope with the loss of my own sense of worth as a respectable human being, while deciding if I was willing to put my job on the line. It's a difficult call in any case, though I think it's not always as easy to spot sexual harassment as it was in these cases. Sexual harassment can be someone purposefully making you uncomfortable solely on the basis of your sex; the harassment need not be lewd remarks made to or about you. The decision to remain silent can be devastating, but I think I would have greater trouble living with never saying anything at all than facing what might come from speaking up. Both the Anita Hill case and *North Country* have the same message: you must stand up for your rights, even if you stand alone.

(2) Historical research paper

Another kind of assignment you may be given in a humanities course is a historical research paper, which is written to reconstruct a past event or era or to profile an individual. Most historians use a combination of primary sources (**16b(1)**) and secondary sources (**16b(2)**) to explain or interpret some feature of the past. Instructors assign historical research papers to see that you understand how to summarize, analyze, and synthesize various primary sources to reconstruct what might have happened during a particular time or to a specific person. A historical research paper also allows you to place your interpretation in the context of others that have been offered, using some sources to support your interpretation and other sources to refute the alternative interpretations.

The introduction to a historical research paper explains the importance of the topic and provides the thesis. Following the introduction and thesis, the body of the paper provides evidence from both primary and secondary sources to support the thesis. Finally, the conclusion of a historical research paper should reconsider the major claim of the paper in terms of its overall significance, inferences, and implications (for research, teaching, practice, and so forth). See **17b** for an example of this kind of humanities paper.

(3) Position paper

Some humanities courses, particularly those in rhetoric, literature, theory, and philosophy, may require you to write a position paper. The purpose of a position paper is to present critical and careful thinking about a specific topic, such as the nature of reality, ethical practices in communication, the existence of objectivity, or the purpose of religious belief. In a position paper, you state what you believe about the topic and provide reasons to support your claim. You may be asked to take a side in an existing philosophical debate or to express your own thoughts on the topic. In either case, you need to consider both what you agree with and what you disagree with.

A position paper is likely to be organized using a variation of the classical arrangement (**7g(1)**). The paper begins with a brief introduction to the topic and its importance and includes a statement of the **claim.** For instance, if you are asked to write about the existence of free will, you might claim that people have some agency to choose their actions but that most actions are based on what society expects, rather than on independent judgments. Following the statement of the claim, you provide an **explication**, which explains the basis for your belief. In this section, you define any terms that are important to your topic (*free will*, for instance) and provide any necessary background information.

The next section in a position paper discusses any possible **counterarguments** to your position. Here, you summarize and synthesize some of the most prominent scholarly positions on the topic, particularly those that are opposed to yours. This section is likely to require some research. Because you are trying to demonstrate your ability to think critically and rationally, you want to present the counterarguments in as fair and unbiased a manner as possible. Following the discussion of counterarguments, you need to provide a **resolution**. After restating your own position, explain what elements of the counterarguments are worth accepting and which are unconvincing or flawed. You concede or refute each counterargument based on its logic or its supporting information. Next, you provide reasons that support your own argument. In the conclusion, briefly restate the purpose of your paper, your major claim, the primary reasons supporting your claim, and the implications of doing so.

As you write your position paper, focus on your purpose and rhetorical audience. What position do you want to defend—and to whom? Choose a feature of the topic that you can reasonably cover in three to five pages. A concise, well-reasoned paper on a narrow topic will be more impressive than a longer paper that offers only shallow proof for its points. As you frame your argument, be sure to avoid any logical fallacies that could weaken it (7i).

The following excerpt from student Kaycee Hulet's position paper on the existence of numbers illustrates an introduction and a claim:

> The metaphysical question of whether or not numbers exist is one that has been debated for hundreds of years. There are two basic positions that have historically been held on the matter: that numbers do exist and are therefore not invented but discovered, and, conversely, that numbers are a human invention that do not exist but yet have a usefulness in describing objects or explaining the relationship of objects in the natural world. I posit that numbers do not exist in the real world but have a value entirely dependent on their relation to objects in the real world. Brief consideration is given to the existence of numbers in the currently dominant schools of thought regarding mathematics: formalism, neo-platonism, and constructivism.

Following her claim that numbers are a human invention, Kaycee gives a definition of *numbers* (her explication) and describes formalist, neo-platonist, and constructivist positions regarding the existence of numbers (potential counterarguments). She then provides a resolution by suggesting that there is no evidence that numbers exist, but that this fact does not diminish their usefulness as symbols.

(4) Critical review

Students in humanities courses, as well as professional writers, are often asked to write reviews of various creative works, including films, literary works, art exhibits, and performances (musical, theatrical, and dance.) The purpose of a critical review is to evaluate the quality of the work for a rhetorical audience who wants to know what the work is about as well as whether it would be worthwhile to experience it themselves. Accordingly, when you write a critical review, begin with some basic information about the work (the title and the artist, composer, or director and perhaps the location where the work can be seen or heard) and make an evaluative statement, or thesis, that gives readers your general opinion of the work. Following this introduction, you may provide a brief summary of the work that helps readers who are unfamiliar with it to understand the review. As you analyze the strengths and weaknesses of the work, be sure to provide examples from it to support your evaluation. Finally, most reviews conclude with a statement that synthesizes the overall evaluation of the work. (See Matthew Marusak's critical review in **16e**.)

(5) Critical analysis

Many researchers in the humanities write critical analyses in which they demonstrate their understanding of a work by arguing for a specific interpretation that will deepen an audience's understanding of and appreciation for that work. Critical analyses usually focus on the work's formal, stylistic, and/or symbolic features and explain how these elements work together to create meaning. (See **16b** for more information on evidence in critical analyses.) Such analyses sometimes explore the ways in which class, gender, or racial relationships are expressed in a work (**12c**).

　　Most critical analyses include the following sections:

- **Introduction.** The introduction provides a brief historical context for the work. It may also explain why the work ought to be reexamined—in terms of the contemporary historical context, recently discovered information, or recent cultural movements. At the end of the introduction, the **thesis**, a clearly focused claim, states the writer's interpretation of the work.

- **Body.** The body of the paper provides the evidence—the formal, stylistic, symbolic, or contextual details that support the writer's interpretation. Many analyses also address differing interpretations of the work, explaining why the writer's interpretation is more convincing or should be considered. This section can be organized in a number of ways—for example, through comparison and contrast of data or artifacts or with chronological, thematic, or emphatic (from less to more familiar or from less to more contestable) arrangement.

- **Conclusion.** The conclusion should review the thesis as well as the most important evidence supporting the writer's interpretation. Frequently, the conclusion also addresses implications—in other words, the writer explains to readers why his or her interpretation is so important, what effect the work may have had on other works or the cultural context, and/or what the writer's interpretation may mean to readers today.

Carla Spohn's critical analysis of two paintings appears in **16f**.

16e | CRITICAL REVIEW OF A THEATER PRODUCTION

In the following critical review, student Matthew Marusak makes an argument for his negative response to a production of Tennessee Williams's play *Suddenly Last Summer.*

1

Not So *Suddenly Last Summer*

Matthew Marusak

Theatre 464

November 15, 2014

The writer introduces the performance and gives a brief evaluation of the production.

I began to nod off halfway through Carla Gugino's over-the-top, twenty-minute monologue at the end of Tennessee Williams's *Suddenly Last Summer* (Roundabout at Laura Pels Theatre, Harold and Miriam Steinberg Center for Theatre; November 4, 2014). It's not that there is anything inherently wrong with the material: Williams's stark, deeply ambiguous play about the dangers of sexual repression, denial, and deception remains as potent as ever. Rather, Roundabout's production turns an urgent and emotionally explosive work into something uncomfortably dull and embarrassingly wearisome.

This paragraph describes the basic plot of the play for readers.

In theory, any revival of this powerful play should be utterly riveting. In its production at the Laura Pels theatre, however, something has gone unmistakably awry. Wealthy widow Violet Venable (an imposing Blythe Danner)—shrouded in a contradictory haze of unrelenting misery and dreamy-eyed idealism—suffers from the loss of her son, Sebastian, who perished under a veil of mystery the previous summer. As her story unfolds, Mrs. Venable does her best to cloud Sebastian's implicit homosexuality and the events surrounding his death by praising him as a great artist—the way she wants him to be remembered. Mrs. Venable sends the sophisticated,

2

Figure 1. Blythe Danner and Gale Howard perform in Tennessee Williams's *Suddenly Last Summer*. Marcus, Joan. *Blythe Danner and Gale Howard in* Suddenly Last Summer, www.playbill.com/news/article/williams-suddenly-last-summer-opens-off-broadway-with-danner-and-gugino-136368.

suspicious Dr. Cukrowicz (a debonair Gale Harold) to evaluate her niece, Catharine Holly (a woefully miscast Carla Gugino), who was committed to a psychiatric hospital after allegedly witnessing Sebastian's death. At the wishes of her manipulative aunt, Catharine is lobotomized against her will. Only under the influence of a powerful truth serum is Catharine able to reveal the shocking circumstances of her cousin's death.

    Suddenly Last Summer can be a staggering dramatic achievement, but this revival, directed with a heavy hand by Mark Brokaw, has little energy, despite its positive features. Noteworthy, though, is Santo Loquasto's dazzling set design. Sebastian's magical greenhouse garden is

The writer cites both positive and negative features of the production as he continues his evaluation.

3

perfectly staged, as are the simple, elegant interior scenes of the Venable house. Loquasto's costume design is also impressive, while Peter Golub's original score is by turns lovely and haunting. A baffling technical aspect, however, is David Weiner's lighting design, which seems inconsistent to the point of becoming inappropriate and peculiar.

Unfortunately, there are problems with the cast as well. Danner gives a perfectly respectable performance, but not a Danner-caliber one. Lost is any nuance of character and wit (so beautifully portrayed by Katharine Hepburn in the 1959 film), because Danner speaks with a maddeningly uneven dialect, embodies a distracting number of nervous tics, and displays an overly rehearsed polished poise. Moreover, Carla Gugino should never have been cast as Catharine. She has neither the stage presence nor the charm to pull off Catharine's fiery passion. Rounding out the leads is Gale Harold, who takes the play's most underwritten role and somehow makes Dr. Cukrowicz at once both charismatic and calculating.

The conclusion summarizes the major strengths and weaknesses of the production and indicates why the weaknesses outweigh the strengths.

Roundabout's technically robust revival of *Suddenly Last Summer* leaves its audience yearning for artistic power. All the characters try too hard to make an impression instead of revealing their genuine talent and allowing Williams's brilliant script to speak for itself. I cannot recommend this production outright, though it might be worth seeing for Gale Harold alone. He's an underrated, underused actor, and watching him is an unmitigated pleasure.

16f CRITICAL ANALYSIS OF TWO PAINTINGS

In the following critical analysis, student Carla Spohn analyzes two early Italian Renaissance paintings by comparing and contrasting stylistic elements of the two works.

1

Two Annunciations

Carla Spohn

Art History 341

April 15, 2015

The introduction provides a brief historical context for the paper and concludes with the thesis.

The Annunciation of Christ's birth to the Virgin Mary by the Angel Gabriel is a sacred scene that is revered and that has been portrayed by many artists throughout the Middle Ages and the Renaissance. Fra Angelico and Leonardo da Vinci, both transitional artists, painted two different Annunciation paintings that reflect the changing artistic styles and techniques of the fifteenth century. However, while Fra Angelico's *Altarpiece of the Annunciation* is still in some ways reminiscent of medieval conventions, Leonardo's *The Annunciation* depicts a complete embracing of Renaissance ideals.

This section provides evidence for the different styles of Fra Angelico and Leonardo da Vinci that supports the writer's thesis statement.

The most obvious difference between the two Annunciations can be seen in their use of color. The medieval influence in Fra Angelico's painting is shown by the bright blue, which contrasts with the lighter primary colors. While this contrast creates bold visual interest, it emphasizes the unreality of the image. Leonardo, however, uses shading to blend the colors, creating subtle hues which provide variation and a much more naturalistic effect than the stark use of dark and light by Fra Angelico. The color used is also affected by the artists' depiction of light. While Fra Angelico's scene is one of bright sunlight that bathes the figures in vibrant luminosity, the solid beam of light upon the Virgin again creates

2

The Annunciation, c. 1430–32 (tempera and gold on panel), Angelico, Fra (Guido di Pietro) (c. 1387–1455)/Prado, Madrid, Spain/Bridgeman Images

Fra Angelico, *Altarpiece of the Annunciation.* Tempera and gold on panel, Prado, Madrid, c. 1430–1432, www. museodelprado.es/en/visit-the-museum/15-masterpieces/ work-card/obra/the-annunciation.

Annunciation, 1472–75 (oil on panel) (post-restoration), Vinci, Leonardo da (1452–1519)/Galleria degli Uffizi, Florence, Italy/Bridgeman Images

Leonardo da Vinci, *The Annunciation. Oil on panel,* Galleria degli Uffizi, Florence, c. 1472–1475, www.virtualuffizi.com/annunciation_3.html.

3

a sense of unreality, with little depth. In contrast, Leonardo creates reality through his use of natural light and atmospheric effects, which allow for greater solidity and substance than in Fra Angelico's depiction.

The setting in which the two scenes are placed also contributes to the paintings' differences. While both use the Annunciation convention of enclosing the figures, Fra Angelico's is much more apparent with a Roman-style portico; Leonardo's is simply implied by the stone wall cornerstones that frame Mary. Both paintings also convey Renaissance characteristics through classical details, such as the Corinthian columns and round arches in Fra Angelico's and the stone table carved with Roman-like designs in Leonardo's. In contrast to these Renaissance attributes, Fra Angelico exercises the medieval tradition of depicting more than one story in a single scene, which in this instance are separated by the Roman architecture; the figures of Adam and Eve being expelled from the Garden combined with the Annunciation of Christ's birth link salvation to the Fall.

The last feature reflecting the artists' use of or departure from Renaissance conventions is their portrayal of the figures. Both Fra Angelico and Leonardo portray naturalistic figures that demonstrate a sculptural quality in themselves and their draperies. Fra Angelico depicts the angel and Mary as devout figures in profile. Their serene religious attitude is conveyed by the soft curve in their bow of reverence toward each other. While the emotions evoked are those of ethereal spirituality and piety, their faces and gestures capture humanity. Mary is depicted as humble and human, and yet still celestial as she receives a vision from a ray of light.

4

Leonardo's figure suggests a slightly more regal Mary; while the angel bows and greets her, Mary remains upright and only raises her left hand in greeting. The Virgin is also turned more, for a frontal view rather than a profile view. This view somewhat recalls the Byzantine and medieval depiction of Mary enthroned as the central figure, so as to completely convey her majesty to the viewer. Leonardo's Mary is the Queen of Heaven, but depicted as beautifully human and realistic, embodying the Renaissance humanistic belief that humanity is God's greatest creation.

Both Fra Angelico's and Leonardo's Annunciations capture the reverential nature of the subject, despite their many differences. Fra Angelico's painting is truly a transitional piece, combining medieval and Renaissance artistic elements. Leonardo, however, demonstrates that he is a true Renaissance man with his skillful mastery of the newly emerging techniques. Their diverse treatments of the Annunciation reveal two separate ideals concerning religious depictions of Mary: Fra Angelico's Mary reflects her ethereal piety and the medieval notion of humanity's ultimate submission to God, whereas Leonardo's Mary exemplifies naturalistic regality and the Renaissance belief in human greatness.

The conclusion reasserts the main argument for the artists' stylistic differences and explains the implications of this argument.

17 ‖ CMS DOCUMENTATION

The Chicago Manual of Style (CMS), now in its sixteenth edition and published by the University of Chicago Press (2010), provides guidelines for writers, editors, and publishers in history and other subject areas in the arts and humanities.

Fully aligned with this professional resource in terms of formatting and style guidelines is Kate L. Turabian's *A Manual for Writers of Research Papers, Theses, and Dissertations* (now in its 8th edition). Shorter and more accessible than the CMS, Turabian is geared toward college-level writers who are preparing and submitting papers, as is this chapter.

The CMS documentation system uses either footnotes or endnotes and, for most assignments, a bibliography. Each of these citations demonstrates that you have conducted relevant research, credited your sources, and provided the details necessary for your reader to locate your source.

This chapter includes

- guidelines for citing sources within a CMS-style research paper and documenting the sources in a bibliography (**17a**) and
- a sample CMS-style research paper (**17b**).

17a ‖ CMS NOTE AND BIBLIOGRAPHIC FORMS

According to CMS style, in-text citations take the form of sequential superscript numbers that refer to **footnotes** (notes at the bottom of each page) or **endnotes** (notes at the end of the text). The information in these notes may be condensed if a bibliography lists all the sources used in the text. The condensed, or short, form for a note includes only the author's last name, the title (sometimes shortened if longer than four words), and the relevant page number(s): Eggers, *Court Reporters*, 312–15.

When a text has no bibliography, the full note form is used for the first citation of each source. For either footnotes or endnotes, place a superscript number in the text wherever documentation of a source is necessary. The number should be as close as possible to whatever it refers to, following most punctuation that appears at the end of the direct quotation or paraphrase but preceding a dash.

TIPS FOR PREPARING FOOTNOTES

- Most word-processing programs will footnote your work automatically. In your software, review the toolbars and menus to locate the tool to allow you to insert a footnote. A superscript number will appear in the cursor's position. A box will also appear at the bottom of your page in which you can insert the requisite information.
- Each note begins with a full-size number followed by a period and a space.
- Indent the first line of a note five spaces or one-half inch.
- Single-space lines within a footnote.
- Double-space between footnotes when more than one appears on a page.
- Use the abbreviation *Ibid.* (not italicized) to indicate that the source cited in an entry is identical to the one in the preceding entry. Include page numbers if they differ from those in the preceding entry: Ibid., 331–32.
- No bibliography is necessary when the footnotes provide complete bibliographic information for all sources.

TIPS FOR PREPARING ENDNOTES

- Place endnotes on a separate page, following the last page of your text and preceding the bibliography (if one is included).
- Center the word *Notes* (not italicized) at the top of the page.
- Use the abbreviation *Ibid.* (not italicized) to indicate that a source cited in an entry is identical to the one in the preceding entry. Include page numbers if they differ from those in the preceding entry: Ibid., 331–32.
- Indent the first line of a note five spaces or one-half inch.
- Single-space within an endnote and leave one blank line between endnotes.
- No bibliography is necessary when the endnotes provide complete bibliographic information for all sources used in the paper.

TIPS FOR PREPARING A BIBLIOGRAPHY

- Start the bibliography on a separate page, following the last page of the body of the text if footnotes are used or following the last page of endnotes.
- Center the word *Bibliography* (not italicized) at the top of your page.
- Alphabetize entries in the bibliography according to the author's last name.
- If a source has more than one author, alphabetize by the last name of the first author.
- For a work without an author, alphabetize the entry according to the first important word in the title.
- To indicate that a source has the same author(s) as in the preceding entry, begin an entry with six hyphens or a three-em dash (———) instead of the name(s) of the author(s). (If you do not know how to create this mark, search for *em dash*, using the Help function of your word processor.)
- Indent the second and subsequent lines of an entry five spaces (that is, use a hanging indent).
- Single-space within an entry and double-space between entries, unless your instructor asks that you double-space within entries.

Directory to CMS Note and Bibliographic Forms

BOOKS

GENERAL DOCUMENTATION GUIDELINES FOR PRINT-BASED SOURCES

Author or Editor

One author—note form. Provide the author's full name, beginning with the first name and following the last name with a comma. For the short note form, use only the last name of the author.

Full note form
1. Jamie Barlowe,

One author—bibliographic form. Invert the author's name so that the last name appears first. Place a period after the first name.

Bibliographic form
Barlowe, Jamie.

Two authors—note form. Use the word *and* between the names.

Full note form
2. Pauline Diaz and Edward Allan,

Two authors—bibliographic form. Invert the first author's name only. Place a comma and the word *and* after the first author's name. A period follows the second author's name.

Bibliographic form
Diaz, Pauline, and Edward Allan.

Three authors—note form. Use commas after the names of the first and subsequent authors. Include *and* before the final author's name.

Full note form
3. Joyce Freeland, John Bach, and Derik Flynn,

Three authors—bibliographic form. Invert the order of the first author's name only. Place a comma after this name and after the second author's name. Use *and* before the final author's name.

Bibliographic form
Freeland, Joyce, John Bach, and Derik Flynn.

Corporate or group author—note and bibliographic forms. Provide the full name of the group in all forms—full note, short note, and bibliographic entry.

Note form
4. Smithsonian Institution,

Bibliographic form
Smithsonian Institution.

Editor—note and bibliographic forms. Place the abbreviation *ed.* or *eds.* after the name(s) of the editor(s).

Full note form
5. Peggy Irmen, ed.,
6. Cheryl Glenn, Margaret Lyday, and Wendy Sharer, eds.,

Bibliographic form
Irmen, Peggy, ed.
Glenn, Cheryl, Margaret Lyday, and Wendy Sharer, eds.

Titles

Italicized titles. Italicize the titles of books, magazines, journals, newspapers, and films. Capitalize all major words (nouns, pronouns, verbs, adjectives, adverbs, and conjunctions except for *and, but, for, or,* and *nor*). A book title is followed by the publication data enclosed in parentheses in the full note form, by a comma and a page number in the short note form, and by a period in the bibliographic form. In the short note form, a title longer than four words is shortened by omitting any article at its beginning and using only important words from the rest of the title.

Full note form
The Great Design of Henry IV from the Memoirs of the Duke of Sully

Short note form
Great Design of Henry IV,

Bibliographic form
The Great Design of Henry IV from the Memoirs of the Duke of Sully.

Titles in quotation marks. Use quotation marks to enclose the titles of journal or magazine articles, selections from anthologies, and other short works (**40b**). In the note form, a title of a short work is followed by a comma. In the bibliographic form, it is followed by a period.

Note form
"The Humor of New England,"

Bibliographic form
"The Humor of New England."

(continued on page 414)

Titles *(continued from page 413)*

Subtitles. Include a subtitle of a book or article (which appears after a colon) in the full note and bibliographic forms but not in the short note form.

Full note form
Appreciations: Painting, Poetry, and Prose
"Cooperation and Trust: Some Theoretical Notes,"

Short note form
Appreciations,
"Cooperation and Trust,"

Bibliographic form
Appreciations: Painting, Poetry, and Prose.
"Cooperation and Trust: Some Theoretical Notes."

Publication Data

For a book, list the city of publication, the publisher's name, and the date of publication (see citation map 17.1, on page 417). A colon follows the city of publication, and a comma follows the publisher's name. In the full note form, this information should be placed within parentheses. No parentheses are needed for the bibliographic form. The short note form does not include publication data.

Full note form
(New York: Alfred A. Knopf, 2015),

Bibliographic form
New York: Alfred A. Knopf, 2015.

Whenever possible, include both the volume number and the issue number for any journal article you use (see citation map 17.2, on page 423). The volume number should appear after the title, and the issue number should appear after the volume

International Social Work 77 (2014)
Journal of Democracy 14, no. 1 (2003)
Time, January 24, 2015

number (preceded by the abbreviation *no.*). Use a comma to separate the two numbers. Place the year of publication in parentheses after the volume or issue number. For a magazine, provide the full date of publication.

City and state. Identify the city in which the main office of the publisher of a book is located. If the city is not widely known, add the appropriate two-letter state abbreviation (or, for a city outside the United States, the abbreviation for the country). If the city of publication is Washington, include the abbreviation for the District of Columbia, *DC* (not italicized). When two or more cities are listed on a book's title page, use only the first in the bibliographic entry. A colon follows the city name or the state or country abbreviation.

Baltimore:

Carbondale, IL:

Waterloo, ON:

Harmondsworth, UK:

Publisher's name. Provide either the full name of a book's publisher, as given on the title page, or an abbreviated version. The style chosen must be consistent throughout the notes and bibliography. Even when the full name is provided, some words may be omitted: an initial *The,* words such as *Company* and *Corporation,* or abbreviations such as *Co.* and *Inc.* The word *University* may be abbreviated to *Univ.* (not italicized).

Univ. of Chicago Press

Penguin Books

HarperCollins

(continued on page 416)

(continued from page 415)
Page Numbers

If you are citing information from a specific page or pages of a book or article, place the page number(s) at the end of the footnote or endnote. If you are citing more than one page, separate the first and last page with an en dash (a short dash, typically created by pressing the Option and hyphen keys simultaneously): 35–38. If the page numbers have the same hundreds or thousands digit, do not repeat it when listing the final page in the range: 123–48. Page numbers are not included in a bibliographic entry for an entire book; however, a bibliographic entry for an article ends with the range of pages on which the article appears.

The following list contains entries for the full note form and the bibliographic form. The short note form is provided only for the first example.

BOOKS
1. Book with one author
Full note form

1. Carlo D'Este, *Eisenhower: A Soldier's Life* (New York: Holt, 2002), 417–18.

Short note form

1. D'Este, *Eisenhower*, 417–18.

Bibliographic form

D'Este, Carlo. *Eisenhower: A Soldier's Life.* New York: Holt, 2002.

2. Book with two authors
Full note form

2. Alice H. Eagly and Linda L. Carli, *Through the Labyrinth: The Truth about How Women Become Leaders* (Boston: Harvard Business School Press, 2007), 28.

CITATION MAP 17.1: BOOK, CMS STYLE

Include the following elements when citing a book.

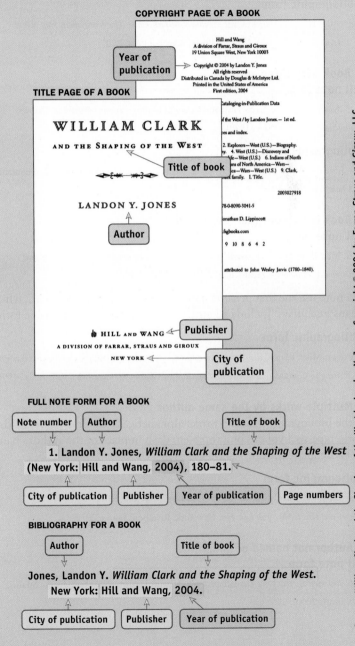

COPYRIGHT PAGE OF A BOOK

Year of publication

Hill and Wang
A division of Farrar, Straus and Giroux
19 Union Square West, New York 10003

Copyright © 2004 by Landon Y. Jones
All rights reserved
Distributed in Canada by Douglas & McIntyre Ltd.
Printed in the United States of America
First edition, 2004

Cataloging-in-Publication Data

of the West / by Landon Jones.— 1st ed.

es and index.

2. Explorers—West (U.S.)—Biography.
y.   4. West (U.S.)—Discovery and
fe—West (U.S.)   6. Indians of North
ns of North America—Wars—
ca—Wars—West (U.S.)   9. Clark,
rk family.   I. Title.

2003027918

78-0-8090-3041-5

onathan D. Lippincott

.fsgbooks.com

9   10   8   6   4   2

attributed to John Wesley Jarvis (1780–1840).

TITLE PAGE OF A BOOK

WILLIAM CLARK

AND THE SHAPING OF THE WEST

Title of book

LANDON Y. JONES

Author

HILL AND WANG   **Publisher**

A DIVISION OF FARRAR, STRAUS AND GIROUX

NEW YORK   **City of publication**

FULL NOTE FORM FOR A BOOK

Note number   **Author**   **Title of book**

1. Landon Y. Jones, *William Clark and the Shaping of the West* (New York: Hill and Wang, 2004), 180–81.

City of publication   **Publisher**   **Year of publication**   **Page numbers**

BIBLIOGRAPHY FOR A BOOK

Author   **Title of book**

Jones, Landon Y. *William Clark and the Shaping of the West.* New York: Hill and Wang, 2004.

City of publication   **Publisher**   **Year of publication**

418 **CMS** CMS Documentation

Bibliographic form

Eagly, Alice H., and Linda L. Carli. *Through the Labyrinth: The Truth about How Women Become Leaders.* Boston: Harvard Business School Press, 2007.

3. Book with three authors
Full note form

3. Karen A. Foss, Sonja K. Foss, and Cindy L. Griffin, *Feminist Rhetorical Theories* (Thousand Oaks, CA: Sage, 1999).

Bibliographic form

Foss, Karen A., Sonja K. Foss, and Cindy L. Griffin. *Feminist Rhetorical Theories.* Thousand Oaks, CA: Sage, 1999.

4. Book with more than three authors
Full note form

4. Mike Palmquist et al., *Transitions: Teaching Writing in Computer-Supported and Traditional Classrooms* (Greenwich, CT: Ablex, 1998), 153.

In a note use the first person's name followed by the phrase *et al.*, which means *and others*. Include all authors' names in the bibliographic form.

Bibliographic form

Palmquist, Mike, Kate Kiefer, James Hartvigsen, and Barbara Goodlew. *Transitions: Teaching Writing in Computer-Supported and Traditional Classrooms.* Greenwich, CT: Ablex, 1998.

5. Multiple works by the same author

In the bibliography, list the works alphabetically by title. After the first work, type six hyphens or a three-em dash in place of the author's name for subsequent entries.

Bibliographic form

Diaz, Junot. *The Brief Wondrous Life of Oscar Wao.* New York: Riverhead Books, 2007.

————. *This Is How You Lose Her.* New York: Riverhead Books, 2012.

6. Author not named or unknown
Full note form

6. *Beowulf: A New Verse Translation,* trans. Seamus Heaney (New York: Farrar, Strauss, and Giroux, 2000), 24.

Bibliography form

Beowulf: A New Verse Translation. Translated by Seamus Heaney. New York: Farrar, Strauss, and Giroux, 2000.

7. Book with an editor
Full note form

7. Hanna Schissler, ed., *The Miracle Years* (Princeton, NJ: Princeton University Press, 2001).

Place the abbreviation *ed.* after the editor's name.

Bibliographic form

Schissler, Hanna, ed. *The Miracle Years.* Princeton, NJ: Princeton University Press, 2001.

8. Book with an author and an editor
Full note form

8. Ayn Rand, *The Art of Fiction,* ed. Tore Boeckmann (New York: Plume, 2000).

Use the abbreviation *ed.* for "edited by."

Bibliographic form

Rand, Ayn. *The Art of Fiction.* Edited by Tore Boeckmann. New York: Plume, 2000.

Write out the words *Edited by.*

9. Translated book

Full note form

9. Orhan Pamuk, *Silent House*, trans. Robert Finn (New York: Knopf, 2012).

Use the abbreviation *trans.* for "translated by."

Bibliographic form

Pamuk, Orhan. *Silent House.* Translated by Robert Finn. New York: Knopf, 2012.

Write out the words *Translated by.*

10. Entry in a reference work
Full note form

10. Robert Cox and Christina R. Foust, "Social Movement Rhetoric," in *The SAGE Handbook of Rhetorical Studies*, ed. Andrea A. Lunsford, Kirt H. Wilson, and Rosa A. Eberly (Thousand Oaks, CA: Sage, 2009), 613.

Bibliographic form

Cox, Robert, and Christina R. Foust. "Social Movement Rhetoric." In *The SAGE Handbook of Rhetorical Studies,* edited by Andrea A. Lunsford, Kirt H. Wilson, and Rosa A. Eberly, 605–27. Thousand Oaks, CA: Sage, 2009.

11. Sacred text
Full note form

11. John 3:16 (New Revised Standard Version).

11. Qur'an 7:1–7.

CMS does not include sacred or religious texts in the bibliography.

12. Source quoted in another source
Full note form

12. Toni Morrison, *Playing in the Dark* (New York: Vintage, 1992), 26, quoted in Jonathan Goldberg, *Willa Cather and Others* (Durham, NC: Duke University Press, 2001), 37.

Bibliographic form

Goldberg, Jonathan. *Willa Cather and Others.* Durham, NC: Duke University Press, 2001.

In the note cite both the original work and the secondary source in which it is quoted. In the bibliography cite the secondary source only.

13. Edition after the first
Full note form

13. Edward O. Wilson, *On Human Nature,* 14th ed. (Cambridge: Harvard University Press, 2001).

Bibliographic form

Wilson, Edward O. *On Human Nature.* 14th ed. Cambridge: Harvard University Press, 2001.

14. One volume in a multivolume work
Full note form

14. Thomas Cleary, *Classics of Buddhism and Zen: The Collected Translations of Thomas Cleary,* (Boston: Shambhala Publications, 2001), 3:116.

Bibliographic form

Cleary, Thomas. *Classics of Buddhism and Zen: The Collected Translations of Thomas Cleary.* Vol. 3. Boston: Shambhala Publications, 2001.

15. Government document
Full note form

15. US Bureau of the Census, *Statistical Abstract of the United States,* 120th ed. (Washington, DC, 2001), 16.

Bibliographic form

US Bureau of the Census. *Statistical Abstract of the United States.* 120th ed. Washington, DC, 2001.

16. Selection from an anthology
Full note form

16. Elizabeth Spencer, "The Everlasting Light," in *The Cry of an Occasion,* ed. Richard Bausch (Baton Rouge: Louisiana State University Press, 2001), 171–82.

Bibliographic form

Spencer, Elizabeth. "The Everlasting Light." In *The Cry of an Occasion,* edited by Richard Bausch, 171–82. Baton Rouge: Louisiana State University Press, 2001.

When only one selection from an anthology is used, inclusive page numbers precede the publication data in the bibliographic entry.

17. Published letter
Full note form

17. Lincoln to George McClellan, Washington, DC, 13 October 1862, in *This Fiery Trial: The Speeches and Writings of Abraham Lincoln,* ed. William E. Gienapp (New York: Oxford University Press, 2002), 178.

Bibliographic form

Lincoln, Abraham. Abraham Lincoln to George McClellan, Washington, DC, 13 October 1862. In *This Fiery Trial: The Speeches and Writings of Abraham Lincoln,* edited by William E. Gienapp, 178. New York: Oxford University Press, 2002.

ARTICLES

18. Article in a journal
Full note form

18. Andreas Schedler, "The Menu of Manipulation," *Journal of Democracy* 13, no. 2 (2002): 48.

Bibliographic form

Schedler, Andreas. "The Menu of Manipulation." *Journal of Democracy* 13, no. 2 (2002):
36–50.

19. Article in a magazine
Full note form

19. John O'Sullivan, "The Overskeptics," *National Review,* June 17, 2002, 23.

Bibliographic form

O'Sullivan, John. "The Overskeptics." *National Review,* June 17, 2002, 22–26.

For a magazine published monthly, include only the month and the
year, with no comma inserted between them.

20. Review or book review
Full note form

20. Anna Seitz Hickey, "Indeed," review of *Yes, Please*, by Amy Poehler, *Centre County
Review of Books* (State College, PA), January 4, 2015, 7.

Bibliographic form

Hickey, Anna Seitz. "Indeed." Review of *Yes, Please*, by Amy Poehler. *Centre County Review of
Books* (State College, PA), January 4, 2015, 7.

In this example, adding the city name to the newspaper title would be
awkward; city and state abbreviation are given in parenthesis.

21. Newspaper article
Full note form

21. Rick Bragg, "An Oyster and a Way of Life, Both at Risk," *New York Times,* June 15,
2002, national edition, sec. A.

If the city of publication is not part of the name, add it at the beginning
(italicized) as part of the name: *St. Paul Pioneer Press.* If the city is not well
known or could be confused with another city of the same name, add
the state name or abbreviation in parentheses after the city's name. If the
paper is a well-known national one, such as the *Wall Street Journal*, it is
not necessary to add the city.

CITATION MAP 17.2: ARTICLE IN A JOURNAL, CMS STYLE

To cite an article from a journal, include the following elements.

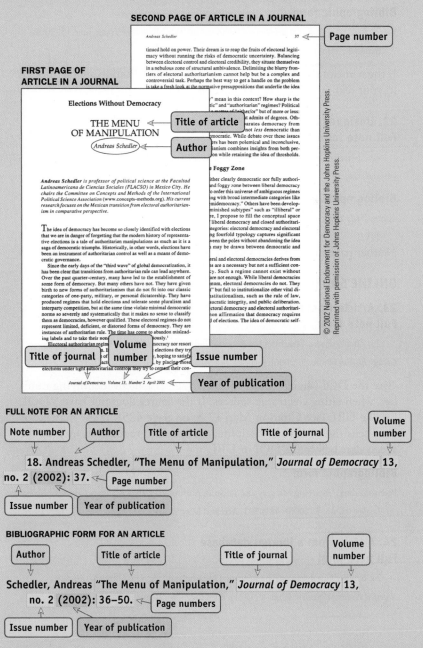

SECOND PAGE OF ARTICLE IN A JOURNAL

Page number

FIRST PAGE OF ARTICLE IN A JOURNAL

Elections Without Democracy

THE MENU OF MANIPULATION — Title of article

Andreas Schedler — Author

Andreas Schedler is professor of political science at the Facultad Latinoamericana de Ciencias Sociales (FLACSO) in Mexico City. He chairs the Committee on Concepts and Methods of the International Political Science Association (www.concepts-methods.org). His current research focuses on the Mexican transition from electoral authoritarianism in comparative perspective.

Title of journal — Volume number — Issue number

Year of publication

Journal of Democracy Volume 13, Number 2 April 2002

© 2002 National Endowment for Democracy and the Johns Hopkins University Press.
Reprinted with permission of Johns Hopkins University Press.

FULL NOTE FOR AN ARTICLE

Note number · Author · Title of article · Title of journal · Volume number

18. Andreas Schedler, "The Menu of Manipulation," *Journal of Democracy* 13, no. 2 (2002): 37.

Issue number · Year of publication · Page number

BIBLIOGRAPHIC FORM FOR AN ARTICLE

Author · Title of article · Title of journal · Volume number

Schedler, Andreas "The Menu of Manipulation," *Journal of Democracy* 13, no. 2 (2002): 36–50.

Issue number · Year of publication · Page numbers

Bibliographic form

Bragg, Rick. "An Oyster and a Way of Life, Both at Risk." *New York Times.* June 15, 2002,
national edition, sec. A.

If the name of the newspaper and the date of publication are mentioned in your text, no bibliographic entry is needed.

22. Unsigned article in a newspaper
Full note form

22. "Nittany Lions Finish with a Flourish," *Centre Daily Times* (State College, PA),
February 26, 2012.

Bibliographic form

Centre Daily Times (State College, PA). "Nittany Lions Finish with a Flourish." February 26,
2012.

Neither page numbers nor section is required.

ONLINE SOURCES

23. Article from an online journal
Full note form

23. Zina Peterson, "Teaching Margery and Julian in Anthropology-Based Survey Courses,"
College English 68, no. 5 (2006): 481–501, accessed May 5, 2010, doi:10.2307/25472167.

Give the DOI (digital object identifier), a permanent identifying number, when citing electronic sources. If the source does not have a DOI, list the URL (see Citation Map 17.3, on page 425). If the material is time-sensitive or if your discipline or instructor requires it, include the access date before the DOI or URL.

Bibliographic form

Peterson, Zina. "Teaching Margery and Julian in Anthropology-Based Survey Courses." *College English* 68, no. 5 (2006): 481–501. Accessed May 5, 2010. doi:10.2307/25472167.

24. Article from a journal database
Full note form

24. Samuel Guy Inman, "The Monroe Doctrine and Hispanic America," *Hispanic America Historical Review* 4, no. 4 (1921): 635, http://www.jstor.org/stable/2505682.

CITATION MAP 17.3: ARTICLE IN A DATABASE, CMS STYLE

Include the following elements when citing an article in a database.

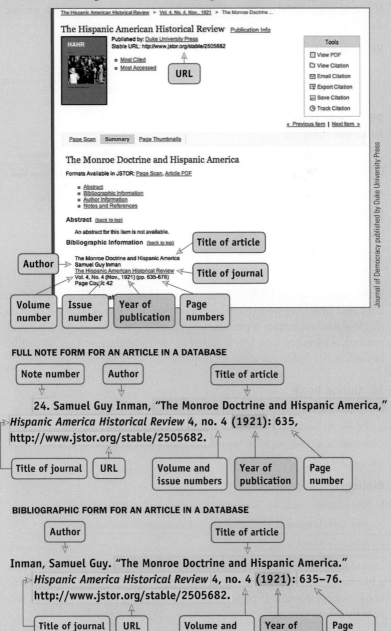

FULL NOTE FORM FOR AN ARTICLE IN A DATABASE

Note number Author Title of article

24. Samuel Guy Inman, "The Monroe Doctrine and Hispanic America," *Hispanic America Historical Review* 4, no. 4 (1921): 635, http://www.jstor.org/stable/2505682.

Title of journal URL Volume and issue numbers Year of publication Page number

BIBLIOGRAPHIC FORM FOR AN ARTICLE IN A DATABASE

Author Title of article

Inman, Samuel Guy. "The Monroe Doctrine and Hispanic America." *Hispanic America Historical Review* 4, no. 4 (1921): 635–76. http://www.jstor.org/stable/2505682.

Title of journal URL Volume and issue numbers Year of publication Page numbers

If there is no DOI, give a stable URL for the article in the online database.

Bibliographic form

Inman, Samuel Guy. "The Monroe Doctrine and Hispanic America." *Hispanic America Historical Review* 4, no. 4 (1921): 635–76. http://www.jstor.org/stable/2505682.

25. Article from an online magazine
Full note form

25. Mark Frank, "Judge for Themselves: Why a Supreme Court Ruling on Sentencing Guidelines Puts More Power Back on the Bench," *Time*, January 24, 2005, http://www.time.com/time/magazine/printout/0,8816,1018063,00.html.

Bibliographic form

Frank, Mark. "Judge for Themselves: Why a Supreme Court Ruling on Sentencing Guidelines Puts More Power Back on the Bench." *Time*, January 24, 2005. http://www.time.com/time/magazine/printout/0,8816,1018063,00.html.

If the source has no DOI, cite the URL. A URL or DOI continued on a second line may be broken *after* a colon or double slash or *before* a single slash, a comma, a period, a hyphen, a question mark, a percent symbol, a number sign (#), a tilde (~), or an underline (_). It can be broken either before or after an ampersand (&) or equals sign.

26. Online book
Full note form

26. Marian Hurd McNeely, *The Jumping-off Place*, illus. William Siegel (New York: Longmans, 1929), 28, http://digital.library.upenn.edu/women/mcneely/place/place.html.

Bibliographic form

McNeely, Marian Hurd. *The Jumping-off Place.* Illustrated by William Siegel. New York: Longmans, 1929. http://digitial.library.upenn.edu/women/mcneely/place/place.html.

Include the same information (author, title, city, publisher, year) as for a book. While some online books provide page images of the original book, others do not. If page numbers vary, use a chapter or other section number instead.

27. Electronic book (e-book)
Full note form

27. S. C. Gwynne, *Empire of the Summer Moon* (New York: Scribner, 2010), chap. 11, Kindle.

Bibliographic form

Gwynne, S. C. *Empire of the Summer Moon*. New York: Scribner, 2012. Kindle.

28. Website
Full note form

28. Jeremy Hylton, The Complete Works of William Shakespeare, *The Tech*, MIT, 1993, http://shakespeare.mit.edu.

Unless no other publication information is available, access dates are not necessary. The citation of an entire website normally appears in the Notes, not in the Bibliography.

29. Work from a website
Full note form

29. Eric Skalac, "BP Well to Stay Sealed after Gulf Spill, Experts Predict," *National Geographic*, last modified April 20, 2011, http://news.nationalgeographic.com/news /Energy/2011/04/110418-oil-spill-anniversary-is-bp-well-sealed/.

Bibliographic form

Skalac, Eric. "BP Well to Stay Sealed after Gulf Spill, Experts Predict." *National Geographic*, last modified April 20, 2011. http://news.nationalgeographic.com/news /Energy/2011/04/110418-oil-spill-anniversary-is-bp-well-sealed/.

See Citation Map 17.4, page 428, for another example of a work from a website.

30. Blog entry
Full note form

30. Megan Slack, "What Is the Sequester?" *The White House Blog*, February 22, 2013, http://www.whitehouse.gov/blog/2013/02/22/what-sequester.

Bibliographic form

Slack, Megan. "What Is the Sequester?" *The White House Blog*. February 22, 2013. http://www.whitehouse.gov/blog/2012/02/22/what-sequester.

CITATION MAP 17.4: WORK FROM A WEBSITE, CMS STYLE

Include the following elements when citing a short work from a website.

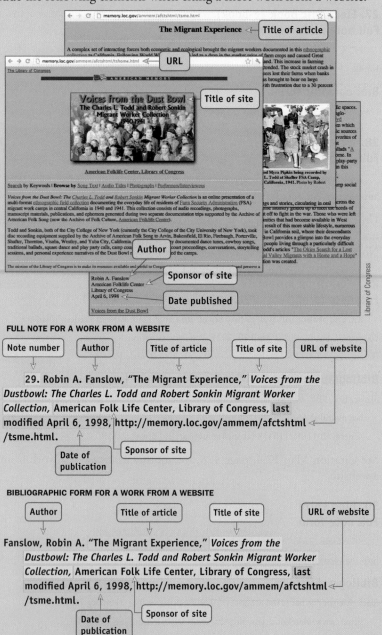

FULL NOTE FOR A WORK FROM A WEBSITE

| Note number | Author | Title of article | Title of site | URL of website |

29. Robin A. Fanslow, "The Migrant Experience," *Voices from the Dustbowl: The Charles L. Todd and Robert Sonkin Migrant Worker Collection,* American Folk Life Center, Library of Congress, last modified April 6, 1998, http://memory.loc.gov/ammem/afctshtml /tsme.html.

Date of publication — Sponsor of site

BIBLIOGRAPHIC FORM FOR A WORK FROM A WEBSITE

| Author | Title of article | Title of site | URL of website |

Fanslow, Robin A. "The Migrant Experience," *Voices from the Dustbowl: The Charles L. Todd and Robert Sonkin Migrant Worker Collection,* American Folk Life Center, Library of Congress, last modified April 6, 1998, http://memory.loc.gov/ammem/afctshtml /tsme.html.

Date of publication — Sponsor of site

If *blog* does not appear as part of the name, add it in parentheses after the name. Although all blogs can be cited in notes, only frequently cited blogs appear in the bibliography.

31. E-mail and other personal communication
Full note form

> 31. Evan Micheals, e-mail message to James Smith, February 22, 2015.

It is not necessary to list personal communications, such as e-mails, letters, and social media communications, in the bibliography.

32. Podcast
Full note form

> 32. Ira Glass, "363: Enforcers," *This American Life*, podcast audio, 57:53, February 22, 2013, http://www.thisamericanlife.org/play_full.php?play=363.

Bibliographic form

> Glass, Ira. "363: Enforcers." *This American Life*. Podcast audio, 57:53. February 22, 2013.
> http://www.thisamericanlife.org/play_full.php?play=363.

After the description of the source type ("podcast audio"), indicate the length of the recording.

33. Video or audio
Full note form

> 33. Adam Savage, *How Simple Ideas Lead to Scientific Discoveries—Adam Savage*, video, 7:31, March 13, 2012, https://www.youtube.com/watch?v+F8UFGu2MgM.

Bibliographic form

> Savage, Adam. *How Simple Ideas Lead to Scientific Discoveries—Adam Savage*. Video, 7:31.
> March 13, 2012. https://www.youtube.com/watch?v+F8UFGu2MgM.

OTHER SOURCES

34. DVD or Blu-ray
Full note form

> 34. *The Girl with the Dragon Tattoo*, directed by David Fincher (Culver City, CA: Sony Pictures Entertainment, 2011), DVD and Blu-ray.

Bibliographic form

The Girl with the Dragon Tattoo. Directed by David Fincher. Culver City, CA: Sony Pictures
Entertainment, 2011. DVD and Blu-ray.

35. Interviews, published and unpublished
Full note form (PUBLISHED)

35. Aldous Huxley, interview by Mike Wallace, *The Mike Wallace Interview: Aldous
Huxley (1958-05-18)*, YouTube video, last modified Aug. 1, 2008, http://www.youtube.com
/watch?v=KGaYXahbcL4.

Bibliographic form (PUBLISHED)

Huxley, Aldous. Interviewed by Mike Wallace. *The Mike Wallace Interview: Aldous Huxley
(1958-05-18).* YouTube video. Last modified Aug. 1, 2008. http://www.youtube.com
/watch?v=KGaYXahbcL4.

Full note form (UNPUBLISHED)

35. John Teodori, interview by James Timothy, November 16, 2007, transcript.

Bibliographic form (UNPUBLISHED)
Unpublished interviews rarely appear in the bibliography, but, if they
do, they should include the name of the person being interviewed, the
interviewer, the place and date of the interview, and the availability of a
transcript or recording.

36. Sound recording
Full note form

36. Frédéric Chopin, *Nocturne Op. 9 No. 2*, with Ivan Moravec (piano), recorded 1966,
Nonesuch B000005J03, 1991, compact disc.

Bibliographic form

Chopin, Frédéric. *Nocturne Op. 9 No. 2.* Ivan Moravec (piano). Recorded 1966. Nonesuch,
B000005J03, 1991. Compact disc.

37. Performance
Full note entry

37. *Proof,* by David Auburn, Walter Kerr Theatre, New York, New York, October 2,
2002.

Bibliographic entry

Auburn, David. *Proof.* Walter Kerr Theatre, New York, New York, October 2, 2002.

38. Work of art
Full note entry

38. *Paul Gaugin, Ancestors of Tehamana*, 1893, oil on canvas, Chicago, IL, Art Institute of
Chicago.

Bibliographic entry

Gaugin, Paul. *Ancestors of Tehamana*, 1893. Oil on canvas. Chicago, IL, Art Institute of
Chicago.

17b   SAMPLE CMS-STYLE PAPER

The following student paper, a historical research project, addresses an
ongoing struggle in South Africa related to electricity usage. Because he
included a full bibliography, Cristian Nuñez supplied endnotes written
in short form. CMS does not provide specific guidelines for a title page
for a student paper, but you can refer to the Turabian-style sample on
page 432 if your instructor requires a title page. Your instructor may
prefer that you format the first page of your paper so that it includes
the information that would appear on a title page (see page 432 for this
format). Only the first pages of his essay, along with portions of his
notes and bibliography, appear here.

Local Politics and National Policy in a Globalized World:

South Africa's Ongoing Electricity Dilemma

Cristian Nuñez

Political Science 87

Professor Stone

December 15, 2014

2

Since its 1994 inception, the South African democracy has struggled
to alleviate national poverty without alienating the global financial
community on which it depends. Even though the government's moderate
pro-business agenda is intended to reduce poverty, it continues to provide
too little support for the nation's poor—an agenda harshly criticized by
citizen-advocate groups. One such group is the Soweto Electricity Crisis
Committee (SECC), a civic organization advocating free basic utilities for
all South Africans, which charges that South Africa's government is not
living up to the human rights core of its Constitution, guaranteeing all
South Africans access to basic resources.[1] The SECC addresses human
rights through its controversial—and illegal—practice of delivering free
electricity to South Africa's poorest people.

The Electricity Crisis

Following the 1993 end of apartheid, the majority (African
National Congress [ANC]) government swept into power with a mandate
to reverse the injustices prevalent in South Africa. Millions of poor
nonwhites hoped that affordable housing, modern education, and basic
utilities would be expanded in their long-neglected neighborhoods.
However, carrying out these goals would prove to be extremely difficult
for the new ANC president Nelson Mandela, who had inherited a huge
financial crisis from the old National Party regime. To avert a spending
crisis of any kind (one that would devalue South African currency both
locally and globally), Mandela's ANC government implemented broad
economic reforms in the hope of directing the foreign investment and
capital inflows necessary for growing the South African economy.[2]

> Although not paginated, the title page is page one

> This introduction establishes the importance of the topic. The thesis statement is the final sentence of the first paragraph.

> Writer explains how the change from apartheid to democracy inadvertently created additional economic woes for nonwhites in South Africa

3

One of the economic reforms included the plan to privatize the

nation's many parastatals (state-owned enterprises). In preparation for

privatization, each parastatal enacted cost-recovery pricing to make itself

more competitive and more attractive to foreign investors. Unfortunately

for the South African poor, such cost-recovery measures eliminated both

subsidized utilities and rent in nonwhite neighborhoods like Soweto,

which is located just outside of Johannesburg and has long been a hotbed

of revolutionary actions and ideas (see Fig. 1). In response, a number of

civics (community action groups) protested the government's economic

reforms, the most brash of them being the SECC.

Figure 1. This township settlement in Soweto typifies the poverty and lack
of access to public services for many South African citizens. Source: Jon
Hrusa, 2005. Kliptown, Soweto: An Anti-Apartheid Symbol. Photograph.
Corbis. http://www.corbisimages.com. (accessed 28 November 2014).

4

By 2001, in an effort to remain financially solvent, South Africa's public utility company, the Electricity Supply Commission (Eskom), was disconnecting twenty thousand households a month for not paying their bills. In response, the SECC illegally reconnected more than three thousand Soweto households in a program called "Reconnect the Power."[3] Because no workable solutions to this problem have yet been discovered since those early disconnections, those illegal reconnections remain in place. In 2009, SECC's electricians were reconnecting nearly forty houses per week, resulting in an estimated 60 percent of Soweto residents receiving electricity without charge. For many of the SECC electricians having electric power is a constitutional right, not a luxury. SECC electrician Levy argues that he and the electricians "are giving back what belongs to the people," thereby justifying the SECC's ongoing activism.[4]

The Legacy of Apartheid and Perceptions of Eskom

Although the SECC was established in 2000, the practice of nonpayment for basic needs has a much longer history in South Africa. During apartheid, the ANC urged residents of Soweto and other townships to stop paying their rent and their electricity and water bills (which were often higher than those of households in upper-class white neighborhoods). The boycott the ANC organized was a powerful weapon against apartheid, eventually bankrupting local authorities. Many people retained this stance of resistance following the end of apartheid. "We did not expect this," said Chris Ngcobo, an organizer of the Soweto boycott under apartheid, who now helps oversee an ANC/Eskom project to reverse

The author breaks his research essay into sections using headings.

5

The rest of the paper describes the ways in which the SECC has intervened in order to provide electricity to poor, nonwhite South Africans.

the culture of nonpayment. "We expected that after the elections people would just pay. But it will not be so easy."[5]

For many residents, nonpayment as protest continued as an intentional act during the Mandela years. During these early post-apartheid years, bill payment was presented as a patriotic gesture in support of the Mandela government.[6] The residents, however, wanted to see improvements first before resuming payment.

6

Notes

1. *Countries of the World.*

2. McNeil, "Shedding State Companies."

3. Bond, *Against Global Apartheid*, 170.

4. Fisher, "South Africa Crisis."

5. Daley, "In South Africa."

6. Ibid.

7

Bibliography

Bond, Patrick. *Against Global Apartheid: South Africa Meets the World Bank, IMF and International Finance.* Cape Town: Univ. of Cape Town Press, 2003.

Chang, Claude V. *Privatisation and Development: Theory, Policy and Evidence.* Hampshire, UK: Ashgate, 2006.

Countries of the World and Their Leaders Yearbook 2015. 2 vols. Detroit: Gale, 2014. http://go.galegroup.com.

Daley, Suzanne. "In South Africa, a Culture of Resistance Dies Hard." *New York Times,* July 19, 1995. http://www.nytimes.com/1995/07/19/world/in-south-africa-a-culture-of-resistance-dies-hard.html.

———. "Seeing Bias in Their Utility Rates, Mixed Race South Africans Riot." *New York Times,* February 7, 1997. http://www.nytimes.com/1997/02/07/world/seeing-bias-in-their-utility-rates-mixed-race-south-africans-riot.html.

Eskom. *Annual Report 1999.* n.d. http://www.eskom.co.za/annreport/main.htm.

Fisher, Jonah. "South Africa Crisis Creates Crusading Electricians." *BBC News,* November 24, 2009. http://news.bbc.co.uk/2/hi/8376400.stm.

Hrusa, Jon. *Kliptown, Soweto: An Anti-Apartheid Symbol.* Corbis, 2005. Photograph. http://www.corbisimages.com.

Kingsnorth, Paul. *One No, Many Yeses.* Sydney: Simon and Schuster, 2003.

McNeil, Donald G., Jr. "Shedding State Companies, if Sometimes Reluctantly." *New York Times,* February 27, 1997. http://www.nytimes.com/1997/02/27/business/shedding-state-companies-if-sometimes-reluctantly.html.

Bibliography begins on a new page

Entries use hanging indent

Two articles by the same author

Unless your instructor specifies double-spacing throughout, bibliographic entries are single-spaced with double-spacing between each entry.

18 ‖ WRITING IN THE NATURAL SCIENCES

The **natural sciences** include mathematics, the biological sciences (biology, botany, and zoology), the physical sciences (chemistry and physics), and the earth sciences (geology and astronomy). They also include **applied sciences** such as engineering, computer science, medicine, and allied health studies. The natural sciences are problem-solving disciplines that report or analyze results derived from meticulous observation and experimentation. For example, Heather Jensen, whose paper appears at the end of this chapter, examined onion root tip cells during five stages of mitosis (cell division). On the basis of her results, she was able to describe how this cell division occurs.

Writing assignments you can expect to receive in natural science courses include literature reviews, field reports, and laboratory reports. To allow you to complete such assignments, this chapter will help you

- determine the audience, purpose, and research question for a paper in the natural sciences (**18a**);
- decide which types of evidence, sources, and reasoning to use in such a paper (**18b**);
- use appropriate language, style, and formatting when writing the paper (**18c**);
- understand typical assignments in the natural sciences (**18d**); and
- learn the conventions for writing a field report (**18e**) and a laboratory report (**18f**).

18a ‖ AUDIENCE, PURPOSE, AND THE RESEARCH QUESTION

Before you start working on a writing assignment for a course in the natural sciences, be sure to consult with your instructor as you determine your audience and your purpose. Your instructor will always be one of your readers, but he or she may ask you to share your work with other readers as well. If you are enrolled in an advanced class, you may be expected to present your work at a local, regional, or national conference. By knowing who constitutes your audience(s), you will be able to gauge how much background information is adequate, how much technical language is appropriate, and what types of evidence and reasoning are necessary.

Researchers in the sciences generally write to inform their readers, either by discussing studies pertaining to a specific topic or by reporting their observations of some phenomenon or the results of an experiment. However, these researchers' purpose may be evaluative if they are critiquing a journal article or argumentative if they are encouraging readers to take a specific action. After you have determined your purpose and audience, formulate a research question that will guide you to sources and help you to use them responsibly (chapters 8–11). The following example research questions focus on global warming:

Questions about cause
What causes global warming?

Questions about consequences
What are the effects of global warming?

Questions about process
How can global warming be stopped?

Questions about definitions or categories
What types of greenhouse gases are responsible for global warming?

Questions about values
What are a scientist's responsibilities concerning the public in the face of global warming?

Research questions in the sciences are often narrowed to enable precise measurements:

Questions about length, distance, frequency, and so on
How far has Mendenhall Glacier receded each year for the past decade, and do the values show any trend?

Questions about comparisons and correlations
How are emission intensities related to the total amount of emissions?

The question Heather Jensen responds to in her laboratory report (**18f**) focuses on a process:

What happens to onion root tip cells during mitosis?

18b   EVIDENCE, SOURCES, AND REASONING

Researchers in the natural sciences attempt to quantify phenomena in the world around them. They look for **empirical evidence**—facts that can be measured or tested—to support their claims. Most of their investigations, then, are set up as experiments. If you conduct an experiment for a course in the natural sciences, you will be expected to start with a **hypothesis**, a prediction that serves as a basis for experimentation. To test the hypothesis, you will follow a procedure—one designed by yourself, established in another study, or specified by your instructor. The results of your experiment will either validate your hypothesis or show it to be in error. This systematic way of proceeding from a hypothesis to verifiable results is called the **scientific method**. Consisting of six steps, this method helps ensure the objectivity and accuracy of experimental findings.

THE SCIENTIFIC METHOD

1. *State a problem*. When you recognize and then state a problem, you establish your rhetorical opportunity (the reason for your writing).
2. *Collect evidence*. Close observation is the key technique for collecting evidence. Be sure to record all details as accurately as you can. Alternatively, you may read the reports of other researchers who have addressed a problem similar to yours. If you draw on observations or experiments, you are using primary sources; if you use scientific articles and statistical charts, you are using secondary sources.
3. *Form a hypothesis*. A hypothesis is a tentative claim, or prediction, about the phenomenon you are studying.
4. *Test the hypothesis*. Although you will have conducted some research before formulating the hypothesis, you continue that research through additional observation or experimentation.
5. *Analyze the results*. Look at your results in light of your hypothesis. Attempt to find patterns, categories, or other relationships.
6. *State the conclusion*. If you have validated your hypothesis, explain why it accounts for *all* of your data. If your hypothesis is disproved, suggest revisions to it or offer a new one.

Reports based on the six steps of the scientific method are **quantitative studies**; their results are presented as numerical data. Heather Jensen's lab report on cell division is a quantitative study. Another type of study performed by scientists, especially those working in the field, is a **qualitative study.** The data in qualitative studies are produced through observation and analysis of natural phenomena. It is not uncommon, however, for studies to have both quantitative and qualitative features.

Regardless of the type of study they perform, scientists depend on previous research to place their work in context. They draw from both primary sources (experiments, observations, surveys, and so on) and secondary sources (books and articles already published on a topic). All sources used in a report or paper in the natural sciences are cited in the body of the text and documented in a reference list. (See chapter **19.**)

18c CONVENTIONS OF LANGUAGE AND ORGANIZATION

(1) Style guidelines

The conventions that most writers in the sciences follow are presented in a manual titled *Scientific Style and Format,* compiled by the Council of Science Editors (CSE). However, you may sometimes be asked to use one of the following manuals:

American Chemical Society. *The ACS Style Guide: Effective Communication of Scientific Information.* 3rd ed. Washington, DC: American Chemical Society, 2006.

American Institute of Physics. *AIP Style Manual.* 4th ed. New York: American Institute of Physics, 1990. (This manual is no longer in print but is available as a free PDF file at http://www.aip.org/pubservs/style/4thed/toc.html.)

American Medical Association. *AMA Manual of Style: A Guide for Authors and Editors.* 10th ed. New York: Oxford Univ. Press, 2007.

United States Geological Society. *Suggestions to Authors of the Reports of the United States Geological Survey.* 7th ed. Washington, DC: Government Printing Office, 1991. (Sections of this manual are available as free PDF files at http://www.nwrc.usgs.gov/lib/lib_sta.htm.)

Style guidelines may also be listed on an organization's website. Before starting any writing project, check with your instructor to see which style manual or website you should use.

The CSE manual says that effective scientific prose has the qualities of accuracy, clarity, conciseness, and fluency. The following tips can help you write in the style recommended by the manual.

TIPS FOR PREPARING A PAPER IN THE NATURAL SCIENCES

- Select words that convey meaning precisely (35a).
- Avoid gender bias (34c).
- If two different wordings are possible, choose the more succinct alternative (36a).
- Clarify noun strings by placing modifiers after the main noun.

  the system for measuring frequency NOT the frequency measuring system

- When using an introductory participial phrase, be sure that it modifies the subject of the sentence (27e). Participial phrases that begin with *based on* are particulary troublesome, so double-check to make sure that such a phrase modifies the subject.

  Based on the promising results, the decision to approve the new medication seemed reasonable.

  NOT Based on the promising results, the new medication was approved.

---

(2) Organization

The most frequent writing assignments in the natural sciences are various types of reports—literature reviews, field reports, and laboratory reports. The specific formats for these reports are presented in **18d–f**.

All scientific reports include headings and often subheadings to help readers find and understand information. Heather Jensen uses three levels of heading in her lab report (**18f**). Writers in the natural sciences also use tables and figures (such as graphs, drawings, and maps) to organize information. Essential for presenting numerical data, tables should be numbered and titled. Each table should be introduced in the text so that readers will understand its purpose. Heather includes two tables in her lab report: one to show the number of cells in each phase of mitosis and one to show the percentage of cells in each phase. She introduces her first table this way: "Table 1 shows the number of cells found in each phase of mitosis." Heather also uses six figures in her report. The first five are drawings that illustrate the five phases of cell division. The sixth is a graph that indicates how much time the onion root tip cells she examined spent in each phase. Like tables, figures should be numbered, titled, and introduced in the text. For instructions on how to create tables and bar graphs with a word processor, see **6c(2)**.

(3) Reference lists

CSE provides three options for citing sources and listing them at the end of a paper: the citation-sequence system, the citation-name system, and the name-year system. You can find specific guidelines for creating a reference list in Chapter **19**.

18d | EXAMPLES OF WRITING IN THE NATURAL SCIENCES

(1) Literature review

A **literature review** is essentially an evaluative overview of research directly related to a specific topic. It focuses on both strengths and weaknesses of previous research—in methodology or interpretation—with the goal of establishing what steps need to be taken to advance research on the topic. A literature review may be assigned as part of a longer paper, in which case the information it contains appears in the introductory section of the paper. In a paper on agate formation, student Michelle Tebbe included the following paragraphs, which provide, respectively, a historical account of research on her topic and a review of relevant current studies:

Scientific interest in agate dates back at least to the 18th century when Collini (1776) contemplated the source of silica for agate formation and suggested a mechanism for producing repetitive banding. In the mid-19th century, Noeggerath (1849) hypothesized that the repetitive banding of agate is indicative of natural, external (to the agate-bearing cavity), rhythmic processes such as bedrock leaching of silica by a fluid that enters into cavities via infiltration canals, forming agate after many separate infiltrations. Other processes such as variation in water-table height (Bauer 1904) and alternating wet-dry seasons (Linck and Heinz 1930) have been credited as responsible for rhythmic infilling of cavities by silica-rich solutions.

These now traditional ideas on agate formation imply fluid-rock interaction at low temperatures (<250 °C). Empirical support for low formation temperatures comes from several published studies. Based on hydrogen and oxygen isotope data, Fallick et al. (1985) estimated the temperature of formation of Devonian and Tertiary basalt-hosted Scottish agate to be approximately 50 °C. Using the same methods, Harris (1989) inferred the temperature of formation for basalt-hosted agate from Namibia to be approximately 120 °C. Lueth and Goodell (2005) performed fluid-inclusion analyses for agate from the Paraná Basalts, Rio do Sul, Brazil, and inferred the temperature of formation to be <50 °C for darker-colored samples and 140–180 °C for lighter-colored samples.

(2) Field report

Field work is research done in a natural environment rather than in a laboratory. Examples of field work range from recording beach erosion to studying avalanche patterns. To record their observations and analyses, researchers working in the field write **field reports**. These reports consist mainly of description and analysis, which may be presented together or in separate sections. A field report sometimes includes a reference list of sources mentioned in the text. (See **18e** for a sample field report.)

(3) Laboratory report

The most common writing assignment in the natural sciences is a **laboratory report**. The purpose of a lab report is to describe an experiment, including the results obtained, so that other researchers understand the procedure used and the conclusions drawn. When writing a lab report, you should explain the purpose of your research, recount the procedure you followed, and discuss your results. The format of this type of report follows the steps of the scientific method by starting with a problem and a hypothesis and concluding with a statement proving, modifying, or disproving the hypothesis.

- The **abstract** states the problem and summarizes the results. (You may not have to include an abstract if your report is short or if your instructor does not require it.)
- The **introduction** states the research question or hypothesis clearly and concisely, explains the scientific basis for the study, and provides

brief background material on the subject of the study and the techniques to be used. The introduction usually includes citations referring to relevant sources.

■ The **methods and materials** section is a narrative that describes how the experiment was conducted. It lists the materials that were used, identifies where the experiment was conducted, and describes the procedures that were followed. (Your lab notes should help you remember what you did.) Anyone who wants to repeat your work should be able to do so by following the steps described in this section.

■ **Results** are reported by describing (but not interpreting) major findings and supporting them with properly labeled tables or graphs showing the empirical data.

■ The **discussion** section includes an analysis of the results and an explanation of their relevance to the goals of the study. This section also reports any problems encountered and offers suggestions for further testing of the results.

■ **References** are listed at the end of the paper. The list includes only works that are referred to in the report. The comprehensiveness and the accuracy of this list allow readers to evaluate the quality of the report and put it into a relevant context.

These sections appear in the sample laboratory report in **18f**.

18e FIELD REPORT ON OBSERVATIONS OF LICHEN DISTRIBUTION

Alyssa Jergens wrote the following field report for a biology course. Her assignment was to form and test a hypothesis on the density and positioning of lichen growth on tree trunks. She worked as a member of a research group, but all the members wrote their own reports. Following the guidelines she was given by her instructor, Alyssa describes the observational study in the Methods section and analyzes the findings in the Results section.

1

Lichen Distribution on Tree Trunks

Alyssa Jergens

General Biology I

October 1, 2014

Method

Our group formulated the hypothesis that lichens grow more densely on higher parts of tree trunks than on lower parts of tree trunks. Our null hypothesis was as follows: there will be no difference in lichen density at various heights on tree trunks. Our hypothesis on lichen density led us to predict that the largest clusters of lichens would be found predominately on higher portions of tree trunks.

The writer describes the observational research.

We conducted our study by sampling 20 trees in a designated area of the Central Washington University campus. Each tree trunk was divided into three sections based on height: from ground level to 0.5 m above the ground; from 0.5 m to 1.0 m above the ground; and from 1.0 m to 1.5 m above the ground. Data were recorded on a diagram (Fig. 1). To the right in the diagram are the height ranges of the sections of tree trunks. The tick marks indicate how many trees had most of their lichens in that section of trunk.

A diagram used for data collection is presented in the Method section.

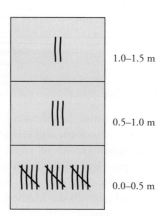

Figure 1 Method for recording lichen density

2

Results

Our observations of lichen growth revealed that lichens are more commonly found on the lower parts of tree trunks. Data from our observational study can be found in Table 1 and Fig. 2. Note that 15 of 20 trees had the densest lichen growth on the lowest section of the trunk (ground level to 0.5 m above the ground).

Table 1 Summary of data

Section of tree trunk	0.0–0.5 m	0.5–1.0 m	1.0–1.5 m
Number of trees with highest lichen density in given trunk section	15	3	2

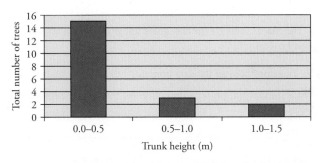

Figure 2 Association of trunk height with lichen distribution

To ensure that the pattern of lichen growth we found was not random, we performed a chi-square test. The observed number, f_o, was determined by counting the total number of trees having the most lichens in each height division. The expected number, f_e, was calculated

3

by taking the total number of trees observed (20) and dividing it by the total number of height divisions (3), to arrive at an expected value of 6.67. The chi-square test results are summarized in Table 2; the calculated value is 15.69.

Table 2 Results of chi-square test

	Observed number (f_o)	Expected number (f_e)	$f_o - f_e$	$(f_o - f_e)^2$	$\dfrac{(f_o - f_e)^2}{f_e}$
0.0–0.5 m	15	6.67	8.33	69.39	10.40
0.5–1.0 m	3	6.67	−3.67	13.47	2.02
1.0–1.5 m	2	6.67	−4.67	21.81	3.27
Total	20	20			15.69

The concluding paragraph acknowledges that the findings did not support the original hypothesis.

The critical value for the chi-square test given to us in class was 5.99. Our calculated chi-square value, 15.69, is greater than the critical value. Therefore, because the data from this observational study do not exhibit a random pattern, it can be concluded that a real nonrandom pattern is present. The results of the chi-square test show that our null hypothesis can be refuted. Although a pattern does exist in the sample of trees we observed, it was not the result we hypothesized. Our hypothesis stated that lichens would grow more densely on the upper portions of tree trunks rather than on the lower portions. Contrary to our expectations, our data and the results of the chi-square test indicate that lichens grow more densely on the lower portions of tree trunks than on the upper portions.

18f   LABORATORY REPORT ON A CELL-DIVISION EXPERIMENT

Heather Jensen's paper is representative of a report based on an experiment outlined in a lab manual for a first-year biology course. It includes section headings and graphics—drawings of the various stages of mitosis and a graph showing the results. The report ends with a reference list formatted according to CSE's citation-sequence system.

1

Observations and Calculations of Onion Root Tip Cells

Heather Jensen

Biology 101

January 9, 2015

Abstract

The first paragraph provides a summary of the experiment.

This laboratory experiment examined *Allium* (onion) root tip cells in the five stages of mitosis. The five stages of mitotic division were identified and recorded, and a 50-cell sample was chosen for closer examination. Of those 50 cells, 64% were found to be in interphase, 20% in prophase, 6% in metaphase, 6% in anaphase, and only 4% in telophase. The results showed that onion root tip cells spend the majority of their life cycle in a rest period (interphase). Prophase was calculated to be the longest phase of active division, while telophase was the shortest. These results were consistent with the experiments completed by other students and scientists.

Introduction

The Introduction section describes the purpose of the experiment.

This lab report outlines a laboratory experiment on mitosis, the division of the nucleus of a cell to form two new cells with the same number of chromosomes as the parent cell. Mitotic cell division consists of five visually identifiable stages: interphase, prophase, metaphase, anaphase, and telophase. The purpose of this experiment was to identify and observe cells in each phase of mitosis, as well as to calculate an estimate of the time involved in each stage of mitosis in an onion root tip cell. The onion root tip was chosen for this experiment because of easy availability and rapid growth. Rapid root growth made it easy to observe

2

multiple cells in the phases of mitosis in a small sample, on one or two slides. Onion root cells complete the entire cycle of division in 80 min, and it was expected that larger numbers of cells would be found in interphase, because the majority of a life cycle is spent performing normal cell functions.

Materials and Methods

The materials required for this experiment include a compound microscope and prepared slides of a longitudinal section of *Allium* (onion) root tip. First, the slides were placed on a compound microscope under low power, a 40× magnification level. The end of the root tip was located; then the cells immediately behind the root cap were examined. These cells appeared as a darker area under low power. This area of cells was identified as the apical meristem,[1] an area of rapid growth and division in the onion root tip. This area of cells was examined, while keeping the microscope on low power, to find and identify cells in interphase, prophase, metaphase, anaphase, and telophase. Then high power, a 400× magnification, was used to further examine and record the appearance of these cells.

After the multiple phases of mitosis were observed, a large area of 50 cells in mitosis was selected for further examination. This area was observed under low power in order to assess rows of cells in an easily countable space. Then the number of cells in each stage of mitosis was counted. These numbers were divided by the total number of cells examined, 50 cells, and multiplied by 100 in order to calculate the percentage of cells in each phase of mitosis. For example, if 10 cells were observed in interphase, then 10/50 = 0.20 and 0.20 • 100 = 20% of cells

The first paragraph in the Materials and Methods section lists the materials used and describes the methodology of the experiment.

A superscript number refers to the first source on the References list.

The writer describes the calculations performed on the data.

3

were in interphase. The actual time of each phase of mitosis in this sample of cells was calculated by multiplying the percentage by the total time of the division cycle, 80 min for the onion root tip cell. For example, if 20% (20/100 = 0.20) of the cells were observed in interphase, then 0.20 • 80 min = 16 min total time were spent in interphase.

The Results section describes the phases of cell division, with labeled drawings as support.

Results

Drawings and Observations

INTERPHASE

    This phase lasts from the completion of a division cycle to the beginning of the next cycle (Fig. 1). All regular cell functions occur in this

The superscript number refers to the second source.

phase (except reproduction). It is not part of mitosis.[2]

Figure 1 Two cells observed in interphase

PROPHASE

    Technically the first phase of mitosis, this stage is marked by the thickening and shortening of chromosomes, which makes them visible under a compound microscope. The nucleus appears grainy at first and then the chromosomes appear more clearly defined as prophase progresses (Fig. 2).

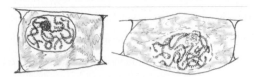

Figure 2 Two cells observed in prophase

4

METAPHASE

This phase is identified by the lining up of double chromosomes along the center line, the equator, of the cell (Fig. 3).

Figure 3 Two cells observed in metaphase

ANAPHASE

This phase is classified by the separation of the double chromosomes. They begin to pull apart to opposite poles of the cell (Fig. 4).

Figure 4 Two cells observed in anaphase

TELOPHASE

In telophase, the chromosomes have reached the opposite poles of the cell, and the connection between the chromosomes begins to break down as the nuclear membrane begins to form around each chromosomal clump (Fig. 5). At the end of telophase, cytokinesis, or the division of the cytoplasm, takes place. In plant cells, a cell plate begins to form in the center of the cell and then grows outward to form a new cell wall, completely dividing the old cell into two new cells, both with a complete set of chromosomes.

Figure 5 Two cells observed in telophase

Table 1 shows the number of cells found in each phase of mitosis.

Table 1 Number of cells in each phase

Interphase	Prophase	Metaphase	Anaphase	Telophase
32 cells	10 cells	3 cells	3 cells	2 cells

Tables summarize findings.

Table 2 shows the calculated percentage of cells in each phase of mitosis.

Table 2 Percentage of cells in each phase

Interphase	Prophase	Metaphase	Anaphase	Telophase
64%	20%	6%	6%	4%

Fig. 6 shows the actual time cells spent in each phase of mitosis.

The writer includes a graph that presents key results clearly.

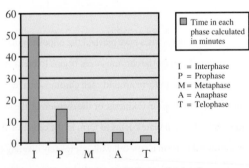

Figure 6 Time spent in each phase of mitosis

6

Discussion

This laboratory experiment provided firsthand experience with the phases of cell division. The five phases became more easily recognizable as each cell was examined and classified. Cells often looked like they could be classified in interphase or prophase or like they were between phases. Observation led to the confirmation that mitosis is a fluid process and not just a series of distinct phases. During the experiment, difficulties with overdyed and gray areas caused uncertainty because visual indications of phase were impossible to detect. This problem was addressed through the careful selection of clear patches of cells for observation. The expectation that a large number of cells would be found in interphase was confirmed by the numbers of cells counted in the cell sample of the onion root tip. Online comparison of the results of this experiment to those of other similar experiments confirmed the results found here as typical of an onion (*Allium*) root tip.[3] This indicated that the careful selection of clear patches of cells for sampling proved an effective method for eliminating error that might have been caused by the incorrect labeling of cells or the poor visibility of cells in overdyed or gray areas. Further studies might include larger samples of cells. Experiments with larger numbers of cells would offer additional evidence to confirm the results found in this experiment.

The writer explains how the results of the experiment fulfilled its purpose.

The writer describes a problem that was encountered.

The superscript number refers to the third source.

7

References

1. Solomon EP, Martin CE, Martin DW, Berg LA. Biology. 10th ed. Stamford (CT): Cengage; 2015. Plant meristems; p. 714–716.

2. The biology project. Tucson (AZ): Department of Biochemistry and Molecular Biophysics, University of Arizona; c1997 [updated 2004; accessed 2015 Jan 9]. http://www.biology.arizona.edu/cell_bio/tutorials /cell_cycle/cells3.html.

3. Yesnik A, Jaster K. The bio 1 super virtual lab book. Washington (DC): Sidwell Friends School; c1998 [updated 2002; accessed 2015 Jan 9]. Mitosis lab. http://classic.sidwell.edu/us/science/vlb/mitosis/.

The list of references is formatted according to the citation-sequence system.

19 | CSE DOCUMENTATION

The Council of Science Editors (CSE) has established guidelines for writers in the life and physical sciences. *Scientific Style and Format: The CSE Manual for Authors, Editors, and Publishers*, eighth edition, covers general style conventions for punctuation, capitalization, and so forth, as well as specific advice for the use of scientific terminology and formulas. In addition, the manual presents three systems for citing and documenting research sources: the citation-sequence system, the name-year system, and the citation-name system. This chapter includes

- guidelines for citing sources and organizing material within a CSE-style research paper (**19a**) and
- guidelines for documenting sources in a CSE-style list of references (**19b**).

A sample CSE-style report is shown in **18f**.

19a | CSE-STYLE IN-TEXT CITATIONS

CSE's guidelines for the citation-sequence system, the name-year system, and the citation-name system differ significantly, so be sure to know which one to use before you get started. Once you know your instructor's preference, follow the guidelines in one of the following boxes as you prepare your in-text references.

These guidelines are for both paraphrases and quotations. If a quotation is brief, incorporate it into a sentence. A comma or period at the end of a quotation is placed inside the quotation marks. A lengthy quotation should be set off as a block quotation.

TIPS FOR PREPARING CITATION-SEQUENCE IN-TEXT REFERENCES

- Place a superscript number after each mention of a source or each use of material from it. This number corresponds to the number assigned to the source in the end references.
- Be sure to place the number immediately after the material used or the word or phrase indicating the source: Herbert's original method[1] was used.
- Use the same number each time you refer to a source.
- Order the numbers according to the sequence in which sources are introduced: Both Li[1] and Holst[2] have shown . . .
- When referring to more than one source, use commas to separate the numbers corresponding to the sources; there is no space after each comma. Use an en dash between two numbers to indicate a sequence of sources: The early studies[1,2,4–7] . . .

TIPS FOR PREPARING NAME-YEAR IN-TEXT REFERENCES

- Place the author's last name and the year of publication in parentheses after the mention of a source: In a more recent study (Karr 2015), these findings were not replicated. Using the author's last name, the reader will be able to find the corresponding entry in the alphabetized reference list.
- Omit the author's name from the parenthetical citation if it appears in the text preceding it: In Karr's study (2015), these findings were not replicated.
- If the source has two authors, use both of their last names: (Phill and Richardson 2015). If there are three or more authors, use the first author's last name and the abbreviation *et al.*: (Drake et al. 2014).
- Use semicolons to separate multiple citations. Order these citations chronologically when the years differ but alphabetically when the years are the same: (Li 2014; Holst 2015) but (Lamont 2014; Li 2014).

TIPS FOR PREPARING CITATION-NAME IN-TEXT REFERENCES

- Arrange your end references alphabetically. Then assign each reference a number. Use the superscript form of this number in the text immediately after the material used or the word or phrase indicating the source: Stress-related illnesses are common among college students.[1]

- Use the same number each time you refer to a source.

- When referring to more than one source, use commas to separate the numbers corresponding to the sources; there is no space after each comma. Use an en dash between two numbers to indicate a sequence of sources: Recent studies of posttraumatic stress disorder[1,2,4–7] . . .

19b   CSE-STYLE LIST OF REFERENCES

On the final page of your paper, list all the sources you have mentioned. The ordering of the entries will depend on which system you have chosen. Both the citation-name system and the name-year system require alphabetical ordering according to the authors' last names; the citation-sequence system requires that the sources be listed in the order they were mentioned in your text.

TIPS FOR PREPARING END REFERENCES

- Center the heading "References" or "Cited References" at the top of the page.

- If you are using the *citation-sequence system*, list the sources in the order in which they were introduced in the text.

- If you are using the *citation-name system*, your end references should be ordered alphabetically according to the first author's last name and then numbered.

- If you are using the *name-year system*, your end references should be ordered alphabetically.

(continued on page 460)

(continued from page 459)

- Entries in citation-sequence and citation-name reference lists differ only in overall organization: citation-sequence references are listed according to the order of occurrence within the text; citation-name references are listed alphabetically. The name-year system differs from both the citation-sequence and citation-name systems only in the placement of the date of publication: the name-year system calls for the date to be placed after the author's name; the citation-sequence and the citation-name systems call for the date to be placed after the publisher's name in entries for books and after the name of the periodical in entries for articles.

- When listing place of publication information, if the city is not well known or could be confused with another city, include an abbreviation for the state or country in parentheses after the name of the city. The name of a country may be spelled out.

The following entries are organized to present the citation-sequence or citation-name system first, followed by entries reflecting the name-year system.

Directory to CSE Reference List Entries

BOOKS

1. Book with one author   465
2. Book with two or more authors   465
3. Book with an organization (or organizations) listed as author   465
4. Book with editor(s)   466
5. Section of a book with an editor   466
6. Chapter or part of an edited book   466
7. Paper or abstract in conference proceedings   467

ARTICLES

8. Article in a scholarly journal   467
9. Article in a weekly journal   467
10. Article in a magazine   468
11. Article in a newspaper   468

ONLINE SOURCES

The following guidelines are for the citation-sequence or the citation-name system. For examples of reference-list entries for the name-year system, see page 465.

GENERAL DOCUMENTATION GUIDELINES FOR PRINT AND ONLINE SOURCES

Author or Editor

One author. Begin the bibliographic entry with the author's last name followed by the initials for the first name and the middle name (if one is given). Notice that there is no comma after the last name and no period or space between initials.	Klemin TK. Laigo MS.
Two or more authors. Invert the names and initials of all authors, using commas to separate the authors' names.	Stearns BL, Sowards JP. Collum AS, Dahl PJ, Steele TP.
Organization as author. If the author is a division in a larger organization, the name of the organization comes before the name of the division.	American Medical Association. United States Department of Agriculture, US Forest Service.

(continued on page 462)

Author or Editor *(continued from page 461)*

Editor. Add the word *editor* or *editors* after the last name.	Walter PA, editor.
	Mednick VB, Henry JP, editors.

Titles

Books. Use the title given on the book's title page. Titles are neither underlined nor italicized. Capitalize only the first word of the title and any proper nouns or adjectives. A subtitle does not begin with a capital letter unless its first word is a proper noun or adjective. If the book is a second or subsequent edition, follow the title with a period and then the number of the edition.	The magpies: the ecology and behaviour of black-billed and yellow-billed magpies. Genetics. 5th ed.

Journals, magazines, and newspapers. For the names of journals and magazines that are longer than one word, use standard abbreviations (for example, *Sci Am* for *Scientific American*). Rules for abbreviating journal names are given in Appendix 29.1 of the CSE manual and can also be found using a search engine (enter "CSE journal abbreviations"). Use full names of newspapers, but any initial *the* may be dropped.	J Mamm. (for *Journal of Mammology*) New York Times.

Publication Data

Books. Include the place of publication, the publisher's name, and the year of publication. The place of publication can usually be found on the title page. If more than one	London: Chatto & Windus; 2015. Orlando (FL): Harcourt; 2011, c2006.

city is mentioned, use the first one listed. If the city is not well known, clarify its location by including an abbreviation for the state, province, or country in parentheses after the name of the city. The publisher's name is separated from the place of publication by a colon and one space. (Standard abbreviations for publishers' names may be used.) List the source's year of publication after the publisher's name, following a semicolon and one space. If the book has both a year of publication and a copyright year, include just the year of publication unless three or more years separate the two, in which case both dates should be used. The copyright year should be marked with the letter *c.* Sometimes only the copyright year will be available.

Journals and magazines. Use one space after the name of the journal or magazine; then provide the year of publication, the volume number, and the issue number. Place a semicolon between the year of publication and the volume number. Put the issue number in parentheses. Notice that there are no spaces separating the year, the volume number, and the issue number.

Nature. 2009;420(6911)

Natl Geogr Mag. 2009;211(3)

Newspapers. Place the year, month, and day of publication (if any) after the name of the newspaper.

New York Times. 2011 Aug 1

(continued on page 464)

(continued from page 463)
Page Numbers

Books. Page numbers are not always required, so ask your instructor for guidance. If page numbers are required, that information is provided at the end of an entry. When you are citing an entire book, list the total number of pages, excluding preliminary pages with roman numerals. If you have used only part of a book, list just the pages you used. Use the abbreviation *p* for *pages* after the total number of pages but before a range of pages.

University of Chicago Press. 315 p.

OR

Taylor and Francis. p. 136–164.

Journals and magazines. Page numbers should be expressed as a range at the end of an entry.

Natl Geogr Mag. 2011;219(4):82–89.

Newspapers. At the end of the entry, include the section letter, the page number, and the column number.

Houston Chronicle. 2010 Apr 19; Sect. A:2 (col. 1).

Electronic Sources

Entries for electronic sources are similar to those for print sources; however, they include some additional pieces of information:

1. The date of any update or revision, preceded by the word *updated* or *modified*, is given in square brackets after the date of publication.

2. The date of access, preceded by the word *accessed*, is also given in square brackets after the date of publication.

Duru M, Ansquer P, Jouany C, Theau JP, Cruz P. Comparison of methods for assessing the impact of different disturbances and nutrient conditions upon functional characteristics of grassland communities. Ann Bot. 2010 [accessed 2015 May 1];106(5):833–842. http://aob.oxfordjournals.org/content/106/5/823.full.

See pages 468–471 for other examples.

If an updated date is included, the date of access follows it.

3. The Internet address (URL) is included at the end of the entry. If the Internet address must continue on an additional line, break the address after a slash or other punctuation mark.

BOOKS

1. Book with one author
Citation-sequence or citation-name system

1. King BJ. How animals grieve. Chicago: University of Chicago Press; 2013. 193 p.

Name-year system

King BJ. 2013. How animals grieve. Chicago: University of Chicago Press. 193 p.

2. Book with two or more authors
Citation-sequence or citation-name system

2. Ohanian HC, Ruffini R. Gravitation and spacetime. 3rd ed. Cambridge (England): Cambridge University Press; 2013.

Name-year system

Ohanian HC, Ruffini R. 2013. Gravitation and spacetime. 3rd ed. Cambridge (England): Cambridge University Press.

3. Book with an organization (or organizations) listed as author
Citation-sequence or citation-name system

3. International Organization for Migration. Migration, environment and climate change: assessing the evidence. Laczko F, Aghazarm C, editors. Geneva (Switzerland): International Organization for Migration; 2009.

Name-year system

International Organization for Migration. 2009. Migration, environment and climate change: assessing the evidence. Laczko F, Aghazarm C, editors. Geneva (Switzerland): International Organization for Migration.

4. Book with editor(s)
Citation-sequence or citation-name system

4. Lund B, Hunter P, editors. The microbiological safety of food in healthcare settings. Malden (MA): Blackwell; 2007.

Name-year system

Lund B, Hunter P, editors. 2007. The microbiological safety of food in healthcare settings. Malden (MA): Blackwell.

5. Section of a book with an editor
Citation-sequence or citation-name system

5. Banich MT. Hemispheric specialization and cognition. In: Whitaker HA, editor. Concise encyclopedia of brain and language. Oxford (England): Elsevier; 2010. p. 224–230.

Name-year system

Banich MT. 2010. Hemispheric specialization and cognition. In: Whitaker HA, editor. Concise encyclopedia of brain and language. Oxford (England): Elsevier. p. 224–230.

6. Chapter or part of an edited book
Citation-sequence or citation-name system

6. Martin DJ. Social data. In: Wilson J, Fotheringham AS, editors. The handbook of geographic information science. Malden (MA): Blackwell; 2008. p. 35–48.

Name-year system

Martin DJ. 2008. Social data. In: Wilson J, Fotheringham AS, editors. The handbook of geographic information science. Malden (MA): Blackwell. p. 35–48.

7. Paper or abstract in conference proceedings
Citation-sequence or citation-name system

7. Barge RA. Using standards to support human factors engineering. In: Anderson M, editor. Contemporary ergonomics and human factors 2013: proceedings of the International Conference on Ergonomics and Human Factors; 2013 Apr 15–18, Cambridge, England. Croydon (England): Taylor & Francis; 2013. p. 135–137.

Name-year system

Barge RA. 2013. Using standards to support human factors engineering. In: Anderson M, editor. Contemporary ergonomics and human factors 2013: proceedings of the International Conference on Ergonomics and Human Factors; 2013 Apr 15–18; Cambridge, England. Croydon (England): Taylor & Francis. p. 135–137.

ARTICLES
8. Article in a scholarly journal
Citation-sequence or citation-name system

8. Kao-Kniffin J, Freyre DS, Balser TC. Increased methane emissions from an invasive wetland plant under elevated carbon dioxide levels. Appl Soil Ecol. 2011;48(3):309–312.

Name-year system

Kao-Kniffin J, Freyre DS, Balser TC. 2011. Increased methane emissions from an invasive wetland plant under elevated carbon dioxide levels. Appl Soil Ecol. 48(3):309–312.

9. Article in a weekly journal
Citation-sequence or citation-name system

9. Mishra SK, Hoon MA. The cells and circuitry for itch responses in mice. Science. 2013 May 24:968–971.

Name-year system

Mishra SK, Hoon MA. 2013 May 24. The cells and circuitry for itch responses in mice. Science. 968–971.

10. Article in a magazine
Citation-sequence or citation-name system

10. McKibben B. Carbon's new math. Natl Geogr. 2007;212(4):33–37.

Name-year system

McKibben B. 2007. Carbon's new math. Natl Geogr. 212(4):33–37.

11. Article in a newspaper
Citation-sequence or citation-name system

11. O'Connor A. Heart attack risk linked to time spent in traffic. New York Times. 2004
    Oct 26;Sect. F:9 (col. 4).

Name-year system

O'Connor A. 2004 Oct 26. Heart attack risk linked to time spent in traffic. New York
Times. Sect. F:9 (col. 4).

ONLINE SOURCES

12. Online book
Citation-sequence or citation-name system

12. Institute of Medicine, Committee on the Effect of Climate Change on Indoor Air
    Quality and Public Health. Climate change, the indoor environment, and health.
    Washington (DC): National Academy Press; 2011 [accessed 2013 May 26].
    http://www.nap.edu/catalog.php?record_id=13115.

Name-year system

Institute of Medicine, Committee on the Effect of Climate Change on Indoor Air
Quality and Public Health. 2011. Climate change, the indoor environment, and health.
Washington (DC): National Academy Press; [accessed 2013 May 26].
http://www.nap.edu/catalog.php?record_id=13115.

13. Article in an online journal
Citation-sequence or citation-name system

13. Miller MR, White A, Boots M. Host life span and the evolution of resistance
    characteristics. Evol. 2007 [accessed 2007 Oct 31];61(1):2–14.
    http://www.blackwell-synergy.com/doi/full/10.1111/j.1558–5646.2007.00001.x.

Name-year system

Miller MR, White A, Boots M. 2007. Host life span and the evolution of resistance characteristics. Evol. [accessed 2007 Oct 31];61(1):2–14. http://www.blackwell-synergy.com/doi/full/10.1111/j.1558–5646.2007.00001.x.

14. Article in a database
Citation-sequence or citation-name system

14. Stave G, Darcey DJ. Prevention of laboratory animal allergy in the United States. J Occup Environ Med. 2012 [accessed 2013 May 17]; 54(5):558–563. Academic Search Complete. Ipswich (MA): EBSCO. http://web.ebscohost.com. Document No.: 75239696.

Because CSE does not provide specific guidelines for citing an article retrieved from a database, this entry follows the guidelines for citing an online journal and a database.

Name-year system

Stave G, Darcey DJ. 2012. Prevention of laboratory animal allergy in the United States. J Occup Environ Med. [accessed 2013 May 17]; 54(5):558–563. Academic Search Complete. Ipswich (MA): EBSCO. http://web.ebscohost.com. Document No.: 75239696.

15. Article in an online magazine
Citation-sequence or citation-name system

15. Shermer M. Weirdonomics and quirkology: how the curious science of the oddities of everyday life yields new insights. Sci Am. 2007 [accessed 2007 Nov 1];1297(5):45. http://www.scientificamerican.com/article/weirdonomics-and-quirkology/.

Name-year system

Shermer M. 2007. Weirdonomics and quirkology: how the curious science of the oddities of everyday life yields new insights. Sci Am. [accessed 2007 Nov 1];1297(5):45. http://www.scientificamerican.com/article/weirdonomics-and-quirkology/.

16. Article in an online newspaper
Citation-sequence or citation-name system

16. Singer N. Making ads that whisper to the brain. New York Times. Online version.
2010 Nov 13 [accessed 2010 Nov 29]. http://www.nytimes.com/2010/11/14/business/
14stream.html?ref=health.

Name-year system

Singer N. 2010 Nov 13. Making ads that whisper to the brain. New York Times.
Online version. [accessed 2010 Nov 29]. http://www.nytimes.com/2010/11/14/business/
14stream.html?ref=health.

17. Website
Citation-sequence or citation-name system

17. Southern California Earthquake Data Center. Pasadena (CA): Caltech; c2013 [updated
2013 Jan 31; accessed 2013 Jun 3]. http://www.data.scec.org/.

Name-year system

Southern California Earthquake Data Center. c2013. Pasadena (CA): Caltech; [updated
2013 Jan 31; accessed 2013 Jun 3]. http://www.data.scec.org/.

18. Short work from a website
Citation-sequence or citation-name system

18. National Wind Institute. Lubbock (TX): Texas Tech University; c2013. The
Enhanced Fujita scale; 2011 Aug 4 [accessed 2013 Jun 3]; [13 paragraphs].
http://www.spc.noaa.gov/efscale/.

Be sure to include both the copyright date for the site and the publication date for the short work.

Name-year system

National Wind Institute. c2013. Lubbock (TX): Texas Tech University. The Enhanced Fujita
scale; 2011 Aug 4 [accessed 2013 Jun 3]; [13 paragraphs]. http://www.spc.noaa.gov/efscale/.

19. Report from a government agency
Citation-sequence or citation-name system

19. Centers for Disease Control and Prevention, Department of Health and Human Services. Fourth National Report on Human Exposure to Environmental Chemicals, 2009. Atlanta (GA): Centers for Disease Control and Prevention; 2009 [accessed 2010 Dec 10]. http://www.cdc.gov/exposurereport/pdf/FourthReport.pdf.

Name-year system

Centers for Disease Control and Prevention, Department of Health and Human Services. 2009. Fourth National Report on Human Exposure to Environmental Chemicals, 2009. Atlanta (GA): Centers for Disease Control and Prevention; [accessed 2010 Dec 10]. http://www.cdc.gov/exposurereport/pdf/FourthReport.pdf.

20. Online video
Citation-sequence or citation-name system

20. Among giants [video]. Rainhouse Cinema. 2011, 12:51 minutes. [accessed 2015 May 1]. https://vimeo.com/66173800.

Name-year system

Among giants. 2011. [video]. Rainhouse Cinema. 12:51 minutes. [accessed 2015 May 1]. https://vimeo.com/66173800.

The following sample entries for a reference list according to the name-year system correspond to those listed as items 1 through 8 on pp.465–467. Notice that the list is alphabetized. Entries in the citation-name system are also alphabetized. Entries in the citation-sequence system, however, are placed in the order in which they were introduced in the paper.

References

Banich MT. 2010. Hemispheric specialization and cognition. In: Whitaker HA, editor. Concise encyclopedia of brain and language. Oxford (England): Elsevier. p. 224–230.

Barge RA. 2013. Using standards to support human factors engineering. In: Anderson M, editor. Contemporary ergonomics and human factors 2013: proceedings of the International Conference on

Ergonomics and Human Factors; 2013 Apr 15–18; Cambridge, England. Croydon (England): Taylor & Francis. p. 135–137.

International Organization for Migration. 2009. Migration, environment and climate change: assessing the evidence. Laczko F, Aghazarm C, editors. Geneva (Switzerland): International Organization for Migration.

Kao-Kniffin J, Freyre DS, Balser TC. 2011. Increased methane emissions from an invasive wetland plant under elevated carbon dioxide levels. Appl Soil Ecol. 48(3):309–312.

King BJ. 2013. How animals grieve. Chicago: University of Chicago Press. 193 p.

Lund B, Hunter P, editors. 2007. The microbiological safety of food in healthcare settings. Malden (MA): Blackwell.

Martin DJ. 2008. Social data. In: Wilson J, Fotheringham AS, editors. The handbook of geographic information science. Malden (MA): Blackwell. p. 35–48.

Ohanian HC, Ruffini R. 2013. Gravitation and spacetime. 3rd ed. Cambridge (England): Cambridge University Press.

20 | WRITING IN BUSINESS

Writing in business, like writing in any other environment, requires close attention to the rhetorical situation: opportunity, audience, purpose, message, and context. It differs from other writing, however, in the nature of authorship: as a business writer, you need to present yourself and your employer as credible and reliable—whether you are writing to explain, solve a problem, gather information, analyze, or argue a point. One way to project that positive image is to follow the conventions and formats expected by the business community.

On the job or in business courses, you will receive a variety of writing assignments: letters, memos and e-mails, PowerPoint presentations, oral reports, and business reports. This chapter will help you

- recognize the stylistic conventions of standard business writing (**20a**),
- draft a business letter (**20b**),
- produce business memos and e-mails (**20c**),
- compose a résumé (**20d**) and a letter of application (**20e**),
- prepare an oral report including a PowerPoint presentation (**20f**), and
- research and write a formal business report (**20g**).

20a | CONVENTIONS OF LANGUAGE AND ORGANIZATION

In any business environment, you will face both anticipated and unexpected deadlines. The following strategies for effective business communication will help you produce comprehensive, concise, and well-organized documents on time.

STRATEGIES FOR EFFECTIVE BUSINESS COMMUNICATION

Be direct.

- Know who your audience members are and consider their needs.
- State the purpose of your document in your opening paragraph.
- Use language that your audience will find easy to understand.
- Avoid informal language unless you know that a casual tone is acceptable.
- Use technical language only when writing for a specialized audience.

Be concise.

- Compose direct, uncomplicated sentences.
- Include only necessary details.
- Use numbers, bullets, or descriptive headings that guide readers to information.
- Use graphs, tables, and other visual elements to convey information succinctly.

Use conventional formatting.

- Follow the standard formats that have been established within a business or industry or use the formats outlined in this chapter (20b–g).
- Edit and proofread your documents carefully.

20b   BUSINESS LETTERS

Though business letters serve a variety of purposes, they all generally follow a standard block format: each element is aligned flush with the left margin (set at one inch), single-spacing between lines and double-spacing between paragraphs and standard elements.

ELEMENTS OF A STANDARD BUSINESS LETTER

- **Return address.** If you are not required to use stationery with a letterhead, type your address one inch from the top of the paper.

- **Date.** If you are using letterhead stationery, type the date one or two lines below the letterhead's last line. Otherwise, type the date beneath your return address.

- **Recipient's name and address.** Provide the full name and address of the recipient. If you do not know the person's name, try to find it by checking the company's website or phoning the company. If you cannot find the recipient's name, use an appropriate title such as *Personnel Director* or *Customer Service Manager* (not italicized).

- **Greeting.** The conventional greeting is *Dear* (not italicized) followed by the recipient's name and a colon. If you and the recipient use first names to address each other, use the person's first name. Otherwise, use *Mr., Ms., Mrs.,* or *Miss* and the last name. (Choose *Ms.* when you do not know a woman's preference.) Use a full name if you are unsure of the recipient's gender (*Dear Chris Leigh*).

- **Body of the letter.** Most business letters fit on a single sheet of paper. If your letter must continue on a second page, include the recipient's last name, the date, and the page number in three single-spaced lines at the top left on the second page.

- **Closing.** Close your letter two lines after the end of the body with an expression such as *Sincerely* or *Cordially* followed by a comma.

- **Signature.** Type your full name four lines below the closing. Then, in the space above your typed name, sign your full name, using blue or black ink. If you have addressed the recipient by his or her first name, sign just your first name.

- **Additional information.** If you are enclosing extra material such as a résumé, type the word *Enclosure* or the abbreviation *Encl.* (not italicized) two lines below your name. You may also note the number of enclosures or the identity of the document(s): for example, *Enclosures (3)* or *Encl.: 2015 Annual Year-End Report.* If you would like the recipient to know the names of people receiving copies of the letter, use the abbreviation *cc* (for "carbon copy") and a colon followed by the other recipients' names. Place this element on the line directly below the enclosure line or, if there is no enclosure, two lines below your name.

The sample **letter of inquiry** (a letter intended to elicit information) in figure 20.1 illustrates the parts of a typical business letter.

Return address and date	550 First Avenue Ellensburg, WA 98926 February 4, 2015
Name and address of recipient	Mr. Mark Russell Bilingual Publications 5400 Sage Avenue Yakima, WA 98907
Greeting	Dear Mr. Russell:
Body of letter	I am a junior in the Bilingual Education Program at Central Washington University. For my coursework, I am investigating positions in publishing that include the use of two languages. Your name and address were given to me by my instructor, Marta Cole, who worked for you from 2010 through 2014. I have learned something about your publications on your website. I am most interested in dual documents—those in both English and Spanish. Could you please send me samples of such documents so that I can have a better idea of the types of publications you produce? I am also interested in finding out what qualifications I would need to work for a business like yours. I am fluent in both Spanish and English and have taken a course in translation. If possible, I would like to ask you a few questions about your training and experience. Would you have time for an interview some day next week?
Closing	Sincerely,
Signature	*Chris Humphrey* Chris Humphrey

Figure 20.1: A sample letter of inquiry. (© 2013 Cengage Learning)

20c | BUSINESS MEMOS AND E-MAILS

A **memo** (short for *memorandum*) is a brief document, usually focusing on one topic, sent within a business to announce a meeting, explain an event or situation, set a schedule, or request information or action (see figure 20.2). Like memos, e-mail messages are used for internal communication, but they are also used for external communication, for initiating and maintaining relationships with clients, prospective employees, or people at other companies. The basic guidelines for writing memos also apply to e-mail messages.

Because it is circulated internally, a memo or e-mail is usually less formal than a letter. Nonetheless, it should still be direct and concise: a memo should be no longer than a page, and an e-mail no longer than a screen. A conversational tone is acceptable for an internal message to a coworker, but a more formal tone is required for an e-mail or a memo to a supervisor, for example. The following guidelines for formatting these kinds of documents are fairly standard, but a particular company or organization may establish its own format.

To:	Intellectual Properties Committee	Heading
From:	Leo Renfrow, Chair of Intellectual Properties Committee	
Date:	March 15, 2015	
Subject:	Review of Policy Statement	

At the end of our last meeting, we decided to have our policy statement reviewed by someone outside our university. Clark Beech, chair of the Intellectual Properties Committee at Lincoln College, agreed to help us. Overall, as his review shows, the format of our policy statement is sound. Dr. Beech believes that some of the content should be further developed, however. It appears that we have used some ambiguous terms and included some conditions that would not hold up in court.

Body of memo

Early next week, my assistant will deliver a copy of Dr. Beech's review to each of you. Please look it over before our next meeting, on March 29. If you have any questions or comments before then, please call me at ext. 1540. I look forward to seeing all of you at the meeting.

Figure 20.2: A sample business memo. (© 2013 Cengage Learning)

ELEMENTS OF A STANDARD BUSINESS MEMO OR E-MAIL

- **Heading.** On four consecutive lines, type *To* (not italicized) followed by a colon and the name(s) of the recipient(s), *From* followed by a colon and your name and title (if appropriate), *Date* followed by a colon and the date, and *Subject* followed by a colon and a few words identifying the memo's subject. (The abbreviation *Re*, for "regarding," is sometimes used instead of *Subject*.) This information should be single-spaced. If you are sending copies to individuals whose names are not included in the *To* line, place those names on a new line beginning with *cc* ("carbon copy") and a colon. Most e-mail software supplies these header lines on any new message.

- **Body.** Use the block format (**20b**), single-spacing lines within each paragraph and double-spacing between paragraphs. Double-space between the heading and the body of the memo. Open your memo with the most important information and establish how it affects your audience. Use your conclusion to establish goodwill.

- **Signature.** It is not strictly necessary to sign a memo or e-mail because your name is in the heading. Some writers, however, do sign their names, often with a polite closing such as *Sincerely* or *Best wishes*. One way to enhance the professional tone of your messages is to use an e-mail signature—a set of information that identifies you and your company or organization.

Regular e-mail users receive a large volume of messages every day. For that reason, most people are in the habit of scanning messages, deleting many without reading them. To ensure that an e-mail receives the attention it merits, you should announce your topic in the subject line and then arrange and present your message in concise, readable chunks (perhaps bulleted or numbered lists) that incorporate white space and guide recipients to important information. Short paragraphs also allow for white space, which helps readers to pay attention and absorb the key points.

TIPS FOR SENDING ATTACHMENTS WITH E-MAIL MESSAGES

- Use attachments only when absolutely necessary. If you plan to attach files, do so before writing your message; that way you will not forget and send your message without the attachments.

- Before you send any attachment, consider the size of the file—many inboxes have limited space and cannot accept large files or multiple files (totalling over 10 MB) or files that contain streaming video, photographs, or sound clips. If there is a chance that a large file might crash a recipient's e-mail program, call or e-mail the recipient to ask permission before sending it.

- When you do not know the type of operating system or software installed on a recipient's computer, send text-only documents in rich text format (indicated by the file suffix **.rtf**), which preserves most formatting and is recognized by many word-processing programs.

- Attachments are notorious for transmitting computer viruses; therefore, never open an attachment sent by someone you do not know or any attachment if your computer does not have active antivirus software. You can get virus-related updates and alerts on the website for your computer's operating system or from suppliers such as McAfee and Symantec.

❶ CAUTION

E-mail messages that you send from or receive at your workplace are not necessarily private or secure. For this reason, avoid using your work e-mail for personal communications, whether you are forwarding someone else's private message to you or sending jokes, chain letters, or petitions for good causes. Employers have been vindicated in cases in which they were charged with privacy violations for reading employees' e-mail. Most companies and organizations have an e-mail policy specifying employees' responsibilities and appropriate employer responses to violations of the policy. Be sure you know what the policy of your employer is.

20d   RÉSUMÉS

A **résumé** is essentially an argument (chapter 7) designed to emphasize a person's job qualifications by highlighting his or her experience
and abilities. Along with its accompanying letter of application (**20e**),
a résumé should command attention and establish a positive first
impression—immediately. Most interviewers say they spend less than a
minute scanning each résumé as they search for what exactly the applicant can contribute to the organization. Thus, your résumé should be
easy to read, with clear headings, adequate white space, and traditional
format. It should also highlight the parts of your education and experience and the particular skills that best suit the specific position you are
applying for.

Once you have listed all of your potentially relevant work and
educational information, decide what to exclude, include, and emphasize by reviewing what the specific job advertisement says about desired
experience and traits. To familiarize yourself with a company's goals and
philosophy, check its website. If you create and save your résumé as a
word-processing file, you can easily tailor it to various positions during
your job search.

The next step is to decide how to organize your résumé. A **chronological résumé** lists positions and activities in *reverse* chronological
order; that is, your most recent experience comes first. This format
works well if you have a steady job history and want to emphasize your
most recent experience because it is closely related to the position for
which you are applying. An alternative way to organize a résumé is to
list experience in terms of job skills rather than jobs held. This format,
called a **functional résumé**, is especially useful when you have the
required skills, but your work history in the particular field is modest or
you are just starting your career.

Regardless of the format you choose, remember that your résumé is,
in effect, going to someone's office for a job interview. Make sure that it
is dressed for success. Effective résumés are brief, so try to design your
résumé to fit on a single page. Use good-quality paper (preferably white
or off-white) and a laser printer. Choose a standard format and a traditional typeface, applying them consistently throughout. Use boldface
or italic type only for headings. Remember that your choices regarding
indentations, spacing, white space, typeface, and margins contribute

to the overall readability and effectiveness of your résumé. Resist the impulse to make the design unnecessarily complicated: when in doubt, opt for simplicity.

◻ TECH SAVVY

When you are ready to create your résumé, you may find it helpful to use a software program (such as Résumé Wizard from Microsoft) that allows you to select the kind of résumé you need and then prompts you to complete the various sections. Such software also allows you to view your completed document in its entirety and redesign any or all of it. Some job applicants create an **online résumé**, a web-based version that may include links to documents representative of the applicant's work. In addition, these applicants create a non-web version to be downloaded and printed out and possibly scanned into a résumé database. If a job advertisement instructs you to e-mail your résumé, you should send both a web-based and a non-web version (in case the recipient wants to print it out for any reason).

Hung-Wei Chun's résumé (figure 20.3) incorporates features of both the chronological and the functional formats. He starts by listing his objective, which he wrote in response to a specific job advertisement. He then mentions his education (pointing out relevant coursework) and experience, both professional and internship. He even includes an award he received for volunteer work. Hung-Wei also includes other evidence to show that he is a well-qualified job candidate: lists of languages spoken and professional memberships. The final list of activities tells an employer something about Hung-Wei's personality (that is, he is both reflective and energetic).

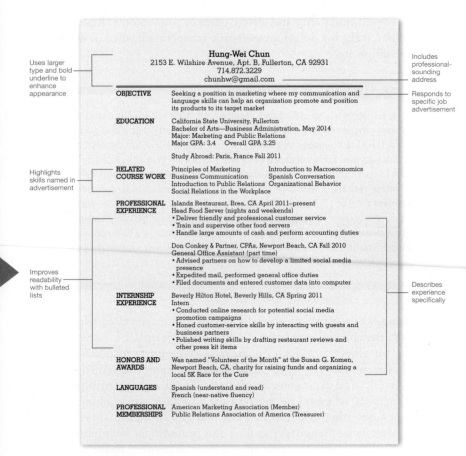

Hung-Wei Chun
2153 E. Wilshire Avenue, Apt. B, Fullerton, CA 92931
714.872.3229
chunhw@gmail.com

Uses larger type and bold underline to enhance appearance

Includes professional-sounding address

OBJECTIVE Seeking a position in marketing where my communication and language skills can help an organization promote and position its products to its target market

Responds to specific job advertisement

EDUCATION California State University, Fullerton
Bachelor of Arts—Business Administration, May 2014
Major: Marketing and Public Relations
Major GPA: 3.4   Overall GPA 3.25

Study Abroad: Paris, France Fall 2011

Highlights skills named in advertisement

RELATED COURSE WORK
Principles of Marketing   Introduction to Macroeconomics
Business Communication   Spanish Conversation
Introduction to Public Relations   Organizational Behavior
Social Relations in the Workplace

PROFESSIONAL EXPERIENCE
Islands Restaurant, Brea, CA April 2011–present
Head Food Server (nights and weekends)
• Deliver friendly and professional customer service
• Train and supervise other food servers
• Handle large amounts of cash and perform accounting duties

Don Conkey & Partner, CPAs, Newport Beach, CA Fall 2010
General Office Assistant (part time)
• Advised partners on how to develop a limited social media presence
• Expedited mail, performed general office duties
• Filed documents and entered customer data into computer

Improves readability with bulleted lists

Describes experience specifically

INTERNSHIP EXPERIENCE
Beverly Hilton Hotel, Beverly Hills, CA Spring 2011
Intern
• Conducted online research for potential social media promotion campaigns
• Honed customer-service skills by interacting with guests and business partners
• Polished writing skills by drafting restaurant reviews and other press kit items

HONORS AND AWARDS
Was named "Volunteer of the Month" at the Susan G. Komen, Newport Beach, CA, charity for raising funds and organizing a local 5K Race for the Cure

LANGUAGES Spanish (understand and read)
French (near-native fluency)

PROFESSIONAL MEMBERSHIPS
American Marketing Association (Member)
Public Relations Association of America (Treasurer)

Figure 20.3: Sample résumé.

ELEMENTS OF A RÉSUMÉ

- **Name, address, phone number(s), and e-mail address.**
- **Career objective(s).** Mention short-term goals and jobs or positions for which you are applying.
- **Educational background.** List your degrees or diplomas, special honors, participation in advanced programs, and possibly your grade point average (either in general or in your major) and relevant coursework.

- **Work experience.** Include all your jobs (paying, volunteer, and internships, as well as military service). List dates, places of employment, and job titles, describing your duties with active verbs that emphasize your initiative and your sense of responsibility.
- **Extracurricular activities.** List your extracurricular activities if they relate directly to the position for which you are applying or demonstrate distinctive leadership, athletic, or artistic abilities.
- **References.** The names and addresses of references (people who have agreed to speak or write on your behalf) are not usually listed on a résumé. Instead, take a list of references to interviews. The list should include their names and addresses as well as their telephone numbers and/or e-mail addresses.

20e   LETTERS OF APPLICATION

Writing a letter of application, or cover letter, is an essential step in applying for a job. Because this letter usually accompanies a résumé (**20d**), it is crucial that it guide the reader to the relevant high points of the résumé, rather than repeating that information. Your letter of application provides you with the chance to sound articulate, interesting, and professional, and to put a personal face on the factual content of the résumé—in other words, to make a good first impression. (See figure 20.4 for a sample letter of application.)

In your opening paragraph, identify the position you are applying for, explain how you learned about it, and—in a single sentence—state why you believe you are qualified to fill it. This statement serves as the thesis for the rest of the letter. In the paragraphs that follow, describe the specific ways your education, experience, and abilities qualify you for the position. Remember, your reader wants to find out quickly what exactly you can contribute to his or her organization. Generally, two body paragraphs follow the introductory paragraph: one describing relevant education, the other relevant work experience. (Many applicants find that their education and their work experience are not equally pertinent to the job at hand. In that case, you might use these two paragraphs to describe two particular course projects or two particular jobs.)

In your closing paragraph, offer any additional useful information and make a direct request for an interview.

Letters of application follow the general format of all business letters (**20b**).

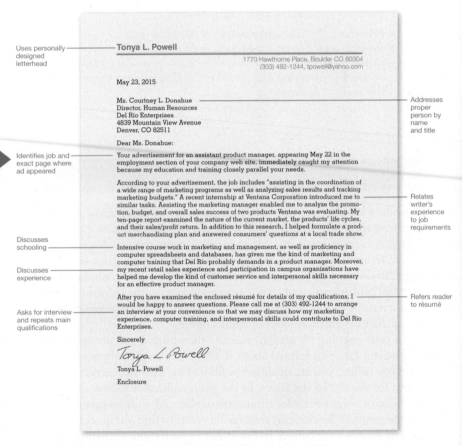

Uses personally designed letterhead

Tonya L. Powell

1770 Hawthorne Place, Boulder CO 80304
(303) 492-1244, tpowell@yahoo.com

May 23, 2015

Ms. Courtney L. Donahue
Director, Human Resources
Del Rio Enterprises
4839 Mountain View Avenue
Denver, CO 82511

Addresses proper person by name and title

Dear Ms. Donahue:

Identifies job and exact page where ad appeared

Your advertisement for an assistant product manager, appearing May 22 in the employment section of your company web site, immediately caught my attention because my education and training closely parallel your needs.

According to your advertisement, the job includes "assisting in the coordination of a wide range of marketing programs as well as analyzing sales results and tracking marketing budgets." A recent internship at Ventana Corporation introduced me to similar tasks. Assisting the marketing manager enabled me to analyze the promotion, budget, and overall sales success of two products Ventana was evaluating. My ten-page report examined the nature of the current market, the products' life cycles, and their sales/profit return. In addition to this research, I helped formulate a product merchandising plan and answered consumers' questions at a local trade show.

Relates writer's experience to job requirements

Discusses schooling

Intensive course work in marketing and management, as well as proficiency in computer spreadsheets and databases, has given me the kind of marketing and computer training that Del Rio probably demands in a product manager. Moreover, my recent retail sales experience and participation in campus organizations have helped me develop the kind of customer service and interpersonal skills necessary for an effective product manager.

Discusses experience

After you have examined the enclosed résumé for details of my qualifications, I would be happy to answer questions. Please call me at (303) 492-1244 to arrange an interview at your convenience so that we may discuss how my marketing experience, computer training, and interpersonal skills could contribute to Del Rio Enterprises.

Refers reader to résumé

Asks for interview and repeats main qualifications

Sincerely

Tonya L. Powell

Tonya L. Powell

Enclosure

Figure 20.4: Model letter of application. (© 2013 Cengage Learning)

TIPS FOR WRITING LETTERS OF APPLICATION

- Address your letter to a specific person. If you are responding to an ad that mentions a department without giving a name, call the company and find out who will be doing the screening. If you cannot obtain a specific name, use an appropriate title such as *Human Resources Director*.

- Be brief. You can assume that the recipient will be screening many applications, so keep your letter to one easy-to-read page.

- Mention that you are enclosing a résumé or refer to it, but do not summarize it. Your goal is to attract the attention of a busy person (who will not want to read the same information in both your letter and your résumé).

- Indicate why you are interested in working for the company or organization to which you are applying. Demonstrating that you already know something about the company and the position, and that you can contribute to it, indicates your seriousness and motivation. If you want more information about the company, locate an annual report and other information by searching the web.

- In your closing, be sure to specify how and where you can be reached and emphasize your availability for an interview.

20f ORAL PRESENTATIONS WITH POWERPOINT

Oral reports accompanied by PowerPoint presentations are commonplace in business. Such reports can be either internal (for supervisors and colleagues) or external (for clients or investors). They may take the form of project status reports, demonstrations of new equipment or software, research reports, or recommendations.

Keep in mind the following guidelines as you compose an oral report and create PowerPoint slides to accompany it.

ELEMENTS OF A STANDARD ORAL PRESENTATION

- **Introduction.** The introduction provides an outline of your main points so that listeners can easily follow your presentation. In no more than one-tenth of your overall presentation time (for example, one minute of a ten-minute presentation), mention who you are, your qualifications, your topic, and the relevance of that topic to your audience.

- **Body.** Make sure the organization of your presentation is clear through your use of transitions. You can number each point (*first, second, third,* and so on) and use cause-and-consequence transitions (*therefore, since, due to*) and chronological transitions (*before, following, next, then*). Provide internal summaries to remind your listeners where you have been and where you are going and offer comments to help your audience sense the weight of various points (for example, *Not many people realize that ...* or *The most important thing I have to share is ...*).

- **Conclusion.** Rather than restating the main ideas, make your conclusion memorable by ending with a proposal for action, a final statistic, recommendations, or a description of the benefits of a certain course of action. Conclusions should be even shorter than introductions.

TIPS FOR INCORPORATING POWERPOINT INTO AN ORAL PRESENTATION

- Design your slides for your audience, not for yourself. If you need speaking notes for your talk, write them on note cards or type them into the notes section provided below each slide in the PowerPoint program.

- Use text and visuals on the PowerPoint slides that complement the oral part of your presentation and do not repeat what you have said. If everything you are saying is on the slides, your audience will skim each slide and then become bored listening as you catch up.

- Be aware of the limitations of PowerPoint. For example, PowerPoint slides do not accommodate large amounts of text. Because PowerPoint tends to encourage oversimplification of information, be sure to tell your audience whenever you had to simplify the information presented on a slide (for example, in order to fit time constraints) and let them know where they can find more details.

- Choose images that support your message. Let visuals (charts, pictures, or graphs) stand alone with just a heading or a title. Use text slides to define terms, to present block quotes that might be difficult to follow orally, and to list the main points you will be making.
- Time your speaking with your presentation of the slides so that the two components are synchronized. Make sure to give your audience enough time to absorb complex visuals.
- PowerPoint is not the only option to consider for use with your oral presentations. Popular alternatives are Prezi and SlideRocket.

By comparing the two slides in figure 20.5, you will see the importance of conciseness, consistency, and parallelism.

Before Revision

Reasons for Selling Online

- Your online business can grow globally.
- Customer convenience.
- You can conduct your business 24/7.
- No need for renting a retail store or hiring employees.
- Reduce inquiries by providing policies and a privacy statement.
- Customers can buy quickly and easily.

After Revision

Figure 20.5: This comparison shows the importance of using not only visuals but also succinct and parallel sentences.

20g BUSINESS REPORTS

Business reports take many forms, including periodic reports, sales reports, progress reports, incident reports, and longer reports that assess relocation plans, new lines of equipment or products, marketing schemes, and so on. The following box describes elements of such reports.

ELEMENTS OF A STANDARD BUSINESS REPORT

- **Front matter.** Depending on the audience, purpose, and length of a given report, the front matter materials may include a letter of transmittal (explaining the relevance of the report), a title page, a table of contents, a list of illustrations, and/or an abstract.

- **Introduction.** This section should identify the problem addressed by the report (the rhetorical opportunity), present background information about it, and include a purpose statement and a description of the scope of the report (a list of the limits that framed the investigation). In a long report, each of these elements may be several paragraphs long, and some may have their own subheadings. An introduction should not take up more than 10 to 15 percent of the length of a report.

- **Body or discussion.** This, the longest section of the report, presents the research findings. It often incorporates charts and graphs to help make the data easy to understand. This section should be subdivided into clear subsections by subheadings or, for a shorter report, paragraph breaks.

- **Conclusion(s).** This section summarizes any conclusions and generalizations deduced from the data presented in the body of the report.

- **Recommendation(s).** Although not always necessary, a section that outlines what should be done with or about the findings is included in many business reports.

- **Back matter.** Like the front matter, the back matter of a report depends on the audience, purpose, and length of the report. Back matter may include a glossary, a list of the references cited, and/or one or more appendixes.

Formal business reports normally examine problems and suggest solutions. In the following report, Martha Montoya discusses the economic impact an industrial park has on the city of Flagstaff, Arizona, so that the city council can make informed decisions about future development of similar industrial parks. Although this professional report is single-spaced, check with your instructor to see whether your assignment should be double-spaced.

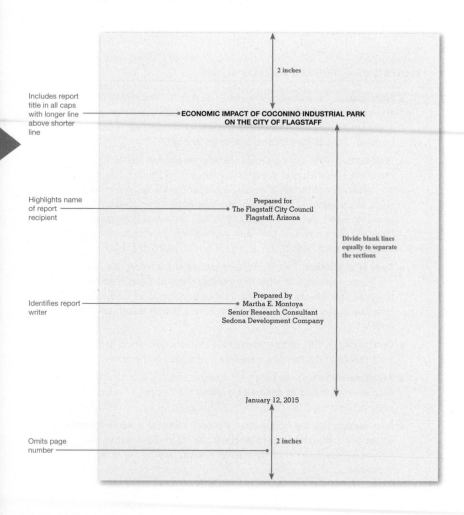

2 inches

Includes report title in all caps with longer line above shorter line

**ECONOMIC IMPACT OF COCONINO INDUSTRIAL PARK
ON THE CITY OF FLAGSTAFF**

Highlights name of report recipient

Prepared for
The Flagstaff City Council
Flagstaff, Arizona

Divide blank lines equally to separate the sections

Identifies report writer

Prepared by
Martha E. Montoya
Senior Research Consultant
Sedona Development Company

January 12, 2015

Omits page number

2 inches

SEDONA DEVELOPMENT COMPANY
426 Saddle Rock Circle   www.sedonadevco.com
Sedona, Arizona 86340   928.450.3348

January 12, 2015

City Council
City of Flagstaff
211 West Aspen Avenue
Flagstaff, AZ 86001

Dear Council Members:

Announces report and identifies authorization

The attached report, requested by the Flagstaff City Council in a letter to Goldman-Lyon & Associates dated October 20, describes the economic impact of Coconino Industrial Park on the city of Flagstaff. We believe you will find the results of this study useful in evaluating future development of industrial parks within the city limits.

Gives broad overview of report purposes

This study was designed to examine economic impact in three areas:

- Current and projected tax and other revenues accruing to the city from Coconino Industrial Park
- Current and projected employment generated by the park
- Indirect effects on local employment, income, and economic growth

Describes primary and secondary research

Primary research consisted of interviews with 15 Coconino Industrial Park (CIP) tenants and managers, in addition to a 2013 survey of over 5,000 CIP employees. Secondary research sources included the Annual Budget of the City of Flagstaff, county and state tax records, government publications, periodicals, books, and online resources. Results of this research, discussed more fully in this report, indicate that Coconino Industrial Park exerts a significant beneficial influence on the Flagstaff metropolitan economy.

Offers to discuss report; expresses appreciation

We would be pleased to discuss this report and its conclusions with you at your request. My firm and I thank you for your confidence in selecting our company to prepare this comprehensive report.

Sincerely,

Martha E. Montoya

Martha E. Montoya
Senior Research Consultant

MEM:coe
Attachment

Uses Roman numerals for prefatory pages

ii

TABLE OF CONTENTS

LIST OF FIGURES

iii

EXECUTIVE SUMMARY

Opens directly
with major
research
findings

The city of Flagstaff can benefit from the development of industrial parks like
the Coconino Industrial Park. Both direct and indirect economic benefits result,
as shown by this in-depth study conducted by Sedona Development Company.
The study was authorized by the Flagstaff City Council when Goldman-Lyon &
Associates sought the City Council's approval for the proposed construction of a
G-L industrial park. The City Council requested evidence demonstrating that an
existing development could actually benefit the city.

Identifies data
sources

Our conclusion that the city of Flagstaff benefits from industrial parks is based on
data supplied by a survey of 5,000 Coconino Industrial Park employees, personal
interviews with managers and tenants of CIP, city and state documents, and
professional literature.

Summarizes
organization
of report

Analysis of the data revealed benefits in three areas:

- **Revenues.** The city of Flagstaff earned over $3 million in tax and other
  revenues from the Coconino Industrial Park in 2013. By 2020 this income is
  expected to reach $5.4 million (in constant 2013 dollars).

- **Employment.** In 2013, CIP businesses employed a total of 7,035 workers, who
  earned an average wage of $56,579. By 2020, CIP businesses are expected to
  employ directly nearly 15,000 employees who will earn salaries totaling over
  $998 million.

- **Indirect benefits.** Because of the multiplier effect, by 2020 Coconino Industrial
  Park will directly and indirectly generate a total of 38,362 jobs in the Flagstaff
  metropolitan area.

Condenses
recommendations

On the basis of these findings, it is recommended that development of additional
industrial parks be encouraged to stimulate local economic growth. The city
would increase its tax revenues significantly, create much-needed jobs, and thus
help stimulate the local economy in and around Flagstaff.

INTRODUCTION: COCONINO AND THE LOCAL ECONOMY

This study was designed to analyze the direct and indirect economic impact of Coconino Industrial Park on the city of Flagstaff. Specifically, the study seeks answers to these questions:

- What current tax and other revenues result directly from this park? What tax and other revenues may be expected in the future?

- How many and what kinds of jobs are directly attributable to the park? What is the employment picture for the future?

- What indirect effects has Coconino Industrial Park had on local employment, incomes, and economic growth?

BACKGROUND: THE ROLE OF CIP IN COMMERCIAL DEVELOPMENT

The development firm of Goldman-Lyon & Associates commissioned this study of Coconino Industrial Park at the request of the Flagstaff City Council. Before authorizing the development of a proposed Goldman-Lyon industrial park, the city council requested a study examining the economic effects of an existing park. Members of the city council wanted to determine to what extent industrial parks benefit the local community, and they chose Coconino Industrial Park as an example.

For those who are unfamiliar with it, Coconino Industrial Park is a 400-acre industrial park located in the city of Flagstaff about 4 miles from the center of the city. Most of the land lies within a specially designated area known as Redevelopment Project No. 2, which is under the jurisdiction of the Flagstaff Redevelopment Agency. Planning for the park began in 1999; construction started in 2001.

The original goal for Coconino Industrial Park was development for light industrial users. Land in this area was zoned for uses such as warehousing, research and development, and distribution. Like other communities, Flagstaff was eager to attract light industrial users because such businesses tend to employ a highly educated workforce, are relatively quiet, and do not pollute the environment (Cohen, 2014). The city of Flagstaff recognized the need for light industrial users and widened an adjacent highway to accommodate trucks and facilitate travel by workers and customers coming from Flagstaff.

1

Uses a bulleted list for clarity and ease of reading

Lists three problem questions

Describes authorization for report and background of study

Includes APA citation with author name and date

The park now contains 14 building complexes with over 1.25 million square feet of completed building space. The majority of the buildings are used for office, research and development, marketing and distribution, or manufacturing uses. Approximately 50 acres of the original area are yet to be developed.

Data for this report came from a 2013 survey of over 5,000 Coconino Industrial Park employees; interviews with 15 CIP tenants and managers; the annual budget of the city of Flagstaff; county and state tax records; and current books, articles, journals, and online resources. Projections for future revenues resulted from analysis of past trends and "Estimates of Revenues for Debt Service Coverage, Redevelopment Project Area 2" (Miller, 2013, p. 79).

DISCUSSION: REVENUES, EMPLOYMENT, AND INDIRECT BENEFITS

The results of this research indicate that major direct and indirect benefits have accrued to the city of Flagstaff and surrounding metropolitan areas as a result of the development of Coconino Industrial Park. The research findings presented here fall into three categories: (a) revenues, (b) employment, and (c) indirect benefits.

Revenues

Coconino Industrial Park contributes a variety of tax and other revenues to the city of Flagstaff, as summarized in Figure 1. Current revenues are shown, along with projections to the year 2020. At a time when the economy is unstable, revenues from an industrial park such as Coconino can become a reliable income stream for the city of Flagstaff.

Figure 1

**REVENUES RECEIVED BY THE CITY OF FLAGSTAFF
FROM COCONINO INDUSTRIAL PARK**

Current Revenues and Projections to 2020

	2013	2020
Sales and use taxes	$1,966,021	$3,604,500
Revenues from licenses	532,802	962,410
Franchise taxes	195,682	220,424
State gas tax receipts	159,420	211,134
Licenses and permits	86,213	201,413
Other revenues	75,180	206,020
Total	$3,015,318	$5,405,901

Source: Arizona State Board of Equalization Bulletin. Phoenix: State Printing Office, 2014, p. 28.

Margin annotations:

Provides specifics for data sources

Uses combination heads

Previews organization of report

Places figure close to textual reference

Sales and Use Revenues

As shown in Figure 1, the city's largest source of revenues from CIP is the sales and use tax. Revenues from this source totaled $1,966,021 in 2013, according to figures provided by the Arizona State Board of Equalization (2014, p. 28). Sales and use taxes accounted for more than half of the park's total contribution to the total income of $3,015,318.

Other Revenues

Other major sources of city revenues from CIP in 2013 include alcohol licenses, motor vehicle in lieu fees, trailer coach licenses ($532,802), franchise taxes ($195,682), and state gas tax receipts ($159,420). Although not shown in Figure 1, other revenues may be expected from the development of recently acquired property. The U.S. Economic Development Administration has approved a grant worth $975,000 to assist in expanding the current park eastward on an undeveloped parcel purchased last year. Revenues from leasing this property may be sizable.

Projections

Total city revenues from CIP will nearly double by 2020, producing an income of $5.4 million. This estimate is based on an annual growth rate of 0.65 percent, as projected by the Bureau of Labor Statistics.

Employment

One of the most important factors to consider in the overall effect of an industrial park is employment. In Coconino Industrial Park the distribution, number, and wages of people employed will change considerably in the next six years.

Distribution

A total of 7,035 employees currently work in various industry groups at Coconino Industrial Park. The distribution of employees is shown in Figure 2. The largest number of workers (58 percent) is employed in manufacturing and assembly operations. The next largest category, computer and electronics, employs 24 percent of the workers. Some overlap probably exists because electronics assembly could be included in either group. Employees also work in publishing (9 percent), warehousing and storage (5 percent), and other industries (4 percent).

Although the distribution of employees at Coconino Industrial Park shows a wide range of employment categories, it must be noted that other industrial parks would likely generate an entirely different range of job categories.

3

Margin annotations:

Continues interpreting figures in table

Includes ample description of electronic reference

Sets stage for next topic to be discussed

Figure 2

EMPLOYMENT DISTRIBUTION OF INDUSTRY GROUPS

Pie chart
shows
proportion
of a whole
and includes
percentage
figures for
clarity

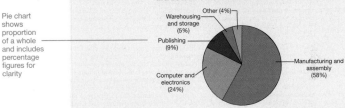

Source: 2013 survey of CIP employees

Wages

Places
figure close
to textual
reference

In 2013 employees at CIP earned a total of $398 million in wages, as shown in Figure 3. The average employee in that year earned $56,579. The highest average wages were paid to employees in white-collar fields, such as computer and electronics ($65,200) and publishing ($61,100). Average wages for workers in blue-collar fields ranged from $48,500 in warehousing and storage to $53,400 in manufacturing and assembly.

Figure 3

AVERAGE ANNUAL WAGES BY INDUSTRY GROUPS

Coconino Industrial Park, 2013

Aligns figures
on the right
and centers
headings
over columns

Industry Group	Employees	Annual Wages	Total
Manufacturing and assembly	4,073	$53,400	$217,498,200
Computer and electronics	1,657	65,200	108,036,400
Publishing	672	61,100	41,059,200
Warehousing and storage	370	48,500	17,945,000
Othe	263	51,300	13,491,900
	7,035		$398,030,700

Source: 2013 Survey of CIP employees

4

Projections

By 2020 Coconino Industrial Park is expected to more than double its number of employees, bringing the total to over 15,000 workers. The total payroll in 2020 will also more than double, producing over $998 million (using constant 2013 dollars) in salaries to CIP employees. These projections are based on a 9 percent growth rate (Miller, 2013, p. 78), along with anticipated increased employment as the park reaches its capacity.

Clarifies information and tells what it means in relation to original research questions

Future development in the park will influence employment and payrolls. One CIP project manager stated in an interview that much of the remaining 50 acres is planned for medium-rise office buildings, garden offices, and other structures for commercial, professional, and personal services (I. M. Novak, personal communication, November 30, 2013). Average wages for employees are expected to increase because of an anticipated shift to higher-paying white-collar jobs. Industrial parks often follow a similar pattern of evolution (Badri, Rivera, & Kusak, 2011, p. 41). Like many industrial parks, CIP evolved from a warehousing center into a manufacturing complex.

CONCLUSIONS AND RECOMMENDATIONS

Combines conclusions and recommendations

Analysis of tax revenues, employment data, personal interviews, and professional literature leads to the following conclusions and recommendations about the economic impact of Coconino Industrial Park on the city of Flagstaff:

1. Sales tax and other revenues produced over $3 million in income to the city of Flagstaff in 2013. By 2020 sales tax and other revenues are expected to produce $5.4 million in city income.

Uses a numbered list for clarity and ease of reading

2. CIP currently employs 7,035 employees, the majority of whom are working in manufacturing and assembly. The average employee in 2013 earned $56,579.

3. By 2020 CIP is expected to employ more than 15,000 workers producing a total payroll of over $998 million.

4. Employment trends indicate that by 2020 more CIP employees will be engaged in higher-paying white-collar positions.

On the basis of these findings, we recommend that the City Council of Flagstaff authorize the development of additional industrial parks to stimulate local economic growth. The direct and indirect benefits of Coconino Industrial Park strongly suggest that future commercial development would have a positive impact on the Flagstaff community and the surrounding region as population growth and resulting greater purchasing power would trigger higher demand.

As the Coconino example shows, gains in tax revenue, job creation, and other direct and indirect benefits would follow the creation of additional industrial parks in and around Flagstaff.

5

Situate Yourself

For your new internship at the magazine *Four Seasons*, you have been asked to edit the following paragraph about snowflakes. Unfortunately, it contains a number of errors. To correct these errors, use your knowledge of the following: fragments, commas splices, fused sentences, subject-verb agreement, clear pronoun reference, and dangling modifiers.

During the winter season in northern climes, snowflakes do not only fall from the sky they are knitted into sweaters, drawn onto cards, and hung as decorations. However, what most people think of as a snowflake, according to Kenneth Libbrecht, is really a snow crystal, the difference between the two are that *snowflake* has a general meaning while *snow crystal* is specific. Similar to the relationship between *flower and tulip*. Snowflakes may consist of a single snow crystal or multiple snow crystals. It is the individual snow crystal that fascinates. Growing six main branches and then sidebranches, the formation of the snow crystal takes place. The numbers of sidebranches vary. This is why some crystals looking feathery while others have rounded edges. Regardless of their shape, each snow crystal is, as Libbrecht notes, "a temporary work of art."

⬛ TECH SAVVY

Using a Grammar Checker

Most word-processing programs have a grammar checker, which can help you identify grammar errors as well as problems with usage and style; however, grammar checkers have significant limitations. A grammar checker will usually identify

- fused sentences, sometimes called run-on sentences (chapter 24),
- some misused prepositions (35c),
- wordy or overly long sentences (33a and 36a), and
- missing apostrophes in contractions (39b).

However, a grammar checker can easily miss

- sentence fragments (chapter 23),
- problems with adverbs or adjectives (27a),
- misplaced or dangling modifiers (27d and 27e),
- problems with pronoun-antecedent agreement (26c),
- errors in subject-verb agreement (25e), and
- misused or missing commas (chapter 37).

Because these errors can weaken your credibility as a writer, you should never rely solely on a grammar checker to find them. Furthermore, grammar checkers can mark as wrong words or phrases that are actually correct. Some of these "errors" may be choices you have made deliberately to suit your rhetorical situation (chapter 1).

Used carefully, a grammar checker can be a helpful tool, but keep the following advice in mind:

- Use a grammar checker only in addition to your own editing and proofreading. When in doubt, consult the appropriate chapters in this handbook.
- Always evaluate any sentences flagged by a grammar checker to determine whether there is, in fact, a problem.
- Adjust the settings on your grammar checker to look for specific types of errors. If you are using Microsoft Word, select Tools; then select either Spelling and Grammar or Options to customize your settings.
- Carefully review the revisions proposed by a grammar checker before accepting them. Sometimes the proposed revisions create new errors.

21 ‖ SENTENCE ESSENTIALS

When you think of the word *grammar*, you might also think of the word *rule*—a regulation that you must obey. But *rule* has another meaning: "a description of what is true in most cases." A grammar rule, then, describes how language is commonly or conventionally used. However, what is appropriate in one rhetorical situation (chapter **1**) may not be appropriate in another. To know which rules to follow, you must first determine your intended audience, overall purpose, and specific context. Once you establish your rhetorical situation, you will be ready to select from the array of words and word arrangements the English language offers. By also learning basic grammar terms and concepts, you will better understand how to choose among the options available to you.

This chapter will help you

- identify the parts of speech (**21a**),
- recognize the essential parts of a sentence (**21b**),
- identify complements (**21c**), and
- recognize basic sentence patterns (**21d**).

21a ‖ PARTS OF SPEECH

When you look up a word in the dictionary, you will often find it followed by one or more of these labels: *adj., adv., conj., interj., n., prep., pron.,* and *v* (or *vb.*). These are the abbreviations for the traditional eight parts of speech: *adjective, adverb, conjunction, interjection, noun, preposition, pronoun,* and *verb*.

(1) Verbs

Verbs that indicate action (*walk, drive, study*) are called **action verbs**. Verbs that express being or experiencing are called **linking verbs**; they include *be, seem,* and *become* and the sensory verbs *look, taste, smell,* *feel,* and *sound.* Both action verbs and linking verbs are frequently accompanied by **auxiliary** or **helping verbs** that add shades of meaning, such as information about time (*will* study this afternoon), ability (*can* study), or obligation (*must* study). See chapter **25** for more details about verbs.

> The dictionary (base) form of most action verbs fits into this frame sentence:
> We should _____ (it). [With some verbs, *it* is not used.]
> The dictionary (base) form of most linking verbs fits into this frame sentence:
> It can _____ good (terrible, fine).

❓ THINKING RHETORICALLY

VERBS

Decide which of the following sentences evokes a clearer image.

The team captain **was** absolutely ecstatic.

Grinning broadly, the team captain **shot** both her arms into the air.

You probably chose the sentence with the action verb *shot* rather than the sentence with *was.* Most writers avoid using the verb *be* in any of its forms (*am, is, are, was, were,* or *been*) when their rhetorical situation calls for vibrant imagery. Instead, they use vivid action verbs.

(2) Nouns

Nouns usually name people, places, things, or ideas. **Proper nouns** are specific names. You can identify them easily because they are capitalized: *Bill Gates, Redmond, Microsoft Corporation.* **Common nouns** refer to any member of a class or category: *person, city, company.* There are three types of common nouns.

■ **Count nouns** refer to people, places, things, and ideas that can be counted. They have singular and plural forms: *boy, boys; park, parks; car, cars; concept, concepts.*

- **Noncount nouns** refer to things or ideas that cannot be counted: *furniture, information.*
- **Collective nouns** are nouns that can be either singular or plural, depending on the context: *The **committee** published its report* [singular]. *The **committee** disagree about their duties* [plural]. (See **25e(7)**.)

Most nouns fit into this frame sentence:

(The) _____ is (are) important (unimportant, interesting, uninteresting).

❓ THINKING RHETORICALLY

NOUNS

Nouns like *entertainment* and *nutrition* refer to concepts. They are called **abstract nouns**. In contrast, nouns like *guitar* and *apple* refer to things perceivable by the senses. They are called **concrete nouns**. When your rhetorical situation calls for the use of abstractions, balance them with tangible details conveyed through concrete nouns. For example, if you use the abstract nouns *impressionism* and *cubism* in an art history paper, also include concrete nouns that will enable readers to visualize the colors, shapes, and brushstrokes of the paintings you are discussing.

---

(3) Pronouns

Pronouns function as nouns, and most pronouns (*it, he, she, they,* and many others) refer to nouns that have already been mentioned. These nouns are called **antecedents** (**26c**).

My <u>parents</u> bought the cheap, decrepit <u>house</u> because **they** thought **it** had charm.

A pronoun and its antecedent may be found either in the same sentence or in separate, though usually adjacent, sentences.

The <u>students</u> collaborated on a research project last year. **They** even presented their findings at a national conference.

The pronouns in the preceding examples are called **personal pronouns**. There are also several other types of pronouns: indefinite, possessive, relative, interrogative, and reflexive/intensive. For a detailed discussion of pronouns, see chapter **26**.

(4) Adjectives

Adjectives most commonly modify nouns: *spicy* food, *cold* day, *special* price. Sometimes they modify pronouns: *blue* ones, anyone *thin*. Adjectives usually answer one of these questions: Which one? What kind of . . . ? How many? What color (or size or shape, and so on)? Although adjectives usually precede the nouns they modify, they occasionally follow them: *enough* time, time *enough*. Adjectives may also follow linking verbs such as *be, seem,* and *become*:

The <u>moon</u> is **full** tonight.   <u>He</u> seems **shy.**

When an adjective follows a linking verb, it modifies the subject of the sentence (**21b**).

> Most adjectives fit into one of these frame sentences:
>   He told us about a/an/the _____ idea (person, place).
>   The idea (person, place) is very _____.

Articles—*a, an,* and *the* —are also used before nouns. The article *a* is used before a consonant sound (**a** yard, **a** university, **a** VIP); *an* is used before a vowel sound (**an** apple, **an** hour, **an** NFL team). Articles are traditionally thought of as a subclass of adjectives; in many current grammars, they are considered a subclass of determiners (chapter **46**).

For a detailed discussion of adjectives, see **27a**.

ñ MULTILINGUAL WRITERS

ARTICLE USAGE

English has two types of articles: indefinite and definite. The **indefinite articles**, *a* and *an*, indicate that a singular noun is used in a general way, as when you introduce the noun for the first time or when you define a word:

> Pluto is **a** dwarf <u>planet</u>.

> There has been **a** <u>controversy</u> over the classification of Pluto.

> **A** <u>planet</u> is a celestial body orbiting a star such as our sun.

The **definite article**, *the*, is used before a noun that has already been introduced or when a reference is obvious. *The* is also used before a noun that is related in form or meaning to a word mentioned previously.

> Scientists distinguish between planets and <u>dwarf planets</u>. Three of **the** <u>dwarf planets</u> in our solar system are Ceres, Pluto, and Eris.

> Scientists were not sure how to <u>classify</u> some celestial bodies. **The** <u>classification</u> of Pluto proved to be particularly controversial.

The definite article also appears before a noun considered unique, such as *moon, universe, solar system, sun, earth,* or *sky.*

> **The** <u>moon</u> is full tonight.

For more information on articles, see chapter **46**.

(5) Adverbs

Adverbs most frequently modify verbs. They provide information about time, manner, place, and frequency, thus answering one of these questions: When? How? Where? How often?

> The conference <u>starts</u> **tomorrow.** [time]

> I **rapidly** <u>calculated</u> the cost. [manner]

We met **here.** [place]

They **often** work late on Thursdays. [frequency]

> Most adverbs of manner fit into this frame sentence:
>   They _____ moved (danced, walked) across the room.

Adverbs that modify verbs can often move from one position in a sentence to another.

He **carefully** removed the radio collar.

He removed the radio collar **carefully.**

Adverbs also modify adjectives and other adverbs by intensifying or otherwise qualifying the meanings of those words.

I was **extremely** curious. [modifying an adjective]

The team played **surprisingly** well. [modifying an adverb]

For more information on adverbs, see **27a.**

❓ THINKING RHETORICALLY

ADVERBS

What do the adverbs add to the following sentences?

The scientist **delicately** places the slide under the microscope.

"You're late," he whispered **vehemently.**

She is **wistfully** hopeful.

Adverbs can help you portray an action, indicate how someone is speaking, and add detail to a description.

(6) Prepositions

A **preposition** generally refers to time, location, or direction. It combines with a noun (and any of its modifiers) to form a prepositional phrase that answers these questions: *Where?* or *When?*

> <u>**In** the early afternoon</u>, we walked <u>**through** our old neighborhood</u>.
> [answer the questions *When?* and *Where?*]

A preposition may also combine with a pronoun.

> We walked <u>**through** it</u>.

SOME COMMON PREPOSITIONS

about	behind	except	of	through
above	beside	for	on	to
after	between	from	out	toward
around	by	in	over	under
as	despite	into	past	until
at	down	like	regarding	up
before	during	near	since	with

Phrasal prepositions consist of more than one word.

> **Except for** the last day, it was a wonderful trip.

> The postponement was **due to** inclement weather.

PHRASAL PREPOSITIONS

according to	except for	in spite of
as for	in addition to	instead of
because of	in case of	with regard to
due to	in front of	with respect to

ñ MULTILINGUAL WRITERS

PREPOSITIONS IN IDIOMATIC COMBINATIONS

Some verbs, adjectives, and nouns combine with prepositions to form idiomatic combinations.

Verb + Preposition	Adjective + Preposition	Noun + Preposition
apply to	fond of	interest in
rely on	similar to	dependence on
trust in	different from	fondness for

(7) Conjunctions

Conjunctions are connectors; they fall into four categories: coordinating, correlative, subordinating, and adverbial. These four types of conjunctions differ from one another, so it is not uncommon to see them listed as separate parts of speech. Each will be described in detail below.

A **coordinating conjunction**, also called a *coordinator*, connects similar words or groups of words; that is, it generally links a word to a word, a phrase to a phrase (**22a**), or a clause to a clause (**22b**).

English **and** Spanish [*And* joins two words and signals addition.]

in school **or** at home [*Or* joins two phrases and marks them as alternatives.]

We did not share a language, **but** somehow we communicated. [*But* joins two independent clauses and signals contrast.]

There are seven coordinating conjunctions. Use the made-up word *fanboys* to help you remember them.

F	A	N	B	O	Y	S
for	and	nor	but	or	yet	so

A coordinating conjunction such as *but* may also link independent clauses (**22b(1)**) that stand alone as sentences.

The momentum in the direction of globalization seems too powerful to buck, the economic logic unmatchable. **But** in a region where jobs are draining away, and where an ethic of self-reliance remains a dim, vestigial, but honored memory, it seems at least an outside possibility.

—**Bill McKibben, "Small World"**

A **correlative conjunction** consists of two parts. The most common correlatives are *both . . . and, either . . . or, neither . . . nor,* and *not only . . . but also.*

either Pedro **or** Sue [*Either . . . or* joins two words and marks them as alternatives.]

neither on the running track **nor** in the pool [*Neither . . . nor* joins two phrases and marks them both as false or impossible.]

Not only did they run ten miles, **but** they **also** swam twenty laps. [*Not only . . . but also* joins two independent clauses and signals addition.]

As the preceding examples show, correlative conjunctions join words, phrases, or clauses, but they do not join sentences. Generally, a correlative conjunction links similar structures. The following sentence needs to be revised because the correlative conjunction links a phrase to a clause:

           did he save
Not only~~saving~~ the lives of the accident victims, **but** he **also** prevented many spinal injuries.

A **subordinating conjunction**, also called a *subordinator*, introduces a dependent clause (**22b(2)**). It also carries a specific meaning; for example, it may indicate cause, concession, condition, purpose, or time. A dependent clause that begins a sentence is followed by a comma.

Unless the project receives more funding, the research will stop. [*Unless* signals a condition.]

The project continued **because** it received additional funding. [*Because* signals a cause.]

SUBORDINATING CONJUNCTIONS		
after	how	than
although	if	though
as if	in case	unless
as though	in that	until
because	insofar as	when, whenever
before	once	where, wherever
even if	since	whether
even though	so that	while

The word *that* can be omitted from the subordinating conjunction *so that* if the meaning remains clear.

> I left ten minutes early **so** I would not be late. [*That* has been omitted.]

However, when *that* is omitted, the remaining *so* can easily be confused with the coordinating conjunction *so*.

> I had some extra time, **so** I went to the music store.

Because sentences with subordinating conjunctions are punctuated differently from sentences with coordinating conjunctions, be careful to distinguish between them. If *so* stands for "so that," it is a subordinating conjunction. If *so* means "thus," it is a coordinating conjunction.

Adverbial conjunctions—such as *however, nevertheless, then,* and *therefore*—link independent clauses (**22b(1)**). These conjunctions, also called **conjunctive adverbs,** signal relationships such as cause, condition, and contrast. Adverbial conjunctions are set off by commas. An independent clause preceding an adverbial conjunction may end in a semicolon instead of a period.

> The senator thought the plan was reasonable**; however,** the voters did not.
>   **. However,** the voters did not.
>   . The voters, **however,** did not.
>   . The voters did not, **however.**

ADVERBIAL CONJUNCTIONS

also	however	moreover	still
consequently	instead	nevertheless	then
finally	likewise	nonetheless	therefore
furthermore	meanwhile	otherwise	thus

(8) Interjections

Interjections most commonly express a simple exclamation or an emotion such as surprise, dread, or resignation. Interjections that come before a sentence end in a period or an exclamation point.

> **Oh.** Now I understand.
> **Wow!** Your design is astounding.

Interjections that begin or interrupt a sentence are set off by commas.

> **Hey,** what are you doing?
> The solution, **alas,** was not as simple as I had hoped it would be.

A NOTE ON GRAMMAR TERMS

Terminology used to discuss grammar has changed over the years. Most of the terms used in this book are considered traditional. However, it is important to realize that if you take advanced courses in grammar, you will encounter new terms and new classification systems.

Exercise 1

Identify the part of speech for each word in the sentences below.

1. Hey, are you a fan of both anime and manga?
2. If you are, you should join the university's Anime and Manga Club.
3. Every Tuesday at noon, we watch current anime or swap favorite manga.
4. Membership is free; however, donations are always welcome.
5. Whenever you have time, you can simply look for us in the Student Union.

21b | SUBJECTS AND PREDICATES

A sentence consists of two parts:

> SUBJECT + PREDICATE

The **subject** is generally someone or something that either performs an action or is described. The **predicate** expresses the action initiated by the subject or gives information about the subject.

The <u>landlord</u> + <u>had</u> <u>renovated</u> the apartment.
[The subject performs an action; the predicate expresses the action.]

The <u>rent</u> + <u>seemed</u> reasonable.
[The subject is described; the predicate gives information about the subject.]

The central components of the subject and the predicate are often called the **simple subject** (the main noun or pronoun) and the **simple predicate** (the main verb and any auxiliary verbs). They are underlined in the examples above.

    Compound subjects and **compound predicates** include a connecting word (conjunction) such as *and, or,* or *but.*

<u>The Republicans</u> **and** <u>the Democrats</u> are debating this issue.
[compound subject]

The candidate <u>stated his views on abortion</u> **but** <u>did not discuss stem-cell research</u>. [compound predicate]

To identify the subject of a sentence, find the verb and then use it in a question beginning with *who* or *what,* as shown in the following examples.

Jennifer works at a clinic.	Meat contains cholesterol.
Verb: **works**	Verb: **contains**
Who works? **Jennifer**	*What* contains? **Meat**
(not the clinic) **works.**	(not cholesterol) **contains.**
Subject: **Jennifer**	Subject: **Meat**

Some sentences begin with an **expletive**—*there* or *it.* Such a word occurs in the subject position, forcing the true subject to follow the verb.

exp   v   s
There were **no exercise machines.**

A subject following the expletive *it* is often an entire clause. You will learn more about clauses in chapter **22.**

exp v   s
It is essential **that children learn about nutrition at an early age.**

ñ MULTILINGUAL WRITERS

BEGINNING A SENTENCE WITH *THERE*

In sentences beginning with the expletive *there,* the verb comes before the subject. The verb *are* is often hard to hear, so be careful to include it when you write a sentence like the following:

are
There﹀ many good books on nutrition.

? THINKING RHETORICALLY

SUBJECT AND PREDICATES

Generally, sentences have the pattern subject + predicate. However, writers often vary this pattern to provide cohesion, emphasis, or both.

He + elbowed his way into the lobby and paused.
[subject + predicate]

From a far corner came + shrieks of laughter.
[predicate + subject]

These two sentences are cohesive because the information in the predicate that begins the second sentence is linked to information in the first sentence. The reversed pattern in the second sentence (predicate + subject) also places emphasis on the subject: *shrieks of laughter.*

21c | COMPLEMENTS

Complements are parts of the predicate required by the verb to make a sentence complete. For example, the sentence *The chair of the committee presented* is incomplete without the complement *his plans.* A complement is generally a pronoun, a noun, or a noun with modifiers.

The chair of the committee introduced
- **her.** [pronoun]
- **Sylvia Holbrook.** [noun]
- **the new <u>member</u>.** [noun with modifiers]

There are four different types of complements: direct objects, indirect objects, subject complements, and object complements.

(1) Direct object

A **direct object** follows an action verb and either receives the action of the verb or identifies the result of the action.

Steve McQueen drove **a Ford Mustang** in the movie *Bullitt.*

I. M. Pei designed **the East Building of the National Gallery.**

Compound direct objects include a connecting word, usually *and.*

Thomas Edison patented **the phonograph <u>and</u> the microphone.**

To identify a direct object, first find the subject and the verb; then use them in a question ending with *what* or *whom.*

Marie Curie discovered radium.	They hired a new engineer.
Subject and verb:	Subject and verb:
Marie Curie discovered	**They hired**
Marie Curie discovered *what?*	They hired *whom?*
radium	**a new engineer**
Direct object: **radium**	Direct object: **a new engineer**

A direct object may be a clause (**22b**).

Researchers found **that patients benefited from the new drug.**

(2) Indirect object

Indirect objects typically name the person(s) receiving or benefiting from the action indicated by the verb. Verbs that often take indirect objects include *bring, buy, give, lend, offer, sell, send,* and *write.*

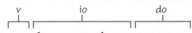

The supervisor gave **the new employees** <u>computers</u>.
[*To whom* were the computers given?]

She wrote **them** <u>recommendation letters</u>.
[*For whom* were the recommendation letters written?]

Like subjects and direct objects, indirect objects can be compound.

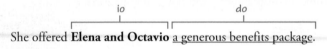

She offered **Elena and Octavio** <u>a generous benefits package</u>.

(3) Subject complement

A **subject complement** follows a linking verb (**21a(1)**) and renames, classifies, or describes the subject. The most common linking verb is *be* (*am, is, are, was, were, been*). Other linking verbs are *become, seem,* and *appear* and the sensory verbs *feel, look, smell, sound,* and *taste.* A subject complement can be a pronoun, a noun, or a noun with modifiers. It can also be an adjective (**21a(4)**).

The winner was

- **you.** [pronoun]
- **Harry Solano.** [noun]
- **the <u>person</u> with the highest score.** [noun with modifiers]
- **ecstatic.** [adjective]

(4) Object complement

An **object complement** renames, classifies, or describes a direct object and helps complete the meaning of a verb such as *call, elect, make, name,* or *paint*. The object complement can be either a noun or an adjective, along with any modifiers.

$$\overset{do}{\overbrace{\text{the rookie}}} \overset{oc}{\overbrace{\textbf{the best \underline{player}}}}$$

Reporters called the rookie **the best \underline{player}.** [noun with modifiers]

His recent performance left the fans **somewhat \underline{disappointed}.** [adjective with modifier]

Exercise 2

Identify the subject and the predicate in each sentence. Then, looking just at the predicate, identify the type of complement underlined. Not all predicates have complements.

1. A naturalist gave <u>us</u> <u>a short lecture on the Cascade Mountains</u>.
2. He showed <u>slides of mountain lakes and heather meadows</u>.
3. Douglas fir predominates <u>in the Cascade forests</u>.
4. Mountaineers and artists consider <u>the North Cascades the most dramatic mountains in the range</u>.
5. Timberlines are <u>low</u> because of the short growing season.
6. Many volcanoes are <u>in the Cascades</u>.
7. Mt. Rainier is <u>the highest volcano in the range</u>.
8. Many visitors to this area hike <u>the Pacific Crest Trail</u>.
9. My friend lent <u>me</u> <u>his map of the trail</u>.
10. The trail begins <u>in southern California</u>, passes <u>through Oregon and Washington</u>, and ends <u>in British Columbia</u>.

21d BASIC SENTENCE PATTERNS

The six basic sentence patterns presented in the following box are based on three verb types: intransitive, transitive, and linking. Notice that *trans* in the words *transitive* and *intransitive* means "over or across."

Thus, the action of a **transitive verb** carries across to an object, but the action of an **intransitive verb** does not. An intransitive verb has no complement, although it is often followed by an adverb (pattern 1). A transitive verb is followed by a direct object (pattern 2), by both a direct object and an indirect object (pattern 3), or by a direct object and an object complement (pattern 4). A linking verb (such as *be, seem, sound,* or *taste*) is followed by a subject complement (pattern 5) or by a phrase that includes a preposition (pattern 6).

BASIC SENTENCE PATTERNS

Pattern 1 SUBJECT + INTRANSITIVE VERB

      s   *v*

Prices dropped.

      s   *v*   *adv*

Prices dropped precipitously.

Pattern 2 SUBJECT + TRANSITIVE VERB + DIRECT OBJECT

      s   *v*   *do*

He writes detective stories.

Pattern 3 SUBJECT + TRANSITIVE VERB + INDIRECT OBJECT + DIRECT OBJECT

      s   *v* *io*   *do*

My father sent me a care package.

Pattern 4 SUBJECT + TRANSITIVE VERB + DIRECT OBJECT + OBJECT COMPLEMENT

      s   *v*   *do*   *oc*

The new leaders declared the country a separate nation.

Pattern 5 SUBJECT + LINKING VERB + SUBJECT COMPLEMENT

      s   *v*   *sc*

Dr. Vargas is the discussion leader.

Pattern 6 SUBJECT + LINKING VERB + PREPOSITIONAL PHRASE

      s *v*   *prep p*

They are in the library.

ñ MULTILINGUAL WRITERS

WORD ORDER

Some languages, such as French and Cantonese, have sentence patterns similar to English sentence patterns. These languages are called **SVO (subject-verb-object) languages,** even though not all sentences have objects. Sentence patterns differ from those of English in **SOV (subject-object-verb) languages** (such as Japanese) and **VSO (verb-subject-object) languages** (such as Arabic). Keep the SVO pattern in mind to help you write English sentences. For more on word order in English, see chapter **48.**

When declarative sentences, or statements, are turned into questions, the subject and the auxiliary verb are usually inverted; that is, the auxiliary verb is moved to the beginning of the sentence, before the subject.

Statement: A Chinese skater (has) won a gold medal.

Question: Has a Chinese skater won a gold medal?

Often, a question word such as *what* or *why* opens a question. As long as the question word is *not* the subject of the sentence, the auxiliary verb precedes the subject.

Question: What has a Chinese skater won? [*What* is the object of *has won.*]

COMPARE: Who has won a gold medal? [*Who* is the subject of the sentence.]

If a statement does not include an auxiliary verb or a form of the linking verb *be,* a form of *do* is added to produce the corresponding question. Again, the auxiliary verb is placed in front of the subject.

Statement: A Chinese skater won a gold medal.

Question: Did a Chinese skater win a gold medal?

As you study sentences more closely, you will find patterns other than the six presented in this section. For example, another pattern requires mention of a destination or location. The sentence *I put the documents* is incomplete without a phrase such as *on your desk.* Other sentences have phrases that are not essential but do add pertinent information. These phrases can sometimes be moved. For example, the phrase *on Friday* can be placed either at the beginning or at the end of the following sentence.

I finished my assignment **on Friday.**
On Friday, I finished my assignment.

To learn how to write effective sentences by varying their structure, see chapter **33**.

ⓝ MULTILINGUAL WRITERS

INVERTING THE SUBJECT AND THE VERB IN QUESTIONS
English is one of a few languages in which the subject and the verb are inverted in questions. Most languages rely on intonation, rather than a change in word order, to indicate that a question is being asked. (English speakers do occasionally use uninverted questions to ask for clarification or to indicate surprise.) In languages other than English, a frequently occurring option for making a statement into a question is to add a particle (see **25a(3)**), such as the Japanese *ka.*

Exercise 3

1. Identify the basic pattern of each sentence in Exercise 2.
2. Write a question corresponding to each of the sentences. Put a check mark next to those questions in which the subject and the verb are inverted.

❓ THINKING RHETORICALLY

SENTENCE PATTERNS

If you want to emphasize a contrast or intensify a feeling, alter the sentence pattern by placing the direct object at the beginning of the sentence.

> I acquired English at home. I learned **French** on the street.

> I acquired English at home. **French** I learned on the street.

A comma is sometimes used after the direct object in such sentences.

> They loved the queen. They despised **the king**.

> They loved the queen. **The king**, they despised.

Exercise 4

Shift the emphasis in the underlined sentences by moving the direct objects to the beginning of the sentence.

1. Leah considers her medical studies her priority. <u>She calls her rock band a hobby</u>.
2. He learned to play the clarinet when he was eight. <u>He mastered the saxophone later on</u>.
3. They renovated the state house. <u>They condemned the old hotel</u>.
4. We played volleyball in the fall. <u>We played basketball in the winter</u>.
5. They named their first child Lewis. <u>They named their second child Clark</u>.

22 ‖ PHRASES, CLAUSES, AND SENTENCES

Within a sentence, groups of words form phrases and clauses. Like single words, these larger units function as specific parts of speech. By understanding how word groups can serve as nouns, verbs, adjectives, or adverbs, you will be able to make your sentences clear, concise, and complete. This chapter will help you

- recognize phrases (**22a**),
- recognize clauses (**22b**), and
- identify sentence forms and functions (**22c** and **22d**).

22a PHRASES

A **phrase** is a sequence of grammatically related words without a subject, a predicate, or both. A phrase is categorized according to its most important word. This section introduces noun phrases, verb phrases, verbal phrases, prepositional phrases, appositives, and absolute phrases.

(1) Noun phrases

A noun phrase consists of a main noun and its modifiers. It can serve as a subject (**21b**) or as a complement (**21c**). It can also be the object of a preposition such as *in, of, on, at,* and *to.* (See **21a(6)** for a longer list of prepositions.)

The heavy frost killed **many fruit trees.** [subject and direct object]

My cousin is **an organic farmer.** [subject and subject complement]

His farm is in **eastern Oregon.** [subject and object of the preposition *in*]

❓ THINKING RHETORICALLY

NOUN PHRASES

In the preceding example sentences, the adjectives *heavy, organic,* and *eastern* add specificity. For example, the noun phrase *an organic farmer* tells the reader more than *farmer* alone would. By composing noun phrases carefully, you will make your sentences more precise.

Much of Greenland lies within the Arctic Circle. ∧The area is
This large island
owned by Denmark. Its∧name is Kaballit Nunaat.
native

[*The area* could refer to either Greenland or the area within the Arctic Circle. *This large island* clearly refers to Greenland. *Its native name* is more precise than just *Its name.*]

ñ MULTILINGUAL WRITERS

NUMBER AGREEMENT IN NOUN PHRASES

Some words must agree in number with the nouns they precede. The words *a, an, this,* and *that* are used before singular nouns; *some, few, these, those,* and *many* are used before plural nouns:

an/that opportunity [singular noun]

some/few/those opportunities [plural noun]

The words *less* and *much* precede nouns representing abstract concepts or masses that cannot be counted (noncount nouns; **21a(2)**):

less freedom, **much** water

For more information, see chapter **46**.

(2) Verb phrases

A verb is essential to the predicate of a sentence (**21b**). It generally expresses action or a state of being. Besides a main verb, a verb phrase includes one or more **auxiliary verbs**, sometimes called *helping verbs,* such as *be, have, do, will,* and *should.*

The passengers **have deplaned.** [auxiliary verb + main verb]

The flight **will be departing** at 7:00 p.m.
[two auxiliary verbs + main verb]

For a comprehensive discussion of verbs, see chapter **25**.

(3) Verbal phrases (gerund, participial, and infinitive phrases)

A **verbal phrase** differs from a verb phrase (**22a(2)**) in that the verb form in a verbal phrase serves as a noun or a modifier rather than as a verb.

He <u>was</u> **reading** the story aloud. [*Reading* is part of the verb phrase *was reading.*]

Reading is fundamental to academic success. [*Reading* serves as a noun. COMPARE: **It** is fundamental to academic success.]

The student **reading** aloud is an education major. [*Reading aloud* modifies *the student.*]

Because of their origin as verbs, verbals in phrases often have their own complements (**21c**) and modifiers (chapter **27**).

He decided **<u>to read</u> the story aloud.** [The object of the verbal *to read* is *the story. Aloud* is a modifier.]

Verbal phrases are divided into three types: gerund phrases, participial phrases, and infinitive phrases.

Gerund phrases include a verb form ending in *-ing* (see **25a(1)**). A gerund phrase serves as a noun, usually functioning as the subject (**21b**) or the object (**21c**) in a sentence.

Writing a bestseller was her only goal. [subject]

My neighbor enjoys **<u>writing</u> about distant places.** [object]

Because gerund phrases act as nouns, pronouns can replace them.

That was her only goal.

My neighbor enjoys **it.**

> **❓ THINKING RHETORICALLY**
>
> **GERUNDS**
>
> What is the difference between the following sentences?
>
> They bundle products together, which often results in higher consumer costs.
>
> Bundling products together often results in higher consumer costs.
>
> In the first sentence, the actor, *they,* is the focus. In the second sentence, the action of the gerund phrase, *bundling products together,* is the focus. As you draft or revise, think about whether you want to emphasize actors or actions.

Participial phrases include either a present participle (a verb form ending in *-ing*) or a past participle (a verb form ending in *-ed* for regular verbs or another form for irregular verbs). (See **25a** for more information on verb forms.)

Planning her questions carefully, she was able to hold fast-paced and engaging interviews. [present participle]

Known for her interviewing skills, she was asked to host her own radio program. [past participle]

Participial phrases function as modifiers (**27a(2)**). They may appear at the beginning, in the middle, or at the end of a sentence. In the following sentences, the participial phrases modify *farmers.*

Fearing a drought, the farmers used less irrigation water.

The farmers, **fearing a drought,** used less irrigation water.

Farmers conserved water, **fearing a drought.**

Remember that gerund phrases and participial phrases have different functions. A gerund phrase functions as a noun; a participial phrase functions as a modifier.

Working together can spur creativity. [gerund phrase]

Working together, the students designed their own software. [participial phrase]

For advice on using punctuation with participial phrases, see **37b** and **37d**.

> **?** **THINKING RHETORICALLY**
>
> **PARTICIPIAL PHRASES**
>
> If some of your sentences sound monotonous or choppy, try combining them by using participial phrases.
>
>> Fans crowded along the city streets. They were celebrating their team's first state championship.
>>
>> REVISED
>>
>> **Crowded along the city streets,** fans celebrated their team's first state championship.
>>
>> OR
>>
>> **Celebrating their team's first state championship,** fans crowded along the city streets.

Infinitive phrases serve as nouns (**21a(2)**) or as modifiers (chapter **27**). The form of an infinitive is distinct—the infinitive marker *to* is followed by the base form of the verb.

> The company intends **to hire twenty new employees.** [noun]
>
> We discussed his plan **to use a new packing process.** [modifier of the noun *plan*]
>
> **To attract customers,** the company changed its advertising strategy. [modifier of the verb *changed*]

Some instructors advise against putting words between the infinitive marker *to* and the base form of the verb.

> Under the circumstances, the
> ∧The jury was unable to, under the circumstances, convict the defendant.

This is good advice to remember if the intervening words create a cumbersome sentence. However, most writers today recognize that a single word splitting an infinitive can provide emphasis.

> He did not expect **to** actually **publish** his work.

ⓝ MULTILINGUAL WRITERS

VERBS FOLLOWED BY GERUNDS AND/OR INFINITIVES

Some verbs in English can be followed by a gerund, some can be followed by an infinitive, and some can be followed by either.

Verbs Followed by a Gerund

admit avoid consider deny dislike enjoy finish suggest

Example: She **enjoys playing** the piano.

Verbs Followed by an Infinitive

agree decide deserve hope need plan promise seem

Example: She **promised to play** the piano for us.

Verbs Followed by Either a Gerund or an Infinitive

begin continue like prefer remember stop try

Examples: She **likes to play** the piano. She **likes playing** the piano.

For more information on verbs and verb forms, see chapters 25 and 47.

(4) Prepositional phrases

Prepositional phrases are modifiers. They provide information about time, place, cause, manner, and so on. They can also answer one of these questions: Which one? What kind of . . . ?

With great feeling, Martin Luther King expressed his dream **of freedom.**
[*With great feeling* describes the way the speech was delivered, and *of freedom* specifies the kind of dream.]

King delivered his most famous speech **at a demonstration in Washington, DC.**
[Both *at a demonstration* and *in Washington, DC* provide information about place.]

A **prepositional phrase** consists of a **preposition** (a word such as *at, of,* or *in*) and a pronoun, noun, or noun phrase (called the **object of the preposition**). A prepositional phrase modifies another element in the sentence.

Everyone **in class** went to the play. [modifier of the pronoun *everyone*]

Some students met the professor **after the play.** [modifier of the verb *met*]

A prepositional phrase sometimes consists of a preposition and an entire clause (**22b**).

They will give the award **to whoever produces the best set design.**

One grammar rule that has been controversial advises against ending a sentence with a preposition. Most professional writers now follow this rule only when they adopt a formal tone. If their rhetorical situation calls for an informal tone, they will not hesitate to place a preposition at the end of a sentence.

He found friends **on** whom he could depend. [formal]

He found friends he could depend **on**. [informal]

(5) Appositives

An **appositive** is most often a noun or a noun phrase that refers to the same person, place, thing, or idea as a preceding noun or noun phrase but in different words. The alternative wording either clarifies the reference or provides extra details. When the appositive simply specifies the referent, no commas are used.

Cormac McCarthy's novel *The Road* won a Pulitzer Prize.

[The appositive specifies which of McCarthy's novels won the award.]

When the appositive provides extra details, commas set it off.

> *The Road,* **a novel by Cormac McCarthy,** won a Pulitzer Prize.
> [The appositive provides extra details about the book.]

For more information on punctuating nonessential appositives, see **37d(2).**

(6) Absolute phrases

An **absolute phrase** is usually a noun phrase modified by a prepositional phrase or a participial phrase (**22a(3)**). It provides descriptive details or expresses a cause or condition.

> **Her guitar in the front seat,** she pulled away from the curb.

> She left town at dawn, **all her belongings packed into a Volkswagen Beetle.**

The preceding absolute phrases provide details; the following absolute phrase expresses cause.

> **Her friend's directions lacking clarity,** she frequently checked her map.

Be sure to use commas to set off absolute phrases.

Exercise 1

Label the underlined phrases in the following sentences as noun phrases, verb phrases, prepositional phrases, or verbal phrases. For verbal phrases, specify the type: gerund, participial, or infinitive. When a long phrase includes a short phrase, identify just the long phrase. Finally, identify any appositive phrases or absolute phrases in the sentences.

1. <u>After the Second World War,</u> <u>fifty-one countries</u> formed <u>the United Nations,</u> <u>an international organization dedicated to peace, tolerance, and cooperation.</u>
2. <u>The Charter of the United Nations</u> <u>was written</u> <u>in 1945.</u>

(continued on page 530)

(continued from page 529)

3. According to this charter, the United Nations may address a wide range of issues.

4. The United Nations devotes most of its energies to protecting human rights, maintaining peace, and encouraging social development.

5. To reach its goals, the United Nations depends on funding from its member states.

6. Its blue flag easily recognized everywhere, the United Nations now includes 192 countries.

7. Symbolizing peace, the emblem on the flag is a map enclosed by olive branches.

22b   CLAUSES

(1) Independent clauses

A **clause** is a group of related words that contains a subject and a predicate. An **independent clause**, sometimes called a *main clause,* has the same grammatical structure as a simple sentence: both contain a subject and a predicate (see **21b**).

$$\overset{\text{s}}{\underbrace{\text{The students}}}\ \overset{\text{pred}}{\underbrace{\text{earned high grades.}}}$$

An independent clause can stand alone as a complete sentence. Other clauses can be added to an independent clause to form a longer, more detailed sentence.

(2) Dependent clauses

A **dependent clause** also has a subject and a predicate (**21b**). However, it cannot stand alone as a complete sentence because of the word introducing it—usually a relative pronoun or a subordinating conjunction.

$$\text{The athlete } \overset{\text{s}}{\underbrace{\textbf{who}}}\ \overset{\text{pred}}{\underbrace{\textbf{placed first}}} \text{ grew up in Argentina. [relative pronoun]}$$

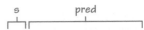

She received the gold medal **because she performed flawlessly.**
[subordinating conjunction]

If it is not connected to an independent clause, a dependent clause is considered a sentence fragment (**23c**).

(a) Noun clauses

Dependent clauses that serve as subjects (**21b**) or objects (**21c**) are called **noun clauses** (or **nominal clauses**). They are introduced by *if, that,* or a *wh-* word such as *what* or *why.* Notice the similarity in usage between noun phrases and noun clauses.

Noun phrases	**Noun clauses**
The testimony may not be true. [subject]	**What the witness said** may not be true. [subject]
We do not understand **their motives.** [direct object]	We do not understand **why they did it.** [direct object]

When no misunderstanding would result, the word *that* can be omitted from the beginning of a noun clause.

The scientist said **she was moving to Australia.** [*that* omitted]

However, *that* should always be retained when there are two noun clauses.

The scientist said **that she was moving to Australia** and **that her research team was planning to accompany her.** [*that* retained in both noun clauses]

(b) Adjectival (relative) clauses

An **adjectival clause**, or **relative clause**, follows a pronoun, noun, or noun phrase and answers one of these questions: Which one? What kind of . . . ? Such a clause usually begins with a **relative pronoun** (*who, whom, that, which,* or *whose*). Notice the similarity in usage between adjectives and adjectival clauses.

Adjectives	Adjectival clauses
Effective supervisors give clear directions. [answers the question *Which supervisors?*]	Supervisors **who give clear directions** earn the respect of their employees. [answers the question *Which supervisors?*]
Long, complicated directions confuse employees. [answers the question *What kind of directions?*]	Directions **that are long and complicated** confuse employees. [answers the question *What kind of directions?*]

An **essential (restrictive) adjectival clause** contains information that is necessary to identify the main noun that precedes the clause. Such a clause is *not* set off by commas. The essential adjectival clause in the following sentence is needed for the reader to know which state carries a great deal of influence in a presidential election.

> The state **that casts the most electoral votes** greatly influences the outcome of a presidential election.

A **nonessential (nonrestrictive) adjectival clause** provides extra details that, even though they may be interesting, are not needed for identifying the preceding noun. An adjectival clause following a proper noun (**21a(2)**) is almost always nonessential. A nonessential adjectival clause should be set off by commas.

> California**, which has fifty-five electoral votes,** greatly influences the outcome of any presidential election.

Many writers use *that* to begin essential clauses and *which* to begin nonessential clauses. Follow this convention if you are required to use APA, CMS, or MLA guidelines. For more information on the use of *which* and *that*, see **26a(3)**.

A relative pronoun can be omitted from an adjectival clause as long as the meaning of the sentence is still clear.

> Mother Teresa was someone **the whole world admired.**
> [*Whom*, the direct object of the clause, has been omitted: the whole world admired *whom*.]

She was someone **who cared more about serving than being served.**
[*Who* cannot be omitted because it is the subject of the clause.]

The relative pronoun is not omitted when the adjectival clause is set off by commas (that is, when it is a nonessential clause).

Mother Teresa**, whom the whole world admired,** cared more about serving than being served.

❓ THINKING RHETORICALLY

ADJECTIVAL CLAUSES

If you find that your sentences tend to be short, try using adjectival clauses to combine them into longer sentences.

> *Dub* is a car magazine. It appeals to drivers with hip-hop attitudes.
> *Dub* is a car magazine **that appeals to drivers with hip-hop attitudes.**
> A Hovercraft can go where many vehicles cannot. It is practically amphibious.
> A Hovercraft, **which can go where many vehicles cannot,** is practically amphibious.

(c) Adverbial clauses

An **adverbial clause** usually answers one of the following questions: Where? When? How? Why? How often? In what manner? Adverbial clauses are introduced by subordinating conjunctions such as *because, although,* and *when.* (For a list of subordinating conjunctions, see **21a(7)**.) Notice the similarity in usage between adverbs and adverbial clauses.

Adverbs	Adverbial clauses
Occasionally, the company hires new writers. [answers the question *How often does the company hire new writers?*]	**When the need arises,** the company hires new writers. [answers the question *How often does the company hire new writers?*]
She acted **selfishly.** [answers the question *How did she act?*]	She acted **as though she cared only about herself.** [answers the question *How did she act?*]

Adverbial clauses can appear at various points in a sentence. Use commas to set off an adverbial clause placed at the beginning or in the middle of a sentence.

Because they disagreed, the researchers made little progress.

The researchers, **because they disagreed,** made little progress.

An adverbial clause at the end of a sentence is rarely preceded by a comma.

The researchers made little progress **because they disagreed.**

However, if a final adverbial clause in a sentence contains an extra detail—information you want the reader to pause before—use a comma to set it off.

I slept soundly that night, **even though a storm raged outside.**

❓ THINKING RHETORICALLY

ADVERBIAL CLAUSES

In an adverbial clause that refers to time or establishes a fact, both the subject and any form of the verb *be* can be omitted. Using such **elliptical clauses** will make your writing more concise.

While fishing, he saw a rare owl.
[COMPARE: **While he was fishing,** he saw a rare owl.]

Though tired, they continued to study for the exam.
[COMPARE: **Though they were tired,** they continued to study for the exam.]

Be sure that the omitted subject of an elliptical clause is the same as the subject of the independent clause. Otherwise, revise either the adverbial clause or the main clause.

While ∧ reviewing your report, a few questions occurred to me.
I was

OR

While reviewing your report, ∧ a few questions ~~occurred to me~~.
I thought of

For more information on the use of elliptical constructions, see **36b.**

Exercise 2

Identify the dependent clauses in the following paragraph.

[1]If you live by the sword, you might die by the sword. [2]However, if you make your living by swallowing swords, you will not necessarily die by swallowing swords. [3]At least, this is the conclusion Brian Witcombe and Dan Meyer reached after they surveyed forty-six professional sword swallowers. [4](Brian Witcombe is a radiologist, and Dan Meyer is a famous sword swallower.) [5]Some of those surveyed mentioned that they had experienced either "sword throats" or chest pains, and others who let their swords drop to their stomachs described perforation of their innards, but the researchers could find no listing of a sword-swallowing mortality in the medical studies they reviewed. [6]The researchers did not inquire into the reasons for swallowing swords in the first place.

22c SENTENCE FORMS

You can identify the form of a sentence by noting the number of clauses it contains and the type of each clause. There are four sentence forms: simple, compound, complex, and compound-complex.

(1) Simple sentences

> ONE INDEPENDENT CLAUSE

A **simple sentence** is equivalent to one independent clause; thus, it must have a subject and a predicate.

The lawyer presented her final argument.

However, you can expand a simple sentence by adding one or more verbal phrases (22a(3)) or prepositional phrases (22a(4)).

Encouraged by the apparent sympathy of the jury, the lawyer presented her final argument. [The verbal phrase adds detail.]

The lawyer presented her final argument **in less than an hour.** [The prepositional phrase adds information about time.]

(2) Compound sentences

> INDEPENDENT CLAUSE + INDEPENDENT CLAUSE

A compound sentence consists of at least two independent clauses but no dependent clauses. The independent clauses of a compound sentence are most commonly linked by a coordinating conjunction. However, punctuation may sometimes serve the same purpose (38a).

The Democrats proposed a new budget, **but** the Republicans opposed it. [The coordinating conjunction *but* links two independent clauses and signals contrast.]

The Democrats proposed a new budget; the Republicans opposed it. [The semicolon serves the same purpose as the coordinating conjunction.]

(3) Complex sentences

> INDEPENDENT CLAUSE + DEPENDENT CLAUSE

A complex sentence consists of one independent clause and at least one dependent clause. A dependent clause in a complex sentence can be a noun clause, an adjectival clause, or an adverbial clause (22b(2)).

Because he was known for architectural ornamentation, no one predicted **that the house <u>he designed for himself</u> would be so plain.** [This sentence has three dependent clauses. *Because he was known for architectural ornamentation* is an adverbial clause. *That the house he designed for himself would be so plain* is a noun clause, and *he designed for himself* is an adjectival clause within the noun clause. The relative pronoun *that* has been omitted from the beginning of the embedded adjectival clause.]

(4) Compound-complex sentences

INDEPENDENT CLAUSE + INDEPENDENT CLAUSE +
DEPENDENT CLAUSE

The combination of a compound sentence and a complex sentence is called a **compound-complex sentence**. A compound-complex sentence consists of at least two independent clauses and at least one dependent clause.

Conflict is essential to good storytelling, **so** fiction writers often create a character **who faces a major challenge.**
[The coordinating conjunction *so* joins the two independent clauses; the relative pronoun *who* introduces the dependent clause.]

❓ THINKING RHETORICALLY

SENTENCE FORMS

If one of your paragraphs has as many simple sentences as the one below, try combining some of your ideas into compound, complex, or compound-complex sentences. As you do, you might need to add extra detail as well.

I rode the school bus every day. I didn't like to, though. The bus smelled bad. And it was always packed. The worst part was the bumpy ride. Riding the bus was like riding in a worn-out sneaker.

REVISED

As a kid, I rode the school bus every day, but I didn't like to. I hated the smell, the crowd, and the bumpy ride itself. Every seat was filled, and many of the kids took their shoes off for the long ride home on roads so bumpy you couldn't even read a comic book. Riding that bus was like riding inside a worn-out sneaker.

Exercise 3

Identify each sentence in the paragraph in Exercise 2 as simple, compound, complex, or compound-complex.

Exercise 4

Vary the sentence forms in the following paragraph. Add details as needed.

> Most people write on a computer. Many still keep a pencil nearby. They most likely use it to jot notes. They rarely think about its role in history. This common writing instrument was invented during the sixteenth century. It was used by George Washington while surveying the Ohio Territory. It was used by Meriwether Lewis and William Clark during their expedition to the Northwest. And Ulysses S. Grant used a pencil to make battle plans. The authors Henry David Thoreau, John Steinbeck, and Ernest Hemingway were other well-known pencil users. The graphite pencil began as an alternative to a stylus made of lead. In fact, we still speak of a pencil lead because the stylus contained this compound. However, the marks a pencil makes are nothing more than flecks of graphite.

22d   SENTENCE FUNCTIONS

Sentences serve a number of functions. Writers commonly state facts or report information with **declarative sentences**. They give instructions with **imperative sentences (commands)**. They use questions, or **interrogative sentences**, to elicit information or to introduce topics. And they express emotion with **exclamative sentences (beginning with *what* or *how*)**. The word *exclamatory* describes sentences with exclamation points.

Declarative	He ran his first marathon. He won!
Imperative	Check the record. Imagine!
Interrogative	What was his time?
Exclamative	What an incredible race that was!

Although most of the sentences you are likely to write will be declarative, an occasional command, question, or exclamation will add variety (33c).

Taking note of end punctuation can help you identify the function of a sentence. Generally, a period indicates the end of a declarative sentence or an imperative sentence (figure 22.1), and a question mark ends an interrogative sentence. To distinguish between an imperative sentence and a declarative sentence, look for a subject (**21b**). If you cannot find one, the sentence is imperative. Because an imperative is directed to another person or persons, the subject *you* is implied:

Expect great things.

Courtesy of United Airlines

Look over there.
[COMPARE: You look over there.]

Figure 22.1: Advertisers often use imperatives to attract the reader's attention.

ñ MULTILINGUAL WRITERS

SENTENCE FUNCTIONS
Declarative, imperative, and interrogative sentences can be used for a variety of purposes. For example, imperative sentences are used not only to give directions but also to make suggestions (*Try using a different screwdriver*), to issue invitations (*Come in*), to extend wishes (*Have a good time*), and to warn others (*Stop there*). Furthermore, a particular purpose, such as getting someone to do something, can be accomplished in more than one way.

Imperative	Close the window, please.
Declarative	You should close the window.
Interrogative	Would you please close the window?

❓ THINKING RHETORICALLY

QUESTIONS

One type of interrogative sentence, the **rhetorical question,** is not a true question, because an answer is not expected. Instead, like a declarative sentence, it is used to state an opinion. However, a positive rhetorical question can correspond to a negative assertion, and vice versa.

Rhetorical questions	Equivalent statements
Should we allow our rights to be taken away?	We should not allow our rights to be taken away.
Isn't it time to make a difference?	It's time to make a difference.

Because they are more emphatic than declarative sentences, rhetorical questions focus the reader's attention on major points.

Exercise 5

Identify each sentence type in the passage below. What type is used most often? Why?

¹Think of the thousand cartoons you have seen—in the *New Yorker* or a multitude of other places—of the marooned human or pair of humans (in whatever combination of sexes) on some microscopic tropical atoll, a little sand, one palm tree, one rock, the vastness of the sea. ²Humor and pathos live together in these scenes. ³Here at last, we think, life is cut down to the bone so that we can see what stuff it is made of. ⁴If two men, they are The Odd Couple; if man and woman, they will find the roots of the old sex wars and quarrel, as they might on a street in New York; if only one [person], there is a message in a bottle, generally with cheerless news. ⁵Do we love this cartoon scene because we imagine we can discover the bedrock of human nature inside it?

—Bill Holm, *Eccentric Islands: Travels Real and Imaginary*

23 ‖ SENTENCE FRAGMENTS

As its name suggests, a **sentence fragment** is only a piece of a sentence; it is not complete. This chapter can help you

- recognize sentence fragments (**23a**) and
- revise fragments resulting from incorrectly punctuated phrases and dependent clauses (**23b** and **23c**).

23a ‖ RECOGNIZING SENTENCE FRAGMENTS

A sentence is considered a fragment when it is incomplete in any of the following ways:

- It is missing a subject or a verb.

  Derived from a word meaning "nervous sleep." Hypnotism actually refers to a type of focused attention. [no subject]

  Alternative medical treatment may include hypnosis. **The placement of a patient into a relaxed state.** [no verb]

- It is missing both a subject and a verb.

  The hypnotic state differs from sleep. **Contrary to popular belief.**

- It is a dependent clause.

  Most people can be hypnotized easily. **Although the depth of the trance for each person varies.**

Note that imperative sentences (**22d**) are not considered fragments. In these sentences, the subject, *you,* is not stated explicitly. Rather, it is implied.

Find out as much as you can about alternative treatments.
[COMPARE: You find out as much as you can about alternative treatments.]

🄝 MULTILINGUAL WRITERS

SUBJECT PRONOUNS
In some languages, subject pronouns are dropped when there is no risk of misunderstanding. In Japanese, a sentence such as *Sushi o tabemasu* ("Eat sushi") is permissible when the subject pronoun can be determined from the context. In Spanish, a verb form reveals information about the subject; unless needed for clarity or emphasis, a subject pronoun can thus be omitted, as in *Trabajo en un banco* ("I work in a bank"). In English, however, subject pronouns must be included in all except imperative sentences.

FOUR METHODS FOR IDENTIFYING FRAGMENTS

If you have trouble recognizing fragments in your own writing, try one or more of these methods:

1. Read each paragraph backwards, sentence by sentence. When you read your sentences out of order, you may more readily note the incompleteness of a fragment.

2. Locate the essential parts of each sentence. First, find the main verb and any accompanying auxiliary verbs. Remember that gerunds and participles cannot function as main verbs (**22a(3)**). After you find the main verb, identify the subject (**21b**). Finally, make sure that the sentence does not begin with a relative pronoun (**22b(2)**) or a subordinating conjunction (**21a(7)**).

   Test sentence 1: The inventor of the Frisbee.

   Test: Main verb? *None.*
   [Because there is no verb, this test sentence is a fragment.]

   Test sentence 2: Walter Frederick Morrison invented the Frisbee.

   Test: Main verb? *Invented.*
   Subject? *Walter Frederick Morrison.*
   Relative pronoun or subordinating conjunction? *None.*
   [The test sentence is complete: it contains a subject and a verb and does not begin with a relative pronoun or a subordinating conjunction.]

3. Put any sentence you think might be a fragment into this frame sentence:

   They do not understand the idea that _____.

Only a full sentence will make sense in this frame sentence. If a test sentence, other than an imperative, does not fit into the frame sentence, it is a fragment.

Test sentence 3: Because it can be played almost anywhere.

Test: They do not understand the idea that *because it can be played almost anywhere.*
[The frame sentence does not make sense, so the test sentence is a fragment.]

Test sentence 4: Ultimate Frisbee is a popular sport because it can be played almost anywhere.

Test: They do not understand the idea that *Ultimate Frisbee is a popular sport because it can be played almost anywhere.*
[The frame sentence makes sense, so the test sentence is complete.]

4. Rewrite any sentence you think might be a fragment as a question that can be answered with *yes* or *no*. Only complete sentences can be rewritten this way.

Test sentence 5: That combines aspects of soccer, football, and basketball.

Test: *Is that combines aspects of soccer, football, and basketball?*
[The question does not make sense, so the test sentence is a fragment.]

Test sentence 6: Ultimate Frisbee is a game that combines aspects of soccer, football, and basketball.

Test: *Is Ultimate Frisbee a game that combines aspects of soccer, football, and basketball?*
[The question makes sense, so the test sentence is complete.]

23b PHRASES AS SENTENCE FRAGMENTS

A phrase is a group of words without a subject and/or a predicate (**22a**). When punctuated as a sentence (that is, with a period, a question mark, or an exclamation point at the end), a phrase becomes a fragment. You can revise such a fragment by attaching it to a related sentence, usually the one preceding it.

Verbal phrase as a fragment

Early humans valued color. ~~Creating~~ **, creating ₌ permanent colors with natural pigments.**

Prepositional phrase as a fragment

For years, the Scottish have dyed sweaters with soot. ~~Originally~~ , *originally* from the chimneys of peat-burning stoves.

Compound predicate as a fragment

Arctic foxes turn white when it snows. ~~And~~ *and* thus conceal themselves from prey.

Appositive phrase as a fragment

During the Renaissance, one of the most highly valued pigments was ultramarine. ~~An~~ *an* extract from lapis lazuli.

Appositive list as a fragment

To derive dyes, we have always experimented with what we find in nature. ~~Shells,~~ *: shells,* roots, insects, flowers.

Absolute phrase as a fragment

The deciduous trees of New England are known for their brilliant autumn color. ~~Sugar~~ *, sugar* maples dazzling tourists with their orange and red leaves.

Instead of attaching a fragment to the preceding sentence, you can recast the fragment as a complete sentence. This method of revision elevates the importance of the information conveyed in the fragment.

Fragment	Humans painted themselves for a variety of purposes. **To attract a mate, to hide themselves from game or predators, or to signal aggression.**
Revision	Humans used color for a variety of purposes. For example, they painted themselves to attract a mate, to hide themselves from game or predators, or to signal aggression.

Exercise 1

Revise each fragment by attaching it to a related sentence or by recasting it as a complete sentence.

1. A brilliant twenty-three-year-old Englishman. Isaac Newton was the first person to study color.
2. By passing a beam of sunlight through a prism. Newton showed that white light comprised all the visible colors of the spectrum.
3. White light passed through the prism. And separated into the colors of the rainbow.
4. Rainbows are arcs of color. Caused by water droplets in the air.
5. Sometimes rainbows contain all the spectrum colors. Red, orange, yellow, green, blue, indigo, and violet.
6. Particles of spray in waterfalls can act as prisms. Producing a variety of colors.
7. Our brains easily fooled. We sometimes see more colors than are actually present.

23c DEPENDENT CLAUSES AS SENTENCE FRAGMENTS

A dependent clause is a group of words with both a subject and a predicate (**22b(2)**), but because it begins with a subordinating conjunction (**21a(7)**) or a relative pronoun (**22b(2)**), it cannot stand alone as a sentence. To revise this type of fragment, attach it to a related sentence, usually the sentence preceding it.

because

The iceberg was no surprise. ~~Because~~ ₍the *Titanic*'s wireless operators had received reports of ice in the area.

, which

More than two thousand people were aboard the *Titanic*. ~~Which~~ ₍was the largest ocean liner in 1912.

You can also recast the fragment as a complete sentence by removing the subordinating conjunction or relative pronoun and supplying any missing elements. This method of revision draws attention to the information originally conveyed in the fragment. Compare the following revisions with the ones above:

The iceberg was no surprise. The *Titanic's* wireless operators had received reports of ice in the area.

More than two thousand people were aboard the *Titanic*. In 1912, this ocean liner was the world's largest.

You can also reduce a clause that is a fragment to a phrase (**22b**) and then attach it to a related sentence.

More than two thousand people were aboard the *Titanic*, the largest ocean liner in 1912. [fragment reduced to an appositive phrase]

If you are unsure of the punctuation to use with phrases or dependent clauses, see chapter **37**.

❓ THINKING RHETORICALLY

FRAGMENTS

When used judiciously, fragments—like short sentences—emphasize ideas or add surprise. However, they are generally permitted only when the rhetorical situation allows the use of a casual tone.

> **May. When the earth's Northern Hemisphere awakens from winter's sleep and all of nature bristles with the energies of new life.** My work has kept me indoors for months now. I'm not sure I'll ever get used to it.
>
> —Ken Carey, *Flat Rock Journal: A Day in the Ozark Mountains*

Exercise 2

Revise each fragment by attaching it to a related sentence or by recasting it as a full sentence.

1. The ship was christened *Titanic.* Which means "of great size."
2. The shipbuilders thought the *Titanic* was unsinkable. Because it had sixteen watertight compartments.
3. The ship sank in less than three hours. Even though the damage caused by the iceberg was not massive.
4. The extent of the damage to the ship's hull was unknown. Until researchers started examining the wreckage in the late 1990s.
5. In 1987, a controversial French expedition recovered dishes, jewelry, and other artifacts from the *Titanic.* Which were later displayed in France and Germany.

Exercise 3

Follow the guidelines in this chapter to locate and revise the fragments in the following paragraph. If you find it necessary, make other improvements as well. Be prepared to explain your revisions.

[1]One of the most popular rides at any county fair or amusement park is the Ferris wheel. [2]The original Ferris wheel, designed by George Washington Gale Ferris, Jr., for a national exposition in 1893. [3]Rose to a height of 264 feet. [4]And accommodated 2,140 passengers. [5]Ferris's goal was to build something that would surpass in effect the Eiffel Tower. [6]Which was constructed just a few years earlier. [7]Though Ferris's plans were not immediately accepted. [8]Once they were, and the wheel opened to the public, it became an immediate success. [9]At times carrying 38,000 passengers a day. [10]Since the nineteenth century. [11]Engineers have designed taller and taller Ferris wheels. [12]The 541-foot Singapore Flyer holds the record, but the Beijing Great Wheel, currently under construction. [13]Will be over 100 feet taller.

24 ‖ COMMA SPLICES AND FUSED SENTENCES

Comma splices and fused sentences are sentence-level mistakes resulting from incorrect or missing punctuation. Both are punctuated as one sentence when they should be punctuated as two sentences (or two independent clauses). By revising comma splices and fused sentences, you indicate sentence boundaries and thus make your writing easier to read. This chapter will help you

- review the rules for punctuating independent clauses (**24a**),
- recognize comma splices and fused sentences (**24b**), and
- learn ways to revise them (**24c** and **24d**).

24a ‖ PUNCTUATING SENTENCES WITH TWO INDEPENDENT CLAUSES

In case you are unfamiliar with or unsure about the conventions for punctuating sentences with two independent clauses, here is a short review.

A comma and a coordinating conjunction can join two independent clauses (**37a**). The coordinating conjunction indicates the relationship between the two clauses. For example, *and* signals addition, whereas *but* and *yet* signal contrast. The comma precedes the conjunction.

INDEPENDENT CLAUSE, **and** INDEPENDENT CLAUSE.

The new store opened this morning, **and** the owners greeted everyone at the door.

A semicolon can join two independent clauses that are closely related. A semicolon generally signals addition or contrast.

> INDEPENDENT CLAUSE; INDEPENDENT CLAUSE.

One of the owners comes from this area; the other grew up in Cuba.

A semicolon may also precede an independent clause that begins with an adverbial conjunction (conjunctive adverb) such as *however* or *nevertheless.* Notice that a comma follows this type of connecting word.

> The store will be open late on Fridays and Saturdays; **however,** it will be closed all day on Sundays.

A comma used to set off an adverbial conjunction (conjunctive adverb) is sometimes omitted when there is no risk that the sentence will be misread.

> The owners remodeled the interior; **then** they put up a new sign outside. [No misreading is possible, so the comma can be omitted.]

A colon can join two independent clauses. The second clause usually explains or elaborates on the first.

> INDEPENDENT CLAUSE: INDEPENDENT CLAUSE.

The owners have announced a special offer: anyone who makes a purchase during the opening will receive a 10 percent discount.

If you are following MLA guidelines, capitalize the first word of a clause following a colon when the clause expresses a rule or principle (**38b(1)**).

A period separates clauses into distinct sentences.

> INDEPENDENT CLAUSE. INDEPENDENT CLAUSE.

The store is located on the corner of Pine Street and First Avenue. It was formerly an insurance office.

Occasionally, commas are used between independent clauses, but only when the clauses are short, parallel in form, and unified in meaning.

They came, they shopped, they left.

For more information on punctuating sentences, see chapters **37**, **38**, and **41**.

| **24b** | RECOGNIZING COMMA SPLICES AND FUSED SENTENCES |

A **comma splice**, or **comma fault**, refers to the incorrect use of a comma between two independent clauses (**22b**).

but
Most stockholders favored the merger,∧ the management did not.

A **fused sentence**, or **run-on sentence**, consists of two independent clauses run together without any punctuation at all.

; however,
The first section of the proposal was approved∧ the budget will have to be resubmitted.

To revise a comma splice or a fused sentence, include appropriate punctuation and any necessary connecting words.

If you have trouble recognizing comma splices or fused sentences, try one of the following methods.

TWO METHODS FOR IDENTIFYING COMMA SPLICES AND FUSED SENTENCES

1. Locate a sentence that may be problematic. Put it into this frame sentence:

They do not understand the idea that _____.

Only complete sentences make sense when placed in the frame sentence. If just part of a test sentence fits, you have probably located a comma splice or a fused sentence.

Test sentence 1: Plasma is the fourth state of matter.

Test: They do not understand the idea that *plasma is the fourth state of matter.*
[The test sentence makes sense in the frame sentence. No revision is necessary.]

> **Test sentence 2:** Plasma is the fourth state of matter, some scientists believe that 99 percent of the universe is made of it.
>
> **Test:** They do not understand the idea that *plasma is the fourth state of matter, some scientists believe that 99 percent of the universe is made of it.*
>
> [The frame sentence does not make sense because there are two sentences completing it, rather than one. The test sentence contains a comma splice and thus should be revised.]
>
> **Revision:** Plasma is the fourth state of matter. Some scientists believe that 99 percent of the universe is made of it.
>
> 2. If you think a sentence may be incorrect, try to rewrite it as a question that can be answered with *yes* or *no.* If just part of the sentence makes sense, you have likely found a comma splice or a fused sentence.
>
> **Test sentence 3:** Plasma is used for a number of purposes.
>
> **Test:** *Is plasma used for a number of purposes?*
> [The question makes sense. No revision is necessary.]
>
> **Test sentence 4:** Plasma is used for a number of purposes it may even power rockets someday.
>
> **Test:** *Is plasma used for a number of purposes it may even power rockets someday?*
> [The question does not make sense because only one part of the test sentence has been made into a question. The test sentence is a fused sentence and thus should be revised.]
>
> **Revision:** Plasma is used for a number of purposes. It may even power rockets someday.

You can also find comma splices and fused sentences by remembering that they commonly occur in certain contexts.

- With transitional words and phrases such as *however, therefore,* and *for example* (see also **24c(5)**)

  Comma splice: The director is unable to meet with you this week, however, next week she will have time on Tuesday.

  [Notice that a semicolon replaces the comma.]

- When an explanation or an example is given in the second sentence

  Fused sentence: The cultural center has a new collection of spear points⌃ ~~many~~ of them were donated by a retired anthropologist.
  (inserted: ". Many")

- When a clause that includes *not* is followed by one without this word, or vice versa

  Comma splice: A World Cup victory is not just an everyday sporting event⌃ ~~it~~ is a national celebration.
  (inserted: ". It")

- When the subject of the second clause is a pronoun whose antecedent is in the preceding clause

  Fused sentence: Lake Baikal is located in southern Russia⌃ ~~it~~ is 394 miles long.
  (inserted: ". It")

24c   REVISING COMMA SPLICES AND FUSED SENTENCES

If you find comma splices or fused sentences in your writing, try one of the following methods to revise them.

(1) Linking independent clauses with a comma and a coordinating conjunction

By linking clauses with a comma and a coordinating conjunction (such as *and* or *but*), you signal the relationship between the clauses (addition or contrast, for example).

Fused sentence: The diplomats will end their discussions on Friday⌃ they will submit their final decisions on Monday.
(inserted: ", and")

Comma splice: Some diplomats applauded the treaty,⌃ others opposed it vehemently.
(inserted: "but")

(2) Linking independent clauses with a semicolon or a colon or separating them with a period

When you link independent clauses with a semicolon, you signal their connection indirectly. There are no explicit conjunctions to use as cues.

The semicolon usually indicates addition or contrast. When you link clauses with a colon, the second clause serves as an explanation or an elaboration of the first. A period indicates that each clause is a complete and separate sentence.

> **Comma splice:** Our division's reports are posted on our web page, hard copies are available by request.

> **Revision 1:** Our division's reports are posted on our web page; hard copies are available by request.

> **Revision 2:** Our division's reports are posted on our web page. Hard copies are available by request.

> **Fused sentence:** Our mission statement is simple ⁀ we aim to provide athletic gear at affordable prices.

(3) Recasting an independent clause as a dependent clause or as a phrase

A dependent clause (22b(2)) includes a subordinating conjunction such as *although* or *because,* which indicates how the dependent and independent clauses are related (in a cause-and-consequence relationship, for example). A prepositional phrase (22a(4)) includes a preposition such as *in, on,* or *because of* that may also signal a relationship directly. Verbal, appositive, and absolute phrases (22a(3), 22a(5), and 22a(6)) suggest relationships less directly because they do not include connecting words.

> **Comma splice:** The wind had blown down trees and power lines, the whole city was without electricity for several hours.

> **Revision 1: Because the wind had blown down power lines,** the whole city was without electricity for several hours. [dependent clause]

> **Revision 2: Because of the downed power lines,** the whole city was without electricity for several hours. [prepositional phrase]

> **Revision 3: The wind having blown down power lines,** the whole city was without electricity for several hours. [absolute phrase]

(4) Integrating one clause into the other

When you integrate clauses, you will generally retain the important details but omit or change some words.

Fused sentence: The proposal covers all but one point it does not describe how the project will be assessed.

Revision: The proposal covers all the points except assessment procedures.

(5) Using transitional words or phrases to link independent clauses

Another way to revise fused sentences and comma splices is to use transitional words and phrases such as *however, on the contrary,* and *in the meantime.* (For other examples, see the list on pages 69–70.)

Fused sentence: Sexual harassment is not just an issue for women . After all, men can be sexually harassed too.

Comma splice: The word *status* refers to relative position within a group ; however, it is often used to indicate only positions of prestige.

If you have questions about punctuating sentences that contain transitional words and phrases, see **38a**.

As you edit fused sentences and comma splices, you will refine the connections between your sentences, helping your readers to follow your train of thought. The following checklist will help you find and fix comma splices and fused sentences.

✔ CHECKLIST for Comma Splices and Fused Sentences

1 **Common Sites for Comma Splices or Fused Sentences**
   - With transitional words such as *however* and *therefore*
   - When an explanation or an example occurs in the second clause
   - When a clause that includes *not* is followed by one without this word, or vice versa
   - When the subject of the second clause is a pronoun whose antecedent is in the first clause

2 **Ways to Fix Comma Splices and Fused Sentences**
   - Link the clauses with a comma and a coordinating conjunction.
   - Link the clauses using a semicolon or a colon.
   - Separate the clauses by punctuating each as a sentence.
   - Make one clause dependent.

- Reduce one clause to a phrase.
- Rewrite the sentence, integrating one clause into the other.
- Use a transitional word or phrase.

Exercise 1

Revise each comma splice or fused sentence by using one of the strategies mentioned in this section.

1. The average human brain weighs about three pounds, the average brain of a sperm whale weighs seventeen pounds.
2. The body of a brain cell can move but most brain cells stay put they extend their axons outward.
3. The brain needs water to function properly dehydration may cause lethargy or learning problems.
4. Researchers studying brain hemispheres have found that many professional musicians process music in their left hemisphere, the notion that musicians and artists depend on the right side of their brain is considered outmoded.
5. Discoveries in neuroscience have yielded many benefits, researchers have developed medication for schizophrenia and Tourette's syndrome.

24d DIVIDED QUOTATIONS

When dividing quotations with signal phrases such as *he said* or *she asked,* use a period between independent clauses.

Comma splice: "Beauty brings copies of itself into being," states Elaine
. "It
Scarry,—"it ∧ makes us draw it, take photographs of it, or describe it to
other people."

[Both parts of the quotation are complete sentences, so the signal phrase is attached to the first, and the sentence is punctuated with a period.]

A comma separates two parts of a single quoted sentence.

"Musing takes place in a kind of meadowlands of the imagination," writes Rebecca Solnit, "a part of the imagination that has not yet been plowed, developed, or put to any immediately practical use."

[Because the quotation is a single sentence, a comma is used.]

Exercise 2

Revise each comma splice or fused sentence in the following paragraph. Some sentences may not need revision.

[1]In *The Politics of Happiness,* Derek Bok, former president of Harvard University, discusses recent findings that researchers studying well-being have reported. [2]He mentions, for example, research showing that measurements of happiness in the United States have not risen much in the last fifty years, people are responding to survey questions about their levels of happiness in much the same way as they did in 1960. [3]Even though average incomes have grown, levels of happiness have not increased. [4]Bok believes that people become accustomed to higher standards of living they do not realize how quickly they adapt and so do not become happier. [5]Bok recognizes that not everyone's income has increased but notes that, strangely enough, the disparity between rich and poor has not caused increased dissatisfaction among the poor, he cites further studies showing that citizens in countries with costly welfare programs are not necessarily happier than citizens in countries with welfare programs that are not as generous. [6]Because of these studies, Bok suggests that our government not focus on economic growth alone as an indicator of well-being and instead take into account current research on what makes people happy. [7]This discussion "is bound to contribute to the evolution of society and the refinement of its values," he explains, "that alone will be an accomplishment of enduring importance to humankind" (212).

25 ‖ VERBS

Choosing verbs to convey your message precisely is the first step toward writing clear sentences. The next step is to ensure that the verbs you choose conform to the conventions your audience expects you to follow. This chapter will help you

- identify conventional verb forms (**25a**),
- use verb tenses to provide information about time (**25b**),
- distinguish between the active voice and the passive voice (**25c**),
- use verbs to signal the factuality or likelihood of an action or event (**25d**), and
- ensure that subjects and verbs agree in number and person (**25e**).

25a ‖ VERB FORMS

Most English verbs have four forms, following the model for *walk*:

walk, walks, walking, walked

However, English also includes irregular verbs, which may have as few as three forms or as many as eight:

let, lets, letting   *be, am, is, are, was, were, being, been*

(1) Regular verbs

Regular verbs have four forms. The **base form** is the form you can find in a dictionary. *Talk, act, change,* and *serve* are all base forms.

The second form of a regular verb is the **-s form**. To derive this form, add to the base form either *-s* (*talks, acts, changes, serves*) or, in some cases, *-es* (*marries, carries, tries*). See **42d** for information on changing *y* to *i* before adding *-es*.

The third form of a regular verb is the **-ing form**, also called the **present participle**. It consists of the base form and the ending *-ing* (*talking, acting*). Depending on the verb, a spelling change may be required when the suffix is added (*changing, chatting*) (**42d**).

The fourth form of a regular verb consists of the base form and the ending *-ed* (*talked, acted*). Again, spelling may vary when the suffix is added (*changed, chatted*) (**42d**). The *-ed* form has two names. When this form is used *without* a form of the auxiliary verb *have* or *be*, it is called the **past form**: We *talked* about the new plan. When the *-ed* form is used *with* one of these auxiliary verbs, it is called the **past participle**: We *have talked* about it several times. A committee *was formed* to investigate the matter.

	Verb Forms of Regular Verbs		
Base Form	***-s* Form (Present Tense, Third Person, Singular)**	***-ing* Form (Present Participle)**	***-ed* Form (Past Form or Past Participle)**
work	works	working	worked
watch	watches	watching	watched
apply	applies	applying	applied
stop	stops	stopping	stopped

❗ CAUTION

When verbs are followed by words with similar sounds, you may find their endings (*-s* or *-ed*) difficult to hear. In addition, these verb endings may seem unfamiliar because your dialect does not have them. Nonetheless, you should use *-s* and *-ed* when you write for an audience that expects you to include these endings.

>   seems
> She ∧ ~~seem~~ satisfied with the report.

>   supposed
> We were ∧ ~~suppose~~ to receive the results yesterday.

(2) Irregular verbs

Most irregular verbs, such as *write,* have forms similar to some of those for regular verbs: base form (*write*), *-s* form (*writes*), and *-ing* form (*writing*). However, the past form (*wrote*) and the past participle (*written*) vary from those of the regular verbs. In fact, some irregular verbs have two acceptable past forms and/or past participles (see *awake, dive, dream,* and *get* in the following chart). Other irregular verbs have only three forms because the same form serves as the base form, the past form, and the past participle (see *set* in the chart). If you are unsure about verb forms not included in the chart, consult a dictionary.

	Verb Forms of Irregular Verbs			
Base Form	-*s* Form (Present Tense, Third Person, Singular)	-*ing* Form (Present Participle)	Past Form	Past Participle
arise	arises	arising	arose	arisen
awake	awakes	awaking	awaked, awoke	awaked, awoken
begin	begins	beginning	began	begun
break	breaks	breaking	broke	broken
bring	brings	bringing	brought	brought
buy	buys	buying	bought	bought
choose	chooses	choosing	chose	chosen
come	comes	coming	came	come
dive	dives	diving	dived, dove	dived
do	does	doing	did	done
dream	dreams	dreaming	dreamed, dreamt	dreamed, dreamt
drink	drinks	drinking	drank	drunk
drive	drives	driving	drove	driven
eat	eats	eating	ate	eaten
forget	forgets	forgetting	forgot	forgotten
forgive	forgives	forgiving	forgave	forgiven

(*continued on page 562*)

(continued from page 561)

Base Form	-s Form (Present Tense, Third Person, Singular)	-ing Form (Present Participle)	Past Form	Past Participle
get	gets	getting	got	gotten, got
give	gives	giving	gave	given
go	goes	going	went	gone
hang (suspend)	hangs	hanging	hung	hung
hang (execute)	hangs	hanging	hanged	hanged
keep	keeps	keeping	kept	kept
know	knows	knowing	knew	known
lay (see the Glossary of Usage)	lays	laying	laid	laid
lead	leads	leading	led	led
lie (see the Glossary of Usage)	lies	lying	lay	lain
lose	loses	losing	lost	lost
pay	pays	paying	paid	paid
rise (see the Glossary of Usage)	rises	rising	rose	risen
say	says	saying	said	said
see	sees	seeing	saw	seen
set (see the Glossary of Usage)	sets	setting	set	set
sink	sinks	sinking	sank	sunk

Base Form	-s Form (Present Tense, Third Person, Singular)	-ing Form (Present Participle)	Past Form	Past Participle
sit (see the Glossary of Usage)	sits	sitting	sat	sat
speak	speaks	speaking	spoke	spoken
stand	stands	standing	stood	stood
steal	steals	stealing	stole	stolen
swim	swims	swimming	swam	swum
take	takes	taking	took	taken
tell	tells	telling	told	told
throw	throws	throwing	threw	thrown
wear	wears	wearing	wore	worn
write	writes	writing	wrote	written

The verb *be* has eight forms:

be	**Be** on time!
am	I **am** going to arrive early tomorrow.
is	Time **is** of the essence.
are	They **are** always punctual.
was	The meeting **was** scheduled for 10 a.m.
were	We **were** only five minutes late.
being	He is **being** delayed by traffic.
been	How long have we **been** here?

> **ñ MULTILINGUAL WRITERS** ▬▬▬▬▬▬

OMISSION OF FORMS OF *BE* IN OTHER LANGUAGES

Forms of the verb *be* can be omitted in some languages. In English, however, they are necessary.

Sentence without an auxiliary verb: The population ˄is growing.

Sentence without a linking verb: It ˄is quite large.

---

(3) Prepositional verbs and phrasal verbs

A **prepositional verb** is a frequently occurring combination of a verb and a preposition. *Rely on, think about, look like,* and *ask for* are all prepositional verbs. A **phrasal verb** is a combination of a verb and a particle such as *up, out,* or *on*. A **particle** resembles an adverb or a preposition, but it is so closely associated with a verb that together they form a unit of meaning. *Carry out, go on, make up, take on,* and *turn out* are phrasal verbs commonly found in college-level writing. Notice that these five phrasal verbs have meanings that can be expressed in one word: *do, continue, form, accept,* and *attend.*

> **ñ MULTILINGUAL WRITERS** ▬▬▬▬▬▬

Definitions of phrasal verbs are often not obvious. For example, *find out* means "to discover." To learn more about phrasal verbs, see chapter 47.

---

(4) Auxiliary verbs

The auxiliary verbs *be, do,* and *have* combine with main verbs, both regular and irregular.

be	am, is, are, was, were surprised
	am, is, are, was, were writing
do	does, do, did call
	doesn't, don't, didn't spend
have	has, have, had prepared
	has, have, had read

When you combine auxiliary verbs with main verbs, you alter the meanings of the main verbs in subtle ways. The resulting verb combinations may provide information about time, emphasis, or action in progress.

Be, do, and *have* are not just auxiliary verbs, though. They may be used as main verbs as well.

be	I **am** from Texas.
do	He **does** his homework early in the morning.
have	They **have** an apartment near a park.

A sentence may even include one of these verbs as both an auxiliary and a main verb.

They **are being** careful.

Did you **do** your taxes by yourself?

She **has** not **had** any free time this week.

Another type of auxiliary verb is called a **modal auxiliary**. There are nine modal auxiliaries: *can, could, may, might, must, shall, should, will,* and *would.* The following box provides examples of common meanings conveyed by modal auxiliaries.

SOME COMMON MEANINGS OF MODAL AUXILIARIES

Meaning	Modal Auxiliary	+	Main Verb	Example(s)
Ability	can, could		afford	They *can afford* to rent an apartment.
				They *could* not *afford* to buy a house.
Certainty	will		leave	We *will leave* tomorrow.
Obligation	must		return	You *must return* your books soon.
Advice	should		talk	He *should talk* with his counselor.
Permission	may		use	You *may use* the computers in the library.

> **!** **CAUTION**
>
> When a modal auxiliary occurs with the auxiliary *have* (*must have forgotten, should have known*), *have* frequently sounds like the word *of*. When you proofread, be sure that modal auxiliaries are not followed by *of*.
>
> >   *have*
> > They **could** ⌃**of taken** another route.
>
> Writers generally do not combine modal auxiliaries unless they want to portray a regional dialect.
>
> >   *be able to*
> > We **might** ⌃~~could~~ plan the meeting for after the holidays.

> **ñ** **MULTILINGUAL WRITERS**
>
> ### MODAL AUXILIARY VERBS
>
> Most modal auxiliary verbs have more than one meaning. *Could* sometimes refers to ability (*I **could** swim a mile when I was sixteen*). However, *could* can also refer to possibility (*Something good **could** happen*). To learn more about modal auxiliary verbs and about phrasal modals such as *be going to* and *have to*, see chapter **47**.

(5) Participles

Present participles (*-ing* verb forms) are used with a form of the auxiliary verb *be*: We *are waiting* for the next flight. It *is arriving* sometime this afternoon. Depending on the intended meaning, past participles can be used with either *be* or *have*: The first flight *was canceled*. We *have waited* for an hour. If a sentence contains only a participle, it is probably a fragment (**23b**).

>   , *dreaming*
> I sit on the same bench every day. ~~Dreaming~~ ⌃of far-off places.

When a participle is part of a verbal phrase, it often appears without an auxiliary verb (**22a(3)**).

> **Swatting** at mosquitoes and **cursing** softly, we packed our gear.
> [COMPARE: We **were swatting** at mosquitoes and **cursing** softly as we packed our gear.]

Exercise 1

Revise the following sentences. Explain any changes you make.

1. Any expedition into the wilderness suffer its share of mishaps.
2. The Lewis and Clark Expedition began in May 1804 and end in September 1806.
3. Fate must of smiled on Meriwether Lewis and William Clark, for there were no fatalities under their leadership.
4. Lewis and Clark lead the expedition from St. Louis to the Pacific Ocean and back.
5. President Thomas Jefferson commission the expedition in 1803 in part because he was interest in finding the Northwest Passage—a hypothetical waterway connecting the Atlantic and Pacific Oceans.
6. By 1805, the Corps of Discovery, as the expedition was call, included thirty-three members.
7. The Corps might of lost all maps and specimens had Sacajawea, a Native American woman, not fish them from the Missouri River.
8. Sacajawea could of went off with her own people in Idaho, but she accompany Lewis and Clark to the Pacific.
9. When the Mandans had finish inspecting York, William Clark's African American servant, they assume he was the expedition's leader.
10. The success of the expedition depend on its members' willingness to help one another.

25b VERB TENSES

Verb tenses provide information about time. For example, the tense of a verb may indicate that an action took place in the past or that an action is ongoing. Verb tenses are labeled as present, past, or future; they are also labeled as simple, progressive, perfect, or perfect progressive. The following chart shows how these labels apply to the tenses of *walk*.

Verb Tenses			
	Present	**Past**	**Future**
Simple	I/you/we/they **walk.** He/she/it **walks.**	walked	will walk
Progressive	I **am walking.** He/she/it **is walking.** You/we/they **are walking.**	I/he/she/it **was walking.** You/we/they **were walking.**	will be walking
Perfect	I/you/we/they **have walked.** He/she/it **has walked.**	had walked	will have walked
Perfect progressive	I/you/we/they **have been walking.** He/she/it **has been walking.**	had been walking	will have been walking

Some of the tenses have more than one form because they depend on the person and the number of the subject (generally, the main noun or the pronoun that precedes the verb). **Person** refers to the role of the subject. First person (expressed by the pronoun *I* or *we*) indicates that the subject of the verb is the writer or writers. Second person (*you*) indicates that the subject is the audience. Third person (*he, she, it,* or *they*) indicates that the subject is someone or something other than the writer or audience. First- and second-person references are pronouns, but third-person references can be either pronouns or nouns (such as *book* or *books*). **Number** signals whether the subject is singular (referring to just one person or thing) or plural (referring to more than one person or thing).

25c VOICE

Voice indicates the relationship between a verb and its subject. When a verb is in the **active voice**, the subject is generally a person or thing performing the action indicated by the verb. When a verb is in the **passive voice**, the subject is usually the *receiver* of the action.

Jen Wilson **wrote** the essay. [active voice]
The essay **was written** by Jen Wilson. [passive voice]

Notice that the actor, Jen Wilson, appears in a prepositional phrase beginning with *by* in the passive sentence. Some sentences, however, do not include a *by* phrase because the actor is unknown or unimportant.

Jen Wilson's essay **was published** in the student newspaper.

In the sentence above, it is not important to know who accepted Jen's essay for publication, only that it was published. The best way to decide whether a sentence is in the passive voice is to examine its verb phrase.

(1) Verbs in the passive voice

The verb phrase in a sentence written in the passive voice consists of a form of the auxiliary verb *be* (*am, is, are, was, were, been*) and a past participle (**25a(1)**). Depending on the verb tense, other auxiliaries such as *have* and *will* may appear as well. The following sentences in the passive voice show which auxiliaries are used with *called*:

Simple present	The meeting *is called* to order.
Simple past	The recruits *were called* to duty.
Present progressive	The council *is being called* to act on the proposal.
Past perfect	Ms. Jones *had been called* for jury duty twice last year, but she was glad to serve again.

If a verb phrase does not include both a form of the auxiliary verb *be* and a past participle, it is in the active voice.

(2) Choosing between the active and the passive voice

Use the active voice for emphasizing an actor and an action. First, make the actor the subject of the sentence, and then choose verbs that will help your readers see what the actor is doing. Notice how the following sentences in the active voice emphasize the role of the students:

Active voice   A group of students planned the graduation ceremony. They invited a well-known columnist to give the graduation address.

Passive voice   The graduation ceremony was planned by a group of students. A well-known columnist was invited to give the graduation address.

Use the passive voice when you want to stress the recipient of the action, rather than the actor, or when the actor's identity is unimportant or unknown. For example, you may want to emphasize the topic of a discussion.

Tuition increases **were discussed** at the board meeting.

Or you may be unable to identify the actor who performed some action.

The lights **were left** on in the building last night.

Writers of scientific prose often use the passive voice to highlight the experiment rather than the experimenter. The following is an excerpt from student Heather Jensen's lab report (see **18f** for the full paper):

First, the slides **were placed** on a compound microscope under low power, a 40X magnification level. The end of the root tip **was located**; then the cells immediately behind the root cap **were examined**.

Exercise 2

Identify the voice in each sentence as active or passive. Remember: if the verb phrase includes a form of the auxiliary verb *be* (*am, is, are, was, were, been*) and a past participle (**25a(1)**), the sentence is in the passive voice.

1. In a *National Geographic* article, Zahi Hawass discusses recent information regarding the life and death of King Tut.

2. King Tut was enthroned at the age of nine.
3. Originally, he was called Tutankhaten.
4. Later he changed his name to Tutankhamun.
5. At nineteen years of age, King Tut died.
6. His mummy was discovered in 1922.
7. Recently, King Tut's DNA was obtained.
8. The findings of the genetic testing reveal that King Tut may have died of malaria.

Exercise 3

Rewrite the sentences in Exercise 2, making sentences in the active voice passive, and vice versa. Add or delete actors when necessary. If one version of a sentence is better than the other, explain why.

25d ‖ MOOD

The **mood** of a verb indicates the writer's attitude concerning the factuality of what is being expressed. The **indicative mood** is used for statements and questions regarding fact or opinion. The **imperative mood** is used to give commands or directions. The **subjunctive mood** is used to state requirements, make requests, and express wishes.

Indicative	I am on the board of directors.
	Were you on the board last year?
	The board will meet in two weeks.
Imperative	Plan on attending the meeting.
	Be on time!

Subjunctive	She suggests that you come early.
	If you came to more meetings, you would understand the issues.
	If I had attended regularly, I would have voted for the plan.

The subjunctive mood is also used to signal hypothetical situations—situations that are not real or not currently true (for example, *If I were president, . . .*).

Verb forms in the subjunctive mood serve a variety of functions. The **present subjunctive** is the base form of the verb. It is used with such verbs as *demand, insist, suggest*, and *recommend* to express necessity.

The manager suggested that he **pay** for his own travel. [active voice]

We demanded that he **be reimbursed.** [passive voice]

The **past subjunctive** has the same form as the simple past (for example, *had, offered,* or *wrote*). However, the past subjunctive form of *be* is *were*, regardless of person or number. This form is used to present hypothetical situations.

If they **offered** me the job, I would take it. [active voice]

Even if I **were promoted,** I would not change my mind. [passive voice]

Although it is called "past," the past subjunctive refers to the present or the future.

The **perfect subjunctive** has the same form as the past perfect tense: *had* + past participle. The perfect subjunctive signals that the action did not occur.

She wishes she **had participated** in the scholarship competition. [active voice]

If she **had been awarded** the scholarship, she would have quit her job. [passive voice]

The following guidelines should help you avoid pitfalls when using the subjunctive.

TIPS FOR USING THE SUBJUNCTIVE

- In clauses beginning with *as if* and *as though*, use the past subjunctive or the perfect subjunctive:

  He acts as if he ⌃**was** the owner.
  were

  She looked at me as though she ⌃**heard** this story before.
  had

- In a dependent clause that begins with *if* and refers to a condition or action that did not occur, use the past subjunctive or the perfect subjunctive. Avoid using *would have* in such an *if* clause.

  If I ⌃**was** rich, I would buy a yacht.
  were

  If the driver ⌃**would have checked** his rearview mirror, the accident would not have happened.
  had

  Notice that an indicative clause beginning with *if* may describe a condition or action that can occur.

  If it is sunny tomorrow, I'm going fishing. [indicative mood]

- In dependent clauses following verbs that express wishes, requirements, or requests, use the past subjunctive or the perfect subjunctive.

  I wish I ⌃**was** taller.
  were

  My brother wishes he ⌃**studied** harder years ago.
  had

Some linguists believe that certain subjunctive forms are disappearing from the English language. It is not unusual to find clauses such as *I wish I was . . .* (instead of *I wish I were . . .*) in the essays of many well-known writers. Nonetheless, appropriate use of verb forms in the subjunctive mood is still expected in most academic rhetorical situations.

Exercise 4

Use subjunctive verb forms to revise the following sentences.
1. The planners of Apollo 13 acted as if the number 13 was a lucky number.
2. Superstitious people think that if NASA changed the number of the mission, the astronauts would have had a safer journey.
3. They also believe that if the lunar landing would have been scheduled for a day other than Friday the Thirteenth, the crew would not have encountered any problems.
4. The crew used the lunar module as though it was a lifeboat.
5. If NASA ever plans a space mission on Friday the Thirteenth again, the public would object.

25e ‖ SUBJECT-VERB AGREEMENT

To say that a verb *agrees* with a subject means that the form of the verb (*-s* form or base form) is appropriate for the subject. For example, if the subject refers to one person or thing (*an athlete*, *a computer*), the *-s* form of the verb is appropriate (*runs*). If the subject refers to more than one person or thing (*athletes, computers*), the base form of the verb is appropriate (*run*). Notice in the following examples that the singular third-person subjects take a singular verb (*-s* form) and all the other subjects take the base form

He, she, it, Joe, a student	has, looks, writes
I, you, we, they, the Browns, the students	have, look, write

The verb *be* has three different present-tense forms and two different past-tense forms:

I	am/was
He, she, it, Joe, a student	is/was
You, we, they, the Browns, the students	are/were

ⓝ MULTILINGUAL WRITERS

ADDING -s TO NOUNS AND VERBS

Standardized English requires the addition of -s to mark most nouns as plural and most verbs as third-person singular. (Modal auxiliaries are the exception.) Be careful not to confuse the verb ending and the noun ending.

The **students** need attention. [noun + -s]

The student **needs** attention. [verb + -s]

You can refer to the following subsections for guidance on subject-verb agreement in particular situations:

- when a word or words come between the subject and the verb (**25e(1)**);
- when two or more subjects are joined by conjunctions (**25e(2)** and **25e(3)**);
- when word order is inverted (**25e(4)**);
- when the subject is a relative pronoun (**25e(5)**), an indefinite pronoun (**25e(6)**), or a collective noun or measurement word (**25e(7)**);
- when the subject is a noun that is plural in form but singular in meaning (**25e(8)**);
- when the subject and its complement differ in number (**25e(9)**); and
- when the subject is a noun clause beginning with *what* (**25e(10)**).

(1) Subject and verb separated by one or more words

When phrases such as the following occur between the subject and the verb, they do not affect the number of the subject or the form of the verb:

accompanied by	as well as	not to mention	including
along with	in addition to	no less than	together with

Her **salary,** together with tips, **is** just enough to live on.

Tips, together with her salary, **are** just enough to live on.

(2) Subjects joined by *and*

A compound subject (two nouns joined by *and*) that refers to a single person or thing takes a singular verb.

> The **founder and president** of the art association **was** elected to the board of the museum.

> **Red beans and rice is** the specialty of the house.

(3) Subjects joined by *or, either . . . or*, or *neither . . . nor*

When singular subjects are linked by *or, either . . . or*, or *neither . . . nor*, the verb is singular as well.

> The **provost or** the **dean** usually **presides** at the meeting.

> **Either** his **accountant or** his **lawyer has** the will.

If the subjects linked by one of these conjunctions differ in person or number, the verb agrees in number with the subject closer to the verb.

> Neither the basket nor the **apples were** expensive. [plural]

> Neither the apples nor the **basket was** expensive. [singular]

(4) Inverted word order

In most sentences, the subject precedes the verb.

> The large **cities** of the Northeast **were** the hardest hit by the winter storms.

The subject and verb can sometimes be inverted for emphasis; however, they must still agree.

> The hardest hit by the winter storms **were** the large **cities** of the Northeast.

When *there* begins a sentence, the subject and verb are always inverted (**21b**); the verb still agrees with the subject, which follows it.

> There **are** several **cities** in need of federal aid.

(5) Clauses with relative pronouns

In an adjectival (relative) clause (**22b(2)**), the subject is generally a relative pronoun (*that, who,* or *which*). To determine whether the relative pronoun is singular or plural, you must find its antecedent (the word or words it refers to). When the antecedent is singular, the relative pronoun is singular; when the antecedent is plural, the relative pronoun is plural. In essence, the verb in the adjectival clause agrees with the antecedent.

sing ant   sing v

The person <u>who</u> reviews applications is out of town this week.

pl ant   pl v

The director met with the **students <u>who</u> are** studying abroad next quarter.

According to rules of traditional grammar, in sentences like the following, which contains the pattern *one + of +* plural noun + adjectival clause, the antecedent for the relative pronoun (*who,* in this case) is the plural noun (*students*). The verb in the adjectival clause is thus plural as well (*plan*).

pl ant   pl v

Julie is one of the **students <u>who</u> plan** to study abroad.

However, professional writers often consider *one,* instead of the plural noun, to be the antecedent of the relative pronoun and thus use the singular verb:

sing ant   sing v

Julie is **one** of the students <u>**who**</u> **plans** to study abroad.

(6) Indefinite pronouns

The indefinite pronouns *each, either, everybody, everyone,* and *anyone* are considered singular and so require singular verb forms.

<u>**Each**</u> of them **is willing** to lead the discussion.

<u>**Everybody**</u> in our class **takes** a turn giving a presentation.

Other indefinite pronouns, such as *all, any, some, none, half,* and *most,* can be either singular or plural, depending on whether they refer to a unit or quantity (singular) or to individuals (plural).

My sister collects comic **books; some are** quite valuable.

pl ant   *pl v*

My sister collects antique **jewelry; some** of it **is** quite valuable.

sing ant   *sing v*

When an indefinite pronoun is followed by a prepositional phrase beginning with the preposition *of,* the verb agrees in number with the object of the preposition.

pl obj pl v

None of **those are** spoiled.

sing obj sing v

None of the **food is** spoiled.

sing obj   *sing v*

More than **half** of the **population** in West Texas **is** Hispanic.

pl obj   *pl v*

More than **half** of the **people** in West Texas **are** Hispanic.

Some grammarians reason that *none*, like *no one*, is singular and thus should be followed by a singular verb.

None of the grant requests **has** been rejected.

Nonetheless, many reputable writers have used *none* with plural verbs, leading to the widespread acceptance of this usage.

None of the grant requests **have** been rejected.

(7) Collective nouns and measurement words

Collective nouns (**21a(2)**) and measurement words require singular verbs when they refer to groups or units. They require plural verbs when they refer to individuals or parts.

Singular (regarded as a group or unit)	Plural (regarded as individuals or parts)
The **majority rules.**	The **majority** of us **are** in favor.

Ten million gallons of oil **is** more than enough.	**Ten million gallons** of oil **were spilled.**
The **number** of errors **is** insignificant.	A **number** of workers **were** absent.

(8) Words ending in -s

Titles of works that are plural in form (for example, *Star Wars* and *Dombey and Son*) are treated as singular because they refer to a single book, movie, recording, or other work.

> *The Three Musketeers* **is** one of the films she discussed in her paper.

A reference to a word is also considered singular.

> *Beans* **is** slang for "the least amount": I don't know beans about football.

Some nouns ending in *-s* are actually singular: *linguistics, news,* and *Niagara Falls.*

> The **news is** encouraging.

Nouns such as *athletics, politics,* and *electronics* can be either singular or plural, depending on their meanings.

> **Statistics is** an interesting subject. [singular]

> **Statistics are** often misleading. [plural]

(9) Subjects and subject complements

Some sentences may have a singular subject (**21b**) and a plural subject complement (**21c**), or vice versa. In either case, the verb agrees with the subject.

> Her primary **concern is** rising health-care **costs.**

> **Rising health-care costs are** her primary **concern.**

❓ THINKING RHETORICALLY

AGREEMENT OF RELATED SINGULAR AND PLURAL NOUNS

When a sentence has two or more nouns that are related, use either the singular form or the plural form consistently.

The **student** raised her **hand.**

The **students** raised their **hands.**

Occasionally, you may have to use a singular noun to retain an idiomatic expression or to avoid ambiguity.

They kept their **word.**

The **participants** were asked to name their favorite **movie.**

(10) Subjects beginning with *what*

In noun clauses (**22b(2)**), *what* may be understood as either "the thing that" or "the things that." If it is understood as "the thing that," the verb in the main clause is singular.

What we need **is** a new policy.
[*The thing that* we need is a new policy.]

If *what* is understood as plural (the things that), the verb in the main clause is plural.

What we need **are** new guidelines.
[*The things that* we need are new guidelines.]

Note that the main noun following the verb in these examples (*policy, guidelines*) also agrees with the verb: *policy* and *is* are singular; *guidelines* and *are* are plural.

According to a traditional grammar rule, a singular verb should be used in both the noun clause beginning with *what* and the main clause.

What **is** needed **is** new guidelines.

However, many writers and editors today consider this rule outmoded.

Exercise 5

In each sentence, choose the correct form of the verb in parentheses. Make sure that the verb agrees with its subject according to the conventions for academic and professional writing.

1. There (is/are) at least two good reasons for changing motor oil: risk of contamination and danger of additive depletion.
2. Reasons for not changing the oil (include/includes) the cost to the driver and the inconvenience of the chore.
3. What I want to know (is/are) the number of miles I can drive before changing my oil.
4. Each of the car manuals I consulted (recommends/recommend) five-thousand-mile intervals.
5. Neither the automakers nor the oil station attendants (know/knows) how I drive, however.
6. My best friend and mechanic (says/say) four thousand miles.
7. But my brother says three thousand miles (is/are) not long enough.

Exercise 6

Complete the following sentences, making sure that subjects and verbs agree.

1. Applying for college and enrolling in courses . . .
2. Erik is one of the students who . . .
3. Either of them . . .
4. The list of volunteers . . .
5. Hidden beneath the stairs . . .
6. The teacher, along with her students, . . .
7. What we requested . . .

26 ‖ PRONOUNS

When you use pronouns effectively, you add clarity and coherence to your writing. However, if you do not provide the words, phrases, or clauses that make your pronoun references clear, you might unintentionally cause confusion. This chapter will help you

- recognize various types of pronouns (**26a**),
- use appropriate pronouns (**26b**),
- make sure that pronouns agree with their antecedents (**26c**),
- provide clear pronoun references (**26d**),
- understand when to use *I, we,* and *you* (**26e**).

26a ‖ RECOGNIZING PRONOUNS

A **pronoun** is commonly defined as a word used in place of a noun that has already been mentioned—its **antecedent**.

John said **he** would guide the trip.

A pronoun may also substitute for a group of words acting as a noun (see **22b(2)**).

The participant with the most experience said **he** would guide the trip.

Most pronouns refer to nouns, but some modify nouns.

This man is our guide.

Pronouns are categorized as personal, reflexive/intensive, relative, interrogative, demonstrative, and indefinite.

(1) Personal pronouns

To understand the uses of personal pronouns, you must first be able to recognize person, number, and case. **Person** indicates whether a pronoun refers to the writer (**first person**), to the reader (**second person**), or to another person, place, thing, or idea (**third person**). **Number** reveals whether a pronoun is singular or plural. **Case** refers to the form a pronoun takes to indicate its function in a sentence. Pronouns can be subjects, objects, or possessives. When they function as subjects (**21b(1)**), they are in the subjective case; when they function as objects (**21b(2)**), they are in the objective case; and when they indicate possession or a related meaning (**39a**), they are in the possessive case. (See **26b** for more information on case.) Possessives can be divided into two groups based on whether they are followed by nouns: *my, your, his, her, its, our,* and *their* are all followed by nouns; *mine, yours, his, hers, ours,* and *theirs* are not. (Notice that *his* is in both groups.)

> **Their** budget is higher than **ours.**

> [*Their* is followed by a noun; *ours* is not.]

CASE:	Subjective		Objective		Possessive	
NUMBER:	Singular	Plural	Singular	Plural	Singular	Plural
First person	I	we	me	us	my mine	our ours
Second person	you	you	you	you	your yours	your yours
Third person	he, she, it	they	him, her, it	them	his, her, hers, its	their theirs

(2) Reflexive/intensive pronouns

Reflexive pronouns direct the action back to the subject (*I saw myself*); **intensive pronouns** are used for emphasis (*I myself questioned the judge*). *Myself, yourself, himself, herself, itself, ourselves, yourselves,* and *themselves* are used as either reflexive pronouns or intensive pronouns. Both types of pronouns are objects and must be accompanied by subjects.

| Reflexive pronoun | **He** was always talking to **himself.** |
| Intensive pronoun | **She herself** delivered the letter. |

Avoid using a reflexive pronoun as a subject. A common error is using *myself* in a compound subject.

Ms. Palmquist and ∧ ~~myself~~ discussed our concern with the senator.

Hisself, themself, and *theirselves* are inappropriate in college or professional writing. Instead, use *himself* and *themselves.*

        themselves
The interns worked by ∧ ~~theirselves~~ on one of the projects.

(3) Relative pronouns

An adjectival clause (or relative clause) ordinarily begins with a relative pronoun: *who, whom, which, that,* or *whose.* To provide a link between this type of dependent clause and the main clause, the relative pronoun corresponds to its antecedent—a word or phrase in the main clause.

           ant   rel pro
The students talked to **a reporter who** had just returned from overseas.

Notice that if you rewrite the dependent clause as a separate independent clause, you use the antecedent in place of the relative pronoun.

A reporter had just returned from overseas.

Who, whose, and *whom* ordinarily refer to people; *which* refers to things; *that* refers to things and, in some contexts, to people. The possessive *whose* (used in place of the awkward *of which*) usually refers to people but sometimes refers to things.

The poem, **whose** author is unknown, has recently been set to music.

	Refers to people	Refers to things	Refers to either
Subjective	who	which	that
Objective	whom	which	that
Possessive			whose

Knowing the difference between an essential clause and a nonessential clause will help you decide whether to use *which* or *that* (see **22b(2)**). A clause that a reader needs in order to identify the antecedent correctly is an **essential clause**.

ant ess cl
The person who presented the award was last year's winner.

If the essential clause were omitted from this sentence, the reader would not know which person was last year's winner.

A **nonessential clause** is *not* needed for correct identification of the antecedent and is thus set off by commas. A nonessential clause often follows a proper noun (a specific name).

ant noness cl
Andrea Bowen, who presented the award, was last year's winner.

Notice that if the nonessential clause were removed from this sentence, the reader would still know the identity of last year's winner.

According to a traditional grammar rule, *that* is used in essential adjectival clauses, and *which* is used in nonessential adjectival clauses.

I need a job **that** pays well.

For years, I have had the same job, **which** pays well enough.

However, some professional writers do not follow both parts of this rule. Although they will not use *that* in nonessential clauses, they will use *which* in essential clauses. See **22b(2)** for more information on the use of *which* and *that*.

(4) Interrogative pronouns

The **interrogative pronouns** *what, which, who, whom,* and *whose* are question words. Be careful not to confuse *who* and *whom* (see **26b(5)**). *Who* functions as a subject; *whom* functions as an object.

Who won the award? [COMPARE: **He** won the award.]

Whom did you see at the ceremony? [COMPARE: I saw **him**.]

(5) Demonstrative pronouns

The **demonstrative pronouns**, *this* and *these,* indicate that someone or something is close by in time, space, or thought. *That* and *those* signal remoteness.

These are important documents; **those** can be thrown away.

Demonstrative pronouns sometimes modify nouns.

These documents should be filed.

(6) Indefinite pronouns

Indefinite pronouns usually do not refer to specific persons, objects, ideas, or events.

anyone	anybody	anything
everyone	everybody	everything
someone	somebody	something
no one	nobody	nothing
each	either	neither

Indefinite pronouns do not refer to an antecedent. In fact, some indefinite pronouns *serve* as antecedents.

Someone forgot **her** purse.

26b   PRONOUN CASE

The term *case* refers to the form a pronoun takes to indicate its function in a sentence. There are three cases: subjective, objective, and possessive. The following sentence includes all three.

He [subjective] wants **his** [possessive] legislators to help **him** [objective].

(1) Pronouns in the subjective case

A pronoun that is the subject of a sentence is in the subjective case. To determine which pronoun form is correct in a compound subject (a noun and a pronoun joined by *and*), say the sentence using the pronoun alone, omitting the noun. For the following sentence, notice that "*Me* solved the problem" is not Standardized English, but "*I* solved the problem" is.

> *and I*
> ~~Me and~~ Marisa ∧ solved the problem.

Place the pronoun last in the sequence. If the compound subject contains two pronouns, test each one by itself.

> *He*
> ∧ ~~Him~~ and I confirmed the results.

Pronouns following a *be* verb (*am, is, are, was, were, been*) should also be in the subjective case.

> *I*
> The first presenters were Kevin and ∧ ~~me~~.

ñ MULTILINGUAL WRITERS

NOUN OR PRONOUN AS SUBJECT
In some languages, a noun in the subject position may be followed by a pronoun. In Standardized English, though, such a pronoun should be omitted.

> My roommate ~~he~~ works in the library three hours a week.

---

(2) Pronouns in the objective case

Whenever a pronoun follows an action verb or a preposition, it takes the **objective case**.

Direct object	The whole staff admired **him**.
Indirect object	The staff sent **him** a card.
Object of a preposition	The staff depended on **him**.

Pronouns in compound objects are also in the objective case.

> They will appoint Tom or ⌃Ⅰ. [direct object]
> _{me}

> They sent Tom and ⌃Ⅰ the appropriate forms. [indirect object]
> _{me}

> The manager sat between Tom and ⌃Ⅰ at the meeting. [object of the
> _{me}
>
> preposition]

To determine whether to use the subjective or objective case, remember to say the sentence with just the pronoun. Notice that "They will appoint *I*" does not sound right. Another test is to substitute *we* and *us.* If *we* sounds fine, use the subjective case. If *us* sounds better, use the objective case, as in "They sent *us* the appropriate forms."

(3) Possessive forms

Its, their, and *whose* are possessive forms. Be sure not to confuse them with common contractions: *it's* (*it is* or *it has*), *they're* (*they are*), and *who's* (*who is*).

(4) Appositive pronouns

Appositive pronouns are in the same case as the nouns they rename. In the following sentence, *the red team* is the subject, so the appositive pronoun should be in the subjective case.

> The red team—Rebecca, Leroy, and ⌃me—won by only one point.
> _I

In the next sentence, *the red team* is the object of the preposition *to,* so the appositive pronoun should be in the objective case.

> A trophy was presented to the red team—Rebecca, Leroy, and ⌃Ⅰ.
> _{me}

When the order is reversed and a pronoun is followed by a noun, the pronoun must still be in the same case as the noun.

> ⌃Us students need this policy.
> _{We}

(5) *Who/whoever* and *whom/whomever*

To choose between *who* and *whom* or between *whoever* and *whomever,* you must first determine whether the word is functioning as a subject (**21b**) or an object (**21c**). A pronoun functioning as the subject takes the subjective case.

Who won the award? [COMPARE: **She** won the award.]

The teachers know **who** won the award.

The student **who** won the award was quite surprised.

Whoever won the award deserves it.

There will be a celebration for whoever wins the award.
[NOTE: *Whoever wins the award* is the object of *for; whoever* is the subject of this embedded clause.]

When the pronoun is an object, use *whom* or *whomever.*

Whom did they hire? [COMPARE: They hired **him.**]

I do not know **whom** they hired.

The student **whom** they hired graduated in May.

Whomever they hired will have to work hard this year.

Whom may be omitted in sentences when no misunderstanding would result.

The friend he relied on moved away.

[*Whom* has been omitted after *friend.*]

Although many writers still prefer *whom* or *whomever* as object pronouns, dictionaries also allow the use of *who* or *whoever* in informal contexts.

I wonder **who** she voted for.

Give the campaign literature to **whoever** you see.

Who do you plan to vote for?

26c | PRONOUN-ANTECEDENT AGREEMENT

A pronoun and its antecedent (the word or word group to which it refers) agree in number (both are singular or both are plural).

The **supervisor** said **he** would help.

[Both antecedent and pronoun are singular.]

My **colleagues** said **they** would help.

[Both antecedent and pronoun are plural.]

A pronoun also agrees with its antecedent in gender (masculine, feminine, or neuter).

Joseph claims **he** can meet the deadline. [masculine antecedent]

Anna claims **she** can meet the deadline. [feminine antecedent]

The **committee** claims **it** can meet the deadline. [neuter antecedent]

ñ MULTILINGUAL WRITERS

POSSESSIVE PRONOUNS
A possessive pronoun (*my, your, our, his, her, its,* or *their*), also called a **possessive determiner**, agrees with its antecedent, not with the noun it precedes.

                                    his
Ken Carlson brought ∧ her young daughter to the office today.

[The possessive pronoun *his* agrees with the antecedent, *Ken Carlson*, not with the following noun, *daughter*.]

---

(1) Indefinite pronouns

Although most antecedents for pronouns are nouns, antecedents can be indefinite pronouns (26a(6)). Notice that an indefinite pronoun such as *everyone, someone,* or *anybody* takes a singular verb form.

Everyone **has** [not *have*] the right to an opinion.

Difficulties arise, however, because words like *everyone* and *everybody* seem to refer to more than one person even though they take a singular verb. Thus, the definition of grammatical number and our everyday notion of number conflict. In conversation and informal writing, a plural pronoun (*they, them,* or *their*) is often used with the singular *everyone*. Nonetheless, when you write for an audience that expects you to follow traditional grammar rules, make sure to use a third-person singular pronoun.

Everyone has the combination to ^his or her ~~their~~ private locker.

You can avoid the awkwardness of using *his or her* by using an article instead, by making both the antecedent and the possessive pronoun plural, or by rewriting the sentence using the passive voice (**25c**).

Everyone has the combination to **a** private locker. [article]

Students have combinations to **their** private lockers. [plural antecedent and plural possessive pronoun]

The combination to a private locker **is issued** to everyone. [passive voice]

(2) Referring to both genders

When an antecedent can refer to people of either gender, rewrite the sentence to make the antecedent plural or use *he or she* or *his or her* if doing so is not too cumbersome.

^Lawyers ~~A lawyer~~ represents ^their ~~his~~ clients. [plural pronoun and plural antecedent]

A lawyer represents the clients **he or she** has accepted.

A lawyer represents **his or her** clients.

(See **34c** for more information on using inclusive language.)

(3) Two antecedents joined by *or* or *nor*

If a singular and a plural antecedent are joined by *or* or *nor,* place the plural antecedent second and use a plural pronoun.

Either the senator **or** her <u>assistants</u> will explain how <u>they</u> devised the plan for tax reform.

Neither the president **nor** the <u>senators</u> stated that <u>they</u> would support the proposal.

(4) Collective nouns

When an antecedent is a collective noun (**21a(2)**) such as *team, faculty,* or *committee,* determine whether you intend the noun to be understood as singular or plural and then make sure that the pronoun agrees in number with the noun.

                                            it
The choir decided that ∧ <s>they</s> would tour during the winter. [Because the choir decided as a group, *choir* should be considered singular. The singular form, *it,* replaces the plural, *they.*]

                                                            they
The committee may disagree on methods, but ∧ <s>it</s> must agree on basic aims. [Because the committee members are behaving as individuals, *committee* is regarded as plural. The plural form, *they,* replaces the singular, *it.*]

Exercise 3

Revise the following sentences so that pronouns and antecedents agree.

1. A researcher relies on a number of principles to help him make ethical decisions.
2. Everyone should have the right to participate in a study only if they feel comfortable doing so.

3. A team of researchers should provide its volunteers with consent forms, in which they describe to the volunteers the procedures and risks involved in participation.
4. Every participant should be guaranteed that the information they provide will remain confidential.
5. Institutions of higher education require that a researcher address ethical issues in their proposal.

26d | CLEAR PRONOUN REFERENCE

The meaning of each pronoun in a sentence should be immediately obvious. In the following sentence, the pronouns *them* and *itself* clearly refer to their antecedents, *shells* and *carrier shell,* respectively.

The **carrier shell** gathers small empty **shells** and attaches **them** to **itself.**

A pronoun may refer to two or more antecedents.

Jack and I have collected shells since **we** were eight years old.

Sometimes an antecedent follows a pronoun.

Because of **their** beauty and rarity, **shells** attract collectors worldwide.

(1) Ambiguous or unclear pronoun references

When a pronoun can refer to either of two antecedents, the ambiguity may confuse readers. To make the antecedent clear, replace the pronoun with a noun or rewrite the sentence. The following revised sentences clarify that Mr. Eggers, not Mr. Anderson, will be in charge of the project.

> Mr. Eggers
> Mr. Anderson told Mr. Eggers that ∧ ~~he~~ would be in charge of the project.

> OR

> Mr. Anderson put Mr. Eggers in charge of the project.

(2) Remote or awkward references

To help readers understand your meaning, place pronouns as close to their antecedents as possible. The following sentence needs to be revised so that the relative pronoun *that* is close to its antecedent, *poem.* Otherwise, the reader would wonder how a new book could be written in 1945.

> that was originally written in 1945
> The **poem** ∧ has been published in a new book **that ~~was originally written~~**
> ~~in 1945~~.

Notice, however, that a relative pronoun does not always have to follow its antecedent directly. In the following example, there is no risk of misunderstanding.

> We slowly began to notice **changes** in our lives **that** we had never expected.

(3) Broad or implied references

Pronouns such as *it, this, that,* and *which* may refer to a specific word or phrase or to the sense of a whole clause, sentence, or paragraph.

> The workload was manageable, once I became used to **it**. [*It* refers specifically to *workload.*]

> Large corporations may seem stronger than individuals, but **that** is not true. [*That* refers to the sense of the whole first clause.]

Unless the meaning is clear, avoid reference to the general idea of a preceding clause or sentence. Instead, clarify the reference by adding necessary words and deleting confusing pronouns. In the following sentence, *this* may refer to the class attendance policy or to the students' feelings about it. The addition of *perception* relieves any confusion caused by two competing interpretations.

When class attendance is compulsory, some students feel that education

                                                                perception
is being forced on them. This ∧ is unwarranted.

Similarly, the next sentence needs to be revised so that the reason for recommending regulations is unambiguous.

Many companies in the tourist industry advertise as being eco-friendly

                                                        . Such disregard
yet ignore requests to develop sustainable practices ∧ , which is the
reason federal and international regulations need to be established and enforced.

In addition, remember to express an idea explicitly rather than using a vague *it* or *they.*

                                    Teaching music
My father is a music teacher. ∧ It is a profession that requires much patience.

Former students
∧ They say my father shows a great deal of patience with everyone.

Be especially careful to provide clear antecedents when you are referring to the work or possessions of others. The following sentence requires revision because *she* can refer to someone other than Jen Norton:

     her   Jen Norton
In ∧ Jen Norton's new book, ∧ she argues for election reform.

(4) The use of *it* without an antecedent

The expletive *it* does not have a specific antecedent (see **21b**). Instead, it is used to postpone, and thus give emphasis to, the subject of a sentence.

A sentence that begins with this expletive can sometimes be wordy or awkward. Revise such a sentence by replacing *it* with the postponed subject.

> Trying to repair the car   useless
>
> ∧~~It~~ was ∧ ~~no use trying to repair the car.~~

Avoid placing one *it* near another *it* with a different meaning.

> Staying in the old apartment
>
> ∧~~It~~ would be simpler ~~to stay in the old apartment~~, but it is too far from my job. [The first *it* is an expletive; the second *it* refers to *apartment*.]

Exercise 4

Edit the following sentences to make all references clear.

1. A singer, songwriter, and human rights activist, it is no wonder that Joan Baez is one of today's most inspirational public figures.
2. Baez's father worked for the United Nations Education, Scientific and Cultural Organization (UNESCO), which meant that as a young girl, she lived in many different countries.
3. Baez made her first record in 1960. It is remarkable that she recorded it when she was only nineteen years old.
4. Baez had a younger sister, Mimi Fariña, who was also a singer-songwriter; sometimes she joined her on tour.
5. In 2011, at a general meeting of the human-rights organization Amnesty International, they gave Baez a special award for her inspirational activism.

| **26e** | USE OF FIRST-PERSON AND SECOND-PERSON PRONOUNS |

Using *I* is appropriate when you are writing about personal experience. In academic and professional writing, the use of the first-person singular pronoun is also a way to distinguish your own views from those of others. However, if you frequently repeat *I feel* or *I think,* your readers may suspect that you do not understand much beyond your own experience.

We, the first-person plural pronoun, is trickier to use correctly. When you use it, make sure that your audience can tell which individuals are included in this plural reference. For example, if you are writing a paper for a college course, does *we* mean you and the instructor, you and your fellow students, or some other group (such as all Americans)? Because you may inadvertently use *we* in an early draft to refer to more than one group of people, as you edit, check to see that you have used this first-person plural pronoun consistently.

If you decide to address readers directly, you will undoubtedly use the second-person pronoun *you* (as we, the authors of this handbook, have done). There is some disagreement, though, over whether to permit the use of the indefinite *you* to mean "a person" or "people in general." Check with your instructor about this usage. If you are told to avoid using the indefinite *you*, recast your sentences. For example, use *one* instead of *you.*

Even in huge, anonymous cities, ∧ one finds ~~you find~~ community spirit.

If the use of *one* sounds too formal, try changing the word order and/or using different words.

Community spirit arises even in huge, anonymous cities.

Exercise 5

Revise the following paragraph to eliminate the use of the first- and second-person pronouns.

¹In my opinion, some animals should be as free as we are. ²For example, I think orangutans, African elephants, and Atlantic bottlenose dolphins should roam freely rather than be held in captivity. ³We should neither exhibit them in zoos nor use them for medical research. ⁴If you study animals such as these you will see that, like us, they show emotions, self-awareness, and intention. ⁵You might even find that some use language to communicate. ⁶It is clear to me that they have the right to freedom.

27 ‖ MODIFIERS

Modifiers are words, phrases, or clauses that modify; that is, they qualify or limit the meaning of other words. For example, if you were to describe a sandwich as "humdrum," as "lacking sufficient mustard," or as something "that might have tasted good two days ago," you would be using a word, a phrase, or a clause to modify *sandwich*. When used effectively, modifiers enliven writing with details and enhance its coherence.

This chapter will help you

- recognize modifiers (**27a**),
- use conventional comparative and superlative forms (**27b**),
- revise double negatives (**27c**), and
- place modifiers effectively (**27d** and **27e**).

27a ‖ RECOGNIZING MODIFIERS

The most common modifiers are adjectives and adverbs. You can distinguish an adjective from an adverb by determining what type of word is modified. **Adjectives** modify nouns and pronouns (**21a(4)**); **adverbs** modify verbs, adjectives, and other adverbs (**21a(5)**).

Adjectives	Adverbs
She looked **curious.** [modifies pronoun]	She looked at me **curiously.** [modifies verb]
productive meeting [modifies noun]	**highly** productive meeting [modifies adjective]
a **quick** lunch [modifies noun]	**very** quickly [modifies adverb]

ñ MULTILINGUAL WRITERS

ADJECTIVE SUFFIXES IN OTHER LANGUAGES

In some languages, adjectives and nouns agree in number. In Spanish, for example, when a noun is plural, the adjective is plural as well: *vistas claras.* In English, however, adjectives do not have a plural form: *clear views.* For more information on adjectives, see chapter 46.

You can also identify a modifier by considering its form. Many adjectives end with one of these suffixes: *-able, -al, -ful, -ic, -ish, -less,* or *-y.*

accept**able**   ren**tal**   event**ful**   ange**lic**   sheep**ish**   effort**less**   sleep**y**

Present and past participles (25a(5)) can also be used as adjectives.

a **determining** factor	a **determined** effort
[present participle]	[past participle]

Be sure to include the complete *-ed* ending of a past participle.

Please see the ∧enclose documents for more details.
    enclosed

? THINKING RHETORICALLY

ADJECTIVES

When your rhetorical situation calls for vivid images or emotional intensity, choose appropriate adjectives to convey these qualities. That is, instead of describing a movie you enjoyed with the overused adjective "great," you could say that it was "exhilarating" or "electrifying," as the reviewers quoted in figure 27.1 do. When you sense that you might be using a lackluster adjective, search for an alternative in a thesaurus. If any of the words listed there are unfamiliar, be sure to look them up in a dictionary so that you use them correctly.

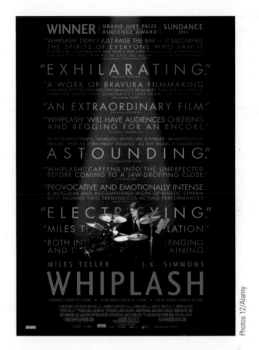

Figure 27.1: Movie posters often include descriptive adjectives.

The easiest type of adverb to identify is the adverb of manner (**21a(5)**). It is formed by adding -*ly* to an adjective.

careful**ly**   unpleasant**ly**   silent**ly**

If the adjective ends in -*y,* the -*y* is changed to -*i* before -*ly* is added.

eas**y** [adjective]   eas**ily** [adverb]

If the adjective ends in -*le,* the -*e* is dropped and just *y* is added.

simp**le** [adjective]   simp**ly** [adverb]

However, not all words ending in -*ly* are adverbs. Certain adjectives related to nouns also end in -*ly* (*friend, friendly; hour, hourly*). In addition, not all adverbs end in -*ly*. Adverbs that indicate time or place (*today, tomorrow, here, there*) do not have the -*ly* ending; neither does the negator *not*. A few words—for example, *fast* and *well*—can function as either adjectives or adverbs.

They like **fast** cars. [adjective]

They ran **fast** enough to catch the bus. [adverb]

(1) Modifiers of linking verbs and action verbs

An adjective used after a sensory linking verb (*look, smell, taste, sound,* or *feel*) modifies the subject of the sentence (**21b**). A common error is to use an adverb after this type of linking verb.

bad

I felt ∧ b̶a̶d̶l̶y̶ about missing the rally. [The adjective *bad* modifies *I.*]

However, when *look, smell, taste, sound,* or *feel* is used as an action verb (**21a(1)**), it can be modified by an adverb.

She looked **angrily** at the referee. [The adverb *angrily* modifies *looked.*]

BUT She looked **angry.** [The adjective *angry* modifies *she.*]

The words *good* and *well* are also easy to confuse. In academic rhetorical situations, *good* is considered an adjective and so is not used with action verbs.

well

The whole team played ∧ g̶o̶o̶d̶.

Another frequent error is the dropping of *-ly* endings from adverbs. Although you may not hear the ending when you speak, be sure to include it when you write.

locally

They bought only ∧ l̶o̶c̶a̶l̶ grown vegetables.

Exercise 1

Revise the following sentences so that all adjectives and adverbs are used in ways considered conventional in academic writing.

1. Relaxation techniques have been developed for people who feel uncomfortably in some way.
2. Meditation is one technique that is real helpful in relieving stress.
3. People searching for relief from tension have found that a breathing meditation works good.
4. They sit quiet and concentrate on both inhaling and exhaling.
5. They concentrate on breathing deep.

(2) Nouns as modifiers

Adjectives and adverbs are the most common modifiers, but nouns (**21a(2)**) can also be modifiers (***movie** critic, **reference** manual*). A string of noun modifiers can be cumbersome. The following example shows how a sentence with too many noun modifiers can be revised.

The ~~Friday afternoon~~ Student Affairs Committee meeting ∧ has been cancelled.

scheduled for Friday afternoon

(3) Phrases and clauses as modifiers

Participial phrases, prepositional phrases, and some infinitive phrases are modifiers (**22a(3)** and **22a(4)**).

> **Growing in popularity every year,** mountain bikes now dominate the market. [participial phrase modifying the noun *bikes*]

> Mountain bikes first became popular **in the 1980s.** [prepositional phrase modifying the verb *became*]

Some people use mountain bikes **to commute to work.** [infinitive phrase modifying the verb *use*]

Adjectival (relative) clauses and adverbial clauses are both modifiers (see **22b(2)**).

BMX bicycles have frames **that are relatively small.** [adjectival clause modifying the noun *frames*]

Although mountain bikes are designed for off-road use, many people use them on city streets. [adverbial clause modifying the verb *use*]

(4) Sentence modifers

Sentence modifiers are generally single-word adverbs that end in *ly*. A sentence modifier indicates the writer's perspective on or attitude toward the information conveyed in the sentence. When such a modifier begins a sentence, it is followed by a comma.

Clearly, some adjustments must be made to the proposal.

Fortunately, the storm veered to the east.

27b COMPARATIVES AND SUPERLATIVES

Many adjectives and adverbs change form to show degrees of quality, quantity, time, distance, manner, and so on. The **positive form** of an adjective or adverb is the word you would look for in a dictionary: *hard, urgent, deserving.* The **comparative form**, which either ends in *-er* or is preceded by *more* or *less*, compares two elements: *I worked **harder** than I ever had before.* The **superlative form**, which either ends in *-est* or is preceded by *most* or *least*, compares three or more elements: *Jeff is the **hardest** worker I have ever met.*

Positive	Comparative	Superlative
hard	harder	hardest
urgent	more/less urgent	most/least urgent
deserving	more/less deserving	most/least deserving

(1) Complete and logical comparisons

When you use the comparative form of an adjective or an adverb, be sure to indicate what two elements you are comparing. The revision of the following sentence makes it clear that a diesel engine and a gas engine are being compared:

A diesel engine is **heavier**$_\wedge$ $^{than\ a\ gas\ engine}$.

Occasionally, the second element in a comparison is implied. The word *paper* does not have to be included after *second* in the sentence below. The reader can infer that the grade on the second paper was better than the grade on the first paper.

She wrote **two** papers; the instructor gave her a **better** grade on the second.

A comparison should also be logical. The following example illogically compares *population* and *Wabasha*:

The **population** of Winona is larger than **Wabasha**.

You can revise this type of faulty comparison in one of three ways:

- Repeat the word that refers to what is being compared.

  The **population** of Winona is larger than the **population** of Wabasha.

- Use a pronoun that corresponds to the first element in the comparison.

The **population** of Winona is larger than **that** of Wabasha.

- Use possessive forms.

Winona's population is larger than **Wabasha's.**

(2) Double comparatives or superlatives

Use either an ending (*-er* or *-est*) or a preceding qualifier (*more* or *most*), not both, to form a comparative or superlative.

The first bridge is **more narrower** than the second.

The **most narrowest** bridge is in the northern part of the state.

Some modifiers have *absolute meanings*. These modifiers name qualities that are either present in full or not at all:

complete   eternal   fatal   finite   identical   perfect   straight   unique

Expressing degrees of such modifiers is illogical, so their comparative and superlative forms are rarely used in academic writing.

a ~~more~~ perfect society   the ~~most~~ unique campus

Exercise 2
================

Provide the correct comparative or superlative form of each modifier within parentheses.

1. Amphibians can be divided into three groups. Frogs and toads are in the (common) group.
2. Because they do not have to maintain a specific body temperature, amphibians eat (frequently) than mammals do.
3. Reptiles may look like amphibians, but their skin is (dry).

4. During the Devonian period, the (close) ancestors of amphibians were fish with fins that looked like legs.
5. In general, amphibians have (few) bones in their skeletons than other animals with backbones have.
6. Color markings on amphibians vary, though the back of an amphibian is usually (dark) than its belly.

27c DOUBLE NEGATIVES

The term **double negative** refers to the use of two negative words to express a single negation. Unless you are portraying dialogue, revise any double negatives you find in your writing.

He did**n't** keep~ *any* **no** records.

OR

He ~ *kept* ~~did**n't** keep~~ **no** records.

Using *not* or *nothing* with *hardly, barely,* or *scarcely* creates a double negative. The following examples show how sentences containing such double negatives can be revised:

I could~n't~ **hardly** quit in the middle of the job.

OR

I could**n't** ~~hardly~~ quit in the middle of the job.

The motion passed with **~~not~~ scarcely** a protest.

OR

The motion passed with~ *little* **~~not scarcely~~** a protest.

ñ MULTILINGUAL WRITERS

NEGATION IN OTHER LANGUAGES
The use of two negative words in one sentence is common in languages such as Spanish:

> *Yo **no** compré **nada**.* ["I didn't buy anything."]

If your native language allows this type of negation, be especially careful to check for and revise any double negatives you find in your English essays.

27d PLACEMENT OF MODIFIERS

Effective placement of modifiers will improve the clarity and coherence of your sentences. A **misplaced modifier** obscures the meaning of a sentence.

(1) Keeping related words together

Place the modifiers *almost, even, hardly, just,* and *only* before the words or word groups they modify. Altering placement can alter meaning.

The committee can **only** nominate two members for the position. [The committee cannot *appoint* the two members to the position.]

The committee can nominate **only** two members for the position. [The committee cannot nominate more than two members.]

Only the committee can nominate two members for the position. [No person or group other than the committee can nominate members.]

(2) Placing phrases and clauses near the words they modify

Readers expect phrases and clauses to modify the nearest grammatical element. The revision of the following sentence clarifies that the prosecutor, not the witness, was skillful:

With great skill, the
∧~~The~~ prosecutor cross-examined the witness ~~with great skill~~.

The following revision makes it clear that the phrase *crouched and ugly* describes the phantom, not the boy:

The   crouched and ugly
∧~~Crouched and ugly, the~~ young boy gasped at the ∧phantom moving

across the stage.

The next sentence is fine as long as Jesse wrote the proposal, not the review. If he wrote the review, the sentence should be recast.

I have not read the review of the proposal Jesse wrote.

Jesse's
I have not read ∧~~the~~ review of the proposal ~~Jesse wrote~~.

(3) Revising squinting modifiers

A **squinting modifier** can be interpreted as modifying either what precedes it or what follows it. To avoid such lack of clarity, you can reposition the modifier or revise the entire sentence.

Even though Erikson lists some advantages **overall** his vision of a successful business is faulty.

Revisions

Even though Erikson lists some **overall** advantages, his vision of a successful business is faulty. [modifer repositioned; punctuation added]

Erikson lists some advantages**; however, overall,** his vision of a successful business is faulty. [sentence revised]

Exercise 3

Improve the clarity of the following sentences by moving the modifiers. Not all sentences require editing.

1. Alfred Joseph Hitchcock was born the son of a poultry dealer in London.

2. Hitchcock was only identified with thrillers after making his third movie, *The Lodger*.

3. Hitchcock moved to the United States in 1939 and eventually became a naturalized citizen.

4. Hitchcock's most famous movies revolved around psychological improbabilities that are still discussed by movie critics today.

5. Although his movies are known for suspense sometimes moviegoers also remember Hitchcock's droll sense of humor.

6. Hitchcock just did not direct movie thrillers; he also produced two television series.

7. Originally a British citizen, Queen Elizabeth knighted Alfred Hitchcock in 1980.

27e ║ DANGLING MODIFIERS

Dangling modifiers are phrases (**22a**) or **elliptical clauses** (clauses without a subject) (**22b(2)**) that lack an appropriate word to modify. To avoid including dangling modifiers in your essays, first look carefully at any sentence that begins with a phrase or an elliptical clause. If the phrase or clause suggests an action, be sure that what follows the modifier is the actor (the subject of the sentence). If there is no actor performing the action indicated in the phrase, the modifier is dangling. To revise this type of dangling modifier, name an actor—either in the modifier or in the main clause.

Lying on the beach, time became irrelevant. [Time cannot lie on a beach.]

Revisions

While **we** were lying on the beach, time became irrelevant. [actor in the modifier]

Lying on the beach, **we** found that time became irrelevant. [actor in the main clause]

While eating lunch, waves lapped at our toes. [Waves cannot eat lunch.]

Revisions

While **we** were eating lunch, waves lapped at our toes. [actor in the modifier]

While eating lunch, **we** noticed the water lapping at our toes. [actor in the main clause]

The following sentences illustrate revisions of other common types of dangling modifiers:

To avoid getting sunburn,ʌ you should apply sunscreen ~~should be applied~~ before going outside. [Sunscreen cannot avoid getting sunburn.]

ʌ Because they were in ~~In~~ a rush to get to the beach, an accident occurred. [An accident cannot be in a rush.]

Although you will most frequently find a dangling modifier at the beginning of a sentence, you may sometimes find one at the end of a sentence.

Good equipment is importantʌ for anyone ~~when~~ snorkeling. [Equipment cannot snorkel.]

Sentence modifiers and absolute phrases are *not* dangling modifiers.

The fog finally lifting, vacationers headed for the beach.

Marcus played well in the final game, **on the whole.**

Exercise 4

Revise the following sentences to eliminate misplaced and dangling modifiers. Some sentences may not require editing.

1. Climbing a mountain, fitness becomes all-important.
2. To make the climb a true adventure, climbers must doubt whether they will reach the summit.
3. Having set their goals, the mountain must challenge the climbers.
4. In determining an appropriate challenge, considering safety precautions is necessary.
5. Taking care to stay roped together, accidents are less likely to occur.
6. Even when expecting sunny weather, rain gear should be packed.
7. Knowing how to rappel, descent from a cliff is easier and safer.
8. Although adding extra weight, climbers should not leave home without a first-aid kit.
9. Climbers should not let themselves become frustrated if they are not immediately successful.
10. By taking pains at the beginning of a trip, agony can be averted at the end of a trip.

Exercise 5

Using what you have learned in this chapter, revise all modifier errors in the following sentences.

1. As a woman of both the nineteenth and twentieth centuries, the life of Gertrude Bell was unusual.

2. Young, wealthy, and intelligent, many people were impressed by the red-headed Bell.

3. Among the first women to graduate from Oxford, she couldn't hardly be satisfied with domestic life.

4. Instead, Bell traveled to what were considered the most remotest countries in the world, saw the wonders of the Ottoman Empire, and explored the desert of Iraq.

5. Several of the Arab sheiks who knew Bell thought that she acted bold.

6. The war in Iraq did not give Bell no time to pursue her research.

7. She became an Arab rebellion supporter.

8. While traveling in Iraq, meetings with important politicians took place.

9. In 1921, Winston Churchill invited Bell to a conference in the Middle East because the other Great Britain conference participants knew little about Iraq.

10. When the photo of the conference participants was taken, Bell looked elegantly in her feathered hat and silk dress among the thirty-six black-suited males.

S

EFFECTIVE SENTENCES

Situate Yourself

After drafting your answer to an essay exam question, you have purposefully allowed yourself ten minutes to proofread and edit what you have written. As you move through your answer below, pay careful attention to such sentence-level issues as sentence unity, consistency, subordination and coordination, parallelism, emphasis, and variety.

Kenneth Burke became a famous rhetorician during the twentieth century. He is famous for defining what it means to be human. He calls humans symbol-using animals, which means that we use language to communicate. Language is symbolic. We are also symbol-making and symbol-misusing animals. We invented the negative and that does not exist in nature and we do not live in our natural condition because we have invented language and technology. We are all goaded by the spirit of hierarchy and social status and order. Finally, Burke defines us as being rotten with perfection, and that means that we all struggle to be better (maybe even perfect) rather than just be.

SENTENCE STYLE

Most professional writers and readers use the following words to describe effective sentences.

- *Exact.* Precise words and word combinations enable readers to come as close as they can to a full understanding of the writer's message.
- *Conventional.* For most assignments, you will be expected to conform to the conventions and usage expectations of the academic community by using Standardized English.
- *Consistent.* A consistent writing style is characterized by the steady use of one type of words and grammatical structure, whether formal, informal, poetic, or technical.
- *Parallel.* Related to consistency, parallelism refers to the alignment of similar ideas with similar grammatical structures.
- *Concise.* Concise prose makes a point effectively with the fewest words possible.
- *Coherent.* Coherence refers to clear connections among adjacent sentences and paragraphs.
- *Varied.* Appealing sentences and paragraphs vary in length, thereby varying in structure, rhythm, and emphasis.

In the following chapters, you will learn to identify the rhetorical options considered effective by most academic and professional writers. Remember, though, that appropriateness varies across rhetorical situations. You may find that it does not make sense to apply a general rule such as "Use the active voice" in all circumstances. For example, you may be expected to write a vigorous description of an event, detailing exactly what happened, but find that you need to use the passive voice when you do not know who was responsible for the event: Several of the campaign signs *were defaced*. Or, as another example, you may need to set aside the rule calling for Standardized English if you are writing dialogue in which the speakers use regional dialects. Analyzing your rhetorical situation, rather than always following general rules, will help you write clear, purposeful sentences that engage your readers.

28 ‖ SENTENCE UNITY

Consistent, clear, and complete sentences serve as the foundation of effective academic and professional writing. Your carefully crafted sentences demonstrate concern for your rhetorical audience and awareness of your rhetorical situation. Such consideration, in turn, gives you a better chance of achieving your rhetorical purpose. This chapter can help you

- choose and arrange details (**28a**),
- revise mixed metaphors and mixed constructions (**28b** and **28c**),
- relate sentence parts (**28d**),
- include necessary words (**28e**), and
- complete comparisons (**28f**) and intensifiers (**28g**).

28a   CHOOSING AND ARRANGING DETAILS

Well-chosen details add interest and credibility to your writing. As you revise, you may occasionally notice a sentence that would be clearer and more believable with the addition of a phrase or two about time, location, or cause.

Missing important detail	An astrophysicist from the Harvard-Smithsonian Center has predicted a galactic storm.
With detail added	An astrophysicist from the Harvard-Smithsonian Center has predicted **that** a galactic storm **will occur within the next 10 million years.**

Without the additional information about time, most readers would wonder when the storm was supposed to occur. The added detail makes the sentence clearer.

The details you include should serve to guide your readers. Just as too few details can leave readers wondering, too many details can leave them confused about your main point. As you compose and then revise, be sure the details included are still meaningful. Upon revision, the writer of the following sentence realized that the mention of her uncle was no longer relevant to the main idea of her essay.

> When I was only sixteen, I left home to attend a college in California ~~that my uncle had graduated from twenty years earlier~~.

When considering how many details to include, be sure that each one contributes to the central thought, as in the following description of brain activity:

> A given mental task may involve a complicated web of circuits, which interact in varying degrees with others throughout the brain—not like the parts in a machine, but like the instruments in a symphony orchestra combining their tenor, volume, and resonance to create a particular musical effect.
> —**James Shreeve, "Beyond the Brain"**

By using parallel structures (see chapter 31) and careful punctuation, James Shreeve has created a long yet focused sentence.

Besides choosing details purposefully, you also need to indicate a clear connection between the details and the main idea of your sentence.

Unrelated	Many tigers facing possible extinction live in India, **where there are many people.**
Related	Many tigers facing possible extinction live in India, **where their natural habitat is shrinking because of human population growth.**

28b REVISING MIXED METAPHORS

When you use language that evokes images, make sure that the images are meaningfully related. Unrelated images that appear in the same sentence are called **mixed metaphors**. The following sentence includes incompatible images.

As he climbed the corporate ladder, he~ ~~sank into a sea of~~ debt.
incurred a large amount of

The combination of two images—climbing a ladder and sinking into a sea—could create a picture in the reader's mind of a man hanging onto a ladder as it disappears into the water. The easiest way to revise such a sentence is to replace the words evoking one of the conflicting images.

28c | REVISING MIXED CONSTRUCTIONS

A sentence that begins with one kind of grammatical structure and shifts to another is a **mixed construction.** To untangle a mixed construction, make sure that the sentence includes a conventional subject—a noun, a noun phrase, a gerund phrase, an infinitive phrase, or a noun clause. Prepositional phrases and adverbial clauses are not typical subjects.

Practicing
~ ~~By practicing~~ a new language daily will help you become proficient. [A gerund phrase replaces a prepositional phrase.]

Her scholarship award
~ ~~Although she won a scholarship~~ does not give her the right to skip classes. [A noun phrase replaces an adverbial clause.]

If you find a sentence that has a mixed construction, you can either revise the subject, as in the previous examples, or leave the beginning of the sentence as a modifier and add a new subject after it.

By practicing a new language daily, **you** will become more proficient.

Although she won a scholarship, **it** does not give her the right to skip classes.

Exercise 1

Revise the following sentences so that details clearly support the main idea. Correct any mixed metaphors or mixed constructions.

1. In the United States, each person has one vote, but there may be problems at the polling booths.

2. Everyone's voting rights should be protected. The federal government has funded the replacement of the punch-card ballot.

3. Many states use optical scanners, which were also used on the standardized tests we took in high school. These scanners sort readable from unreadable ballots.

4. Some voters question the use of touch-screen voting systems. These systems leave no paper trail of all the ballots election officers need to swim through during a recount.

5. By providing educational materials helps citizens learn where and how to vote.

28d | RELATING SENTENCE PARTS

When drafting, writers sometimes compose sentences in which the subject and predicate are mismatched. In other words, the subject is completed in the predicate as *being* something or *doing* something that is not logically possible. This breakdown in meaning is called **faulty predication**. Similarly, mismatches between a verb and its complement (21c) can obscure meaning.

(1) Mismatch between subject and verb

The joining of a subject and a verb must create a meaningful idea.

Mismatch	The absence of detail screams out at the reader. [An *absence* cannot scream.]
Revision	The reader immediately notices the absence of detail.

(2) Illogical equation with *be*

When a form of the verb *be* joins two parts of a sentence (the subject and the subject complement), these two parts need to be logically related.

Free speech
∧ The importance of free speech is essential to a democracy.
[*Importance* cannot be essential.]

(3) Mismatches in definitions

When you write a sentence that states a formal definition, the term you are defining should be followed by a noun or a noun phrase, not an adverbial clause (**22b**). Avoid using *is when* or *is where*.

the   of
Ecology is ∧ when you study ∧ the relationships among living organisms and between living organisms and their environment.

the contest between   vying
Exploitative competition is ∧ where two or more organisms ∧ vie for a limited resource such as food.

(4) Mismatch of *reason* with *is because*

You can see why *reason* and *is because* are a mismatch by looking at the meaning of *because*: "for the reason that." Saying "the reason is for the reason that" is redundant. Be sure to revise any sentence containing the construction *the reason is . . . because*.

The reason the old train station was closed is because it had fallen into disrepair.

(5) Mismatch between verb and complement

A verb and its complement should fit together meaningfully.

Mismatch   Only a few students used the incorrect use of *there*.
                  [To "use an incorrect use" is not logical.]

Revision   Only a few students used *there* incorrectly.

To make sure that a relative pronoun (26a(3)) in the object position is connected logically to a verb, replace that relative pronoun with its antecedent (21a(3)). Then check that the subject and verb have a logical connection. In the following sentence, *the inspiration* is the antecedent for *that*.

Mismatch   The inspiration that the author created touched young writers. ["The author created the inspiration" does not make sense.]

Revision   The author inspired young writers.

Verbs used to integrate information appear in *attributive tags* and are often followed by specific types of complements. Some of the verbs used in this way are listed with their typical complements in the box below. (Some verbs such as *explain* fall into more than one category.)

VERBS FOR ATTRIBUTIVE TAGS AND THEIR COMPLEMENTS

Verb + *that* noun clause

agree	claim	explain	report	suggest
argue	demonstrate	maintain	state	think

Example: The researcher **reported** that the weather patterns had changed.

Verb + noun phrase + *that* noun clause

assure	convince	inform	remind	tell

Example: He **told** the reporters that he was planning to resign.

Verb + *wh-* noun clause

demonstrate	discover	explain	report	suggest
describe	discuss	investigate	state	wonder

Example: She **described** what had happened.

Exercise 2

Revise the following sentences so that each verb is followed by a conventional complement.

1. The speaker discussed that applications had specific requirements.
2. He convinced that mass transit was affordable.
3. The two groups agreed how the problem could be solved.
4. Brown described that improvements had been made to the old house.
5. They wondered that such a catastrophe could happen.

28e ‖ INCLUDING NECESSARY WORDS

When we speak or write quickly, we often omit small words. As you revise, be sure to include all necessary articles, prepositions, verbs, and conjunctions.

Graduation will take place in ∧ Bryce Jordan Center. [missing an article]
the

We discussed a couple ∧ issues. [missing a preposition]
of

When a sentence has a **compound verb** (two verbs linked by a conjunction), you may need to supply a different preposition for each verb to make your meaning clear.

He neither **believes** ∧ nor **approves of** the plan.
in

All verbs, both auxiliary and main (**25a(4)**), should be included to make sentences complete.

She ∧ spoken with all the candidates.
has

Voter turnout has never ∧ and will never be 100 percent.
been

When a sentence consists of two short clauses and the verb in both clauses is the same, the verb in the second clause may be omitted.

> The wind **was** fierce and the thunder [was] deafening.

Include the word *that* before a clause when it makes the sentence easier to read. Without the added *that* in the following sentence, a reader may stumble over *discovered the fossil* before understanding that *the fossil* is linked to *provided.*

> The paleontologists discovered ∧ that the fossil provided a link between the dinosaur and the modern bird.

When a sentence has two *that* clauses, *that* should begin each one.

> The graph indicated **that the population had increased** but **that the number of homeowners had not.**

⬛ TECH SAVVY

A grammar checker will sometimes alert you to a missing word, but it will just as often fail to do so. It may also tell you that a word is missing when it is not. You are better off proofreading your work yourself.

28f COMPLETING COMPARISONS

A comparison has two parts: someone or something is compared to someone or something else. As you revise your writing, make sure that your audience knows who or what is being compared. To revise incomplete comparisons, add necessary words, phrases, or clauses.

> Printers today are quite different ∧ from those sold in the early 1990s.

> His first novel was better ∧ than the one just published.

After you are sure that your comparisons are complete, check to see that they are also logical.

those of

Her test scores are higher than ∧ the other students.

In the original sentence, *scores* were being compared to *students*. You could also rewrite this sentence as follows:

Her test scores are higher than the other students'.

Because *test scores* have already been mentioned, it is clear that *students'* (with an apostrophe) is short for *students' test scores*.

28g COMPLETING INTENSIFIERS

In speech, the intensifiers *so, such,* and *too* are used to mean "very," "unusually," or "extremely."

That movie was **so** funny.

In academic and professional writing, however, the intensifiers *so, such,* and *too* require a completing phrase or clause.

That movie was **so** funny **that I watched it twice.**

Julian has **such** a hearty laugh **that it makes everyone else laugh with him.**

Child custody is just **too** complex an issue **to cover in one class discussion.**

Exercise 3

Revise the following sentences to make them clear and complete.

1. Ralph McQuarrie sketched designs for R2D2 and Darth Vader, including his mask. Iain McCaig wanted to create something scarier for *The Phantom Menace*.
2. He drew generic male face with metal teeth and long red ribbons of hair falling in front of it.
3. He designed a face that looked as though it had been flayed.
4. The evil visage of Darth Maul was so horrible.
5. The reason McCaig added elegant black feathers is because he wanted to balance the effect.

29 ‖ CONSISTENCY

A consistent writing style will make it easier for readers to understand your message and rhetorical purpose. This chapter will help you maintain consistency

- in verb tense (**29a**),
- in point of view (**29b**), and
- in tone (**29c**).

29a ‖ VERB TENSE

By using verb tenses consistently, you help your readers understand when the actions or events you are describing took place. Verb tenses convey information about time frames and grammatical aspect. *Time frame* refers to whether the tense is present, past, or future (refer to the columns of the chart on page 568). *Aspect* refers to whether it is simple, progressive, perfect, or perfect progressive (refer to the rows in the chart on page 568). Consistency in the time frame of a verb, though not necessarily in its aspect, ensures that any sequence of reported events is clearly and accurately portrayed. In the following paragraph, notice that the time frame remains in the past, but the aspect varies among simple, perfect, and progressive:

past perfect

In the summer of 1983, I **had** just **finished** my third year of architecture

simple past   *past perfect (compound predicate)*

school and **had** to find a six-month internship. I **had grown** up and **gone**

past perfect

through my entire education in the Midwest, but I **had been** to

simple past · simple past

New York City once on a class field trip and I **thought** it **seemed** like

a pretty good place to live. So, armed with little more than an inflated

simple past

ego and my school portfolio, I **was** off to Manhattan, oblivious to the bad

past progressive

economy and the fact that the city **was overflowing** with young architects.

—Paul K. Humiston, "Small World"

If you do need to shift to another time frame within a paragraph, you can use a time marker:

now, then, today, yesterday

in two years, during the 1920s

after you finish, before we left

For example, in the following paragraph, the time frame shifts back and forth between present and past—between today, when Edward O. Wilson is studying ants in the woods around Walden Pond, and the nineteenth century, when Thoreau lived there. The time markers are bracketed.

simple present · simple past

These woods **are** not wild; indeed, they **were** not wild [in Thoreau's day].

simple present

[Today], the beach and trails of Walden Pond State Reservation **draw**

simple present

about 500,000 visitors a year. Few of them **hunt** ants, however. Underfoot

simple present · simple past

and under the leaf litter there **is** a world as wild as it **was** [before human

simple past

beings **came** to this part of North America].

—James Gorman, "Finding a Wild, Fearsome World beneath Every Fallen Leaf"

On occasion, a shift in time is indicated implicitly—that is, without an explicit time marker. A writer may change tenses without using any time marker (1) to explain or support a general statement with information about the past, (2) to compare and contrast two different time periods, or (3) to comment on a topic. Why do you think the author of the following paragraph varies verb tenses?

> Thomas Jefferson, author of the Declaration of Independence, **is** considered one of our country's most brilliant citizens. His achievements **were** many, as **were** his interests. Some historians **describe** his work as a naturalist, scientist, and inventor; others **focus** on his accomplishments as an educator and politician. Yet Jefferson **is** best known as a spokesman for democracy.

Except for the two uses of *were* in the second sentence, all verbs are in the present tense. The author uses the past tense in the second sentence to provide evidence from the past that supports the topic sentence.

Before you turn in a final draft, check the verb tenses you have used to ensure that they are logical and consistent. Revise any that are not.

The white wedding dress ∧came ~~comes~~ into fashion when Queen Victoria wore a white gown at her wedding to Prince Albert of Saxe. Soon after, brides who could afford them bought stylish white dresses for their weddings. Brides of modest means, however, ∧continued ~~continue~~ to choose dresses they could wear more than once.

Exercise 1

Locate the shifts in tense in this passage and decide whether they are effective. Be prepared to state your reasoning.

¹Dave Rahm lived in Bellingham, Washington, north of Seattle. ²Bellingham, a harbor town, lies between the alpine North Cascade Mountains and the San Juan Islands in Haro Strait above Puget Sound. ³The latitude is that of Newfoundland. ⁴Dave Rahm was a stunt pilot, the air's own genius.

—**Annie Dillard, "The Stunt Pilot"**

Exercise 2

Revise the following paragraph so that there are no unnecessary shifts in verb tense.

I **had** already **been walking** for a half hour in the semidarkness of Amsterdam's early-morning streets when I **came** to a red light. I **am** in a hurry to get to the train station and no cars **were** out yet, so I **cross** over the cobblestones, passing a man waiting for the light to change. I never **look** back when he **scolds** me for breaking the law. I **had** a train to catch. I **was** going to Widnau, in Switzerland, to see Aunt Marie. I **have** not **seen** her since I **was** in second grade.

29b	POINT OF VIEW

Whenever you write, you must establish your point of view (perspective). Your point of view will be evident in the pronouns you choose. *I* or *we* indicates a first-person point of view, which is appropriate for writing that includes personal views or experiences. If you decide to address the reader as *you*, you are adopting a second-person point of view. However, because a second-person point of view is rare in academic writing, avoid using *you* unless you are purposefully addressing the reader. If you select the pronouns *he, she, it, one,* and *they,* you are writing with a third-person point of view. The third-person point of view is the most common point of view in academic writing.

Although you may find it necessary to use different points of view in a paper, especially if you are comparing or contrasting other people's views with your own, be careful not to confuse readers by shifting perspective unnecessarily. The following paragraph has been revised to ensure consistency of point of view.

To an observer, a sleeping person appears passive, unresponsive, and essentially isolated from the rest of the world and its barrage of stimuli. While it is true that ∧ ~~you are~~ unaware of most surrounding noises ∧ ~~when you are asleep, our~~ brain is far from inactive. In fact, the brain can be as active during sleep as it is ∧ ~~when you are awake.~~ When ∧ ~~our brains are~~ asleep, the rate and type of electrical activity change.

[annotations above the line: "someone asleep is" inserted before "unaware"; ", that person's" inserted before "brain"; "in a waking state." inserted; "a person is" inserted before "asleep"]

29c | TONE

The tone of a piece of writing conveys a writer's attitude toward a topic (3a(3)). The words and phrases a writer chooses affect the tone he or she creates. Notice the difference in tone in the following excerpts describing the same scientific experiment. The first paragraph was written for the general public and uses the second-person point of view; the second was written in third-person for other researchers.

Imagine that I asked you to play a very simple gambling game. In front of you, are four decks of cards—two red and two blue. Each card in those four decks either wins you a sum of money or costs you some money, and your job is to turn over cards from any of the decks, one at a time, in such a way that maximizes your winnings. What you don't know at the beginning, however, is that the red decks are a minefield. The rewards are high, but when you lose on red, you lose *a lot*. You can really only win by taking cards from the blue decks, which offer a nice, steady diet of $50 and $100 payoffs. The question is: how long will it take you to figure this out? —**Malcolm Gladwell,** *Blink*

In a gambling task that simulates real-life decision-making in the way it factors uncertainty, rewards, and penalties, the players are given four decks of cards, a loan of $2000 facsimile U.S. bills, and asked to play so that they can lose the least amount of money and win the most (1). Turning each card carries an immediate reward ($100 in decks A and B and $50 in decks C and D). Unpredictably, however, the turning of some cards also carries a penalty (which is large in decks A and B and small in decks C and D). Playing mostly from the disadvantageous decks (A and B) leads to an overall loss. Playing from the advantageous decks (C and D) leads to an overall gain. The players have no way of predicting when a penalty will arise in a given deck, no way to calculate with precision the net gain or loss from each deck, and no knowledge of how many cards they must turn to end the game (the game is stopped after 100 card selections).

—Antoine Bechara, Hanna Damasio, Daniel Tranel, and Antonio R. Damasio, "Deciding Advantageously before Knowing the Advantageous Strategy"

In the excerpt from *Blink*, Malcolm Gladwell addresses readers directly: "Imagine that I asked you to play a very simple gambling game." In the excerpt aimed at an audience of researchers, Antoine Bechara and his coauthors describe their experiment without directly addressing the reader. Gladwell also uses less formal language than Bechara and his colleagues do. The scientists use words such as "immediate reward" and "penalty," while Gladwell conveys the same information informally: "wins you a sum of money or costs you some money." Finally, the scientists include a reference citation in their paragraph (the number *1* in parentheses), but Gladwell does not.

Neither of these excerpts is better than the other. The tone of each is appropriate for the given rhetorical situation. However, shifts in tone can be distracting. The following paragraph was revised to ensure consistency of tone:

Scientists at the University of Oslo (Norway) ∧have evidence that ~~think they know why~~ the common belief about the birth order of ∧children carries some truth. ~~kids has some truth to it.~~ Using as data IQ tests taken from military records, the scientists found that older children ∧score ~~have~~ significantly ∧higher than their siblings. ~~more on the ball than kids in second or third place.~~ According to the researchers, the average variation in scores is large enough to account for differences in college admission.

Exercise 3

Revise the following paragraph so that there are no unnecessary shifts in tone.

[1]Many car owners used to grumble about deceptive fuel-economy ratings. [2]They often found, after they had already purchased a car, that their mileage was lower than that on the car's window sticker. [3]The issue remained pretty much ignored until our gas prices started to go up like crazy. [4]Because of increased pressure from consumer organizations, the Environmental Protection Agency reviewed and then changed the way it was calculating fuel-economy ratings. [5]The agency now takes into account factors such as quick acceleration, changing road grades, and the use of air conditioning, so the new ratings should reflect your real-world driving conditions. [6]Nonetheless, the ratings can never be right on target given that we all have different driving habits.

30 ‖ SUBORDINATION AND COORDINATION

Your understanding of subordination and coordination enhances the connections you make among ideas and adds variety to your sentences (chapter **33**). This chapter will help you

- use subordination effectively (**30a**),
- use coordination effectively (**30b**), and
- avoid faulty or excessive subordination and coordination (**30c**).

30a ‖ USING SUBORDINATION EFFECTIVELY

Subordinate means "being of lower rank." Because a subordinate grammatical structure cannot stand alone, it is dependent on the main (independent) clause (like the two parts of this sentence). The most common subordinate structure is the dependent clause (**22b(2)**), which usually begins with a subordinating conjunction (**21a(7)**) or a relative pronoun (**26a(3)**).

(1) Subordinating conjunctions

A **subordinating conjunction** specifies the relationship between a dependent clause and an independent clause. For example, it might signal a causal relationship.

> Our team won the swim meet **because the members inspire one another.**

Here are a few of the most frequently used subordinating conjunctions:

Cause	*because*
Concession	*although, even though*
Condition	*if, unless*
Effect	*so that*

Sequence	*before, after*
Time	*when*

By using subordinating conjunctions, you can combine short sentences and indicate how they are related.

> ~~We spent~~ all day Saturday studying, I still managed to hear Kofi Annan at Schwab Auditorium that evening.

(with handwritten insertion: "Even though we" at start, and a comma/semicolon change after "studying")

If the subjects of the two clauses are the same, the dependent clause can often be shortened to a phrase.

> After ~~we ate~~ our breakfast, we headed back to the construction site.

(with handwritten insertion: "eating")

(2) Relative pronouns

A **relative pronoun** (*who, whom, which, that,* or *whose*) introduces a dependent clause that, in most cases, modifies the pronoun's antecedent (**26a(3)**). By using this type of dependent clause, called an **adjectival clause,** or a **relative clause,** you can embed details into a sentence.

> The Roman temple has a <u>portico</u> **that opens to the morning sun.**

> Steven Spielberg produced and directed a <u>film</u> about Abraham Lincoln, **which quickly won many awards.**

---

❶ CAUTION

A relative clause beginning with *which* sometimes refers to an entire independent clause rather than modifying a specific word or phrase. Because this type of reference can be vague, you should avoid it if possible.

> ~~He is~~ a graduate of a top university, ~~which should provide him with~~ many opportunities.

(with handwritten insertions: "As" at start, and "he should have" above "which should provide him with")

An adjectival clause can be shortened as long as the meaning of the sentence remains clear.

The Parthenon is the Greek temple ~~that was~~ dedicated to Athena.

30b USING COORDINATION EFFECTIVELY

Coordinate means "being of equal rank." Coordinate grammatical elements have the same form. For example, they may be two words that are both adjectives, two phrases that are both prepositional, or two clauses that are both independent.

a **stunning** and **satisfying** conclusion [adjectives]

in the attic or **in the basement** [prepositional phrases]

The company was losing money, yet **the employees suspected nothing.** [independent clauses]

To indicate the relationship between coordinate words, phrases, or clauses, choose an appropriate coordinating or correlative conjunction (**21a(7)**).

Addition	*and, both . . . and, not only . . . but also*
Alternative	*or, nor, either . . . or, neither . . . nor*
Cause	*for*
Contrast	*but, yet*
Result	*so*

By using coordination, you can avoid unnecessary repetition.

The hike to the top of Angels Landing has countless

switchbacks. ~~It also has~~ ^{and} long drop-offs.

A semicolon can also be used to link coordinate independent clauses:

Hikers follow the path; climbers scale the cliff wall.

ñ MULTILINGUAL WRITERS

CHOOSING CONJUNCTIONS

In English, use either a coordinating conjunction or a subordinating conjunction, but not both, to signal a connection between clauses.

- Because he had a severe headache, ~~so~~ he went to the health center.

- He
  ∧~~Because he~~ had a severe headache, so he went to the health center.

Exercise 1

===

Using subordination and coordination, revise the sentences in the following paragraph to emphasize ideas you consider important.

¹The Lummi tribe lives in the Northwest. ²The Lummis have a belief about sorrow and loss. ³They believe that grief is a burden. ⁴According to their culture, this burden should not be carried alone. ⁵After the terrorist attack on the World Trade Center, the Lummis wanted to help shoulder the burden of grief felt by others. ⁶Some of the Lummis carve totem poles. ⁷These carvers crafted a healing totem pole. ⁸They gave this pole to the citizens of New York. ⁹Many of the citizens of New York had family members who were killed in the terrorist attacks. ¹⁰The Lummis do not believe that the pole itself heals. ¹¹Rather, they believe that healing comes from the prayers and songs said over it. ¹²For them, healing is not the responsibility of a single person. ¹³They believe that it is the responsibility of the community.

> **30c** | AVOIDING FAULTY OR EXCESSIVE SUBORDINATION AND COORDINATION

(1) Choosing precise conjunctions

Effective subordination requires choosing subordinating conjunctions carefully. In the following sentence, the use of *as* is distracting because it can mean either "because" or "while."

> Because
> ^~~As~~ time was running out, I randomly filled in the remaining circles on the exam sheet.

Your choice of coordinating conjunction should also convey your meaning precisely. For example, to indicate a cause-and-consequence relationship, *so* is more precise than *and*.

> so
> The rain continued to fall, ^~~and~~ the concert was cancelled.

(2) Avoiding excessive subordination and coordination

As you revise your writing, make sure that you have not overused subordination or coordination. In the following ineffective sentence, two dependent clauses compete for the reader's focus. The revision is clearer because it eliminates one of the dependent clauses.

Ineffective subordination

Although researchers used to believe that ancient Egyptians were the first to domesticate cats, they now think that cats may have provided company for humans 5,000 years earlier **because** the intact skeleton of a cat has been discovered in a Neolithic village on Cyprus.

Revised

Although researchers used to believe that ancient Egyptians were the first to domesticate cats, they now think that cats may have provided company for humans 5,000 years earlier. They base their revised estimate on the discovery of an intact cat skeleton in a Neolithic village on Cyprus.

Overuse of coordination results in a rambling sentence in need of revision.

Ineffective coordination

The lake was surrounded by forest, and it was large and clean, so it looked refreshing.

Revised

Surrounded by forest, the large, clean lake looked refreshing.

The following strategies should help you avoid overusing coordinating conjunctions.

(a) Using a more specific subordinating conjunction or an adverbial conjunction

I worked all summer to earn tuition money, ~~and I didn't~~ *so that I wouldn't*∧ have to work during the school year.

OR

I worked all summer to earn tuition money, ~~and~~ *; thus*∧ I didn't have to work during the school year.

(b) Using a relative clause to embed information

Seafood ∧ *, which is nutritious and low in fat,* ~~is nutritious, and it is low in fat, and it~~ has become available in greater variety.

(c) Allowing two or more verbs to share the same subject

Marie quickly grabbed a shovel, ~~and then she~~ ran to the edge of the field, and ~~then she~~ put out the fire before it could spread to the trees.

(d) Placing some information in an appositive phrase

, a researcher in astronomy at Johns Hopkins University,
Karl Glazebrook ∧is a researcher in astronomy at Johns Hopkins University, and he has questioned the conventional theory of galaxy formations.

(e) Placing some information in a prepositional or verbal phrase

In the thick snow,
∧The snow was thick, and we could not see where we were going.

After pulling   the plane
∧The plane pulled away from the gate on time, ∧and then it sat on the runway for two hours.

Exercise 2

Revise the following sentences to eliminate faulty or excessive co-ordination and subordination. Be prepared to explain why your sentences are more effective than the originals.

1. The Duct Tape Guys usually describe humorous uses for duct tape, providing serious information about the history of duct tape on their website.

2. Duct tape was invented for the U.S. military during World War II to keep the moisture out of ammunition cases because it was strong and waterproof.

3. Duct tape was originally called "duck tape" as it was waterproof and ducks are like that too and because it was made of cotton duck, which is a durable, tightly woven material.

4. Duck tape was also used to repair jeeps and to repair aircraft, its primary use being to protect ammunition cases.

5. When the war was over, house builders used duck tape to connect duct work together, and the builders started to refer to duck tape as "duct tape" and eventually the color of the tape changed from the green that was used during the war to silver, which matched the ducts.

31 ‖ PARALLELISM

When you join two or more ideas, whether each is encapsulated in a word or expressed in an entire sentence, the linked ideas need to be parallel in form—that is, formed with all adjectives, with all prepositional phrases, with all nominal clauses, and so on. **Parallelism** is the use of grammatically equivalent forms to clarify meaning and to emphasize ideas. This chapter will help you

- create parallelism by repeating words and grammatical forms (**31a**),
- link parallel forms with correlative conjunctions (**31b**), and
- use parallel forms to ensure clarity or provide emphasis (**31c**).

31a ‖ CREATING PARALLELISM

Recognizing parallel grammatical forms is easiest when you look for the repetition of certain words. The repetition of a preposition, the infinitive marker *to,* or the introductory word of a clause is a good clue that parallel grammatical forms will follow.

Preposition	My embarrassment stemmed not **from** the money lost but **from** the notoriety gained.
Infinitive marker *to*	She wanted her audience **to** remember the protest song and **to** understand its origin.
Introductory word of a clause	The team members vowed **that** they would support each other, **that** they would play their best, and **that** they would win the tournament.

The infinitive marker *to* does not need to be repeated as long as the sentence remains clear.

She wanted her audience **to remember** the protest song and **understand** its origin.

To recognize parallelism in sentences that do not include repeated words, look for a coordinating conjunction: *and, but, or, yet, so, nor,* or *for* (**21a(7)**). The parts of a sentence that such a conjunction joins are parallel if they have similar grammatical forms (all nouns, all participial phrases, and so on).

Words	The young actor was **shy** <u>yet</u> **determined.** [two adjectives joined by *yet*]
Phrases	Her goals include **publicizing student and faculty research, increasing the funding for that research,** <u>and</u> **providing adequate research facilities.** [three gerund phrases joined by *and*]
Clauses	Our instructor explained **what the project had entailed** <u>and</u> **how the researchers had used the results.** [two noun clauses joined by *and*]

As you edit a draft, look for sentences that include two or three words, phrases, or clauses joined by a conjunction and make sure the grammatical forms being linked are parallel.

People all around me are **buying, remodeling,** or ∧~~they want to sell~~ ~~their~~ houses. *[selling]*

Whether **mortgage rates rise** or ~~the~~ **building codes** ∧~~are changed,~~ the real estate market should remain strong this spring. *[change]*

Exercise 1

Identify the parallel structures in the following sentences.

1. The conservation group's goals are to raise awareness of the natural area, to build a walking path near the creek running through it, and to construct a nature center at the east end of the parking lot.
2. She is dedicated to freedom, development, diversity, and justice.
3. Some say voting is a right, but others say it is a responsibility.
4. Because the season was over and, more important, because their team was victorious, fans flooded the streets and celebrated until midnight.
5. He said that we would conduct a similar project but that we would likely get different results.

31b ║ LINKING PARALLEL FORMS WITH CORRELATIVE CONJUNCTIONS

Correlative conjunctions (or **correlatives**) are pairs of words that link other words, phrases, or clauses (**21a(7)**).

both . . . and

either . . . or

neither . . . nor

not only . . . but also

whether . . . or

Notice how the words or phrases following each of the paired conjunctions are parallel.

The new teacher is **both** <u>determined</u> **and** <u>dedicated</u>.

Whether her goals include <u>publicizing student and faculty research</u> **or** <u>increasing research funding</u>, she always works to improve research facilities.

Be especially careful when using *not only . . . but also.*

His team practices not only
∧ ~~Not only practicing~~ at 6 a.m. during the week, but ~~his team~~ also ~~scrimmages~~ on Sunday afternoons.

OR

       does his team practice   it
Not only ∧ ~~practicing~~ at 6 a.m. during the week, but ∧ ~~the team~~ also scrimmages on Sunday afternoons.

In the first revised example, each conjunction is followed by a prepositional phrase (**22a(4)**). In the second revised example, each conjunction accompanies a clause (**22b**).

31c	USING PARALLELISM TO PROVIDE CLARITY AND EMPHASIS

Repeating a pattern emphasizes the relationship of ideas. The following three sentences, all including parallelism, come from a public speech by political leader Jesse Jackson:

Today's students can put <u>dope in their veins</u> or <u>hope in their brains</u>. If **they** can <u>conceive it</u> and <u>believe it</u>, **they** can <u>achieve it</u>. **They** must know it is not <u>their aptitude</u> but <u>their attitude</u> that will determine <u>their altitude</u>.

To create parallelism, Jackson repeats words (*they*), uses rhymes (*dope/ hope, veins/brains, conceive/believe/achieve*), and employs similar grammatical forms (*their aptitude, their attitude, their altitude*).

> **❷ THINKING RHETORICALLY**

PARALLELISM

Parallel elements make your writing easy to read. But consider breaking from the parallel pattern on occasion to emphasize a point. For example, to describe a friend, you could start with two adjectives and then switch to a noun phrase.

> My friend Alison is **kind, modest**—and **the smartest mathematician in the state.**

By expressing key ideas in parallel structures, you emphasize them. However, if you overuse parallel patterns, they will lose their impact. Parallelism is especially effective in the introduction to a paragraph or an essay. The following passage from the introduction to a chapter of a book on advertising contains three examples of parallel forms:

> While **men are encouraged to fall in love with their cars, women are more often invited to have a romance,** indeed an erotic experience, with **something closer to home, something that truly does pump the valves of our hearts**—the food we eat. And the consequences become even more severe as we enter into the territory of **compulsivity** and **addiction.**
>
> —Jean Kilbourne, *Deadly Persuasion*

Parallel structures can also be effective in the conclusion to an essay.

> **Because these men work** with **animals,** not **machines, because they live** outside in landscapes of torrential beauty, **because they are confined** to **a place** and **a routine** embellished with awesome variables, **because calves die** in the arms that pulled others into life, **because they go to** the mountains as if on a pilgrimage to find out what makes a herd of elk tick, **their strength** is also **a softness, their toughness, a rare delicacy.**
>
> —Gretel Ehrlich, "About Men"

Exercise 2

Make the structures in each sentence parallel. In some sentences, you may have to use different wording.

1. Helen was praised by the vice president, and her assistant admired her.

2. Colleagues found her genial and easy to schedule meetings with.

3. When she hired new employees for her department, she looked for applicants who were intelligent, able to stay focused, and able to speak clearly.

4. At meetings, she was always prepared, participating actively yet politely, and generated innovative responses to department concerns.

5. In her annual report, she wrote that her most important achievements were attracting new clients and revenues were higher.

6. When asked about her leadership style, she said that she preferred collaborating with others rather than to work alone in her office.

7. Although dedicated to her work, Helen also recognized that parenting was important and the necessity of cultivating a life outside of work.

8. She worked hard to save money for the education of her children, for her own music lessons, and investing for her retirement.

9. However, in the coming year, she hoped to reduce the number of weekends she worked in the office and spending more time at home.

10. She would like to plan a piano recital and also have the opportunity to plan a family vacation.

32 ‖ EMPHASIS

In any rhetorical situation, some ideas are more important than others. You can energize your writing and direct the reader's attention by emphasizing those ideas. This chapter will help you create emphasis as you

- place words where they receive emphasis (**32a**),
- use cumulative and periodic sentences (**32b**),
- arrange ideas in emphatic order (**32c**),
- repeat important words (**32d**),
- invert word order in sentences (**32e**), and
- use an occasional short sentence (**32f**).

Subordination and coordination (chapter **30**), parallelism (chapter **31**), and precise word choice (chapter **35**) also offer you ways to emphasize your ideas.

32a ‖ PLACING WORDS FOR EMPHASIS

Words at the beginning or the end of a sentence receive emphasis. When you read aloud the brief sentence *We discussed the film*, you will likely stress *film*. Take advantage of this tendency by starting or finishing a sentence with the most important information—usually an idea that is new to the reader.

Many viewers   the film's stop-motion animation.

 ‸The film's stop-motion animation was raved about ‸by many viewers.

To ensure that readers focus on the end of the sentence, use an occasional dash (**41d**) or colon (**38b**) to set off the information.

By 1857, miners had extracted 760 tons of gold from these hills—and left behind more than ten times as much mercury, as well as devastated forests, slopes and streams.

—Rebecca Solnit, *Storming the Gates of Paradise: Landscapes for Politics*

The everyday episodes of online cruelty, added together, became what he was warned about: bullying.

Words that come before commas, especially if they are nouns, receive stress. (Consider the emphasis on the words *commas* and *nouns* in the preceding sentence.) In the following passage, the emphasis on *day, astronomy, mathematics, optics,* and *Laws* is due, in part, to comma placement.

One of the most brilliant and influential scientists of his day, [Johannes] Kepler made numerous contributions to astronomy, mathematics, and optics, including his famous discovery of what are now called Kepler's Laws, describing the motions of the planets round the sun.

—Kenneth Libbrecht, *The Snowflake: Winter's Secret Beauty*

Exercise 1

Below are five versions of a sentence. Decide which words receive more stress than the others in each version. Explain why.

1. The stunt double is essential to any action movie; that person may have to ride a horse backwards, jump from a tall building, or leap between speeding cars.

2. Essential to any action movie is the person riding a horse backwards, jumping from a tall building, or leaping between speeding cars: the stunt double.

3. The stunt double—essential to any action movie—may have to ride a horse backwards, jump from a tall building, or leap between speeding cars.

4. The stunt double, who may have to ride a horse backwards, jump from a tall building, or leap between speeding cars, is essential to any action movie.

5. In an action movie, a stunt double may have to leap between speeding cars, jump from a tall building, or ride a horse backwards.

32b USING CUMULATIVE AND PERIODIC SENTENCES

In a **cumulative sentence**, the main idea (the independent clause) comes first, followed by supporting ideas and supplementary details that expand on that main idea.

> **The day was hot for June**, a pale sun burning in a cloudless sky, wilting the last of the irises, the rhododendron blossoms drooping.
>
> —Adam Haslett, "Devotion"

In a **periodic sentence,** however, the main idea comes last, just before the period, as though the writer is warming up to the main point.

> Because the scar resulting from the burn is typically much larger than the original lesion, allowing for less intricacy, **the designs tend to be much simpler than those used in tattoos**.
>
> —Nina Jablonski, *Skin: A Natural History*

Both of these types of sentences can be effective. But because cumulative sentences are more common, the infrequently encountered periodic sentence tends to provide greater emphasis.

32c ORDERING IDEAS FROM LEAST TO MOST IMPORTANT

Just as you arrange paragraphs in **emphatic order** (3c), you can also arrange ideas and words in emphatic order. By arranging your ideas from least important to most important, you build up suspense, work toward a climax. If the most important idea appears first, a sentence may seem to trail off. If that idea appears in the middle of the sentence, readers may not recognize its significance. If, however, the most important idea appears at the end of the sentence, it will not only receive emphasis but also provide a springboard to the next sentence. In the following example, the writer emphasizes a doctor's desire to help the disadvantaged and then implies that this desire has been realized through work with young Haitian doctors:

> While he was in medical school, the soon-to-be doctor discovered his calling: to diagnose infectious diseases, to find ways of curing people with these diseases, and **to bring the lifesaving knowledge of modern medicine to the disadvantaged**. Most recently, he has been working with a small group of young doctors in Haiti.

EMPHATIC ORDER

Placing the least important idea at the end of the sentence can be effective when you are trying to be humorous, as in the following example:

> Contemporary man, of course, has no such peace of mind. He finds himself in the midst of a crisis of faith. He is what we fashionably call "alienated." He has seen the ravages of war, he has known natural catastrophes, he has been to singles bars.
>
> —Woody Allen, *Side Effects*

32d REPEATING IMPORTANT WORDS

Effective writers avoid unnecessary repetition but often use deliberate repetition to emphasize key words or ideas.

> We **forget** all too soon the things we thought we could never **forget**. We **forget** the loves and betrayals alike, **forget** what we whispered and what we screamed, **forget** who we are.   —Joan Didion, "On Keeping a Notebook"

In this case, the emphatic repetition of *forget* reinforces the author's point—that we do not remember many things that once seemed impossible to forget.

32e INVERTING WORD ORDER

Most sentences begin with a subject and end with a predicate. When you move words out of their normal order, you draw attention to them.

<u>**At the back of the crowded room**</u> sat **a newspaper reporter**.
[COMPARE: **A newspaper reporter** sat <u>**at the back of the crowded room**</u>.]

Notice the inverted word order in the second sentence of the following passage:

> [1]The Library Committee met with the City Council on several occasions to persuade them to fund the building of a library annex. [2]So successful were their efforts that a new wing will be added by next year. [3]This wing will contain archival materials that were previously stored in the basement.

The modifier *so successful* appears at the beginning of the sentence, rather than in its normal position, after the verb: *Their efforts were* so successful *that . . . .* The inverted word order emphasizes the committee's accomplishment.

ñ MULTILINGUAL WRITERS

INVERTING WORD ORDER

English sentences are inverted in various ways. Sometimes the main verb in the form of a participle is placed at the beginning of the sentence. The subject and the auxiliary verb(s) are then inverted.

part   aux   s

Carved into the bench **were someone's initials.**
[COMPARE: Someone's initials were carved into the bench.]

For more information on English word order, see chapter **48**.

32f   USING AN OCCASIONAL SHORT SENTENCE

In a paragraph of mostly long sentences, try using a short sentence for emphasis. To optimize the effect, lead up to the short sentence with an especially long sentence.

> After buying the groceries, cleaning the vegetables, marinating the beef, baking a cake, hanging the decorations, and setting the table, I showered and got myself ready to have a good time with my invited guests. **Then the phone rang.**

Exercise 2

Add emphasis to each of the following sentences by using the technique indicated at the beginning. You may have to add some words and/or delete others.

1. (climactic order) In the 1960 Olympics, Wilma Rudolph tied the world record in the 100-meter race, she tied the record in the 400-meter relay, she won the hearts of fans from around the world, and she broke the record in the 200-meter race.

2. (periodic sentence) Some sports reporters described Rudolph as a gazelle because of her beautiful stride.

3. (inversion) Rudolph's Olympic achievement is impressive, but her victory over a crippling disease is even more spectacular.

4. (final short sentence) Rudolph was born prematurely, weighing only four and one-half pounds. As a child, she suffered from double pneumonia, scarlet fever, and then polio.

5. (cumulative sentence) She received help from her family. Her brothers and sister massaged her legs. Her mother drove her to a hospital for therapy.

6. (inversion) Her siblings' willingness to help was essential to her recovery, as were her mother's vigilant care and her own determination.

7. (periodic sentence) Her passions became basketball and track after she recovered, built up her strength, and gained self-confidence.

8. (climactic order) Rudolph set a scoring record in basketball, she set the standard for future track and field stars, and she set an Olympic record in track.

33 || VARIETY

To make your writing lively and distinctive, include a variety of sentence types and lengths. Notice how the sentences in the following paragraph vary in length, form (simple, compound, and compound-complex), and function (statements, questions, and commands). The variety of sentences makes this paragraph about pleasure pleasurable to read.

> Start with the taste. Imagine a moment when the sensation of honey or sugar on the tongue was an astonishment, a kind of intoxication. The closest I've ever come to recovering such a sense of sweetness was secondhand, though it left a powerful impression on me even so. I'm thinking of my son's first experience with sugar: the icing on the cake at his first birthday. I have only the testimony of Isaac's face to go by (that, and his fierceness to repeat the experience), but it was plain that his first encounter with sugar had intoxicated him—was in fact an ecstasy, in the literal sense of the word. That is, he was beside himself with the pleasure of it, no longer here with me in space and time in quite the same way he had been just a moment before. Between bites Isaac gazed up at me in amazement (he was on my lap, and I was delivering the ambrosial forkfuls to his gaping mouth) as if to exclaim, "Your world contains *this*? From this day forward I shall dedicate my life to it." (Which he basically has done.) And I remember thinking, this is no minor desire, and then wondered: Could it be that sweetness is the prototype of *all* desire?   —**Michael Pollan**, *The Botany of Desire*

This chapter will help you

- revise sentence length and form (**33a**);
- vary sentence openings (**33b**); and
- use an occasional question, command, or exclamation (**33c**).

If you have difficulty distinguishing between various types of sentence structures, review the fundamentals in chapters **21** and **22**.

33a REVISING SENTENCE LENGTH AND FORM

To avoid the choppiness of a series of short sentences, combine some of them into longer sentences. You can combine sentences by using a coordinating conjunction (such as *and, but,* or *or*), a subordinating conjunction (such as *because, although,* or *when*), or a relative pronoun (such as *who, that,* or *which*).

Short	Americans typically eat popcorn at movie theaters. They also eat it at sporting events.
Combined	Americans typically eat popcorn at movie theaters **and** sporting events. [coordinating conjunction (**21a(7)**)]
Short	Researchers have found thousand-year-old popcorn kernels. These kernels still pop.
Combined	Researchers have found thousand-year-old popcorn kernels **that** still pop. [relative pronoun (**26a(3)**)]
Short	Popcorn was in demand during the Great Depression. Impoverished families could afford it.
Combined	**Because** impoverished families could afford it, popcorn was in demand during the Great Depression. [subordinating conjunction (**21a(7)**)]

You may sometimes be able to use both a subordinating and a coordinating conjunction.

Short	Sugar was sent abroad during World War II. Little sugar was left for making candy. Americans started eating more popcorn.
Combined	**Because** sugar was sent abroad during World War II, little was left for making candy, **so** Americans started eating more popcorn. [subordinating and coordinating conjunctions (**21a(7)**)]

It is also possible to combine sentences by condensing one of them into a phrase (**22a**).

Short	Some colonial families ate popcorn for breakfast. They ate it with sugar and cream.
Combined	Some colonial families ate popcorn **with sugar and cream** for breakfast. [prepositional phrase (**22a(4)**)]
Short	The world's largest popcorn ball measured twelve feet in diameter. It took two thousand pounds of popcorn to create.
Combined	**Measuring twelve feet in diameter,** the world's largest popcorn ball took two thousand pounds of popcorn to create. [participial phrase (**22a(3)**)]

❓ THINKING RHETORICALLY

SHORT SENTENCES

Occasionally, a series of brief sentences produces a special effect. The short sentences in the following passage capture the quick actions taking place as an accident is about to occur:

"There's a truck in your lane!" my friend yelled. I swerved toward the shoulder. "Watch out!" she screamed. I hit the brakes. The wheel locked. The back of the car swerved to the right.

33b VARYING SENTENCE OPENINGS

Most writers begin more than half of their sentences with a subject. Although this pattern is common, relying on it too heavily can make writing seem predictable. Experiment with the following alternatives for starting your sentences.

(1) Beginning with an adverb

Immediately, the police officer got out of the car and asked for my driver's license.

(2) Beginning with a phrase

In the arena, fans stood with their hands over their hearts and sang the National Anthem. [prepositional phrase (**22a(4)**)]

A town of historic interest, Santa Fe also has many art galleries and restaurants. [appositive phrase (**22a(5)**)]

To win, candidates need to convey a clear message that is not contaminated by the opposition. [infinitive phrase (**22a(3)**)]

Tapping the power of being seen, the Oscar nominees appeared on late-night television, morning news programs, and in glossy magazines. [participial phrase (**22a(3)**)]

The awards now over, we understood clearly how the power of the movie's story itself affects the Academy's voting in all categories. [absolute phrase (**22a(6)**)]

(3) Beginning with a transitional word or phrase

In each of the following examples, the transitional word or phrase shows the relationship between the ideas in the pair of sentences. (See also **3d**.)

Many restaurants close within a few years of opening. **But** others, which offer good food at reasonable prices, become well established.

Difficulty in finding a place to park keeps some people from going out to lunch downtown. **However,** that problem may be alleviated with the construction of a new underground parking garage.

Independently owned restaurants struggle to get started for a number of reasons. **First of all,** they have to compete against successful restaurant chains.

(4) Beginning with a word that usually comes after the verb

I was an abysmal football player. **Soccer,** though, I could play well. [direct object]

Vital to any success I had were my mother's early lessons. [predicate adjective]

Exercise 1

Convert each set of short sentences into a single longer sentence.

1. On May 29, 1953, Edmund Hillary reached the summit of Mt. Everest. Hillary was a mountaineer from New Zealand. Tenzing Norgay was his Sherpa guide. Mt. Everest is the highest mountain in the world.

2. Hillary had been a member of a Swiss expedition. The Swiss expedition tried to reach the top of Mt. Everest in 1952. Bad weather stopped them eight hundred feet from the summit.

3. In March of 1953, Hillary joined an expedition from Great Britain. This expedition was led by John Hunt.

4. The expedition approached the peak. Conditions were worsening. Hunt directed Hillary and Norgay to continue to the summit.

5. Hillary thawed out his frozen boots on the morning of May 29. The two climbers then made the final ascent.

Exercise 2

Rewrite each sentence so that it does not begin with a subject.

1. John Spilsbury was an engraver and mapmaker from London who made the first jigsaw puzzle in about 1760.

2. He pasted a map onto a piece of wood and used a fine-bladed saw to cut around the borders of the countries.

3. The jigsaw puzzle was first an educational toy and has been a mainstay in households all over the world ever since its invention.

4. The original puzzles were quite expensive because the wooden pieces were cut by hand.

5. Most puzzles are made of cardboard today.

33c USING QUESTIONS, EXCLAMATIONS, AND COMMANDS

You can vary sentences in a paragraph by introducing an occasional question, exclamation, or command (**22d**).

(1) Raising a question or two for variety

> It can be uncomfortable for a boy to watch the frenzied, uninhibited enthusiasm of girl fans screaming for their idols, whether it's Sinatra, the Beatles, or Michael Jackson. That is partly jealousy too—*who wouldn't want to be the one who inspires girls to make that kind of noise?* But it's also partly because we envy that enthusiasm.
>
> —**Rob Sheffield,** *Talking to Girls about Duran Duran*

You can either answer the question you pose or let readers answer it for themselves, in which case it is called a **rhetorical question** (**22d**).

(2) Adding an exclamatory sentence for variety

> But at other moments, the classroom is so lifeless or painful or confused— and I so powerless to do anything about it—that my claim to be a teacher seems a transparent sham. Then the enemy is everywhere: in those students from some alien planet, in the subject I thought I knew, and in the personal pathology that keeps me earning my living this way. *What a fool I was to imagine that I had mastered this occult art—harder to divine than tea leaves and impossible for mortals to do even passably well!*
>
> —**Parker Palmer,** *The Courage to Teach*

Although you can make sentences emphatic without using exclamation points (chapter **32**), the introduction of an exclamatory sentence can break up a regular pattern of declarative sentences.

(3) Including a command for variety

> Now I stare and stare at people shamelessly. *Stare.* It's the way to educate your eye.
>
> —**Walker Evans,** *Unclassified*

In this case, a one-word command, "Stare," provides variety.

Exercise 3

Explain how questions and commands add variety to the following paragraph. Describe other ways in which this writer varies his sentences.

¹The gods, they say, give breath, and they take it away. ²But the same could be said—couldn't it?—of the humble comma. ³Add it to the present clause, and, of a sudden, the mind is, quite literally, given pause to think; take it out if you wish or forget it and the mind is deprived of a resting place. ⁴Yet still the comma gets no respect. ⁵It seems just a slip of a thing, a pedant's tick, a blip on the edge of our consciousness, a kind of printer's smudge almost. ⁶Small, we claim, is beautiful (especially in the age of the microchip). ⁷Yet what is so often used, and so rarely recalled, as the comma—unless it be breath itself?

—Pico Iyer, "In Praise of the Humble Comma"

**EFFECTIVE
LANGUAGE**

Situate Yourself

Even grammatically correct sentences can be improved by more effective language—that is by using the appropriate language, precise words, and to-the-point sentences. Revise the following letter to Professor Glenn so that it guides her to knowing exactly who you are, what problem you would like to resolve, and how. Your goal is to be clear, concise, and respectful.

Dear Cheryl,

It's me, Terry, who is in your class and I want to tell you how much I like it. You do talk about girls and other minorities and their problems a lot, but other than that it's a pretty cool class. But I've got a problem, too, even though I'm not a minority. I've gotta miss class next Wednesday, Thursday, and Friday because I'm going home for my dad's 50th birthday. He and his girlfriend are having a big bash, and they need my help in organizing it especially since they're both getting up there. I need to help them with food and other stuff.

You're probably around my dad's age, so I know you'll understand. You said you wanted to know when we are going to miss class, so I'm telling you.

Terry

34 ‖ GOOD USAGE

Using the right words at the right time can make the difference between having your ideas taken seriously and seeing them brushed aside. Using the right words demonstrates that you are keeping your audience in mind. This chapter will help you

- write in a clear, straightforward style (**34a**);
- choose words that are appropriate for your audience, purpose, and context (**34b**);
- use inclusive language (**34c**); and
- find information in dictionaries (**34d**) and thesauruses (**34e**).

34a ‖ CLEAR STYLE

The right words make your writing easy and pleasurable to read: the right words achieve a clear style that your audience understands and that is appropriate for the occasion. Ornate sentences that include flowery or overly technical language may not be understood by a broad audience.

Ornate   The majority believes that achievement derives primarily from the diligent pursuit of allocated tasks.

Clear   Most people believe that success results from hard work.

If you want readers to take your writing seriously, you must show them respect by not using obscure words when common words will do and by not using more words than necessary. Using words that are precise (**35a**) and sentences that are concise (chapter **36**) can also help you achieve a clear style.

Exercise 1

Revise the following sentences for an audience that prefers a clear, straightforward style.

1. Expert delineation of character in a job interview is a goal that is not always possible to achieve.

2. In an employment situation, social pleasantries may contribute to the successful functioning of job tasks, but such interactions should not distract attention from the need to complete all assignments in a timely manner.

3. Commitment to an ongoing and carefully programmed schedule of physical self-management can be a significant resource for stress reduction in the workplace.

34b APPROPRIATE WORD CHOICE

You may find yourself writing for an audience that you know will welcome slang and colloquial expressions or for a specialized audience who will immediately understand technical jargon. When you are uncertain about a word, turn to a good dictionary. Words labeled *dialect, slang, colloquial, nonstandard,* or *unconventional* are generally inappropriate for academic and professional writing. If a word has no label, you can safely assume that it can be used in writing for school or work. Otherwise, the following advice can help you determine which words to use and which to avoid.

(1) Slang

The term **slang** covers a wide range of words or expressions that are used in informal situations or are considered fashionable by people in a particular age group, locality, or profession. Although such words are often used in private conversation or in writing intended to mimic conversation, they are usually out of place in academic or professional writing.

(2) Conversational (or colloquial) words

Words labeled *colloquial* in a dictionary are fine for casual conversation and for written dialogues or personal essays on a light topic. Such words are sometimes used for special effect in academic writing, but you should usually replace them with more appropriate words. For example, the conversational words *dumb* and *kid around* could be replaced by *illogical* and *tease.*

> **❶ CAUTION**
>
> Because contractions (such as *you'll* for "you will" and *she's* for "she is") reflect the sound of conversation, you can use them in certain types of writing to create a friendly tone. However, some of your instructors or supervisors may consider them too informal for academic or professional writing.

(3) Regionalisms

Regionalisms—such as *sack* for "bag" and *sweeper* for "vacuum cleaner"—can make writing lively and distinctive, but they are often considered too informal for academic and professional writing.

(4) Technical words or jargon

When writing for a diverse audience, an effective writer will not refer to the need for bifocals as *presbyopia.* However, technical language is appropriate when the audience can understand it (as when one physician writes to another) or when the audience would benefit by learning the terms in question. Sometimes, terms that originated as jargon enter mainstream usage. As computer use has grown, for example, technical terms such as *application (app)* and *cloud computing* have become commonly used and widely understood.

34c   INCLUSIVE LANGUAGE

By choosing words that are inclusive rather than exclusive, you invite readers into your writing. Prejudiced or derogatory language has no place in academic or professional writing; using it undermines your

Figure 34.1: Photographs and statements on the websites of many companies indicate a commitment to an inclusive work environment.

authority and credibility. It is best to use language that will engage, not alienate, your readers (figure 34.1).

(1) Nonsexist language

Effective writers show equal respect for all people, all genders. For example, they avoid using *man* to refer to people in general because they understand that the word excludes everyone else.

Achievements [OR Human achievements]

Man's achievements in science are impressive.

People of all genders can be *firefighters* or *police officers*—words that have become gender-neutral alternatives to *firemen* and *policemen*. Use the following tips to ensure that your writing is respectful.

TIPS FOR AVOIDING SEXIST LANGUAGE

When reviewing drafts, check for and revise the following types of sexist language.

- **Generic *he:*** A senator should listen to *his* constituents.

  A senator should listen to **his or her** constituents. [use of the appropriate form of *he or she*]

  Senators should listen to **their** constituents. [use of plural forms]

  By listening to their constituents, **senators obtain important information on the consequences of their votes and decisions.** [elimination of *his* by revising the sentence]

- **Occupational stereotype:** Glenda James, a *female* engineer at Howard Aviation, won the best-employee award.

  Howard Aviation engineer Glenda James won the best-employee award. [removal of the unnecessary gender reference]

- **Terms such as *man* and *mankind* or those with *-ess* or *-man* endings:** Labor laws benefit the common *man*. *Mankind* benefits from philanthropy. The *stewardess* brought me some orange juice.

  Labor laws benefit **working people.** [replacement of the stereotypical term with a gender-neutral term]

  Everyone benefits from philanthropy. [use of an indefinite pronoun]

  The **flight attendant** brought me some orange juice. [use of a gender-neutral term]

- **Stereotypical gender roles:** I was told that the university offers free tuition to faculty *wives*. The minister pronounced them *man* and *wife*.

  I was told that the university offers free tuition to faculty **spouses.** [replacement of the stereotypical term with a gender-neutral term]

  The minister pronounced them **husband** and wife. [use of a term equivalent to *wife*]

  The minister pronounced them husband and husband.

- **Inconsistent use of titles:** *Mr.* Holmes and his *wife,* Mary, took a long trip to China.

  Mr. and Mrs. [or Ms.] Holmes took a long trip to China. [consistent use of titles]

(continued on page 668)

(continued from page 667)

Peter and Mary Holmes took a long trip to China. [removal of titles]

Peter Holmes and **Mary Wolfe** took a long trip to China. [use of full names]

- **Unstated gender assumption:** Have your *mother make your costume* for the school pageant.

Have your **parents provide you with a costume** for the school pageant. [replacement of the stereotypical words with gender-neutral ones]

Exercise 2

Make the following sentences inclusive by eliminating sexist language.

1. A special code of ethics guides a nurse in fulfilling her responsibilities.
2. According to the weatherman, this summer will be unseasonably cold.
3. Dr. William Avery and his wife donated money to the scholarship fund.
4. Professor Garcia mapped the journey of modern man.
5. While in college, she worked as a waitress in a diner.

(2) Nonracist language

Rarely is it necessary to identify anyone's race or ethnicity in academic or professional writing. However, you may need to use appropriate racial or cultural-ethnic terms if you are writing a demographic report, an argument against existing racial inequities, or a historical account of a particular event involving ethnic groups. Determining which terms a particular group prefers can be difficult because preferences sometimes vary within a group and change over time. One conventional way to refer to Americans of a specific descent is to include an adjective before the word *American*: *African American, Asian American, European American, Latin American, Mexican American, Native American*. These words are widely used; however, members of a particular group may identify themselves in more than one way. In addition to *African American* and *European American, Black* (or *black*) and *White* (or *white*) have long been used. People of Spanish-speaking descent may prefer *Chicano/Chicana, Hispanic, Latino/Latina, Puerto Rican,* or other terms. Members of cultures that are indigenous to North America may prefer a specific name such as *Cherokee, Inuit,* or *Haida,* though some also accept *American Indians* or *Native People.* An up-to-date dictionary that includes notes on usage can help you choose appropriate terms.

(3) Respectful language about differences

If a writing assignment requires you to distinguish people based on age, ability, geographical area, religion, or sexual orientation, show respect to the groups or individuals you discuss by using the terms they prefer.

(a) Referring to age

Although some people object to the term *senior citizen,* a better alternative has not emerged. When used respectfully, the term refers to a person who has reached the age of retirement (but may not have decided to retire) and is eligible for certain privileges granted by society. However, if you know your audience would object to this term, find out which alternative is preferred.

(b) Referring to disability or illness

In references to disabilities and illnesses, it is appropriate to put the person first. In this way, the focus is placed on the individual rather than on the limitation. Thus, the phrase *persons with disabilities* is preferred over *disabled persons.* You can find out whether such person-first expressions are preferred by noting whether they are used in the articles and books (or by the people) you consult. Be aware, though, that some writers and readers think that these types of expressions sound unnatural, and others maintain that they do not serve their intended purpose because the last word in a phrase can carry the greater weight, especially at the end of a sentence.

(c) Referring to geographical areas

Certain geographical terms need to be used with special care. Though most frequently used to refer to people from the United States, the term *American* may also refer to people from Canada, Mexico, Central America, or South America. If your audience may be confused by this term, use *people from the United States* or *U.S. citizens* instead.

The term *Arab* refers to people who speak Arabic. If you cannot use specific terms such as *Iraqi* or *Saudi Arabian,* be sure you know that a country's people speak Arabic and not another language. Iranians, for example, are not Arabs because they speak Farsi.

British, rather than *English,* is the preferred term for referring to people from the island of Great Britain or from the United Kingdom (England, Scotland, Wales, and Northern Ireland).

(d) Referring to religion

Reference to a person's religion should be made only if it is relevant. If you must mention religious affiliation, use only those terms considered respectful. Because religions have both conservative and liberal followers, be careful not to make generalizations (7i(12)) about political stances.

(e) Referring to sexual orientation

If your rhetorical situation calls for identifying sexual orientation, choose terms used by the people you are discussing. For instance, LGBTQ includes preferred terms for all the people who are not firmly heterosexual: lesbian, gay, bisexual, transgender, or questioning.

✔ **CHECKLIST** for Assessing Usage within a Rhetorical Situation

- Do your words convey the meaning you intend? Do they help you fulfill your purpose?
- Do any of your words sound too casual or too formal?
- Can your audience understand the words you have used? Do you explain any words your readers might not understand? Have you used any words that could offend readers?
- Are your words appropriate for the context in which they will be read?

34d ▌ DICTIONARIES

A good dictionary is an indispensable tool for a writer. Some online dictionaries are very good. Desk dictionaries such as *The American Heritage Dictionary* and *Merriam-Webster's Collegiate Dictionary* do much more than provide the correct spellings of words; they also give meanings, parts of speech, plural forms, and verb tenses, as well as information about pronunciation and origin. As noted above, a reliable dictionary includes labels (for example, *dialect, slang, colloquial, nonstandard,* or *unconventional)* that can help you decide whether words are appropriate for your purpose, audience, and context. Because meanings of words change and because new words are constantly introduced into English, it is important to choose a dictionary, whether print or electronic, that has a recent copyright date.

(1) Unabridged or specialized dictionaries

An **unabridged dictionary** provides a comprehensive survey of English words, including detailed information about their origins. A **specialized dictionary** presents words related to a specific discipline or to some aspect of usage.

Unabridged Dictionaries

The Oxford English Dictionary. 2nd ed. 20 vols. 1989–. CD-ROM. 4.0. 2009.

Webster's Third New International Dictionary of the English Language. CD-ROM. 3.0. 2002.

These dictionaries also have regularly updated online versions.

Specialized Dictionaries

The American Heritage Guide to Contemporary Usage and Style. 2005.

The Cambridge Guide to English Usage. 2004.

Fowler's Modern English Usage. 2004.

The Oxford Dictionary of Idioms. 2007.

> **ñ MULTILINGUAL WRITERS**

DICTIONARIES AND OTHER RESOURCES
The following dictionaries are recommended for nonnative speakers of English.

> *The American Heritage Dictionary of Phrasal Verbs.* 2005.
>
> *Collins Cobuild Student's Dictionary plus Grammar.* 2005.
>
> *Longman Advanced American Dictionary.* 2013.
>
> *Longman Advanced American English.* 2009.
>
> *Merriam-Webster's Advanced Learner's English Dictionary.* 2008.
>
> Swan, Michael. *Practical English Usage.* 3rd ed. 2005. (This is a guide to problems encountered by multilingual writers.)

(2) Dictionary entries

Dictionary entries provide a range of information. Figure 34.2 shows sample entries from *The Newbury House Dictionary.* Notice that *cool* is listed three times: as an adjective, a noun, and a verb. The types of information these entries provide can be found in almost all desk dictionaries, though sometimes in a different order.

TYPES OF INFORMATION PROVIDED BY DICTIONARY ENTRIES

- **Spelling, syllabication (word division), and pronunciation.** Dictionary entries begin with the correctly spelled word, divided into syllables, followed by the pronunciation.

- **Parts of speech and word forms.** Dictionaries identify parts of speech—for instance, with *n* for "noun" or *vi* for "intransitive verb." Meanings will vary depending on the part of speech identified. Dictionaries also indicate irregular forms of verbs, nouns, and adjectives: *fly, flew, flown, flying, flies; child, children; good, better, best.*

- **Word origin.** English has a rich heritage. A dictionary entry indicates whether a word has roots in an older version of English (Old English, roughly CE 700–1100, or Middle English, 1100–1500), has even deeper roots in another language (Latin, Greek, German, French, and so on), or has been added more recently from another language.

- **Date of first occurrence.** Most entries include the date when the use of the word (in the first sense listed in the entry) was initially recorded.
- **Definition(s).** Generally, the oldest meaning is given first. However, meanings can also be ordered according to frequency of usage, with the most common usage listed first.
- **Usage.** Quotations show how the word can be used in various contexts. Sometimes a comment on usage problems is placed at the end of an entry.
- **Idioms.** When the word is part of a common idiom (35c), the idiom is listed and defined.
- **Synonyms.** Some dictionaries provide explanations of subtle differences in meaning among a word's synonyms.

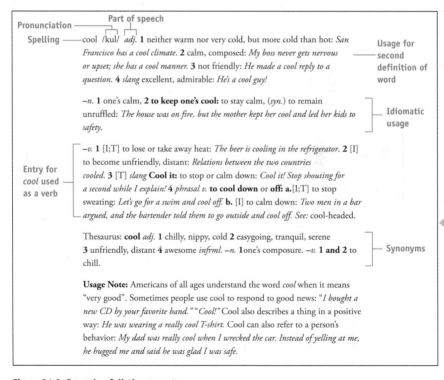

Pronunciation ———
Part of speech

Spelling ——— cool /kul/ *adj.* **1** neither warm nor very cold, but more cold than hot: *San Francisco has a cool climate.* **2** calm, composed: *My boss never gets nervous or upset; she has a cool manner.* **3** not friendly: *He made a cool reply to a question.* **4** *slang* excellent, admirable: *He's a cool guy!*

Usage for second definition of word

—*n.* **1** one's calm, **2 to keep one's cool:** to stay calm, (*syn.*) to remain unruffled: *The house was on fire, but the mother kept her cool and led her kids to safety.*

Idiomatic usage

Entry for *cool* used as a verb

—*v.* **1** [I;T] to lose or take away heat: *The beer is cooling in the refrigerator.* **2** [I] to become unfriendly, distant: *Relations between the two countries cooled.* **3** [T] *slang* **Cool it:** to stop or calm down: *Cool it! Stop shouting for a second while I explain!* **4** *phrasal v.* **to cool down** or **off: a.** [I;T] to stop sweating: *Let's go for a swim and cool off.* **b.** [I] to calm down: *Two men in a bar argued, and the bartender told them to go outside and cool off. See:* cool-headed.

Thesaurus: **cool** *adj.* **1** chilly, nippy, cold **2** easygoing, tranquil, serene **3** unfriendly, distant **4** awesome *infrml.* —*n.* **1** one's composure. —*v.* **1 and 2** to chill.

Synonyms

Usage Note: Americans of all ages understand the word *cool* when it means "very good". Sometimes people use cool to respond to good news: *"I bought a new CD by your favorite band." "Cool!"* Cool also describes a thing in a positive way: *He was wearing a really cool T-shirt.* Cool can also refer to a person's behavior: *My dad was really cool when I wrecked the car. Instead of yelling at me, he hugged me and said he was glad I was safe.*

Figure 34.2: Example of dictionary entry.

34e | THESAURUSES

A **thesaurus** provides alternatives for frequently used words. Unlike a dictionary, which explains what a word means and how it evolved, a thesaurus provides only a list of words that serve as possible synonyms for each term it includes. A thesaurus can be useful, especially when you want to jog your memory about a word you know but cannot recall. You may, however, use a word incorrectly if you simply pick it from a list in a thesaurus. If you find an unfamiliar yet intriguing word, make sure that you are using it correctly by looking it up in a dictionary.

Exercise 3

Find definitions for the pairs of words in parentheses. Then choose the word you think best completes each sentence. Be prepared to explain your answers.

1. Sixteen prisoners on death row were granted (mercy/clemency).
2. The outcome of the election (excited/provoked) a riot.
3. The young couple was (covetous/greedy) of their neighbors' estate.
4. While she was traveling in Muslim countries, she wore (modest/chaste) clothing.
5. The president of the university (authorized/confirmed) the rumor that tuition would be increasing next year.

35 | PRECISE WORD CHOICE

Make words work for you. By choosing the right word and putting it in the right place, you can communicate exactly what you mean and make your writing distinctive. This chapter will help you

- choose words appropriate for your purpose, audience, and context (**35a**);
- create fresh, clear expressions (**35b**);
- use idioms and collocations (**35c**); and
- compose clear definitions (**35d**).

35a | ACCURATE AND PRECISE WORD CHOICE

(1) Denotations and connotations

Denotations are definitions of words, such as those that appear in dictionaries. For example, the noun *beach* denotes a sandy or pebbly shore. However, some words have more than one definition or one definition that can be interpreted in a number of ways. Select words whose denotations convey your point exactly.

Padre Island National Seashore ˄ is really great. *astounds even an indifferent tourist like me.*

[Because *great* can mean "extremely large" as well as "outstanding" or "powerful," its use in this sentence is imprecise.]

Denotations of words can also sometimes be confused.

The park ranger ˄ inferred *implied* that the Kemp's ridley sea turtle may become extinct.

[*Imply* means "to suggest," so *implied* is the exact word for this sentence. *Infer* means "to draw a conclusion from evidence": From the park ranger's comments, I *inferred* that the Kemp's ridley sea turtle may become extinct.]

The **Glossary of Usage** at the back of this book includes the definitions of many words that are commonly confused.

Connotations are the associations evoked by a word. *Beach,* for instance, may connote natural beauty, surf, shells, swimming, tanning, sunburn, and/or crowds. The context in which a word appears affects the associations it evokes. In a treatise on shoreline management, *beach* has scientific and geographic connotations; in a fashion magazine, this word is associated with bathing suits, sunglasses, and sunscreen. The challenge for writers is to choose the words that are most likely to spark the appropriate connotations in their readers' minds.

resilience
The ~~obstinacy~~ of the Kemp's ridley sea turtle has delighted park rangers.

[*Obstinacy* has negative connotations, which make it an unlikely quality to cause delight.]

ñ MULTILINGUAL WRITERS

CONNOTATIONS
Your ability to recognize connotations will improve as your vocabulary increases. When you encounter a new word that seems to mean exactly what another word means, study the context in which each word is used. Then, to help yourself learn the new word and its context, create a phrase or a sentence that you can easily remember. If you are confused about the connotations of specific words, consult an ESL dictionary (see page 674).

---

(2) Specific, concrete words

A **general word** is all-inclusive, indefinite, and sweeping in scope. A **specific word** is precise, definite, and limited in scope.

General	Specific	More Specific/Concrete
food	fast food	cheeseburger
media	newspapers	*The Miami Herald*
place	city	Atlanta

An **abstract word** refers to a concept or idea, a quality or trait, or anything else that cannot be touched, heard, or seen. A **concrete word** signifies a particular object, a specific action, or anything that can be touched, heard, or seen.

Abstract   democracy, evil, strength, charity

Concrete   mosquito, hammer, plastic, fog

As you select words to fit your context, be as specific and concrete as you can. For example, instead of the word *bad,* consider using a more precise adjective.

bad neighbors: rowdy, snobby, nosy, fussy, sloppy, threatening

bad meat: tough, tainted, overcooked, undercooked, contaminated

bad wood: rotten, warped, scorched, knotty, termite-ridden

To test whether or not a word is specific, you can ask one or more of these questions about what you want to say: Exactly who? Exactly what? Exactly when? Exactly where? Exactly how? In the following examples, notice what a difference concrete words can make in expressing an idea and how adding details can expand or develop it.

Vague   She has kept no reminders of performing in her youth.

Specific   She has kept no sequined costume, no photographs, no fliers or posters from that part of her youth.

—LOUISE ERDRICH, "The Leap"

The word *thing* may refer to a task, an errand, an implement, a concept, an utterance, and so on. Because this word has so many referents, replace it with a specific word whenever possible.

We did not say a ~~thing~~ word.

Fear and horror are not the same ~~thing~~ emotion.

(3) Figurative language

Figurative language is the use of words in an imaginative rather than a literal sense. Similes and metaphors are the chief **figures of speech.** A **simile** is a comparison of dissimilar things using *like* or *as.* A **metaphor** is an implied comparison of dissimilar things, without *like* or *as.*

Similes

Norms live in the culture **like genes, manifesting themselves unexpectedly, the way a child's big ears appear from an ancestor of whom no picture or name remains.**

—CHARLES WOHLFORTH, "Conservation and Eugenics:
The Environmental Movement's Dirty Secret"

When **her body was hairless as a baby's,** she adjusted the showerhead so that the water burst forth in pelting streams.

—LOIDA MARITZA PÉREZ, *Geographies of Home*

Metaphors

His **money was a sharp pair of scissors** that snipped rapidly through tangles of red tape.

—HISAYE YAMAMOTO, "Las Vegas Charley"

Making tacos is a graceful dance.

—DENISE CHÁVEZ, *A Taco Testimony*

Single words can be used metaphorically.

These roses must be **planted** in good soil. [literal]

Keep your life **planted** wherever you can put down the most roots. [metaphorical]

Similes and metaphors are especially valuable when they are concrete and describe or evoke essential relationships that cannot otherwise be communicated. Similes or metaphors can be extended throughout a paragraph of comparison, but be careful not to mix them (**28b**).

Exercise 1

Study the passage below, and prepare to discuss the author's use of exact and figurative language to communicate her ideas.

^{1}The kitchen where I'm making dinner is a New York kitchen. ^{2}Nice light, way too small, nowhere to put anything unless the stove goes. ^{3}My stove is huge, but it will never go. ^{4}My stove is where my head clears, my impressions settle, my reporter's life gets folded into my life, and whatever I've just learned, or think

I've learned—whatever it was, out there in the world, that had seemed so different and surprising—bubbles away in the very small pot of what I think I know and, if I'm lucky, produces something like perspective.

—**JANE KRAMER, "The Reporter's Kitchen"**

Exercise 2

Use figurative language to provide details about each of the following topics.

1. the look on someone's face
2. a cold rainy day
3. studying for an exam
4. your favorite food
5. buying textbooks
6. a busy street
7. waiting in a long line to see a movie
8. the way someone talks

35b   CLICHÉS AND EUPHEMISMS

When forced or overused, certain expressions lose their impact. For example, the expressions *bite the dust, breath of fresh air,* and *smooth as silk* were once striking and thus effective. Excessive use, though, has drained them of their original force and made them **clichés.** Newer expressions such as *put a spin on something* and *think outside the box* have also lost their vitality because of overuse. Nonetheless, clichés are so much a part of the language, especially the spoken language, that nearly every writer uses them from time to time. But effective writers often give a fresh twist to an old saying.

I seek a narrative, a fiction, to order days like the one I spent several years ago, on a gray June Saturday in Chicago, when I took a roller-coaster ride on the bell curve of my experience.

—**GAYLE PEMBERTON, "The Zen of Bigger Thomas"**

[Notice how much more effective this expression is than a reference to "being on an emotional roller coaster."]

Variations on familiar expressions from literature and history, many of which have become part of everyday language, can often be used to good effect.

We have met the enemy and he is us.

—WALT KELLY, Earth Day poster, 1970

[This statement is a variation on one made by American naval officer Oliver Hazard Perry during the War of 1812: "We have met the enemy and they are ours."]

Good writers, however, do not rely too heavily on the words of others; they choose their own words to communicate their ideas.

Sometimes writers coin new expressions to substitute for words that have coarse or unpleasant connotations. These expressions, called **euphemisms**, occasionally become standardized. To avoid the word *dying*, for example, a writer might say that someone was *terminally ill*. Although euphemisms sound more pleasant than the words they replace, they can sometimes obscure facts. Euphemisms such as *revenue enhancement* for *tax hike* and *pre-owned* for *used* are considered insincere or deceitful.

Exercise 3

Replace the following overused expressions with carefully chosen words. Then use the replacements in sentences.

EXAMPLE

beyond the shadow of a doubt

undoubtedly   **OR**   with total certainty

1. reality check
2. global village
3. shout-out
4. face time
5. it is what it is

6. bottom line
7. in the loop
8. over the top
9. win by a landslide
10. call the shots

35c IDIOMS AND COLLOCATIONS

Idioms are fixed expressions whose meanings cannot be entirely determined by knowing the meanings of their parts—examples are *bear in mind, fall in love,* and *stand a chance.* **Collocations** are combinations of words that frequently occur together. Unlike idioms, they have meanings that *can* be determined by knowing the meanings of their parts—think of *depend on, fond of, little while,* or *right now.* Regardless of whether you are using an idiom or a collocation, if you make even a small change to the expected wording, you may distract or confuse your readers.

She tried to keep a ~~small~~ profile.
                    low

They had ~~an invested~~ interest in the project.
         a vested

As you edit your writing, keep an eye out for idioms or collocations that might not be worded correctly. Then check a general dictionary, a dictionary of idioms (see page 671), or the **Glossary of Usage** at the end of this book to ensure that your usage is appropriate. Use idioms with care, though. If overused, they may be considered clichés.

Because prepositions are often small, unstressed words, writers sometimes confuse them. The following is a list of common collocations containing prepositions.

CHOOSING THE RIGHT PREPOSITION

according **to** the source	intend **to** finish his degree
accused **of** the crime	opposition **to** the idea
based **on** the novel	parallel **to** the road
bored **by** it	perspective **on** the topic
conform **to/with** standards	plan **to** attend
connected **to** each other	prior **to** the ruling
consists **of** cards and letters	relevant **to** the discussion
different **from** the first draft	substitute beans **for** meat
happened **by** accident	superior **to** others
in accordance **with** policy	sure **to** see the movie
independent **of** his family	try **to** be on time
insist **on** repayment	typical **of** that period

ⓝ MULTILINGUAL WRITERS

UNDERSTANDING AND USING IDIOMS

The context in which an idiom appears can often help you understand the meaning. For example, if you read "When they learned that she had accepted illegal campaign contributions, several political commentators raked her over the coals," you would probably understand that *to rake over the coals* means "to criticize severely." As you learn new idioms from your reading, make a list of those you might want to use in your own writing. If you are confused about the meaning of a particular idiom, check a dictionary of idioms (see page 671).

Exercise 4

Write a sentence using each idiom or collocation correctly.

1. pass muster, pass the time
2. do one's best, do one's part, do one's duty
3. in a pinch, in a rut, in a way
4. cut down, cut back, cut corners
5. make time, make sure, make sense

35d CLEAR DEFINITIONS

When words have more than one meaning, establish which meaning you have in mind. A definition can set the terms of the discussion.

> In this paper, I use the word *communism* **in the Marxist sense of social organization based on the holding of all property in common.**

A **formal definition** first states the term to be defined, then puts it into a class, and finally differentiates it from other members of that class.

A *phosphene* [term] is **a luminous visual image** [class] that **results from applying pressure to the eyeball** [differentiation].

A short dictionary definition may be adequate when you need to convey the meaning of a word unfamiliar to readers.

Here, *galvanic* means **"produced as if by electric shock."**

Giving a synonym may also clarify the meaning of a term. Such synonyms are often used as appositives (**22a(5)**).

Machismo, **confidence with an attitude,** can be a pose rather than a reality.

Writers frequently show—rather than tell—what a word means by giving examples.

Many homophones (**such as** *be* **and** *bee* **or** *see* **and** *sea*) **are not spelling problems.**

Sometimes, your own definition can clarify a concept.

Clichés could be defined as **thoughts that have hardened.**

When writing definitions, do not confuse readers by placing a predicate with a subject that is not logically connected to it (**28d(3)**). Constructions that combine *is* or *are* with *when,* *where,* or *because* are often illogical because forms of *be* signify identity or equality between the subject and what follows.

The Internet ^allows ~~is when~~ you ^to look at text and images from across the world.

Exercise 5

Using your own words, define each of the following terms in full sentences.

1. audacity
2. professionalism
3. dilemma
4. indifference
5. ambiguity
6. equal opportunity

36 ‖ CONCISENESS

To facilitate readers' understanding, effective writers convey their thoughts clearly and efficiently. Clear and effective sentences are not always short; rather, they are wisely constructed. This chapter will help you

- make each word count (**36a**) and
- use elliptical constructions (**36b**).

36a ‖ ELIMINATING REDUNDANCY AND WORDINESS

Throughout your writing process, review your sentences to make sure that they contain only the words necessary to make your point.

(1) Redundancy

Restating a key point in different words can help readers understand it. But if you rephrase readily understood terms, your work will suffer from **redundancy**—repetition for no good reason.

Ballerinas auditioned ~~in the tryouts~~ for *The Nutcracker*.

Each student had a unique talent_∧for ~~and ability that he or she used in his or her~~ acting.

You should also avoid grammatical redundancy, as in double subjects (*my sister* [*she*] *is*), double comparisons ([*more*] *easier than*), and double negatives (*could*[*n't*] *hardly*).

(2) Wordiness

As you edit a draft, look for ways to rewrite sentences in fewer words, without risking the loss of important details. One exact word often says as much as several inexact ones.

spoke in a low and hard-to-hear voice	**mumbled**
a person who gives expert advice	**consultant**

Some unscrupulous brokers are ~~taking money and savings from~~ _{cheating} elderly people ~~who need that money because they planned to use it as a retirement pension.~~ _{out of their pensions.}

_{if} ~~In the event that~~ taxes are raised, ~~expect complaints on the part of the voters.~~ _{voters will complain.}

REPLACEMENTS FOR WORDY EXPRESSIONS

Instead of	Use
at this moment (point) in time	now, today
due to the fact that	because
in view of the fact that	because
for the purpose of	for
it is clear (obvious) that	clearly (obviously)
there is no question that	unquestionably, certainly
without a doubt	undoubtedly
beyond the shadow of a doubt	certainly, surely
it is my opinion that	I think (believe) that
in this day and age	today
in the final analysis	finally

In addition, watch for vague words such as *area, aspect, factor, feature, kind, situation, thing,* and *type.* They may signal wordiness.

~~In an employment situation, effective~~ _{Effective} communication is essential at work.

WORDINESS IN COMMON PHRASES

yellow [in color]	circular [in shape]
at 9:45 a.m. [in the morning]	return [back]
[basic] essentials	rich [and wealthy] nations
bitter[-tasting] salad	small[-sized] potatoes
connect [up together]	[true] facts
because [of the fact that]	was [more or less] hinting
[really and truly] fearless	by [virtue of] his authority

(3) *There are* and *it is*

There or *it* may function as an **expletive**—a word that signals that the subject of the sentence will follow the verb, usually a form of *be* (**20b**). Writers use expletives to emphasize words that would not be emphasized in the typical subject-verb order. Notice the difference in rhythm between the following sentences:

Two children were playing in the yard. [typical order]

There were two children playing in the yard. [use of expletive]

However, expletives are easily overused. If you find that you have drafted several sentences that begin with expletives, revise a few of them.

> Hundreds   were
> ∧There were hundreds of fans∧crowding onto the field.

> Joining the crowd
> ∧It was frightening to join the crowd.

(4) Relative pronouns

The relative pronouns *who, which,* or *that* can frequently be deleted without affecting the meaning of a sentence. If one of these pronouns is followed by a form of the verb *be* (*am, is, are, was,* or *were*), you can often omit the pronoun and sometimes the verb as well.

The change that the young senator proposed yesterday angered most legislators.

The Endangered Species Act, which was passed in 1973, protects the habitat of endangered plants and animals.

When deleting a relative pronoun, you might have to make other changes to a sentence as well.

Nations _∧ *providing* ~~that provide~~ protection for endangered species often create preserves and forbid hunting of these species.

ñ **MULTILINGUAL WRITERS**

USING RELATIVE PRONOUNS

Review your sentences to make sure that no clause includes both a personal pronoun (**26a(1)**) and a relative pronoun (**26a(3)**) referring to the same antecedent (**26c**).

> The drug **that** we were testing ~~it~~ has not been approved by the Food and Drug Administration.

> The principal investigator, **whom** we depended on ~~her~~ for guidance, had to take a medical leave before the project was completed.

For more information on relative (adjectival) clauses, see chapter **48**.

36b USING ELLIPTICAL CONSTRUCTIONS

An **elliptical construction** is one that deliberately omits words that can be understood from the context.

> Speed is the goal for some swimmers, endurance ~~is the goal~~ for others, and relaxation ~~is the goal~~ for still others.

Sometimes, as an aid to clarity, commas mark omissions in elliptical constructions.

> My family functioned like a baseball team: my mom was the coach; my brother**,** the pitcher; and my sister**,** the shortstop. [Use semicolons to separate items with internal commas (**38a**).]

37 | THE COMMA

Punctuation lends to written language the same flexibility that facial expressions, pauses, and variations in voice pitch offer spoken language. The following sentences illustrate that flexibility:

When the recruiter called, Kenneth Martin answered.

When the recruiter called Kenneth, Martin answered.

When the first sentence is spoken, a pause after *called* makes it clear that the sentence refers to only two people: the recruiter and Kenneth Martin. In the second example, a pause after *Kenneth* lets the listener know that the sentence refers to three people: the recruiter, Kenneth, and Martin. In written text, the same intended meanings can be established by commas.

Pauses and commas are not always paired, however. Pauses are not a reliable guide for comma placement: commas are often called for where speakers do not pause, and pauses can occur where no comma is necessary. Thus, it is important to understand the basic principles of comma usage. This chapter will help you use commas to

- separate independent clauses joined by coordinating conjunctions (**37a**),
- set off introductory clauses and phrases (**37b**),
- separate items in a series (**37c**),
- set off nonessential (nonrestrictive) elements (**37d**),
- set off geographical names and items in dates and addresses (**37e**), and
- set off direct quotations (**37f**),

as well as help you to

- recognize unnecessary or misplaced commas (**37g**).

37a	BEFORE A COORDINATING CONJUNCTION LINKING INDEPENDENT CLAUSES

Use a comma before a coordinating conjunction (*and, but, for, nor, or, so,* or *yet*) that links two independent clauses. (Some people use *fanboys,* a made-up word formed of the first letters of the coordinating conjunctions, as an aid to remembering them; see **21a(7)**.) An **independent clause** is a group of words that can stand as a sentence (**22b(1)**).

INDEPENDENT CLAUSE**,** COORDINATING CONJUNCTION INDEPENDENT CLAUSE.

	and	
	but	
	for	
Subject + predicate,	**nor**	subject + predicate.
	or	
	so	
	yet	

The Iditarod Trail Sled Dog Race begins in March**,** **but** training starts much sooner.

In the 1960s, Dorothy Page wanted to spark interest in the role of dog sledding in Alaskan history**,** **so** she proposed staging a long race.

No matter how many clauses are in a sentence, a comma comes before each coordinating conjunction.

The race takes several days to complete**,** **and** training is a year-round activity**,** **but** the mushers do not complain.

When the independent clauses are short, the comma is often omitted before *and, but,* or *or.*

My friend races **but** I don't.

If a coordinating conjunction joins two parts of a compound predicate (which means there is only one subject), a comma is not normally used before the conjunction. (See **21b** and **37g(3)**.)

The race starts in Anchorage₆and ends in Nome.

A semicolon, instead of a comma, precedes a conjunction joining two independent clauses when at least one of the clauses already contains a comma. (See also **38a**.)

When running long distances, sled dogs burn more than ten thousand calories a day⨾ **so** they must be fed well.

Exercise 1

Insert commas where needed.

1. When people get goose bumps, they may be reacting to a sudden drop in the temperature or they may be responding to a strong emotion.
2. In general, people notice goose bumps on their forearms but some people also report having goose bumps on their legs.
3. When a goose is plucked, its flesh protrudes and these protrusions are what goose bumps supposedly resemble but the technical term for goose bumps is *piloerection*.
4. The German and Italian languages also have words that refer to goose flesh but French and Spanish translations refer to hens.
5. Many people report that they get goose bumps when they hear about heroic behavior yet is not uncommon for people to have a similar response to beauty in art or nature.

37b | AFTER INTRODUCTORY CLAUSES, PHRASES, OR WORDS

(1) Following an introductory dependent clause

If you begin a sentence with a dependent (subordinate) clause (**22b(2)**), place a comma after it to set it off from the independent (main) clause (**22b(1)**).

> INTRODUCTORY CLAUSE, INDEPENDENT CLAUSE.

Although the safest automobile on the road is expensive, the protection it offers justifies the cost.

(2) Following an introductory phrase

Place a comma after an introductory phrase to set it off from the independent clause.

> INTRODUCTORY PHRASE, INDEPENDENT CLAUSE.

(a) Introductory prepositional phrases

Despite a downturn in the national economy, the number of students enrolled in this university has increased.

If you begin a sentence with a short introductory prepositional phrase (**22a(4)**), you may omit the comma as long as the resulting sentence is not difficult to read.

In 2015 the enrollment at the university increased.

BUT

In 2015, 625 new students enrolled in courses.
[A comma separates two numbers.]

A comma is not used after a prepositional phrase that begins a sentence in which the subject and predicate (**21b**) are inverted.

With children came responsibilities.
[The subject of the sentence is *responsibilities*: Responsibilities came with children.]

(b) Other types of introductory phrases

If you begin a sentence with a participial phrase (**22a(3)**) or an absolute phrase (**22a(6)**), place a comma after the phrase.

Having never left home, she imagined the outside world to be fantastic, almost magical. [participial phrase]

The language difference aside, life in Germany did not seem much different from life in the United States. [absolute phrase]

(3) Following an introductory word

INTRODUCTORY WORD, INDEPENDENT CLAUSE.

Use a comma to set off an interjection, a **vocative** (a word used to address someone directly), or a transitional word that begins a sentence.

Yikes, I forgot to pick him up from the airport. [interjection]

Bob, I want you to know how very sorry I am. [vocative]

Moreover, I insist on paying for your taxi. [transitional word]

When there is no risk of misunderstanding, some introductory adverbs and transitional words do not need to be set off by a comma (see also **38a(1)**).

Sometimes even a good design is rejected by the board.

Exercise 2

Insert commas where necessary in the following paragraph. Explain why each comma is needed. Some sentences may not require editing.

¹If you had to describe sound would you call it a wave? ²Although sound cannot be seen people have described it this way for a long time. ³In fact the Greek philosopher Aristotle believed that sound traveling through air was like waves in the sea. ⁴Envisioning waves in the air he hypothesized that sound would not be able to pass through a vacuum because there would

(continued on page 696)

(continued from page 695)

be no air to transmit it. [5]Aristotle's hypothesis was not tested until nearly two thousand years later. [6]In 1654 Otto von Guericke found that he could not hear a bell ringing inside the vacuum he had created. [7]Thus Guericke established the necessity of air for sound transmission. [8]However although most sound reaches us through the air it travels faster through liquids and solids.

| **37c** | SEPARATING ELEMENTS IN A SERIES OR COORDINATE ADJECTIVES |

A **series** contains three or more parallel elements. To be parallel, elements must be grammatically equal; all of them must be words, phrases, or clauses. (See chapter 31.)

(1) Words, phrases, or clauses in a series

A comma appears after each item in a series except the last one.

Ethics are based on **moral, social,** or **cultural values.** [words in a series]

The company's code of ethics encourages **seeking criticism of work, correcting mistakes,** and **acknowledging the contributions of everyone.** [phrases in a series]

Several circumstances can lead to unethical behavior: **people are tempted by a desire to succeed, they are pressured by others into acting inappropriately,** or **they are simply trying to survive.** [clauses in a series]

If elements in a series contain internal commas, you can prevent misreading by separating the items with semicolons.

According to their code of ethics, researchers must disclose all results, without omitting any data; indicate various interpretations of the data; and make the data and methodology available to other researchers, some of whom may choose to replicate the study.

❓ THINKING RHETORICALLY

SERIES COMMAS VERSUS CONJUNCTIONS

How do the following sentences differ?

We discussed them all: life, liberty, **and** the pursuit of happiness.

We discussed them all: life **and** liberty **and** the pursuit of happiness.

We discussed them all: life, liberty, the pursuit of happiness.

The first sentence follows conventional guidelines; that is, a comma and a conjunction precede the last element in the series. The less conventional second and third sentences do more than convey information. With two conjunctions and no commas, the second sentence slows down the pace of the reading, causing stress to be placed on each of the three elements in the series. In contrast, the third sentence, with commas but no conjunctions, speeds up the reading, as if to suggest that the rights listed do not need to be stressed because they are so familiar. To get a sense of how your sentences will be read and understood, try reading them aloud.

(2) Coordinate adjectives

Two or more adjectives that precede the same noun are called **coordinate adjectives**. To test whether adjectives are coordinate, either interchange them or put *and* between them. If the altered version of the adjectives-and-noun combination is acceptable, the adjectives are coordinate and should be separated by a comma or commas.

Crossing the **rushing, shallow** creek, I slipped off a rock and fell into the water.
[COMPARE: a rushing and shallow creek OR a shallow, rushing creek]

The adjectives in the following sentence are not separated by a comma. Notice that they cannot be interchanged or joined by *and*.

Sitting in the water, I saw an **old wooden** bridge.
[NOT a wooden old bridge OR an old and wooden bridge]

37d WITH NONESSENTIAL ELEMENTS

Nonessential (nonrestrictive) elements provide supplemental information, that is, information a reader does not need in order to identify who or what is being discussed (see also **22b(2)**). Use commas to set off a nonessential word or word group: one comma precedes a nonessential element at the end of a sentence; two commas set off a nonessential element in the middle of a sentence.

> The Annual Hilltop Folk Festival**,** **planned for late July,** should attract many tourists.

In the preceding sentence, the phrase placed between commas, *planned for late July,* conveys nonessential information: the reader knows which festival will attract tourists without being told when it will be held. When a phrase follows a proper noun (**21a(2)**), such as *The Annual Hilltop Folk Festival,* it is usually nonessential. Note, however, that in the following sentence, the phrase *planned for late July* is necessary for the reader to identify the festival as the one scheduled to occur in late July, not another time:

> The festival **planned for late July** should attract many tourists.

In the preceding sentence, the phrase is an **essential (restrictive) element** because without it, the reader will not know which festival the writer has in mind. Essential elements are not set off by commas; they are integrated into sentences (**22b(2)**).

(1) Setting off nonessential elements used as modifiers

(a) Adjectival clauses

Nonessential modifiers are often **adjectival (relative) clauses,** which are usually introduced by a relative pronoun, *who, which,* or *that* (**22b(2)**). In the following sentence, a comma sets off the adjectival clause because the reader does not need the content of that clause in order to identify the mountain:

> We climbed Denali**,** **which is over 15,000 feet high.**

(b) Participial phrases

Nonessential modifiers also include **participial phrases** (phrases that begin with a present or past participle of a verb) **(22a(3))**.

Denali, **towering above us,** brought to mind our abandoned plan for climbing it. [participial phrase beginning with a present participle]

My sister, **slowed by a knee injury,** rarely hikes anymore. [participial phrase beginning with a past participle]

(c) Adverbial clauses

An **adverbial clause (22b(2))** begins with a subordinating conjunction that signals cause (*because*), purpose (*so that*), or time (*when, after, before*). This type of clause is usually considered essential and thus is not set off by a comma when it appears at the end of a sentence.

Dinosaurs may have become extinct **because their habitat was destroyed.**

In contrast, an adverbial clause that provides nonessential information, such as an aside or a comment, should be set off from the main clause.

Dinosaurs are extinct, **though they are alive in many people's imaginations.**

(2) Setting off nonessential appositives

Appositives refer to the same person, place, object, idea, or event as a nearby noun or noun phrase but in different words **(22a(5))**. Nonessential appositives provide extra details about nouns or noun phrases **(22a(1))** and are set off by commas; essential appositives are not. In the following sentence, the title of the article is mentioned, so the reader does not need the information provided by the appositive in order to identify the article. The appositive is thus set off by commas.

"Living on the Line," **Joanne Hart's most recent article,** describes the lives of factory workers in China.

In the next sentence, *Joanne Hart's article* is nonspecific, so an essential appositive containing the specific title of the article is integrated into the sentence. It is not set off by commas. Without the appositive, the reader would not know which of Hart's articles describes the lives of factory workers in China.

> Joanne Hart's article "Living on the Line" describes the lives of factory workers in China.

If Hart had written only this one article, the title would be set off by commas. The reader would not need the information in the appositive to identify the article.

Abbreviations of titles or degrees after names are treated as nonessential appositives.

> Was the letter from Frances Evans**,** PhD**,** or from Francis Evans**,** MD?

Increasingly, however, *Jr., Sr., II,* and *III* are considered part of a name, and the comma is thus often omitted.

> William Homer Barton**,** Jr.   OR   William Homer Barton Jr.

(3) Setting off absolute phrases

An **absolute phrase** (the combination of a noun and a modifying word or phrase; see **22a(6)**) provides nonessential details and so should always be set off by a comma or commas.

> The actor**,** **his hair wet and slicked back,** began his audition.

> The director stared at him**,** **her mind flipping through the photographs she had viewed earlier.**

(4) Setting off transitional expressions and other parenthetical elements

Commas customarily set off transitional words and phrases such as *for example, that is,* and *namely.*

> An airline ticket**,** **for example,** can be delivered electronically.

Some transitional words and short phrases such as *also, too, at least,* and *thus* need not be set off by commas.

> Traveling has **thus** become easier in recent years.

Use commas to set off other parenthetical elements, such as words or phrases that provide commentary you wish to stress.

Over the past year, my flights have**,** **miraculously,** been on time.

(5) Setting off contrasted elements

Commas set off sentence elements in which words such as *never* and *unlike* express contrast.

A planet**,** **unlike** a star**,** reflects rather than generates light.

In sentences in which contrasted elements are introduced by *not only . . . but also,* place a comma before *but* if you want to emphasize what follows it. Otherwise, leave the comma out.

Planets **not only** vary in size**,** **but also** travel at different speeds. [Comma added for emphasis.]

Exercise 3

Set off nonessential elements with commas.

1. Maine Coons long-haired cats with bushy tails are known for their size.
2. The largest cat on record for example was forty-eight inches long.
3. These animals which are extremely gentle despite their large size often weigh twenty pounds.
4. Most Maine Coons have exceptionally high intelligence for cats which enables them to recognize language and even to open doors.
5. Unlike most cats Maine Coons will play fetch with their owners.
6. According to a legend later proven to be false Maine Coons are descendants from Turkish Angora cats owned by Marie Antoinette.

37e | WITH GEOGRAPHICAL NAMES AND ITEMS IN DATES AND ADDRESSES

Use commas to make geographical names, dates, and addresses easy to read.

(1) City and state

Nashville, Tennessee, is the capital of country-and-western music in the United States.

(2) Day and date

Martha left for Peru on **Wednesday, February 12, 2015,** and returned on March 12.

OR

Martha left for Peru on **Wednesday, 12 February 2015,** and returned on 12 March.

In the style used in the second sentence (which is not as common in the United States as the style in the first example), one comma is omitted because *12* precedes *February* and is thus clearly separate from *2015*.

(3) Addresses

In a sentence containing an address, the name of the person or organization, the street address, and the name of the town or city are all followed by commas, but the abbreviation for the state is not.

I had to write to **Ms. Melanie Hobson, Senior Analyst, Hobson Computing, 2873 Central Avenue, Orange Park, FL 32065.**

37f | WITH DIRECT QUOTATIONS

Many sentences containing direct quotations also contain attributive tags such as *The author claims* or *According to the author* (11c). Use commas to set off these attributive tags whether they occur at the beginning, in the middle, or at the end of a sentence.

(1) Attributive tag at the beginning of a sentence

Place the comma directly after the attributive tag, before the quotation marks.

> As Jacques Barzun claims**,** "It is a false analogy with science that makes one think latest is best."

(2) Attributive tag in the middle of a sentence

Place the first comma inside the quotation marks that precede the attributive tag; place the second comma directly after the attributive tag, before the next set of quotation marks.

> "It is a false analogy with science**,**" claims Jacques Barzun**,** "that makes one think latest is best."

(3) Attributive tag at the end of a sentence

Place the comma inside the quotation marks before the attributive tag.

> "It is a false analogy with science that makes one think latest is best**,**" claims Jacques Barzun.

37g UNNECESSARY OR MISPLACED COMMAS

Although a comma may signal a pause, not every pause calls for a comma. As you read the following sentence aloud, you may pause naturally at several places, but no commas are necessary.

> Heroic deeds done by ordinary people inspire others to act in ways that are not only moral but courageous.

(1) No comma between a subject and its verb or a verb and its object

Although speakers often pause after the subject (**21b**) or before the object (**21c**) of a sentence, such a pause should not be indicated by a comma.

> In this climate, rain at frequent intervals⌒produces mosquitoes.
> [no separation between the subject (*rain*) and the verb (*produces*)]

The forecaster said˅that rain was likely. [no separation between the verb (*said*) and the direct object (the noun clause *that rain was likely*)]

(2) No comma following a coordinating conjunction

Avoid using a comma after a coordinating conjunction (*and, but, for, nor, or, so,* or *yet*).

We worked very hard on her campaign for state representative **,** but˅ the incumbent was too strong to defeat in the northern districts.

(3) No comma separating elements in a compound predicate

In general, avoid using a comma between two elements of a compound predicate (**21b**).

I read the comments carefully˅and then started my revision.

However, if you want to place stress on the second element in a compound predicate, you may place a comma after the first element. Use this option sparingly, or it will lose its effect.

I read the comments word by word**,** and despaired.

(4) No comma setting off essential words, phrases, and clauses

In the following sentences, the elements in boldface are essential and so should not be set off by commas (**37d**).

Zoe was born˅**in Chicago during the Great Depression.**

Perhaps˅the thermostat is broken.

Everyone˅**who has a mortgage**˅is required to have fire insurance.

Someone˅**wearing an orange wig**˅greeted us at the door.

(5) No comma preceding the first item of a series or following the last

Make sure that you place commas only between elements in a series, not before or after the series.

She was known for⌣her photographs, sketches, and engravings.

The exhibit included her most exuberant, exciting, and expensive⌣ photographs.

Exercise 4

Explain the use of each comma in the following paragraph.

[1]There is some evidence that musical training may enhance performance on some tests of mental abilities, but the effects are not great. [2]To some extent, this is another chicken-and-egg problem. [3]Does musical training enhance performance on the tests, or do children who take musical training exhibit enhanced performance on tests because of their particular interests and abilities? [4]But early musical training perhaps increases the possibility the child will have perfect pitch, as we noted, presumably enhancing later musical capabilities. [5]Actually, one recent and carefully done study found a greater increase in the IQ scores of children after taking music lessons than after taking drama or no lessons.

—**Richard F. Thompson and Stephen A. Madigan**
Memory: The Key to Consciousness

38 ‖ THE SEMICOLON AND THE COLON

Although semicolons and colons can both link independent clauses, the use of these punctuation marks in this way is determined by the purpose of the second clause and the relation between the two clauses. In addition, semicolons and colons each have unique uses. This chapter will help you

- use semicolons correctly (**38a**) and
- use colons correctly (**38b**).

38a ‖ THE SEMICOLON

The semicolon indicates that the phrases or clauses on either side of it are closely related. It most frequently connects two independent clauses when the second clause supports or contrasts with the first, but it can be used for other purposes as well.

(1) Connecting independent clauses

A semicolon placed between two independent clauses indicates that they are closely related. The second of the two clauses generally supports or contrasts with the first.

> For many cooks, basil is a key ingredient; it appears in recipes worldwide. [support]

> Sweet basil is used in many Mediterranean dishes; Thai basil is used in Asian and East Indian recipes. [contrast]

Although *and, but*, and similar words can signal these kinds of relationships, consider using an occasional semicolon for variety.

Sometimes, a transitional expression such as *for example* or *however* (24c(5)) accompanies a semicolon and further establishes the exact relationship between the ideas in the linked clauses.

Basil is omnipresent in the cuisine of some countries; **for example,** Italians use basil in salads, soups, and many vegetable dishes.

The culinary uses of basil are well known; **however,** this herb also has medicinal uses.

A comma is usually inserted after a transitional word, but it can be omitted if doing so will not lead to a misreading.

Because *basil* comes from a Greek word meaning "king," it suggests royalty; **indeed** some cooks accord basil royal status among herbs.

(2) Separating elements that contain commas

In a series of phrases or clauses (chapter 22) that contain commas, semicolons indicate where each phrase or clause ends and the next begins. In the following sentence, the semicolons help the reader distinguish three separate phrases.

To survive, mountain lions need a large area in which to range; a steady supply of deer, skunks, raccoons, foxes, and opossums; and the opportunity to find a mate, establish a den, and raise a litter.

Exercise 1

Revise the following sentences, using semicolons to separate independent clauses or elements that contain internal commas.

1. Soccer is a game played by two teams on a rectangular field, each team tries to knock a ball, roughly twenty-eight inches in circumference, through the opponent's goal.
2. The game is called *soccer* only in Canada and the United States, elsewhere it is known as *football*.

(*continued on page 708*)

(*continued from page 707*)

3. Generally, a team consists of eleven players: fullbacks, who defend the goal by trying to win control of the ball, halfbacks, who play both defense and offense, forwards, whose primary responsibility is scoring goals; and a goalie, who guards the goal.

4. In amateur matches, players can be substituted frequently, however, in professional matches, the number of substitutions is limited.

5. Soccer players depend on five skills: kicking, which entails striking the ball powerfully with the top of the foot, dribbling, which requires tapping or rolling the ball while running, passing, which is similar to kicking but with more control, heading, which involves striking the ball with the forehead, and trapping, which is the momentary stopping of the ball.

(3) Revising common semicolon errors

Semicolons do not set off phrases (**22a**) or dependent clauses (**22b(2)**) unless those elements contain commas. Use commas to set off a phrase or a dependent clause.

We consulted Alinka Kibukian; ⌃ the local horticulturalist.

Needing summer shade; ⌃ we planted two of the largest trees we could afford.

We learned that young trees need care; ⌃ which meant we had to do some extra chores after dinner each night.

Our trees have survived; ⌃ even though we live in a harsh climate.

Exercise 2

Use a comma to replace any semicolon that sets off a phrase or a dependent clause in the following sentences. Do not change properly used semicolons.

1. The vice president of the United States walks along the fenced-in crowd; regularly stopping to shake a hand, pose for the camera, or hold a baby; a man who has held elected office for over forty years, he relishes being in the public eye.

2. He has gone into the Grange Hall, where he sits with a group of family farmers; peppering them with questions about the future of the farm, whether the corporate farm, the family farm, or some combination of the two bodes best for our nation's future; he leaves the hall, thanks his hosts, and makes his way to his next commitment.

38b THE COLON

A colon calls attention to what follows, whether the grammatical unit is a clause, a phrase, or words in a series. It also separates numbers in parts of scriptural references and titles from subtitles. Leave only one space after a colon.

(1) Directing attention to an explanation, a summary, or a quotation

When a colon appears between two independent clauses, it signals that the second clause will explain or expand on the first.

> No one expected the game to end as it did: after seven extra innings, the favored team collapsed.

A colon is also used after an independent clause to introduce a direct quotation.

The Dalai Lama explained the importance of forgiveness: "When other beings, especially those who hold a grudge against you, abuse and harm you out of envy, you should not abandon them, but hold them as objects of your greatest compassion and take care of them."

❶ CAUTION

The rules for using an uppercase or a lowercase letter to begin the first word of an independent clause that follows a colon vary across style manuals.

MLA	The first letter should be lowercase unless (1) it begins a word that is normally capitalized, (2) the independent clause is a quotation, or (3) the clause expresses a rule or principle.
APA	The first letter should be uppercase.
CMS	The first letter should be lowercase unless (1) it begins a word that is normally capitalized, (2) the independent clause is a quotation or a direct question, or (3) two or more sentences follow the colon.

A colon at the end of an independent clause is sometimes followed by a phrase rather than another clause. This use of the colon puts emphasis on the phrase.

I was finally confronted with what I had dreaded for months: the due date for the final balloon payment on my car loan.

All the style manuals advise using a lowercase letter to begin a phrase following a colon.

(2) Signaling that a list follows

Writers frequently use colons to introduce lists (which add to or clarify the information preceding the colon).

Three students received internships: Asa, Vanna, and Jack.

Avoid placing a colon between a verb and its complement (**21c**) or after the words *including* and *such as*.

The winners were꞉Asa, Vanna, and Jack.

Vegans do not eat dairy products such as꞉butter and cheese.

(3) Separating a title and a subtitle

Use a colon between a work's title and its subtitle.

Collapse꞉ How Societies Choose to Fail or Succeed

(4) In reference numbers

Colons are often used between numbers in scriptural references.

Ps. 3꞉5   Gen. 1꞉1

However, MLA prefers periods instead of colons in such references.

Ps. 3.5   Gen. 1.1

MLA does use colons to separate units of time in in-text citations for time-based media.

("Scarecrow" 00꞉33꞉22-24)

(5) Specialized uses in business correspondence

A colon follows the salutation of a business letter and any notations.

Dear Dr. Hodges꞉   Dear Imogen꞉   Encl꞉

A colon introduces the headings in a memo.

To꞉   From꞉   Subject꞉   Date꞉

Exercise 3

Insert colons where they are needed in the following sentences.

1. Before we discuss marketing, we need to outline the behavior of consumers consumer behavior is the process individuals go through as they select, buy, or use products or services to satisfy their needs and desires.

2. The process consists of six stages recognizing a need or desire, finding information, evaluating options, deciding to purchase, purchasing, and assessing purchases.

3. Many consumers rely on one popular publication for product information *Consumer Reports*.

4. When evaluating alternatives, a consumer uses criteria; for example, a house hunter might use some of the following price, location, size, age, style, and landscaping design.

5. The post-purchase assessment has one of two results satisfaction or dissatisfaction with the product or service.

39 | THE APOSTROPHE

Apostrophes serve a number of purposes. You can use them to show that someone owns something *(my neighbor's television),* that someone has a specific relationship with someone else *(my neighbor's children),* or that someone has produced or created something *(my neighbor's recipe).* Apostrophes are also used in contractions *(can't, don't)* and in a few plural forms *(x's and y's).* This chapter will help you use apostrophes to

- indicate ownership and other relationships (**39a**),
- mark omissions of letters or numbers (**39b**), and
- form certain plurals (**39c**).

39a | INDICATING OWNERSHIP AND OTHER RELATIONSHIPS

An apostrophe, often followed by an *s,* signals the possessive case of nouns. (For information on case, see **26a(1)** and **26b**.) Possessive nouns are used to express a variety of meanings.

Ownership	**Dyson's** sermon, the **minister's** robe
Origin	**Leakey's** research findings, the **guide's** decision
Human relationships	**Helen's** sister, the **teacher's** students
Possession of physical or psychological traits	**Mona Lisa's** smile, the **team's** spirit
Association between abstractions and attributes	**democracy's** struggles, **tyranny's** influence
Identification of documents and credentials	**driver's** license, **bachelor's** degree
Identification of things named after people	**St. John's** Cathedral, **Rubik's** Cube

Specification of amounts	a **day's** wages, an **hour's** delay
Holidays	Mother's/Father's Day, New Year's Day, Presidents' Day [BUT Veterans Day]

ⓝ MULTILINGUAL WRITERS

WORD WITH APOSTROPHE AND S VERSUS PHRASE BEGINNING WITH OF

In many cases, to indicate ownership, origin, and other meanings discussed in this chapter, you can use either a word with an apostrophe and an *s* or a prepositional phrase beginning with *of*.

Louise Erdrich's novels   OR   the novels **of** Louise Erdrich

the plane's arrival   OR   the arrival **of** the plane

However, the ending -'*s* is more commonly used with nouns referring to people, and a phrase beginning with *of* is used with most nouns referring to location.

my **uncle's** workshop, **Edward's** truck, the **student's** paper [nouns referring to people]

the **end of** the movie, the **middle of** the day, the **front of** the building [nouns referring to location]

(1) Forming the possessive of singular nouns, indefinite pronouns, acronyms, and abbreviations

Add -'*s* to form the possessive case of most singular nouns, indefinite pronouns, acronyms (words formed by letters or initial word parts of phrases), and abbreviations.

the instructor's office [noun]   Dickinson's poems [noun]

someone's billfold [indefinite pronoun]

sonar's strength [an acronym of *sound, navigation, ranging*]
FAQ's usefulness [an acronym for *frequently asked question*]

Luther Liggett Jr.'s letter [Notice that no comma precedes the abbreviation *Jr.* here, although *Jr.* is sometimes set off by a comma (**37d(2)**).]

To form the possessive of most singular proper nouns, add an apostrophe and an *s: Iowa's governor.* When a singular proper noun ends in *-s*, though, you will have to consult the style guide for the discipline in which you are writing. Some style guides recommend always using *-'s*, as in *Illinois's legislature, Dickens's novels, Ms. Jones's address,* and *Descartes's reasoning.* The *Chicago Manual of Style,* however, notes some exceptions to this rule. An apostrophe without an *s* is appropriate when a singular common noun ends in *-s (physics' contribution)* and when the name of a place or an organization ends in *-s* but refers to a single entity *(United States' foreign aid).*

Possessive pronouns *(my, mine, our, ours, your, yours, his, her, hers, its, their, theirs,* and *whose)* are not written with apostrophes (**26b(3)**).

South Africa's democracy differs from **ours.**

The committee concluded **its** discussion.

---

❶ CAUTION

Be careful not to confuse possessive pronouns with contractions. Confusing *its* and *it's* is a very common mistake. Keep in mind that whenever you write a contraction, you should be able to substitute the complete words for it without changing the meaning.

Possessive pronoun	Contraction
Its motor is small.	**It's** [It is] a small motor.
Whose turn is it?	**Who's** [Who is] representing us?

Its is the possessive form of *it. It's* is a contraction for *it is* or *it has.*

---

(2) Forming the possessive of plural nouns ending in -s

Plural nouns ending in *-s* require only an apostrophe to form the possessive.

the boys' game   the babies' toys   the Joneses' house

Plural nouns that do not end in *-s* need both an apostrophe and an *s.*

men's lives   women's health   children's projects

---

❶ CAUTION

An apostrophe is not needed to make a noun plural. To make most nouns plural, add *-s* or *-es*. Add an apostrophe only to signal ownership, origin, and other similar relationships.

> protesters
> The ∧ ~~protesters~~' swarmed the conference center.

> The protesters' gathering was on Wednesday.

Likewise, to form the plural of a family name, use *-s* or *-es,* not an apostrophe.

> Johnsons
> The ∧ ~~Johnson's~~ participated in the study.

> [COMPARE: The Johnsons' participation in the study was crucial.]

> Jameses
> The ∧ ~~James's~~ live in the yellow house on the corner.

> [COMPARE: The Jameses' house is the yellow one on the corner.]

---

(3) Showing collaboration or joint ownership

In the first example below, the ending -'s has been added to the second singular noun (*plumber*). In the second example, just an apostrophe has been added to the second plural noun (*Lopezes*), which already ends in *s.*

the carpenter and the **plumber's** decision [They made the decision collaboratively.]

the Becks and the **Lopezes'** cabin [They own one cabin jointly.]

(4) Showing separate ownership or individual contributions

In the examples below, the possessive form of each plural noun ends with an apostrophe, and that of each singular noun has the ending -'s.

the **Becks'** and the **Lopezes'** cars [Each family owns a car.]

the **carpenter's** and the **plumber's** proposals [They each made a proposal.]

(5) Forming the possessive of a compound noun

Add -'s to the last word of a compound noun.

> my brother-in-**law's** friends, the attorney **general's** statements [singular]
>
> my brothers-in-**law's** friends, the attorneys **general's** statements [plural]

To avoid awkward constructions such as the last two, consider using a prepositional phrase beginning with *of* instead: *a friend of my brothers-in-law* and *the statements of the attorneys general*.

(6) Forming the possessive of a noun preceding a gerund

Depending on its number, a noun that precedes a gerund takes either -'s or just an apostrophe.

> Lucy**'s having** to be there seemed unnecessary. [singular noun preceding a gerund]
>
> The family appreciated the lawyers' **handling** of the matter. [plural noun preceding a gerund]

ñ MULTILINGUAL WRITERS

GERUND PHRASES

When a gerund appears after a possessive noun, the noun is the subject of the gerund phrase.

> **Lucy's having to be there** [COMPARE: **Lucy** has to be there.]
>
> **The lawyers' handling of the matter** [COMPARE: **The lawyers** handled the matter.]

A gerund phrase may serve as the subject or the object in a sentence (**22a(3)**).

> s
>
> **Lucy's having to be there** seemed unnecessary.
>
> obj
>
> The family appreciated **the lawyers' handling of the matter.**

Sometimes you may find it difficult to distinguish between a gerund and a present participle (**22a(3)**). A good way to tell the difference is to note whether the emphasis is on an action or on a person. In a sentence containing a gerund, the emphasis is on the action; in a sentence containing a participle, the emphasis is on the person.

Our successful completion of the project depends on **Terry's providing** the illustrations. [gerund; the emphasis is on the action, *providing*]

I remember **my brother telling** me the same joke last year. [participle; the emphasis is on the person, *my brother*]

(7) Naming products and geographical locations

Follow an organization's preference for the use of an apostrophe in its name or the name of a product (figure 39.1). Follow local conventions for an apostrophe in the name of a geographical location.

Consumers Union   Actors' Equity   Shoppers Choice   Taster's Choice

Devil's Island   Devils Tower   Devils Mountain

Figure 39.1: Whether an apostrophe is used in a brand name is determined by the organization that owns that name.

Exercise 1

Following the pattern of the examples, change the modifier after each noun to a possessive form that precedes the noun.

EXAMPLES

proposals made by the committee   *the committee's proposals*

poems written by Keats   *Keats's poems*

1. the day named after St. Patrick
2. a leave of absence lasting six months
3. the position taken by HMOs
4. the report given by the eyewitness
5. the generosity of the Lees
6. a new book coauthored by Pat and Alan
7. the weights of the children
8. the spying done by the neighbors
9. the restaurants in Santa Fe
10. coffee roasted by Peet

39b   MARKING OMISSIONS OF LETTERS OR NUMBERS

Apostrophes signal contractions and other omissions in numbers and in words representing speech.

they're [they are]   class of '15 [class of 2015]

y'all [you all]   singin' [singing]

Contractions are not always appropriate for formal contexts. Your audience may expect you to use full words instead (for example, *cannot* instead of *can't* and *will not* instead of *won't*).

39c FORMING CERTAIN PLURALS

In the past, an apostrophe and an *s* were used to form the plural of a number, an abbreviation, or a word referred to as a term. Today, the apostrophe is rarely used in plural forms except for those of abbreviations that take periods or that contain lowercase letters or symbols.

The following plurals are generally formed by simply adding an *s:*

| 1990s | fours and fives | YWCAs | two *and*s | the three Rs |

A few plural forms still include an apostrophe:

| D.D.S.'s | *x*'s and *y*'s | +'s and −'s |

Exercise 2

Insert apostrophes where needed in the following sentences. Be prepared to explain why they are necessary.

1. Whos in charge here?
2. Hansons book was published in the early 1920s.
3. They hired a rock n roll band for their engagement party.
4. NPRs fund drive begins this weekend.
5. Youll have to include the ISBNs of the books youre going to purchase.
6. Only three of the proposals are still being considered: yours, ours, and the Wilbers.
7. Its always a big deal when your children leave for college.
8. Not enough students enrolled in the summer 15 course.
9. The students formed groups of twos and threes.
10. Laquisha earned two As and two Bs this semester.

40 ‖ QUOTATION MARKS

Quotation marks enclose sentences or parts of sentences that play a special role. They can indicate that the words between them were first written or spoken by someone else or that they are being used in an unconventional way. This chapter will help you use quotation marks

- with direct quotations (**40a**),
- with titles of short works (**40b**),
- to indicate that words or phrases are used ironically or unconventionally (**40c**), and
- in combination with other punctuation marks (**40d**).

40a ‖ DIRECT QUOTATIONS

Double quotation marks set off direct quotations, including those in dialogue. Single quotation marks set off a quotation within a quotation.

(1) Double quotation marks with direct quotations

Quotation marks enclose only a direct quotation, not any accompanying attributive tag such as *she said* or *he replied*. When a sentence ends with quoted material, place the period inside the quotation marks. For guidelines on comma placement, see **40d(1)**.

> "I believe that we learn by practice," writes Martha Graham in "An Athlete of God." "Whether it means to learn to dance by practicing dancing or to learn to live by practicing living, the principles are the same."

When using direct quotations, reproduce all quoted material exactly as it appears in the original, including capitalization and punctuation. To learn how to set off long quotations as indented blocks, see **13a(2)**.

(2) No quotation marks for indirect quotations or paraphrases

Indirect quotations and paraphrases (**11e**) are restatements of what someone else has said or written.

> Martha Graham believes that practice is necessary for learning, regardless of what we are trying to learn.

(3) Single quotation marks for quotations within quotations

If the quotation you are using includes another direct quotation, use single quotation marks with the embedded quotation.

> According to Anita Erickson, "when the narrator says, 'I have the right to my own opinion,' he means that he has the right to his own delusion."

However, if an embedded quotation appears within a block quotation, it should be enclosed in double quotation marks. (Keep in mind that double quotation marks are not used at the beginning or the end of a block quotation.)

Anita Erickson claims that the narrator uses the word *opinion* deceptively.

> Later in the chapter, when the narrator says, "I have the right to my own opinion," he means that he has the right to his own delusion. Although it is tempting to believe that the narrator is making decisions based on a rational belief system, his behavior suggests that he is more interested in deception. With poisonous lies, he has already deceived his business partner, his wife, and his children.

(4) Dialogue in quotation marks

When creating or reporting a dialogue, enclose in quotation marks what each person says, no matter how short. Use a separate paragraph for each speaker, beginning a new paragraph whenever the speaker changes. Narrative details can be included in the same paragraph as a direct quotation.

> Farmer looked up, smiling, and in a chirpy-sounding voice he said, "But that feeling has the disadvantage of being . . . " He paused a beat. "Wrong."
>
> "Well," I retorted, "it depends on how you look at it."
>
> —**TRACY KIDDER,** *Mountains Beyond Mountains*

When quoting more than one paragraph by a single speaker, put quotation marks at the beginning of each paragraph. However, do not place closing quotation marks at the end of each paragraph—only at the end of the last paragraph.

(5) Thoughts in quotation marks

Quotation marks set off thoughts that resemble speech.

"He's already sulking about the outcome of the vote," I thought, as I watched the committee chair work through the agenda.

Thoughts are usually marked by such phrases as *I thought, he felt*, and *she believed*. Remember, though, that quotation marks are not used with thoughts that are reported indirectly (**40a(2)**).

I wondered why he had not responded to my memo.

(6) Short excerpts of poetry within a sentence in quotation marks

When quoting fewer than four lines of poetry, enclose them in quotation marks and use a slash (**41h**) to indicate the line division.

Together, mother and daughter recited their favorite lines: "Shall I compare thee to a summer's day? / Thou art more lovely and more temperate."

To learn how to format longer quotations of poetry, see **12e(4)**.

40b   TITLES OF SHORT WORKS

Quotation marks enclose the title of a short work, such as a story, an essay, a poem, or a song. The title of a longer work, such as a book, a magazine, a newspaper, or a play, should be italicized.

"The Girls of Summer" first appeared in the *New Yorker*.

Short story	"The Lottery"	"A Good Man Is Hard to Find"
Essay	"Walden"	"A Modest Proposal"

Article	"Small World"	"Arabia's Empty Quarter"
Book chapter	"Rain"	"Cutting a Dash"
Short poem	"Orion"	"Where the Sidewalk Ends"
Song	"Lazy River"	"Like a Rolling Stone"
TV episode	"Show Down!"	"The Last Time"

Use double quotation marks around the title of a short work embedded in a longer italicized title.

Interpretations of "*Young Goodman Brown*" [book about a short story]

Use single quotation marks for a title within a longer title that is enclosed in double quotation marks.

"Irony in 'The Road Not Taken' " [article about a poem]

ñ MULTILINGUAL WRITERS

DIFFERING USES OF QUOTATION MARKS
In works published in Great Britain, the use of quotation marks differs in some ways from the U.S. style presented here. For example, single quotation marks are always used to set off direct quotations and the titles of short works. A period is placed outside a quotation mark ending a sentence. Double quotation marks indicate a quotation within a quotation. When writing in the United States, be sure to follow the rules for American English.

British usage	In class, we compared Wordsworth's 'Upon Westminster Bridge' with Blake's 'London'.
American usage	In class, we compared Wordsworth's "Upon Westminster Bridge" with Blake's "London."

40c | FOR IRONIC TONE OR UNUSUAL USAGE

Writers sometimes use quotation marks to indicate that they are using a word or phrase ironically. The word *gourmet* is used ironically in the following sentence.

> His "gourmet" dinner turned out to be processed turkey and instant mashed potatoes.

❶ CAUTION

Avoid using quotation marks around words that may not be appropriate for your rhetorical situation. Instead, take the time to choose suitable words. The revised sentence in the following pair is more effective than the first.

| **Ineffective** | He is too much of a "wimp" to be a good leader. |
| **Revised** | He is too indecisive to be a good leader. |

Similarly, putting a cliché (35b) in quotation marks may make readers conclude that you do not care enough about conveying your meaning to think of a fresh expression.

40d | WITH OTHER PUNCTUATION MARKS

To decide whether to place some other punctuation mark inside or outside quotation marks, determine whether the particular mark functions as part of the quotation or part of the surrounding context.

(1) With commas and periods

Quoted material is usually accompanied by an attributive tag such as *she said* or *he replied*. When a sentence starts with such an expression, place a comma after it to separate the attributive tag from the quotation.

> She replied, "There's more than one way to slice a pie."

If the sentence starts with the quotation instead, place the comma inside the closing quotation marks.

> "There's more than one way to slice a pie," she replied.

Place a period inside closing quotation marks, whether single or double, if a quotation ends a sentence.

> Jeff responded, "I didn't understand 'An Algorithm for Life.'"

When quoting material from a source, provide the relevant page number(s). If you are following MLA guidelines, note the page number(s) in parentheses after the final quotation marks. Place the period that ends the sentence after the final parenthesis, unless the quotation is a block quotation (13a(2)).

> According to Diane Ackerman, "Love is a demanding sport involving all the muscle groups, including the brain" (86).

---

❶ CAUTION

Do not put a comma after *that* when it precedes a quotation.

Diane Ackerman claims that⌀"[l]ove is a demanding sport involving all the muscle groups, including the brain" (86).

---

(2) With semicolons and colons

Place semicolons and colons outside quotation marks.

> His favorite song was "Cyprus Avenue"; mine was "Astral Weeks."

> Because it is repeated, one line stands out in "The Conductor": "We are never as beautiful as now."

(3) With question marks, exclamation points, and dashes

If the direct quotation includes a question mark, an exclamation point, or a dash, place that punctuation *inside* the closing quotation marks.

> Jeremy asked, "What is truth?"

> Gordon shouted "Congratulations!"

> Laura said, "Let me tell—" Before she could finish her sentence, Dan walked into the room.

Use just one question mark inside the quotation marks when a question you write ends with a quoted question.

> Why does the protagonist ask, "Where are we headed?"

If the punctuation is not part of the quoted material, place it *outside* the closing quotation marks.

> Who wrote "The Figure a Sentence Makes"?

> You have to read "Awareness and Freedom"!

> She called me a "toaster head"—perhaps justifiably under the circumstances.

Exercise 1

Revise sentences in which quotation marks are used incorrectly and insert quotation marks where they are needed. Do not alter sentences that are written correctly.

1. Have you read On Women's Right to Vote by Susan B. Anthony?

2. In a speech delivered after she was arrested for casting an illegal vote, Anthony asked this question: Are women persons?

3. She acknowledges that she has been indicted for "the alleged crime of having voted in the last presidential election".

4. Anthony suggests that not allowing women to vote is a violation of 'the supreme law of the land'.

5. According to the author, "We, the whole people, . . . formed the Union."

6. She points out that Webster, Worcester, and Bouvier all define a citizen to be a person in the United States, entitled to vote and hold office.

7. Anthony maintains, Being persons, then, women are citizens; and no state has a right to make any law . . . that shall abridge their privileges or immunities.

41 ‖ THE PERIOD AND OTHER PUNCTUATION MARKS

To indicate the end of a sentence, you can use one of three punctuation marks: the period, the question mark, or the exclamation point. Which one you use depends on your meaning: do you want to make a statement, ask a question, or express an exclamation?

Everyone passed the exam.

Everyone passed the exam? [informal usage]

Everyone passed the exam!

Within sentences, you can use colons, dashes, parentheses, square brackets, ellipsis points, and slashes to emphasize, downplay, or clarify the information you want to convey. (For use of the colon, see **38b**; for use of the hyphen, see **42f**.) This chapter will help you use

- end punctuation marks (the period (**41a**), the question mark (**41b**), and the exclamation point (**41c**)),
- the dash (**41d**),
- parentheses (**41e**),
- square brackets (**41f**),
- ellipsis points (**41g**), and
- the slash (**41h**).

To accommodate computerized typesetting, both CMS and APA guidelines call for only one space after a period, a question mark, an exclamation point, and a colon. According to these manuals, there should be no space preceding or following a hyphen or a dash. The MLA style manual recommends using only one space after end punctuation marks but allows two spaces if they are used consistently.

41a THE PERIOD

(1) Marking the end of a sentence

Use a period at the end of a declarative sentence.

> Many adults in the United States are overfed yet undernourished.
>
> Soft drinks account for 7 percent of their average daily caloric intake.

In addition, place a period at the end of an instruction or recommendation written as an imperative sentence (**22d**).

> Eat plenty of fruits and vegetables. Drink six to eight glasses of water a day.

Indirect questions are phrased as statements, so be sure to use a period, rather than a question mark, at the end of such a sentence.

> The researcher explained why people eat so much junk food.
> [COMPARE: Why do people eat so much junk food?]

(2) Following some abbreviations

> Dr. Jr. a.m. p.m. vs. etc. et al.

Only one period follows an abbreviation that ends a sentence.

> The tour begins at 1:00 p.m.

Periods are not used with many common abbreviations (for example, *MVP, mph,* and *FM*). (See chapter **45**.) A dictionary lists the conventional form of an abbreviation as well as any alternatives.

41b THE QUESTION MARK

Place a question mark after a direct question.

> How does the new atomic clock work? Who invented this clock?

Use a period, instead of a question mark, after an indirect question—that is, a question embedded in a statement.

I asked whether the new atomic clock could be used in cell phones. [COMPARE: Can the new atomic clock be used in cell phones?]

ⓝ MULTILINGUAL WRITERS

INDIRECT QUESTIONS

In English, indirect questions are written as declarative sentences. The subject and verb are not inverted as they would be in the related direct question.

We do not know when ~~will~~ the meeting ⌄will end.

[COMPARE: When will the meeting end?]

For more on word order and questions, see chapter 48.

Place a question mark after each question in a series of related questions, even when they are not full sentences.

Will the new atomic clock be used in cell phones? word processors? car navigation systems?

If a direct quotation is a question, place the question mark inside the final quotation marks.

Tony asked, "How small is this new clock?"

In contrast, if you include quoted material in a question of your own, place the question mark outside the final quotation marks.

Is the clock really "no larger than a sugar cube"?

If you embed in the middle of a sentence a question not attributable to anyone in particular, place a comma before it and a question mark after it.

When the question, how does the clock work? arose, the researchers described a technique used by manufacturers of computer chips.

The first letter of such a question should not be capitalized unless the question is extremely long or contains internal punctuation.

To indicate uncertainty about a fact such as a date of birth, place a question mark inside parentheses directly after the fact in question.

> Chaucer was born in 1340 (?) and died in 1400.

41c   THE EXCLAMATION POINT

An exclamation point often marks the end of a sentence, but its primary purpose is rhetorical—to create emphasis.

> Wow! What a game!

When a direct quotation ends with an exclamation point, no comma or period is placed immediately after it.

> "Get a new pitcher!" he yelled.

> He yelled, "Get a new pitcher!"

Use the exclamation point sparingly so that you do not diminish its impact. If you do not intend to signal strong emotion, place a comma after an interjection and a period at the end of the sentence.

> Well, no one seriously expected this victory.

Exercise 1

Compose and punctuate brief sentences of the following types.
1. a declarative sentence containing a quoted exclamation
2. a sentence beginning with an interjection
3. a direct question
4. a declarative sentence containing an indirect question
5. a declarative sentence containing a direct question

41d THE DASH

A dash (or em dash) marks a break in thought, sets off a nonessential element for emphasis or clarity, or follows an introductory list or series. The short dash (or en dash) is used mainly in number ranges (45g(2)).

⬤ TECH SAVVY

To use your keyboard to create a dash, type two hyphens with no spaces between, before, or after them. Most word-processing programs can be set to convert these hyphens automatically to an em dash. In Microsoft Word, you can also hold down the Option and Shift keys while typing a hyphen (Mac) or the Control and Alt keys while typing the minus symbol (PC).

(1) To mark a break in the normal flow of a sentence

Use a dash to indicate a shift in thought or tone.

I was awed by the almost superhuman effort Stonehenge represents—but who wouldn't be?

(2) To set off a nonessential element

A dash or a pair of dashes sets off a nonessential element for emphasis or clarity.

Dr. Kruger's specialty is mycology—the study of fungi.

The trail we took into the Grand Canyon—steep, narrow, winding, and lacking guardrails—made me wonder whether we could call a helicopter to fly us out.

(3) To set off an introductory list or series

If you decide to place a list or series at the beginning of a sentence in order to emphasize it, the main part of the sentence (after the dash) should sum up the meaning of the list or series.

Eager, determined to succeed, and scared to death—all of these describe how I felt on the first day at work.

❓ THINKING RHETORICALLY

COMMAS, DASHES, AND COLONS

Although a comma, a dash, or a colon may be followed by an explanation, an example, or an illustration, the rhetorical impact of each of these punctuation marks differs.

He never failed to mention what was most important to him, the bottom line.

He never failed to mention what was most important to him—the bottom line.

He never failed to mention what was most important to him: the bottom line.

The comma, one of the most common punctuation marks, barely draws attention to what follows it. The dash, in contrast, signals a longer pause and so causes more emphasis to be placed on the information that follows. The colon is more direct and formal than either of the other two punctuation marks. (See **38b** for more about the colon.)

41e   PARENTHESES

Use parentheses to set off information that is not closely related to the main point of a sentence or paragraph but that provides an interesting detail, an explanation, or an illustration.

One of the most striking peculiarities of the human brain is the great development of the frontal lobes—they are much less developed in other primates and hardly evident at all in other mammals. They are the part of the brain that grows and develops most after birth (and their development is not complete until about the age of seven).

—**Oliver Sacks,** *An Anthropologist on Mars*

Place parentheses around an acronym or an abbreviation when introducing it after its full form.

The Search for Extraterrestrial Intelligence (SETI) uses the Very Large Array (VLA) outside Socorro, New Mexico, to scan the sky.

If you use numbers or letters in a list within a sentence, set them off by placing them within parentheses.

Your application should include (1) a current résumé, (2) a statement of purpose, and (3) two letters of recommendation.

For information on the use of parentheses in bibliographies and in-text citations, see Chapters **13**, **15**, **17**, and **19**.

❓ THINKING RHETORICALLY

DASHES AND PARENTHESES

Dashes and parentheses are both used to set off part of a sentence, but they differ in the amount of emphasis they signal. Whereas dashes call attention to the material that is set off, parentheses usually de-emphasize such material.

Her grandfather—born during the Great Depression—was appointed by the president to the Securities and Exchange Commission.

Her grandfather (born in 1930) was appointed by the president to the Securities and Exchange Commission.

41f SQUARE BRACKETS

Square brackets set off additions or alterations that clarify direct quotations. In the following example, the bracketed noun specifies what is meant by the pronoun *They*:

"They [hyperlinks] are what turn the Web from a library of pages into a web" (Weinberger 170).

Square brackets also indicate that a letter at the beginning of a quotation has been changed from uppercase to lowercase, or vice versa.

David Weinberger claims that "[e]ven our notion of self as a continuous body moving through a continuous map of space and time is beginning to seem wrong on the Web" (10).

To avoid the awkwardness of using brackets in this way, you may be able to quote only part of a sentence and thus not need to change the capitalization.

David Weinberger claims that "our notion of self as a continuous body moving through a continuous map of space and time is beginning to seem wrong on the Web" (10).

Within parentheses, square brackets are used because having two sets of parentheses could be confusing.

The Web has broken the traditional model for publishing. (See, for example, David Weinberger's *Small Pieces Loosely Joined* [Cambridge: Perseus, 2002].)

41g ║ ELLIPSIS POINTS

Ellipsis points indicate an omission from a quoted passage or a reflective pause or hesitation.

(1) To mark an omission within a quoted passage

Whenever you omit anything from material you quote, replace the omitted material with ellipsis points—three equally spaced periods. Be sure to compare your quoted sentence to the original, checking to see that your omission does not change the meaning of the original.

To avoid excessive use of ellipses, replace some direct quotations with paraphrases (11e).

The following examples illustrate how to use ellipsis points in quotations from a passage by Patricia Gadsby.

Original

Cacao doesn't flower, as most plants do, at the tips of its outer and uppermost branches. Instead, its sweet white buds hang from the trunk and along a few fat branches, popping out of patches of bark called cushions, which form where leaves drop off. They're tiny, these flowers. Yet once pollinated by midges, no-see-ums that flit in the leafy detritus below, they'll make pulp-filled pods almost the size of rugby balls.

—Patricia Gadsby, "Endangered Chocolate"

(a) Omission within a quoted sentence

Patricia Gadsby notes that cacao flowers "once pollinated by midges . . . make pulp-filled pods almost the size of rugby balls."

Retain a comma, colon, or semicolon that appears in the original text if it makes a quoted sentence easier to read. If no misreading will occur, the punctuation mark can be omitted.

Patricia Gadsby describes the outcome of pollinating the cacao flowers: "Yet once pollinated by midges, . . . they'll make pulp-filled pods almost the size of rugby balls." [The comma after "midges" is retained.]

According to Gadsby, "Cacao doesn't flower . . . at the tips of its outer and uppermost branches." [The comma after "flower" is omitted]

(b) Omission at the beginning of a quoted sentence

Do not use ellipsis points to indicate that you have deleted words from the beginning of a quotation, whether it is run into the text or set off in a block. The opening part of the original sentence has been omitted in the following quotation.

According to Patricia Gadsby, cacao flowers will become "pulp-filled pods almost the size of rugby balls."

Note that the first letter of the integrated quotation is not capitalized.

(c) Omission at the end of a quoted sentence

To indicate that you have omitted words from the end of a sentence, put a single space between the last word and the set of three spaced ellipsis points. Then add the end punctuation mark (a period, a question mark, or an exclamation point). If the quoted material is followed by a parenthetical source or page reference, the end punctuation comes after the second parenthesis.

> Claiming that cacao flowers differ from those of most plants, Patricia Gadsby describes how "the sweet white buds hang from the trunk and along a few fat branches . . . ."
>
> OR ". . . a few fat branches . . ." (2).

(d) Omission of a sentence or more

To signal the omission of a sentence or more (even a paragraph or more), place an end punctuation mark (usually a period) before the ellipsis points.

> Patricia Gadsby describes the flowering of the cacao plant: "Its sweet white buds hang from the trunk and along a few fat branches, popping out of patches of bark called cushions, which form where leaves drop off. . . . Yet once pollinated by midges, no-see-ums that flit in the leafy detritus below, they'll make pulp-filled pods almost the size of rugby balls."

(e) Omission of a line or more of a poem

To signal the omission of a full line or more in quoted poetry, use spaced periods extending the length of either the line above it or the omitted line.

> The yellow fog that rubs its back upon the window-panes,
>
> . . . .
>
> Curled once about the house, and fell asleep.
>
> —T. S. Eliot, "The Love Song of J. Alfred Prufrock"

(2) To mark an incomplete sentence

Ellipsis points show that a sentence has been intentionally left incomplete.

> Read aloud the passage that begins "The yellow fog . . ." and explain the imagery.

(3) To mark hesitation in a sentence

Ellipsis points can mark a reflective pause or a hesitation.

Keith saw four menacing youths coming toward him . . . and ran.

A dash can also be used to indicate this type of a pause.

41h THE SLASH

A slash between words, as in *and/or*, *young/old*, and *heaven/hell*, indicates that either word is applicable in the given context. There are no spaces before and after a slash used in this way. Because extensive use of the slash can make writing choppy, use it judiciously and sparingly. Most style sheets recommend avoiding the use of *him/her*, and so on. MLA style uses the slash in works-cited entries between co-publishers (see 13b).

A slash is also used to mark line divisions in quoted poetry. A slash used in this way is preceded and followed by a space.

Wallace Stevens refers to the listener who, "nothing himself, beholds **/** Nothing that is not there and the nothing that is."

Exercise 2

Add appropriate dashes, parentheses, square brackets, and slashes to the following sentences. Be ready to explain the reason for each mark you add.

1. The three recognized autism spectrum disorders ASDs are autism, Asperger syndrome, and pervasive developmental disorder–not otherwise specified PDD-NOS.
2. Disagreement concerning the causes of autism environmental, medical, and or genetic continues to flourish.
3. The rise in diagnoses of autism might be due to better diagnostic practices or an increase in the disorder itself.

Exercise 3

Punctuate the following sentences with appropriate end marks, commas, colons (38b), dashes, and parentheses. Do not use unnecessary punctuation. Give a justification for each mark you add, especially where more than one type of mark (for example, commas, dashes, or parentheses) is acceptable.

1. Many small country towns are very similar a truck stop a gas station a crowded diner and three bars

2. The simple life a nonexistent crime rate and down-home values these are some of the advantages these little towns offer

3. Why do we never see these quaint examples of pure Americana when we travel around the country on the interstates

4. Rolling across America on one of the big interstates I-20 I-40 I-70 I-80 or I-90 you are likely to pass within a few miles of a number of these towns

5. Such towns almost certainly will have a regional or perhaps an ethnic flavor Hispanic in the southwest Scandinavian in the north

6. When I visit one of these out-of-the-way places I always have a sense of well really a feeling of safety

7. There's one thing I can tell you small-town life is not boring

8. My one big question however is what do you do to earn a living in these towns

MECHANICS

Situate Yourself

Your internship with the National Park Service requires you to work on a project describing national monuments and their presence in popular culture. While visiting the Statue of Liberty, you jotted down the following important points into the notes app on your cell phone. Now your job is to put those notes into standard paragraph form. (Remember to use what you know about spelling, capitalization, italics, abbreviation, acronyms, and numbers.)

Gift to U.S. from France

Work of art title—liberty enlightening the world

Assembled on Liberty Island, was Bedloe's Is

Dedicated 1886

Symbol of freedom

Height, base to tip of torch—151 ft—appears taller because of pedastle—154 ft

Prominence in New York Harbor

Important role in pop culture—films—saboteur, planet of the apes, independence day

42 || SPELLING, THE SPELL CHECKER, AND HYPHENATION

When you first draft a paper, you might not pay close attention to spelling words correctly. After all, the point of drafting is to generate and organize ideas. However, proofreading for spelling mistakes is essential as you near the end of the writing process. You want to submit the kind of writing your teacher, employer, or supervisor expects to read: polished work that is as nearly perfect as you can make it.

You can train yourself to be a good proofreader by checking a dictionary every time you question the spelling of a word. If two spellings are listed, such as *fulfill* and *fulfil*, either form is correct, although the first option provided is generally considered more common. Once you choose between such options, be sure to use the spelling you pick consistently. You can also learn to be a better speller by studying a few basic strategies. This chapter will help you

- use a spell checker (**42a**),
- spell words according to pronunciation (**42b**),
- spell words that sound alike (**42c**),
- understand how prefixes and suffixes affect spelling (**42d**),
- use *ei* and *ie* correctly (**42e**), and
- use hyphens to link and divide words (**42f**).

42a | SPELL CHECKER

The spell checker is a wonderful invention, but only when you use it with care. A spell checker will usually flag

- misspellings of common words,
- some commonly confused words (such as *affect* and *effect*), and
- obvious typographical errors (such as *tge* for *the*).

However, a spell checker generally will *not* detect

- specialized vocabulary or foreign words not in its dictionary,

- typographical errors that are still correctly spelled words (such as *was* for *saw*), and
- misuses of words that sound alike but are not on the spell checker's list of commonly confused words.

The following strategies can help you use a spell checker effectively.

TIPS FOR USING A SPELL CHECKER

- If a spell checker regularly flags a word that is not in its dictionary but is spelled correctly, add that word to its dictionary by clicking on the Add button. From that point on, the spell checker will accept the word.
- Reject any offers the spell checker makes to correct all instances of a particular error.
- Use a dictionary to evaluate the alternative spellings the spell checker provides; some of them may be erroneous.

42b SPELLING AND PRONUNCIATION

Many words in English are not spelled the way they are pronounced, so pronunciation is not a reliable guide to correct spelling. Sometimes, people skip over an unstressed syllable, as when *February* is pronounced "Febuary," or they slide over a sound that is hard to articulate, as when *library* is pronounced "libary." Other times, people add a sound—for instance, when they pronounce *athlete* as "athalete." And people may switch sounds around, as in "irrevelant" for *irrelevant.* Such mispronunciations can lead to misspellings.

You can help yourself remember the spellings of some words by considering the spellings of their root words—for example, the root word for *irrelevant* is *relevant.* You can also teach yourself the correct spellings of words by pronouncing them the way they are spelled, that is, by pronouncing each letter mentally so that you "hear" even silent letters. You are more likely to remember the *b* in *subtle* if you pronounce it when spelling that word. Here are a few words typically misspelled because they include unpronounced letters:

condem*n*   forei*g*n   lab*o*ratory   mus*c*le   solem*n*

Here are a few more that include letters that are often not heard in rapid speech, though they can be heard when carefully pronounced:

can*d*idate   diff*e*rent   enviro*n*ment   gover*n*ment   sep*a*rate

---

> **❶ CAUTION**
>
> Because the words *and, have,* and *than* are often not stressed in speech, they are often spelled as words they sound like.
>
> They would rather₍have₎of written two papers₍than₎then taken midterm₍and₎an final exams.
>
> Watch for these misspellings when you proofread your papers.

42c   WORDS THAT SOUND ALIKE

Pairs of words such as *forth* and *fourth* or *sole* and *soul* are **homophones**: they sound alike but have different meanings and spellings. Some words that have different meanings sound exactly alike (*break/brake*); others sound alike in certain dialects (*marry/merry*). If you are unsure about the difference in meaning between any two words that sound alike, consult a dictionary. A number of frequently confused words are listed with explanations in this handbook's **Glossary of Usage**.

Also troublesome are two-word sequences that can be written as compound words or as separate words. The following are examples:

Everyday life was grueling.	She attended class **every day.**
They do not fight **anymore.**	They could not find **any more** evidence.

Other examples are *awhile/a while, everyone/every one, maybe/may be,* and *sometime/some time.*

A lot and *all right* are still spelled as two words. *Alot* is always considered incorrect; *alright* is also considered incorrect except in some newspapers and magazines. (See the **Glossary of Usage**.)

Singular nouns ending in *-nce* and plural nouns ending in *-nts* are easily confused.

Assistance is available.   I have two **assistants.**

His **patience** wore thin.   Some **patients** waited for hours.

Contractions and possessive pronouns are also often confused. In contractions, an apostrophe indicates an omitted letter (or letters). In possessive pronouns, there is no apostrophe. (See also **26b** and **39a(1)**.)

Contraction	**Possessive**
It's my turn next.	Each group waited **its** turn.
You're next.	**Your** turn is next.
There's no difference.	**Theirs** is no different.

TIPS FOR SPELLING WORDS THAT SOUND ALIKE

- Be alert for words that are commonly confused (*accept/except*).
- Distinguish between two-word sequences and single words that sound similar (*may be/maybe*).
- Use *-nts*, not *-nce*, for plural words (*instants/instance*).
- Mark contractions, but not possessive pronouns, with apostrophes (*who's/whose*).

42d PREFIXES AND SUFFIXES

When a prefix is added to a base word (often called the **root**), the spelling of the base word is unaffected.

necessary, **un**necessary   moral, **im**moral

However, adding a suffix to the end of a base word often changes the spelling.

beauty, beauti**ful**   describe, descri**ption**   BUT   resist, resist**ance**

Although spellings of words with suffixes are irregular, they follow certain conventions.

(1) Dropping or retaining a final *e*

- If a suffix begins with a vowel, the final *e* of the base word is dropped: bride, brid**al**; come, com**ing**; combine, combin**ation**; prime, prim**ary**. However, to keep the /s/ sound of *ce* or the /j/ sound of *ge*, retain the final *e* before *-able* or *-ous:* courag**eous**, manag**eable**, notic**eable**.
- If a suffix begins with a consonant, the final *e* of the base word is usually retained: entire, entire**ly**; rude, rude**ness**; place, place**ment**; sure, sure**ly**. Exceptions include *argument, awful, ninth, truly,* and *wholly.*

(2) Doubling a final consonant when a suffix begins with a vowel

- If a one-syllable word with a single vowel or a stressed syllable with a single vowel ends with a consonant, double the final consonant: stop, sto**pped**, sto**pping**; omit, omi**tted**, omi**tting**.
- If there are two vowels before the consonant, the consonant is not doubled: seat, seat**ed**, seat**ing**; remain, remain**ed**, remain**ing**.
- If the final syllable is not stressed, the consonant is not doubled: edit, edit**ed**, edit**ing**; picket, picket**ed**, picket**ing**.

(3) Changing or retaining a final *y*

- Change a final *y* following a consonant to *i* when adding a suffix (except *-ing*): lazy, laz**ily**; defy, def**ies**, def**ied**, def**iance** BUT defy**ing**; modify, modif**ies**, modif**ied**, modif**ier** BUT modify**ing**.
- Retain the final *y* when it follows a vowel: gray, gray**ish**; stay, stay**s**, stay**ed**; obey, obey**s**, obey**ed**.
- Some verb forms are irregular and thus can cause difficulties: *lays, laid; pays, paid.* For a list of irregular verbs, see pages 561–563.

(4) Retaining a final *l* when *-ly* is added

cool, coo**lly**   formal, forma**lly**   real, rea**lly**   usual, usua**lly**

Exercise 1

Add the specified suffixes to the words that follow. Be prepared to explain the reason for the spelling of each resulting word.

EXAMPLE

-ly: late, casual, psychological   *lately   casually   psychologically*

1. -ing: put, admit, write, use, try, play
2. -ment: manage, commit, require, argue
3. -ous: continue, joy, acrimony, libel
4. -ed: race, tip, permit, carry, pray
5. -able: desire, read, trace, knowledge
6. -ly: true, sincere, normal, general

(5) Making a noun plural by adding -s or -es to the singular form

- If the sound in the plural form of a noun ending in *f* or *fe* changes from /f/ to /v/, change the ending to *-ve* before adding *-s:* thie**f**, thie**ves**; li**fe**, li**ves** BUT roof, roo**fs**.
- Add *-es* to most nouns ending in *s, z, ch, sh,* or *x:* box, box**es**; peach, peach**es**.
- If a noun ends in a consonant and *y,* change the *y* to *i* and add *-es:* company, compan**ies**; ninety, ninet**ies**; territory, territor**ies**. (See also **42d(3)**.)
- If a noun ends in a consonant and *o,* add *-es:* hero, hero**es**; potato, potato**es**. However, note that sometimes just *-s* is added (photo, pho**tos**; memo, memo**s**) and other times either an *-s* or *-es* suffix can be added (motto**s**, motto**es**; zero**s**, zero**es**).
- Certain nouns have irregular plural forms: woman, wom**en**; child, child**ren**; foot, f**eet**.
- Add *-s* to most proper nouns: the Lee**s**; the Kennedy**s**. Add *-es* to most proper nouns ending in *s, z, ch, sh,* or *x:* the Rodriguez**es**, the Jones**es** BUT the Bach**s** (in which *ch* is pronounced /k/).

> **❗ CAUTION**
>
> Words borrowed from Latin or Greek generally form their plurals as they did in the original language.
>
> | **Singular** | criterion | alumnus, alumna | analysis | datum | species |
> |---|---|---|---|---|---|
> | **Plural** | criteria | alumni, alumnae | analyses | data | species |
>
> Many words with such origins gradually come to be considered part of the English language, and during this process, two plural forms will be listed in dictionaries as acceptable: *syllabus/syllabuses, syllabi.* Be sure to use only one of the acceptable plural forms in a paper you write.

Exercise 2

Provide the plural forms for the following words. If you need extra help, check a dictionary.

1. virus
2. committee
3. phenomenon
4. copy
5. hero
6. embargo
7. shelf
8. belief
9. foot
10. portfolio
11. cactus
12. census

42e CONFUSION OF *EI* AND *IE*

An old rhyme will help you remember the order of letters in most words containing *e* and *i:*

Put *i* before *e*

Except after *c*

Or when sounded like *a*

As in *neighbor* and *weigh.*

Words with *i* before *e*: bel**ie**ve, ch**ie**f, pr**ie**st, y**ie**ld

Words with *e* before *i*, after *c*: conc**ei**t, perc**ei**ve, rec**ei**ve

Words with *ei* sounding like *a* in *cake*: **ei**ght, r**ei**n, th**ei**r, h**ei**r

Words that are exceptions to the rules in the rhyme include *either, neither, species, foreign*, and *weird*.

ñ MULTILINGUAL WRITERS

AMERICAN AND BRITISH SPELLING DIFFERENCES
Although most words are spelled the same in both the United States and Great Britain, some are spelled differently, including the following.

American	check	realize	color	connection
British	cheque	realise	colour	connexion

Use the American spellings when writing for an audience in the United States.

42f   HYPHENS

Hyphens link two or more words functioning as a single word and separate word parts to clarify meaning. They also have many conventional uses in numbers, fractions, and measurements. (Do not confuse the hyphen with a dash; see **41d** and **45g(2)**.)

(1) Between two or more words that form a compound

Some compounds are listed in the dictionary with hyphens (*eye-opener, cross-examination*), others are written as two words (*eye chart, cross fire*), and still others appear as one word (*eyewitness, crossbreed*). If you have questions about the spelling of a compound word, a dictionary is a good resource. However, it is also helpful to learn a few basic patterns.

- If two or more words serve as a single adjective before a noun, they should be hyphenated. If the words follow the noun, they are not hyphenated.

You submitted an **up-to-date** report. The report was **up to date.**

A **well-known** musician is performing tonight. The musician is **well known.**

- When the second word in a hyphenated expression is omitted, the first word is still followed by a hyphen.

They discussed both **private-** and **public-sector** partnerships.

- A hyphen is not used after adverbs ending in *-ly* (*poorly planned event*), in names of chemical compounds (*sodium chloride solution*), or in modifiers with a letter or numeral as the second element (*group C homes, type IV virus*).

(2) Between a prefix and a word to clarify meaning

- To avoid ambiguity or an awkward combination of letters or syllables, place a hyphen between the base word and its prefix: *anti-intellectual, de-emphasize, re-sign the petition* [COMPARE: *resign the position*].
- Place a hyphen between a prefix and a word beginning with a capital letter and between a prefix and a word already containing a hyphen: *anti-American, non-self-promoting.*
- Place a hyphen after the prefix *all-, e-, ex-,* or *self-*: *all-inclusive, e-commerce, ex-husband, self-esteem.* Otherwise, most words with prefixes are not hyphenated. (The use of the unhyphenated *email* has become very common, but *e-mail* is the spelling preferred by APA, CMS, and MLA. The prefix *e-* is sometimes used without a hyphen in trade names, such as eBay.)

(3) In numbers, fractions, and units of measure

- Place a hyphen between two numbers when they are spelled out: *thirty-two, ninety-nine.* However, no hyphen is used before or after the words *hundred, thousand,* and *million: five hundred sixty-three, forty-one million.*
- Hyphenate fractions that are spelled out: *three-fourths, one-half.*
- When you form a compound modifier that includes a number and a unit of measurement, place a hyphen between them: *twenty-first-century literature, twelve-year-old boy, ten-year project.*

Exercise 3

Convert the following groups of words into hyphenated compounds.

EXAMPLE

a movie lasting two hours   *a two-hour movie*

1. a boss who is well liked
2. a television screen that is forty-eight inches across
3. a highway with eight lanes
4. a painting from the seventeenth century
5. a chemist who won the Nobel Prize
6. a virus that is food borne

43 | CAPITALS

When you look at an advertisement, an e-mail message, or a paragraph in this book, you can easily pick out capital letters (see figure 43.1, for example). These beacons draw your attention to significant details—for example, the beginnings of sentences or the names of particular people, places, and products. Although most capitalization conventions apply to any rhetorical situation, others are specific to a discipline or a profession. In this chapter, you will learn the conventions that are followed in most academic and professional settings. This chapter will help you

- use capitals for proper names (**43a**);
- capitalize words in titles and subtitles of works (**43b**);
- capitalize the first letter of a sentence (**43c**);
- use capitals for computer keys, menu items, and icon names (**43d**); and
- avoid unnecessary capitalization (**43e**).

---

❶ CAUTION

You may have noticed that capitalization styles differ in various types of publications. For instance, the word *president* is always capitalized in documents published by the U.S. Government Printing Office, but it is capitalized in most newspapers only when it is followed by a specific name:

The delegates met with **P**resident Truman.

The delegates met with the **p**resident.

Be careful to use an appropriate capitalization style for your rhetorical situation.

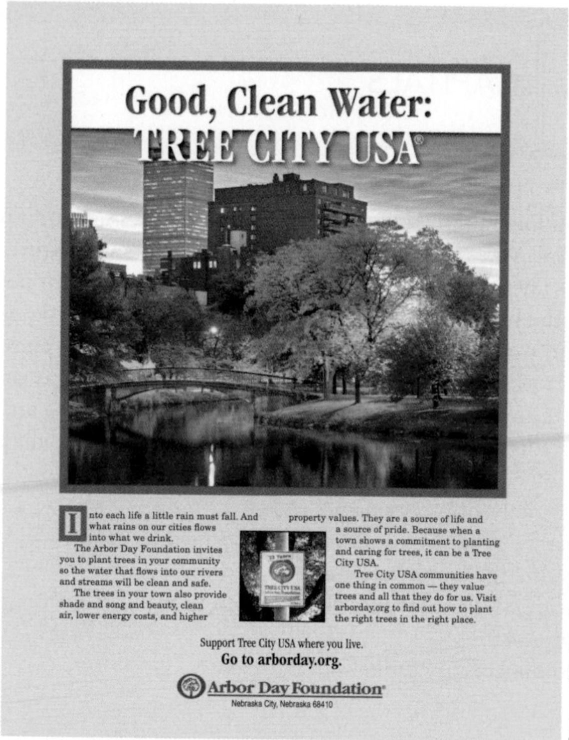

Courtesy of the Arbor Day Foundation

Figure 43.1: Advertisers often highlight important words by capitalizing them.

43a PROPER NAMES

When you capitalize a word, you emphasize it. That is why names of people and places are capitalized, even when they are used as modifiers (*Mexico, Mexican government*). Some words, such as *college, company, park,* and *street,* are capitalized only if they are part of a name (*a university* but *University of Pennsylvania*). The following names and titles should be capitalized.

(1) Names of specific persons or things

Zora Neale Hurston	Flight 224	Honda Accord
John Paul II	Academy Award	USS *Cole*
Skylab	Nike	Microsoft Windows

For a brand name such as eBay or iPhone that begins with a lowercase letter, do not change that letter to a capital when the name begins a sentence.

Many people like to shop on eBay.

eBay attracts many shoppers.

A word denoting a family relationship is capitalized only when it substitutes for the person's proper name.

I told **Mom** about the event. [I told Virginia about the event.]

I told my **mom** about the event. [NOT I told my Virginia about the event.]

(2) Titles accompanying proper names

A title is capitalized when it precedes the name of a person but not when it follows the name or stands alone.

Governor Bill Haslam	Bill Haslam, the governor
Captain Ray Machado	Ray Machado, our captain
Aunt Helen	Helen, my aunt
President Lincoln	Abraham Lincoln, the president of the United States

(3) Names of ethnic or cultural groups and languages

Asians	African Americans	Latinos/Latinas	Poles
Arabic	English	Korean	Spanish

(4) Names of bridges, buildings, monuments, and geographical features

Golden Gate Bridge   Empire State Building   Lincoln Memorial

Arctic Circle   Mississippi River   Grand Canyon

When referring to two or more geographical features, do not capitalize the generic term: *Lincoln and Jefferson memorials, Yellowstone and Olympic national parks.*

(5) Names of organizations, government agencies, institutions, and companies

B'nai B'rith   National Endowment for the Humanities

Phi Beta Kappa   Internal Revenue Service

Howard University   Ford Motor Company

When used as common nouns, *service, company,* and *university* are not capitalized. However, universities and other organizations often capitalize these words when they are used as shortened forms of the institutions' full names.

> The policies of Hanson University promote the rights of all individuals to equal opportunity in education. The University complies with all applicable federal, state, and local laws.

(6) Names of days of the week, months, and holidays

Wednesday   August   Fourth of July

The names of the seasons—spring, summer, fall, winter—are not capitalized.

ⓝ MULTILINGUAL WRITERS

CAPITALIZING DAYS OF THE WEEK

Capitalization rules vary according to language. For example, in English, the names of days and months are capitalized, but in some other languages, such as Spanish and Italian, they are not.

(7) Designations for historical documents, periods, events, movements, and styles

Declaration of Independence   Renaissance   Industrial Revolution

A historical period that includes a number is not capitalized unless it is considered a proper name.

twentieth century	the Roaring Twenties
the seventies	the Gay Nineties

The name of a cultural movement or style is capitalized if it is derived from a person's name or if capitalization distinguishes the name of the movement or style from the ordinary use of the word or phrase.

Platonism   Reaganomics   New Criticism

Most names of cultural movements and styles are not capitalized.

art deco   impressionism   realism   deconstruction

(8) Names of religions, their adherents, holy days, titles of holy books, and words denoting a Supreme Being

Buddhism, Christianity, Islam, Judaism

Buddhist, Christian, Muslim, Jew

Bodhi Day, Easter, Ramadan, Yom Kippur

Sutras, Bible, Koran, Talmud BUT biblical, talmudic

Buddha, God, Allah, Yahweh

Some writers always capitalize personal pronouns (26a(1)) that refer to a Supreme Being; others capitalize such words only when capitalization is needed to prevent ambiguity:

The Lord commanded the prophet to warn His people.

(9) Words derived from proper names

Americanize [verb]   Orwellian [adjective]   Marxism [noun]

When a proper name becomes the name of a general class of objects or ideas, it is no longer capitalized. For example, the word *zipper* was originally the trademarked name of the fastening device and was capitalized;

it now refers to the class of such devices and is written with a lowercase letter. A word derived from a brand name, such as *Xerox* or *Kleenex*, should be capitalized. If possible, avoid using brand names and choose generic terms such as *photocopy* and *tissue* instead. If you are not sure whether a proper name or derivative has come to stand for a general class, look up the word in a dictionary.

(10) Abbreviations and acronyms

These forms are derived from the initial letters of capitalized word groups:

AMEX   AT&T   CBS   CST   NFL   OPEC   UNESCO   YMCA

(See also **41a(2)** and chapter **45**.)

(11) Military terms

Names of forces and special units are capitalized, as are names of wars, battles, revolutions, and military awards.

United States Army   Marine Corps   Secret Service   Green Berets

Russian Revolution   Gulf War   Operation Overlord   Purple Heart

Military words such as *army, navy,* and *war* are not capitalized when they stand alone.

My sister joined the navy in 2015.

STYLE SHEET FOR CAPITALIZATION

Capitals	No capitals
the West [geographical region]	driving west [compass point]
a Chihuahua [a breed of dog named after a state in Mexico]	a poodle [a breed of dog]
Washington State University [a specific institution]	a state university
Revolutionary War [a specific war]	an eighteenth-century war
U.S. Army [a specific army]	a peacetime army

Declaration of Independence [title of a document]	a declaration of independence
May [specific month]	spring [general season]
Memorial Day [specific day]	a holiday
two Democratic candidates [refers to a political party]	democratic procedures [refers to a form of government]
a Ford tractor [brand name]	a farm tractor
Parkinson's disease [a disease named for a person]	flu, asthma, leukemia
Governor Clay [a person's title]	the governor of this state

43b TITLES AND SUBTITLES

The first and last words in titles and subtitles are capitalized, as are major words—that is, all words other than articles (*a, an,* and *the*), coordinating conjunctions (*and, but, for, nor, or, so,* and *yet*), prepositions (see the list on page 510), and the infinitive marker *to*. (For more information on titles, see **40b** and **44a**.)

From Here to Eternity

"To Be a Student or Not to Be a Student"

APA guidelines differ slightly from other style guidelines: APA recommends capitalizing any word in a title, including a preposition, that has four or more letters.

Southwestern Pottery from Anasazi to Zuni [MLA and CMS]

Southwestern Pottery From Anasazi to Zuni [APA]

MLA, APA, and CMS advise capitalizing all words in a hyphenated compound, except for articles, coordinating conjunctions, and prepositions.

"The Arab-Israeli Dilemma" [compound proper adjective]

"Stop-and-Go Signals" [lowercase for the coordinating conjunction]

When a hyphenated word containing a prefix appears in a title or subtitle, capitalize both elements when the second element is a proper noun (**21a(2)**) or adjective (*Pre-Columbian*). However, if the word following the prefix is a common noun (as in *anti-independence*), capitalize it only if you are following APA guidelines.

"Pre-Columbian Artifacts in Peruvian Museums" [MLA, APA, and CMS]

"Anti-Independence Behavior in Adolescents" [APA]

"Anti-independence Behavior in Adolescents" [MLA and CMS]

When you write bibliographic entries requiring MLA and CMS standards, follow the conventions mentioned in this section. For APA bibliographic entries, capitalize only proper nouns and the first word of the title and subtitle of books and articles.

43c   BEGINNING A SENTENCE

It is not difficult to remember that a sentence begins with a capital letter, but there are certain types of sentences that deserve special note.

(1) A quoted sentence

If a direct quotation is a full sentence, the first word should be capitalized.

> When asked to name the books she found most influential, Nadine Gordimer responded, "**I**n general, the works that mean most to one—change one's thinking and therefore maybe one's life—are those read in youth."

Even if you interrupt a quoted sentence with commentary, only the first letter should be capitalized.

> "**O**ddly," states Ved Mehta, "like my earliest memories, the books that made the greatest impression on me were the ones I encountered as a small child."

However, if you integrate someone else's sentence into a sentence of your own, the first letter should be lowercase—and placed in brackets if you are following MLA guidelines.

> Nadine Gordimer believes that "**[i]**n general, the works that mean most to one—change one's thinking and therefore maybe one's life—are those read in youth" (102).

(2) A freestanding parenthetical sentence

If you place a full sentence inside parentheses, and it is not embedded in a sentence of your own, be sure to capitalize the first word.

> The recordings used in the study were made in the 1980s. (**T**itles of the recordings can be found in the appendix.)

If the sentence inside the parentheses occurs within a sentence of your own, the first word should not be capitalized.

> The recordings used in the study were made in the 1980s (**t**itles of the recordings can be found in the appendix).

(3) An independent clause following a colon

According to *The Chicago Manual of Style*, if there is only one independent clause (**22b(1)**) following a colon, the first word should be lowercased. However, if two or more independent clauses follow the colon, the first word of each clause is capitalized.

> The ear thermometer is used quite frequently now: **t**his type of thermometer records a temperature more accurately than a glass thermometer.

> Two new thermometers are replacing the old thermometers filled with mercury: **T**he digital thermometer uses a heat sensor to determine body temperature. **T**he ear thermometer is actually an infrared thermometer that detects the temperature of the eardrum.

The APA manual recommends capitalizing the first word of any independent clause following a colon.

Think of fever as a symptom, not as an illness: **I**t is the body's response to infection. [APA]

He has two basic rules for healthy living: **E**at sensibly and exercise strenuously at least three times a week. [APA and MLA]

A grammar checker will flag a word at the beginning of a sentence that should be capitalized, but it will not be able to determine whether a word following a colon should be capitalized.

(4) Abbreviated questions

In a series of abbreviated questions, the first words of all the questions are capitalized when the intent is to draw attention to the individual questions. Otherwise, questions in a series begin with lowercase letters.

How do we distinguish the legal codes for families? For individuals? For genetic research?

Did you remember to include your application? résumé? letters of recommendation?

43d   COMPUTER KEYS, MENU ITEMS, AND ICON NAMES

When referring to a specific computer key, menu item, or icon name, capitalize the first letter.

To find the thesaurus, press Shift and the function key F7.

Instead of choosing Copy from the Edit menu, you can press Ctrl+C.

For additional information, click on Resources.

43e   UNNECESSARY CAPITALS

(1) Capitalizing common nouns

Many nouns can be either common or proper, depending on the context. A **proper noun** (21a(2)), also called a *proper name*, identifies a specific entity. A **common noun** (**21a(2)**), which is usually preceded by a word such as *the, a, an, this,* or *that,* is not capitalized.

> a speech course in theater and television [COMPARE: Speech 324: Theater and Television]

> a university, this high school [COMPARE: University of Michigan, Elgin High School]

(2) Overusing capitalization to signal emphasis

Occasionally, a common noun is capitalized for emphasis.

> Some politicians will do anything they can for Power.

If you use capitals for emphasis, do so sparingly; overuse will weaken the effect. For other ways to achieve emphasis, see chapter **32**.

(3) Signaling emphasis online

For online writing in academic and professional contexts, capitalize as you normally do. Be careful not to capitalize whole words for emphasis because your reader may feel as though you are SHOUTING (which is the term used for this rude and undesirable practice).

Exercise 1

Write a sentence using each of the following words correctly.

1. first lady	5. west	9. independent
2. First Lady	6. West	10. Independent
3. mountains	7. avenue	11. doctor
4. Mountains	8. Avenue	12. Doctor

Exercise 2

Edit the capitalization errors in the following paragraph. Be prepared to explain any changes that you make.

[1]Swimmer michael phelps holds the record as the most decorated olympian. [2]By the end of the 2012 olympics in london, england, he had earned twenty-two medals (The previous record holder had eighteen). [3]In the 2008 summer olympic games in beijing, china, phelps finished first eight times. [4]Afterwards, with a bonus he was given by the sports company speedo, phelps established a Foundation to promote healthy lifestyles and the sport of swimming, especially among children. [5]According to phelps, the swimming pool provided a place for him "To have fun, stay healthy, set goals, work hard and gain confidence."

44 | ITALICS

Italics indicate that a word or a group of words is being used in a special way. For example, the use of italics can clear up the ambiguity in the following sentence:

The linguistics students discussed the word stress.

Does this sentence mean that the students discussed a particular word or that they discussed the correct pronunciation of words? By italicizing *stress,* the writer indicates that it was the word itself, not an accent pattern, that the students discussed.

The linguistics students discussed the word *stress.*

This chapter will help you use italics for

- the titles of separate works (44a);
- foreign words (44b);
- the names of legal cases (44c);
- the names of ships, submarines, aircraft, spacecraft, and satellites (44d);
- words, letters, or numerals used as such or letters used in mathematical expressions (44e); and
- words receiving emphasis (44f).

Word-processing programs make it easy to use italics. In handwritten documents, you can indicate italics by underlining.

Donna Tartt's novel <u>The Goldfinch</u> won the 2015 Pulitzer Prize for fiction.

The use of italics instead of underlining is now widely accepted in business writing and academic writing. MLA, APA, and CMS all call for italics.

44a ‖ TITLES OF WORKS PUBLISHED OR PRODUCED SEPARATELY

By convention, italics indicate the title of a longer work, while quotation marks indicate the title of a shorter work. For instance, the title of a collection of poetry published as a book (a longer work) is italicized, and the title of any poem (shorter work) included in the book is enclosed in quotation marks (**40b**). These conventions help readers recognize the nature of a work and sometimes its relationship to another work.

Walt Whitman's "I Sing the Body Electric" first appeared in 1855 in the collection *Leaves of Grass*.

The titles of the following kinds of works are italicized:

Books	*The Little Prince*	*Huck Finn*
Magazines	*Wired*	*Rolling Stone*
Newspapers	*USA Today*	*Wall Street Journal*
Plays, films, DVDs	*The Lion King*	*Boyhood*
Television and radio shows	*Mad Men*	*A Prairie Home Companion*
Recordings	*Can't Be Tamed*	*Great Verdi Overtures*
Works of art	*American Gothic*	*David*
Long poems	*Paradise Lost*	*The Divine Comedy*
Pamphlets	*Saving Energy*	*Tips for Gardeners*
Comic strips	*Peanuts*	*Doonesbury*

According to MLA guidelines, titles of websites are also italicized.

When an italicized title includes the title of a longer work within it, the embedded title is not italicized.

Modern Interpretations of Paradise Lost

If the italicized title includes the title of a short work within it, both titles are italicized, and the short work is also enclosed in quotation marks.

Willa Cather's "Paul's Case"

Titles are not placed in italics or between quotation marks when they stand alone on a title page, a book cover, or a newspaper page. Furthermore, neither italics nor quotation marks are necessary for titles of major historical documents or religious texts.

The Bill of Rights contains the first ten amendments to the U.S. Constitution.

The Bible, a sacred text just as the Koran or the Torah is, begins with the Book of Genesis.

According to CMS guidelines, an initial *the* in a newspaper or periodical title is not italicized. Nor is it capitalized, unless it begins a sentence.

The story was published in the *New York Times.*

However, MLA guidelines call for this initial *The* to be capitalized and italicized: *The Wall Street Journal.*

In any style, omit an article (*a, an,* or *the*) at the beginning of such a title when it would make a sentence awkward.

The report will appear in Thursday's ~~the~~ *Wall Street Journal.*

44b   FOREIGN WORDS

Use italics to indicate foreign words.

Japan has a rich store of traditional folktales, *mukashibanashi,* "tales of long ago."   **—Gary Snyder, *Back on the Fire***

A foreign word used frequently in a text should be italicized only once—at its first occurrence.

The Latin words used to classify plants and animals according to genus and species are italicized.

Homo sapiens   *Rosa setigera*   *Ixodes scapularis*

Countless words borrowed from other languages have become part of English and are therefore not italicized.

bayou (Choctaw)   karate (Japanese)   arroyo (Spanish)

If you are not sure whether a word has been accepted into English, look for it in a standard dictionary (**34d**).

44c   LEGAL CASES

Italics identify the names of legal cases.

Miranda v. Arizona   *Roe v. Wade*

The abbreviation *v.* (for "versus") may appear in either italic or nonitalic type, as long as the style is used consistently. Italics are also used for the shortened name of a well-known legal case.

According to the *Miranda* decision, suspects must be informed of their right to remain silent and their right to legal advice.

Italics are not used to refer to a case by other than its official name.

All the major networks covered the O. J. Simpson trial.

44d   NAMES OF SHIPS, SUBMARINES, AIRCRAFT, SPACECRAFT, AND SATELLITES

Italicize the names of specific ships, submarines, aircraft, spacecraft, and satellites.

USS *Enterprise*   USS *Hawkbill*   *Enola Gay*   *Atlantis*   *Aqua*

The names of trains, the models of vehicles, and the trade names of aircraft are not italicized.

Orient Express   Ford Mustang   Boeing 747

44e WORDS, LETTERS, OR NUMERALS REFERRED TO AS SUCH AND LETTERS USED IN MATHEMATICAL EXPRESSIONS

When you refer to a specific word, letter, or numeral as itself, you should italicize it.

The word *love* is hard to define. [COMPARE: They were in love.]

The *b* in *bat* is not aspirated. [COMPARE: He earned a B+.]

The *2* on the sign has faded, and the *5* has disappeared. [COMPARE: She sent 250 cards.]

Statistical symbols and variables in algebraic expressions are also italicized.

The Pythagorean theorem is expressed as $a^2 + b^2 = c^2$.

44f WORDS RECEIVING EMPHASIS

Used sparingly, italics can signal readers to stress certain words (figure 44.1).

These *are* the right files. [The verb *are* receives more emphasis than it normally would.]

Italics can also emphasize emotional content.

We have to go *now*. [The italicized word signals urgency.]

Figure 44.1: This web banner uses italics to emphasize the importance of the individual in effecting change.

If overused, italics will lose their impact. Instead of italicizing words, substitute more specific words (chapter 35) or vary sentence structures (chapter 33).

Exercise 1

Identify all words that should be italicized in the following sentences. Explain why italics are necessary in each case.

1. Information about museum collections and exhibits can be found in art books, museum websites, and special sections of magazines and newspapers such as Smithsonian Magazine and the New York Times.

2. The website for the Metropolitan Museum of Art has pictures of Anthony Caro's sculpture Odalisque and Charles Demuth's painting The Figure 5 in Gold.

3. The title page of William Blake's Songs of Innocence is included in Masterpieces of the Metropolitan Museum of Art.

4. This book includes a photograph of a beautiful script used in the Koran; the script is known as the maghribi, or Western, style.

5. The large Tyrannosaurus rex discovered by Sue Hendrickson in South Dakota is on display at the Field Museum.

6. The International Museum of Cartoon Art provides information about the designers of such comic strips as Blondie, Peanuts, Mutt and Jeff, and Li'l Abner.

7. The Great Train Robbery, It Happened One Night, and Grand Illusion are in the collection at the Celeste Bartos Film Preservation Center.

8. In 1998, the Songwriters Hall of Fame honored John Williams, who has written music for such movies as Jaws, Star Wars, and E.T.

9. The Smithsonian Institution's National Air and Space Museum houses an impressive collection of aircraft and spacecraft, including Spirit of St. Louis and Gemini 4.

10. The digital collection listed on the website Experience Music Project includes music from the albums Fresh Cream and Bluesbreakers with Eric Clapton.

45 ‖ ABBREVIATIONS, ACRONYMS, AND NUMBERS

Abbreviations, acronyms, and numbers facilitate easy recognition (figure 45.1) and effective communication in both academic papers and business documents. An **abbreviation** is a shortened version of a word or phrase: *assn.* (association), *dept.* (department), *et al.* (*et alii,* or "and others"). An **acronym** is a word formed by combining the initial letters and/or syllables of a series of words: *AIDS* (**a**cquired **i**mmune **d**eficiency **s**yndrome), *sonar* (**so**und **na**vigation **r**anging). This chapter will help you learn

- how and when to abbreviate (**45a–d**),
- when to explain an acronym (**45e**), and
- whether to spell out a number or use numerals (**45f** and **45g**).

Figure 45.1: Abbreviated brand names create instant recognition for products or services.

45a   ABBREVIATIONS WITH NAMES

The abbreviations *Ms., Mr., Mrs.,* and *Dr.* appear before names, whether given as full names or only surnames.

Ms. Sandy Scharnhorst   **Mrs.** Campbell

Mr. Alfredo Luján   **Dr.** Bollinger

Civil or military titles should not be abbreviated in academic writing.

Senator Bob Corker   Captain Derrick   Professor Kirsten Benson

Abbreviations such as *Jr., Sr.,* and *MD* appear after names.

Samuel Levy **Jr.**   Imogen Hickey, **MD**

Mark Ngo **Sr.**   Joan Richtsmeier, **PhD**

In the past, periods were customarily used in abbreviations for academic degrees, but MLA and CMS now recommend omitting periods from abbreviations such as *MA, PhD,* and *MD.* Although MLA still follows the convention calling for commas to set off *Jr.* or *Sr.,* these abbreviations are increasingly considered part of the names they follow and thus need not be set off by commas unless you are following MLA style.

Note that when two designations are possible, only one should be used.

Dr. Kristin Grine OR Kristin Grine, **MD** [NOT Dr. Kristin Grine, MD]

Abbreviations of plural proper nouns are often formed by simply adding *s* before the period: *Drs.* Grine and Hickey. But there are exceptions: the plural of *Mr.* is *Messrs.,* and the plural of *Mrs.* is *Mesdames,* for which there is no abbreviated form.

45b   ADDRESSES IN CORRESPONDENCE

The names of states and words such as *Street, Road, Company,* and *Corporation* are usually written out when they appear in a letter, including in the address at the top of the page. However, they may be abbreviated when used in the address on an envelope.

Sentence　　　Derson Manufacturing Company is located on
　　　　　　　　Madison Street in Watertown, Minnesota.

Address　　　Derson Manufacturing Co.
　　　　　　　　200 Madison St.
　　　　　　　　Watertown, MN 55388

When addressing correspondence within the United States, use the two-letter state abbreviations established by the U.S. Postal Service. (No period follows these abbreviations.) If you do not know an appropriate state abbreviation or zip code, you can find it on the Postal Service's website.

45c ABBREVIATIONS IN SOURCE DOCUMENTATION

Abbreviations are commonly used when citing research sources in bibliographies, footnotes, and endnotes. Common abbreviations include the following (not all citation styles accept all of these abbreviations).

Bibliographies and Notes

anon., Anon.	anonymous, Anonymous
biog.	biography, biographer, biographical
bull.	bulletin
c. or ca.	circa, about (for example, *c. 1920*)
col., cols.	column, columns
cont.	contents OR continues, continued
et al.	*et alii* ("and others")
fig.	figure
fwd.	foreword, foreword by
illus.	illustrated by, illustrator, illustration
inc., Inc.	including, Incorporated
intl.	international
introd.	introduction, introduction by
ms., mss.	manuscript, manuscripts
natl.	national

n.d.	no date, no date of publication
n.p.	no place of publication, no publisher
n. pag.	no pagination
no., nos.	number, numbers
p., pp.	page, pages
P, Pr.	Press
pref.	preface
pt., pts.	part, parts
trans. or tr.	translation, translated by
U, Univ.	University

Computer Terms

doi	Digital Object Identifier (DOI)
FTP	file transfer protocol
HTML	hypertext markup language
http	hypertext transfer protocol
KB	kilobyte
MB	megabyte
MOO	multiuser domain, object-oriented
PDF	portable document format
URL	uniform resource locator

Divisions of Government

Cong.	Congress
dept.	department
div.	division
govt.	government
GPO	Government Printing Office
HR	House of Representatives

45d ACCEPTABLE ABBREVIATIONS IN ACADEMIC AND PROFESSIONAL WRITING

Abbreviations are usually too informal for use in sentences, although some have become so familiar that they are considered acceptable substitutes for full words.

(1) Abbreviations for special purposes

The names of months, days of the week, and units of measurement are usually written out (not abbreviated) when they are included in sentences, as are words such as *Street* and *Corporation.*

> On a Tuesday in September, we drove ninety-nine miles to San Francisco, California, where we stayed in a hotel on Market Street.

Words such as *volume, chapter,* and *page* are abbreviated (*vol., ch.,* and *p.*) in bibliographies and in citations of research sources, but they are written out within sentences.

> I read the introductory chapter and the three final pages in the first volume of the committee's report.

(2) Clipped forms

A word shortened by common usage, a **clipped form,** does not end with a period. Some clipped forms—such as *rep* (for *representative*), *exec* (for *executive*), and *info* (for *information*)—are too informal for use in college writing. Others—such as *exam, lab,* and *math*—have become acceptable because they have been used so frequently that they no longer seem like shortened forms.

(3) Abbreviations for time periods and zones

> 82 BC for *before Christ* [OR 82 BCE for *before the Common Era*]

> AD 95 for *anno Domini,* "in the year of our Lord" [OR 95 CE for *of the Common Era*]

> 7:40 a.m. for *ante meridiem,* "before noon"

> 4:52 EST for *Eastern Standard Time*

Words designating units of time, such as *minute* and *month,* are written out when they appear in sentences. They can be abbreviated in tables or charts.

sec.	min.	hr.	wk.	mo.	yr.

(4) The abbreviation U.S. or US as an adjective

the U.S. Navy, the US economy
[COMPARE: They moved to the United States in 2010.]

The abbreviation *U.S.* or *US* should be used only as an adjective in academic and professional writing. When using *United States* as a noun, spell it out. The choice of *U.S.* or *US* will depend on the discipline in which you are writing: MLA lists US as the preferred form, but APA uses U.S., and CMS accepts either form.

(5) Individuals known by their initials

JFK   LBJ   E. B. White   B. B. King

In most cases, however, first and last names should be written out in full.

Oprah Winfrey   Peyton Manning   Donald Trump

(6) Some abbreviations for Latin expressions

Certain abbreviations for Latin expressions are common in academic writing.

cf. [compare]   et al. [and others]   i.e. [that is]

e.g. [for example]   etc. [and so forth]   vs. OR v. [versus]

45e   ACRONYMS

The ability to identify a particular acronym will vary from one audience to another. Some readers will know that NAFTA stands for the North American Free Trade Agreement; others may not. By spelling out acronyms the first time you use them, you are being courteous and clear. Introduce the acronym by placing it in parentheses after the group of words it stands for.

The Federal Emergency Management Administration (FEMA) was criticized by many after Hurricane Katrina.

🔵 MULTILINGUAL WRITERS

USING ARTICLES WITH ABBREVIATIONS, ACRONYMS, OR NUMBERS

When you use an abbreviation, an acronym, or a number, you sometimes need an indefinite article. Choose *a* or *an* based on the pronunciation of the initial sound of the abbreviation, acronym, or number: use *a* before a consonant sound and *an* before a vowel sound.

A picture of **a UN** delegation is on the front page of today's newspaper. [*UN* begins with a consonant sound.]

I have **an IBM** computer. [*IBM* begins with a vowel sound.]

The reporter interviewed **a NASA** engineer. [*NASA* begins with a consonant sound.]

My friend drives **a 1964** Mustang. [*1964* begins with a consonant sound.]

Exercise 1

Decide whether the following sentences use forms appropriate for college essays. Correct any usage that is not appropriate.

1. I always wake up before 6 a.m.
2. The pope was buried in 670 anno Domini.
3. The Walkers live on Sandy Ridge Rd.
4. We live six blocks from Sunset Lane.
5. My parents always go to Florida in Feb.
6. Easter is sometimes celebrated during the third month of the yr.
7. Knoxville is in TN.
8. We can meet at the UPS shipping store.
9. She prefers to be addressed as Ms. Terry Campbell.
10. He is not very impressive as a state rep.

45f   GENERAL USES OF NUMBERS

Depending on their uses, numbers are treated in different ways. MLA recommends spelling out numbers that are expressed in one or two words (*nine, ninety-one, nine hundred, nine million*). A numeral is used for any other number ($9\frac{1}{2}$, *9.9, 999*), unless it begins a sentence. CMS advises spelling out whole numbers from zero through one hundred and any number followed by the word *hundred, thousand, hundred thousand,* or *million*.

> The register recorded 164 names.

APA advises spelling out numbers below ten, common fractions, and numbers that are spelled out in universally accepted usage (for example, the Twelve Apostles). All three of these style manuals recommend using words rather than numerals at the beginning of a sentence.

> One hundred sixty-four names were recorded in the register.
> [Notice that *and* is not used in numbers greater than one hundred.
> NOT One hundred and sixty-four names . . . .]

When numbers or amounts refer to the same entities throughout a passage, use numerals when any of the numbers would be more than two words long if spelled out.

> Only 5 of the 134 delegates attended the final meeting. The remaining 129 delegates will be informed by e-mail.

In scientific or technical writing, numerals are used before abbreviations of units of measurement (*2 L, 30 cc*).

45g   SPECIAL USES OF NUMBERS

(1) Expressing specific times of day in either numerals or words

Numerals or words can be used to express times of day. They should be used consistently.

4 p.m. OR four o'clock in the afternoon

9:30 a.m. OR half-past nine in the morning OR nine-thirty in the morning [Notice the use of hyphens.]

(2) Using numerals and words for dates

Months are written as words, years as numerals, and days and decades as either words or numerals. However, 9/11 is an acceptable alternative to September 11, 2001.

May 20, 1998 OR 20 May 1998 [NOT May 20th, 1998]

the fourth of December OR December 4

the fifties OR the 1950s

from 2010 to 2015 OR 2010–2015 [Sometimes a hyphen is used instead of an en dash.]

⬛ TECH SAVVY

To create an en dash, press Option and the hyphen key simultaneously.

ⓝ MULTILINGUAL WRITERS

DIFFERENT WAYS OF WRITING DATES

Many cultures invert the numerals for the month and the day: *14/2/2015* or *14 February 2015*. In publications from the United States, the month generally precedes the day: *2/14/2015* or *February 14, 2015*.

(3) Using numerals in addresses

Numerals are commonly used in street addresses and for zip codes.

25 Arrow Drive, Apartment 1, Columbia, MO 78209

OR, for a mailing envelope, 25 Arrow Dr., Apt. 1, Columbia, MO 78209

(4) Using numerals for identification

A numeral may be used as part of a proper noun (21a(2)).

Channel 10   Edward III   Interstate 40   Room 311

(5) Referring to pages and divisions of books and plays

Numerals are used to designate pages and other divisions of books and plays.

page 15   Chapter 8   Part 2   in act 2, scene 1 OR in Act II, Scene I

(6) Expressing decimals and percentages numerically

Numerals are used to express decimals and percentages.

a 2.5 average   12 percent   0.853 metric ton

(7) Using numerals for large fractional numbers

Numerals with decimal points can be used to express large fractional numbers.

5.2 million inhabitants   1.6 billion years

ñ MULTILINGUAL WRITERS

COMMAS AND PERIODS WITH NUMERALS

Cultures differ in their use of the period and the comma with numerals. In American usage, a decimal point (period) indicates a number or part of a number that is smaller than one, and a comma divides large numbers into units of three digits.

7.65 (seven and sixty-five   10,000
one-hundredths)   (ten thousand)

In some other cultures, these usages of the decimal point and the comma are reversed.

7,65 (seven and sixty-five   10.000
one-hundredths)   (ten thousand)

(8) Different ways of writing monetary amounts

Monetary amounts should be spelled out if they occur infrequently in a piece of writing. Otherwise, numerals and symbols can be used.

two million dollars $2,000,000

ninety-nine cents   99¢ OR $0.99

Exercise 2

Edit the following sentences to correct the usage of abbreviations and numbers.

1. A Natl. Historic Landmark, Hoover Dam is located about 30 miles s.e. of Las Vegas, Nev.
2. The dam is named after Herbert Hoover, the 31st pres. of the U.S.
3. It is administered by the U.S. Dept. of the Interior.
4. Built by the fed. gov. between nineteen thirty-three and 1935, this dam is still considered one of the greatest achievements in the history of civ. engineering.
5. Construction of the dam became possible after several states in the Southwest (namely, AZ, CA, CO, NV, NM, UT, and WY) agreed on a plan to share water from the river.
6. The concrete used in the dam would have built a highway 16 ft. wide, stretching all the way from San Francisco to NYC.
7. 3,500 men worked on the dam during an average month of construction; this work translated into a monthly payroll of $500,000.

8. Spanning the Colorado River, Hoover Dam created Lake Mead—a reservoir covering 247 sq. miles.

9. A popular tourist attraction, Hoover Dam was closed to the public after terrorists attacked the U.S. on 9/11/01.

10. Today, certain pts. of the dam remain closed to the public as part of the effort to improve U.S. security.

ADVICE for MULTILINGUAL WRITERS

Situate Yourself

In the United States, candidates for job interviews are often asked to talk about their strengths. Depending on your country of origin, such a request may seem strange because you are, in a way, being asked to boast about your abilities and experiences. However, instead of thinking of highlighting your strengths as boasting, consider the job interview as an opportunity for you to explain how your strengths align with the needs of a company or organization.

For this activity, imagine a particular employer you would like to work for. Write a response to this question: What is your greatest strength? Include an example of how that strength was a benefit in the past and how it could benefit the company or organization you are interviewing with. As you write, make note of any sections in chapters 46–48 that are particularly helpful to you.

(continued from page 789)

- The article *an* is used before an adjective that begins with a vowel sound.

    We went to *an* **o**utdoor cafe.

- Plural count nouns are preceded by *some, many,* or *few* when the quantity is a consideration.

    Some/Many/Few students have volunteered.

- Plural count nouns take no determiner at all when quantity is not a consideration.

    Students have volunteered.

    Potatoes are grown in Idaho.

46c DETERMINERS AND NONCOUNT NOUNS

A **noncount noun** names something that cannot be counted; it has neither a singular nor a plural form. Some noncount nouns never take determiners.

TYPES OF NONCOUNT NOUNS THAT TAKE NO DETERMINERS

- **Games and sports:** baseball, basketball, chess, football, poker, tennis, soccer

    Soccer is my favorite sport.

- **Subjects of study:** biology, chemistry, economics, English, history, mathematics, psychology, sociology

    English is my favorite subject.

Other types of noncount nouns may or may not take determiners.

TYPES OF NONCOUNT NOUNS THAT MAY OR MAY NOT TAKE DETERMINERS

- **Abstractions:** confidence, democracy, education, happiness, health, honesty, importance, knowledge, love, news, wisdom

    An **education** is of utmost importance.

    Education is crucial to economic security.

- **Groups of things:** clothing, equipment, garbage, homework, money, scenery, traffic, transportation, vocabulary

  The **homework** for French class is time-consuming.

  I spend a lot of time doing **homework.**
- **Substances:** air, blood, coffee, ice, rice, tea, water, wood

  This **tea** is watery.

  She prefers **tea** for breakfast.

To decide which determiner to use with a noun referring to an abstraction, a group, or a substance, begin with the question you asked about count nouns: **Is the noncount noun referring to something specific?** If it is, use the determiners in the following list.

DETERMINERS WITH NONCOUNT NOUNS THAT REFER TO SPECIFIC ABSTRACTIONS, GROUPS OF THINGS, OR SUBSTANCES

Use *the, this, that,* or a possessive before a noncount noun making a specific reference.

> *The/This/That/Our* information is important.

If the noncount noun is *not* referring to something specific, use the following guidelines.

DETERMINERS WITH NONCOUNT NOUNS THAT DO NOT REFER TO SPECIFIC ABSTRACTIONS, GROUPS OF THINGS, OR SUBSTANCES

A noncount noun is preceded by the determiner *some, much,* or *little* when quantity is a consideration.

> We drank *some/much/little* water.

A noncount noun takes no determiner at all when quantity is not a consideration.

> We drank only water.

Because noncount nouns do not have singular and plural forms, sentences like the following should be edited:

We learned to use a lot of equipments. [An *s* is not added to a noncount noun.]

assignments
I finished two homeworks today. [Numbers are not used with noncount nouns.]

The job requires a̶ special machinery. [*A* and *an* are not used with noncount nouns.]

is
The vocabulary a̶r̶e̶ difficult. [Use a singular verb with a noncount noun.]

Some words can be used as either a count noun or a noncount noun.

They believed **life** was sacred. [noncount noun]

He led *an* interesting **life.** [count noun]

46d   DETERMINERS AND ADJECTIVES

Some adjectives add specificity to nouns. Use *the* before the following types of adjectives.

ADJECTIVES AND DETERMINERS: SPECIFIC REFERENCES

- Adjectives indicating sequence, such as *first, next, last,* and so forth
    The **first/next/last** person in line will win a prize.
- Adjectives indicating a single person or item, such as *right, only,* and so forth
    She had *the* **right/only** answer.

When describing how one of two individuals or entities differs from or surpasses the other, use the comparative form of an adjective (**27b**). The comparative form has the suffix *-er* or the word *more* or *less*:

Cars are cheap*er* here. Cars are *more* expensive there.

Use the article *the* before the comparative form in this phrase: *the* [comparative form] *of the two* [plural noun].

The older *of the two* sons is now a doctor.

She bought *the* less expensive *of the two* cars.

When describing how one of three or more individuals or entities surpasses all the others, use the superlative form of an adjective (**27b**). There are two superlative forms: (1) the adjective has the suffix *-est* and is preceded by the article *the*, or (2) the adjective does not have that suffix and is preceded by *the most* or *the least*.

Cars are *the* cheap*est* here. Cars are *the most* expensive there.

Use the following guidelines to help you choose which form to use.

GUIDELINES FOR FORMING COMPARATIVES AND SUPERLATIVES

- One-syllable words generally take the ending *-er* or *-est*: *fast, faster, fastest.*
- Two-syllable words ending in a consonant and *-y* also generally take the ending *-er* or *-est*, with the *y* changed to an *i*: *noisy, noisier, noisiest.*
- Two-syllable adjectives ending in *-ct*, *-nt*, or *-st* are preceded by *more/less* or *most/least*: *less exact, least exact; more recent, most recent; more honest, most honest.* Two-syllable adjectives with a suffix such as *-ous, -ish, -ful, -ing,* or *-ed* are also preceded by *more/less* or *most/least*: *more/most famous; more/most squeamish; less/least careful; more/most lasting, less/least depressed.*
- Two-syllable adjectives ending in *-er, -ow,* or *-some* either take the ending *-er* or *-est* or are preceded by *more/less* or *most/least*: *narrower, more narrow, less narrow, narrowest, most narrow, least narrow.*
- Words of three or more syllables are preceded by *more/less* or *most/least*: *less/least fortunate; more/most intelligent.*
- Some modifiers have irregular comparative and superlative forms:

    little, less, least

    good/well, better, best

    bad, worse, worst

46e	SHIFTING FROM NONSPECIFIC TO SPECIFIC REFERENCES

In writing, you usually introduce an individual or an entity with a non-specific reference. After you have mentioned the individual or entity, you can use specific references.

First mention
A tsunami <u>warning</u> was issued last night.

Subsequent mention
This <u>warning</u> affected all low-lying areas.

A subsequent mention does not have to repeat the word used in the first mention. However, the word chosen must be closely related to the one introduced first.

The weather service <u>warned</u> people about possible flooding. **The** <u>warning</u> included possible evacuation routes.

Exercise 1

Edit the following common sayings so that determiners are used correctly.
1. The absence makes a heart grow fonder.
2. The actions speak louder than the words.
3. The bad news travels fast.
4. Best things come in the small packages.
5. The blood is thicker than the water.
6. Don't cry over the spilled milk.

47 | VERBS AND VERB FORMS

Learning how to use verbs effectively involves more than looking up their meanings in a dictionary. You must also understand how the *form* of a verb affects its meaning. Building on the discussion in chapter 25, this chapter gives more information about

- verb tenses (47a),
- auxiliary verbs (47b),
- prepositional and phrasal verbs (47c), and
- participles used as adjectives (47d).

47a | VERB TENSES

English verbs are either regular verbs (25a(1)) or irregular verbs (25a(2)). This distinction is based on the forms of a verb. The forms of irregular verbs do not follow the set pattern that the forms of regular verbs do. If you have trouble choosing the right verb forms, study the charts on pages 560 and 561–563. As you become more familiar with English verb forms, you will understand how they provide information about time. Keep in mind that, although the words *present, past,* and *future* may lead you to think that these tenses refer to actions or events occurring now, in the past, and in the future, respectively, this strict separation is not always the case.

(1) Simple tenses

Simple tenses have many uses, which are not limited to indicating specific times. The conjugation of the **simple present tense** of a regular verb includes two forms of the verb: the base form and the -*s* form. Notice that the third-person singular form is the only form with the -*s* ending.

Simple Present Tense

	Singular	Plural
First person	I **work**	We **work**
Second person	You **work**	You **work**
Third person	He, she, it **works**	They **work**

Use the simple present tense for the following purposes.

USES OF THE SIMPLE PRESENT TENSE

- To indicate a current state: We **are** ready.
- To report a general fact: The sun **rises** in the east.
- To describe a habitual action: Dana **uses** common sense.
- To add a sense of immediacy to a description of a historical event: In 1939, Hitler's armies **attack** Poland.
- To discuss literary and artistic works: Joseph Conrad **writes** about what he sees in the human heart.
- To refer to future events: The festival **begins** next month.

The simple past tense of a regular verb has only one form: the base form with the *-ed* ending. The past tense forms of irregular verbs vary (see **25a(2)**).

Simple Past Tense

I, you, he, she, it, we, they **worked**

The simple past tense is used to refer to completed actions or past events.

USES OF THE SIMPLE PAST TENSE

- To indicate a completed action: He **traveled** to the Philippines.
- To report a past event: The accident **occurred** several weeks ago.

The simple future tense of a regular verb also has only one form: the base form accompanied by the auxiliary *will.*

Simple Future Tense
I, you, he, she, it, we, they **will work**

The simple future tense refers to future actions or states.

USES OF THE SIMPLE FUTURE TENSE

- To promise to perform an action: I **will call** you tonight.
- To predict a future action: They **will finish** the project soon.
- To predict a future state of being: Everyone **will be** weary.

It is also possible to use a form of *be going to* when referring to the future (47b(2)).

I **am going to** study in Russia next year.

(2) Progressive tenses

Progressive tenses indicate that actions or events are repetitive, ongoing, or temporary. The present progressive tense consists of a present-tense form of the auxiliary verb *be* and the present participle (*-ing* form) of the main verb, whether that verb is regular or irregular. Notice that the present participle remains the same regardless of person and number, but the auxiliary *be* appears in three forms: *am* for first-person singular, *is* for third-person singular, and *are* for other person-number combinations.

Present Progressive Tense		
	Singular	**Plural**
First person	I am working	We **are working**
Second person	You **are working**	You **are working**
Third person	He, she, it **is working**	They **are working**

The present progressive tense signals an activity in progress or a temporary situation.

USES OF THE PRESENT PROGRESSIVE TENSE

- To show that an activity is in progress: The doctor **is attending** a conference in Nebraska.
- To indicate that a situation is temporary: We **are living** in a yurt right now.
- To refer to an action that will occur at a specific time in the future: They **are leaving** for Alaska next week.

Like the present progressive, the past progressive tense is a combination of the auxiliary verb *be* and the present participle (*-ing* form) of the main verb. However, the auxiliary verb is in the past tense, rather than in the present tense.

Past Progressive Tense

	Singular	Plural
First person	I **was working**	We **were working**
Second person	You **were working**	You **were working**
Third person	He, she, it **was working**	They **were working**

The past progressive tense signals that an action or event occurred in the past and was repeated or ongoing.

USES OF THE PAST PROGRESSIVE TENSE

- To indicate that a past action was repetitive: The new member **was** constantly **interrupting** the discussion.
- To signal that a past action was occurring when something else happened: We **were eating** dinner when we heard the news.

A verb in the future progressive tense has only one form. Two auxiliaries, *will* and *be,* are used with the *-ing* form of the main verb.

Future Progressive Tense

I, you, he, she, it, we, they **will be working**

The future progressive tense indicates that actions will occur over some period of time in the future.

> **USE OF THE FUTURE PROGRESSIVE TENSE**
>
> ■ To indicate that an action will occur over a span of time in the future:
> She **will be giving** her report at the end of the meeting.

❗ CAUTION

Some verbs do not express actions but rather mental states, emotions, conditions, or relationships. These verbs are not used in progressive forms; they include *believe, belong, contain, cost, know, like, own, prefer,* and *want.*

       contains
The book ∧ is containing many Central American folktales.

     knows
He ∧ is knowing many old myths.

(3) Perfect tenses

Perfect tenses indicate actions that were performed or events that occurred before a particular time. The present perfect tense is formed by combining the auxiliary *have* with the past participle of the main verb. The participle remains the same regardless of person and number; however, the auxiliary has two forms: *has* for third-person singular and *have* for the other person-number combinations.

	Present Perfect Tense	
	Singular	**Plural**
First person	I **have worked**	We **have worked**
Second person	You **have worked**	You **have worked**
Third person	He, she, it **has worked**	They **have worked**

The present perfect tense is used for the following purposes.

USES OF THE PRESENT PERFECT TENSE

- To signal that a situation originating in the past is continuing into the present: They **have lived** in New Zealand for twenty years.
- To refer to a past action that has current relevance: I **have read** that book already, but I could certainly read it again.

The past perfect tense is also formed by combining the auxiliary *have* with the past participle. However, the auxiliary is in the past tense. There is only one form of the past perfect.

Past Perfect Tense

I, you, he, she, it, we, they **had worked**

The past perfect tense specifies that an action was completed at a time in the past prior to another time or before another past action.

USES OF THE PAST PERFECT TENSE

- To indicate that a past action occurred prior to a given time in the past: By the time he turned forty, he **had earned** enough money for retirement.
- To indicate that a past action occurred prior to another past action: She **had** already **mailed** the letter when she realized her mistake.
- To emphasize the point of preceding discourse: I spent the morning in my office. I shelved all my books, arranged the furniture, hung a few photographs, and learned to use the computer. My new job **had begun.**

The future perfect tense consists of two auxiliaries, *will* and *have*, along with the past participle of the main verb. There is only one form of the future perfect tense.

Future Perfect Tense

I, you, he, she, it, we, they **will have worked**

The future perfect tense refers to an action that is to be completed prior to a future time.

- To refer to future completion of an action: By this time next year, I **will have finished** medical school.

(4) Perfect progressive tenses

Perfect progressive tenses combine the forms and meanings of the progressive and the perfect tenses. The present perfect progressive form consists of two auxiliaries, *have* and *be,* plus the present participle (*-ing* form) of the main verb. The form of the auxiliary *have* varies with person and number. The auxiliary *be* appears as the past participle, *been.*

Present Perfect Progressive Tense		
	Singular	Plural
First person	I **have been working**	We **have been working**
Second person	You **have been working**	You **have been working**
Third person	He, she, it **has been working**	They **have been working**

The present perfect progressive signals that an action, state, or event originating in the past is ongoing or incomplete.

USES OF THE PRESENT PERFECT PROGRESSIVE TENSE

- To signal that a state of being is ongoing: I **have been feeling** tired for a week.
- To indicate that an action is incomplete: We **have been organizing** the conference since April.

The past perfect progressive tense follows the pattern *had + been +* present participle (*-ing* form) of the main verb. (The auxiliary *have* is in the past tense.)

Past Perfect Progressive Tense
I, you, he, she, it, we, they **had been working**

The past perfect progressive tense refers to a situation or an action occurring over a period of time in the past and prior to another past action.

USE OF THE PAST PERFECT PROGRESSIVE TENSE

- To indicate that an ongoing action occurred prior to a past action: She **had been living** so frugally all year that she saved enough money for a new car.

The future perfect progressive form has the pattern *will* + *have* + *been* + present participle (*-ing* form) of the main verb.

Future Perfect Progressive Tense

I, you, he, she, it, we, they **will have been working**

The future perfect progressive tense refers to an action that is occurring in the present and will continue to occur for a specific amount of time.

USE OF THE FUTURE PERFECT PROGRESSIVE TENSE

- To indicate that an action will continue until a specified time: In one month, I **will have been working** on this project for five years.

Exercise 1

Explain how the meaning of each sentence changes when the verb tense changes.

1. In "Fiji's Rainbow Reef," Les Kaufman (describes/described) the coral reefs of Fiji and (discusses/discussed) the factors affecting their health.
2. Rising water temperatures (damaged/have damaged/did damage) the reefs.

3. The algae that (provide/provided) color (do not survive/did not survive) in the warmer water.
4. The lack of algae (has left/had left) the coral "bleached."
5. Strangely, though, new life (is flourishing/was flourishing/has been flourishing) in some of these areas.
6. Scientists (study/will study) this area to understand its resilience.

(5) Using verb tenses to convey the duration or time sequence of actions and events

When you use more than one tense in a single sentence, you give readers information about how actions or events are related in time and duration.

> Whenever the teacher **calls** on me, I **stutter** nervously.
> [Verbs in the present tense indicate habitual actions.]

> When the speaker **had finished,** everyone **applauded.**
> [The past perfect tense *had finished* indicates a time before the action expressed by *applauded*.]

Infinitives and participles can be used to express time relations within a sentence. The present infinitive (*to* + base form) of a verb expresses action occurring later than the action expressed by the main verb.

> They **want to design** a new museum. [The action of designing will take place in the future.]

The perfect infinitive (*to* + *have* + past participle) signals that an action, state, or event is potential or hypothetical or that it did not occur.

> She **hopes to have earned** her degree by the end of next year.
> [Earning the degree has the potential to occur.]

> The governor **would like to have postponed** the vote.
> [The postponement did not occur.]

The present participle (*-ing* form) indicates simultaneous or previous action.

> **Laughing** loudly, the old friends **left** the restaurant arm in arm.
> [The friends were laughing as they were leaving.]

> **Hearing** that she was ill, I **rushed** right over.
> [The action of hearing occurred first.]

The perfect participle (*having* + past participle) expresses action completed before the action conveyed by the main verb.

> **Having learned** Spanish at an early age, she **spoke** to the Mexican diplomats in their native language.

The past participle can be used to express either simultaneous action or previous action.

> **Led** by a former Peace Corps worker, the volunteers **provided** medical assistance. [The two actions occurred simultaneously.]

> **Encouraged** by job prospects, he **moved** to Atlanta. [The encouragement preceded the move.]

Exercise 2

Revise the following sentences so that all verbs express logical time sequences.

1. We expected the storm to have bypassed our town, but it made a direct hit.
2. We would like to have prior notice; however, even the police officers were taken by surprise.
3. Not having known much about flooding, the emergency crew was at a disadvantage.
4. Having thrown sandbags all day, the volunteers had been exhausted by 5 p.m.
5. They went home, succeeding in preventing a major disaster.

47b AUXILIARY VERBS

Auxiliary verbs add nuances of meaning to main verbs (25a(4)). Some provide information about time (47a), while others are used to provide emphasis, to form questions, or to indicate ability, certainty, obligation, and so on.

(1) The auxiliary verb *do*

Unlike *be* and *have*, the auxiliary verb *do* does not occur with other verbs to indicate tense. Instead, it is used in questions, negations, and emphatic sentences.

Do you have any questions? [question]

I **do** not have any questions. [negation]

I **do** have a few comments. [emphatic sentence]

The auxiliary *do* is used only in the simple present (*do, does*) and the simple past (*did*).

(2) Modal verbs

The modal auxiliary verbs in English are *can, could, may, might, must, shall, should, will,* and *would* (25a(4)). English also has **phrasal modals**, which are modal auxiliaries consisting of more than one word. They have meanings similar to those of one-word modals.

be able to (ability): We **were able to** find the original document.

have to (obligation): You **have to** report your test results.

Other common phrasal modals are *be going to, be supposed to, had better, need to,* and *used to*. Modal auxiliaries and phrasal modals can sometimes be combined. The modal precedes the phrasal modal.

I <u>**should**</u> **be able to** finish the project by Tuesday.

He <u>**may**</u> **have to** move to another city.

Both modal auxiliaries and phrasal modals indicate a variety of meanings, including obligation, permission, and probability. Modal auxiliaries have only two forms: the base form and the perfective form (base form + *have* + past participle). Most phrasal modals have more than two forms (*am able to, is able to, were able to, has been able to*). Only *had better* and *used to* have a single form. The following box shows the most common uses of modal verbs in academic writing.

USING MODAL VERBS

Modal Auxiliaries

Verb	Meaning	Example(s)
can	Ability or possibility	New legislation **can** change tax rates. Anything **can** happen.
could	Possibility	The announcement **could** cause unrest.
may	Possibility	Funding **may** be the problem.
must	Obligation or necessity	Judges **must** be neutral. There **must** be a better answer.
should	Obligation or advice	Dissent **should** be acknowledged. You **should** pay off your credit-card balance.
will	Prediction or certainty	She **will** perform the experiment herself. A statistical analysis **will** be performed.
would	Prediction	All **would** benefit from fewer obligations.

Modal Auxiliaries with *Have* + Past Participle

Verb	Meaning	Example
may have	Conjecture	The tank **may have** leaked.
might have	Conjecture	The accident **might have** caused the delay.
must have	Conjecture	The police **must have** known about the protest.
should have	Criticism	Monitors **should have** reported the incident.

Phrasal Modals in the Present Tense

Verb	Meaning	Example(s)
be able to	Ability	They **are able to** respond quickly to emergencies.
have to	Obligation or necessity	The president **has to** attend the meeting. The water for the experiment **has to** be cold.

need to	Obligation or necessity	Students **need to** register for class this week.
		A good summary **needs to** be objective.

Phrasal Modals in the Past Tense

Verb	Meaning	Example
was/were able to	Ability	They **were able to** finish on time.
had to	Obligation	The journalist **had to** divulge his sources.

---

❶ CAUTION

Although English verbs are often followed by the infinitive marker *to* (as in *want to go* and *plan to leave*), modal auxiliaries are not.

We **should to** finish our report by Friday.

Exercise 3

Fill in the blank with a modal auxiliary or a phrasal modal and describe the meaning it conveys.

1. Nations at war _____ follow the Geneva Conventions.
2. Everyone _____ be treated humanely.
3. In various wars, humanitarian groups _____ protect innocent victims.
4. Without humanitarian groups, many more people _____ lost their lives.
5. Critics of past wars state that more aid _____ been provided.

47c PREPOSITIONAL VERBS AND PHRASAL VERBS

Prepositional verbs and phrasal verbs are both combinations of verbs with other words. A prepositional verb consists of a verb followed by a preposition; a phrasal verb consists of a verb followed by a particle.

(1) Prepositional verbs

Some verbs are typically followed by prepositions. Such verbs can be used in either the active voice or the passive voice (25c). Following are ten prepositional verbs that commonly occur in academic writing. Some are more often used in the active voice; others are more often used in the passive voice.

TEN PREPOSITIONAL VERBS COMMON IN ACADEMIC WRITING

Active Voice	Passive Voice
depend on	be applied to
lead to	be derived from
look at	be divided into
refer to	be known as
result in	be used in

When you are reading, take note of prepositions that are combined with specific verbs.

(2) Phrasal verbs

A **phrasal verb** consists of a verb and a particle such as *up, out,* or *on.* A phrasal verb is often idiomatic, conveying a meaning that differs from the common meanings of the individual words. For example, the definitions that first come to mind for the words *blow* and *up* are not likely to help you understand the phrasal verb *blow up* when it means "to enlarge."

She **blew up** the photograph so that she could see the faces better.

Like verbs in general, phrasal verbs may have more than one meaning. *To blow up* means not only "to enlarge" but also "to inflate" or "to explode."

It is also important to note that a given verb can combine with several different particles. *Take* occurs with various particles to form the phrasal verbs *take in* ("understand"), *take on* ("undertake"), *take out* ("remove"), *take up* ("consume"), and *take down* ("dismantle"). In addition to *take*, the following verbs often appear in academic writing as phrasal verbs: *go, come, get, set, carry, turn, bring, look,* and *put.* The meanings of the phrasal verbs depend on the specific particle they include.

A small group of phrasal verbs have meanings that are similar to common definitions of the verbs themselves; their particles just add a sense of completion or emphasis.

They **wrote up** the report by six o'clock.

The particle *up* in *wrote up* does not refer to a direction; instead, it emphasizes the completion of the report. Still other phrasal verbs retain the common meanings of the verb and the particle.

The protesters **hung up** a banner.

The verb and particle in most phrasal verbs may be separated by a short noun phrase (**22a(1)**).

She **called** the meeting **off.**   OR   She **called off** the meeting.

If you use a pronoun with a phrasal verb, always place it between the verb and the particle.

The student **turned** <u>it</u> **in** yesterday.

Some phrasal verbs are not separable, however.

The group **went over** the proposal.

I **came across** an interesting fact.

You should be able to find the definitions of phrasal verbs in a conventional dictionary; however, a specialized dictionary will also provide information about the separability of these verbs. (See **34d** for a list of dictionaries.)

Exercise 4

Insert an appropriate preposition or particle after the verb in each sentence.

1. Overpopulation has brought _____ great changes on earth.
2. Deforestation often leads _____ extinctions.
3. High levels of carbon dioxide result _____ increased global temperatures.
4. Proposals for curbing emissions should be looked _____ closely.
5. Scientists have taken _____ the challenge of slowing the destruction.

47d PARTICIPLES USED AS ADJECTIVES

Both present participles (such as *amazing* and *interesting*) and past participles (*amazed* and *interested*) can be used as adjectives; however, they are not interchangeable. For example, when you want to indicate an emotion, use a present participle with a noun referring to someone or something that is the cause of the emotion. In the phrase *the exciting tennis match,* the tennis match is the cause of the excitement. Use the past participle with a noun referring to someone who experiences an emotion. In the phrase *the excited crowd,* the crowd is experiencing the excitement.

The following participles are commonly used as adjectives describing emotions.

PRESENT AND PAST PARTICIPLES USED AS ADJECTIVES

Causing the emotion	Experiencing the emotion
amazing	amazed
annoying	annoyed
boring	bored
confusing	confused
embarrassing	embarrassed
exciting	excited
interesting	interested
surprising	surprised
tiring	tired

Exercise 5

Choose the correct form of each participle.

1. My uncle is interesting/interested in most but not all sports.
2. He was exciting/excited by the World Cup matches in South Africa.
3. However, he did not like the annoying/annoyed sound of the vuvuzelas.
4. Soccer is his favorite sport; baseball he finds boring/bored.
5. He jokes that being a sports fan is a tiring/tired job.

48 ‖ WORD ORDER

The general order in an English sentence is subject-verb-object; how-ever, few sentences consist of just three words. To help you under-stand and write sentences that are longer and more varied, this chapter discusses

- the appropriate sequence for adjectives (**48a**),
- the placement of adverbs of frequency (**48b**),
- the order of adverbs and direct objects (**48c**), and
- the order of words within certain clauses (**48d**).

48a ‖ ORDERING ADJECTIVES

In English, two or three adjectives modifying the same noun are used in a particular order based on their meanings. (The use of more than two consecutive adjectives is rare.) The following list shows the usual order for adjectives of different types and gives examples of each type:

Evaluator	*fascinating, painful, content*
Size	*large, long, small, short*
Shape	*square, round, triangular*
Age	*young, old, aged, newborn, antique*
Color	*black, white, green, brown*
Origin	*Arabian, Cuban, Peruvian, Slavic*
Material	*silk, paper, pine, rubber*

We visited a **fascinating Italian** village. [evaluator, origin]

An **old black** dog stared at us. [age, color]

48b | PLACING ADVERBS OF FREQUENCY

Adverbs of frequency (such as *always, never, sometimes,* and *often*) appear before one-word verbs.

He **rarely** <u>goes</u> to horror movies.

However, these adverbs appear after a form of *be* when it is the main verb.

Novels written by Stephen King <u>are</u> **always** popular.

When a sentence contains more than one verb in a verb phrase, the adverb of frequency is placed after the first auxiliary verb.

My friends <u>have</u> **never** <u>read</u> *The Shining*.

48c | PLACING ADVERBS AND DIRECT OBJECTS

An adverb may be placed after a verb when the verb has no direct object (**21c**).

They worked **efficiently.**

Revise any sentence that includes an adverb before a direct object.

quickly

I read <s>quickly</s> the letter ∧.   OR   I ∧ read <s>quickly</s> the letter.

Exercise 1

Correct the misplaced words in the following sentences.

1. Sam made a short amazing video.
2. He never has made a better video than this one.
3. He posted immediately it on his blog.
4. He used green strange lighting in all the action scenes.
5. Sam uses always a handheld camera.

48d ORDERING WORDS WITHIN CLAUSES

The word order of embedded questions and adjectival clauses (**22b**) differs from the standard subject-verb-object order of clauses.

(1) Embedded questions

The word order of questions and embedded questions is not the same. Notice the difference in each of the following pairs of sentences:

Is the source reliable? [question]

I do not know whether **the source is** reliable. [embedded question]

How **was the source evaluated?** [question]

He explained how **the source was evaluated.** [embedded question]

Does the author make a good argument? [question]

We should decide whether **the author makes** a good argument. [embedded question]

In the question in each pair, the subject and the verb (or the auxiliary verb if there is one) are inverted; in the embedded question, they are not. The auxiliary verb *do* is not used in embedded questions.

If a question begins with an interrogative pronoun such as *who* or *what* as the subject, the order of the question and the embedded question are the same.

Who worked on the project? [question]

They did not mention **who worked on the project.** [embedded question]

(2) Adjectival clauses

When a clause is used to modify a noun or pronoun, it is an adjectival clause. An adjectival clauses begins with a relative pronoun such as *that, which,* or *who* (**22b**). If the relative pronoun is the subject of the clause, the word order of the clause is standard.

s   v

Twitter is based in San Francisco, California.

s   v

Twitter, **which is based** in San Francisco, California, has users from around the world.

If the relative pronoun is *not* the subject of the adjectival clause, the word that is the subject will not be the first word in the clause.

do

Protestors sent **tweets.**

do   s   v

Tweets **that protestors sent** to journalists were highly effective.

Notice in the preceding sentence that the adjectival clause "that protestors sent" begins with the direct object, so no direct object follows the verb *sent.*

Tweets **that** protestors sent ~~them~~ to journalists were highly effective.

Exercise 2

Revise the word order of each sentence. You may have to add or delete words.

1. The Human Genome Project, which Francis Collins initiated it, turned into an international effort.

2. Prior to 1953, scientists did not know for certain was the structure of DNA a double helix.

3. The discovery of the double helix, which James D. Watson and Francis Crick described it in 1953, eventually led to the study of human genetics.

4. Without an understanding of gene sequences, scientists would not know how do people inherit traits.

5. No one can predict with certainty how will people in the future use this knowledge.

Glossary of Usage

The term *usage* refers to the ways words are used in specific contexts. As you know from speaking and writing every day, the words you choose depend on your audience and your purpose. By consulting the entries in this glossary, you will increase your ability to use words effectively. Many of the entries describe the contexts in which words are used; others distinguish between words that sound or look similar.

The labels below will help you choose appropriate words for your rhetorical situation. Be aware that the idea of standard usage may carry with it the assumption that words not considered standard are inferior. Words labeled "nonstandard" are commonly condemned, even though they may be words some people have grown up hearing and using. A better way to describe usage is to identify what is conventional, or accepted practice, for a specific rhetorical situation.

Conventional   Words or phrases listed in dictionaries without special usage labels; generally considered appropriate in academic and professional writing.

Conversational   Words or phrases that dictionaries label *informal, slang,* or *colloquial;* although often used in informal speech and writing, not generally appropriate for formal writing assignments.

Unconventional   Words or phrases not generally considered appropriate in academic or professional writing and often labeled *nonstandard* in dictionaries; best avoided in formal contexts.

Agreement on usage occurs slowly, often after a period of debate. In this glossary, entries are marked with an asterisk (*) when new usages have been reported by dictionary editors but may not yet be accepted by everyone.

a lot of *A lot of* is conversational for *many, much,* or *a great deal of:* They do not have ~~a lot of~~ **much** time. *A lot* is sometimes misspelled as *alot.*

a while, awhile *A while* means "a period of time." It is often used with the prepositions *after, for,* and *in:* We rested for **a while.** *Awhile* means "a short time." It is not preceded by a preposition: We rested **awhile.**

accept, except The verb *accept* means "to receive": I **accept** your apology. The verb *except* means "to exclude": The policy was to have everyone wait in line, but parents with small children were **excepted.** The preposition *except* means "other than": Everyone **except** Joe will attend the conference.

advice, advise *Advice* is a noun: They asked their attorney for **advice.** *Advise* is a verb: The attorney **advised** us to save all relevant documents.

affect, effect *Affect* is a verb that means "to influence": The lobbyist's pleas did not **affect** the politician's decision. The noun *effect* means "a result": The **effect** of his decision on the staff's morale was positive and long lasting. When used as a verb, *effect* means "to produce" or "to cause": The activists believed that they could **effect** real political change.

agree on, agree to, agree with *Agree on* means "to be in accord with others about something": We **agreed on** a date for the conference. *Agree to* means "to accept something" or "to consent to do something": The customer **agreed to** our terms. The negotiators **agreed to** conclude talks by midnight. *Agree with* means "to share an opinion with someone" or "to approve of something": I **agree with** you on this issue. No one **agreed with** his position.

all ready, already *All ready* means "completely prepared": The rooms are **all ready** for the conference. *Already* means "by or before the time specified": She has **already** taken her final exams.

****all right** *All right* means "acceptable": The students asked whether it was **all right** to use dictionaries during the exam. *Alright* is not yet a generally accepted spelling of *all right,* although it is becoming more common in journalistic writing.

all together, altogether *All together* means "as a group": The cast reviewed the script **all together.** *Altogether* means "wholly, thoroughly": That game is **altogether** too difficult.

allude, elude *Allude* means "to refer to indirectly": The professor **alluded** to a medieval text. *Elude* means "to evade" or "to escape from": For the moment, his name **eludes** me.

allusion, illusion An *allusion* is a casual or indirect reference: The **allusion** was to Shakespeare's *Twelfth Night.* An *illusion* is a false idea or an unreal image: His idea of college is an **illusion.**

alot See **a lot of.**

already See **all ready, already.**

alright See **all right.**

altogether See **all together, altogether.**

a.m., p.m. Use these abbreviations only with numerals: The show will begin at 7:00 **p.m.** [COMPARE: The show will begin at seven *in the evening.*]

*__among, between__ To follow traditional usage, use *among* with three or more entities (a group): The snorkelers swam **among** the fish. Use *between* when referring to only two entities: The rivalry **between** the two teams is intense. Current dictionaries also note the possibility of using *between* to refer to more than two entities, especially when these entities are considered distinct: We have strengthened lines of communication **between** various departments.

amount of, number of Use *amount of* before nouns that cannot be counted: The **amount of** rain that fell last year was insufficient. Use *number of* with nouns that can be counted: The **number of** students attending college has increased.

and/or This combination denotes three options: one, the other, or both. These options can also be presented separately with *or:* The student's application should be signed by a parent **and/or** a teacher. The student's application should be signed by a parent, a teacher, **or** both.

*__angry at, angry with__ Both *at* and *with* are commonly used after *angry,* although according to traditional guidelines, *with* should be used when a person is the cause of the anger: She was **angry with** me because I was late. Many voters were **angry at** the newspaper's coverage of the debate.

another, other, the other *Another* is followed by a singular noun: **another** book. *Other* is followed by a plural noun: **other** books. *The other* is followed by either a singular or a plural noun: **the other book, the other books.**

anymore, any more *Anymore* meaning "any longer" or "now" most frequently occurs in negative sentences: Sarah doesn't work here **anymore.** Its use in positive sentences is considered conversational; *now* is generally used instead: All he ever does ~~anymore~~ **now** is watch television. As two words, *any more* appears with *not* to mean "no more": We do not have **any more** time.

anyone, any one *Anyone* means "any person at all": We did not know **anyone.** *Any one* refers to one of a group: **Any one** of the options is better than the current situation.

*anyplace, everyplace, someplace These words are becoming increasingly common in academic writing. However, according to traditional usage rules, they should be replaced by *anywhere, everywhere,* and *somewhere.*

as Conversational when used after such verbs as *know, say,* and *see.* Use *that, if,* or *whether* instead: I do not know ~~as~~ **whether** my application is complete. Also considered conversational is the use of *as* instead of *who, which,* or *that:* Many of the performers **as who** have appeared on our program will be giving a concert this evening.

as, because The use of *as* to signal a cause may be vague; if it is, use *because* instead: ~~As~~ **Because** we were running out of gas, we turned around.

*as, like According to traditional usage, *as* begins either a phrase or a clause; *like* begins only a phrase: My brother drives too fast, just ~~like~~ **as** my father did. Current dictionaries note the informal use of *like* to begin clauses, especially after verbs such as *look, feel,* and *sound.*

assure, ensure, insure *Assure* means "to state with confidence, alleviating any doubt": The flight attendant **assured** us that our flight would arrive on time. *Ensure* and *insure* are usually interchangeable to mean "make certain," but only *insure* means "to protect against loss": The editor **ensured** [OR **insured**] that the reporter's facts were accurate. Physicians must **insure** themselves against malpractice suits.

awhile See **a while, awhile.**

bad Unconventional as an adverb; use *badly* instead. The team played **badly.** However, the adjective *bad* is used after sensory verbs such as *feel, look,* and *smell:* I feel **bad** that I forgot to return your book yesterday.

because See **as, because.**

being as, being that Unconventional; use *because* instead. ~~Being as~~ **Because** the road was closed, traffic was diverted to another route.

*beside, besides According to traditional usage, these two words have different meanings. *Beside* means "next to": The president sat **beside** the prime minister. *Besides* means "in addition to" or "other than": She has written many articles **besides** those on political reform. Current dictionaries report that professional writers regularly use *beside* to convey this meaning, as long as there is no risk of ambiguity.

better, had better *Better* is conversational. Use *had better* instead: We ~~better~~ **had better** finish the report by five o'clock.

between See **among, between.**

*bring, take Both words describe the same action but from different standpoints. *Bring* indicates movement toward the writer: She **brought** me some flowers. *Take* implies movement away from the writer: He **took** my overdue books to the library. Dictionaries report that this distinction is often blurred when the writer's position is ambiguous or irrelevant: He **brought** [OR **took**] her some flowers.

bunch Conversational to refer to a group: A ~~bunch~~ **group** of students participated in the experiment.

****can, may** *Can* refers to ability, and *may* refers to permission: You **can** [are able to] drive seventy miles an hour, but you **may** not [are not permitted to] exceed the speed limit. Current dictionaries report that in contemporary usage *can* and *may* are used interchangeably to denote possibility or permission, although *may* is used more frequently in formal contexts.

can't hardly, can't scarcely Unconventional. Use *can hardly* or *can scarcely*: The students **can't hardly** wait for summer vacation.

capital, capitol As a noun, *capital* means either "a governing city" or "funds": The **capital** of Minnesota is St. Paul. An anonymous donor provided the **capital** for the project. As a modifier, *capital* means "chief" or "principal": This year's election is of **capital** importance. It may also refer to the death penalty: **Capital** punishment is legal in some states. A *capitol* is a statehouse; the *Capitol* is the U.S. congressional building in Washington, DC.

censor, censure, sensor As a verb, *censor* means "to remove or suppress because of immoral or otherwise objectionable ideas": Do you think a ratings board should **censor** films? As a noun, *censor* refers to a person who is authorized to remove material considered objectionable: The **censor** recommended that the book be banned. The verb *censure* means "to blame or criticize"; the noun *censure* is an expression of disapproval or blame. The Senate **censured** Joseph McCarthy. He received a **censure** from the Senate. A *sensor* is a device that responds to a stimulus: The **sensor** detects changes in light.

center around Conversational for "to center on" or "to revolve around": The discussion **centered ~~around~~ on** the public's response to tax-reform initiatives.

cite, site, sight *Cite* means "to mention": Be sure to **cite** your sources. *Site* is a location: The president visited the **site** for the new library. As a verb, *site* also means "to situate": The builder **sited** the factory near the freeway. The verb *sight* means "to see": The crew **sighted** land. As a noun, *sight* refers to the ability to see or to a view: Her **sight** worsened as she aged. What an incredible **sight!**

climactic, climatic *Climactic* refers to a climax, or high point: The actors rehearsed the **climactic** scene. *Climatic* refers to the *climate:* Many environmentalists are worried about the recent **climatic** changes.

coarse, course *Coarse* refers to roughness: The jacket was made of **coarse** linen. *Course* refers to a route: Our **course** to the island was indirect. *Course* may also refer to a plan of study: I want to take a **course** in nutrition.

compare to, compare with *Compare to* means "to regard as similar," and *compare with* means "to examine for similarities and/or differences": She **compared** her mind **to** a dusty attic. The student **compared** the first draft **with** the second.

complement, complementary, compliment, complimentary *Complement* means "to complete" or "to balance": Their personalities **complement** each other. They have **complementary** personalities. *Compliment* means "to express praise": The professor **complimented** the students on their first drafts. Her remarks were **complimentary.** *Complimentary* may also mean "provided free of charge": We received **complimentary** tickets.

*****compose, comprise** *Compose* means "to make up": That collection **is composed** of medieval manuscripts. *Comprise* means "to consist of": The anthology **comprises** many famous essays. Dictionary editors have noted the increasing use of *comprise* in the passive voice to mean "to be composed of."

conscience, conscious, consciousness *Conscience* means "the sense of right and wrong": He examined his **conscience** before deciding whether to join the protest. *Conscious* means "awake": After an hour, the patient was fully **conscious.** After an hour, the patient regained **consciousness.** *Conscious* may also mean "aware": We were **conscious** of the possible consequences.

continual, continually, continuous, continuously *Continual* means "constantly recurring": **Continual** interruptions kept us from completing the project. Telephone calls **continually** interrupted us. *Continuous* means "uninterrupted": The job applicant had a record of ten years' **continuous** employment. The job applicant worked **continuously** from 2000 to 2009.

*****convince, persuade** *Convince* means "to make someone believe something": His passionate speech **convinced** us that school reform was necessary. *Persuade* means "to motivate someone to act": She **persuaded** us to stop smoking. Dictionary editors note that many speakers now use *convince* as a synonym for *persuade.*

could of *Of* is often mistaken for the sound of the unstressed *have:* They **could of have** [OR might **have,** should **have,** would **have**] gone home.

couldn't care less *Couldn't care less* expresses complete lack of concern: She **couldn't care less** about her reputation. *Could care less* is considered unconventional in academic writing.

council, counsel A *council* is an advisory or decision-making group: The student **council** supported the new regulations. A *counsel* is a legal adviser: The defense **counsel** conferred with the judge. As a verb, *counsel* means "to give advice": She **counsels** people with eating disorders.

criteria, criterion *Criteria* is a plural noun meaning "a set of standards for judgment": The teachers explained the **criteria** for the assignment. The singular form is *criterion:* Their judgment was based on only one **criterion.**

****data** *Data* is the plural form of *datum,* which means "piece of information" or "fact": When the **data are** complete, we will know the true cost. However, current dictionaries also note that *data* is frequently used as a mass entity (like the word *furniture*), appearing with a singular verb.

desert, dessert *Desert* can mean "a barren land": Gila monsters live in the **deserts** of the Southwest. As a verb, *desert* means "to leave": I thought my friends had **deserted** me. *Dessert* refers to something sweet eaten at the end of a meal: They ordered apple pie for **dessert.**

device, devise *Device* is a noun: She invented a **device** that measures extremely small quantities of liquid. *Devise* is a verb: We **devised** a plan for work distribution.

dialogue Many readers consider the use of *dialogue* as a verb to be an example of unnecessary jargon. Use *discuss* or *exchange views* instead: The committee members ~~dialogued about~~ discussed the issues.

differ from, differ with *Differ from* means "to be different": A bull snake **differs from** a rattlesnake in a number of ways. *Differ with* means "to disagree": Senator Brown has **differed with** Senator Owen on several issues.

different from, different than *Different from* is generally used with nouns, pronouns, and noun phrases. The school was **different from** most others. It may also be used with a noun clause: It was **different from** what we had expected. *Different than* is used with adverbial clauses; *than* is the conjunction: We are no **different than** they are.

discreet, discrete *Discreet* means "showing good judgment or self-restraint": His friends complained openly, but his comments were quite **discreet.** *Discrete* means "distinct": The participants in the study came from three **discrete** groups.

disinterested, uninterested *Disinterested* means "impartial": A **disinterested** observer will give a fair opinion. *Uninterested* means "lacking interest": She was **uninterested** in the outcome of the game.

distinct, distinctive *Distinct* means "easily distinguished or perceived": Each proposal has **distinct** advantages. *Distinctive* means "characteristic" or "serving to distinguish": We studied the **distinctive** features of hawks.

*****due to** Traditionally, *due to* was not synonymous with *because of:* ~~Due to~~ **Because of** holiday traffic, we arrived an hour late. However, dictionary editors now consider this usage of *due to* acceptable.

dyeing, dying *Dyeing* comes from *dye,* meaning "to color something, usually by soaking it": As a sign of solidarity, the students are **dyeing** their shirts the same color. *Dying* refers to the loss of life: Because of the drought, the plants are **dying.**

effect See **affect, effect.**

e.g. Abbreviation of *exempli gratia,* meaning "for example." Use only within parentheses: Digestive problems may be treated with herbs (**e.g.,** peppermint and fennel). Otherwise, replace *e.g.* with the English equivalent, *for example:* Social media differ from traditional media, ~~e.g.,~~ **for example,** television and newspapers. Do not confuse *e.g.* with *i.e.,* meaning "that is."

elicit, illicit *Elicit* means "to draw forth": He is **eliciting** contributions for a new playground. *Illicit* means "unlawful": The newspaper reported their **illicit** mishandling of public funds.

elude See **allude, elude.**

emigrate from, immigrate to *Emigrate* means "to leave one's own country": My ancestors **emigrated from** Ireland. *Immigrate* means "to arrive in a different country to settle": The Ulster Scots **immigrated to** the southern United States.

eminent, imminent *Eminent* means "distinguished": An **eminent** scholar in physics will be giving a public lecture tomorrow. *Imminent* means "about to happen": The merger of the two companies is **imminent.**

ensure See **assure, ensure, insure.**

enthuse Many readers object to the use of *enthuse.* Use *enthusiastic* or *enthusiastically* instead: Students ~~enthused~~ **spoke enthusiastically** about the new climbing wall. They were ~~enthused~~ **enthusiastic** about the new climbing wall.

especially, specially *Especially* emphasizes a characteristic or quality: Some people are **especially** sensitive to the sun. *Especially* also means "particularly": Wildflowers are abundant in this area, **especially** during May. *Specially* means "for a particular purpose": The classroom was **specially** designed for music students.

etc. Abbreviation of *et cetera,* meaning "and others of the same kind." Use only within parentheses: Be sure to bring appropriate camping gear (tent, sleeping bag, mess kit, **etc.**). Because *and* is part of the meaning of *etc.,* avoid using the combination *and etc.*

eventually, ultimately *Eventually* refers to some future time: She has made so many valuable contributions that I am sure she will **eventually** become the store supervisor. *Ultimately* refers to the final outcome after a series of events: The course was difficult but **ultimately** worthwhile.

everyday, every day *Everyday* means "routine" or "ordinary": These are **everyday** problems. *Every day* means "each day": I read the newspaper **every day.**

everyone, every one *Everyone* means "all": **Everyone** should attend. *Every one* refers to each person or item in a group: **Every one** of you should attend.

everyplace See **anyplace, everyplace, someplace.**

except See **accept, except.**

explicit, implicit *Explicit* means "expressed clearly and directly": Given his **explicit** directions, we knew how to proceed. *Implicit* means "implied or expressed indirectly": I mistakenly understood his silence to be his **implicit** approval of the project.

farther, further Generally, *farther* refers to geographic distance: We will have to drive **farther** tomorrow. *Further* means "more": If you need **further** assistance, please let me know.

*****feel** Traditionally, *feel* was not synonymous with "think" or "believe": I **feel think** that more should be done to protect local habitat. Dictionary editors now consider this use of *feel* to be a standard alternative.

fewer, less *Fewer* occurs before nouns that can be counted: **fewer** technicians, **fewer** pencils. *Less* occurs before nouns that cannot be counted: **less** milk, **less** support. *Less than* may be used with measurements of time or distance: **less than** three months, **less than** twenty miles.

*****first, firstly; second, secondly** Many college instructors prefer the use of *first* and *second.* However, dictionary editors state that *firstly* and *secondly* are also well-established forms.

foreword, forward A *foreword* is an introduction: The **foreword** to the book provided useful background information. *Forward* refers to a frontward direction: To get a closer look, we moved **forward** slowly.

former, latter Used together, *former* refers to the first of two; *latter* to the second of two. John and Ian are both English. The **former** is from Manchester; the **latter** is from Birmingham.

further See **farther, further.**

get Considered conversational in many common expressions: The weather ~~got better~~ **improved** overnight. I did not know what he ~~was getting at~~ **meant.**

good, well *Good* is an adjective, not an adverb: He pitched ~~good~~ **well** last night. *Good* in the sense of "in good health" may be used interchangeably with *well:* I feel **good** [OR **well**] this morning.

had better See **better, had better.**

half *A half a* or *a half an* is unconventional; use *half a/an* or *a half:* You should be able to complete the questionnaire in **a half ~~an~~** hour.

hanged, hung *Hanged* means "put to death by hanging": The prisoner was **hanged** at dawn. For all other meanings, use *hung:* He **hung** the picture above his desk.

hardly See **can't hardly, can't scarcely.**

has got, have got Conversational; omit *got:* I **have ~~got~~** a meeting tomorrow.

he/she, his/her As a solution to the problem of sexist language, these combinations are not universally accepted. Consider using *he or she* and *his or her.* See **34c.**

herself, himself, myself, yourself Unconventional as subjects in a sentence. Joe and ~~myself~~ **I** will lead the discussion. See **26a(2).**

hopefully According to traditional usage, *hopefully* means "with hope," not "it is hoped": **Hopefully,** the negotiators discussed the proposed treaty. However, dictionary editors have accepted the use of *hopefully* as a sentence modifier: **Hopefully,** the treaty will be ratified. If your instructor prefers that you follow traditional usage, use *I hope* in such a sentence: **I hope** the treaty will be ratified.

hung See **hanged, hung.**

i.e. Abbreviation of *id est,* meaning "that is." Use only within parentheses: All participants in the study ran the same distance (**i.e.,** six kilometers). Otherwise, replace *i.e.* with the English equivalent, *that is:* Assistance was offered to those who might have difficulty boarding, ~~i.e.,~~ **that is,** the elderly, people with disabilities, and parents with small children. Do not confuse *i.e.* with *e.g.,* meaning "for example."

illicit See **elicit, illicit.**

illusion See **allusion, illusion.**

immigrate See **emigrate from, immigrate to.**

imminent See **eminent, imminent.**

*****impact** Though *impact* is commonly used as a verb in business writing, many college teachers still use it as a noun only: The new tax ~~impacts~~ **affects** everyone.

implicit See **explicit, implicit.**

imply, infer *Imply* means "to suggest without actually stating": Though he never mentioned the statistics, he **implied** that they were questionable. *Infer* means "to draw a conclusion based on evidence": Given the tone of his voice, I **inferred** that he found the work substandard.

in regards to Unconventional; see **regard, regarding, regards.**

inside of, outside of Drop *of* when unnecessary: Security guards stood ~~out-side of~~ the front door.

insure See **assure, ensure, insure.**

irregardless Unconventional; use *regardless* instead.

its, it's *Its* is a possessive form: The committee forwarded **its** recommendation. *It's* is a contraction of *it is* or *it has:* **It's** a beautiful day. **It's** been sunny for days.

-ize Some readers object to using this ending to create new verbs: *enronize.* Some of these new verbs, however, have already entered into common usage: *computerize.*

kind of a, sort of a The word *a* is unnecessary: This **kind of a** book sells well. *Kind of* and *sort of* are not conventionally used to mean "somewhat": The report was ~~kind of~~ **somewhat** difficult to read.

later, latter *Later* means "after a specific time" or "a time after now": The concert ended **later** than we had expected. *Latter* refers to the second of two items: Of the two versions described, I prefer the **latter.**

lay, lie *Lay* (*laid, laying*) means "to put" or "to place": He **laid** the book aside. *Lie* (*lay, lain, lying*) means "to rest" or "to recline": I had just **lain** down when the alarm went off. *Lay* takes an object (to **lay** something); *lie* does not. These verbs may be confused because the present tense of *lay* and the past tense of *lie* are spelled the same way.

lead, led As a noun, *lead* means "a kind of metal": The paint had **lead** in it. As a verb, *lead* means "to conduct": A guide will **lead** a tour of the ruins. *Led* is the past tense of the verb *lead:* He **led** the country from 1949 to 1960.

less, less than See **fewer, less.**

lie See **lay, lie.**

like See **as, like.**

literally Conversational when used to emphasize the meaning of another word: I was ~~literally~~ **nearly** frozen after I finished shoveling the sidewalk. *Literally* is conventionally used to indicate that an expression is not being used figuratively: My friend **literally** climbs the walls after work; his fellow rock climbers join him at the local gym.

lose, loose *Lose* is a verb: She does not **lose** her patience often. *Loose* is chiefly used as an adjective: A few of the tiles are **loose.**

lots, lots of Conversational for *many* or *much:* He has ~~lots of~~ **many** friends. We have ~~lots~~ **much** to do before the end of the quarter.

mankind Considered sexist because it excludes women: All ~~mankind~~ **humanity** will benefit from this new discovery.

many, much *Many* is used with nouns that can be counted: **many** stores, too **many** assignments. *Much* is used with nouns that cannot be counted: **much** courage, not **much** time.

may See **can, may.**

may of, might of See **could of.**

maybe, may be *Maybe* is an adverb: **Maybe** the negotiators will succeed this time. *May* and *be* are verbs: The rumor **may be** true.

***media, medium** According to traditional definitions, *media* is a plural word: The **media** have sometimes created the news in addition to reporting it. The singular form is *medium:* The newspaper is one **medium** that people seem to trust. Dictionary editors note the frequent use of *media* as a collective noun taking a singular verb, but this usage is still considered conversational.

might could Conversational for "might be able to": The director **might** ~~could~~ **be able to** review your application next week.

most Unconventional to mean "almost": We watch the news ~~most~~ **almost** every day.

much See **many, much.**

myself See **herself, himself, myself, yourself.**

neither . . . or *Nor,* not *or,* follows *neither:* The book is **neither** as funny ~~or~~ **nor** as original as critics have reported.

nothing like, nowhere near Unconventional; use *not nearly* instead: Her new book is ~~nowhere near~~ **not nearly** as mysterious as her previous novel.

number of When the expression *a number of* is used, the reference is plural: **A number of** positions **are** open. When *the number of* is used, the reference is singular: **The number of** possibilities **is** limited. See also **amount of, number of.**

off of   Conversational; omit *of:* He walked **off ~~of~~** the field.

on account of   Conversational; use *because of:* The singer canceled her engagement ~~on account of~~ **because of** a sore throat.

on the other hand   If you use *on the one hand* to introduce the first of two contrasting points, make sure that *on the other hand* introduces the second. However, *on the other hand* may be used to introduce a contrasting point even if it is not preceded by *on the one hand.*

other   See **another, other, the other.**

passed, past   *Passed* is the past tense of the verb *pass:* Deb **passed** the other runners right before the finish line. *Past* means "beyond a time or location": We walked **past** the high school.

per   In ordinary contexts, use *a* or *an:* You should drink at least six glasses of water ~~per~~ **a** day.

percent, percentage   *Percent* (also spelled *per cent*) is used with a specific number: **Sixty percent** of the students attended the ceremony. *Percentage* refers to an unspecified portion: The **percentage** of high school graduates attending college has increased in recent years.

perspective, prospective   *Perspective* means "point of view": We discussed the issue from various **perspectives.** *Prospective* means "likely to become": **Prospective** journalists interviewed the editor in chief.

persuade   See **convince, persuade.**

phenomena, phenomenon   *Phenomena* is the plural form of *phenomenon:* Natural **phenomena** were given scientific explanations.

*****plus**   *Plus* joins nouns or noun phrases to make a sentence seem like an equation: Her endless curiosity **plus** her boundless energy makes her the perfect camp counselor. Note that a singular form of the verb is required (e.g., *makes*). In the past, plus was not used to join clauses: The candidate had three advanced degrees. **~~Plus~~ In addition**, she had experience working abroad. The use of *plus* at the beginning of a clause is now considered acceptable by some dictionaries.

p.m.   See **a.m., p.m.**

precede, proceed   To *precede* is to "go before": A moment of silence **preceded** the applause. To *proceed* is to "go forward": After stopping for a short rest, we **proceeded** to our destination.

prejudice, prejudiced   *Prejudice* is a noun: They were unaware of their **prejudice.** *Prejudiced* is an adjective: She accused me of being **prejudiced.**

pretty *Pretty* means "attractive," not "rather" or "fairly": We were ~~pretty~~ **fairly** tired after cooking all day.

principal, principle As a noun, *principal* means "chief official": The **principal** greeted the students every day. It also means "capital": The loan's **principal** was still quite high. As an adjective, *principal* means "main": Tourism is the country's **principal** source of income. The noun *principle* refers to a rule, standard, or belief: She explained the three **principles** supporting the theory.

proceed See **precede, proceed.**

prospective See **perspective, prospective.**

quotation, quote In academic writing, *quotation,* rather than *quote,* refers to a sentence or passage repeated or copied from another source: She began her speech with a ~~quote~~ **quotation** from *Othello. Quote* expresses an action: My friend sometimes **quotes** lines from television commercials.

raise, rise *Raise* (*raised, raising*) means "to lift or cause to move upward, to bring up or increase": Retailers **raised** prices. *Rise* (*rose, risen, rising*) means "to get up" or "to ascend": The cost of living **rose** sharply. *Raise* takes an object (to **raise** something); *rise* does not.

real, really *Really* rather than *real* is used to mean "very": He is from a ~~real~~ **really** small town. To ensure this word's effectiveness, use it sparingly.

***reason why** Traditionally, this combination was considered redundant: No one explained the reason ~~why~~ the negotiations failed. [OR No one explained ~~the reason~~ why the negotiations failed.] However, dictionary editors report its use by highly regarded writers.

regard, regarding, regards These forms are used in the following expressions: *in regard to, with regard to, as regards,* and *regarding* [NOT *in regards to, with regards to,* or *as regarding*].

***relation, relationship** According to traditional definitions, *relation* is used to link abstractions: We studied the **relation** between language and social change. *Relationship* is used to link people: The **relationship** between the two friends grew strong. However, dictionary editors now label as standard the use of *relationship* to connect abstractions.

respectfully, respectively *Respectfully* means "showing respect": The children learned to treat one another **respectfully.** *Respectively* means "in the order designated": We discussed the issue with the chair, the dean, and the provost, **respectively.**

rise See **raise, rise.**

sensor See **censor, censure, sensor.**

sensual, sensuous *Sensual* refers to gratification of the physical senses, often those associated with sexual pleasure: Frequently found in this music are **sensual** dance rhythms. *Sensuous* refers to gratification of the senses in response to art, music, nature, and so on: **Sensuous** landscape paintings lined the walls of the gallery.

shall, will Traditionally, *shall* was used with *I* or *we* to express future tense, and *will* was used with the other personal pronouns, but *shall* has almost disappeared in contemporary American English. *Shall* is still used in legal writing to indicate an obligation.

should of See **could of.**

sight See **cite, site, sight.**

sit, set *Sit* means "to be seated": Jonathan **sat** in the front row. *Set* means "to place something": The research assistant **set** the chemicals on the counter. *Set* takes an object (to **set** something); *sit* does not.

site See **cite, site, sight.**

so *So* intensifies another word when it is used with *that:* He was **so** nervous **that** he had trouble sleeping. Instead of using *so* alone, find a precise modifier: She was **so intensely** focused on her career. See **28g.**

someplace See **anyplace, everyplace, someplace.**

sometime, sometimes, some time *Sometime* means "at an unspecified time": They will meet **sometime** next month. *Sometimes* means "at times": **Sometimes** laws are unfair. *Some time* means "a span of time": They agreed to allow **some time** to pass before voting on the measure.

sort of a See **kind of a, sort of a.**

specially See **especially, specially.**

stationary, stationery *Stationary* means "in a fixed position": Traffic was **stationary** for an hour. *Stationery* means "writing paper and envelopes": The director ordered new department **stationery.**

supposed to, used to Be sure to include the frequently unsounded *d* at the end of the verb form: We are **supposed to** leave at 9:30 a.m. We **used to** leave earlier.

take See **bring, take.**

than, then *Than* is used in comparisons: The tape recorder is smaller **than** the radio. *Then* refers to a time sequence: Go straight ahead for three blocks; **then** turn left.

***that, which** *Which* occurs in nonessential (nonrestrictive) clauses: Myanmar, **which** borders Thailand, was formerly called Burma. Both *that* and *which* occur in essential (restrictive) clauses, although traditionally only *that* was considered acceptable: I am looking for an atlas **that** [OR **which**] includes demographic information. (For more information on essential and nonessential clauses, see **37d** and **37g**.)

***that, which, who** In essential (restrictive) clauses, *who* and *that* refer to people. We want to hire someone **who** [OR **that**] has had experience programming. Traditionally, only *who* was used to refer to people. *That,* as well as *which,* refers to things: He proposed a design **that** [OR **which**] will take advantage of solar energy.

their, there, they're *Their* is the possessive form of *they:* They will give **their** presentation tomorrow. *There* refers to location: I lived **there** for six years. *There* is also used as an expletive (see **36a(3)**): **There** is no explanation for the phenomenon. *They're* is a contraction of *they are:* **They're** leaving in the morning.

theirself, theirselves Unconventional; use *themselves.* The students finished the project by ~~theirself~~ **themselves.**

then See **than, then.**

thru *Through* is preferred in academic and professional writing: We drove ~~thru~~ **through** the whole state of South Dakota in one day.

thusly Unconventional; use *thus, in this way,* or *as follows* instead: He accompanied his father on archeological digs and **thusly** discovered his interest in ancient cultures.

time period Readers are likely to consider this combination redundant; use one word or the other, but not both: During this **time period,** the economy was strong.

to, too, two *To* is an infinitive marker: She wanted **to** become an actress. *To* is also used as a preposition, usually indicating direction: They walked **to** the memorial. *Too* means either "also" or "excessively": I voted for her **too.** They are **too** busy this year. *Two* is a number: She studied abroad for **two** years.

toward, towards Although both are acceptable, *toward* is preferred in American English.

try and Conversational for *try to:* The staff will **try ~~and~~ to** finish the project by Friday.

ultimately See **eventually, ultimately.**

uninterested See **disinterested, uninterested.**

*****unique** Traditionally, *unique* meant "one of a kind" and thus was not preceded by a qualifier such as *more, most, quite,* or *very:* Her prose style is ~~quite~~ **unique.** However, dictionary editors note that *unique* is also widely used to mean "extraordinary."

use, utilize In most contexts, *use* is preferred to *utilize:* We ~~utilized~~ **used** a special dye in the experiment. However, *utilize* may suggest an effort to employ something for a purpose: We discussed how to **utilize** the resources we had been given.

used to See **supposed to, used to.**

very To ensure this word's effectiveness, use it sparingly. Whenever possible, choose a stronger word: She was ~~very satisfied~~ **delighted** with her new digital camera.

ways Conversational when referring to distance; use *way* instead: She's a long ~~ways~~ **way** from home.

well See **good, well.**

where Conversational for *that:* I noticed ~~where~~ **that** she had been elected.

where . . . at, where . . . to Conversational; omit *at* and *to:* **Where** is the library ~~at~~? **Where** are you moving ~~to~~?

which See **that, which** and **that, which, who.**

*****who, whom** *Who* is used as the subject or subject complement in a clause: We have decided to hire Marian Wright, ~~whom~~ **who** I believe is currently finishing her degree in business administration. [*Who is the subject in who is currently finishing her degree in business administration.*] See also **that, which, who.** *Whom* is used as an object: Jeff Kruger, ~~who~~ **whom** we hired in 2007, is now our top sales representative. [*Whom is the object in whom we hired.*] Dictionary editors note that in conversation *who* is commonly used as an object as long as it does not follow a preposition. See **26b(5).**

whose, who's *Whose* is a possessive form: **Whose** book is this? The book was written by a young Mexican-American woman **whose** family still lives in Chiapas. *Who's* is the contraction of *who is:* **Who's** going to run in the election? See **26b(3).**

will See **shall, will.**

with regards to Unconventional; see **regard, regarding, regards.**

would of See **could of.**

your, you're *Your* is a possessive form: Let's meet in **your** office. *You're* is a contraction of *you are:* **You're** gaining strength.

yourself See **herself, himself, myself, yourself.**

Glossary of Terms

This glossary provides brief definitions of frequently used terms. Consult the index for references to terms not listed here.

absolute phrase A sentencelike structure containing a subject and its modifiers. Unlike a sentence, an absolute phrase has no verb marked for person, number, or tense: *The ceremony finally over,* the graduates tossed their mortarboards in the air. See **22a(6)**.

acronym A word formed by combining the initial letters or syllables of a series of words and pronounced as a word rather than as a series of letters: *NATO* for North Atlantic Treaty Organization. See **45e**.

active voice See **voice.**

adjectival clause A dependent clause, also called a **relative clause,** that modifies a noun or a pronoun. See **22b(2).**

adjectival phrase A phrase that modifies a noun or a pronoun.

adjective A word that modifies a noun or a pronoun. Adjectives typically end in suffixes such as *-al, -able, -ant, -ative, -ic, -ish, -less, -ous,* and *-y.* See **21a(4)** and **27a. Coordinate adjectives** are two or more adjectives modifying the same noun and separated by a comma: *a brisk, cold* walk. See **37c(2).**

adverb A word that modifies a verb, a verbal, an adjective, or another adverb. Adverbs commonly end in *-ly.* Some adverbs modify entire sentences: *Perhaps* the meeting could be postponed. See **21a(5)** and **27a.**

adverbial clause A dependent clause that modifies a verb, an adjective, or an adverb. See **22b(2).**

adverbial conjunction A word such as *however* or *thus* that joins one independent clause to another; also known as a **conjunctive adverb.** See **22c(4).** COMPARE: **conjunction.**

alt tags Descriptive lines of text for each visual image in an electronic document. Because these lines can be read by screen-reading software, they can assist visually impaired users. See **5d(3)**.

antecedent A word or group of words referred to by a pronoun. See **21a(3)** and **26c**.

appositive A pronoun, noun, or noun phrase that identifies, describes, or explains an adjacent pronoun, noun, or noun phrase. See **22a(5)** and **26b(4)**.

article A word used to signal a noun. *The* is a definite article; *a* and *an* are indefinite articles. See **21a(4)**.

attributive tag A short phrase that identifies the source of a quotation: *according to Jones, Jones claims.* Also called **signal phrase**. See **11d**.

auxiliary verb, auxiliary A verb that combines with a main verb. *Be, do,* and *have* are auxiliary verbs when they are used with main verbs. Also called **helping verbs. Modal auxiliaries** include *could, should,* and *may* and are used for such purposes as expressing doubt or obligation and making a request. See **21a(1)** and **25a(4)**.

Boolean operators Words used to broaden or narrow searches. These include *or, and, not,* and *near.* Also called logical operators. See **9b**.

case The form of a noun or a pronoun that indicates its relationship to other words in a sentence. Nouns and pronouns can be subjects or subject complements **(subjective case)**, objects **(objective case)**, or markers of possession and other relations **(possessive case)**. See **26b**.

claim A statement that a writer wants readers to accept; also called a **proposition.** See **7d**.

clause A sequence of related words forming an independent unit **(independent clause,** or **main clause)** or an embedded unit **(dependent clause** used as an adverb, adjective, or noun). A clause has both a subject and a predicate. See **22b**.

cliché An expression that has lost its power to interest readers because of overuse. See **35b**.

clipped form A word that is a shortened form of another word: *bike* for *bicycle.* See **45d(2)**.

collective noun A noun that refers to a group: *team, faculty, committee.* See **21a(2)**.

collocation Common word combination such as *add to, adept at,* or *admiration for.* See **35c**.

colloquial A label for any word or phrase that is characteristic of informal speech. *Kid* is colloquial; *child* is used in formal contexts. See **34b**.

common noun A noun referring to any or all members of a class or group (*woman, city, holiday*) rather than to specific members (*Susan, Reno, New Year's Day*). COMPARE: **proper noun.** See **21a(2)**.

complement A word or words used to complete the meaning of a verb. A **subject complement** is a word or phrase that follows a linking verb and categorizes or describes the subject. An **object complement** is a word or phrase that categorizes or describes a direct object when it follows such verbs as *make, paint, elect,* and *consider.* See **21c.**

complete predicate See **predicate.**

complete subject See **subject.**

complex sentence A sentence containing one independent clause and at least one dependent clause. See **22c(3)**.

compound-complex sentence A sentence containing at least two independent clauses and one or more dependent clauses. See **22c(4)**.

compound predicate A predicate that has two parts joined by a connecting word such as *and, or,* or *but;* each part contains a verb: Clara Barton *nursed the injured during the Civil War* and *later founded the American Red Cross.* See **21b.**

compound sentence A sentence containing at least two independent clauses and no dependent clauses. See **22c(2)**.

compound subject Two subjects joined by a connecting word such as *and, or,* or *but: Students* and *faculty* are discussing the issue of grade inflation. See **21b.**

compound word Two or more words functioning as a single word: *ice cream, double-check.* See **42f(1)**.

conditional clause An adverbial clause (**22b(2)**), usually beginning with *if,* that expresses a condition: *If it rains,* the outdoor concert will be postponed.

conjunction A word used to connect other words, phrases, clauses, or sentences. **Coordinating conjunctions** (*and, but, or, nor, for, so,* and *yet*) connect and relate words and word groups of equal grammatical rank. See **21a(7)** and **22c**. A **subordinating conjunction** such as *although, if,* or *when* begins a dependent clause and connects it to an independent clause. See **21a(7)** and **22c**. COMPARE: **adverbial conjunction.**

conjunctive adverb See **adverbial conjunction.**

convention, conventional Refers to language or behavior that follows the customs of a community such as the academic, medical, or business community.

coordinate adjective See **adjective.**

coordinating conjunction See **conjunction.**

coordination The use of grammatically equivalent constructions to link or balance ideas. See chapter **30.**

correlative conjunctions, correlatives Two-part connecting words such as *either . . . or* and *not only . . . but also.* See **21a(7)** and **22c.**

count nouns Nouns naming things that can be counted (*word, student, remark*). See **21a(2).** COMPARE: **noncount nouns.**

dangling modifier A word or phrase that does not clearly modify another word or word group. See **27e.** COMPARE: **misplaced modifier.**

dangling participial phrase A verbal phrase that does not clearly modify another word or word group.

deductive reasoning A form of logical reasoning in which a conclusion is formed after relating a specific fact (minor premise) to a generalization (major premise). See **7h(2).** COMPARE: **inductive reasoning.**

demonstratives Four words (*this, that, these,* and *those*) that distinguish one individual, thing, event, or idea from another. Demonstratives may occur with or without nouns: *This* [demonstrative determiner] *law* will go into effect in two years. *This* [demonstrative pronoun] will go into effect in two years. See **26a(5).**

dependent clause See **clause.**

determiner A word that signals the approach of a noun. A determiner may be an article, a demonstrative, a possessive, or a quantifier: *a reason, this reason, his reason, three reasons.*

direct address See **vocative.**

direct object See **object.**

direct quotation See **quotation.**

ellipsis points Three spaced periods that indicate either a pause or the omission of material from a direct quotation. See **41g.**

elliptical clause A clause missing one or more words that are assumed to be understood. See **22b(2).**

essential element A word or word group that modifies another word or word group, providing information that is essential for identification.

Essential elements are not set off by commas, parentheses, or dashes: The woman *who witnessed the accident* was called to testify. Also called a **restrictive element.** COMPARE: **nonessential element.** See **22b(2)** and **37d.**

ethos One of the three classical appeals; the use of language to demonstrate the writer's trustworthy character, good intentions, and substantial knowledge of a subject. Also called an **ethical appeal.** See **7f(1).** See also **logos** and **pathos.**

expletive A word signaling a structural change in a sentence, usually used so that new or important information is given at the end of the sentence: *There* were over four thousand runners in the marathon. See **21b(1).**

faulty predication A sentence error in which the predicate does not logically belong with the given subject. See **28d(2).**

figurative language The use of words in an imaginative rather than in a literal sense. See **35a(3).**

first person See **person.**

flaming A personal attack that occurs in an online exchange. See **5c.**

gender The grammatical label that distinguishes nouns or pronouns as masculine, feminine, or neuter. This term is also used in biological and sociocultural contexts. See **26c(2)** and **34c(1).**

generic noun See **common noun.**

genre A purposeful form of communication distinguished by features and formatting. In literature, genres include categories such as drama and poetry. See **1a** and **12a.**

gerund A verbal that ends in *-ing* and functions as a noun: *Snowboarding* is a popular winter sport. See **22a(3).**

gerund phrase A verbal phrase that employs the *-ing* form of a verb and functions as a noun: Some students prefer *studying in the library.* See **22a(3).**

helping verb See **auxiliary verb.**

homophones Words that have the same sound and sometimes the same spelling but differ in meaning: *their, there,* and *they're* or *capital* meaning "funds" and *capital* meaning "the top of a pillar." See **42c.**

idiom An expression whose meaning often cannot be derived from its elements. *Burning the midnight oil* means "staying up late studying." See **35c.**

imperative mood See **mood.**

indefinite article See **article.**

indefinite pronoun A pronoun such as *everyone* or *anything* that does not refer to a specific person, place, thing, or idea. See **26c(1)**.

independent clause See **clause.**

indicative mood See **mood.**

indirect object See **object.**

indirect question A sentence that includes an embedded question, punctuated with a period instead of a question mark: My friends asked me *why I left the party early.* See **41a(1)**.

indirect quotation See **quotation.**

inductive reasoning The reasoning process that begins with facts or observations and moves to general principles that account for those facts or observations. See **7h(1)**. COMPARE: **deductive reasoning.**

infinitive A verbal that consists of the base form of the verb, usually preceded by the infinitive marker *to.* An infinitive is used chiefly as a noun, less frequently as an adjective or adverb: My father likes *to golf.* See **22a(3)** and **26b(6)**.

infinitive phrase A verbal phrase that contains the infinitive form of a verb: They volunteered *to work at the local hospital.* See **22a(3)**.

inflection A change in the form of a word that indicates a grammatical feature such as number, person, tense, or degree. For example, *-ed* added to a verb indicates the past tense, and *-er* indicates the comparative degree of an adjective or adverb.

intensifier See **qualifier.**

intensive pronoun See **reflexive pronoun.**

interjection A word expressing a simple exclamation: *Hey! Oops!* When used at the beginnings of sentences, mild interjections are set off by commas. See **21a(8)**.

intransitive verb A verb that does not take an object: Everyone *laughed.* See **21d**. COMPARE: **transitive verb.**

invention Using strategies to generate ideas for writing.

inversion A change in the usual subject-verb order of a sentence: *Are you* ready? See **21d**.

keywords Specific words used with a search tool (such as Google) to find information. See **9b**.

linking verb A verb that relates a subject to a subject complement. Examples of linking verbs are *be, become, seem, appear, feel, look, taste, smell,* and *sound.* See **21a(1)**.

logos One of the three classical appeals; the use of language to show clear reasoning. Also called a **logical appeal.** See **7f(2)**. See also **ethos** and **pathos.**

major premise See **premise.**

main clause Also called **independent clause.** See **clause.**

minor premise See **premise.**

misplaced modifier A descriptive or qualifying word or phrase placed in a position that confuses the reader: I read about a wildfire that was out of control *in yesterday's paper.* [The modifier belongs after *read.*] See **27d.**

mixed construction A confusing sentence that is the result of an unintentional shift from one grammatical pattern to another: When police appeared who were supposed to calm the crowds showed up, most people had already gone home. [The sentence should be recast with either *appeared* or *showed up,* not with both.] See **28c.**

mixed metaphor A construction that includes parts of two or more unrelated metaphors: Her *fiery* personality *dampened* our hopes of a compromise. See **28b.**

modal auxiliary See **auxiliary verb.**

modifier A word or word group that describes, limits, or qualifies another. See chapter **27.**

mood A set of verb forms or inflections used to indicate how a speaker or writer regards an assertion: as a fact or opinion (**indicative mood**); as a command or instruction (**imperative mood**); or as a wish, hypothesis, request, or condition contrary to fact (**subjunctive mood**). See **25d.**

netiquette Word formed from *Internet* and *etiquette* to refer to guidelines for writing e-mail messages and other online postings and for online behavior in general. See **5c.**

nominalization Formation of a noun by adding a suffix to a verb or an adjective: *require, requirement; sad, sadness.*

nominative case Also called **subjective case.** See **case.**

noncount nouns Nouns naming things that cannot be counted (*architecture, water*). See **21a(2)**. COMPARE: **count nouns.**

nonessential element A word or word group that modifies another word or word group but does not provide information essential for identification. Nonessential elements are set off by commas, parentheses, or dashes: Carol Lee, *president of the university,* met with alumni representatives. Also called a **nonrestrictive element.** See **22b(2)** and **37d.** COMPARE: **essential element.**

nonrestrictive element See **nonessential element.**

nonstandard, nonstandardized Refers to speech forms that are not considered conventional in many academic and professional settings. See the **Glossary of Usage.**

noun A word that names a person, place, thing, idea, animal, quality, event, and so on: *Alanis, America, desk, justice, dog, strength, departure.* See **21a(2).** See also **collective noun, common noun, count noun, noncount noun,** and **proper noun.**

noun clause A dependent clause used as a noun. See **22b(2).**

noun phrase A noun and its modifiers. See **22a(1).**

number The property of a word that indicates whether it refers to one **(singular)** or to more than one **(plural).** Number is reflected in the word's form: *river/rivers, this/those, he sees/they see.* See **26a, 46a,** and **47a.**

object A noun, pronoun, noun phrase, or noun clause that follows a preposition or a transitive verb or verbal. A **direct object** names the person or thing that receives the action of the verb: I sent the *package.* An **indirect object** usually indicates to whom the action was directed or for whom the action was performed: I sent *you* the package. See **21c(1)** and **21c(2).** The **object of a preposition** follows a preposition: I sent the package to *you.* See **22a(4).**

object complement See **complement.**

object of a preposition See **object.**

objective case See **case.**

parenthetical element Any word, phrase, or clause that adds detail to a sentence or any sentence that adds detail to a paragraph but is not essential for understanding the core meaning. Commas, dashes, or parentheses separate these elements from the rest of the sentence or paragraph. See **37d, 41d,** and **41e.**

participial phrase A verbal phrase that includes a participle: The stagehand *carrying the trunk* fell over the threshold. See **22a(3).** See also **participle** and **phrase.**

participle A verb form that may function as part of a verb phrase (had *determined,* was *thinking*) or as a modifier (a *determined* effort; the couple, *thinking* about their past). A **present participle** is formed by adding *-ing* to the base form of a verb. A **past participle** is usually formed by adding *-ed* to the base form of a verb (*walked, passed*); however, many verbs have irregular past-participle forms (*written, bought, gone*). See **25a(1)** and **25a(2)**.

particle A word such as *across, away, down, for, in, off, out, up, on,* or *with* that combines with a main verb to form a phrasal verb: *write down, look up.* See **25a(3)**.

parts of speech The classes into which words may be grouped according to their forms and grammatical relationships. The traditional parts of speech are verbs, nouns, pronouns, adjectives, adverbs, prepositions, conjunctions, and interjections.

passive voice See **voice.**

past participle See **participle.**

pathos One of the three classical appeals; the use of language to stir the feelings of an audience. Also called an **emotional appeal** or a **pathetic appeal.** See **7f(3)**. See also **ethos** and **logos.**

person The property of nouns, pronouns, and their corresponding verbs that distinguishes the speaker or writer **(first person)**, the individuals addressed **(second person)**, and the individuals or things referred to **(third person)**. See **25b.**

personal pronoun A pronoun that refers to a specific person, place, thing, and so on. Pronoun forms correspond to three cases: subjective, objective, and possessive. See **26a(1)**.

phrasal verb A grammatical unit consisting of a verb and a particle such as *after, in, up, off,* or *out: fill in, sort out.* See **25a(3)**.

phrase A sequence of grammatically related words that functions as a unit in a sentence but lacks a subject, a predicate, or both: *in front of the stage.* See **22a.**

point of view The vantage point from which a topic is viewed; also, the stance a writer takes: objective or impartial (third person), directive (second person), or personal (first person). See **29b.**

possessive case See **case.**

predicate The part of a sentence that expresses what a subject is, does, or experiences. It consists of the main verb, its auxiliaries, and any complements and modifiers. The **simple predicate** consists of only the main verb and any accompanying auxiliaries. See **21b** and **21c.** COMPARE: **subject.**

premise An assumption or a proposition on which an argument or explanation is based. In logic, premises are either **major** (general) or **minor** (specific); when combined correctly, they lead to a conclusion. See **7h(2)**. See also **syllogism.**

preposition A word such as *at, in, by,* or *of* that combines with a noun and any of its modifiers to form a prepositional phrase, which usually provides information about time, location, or direction. See **21a(6)**.

prepositional phrase A preposition with its object and any modifiers: *at* the nearby airport, *by* the sea. See **22a(4)**.

present participle See **participle.**

primary source A source that provides firsthand information. See **9a(1)**. COMPARE: **secondary source.**

pronoun A word that takes the position of a noun, noun phrase, or noun clause and functions as that word or word group does: *it, that, he, them.* See **21a(3)** and chapter **26**.

proper adjective An adjective that is derived from the name of a person or place: *Marxist* theories. See **42a(9)**.

proper noun The name of a specific person, place, organization, and so on: *Dr. Pimomo, Fargo, National Education Association.* Proper nouns are capitalized. See **21a(2)**. COMPARE: **common noun.**

proposition See **claim.**

qualifier A word that intensifies or moderates the meaning of an adverb or adjective: *quite* pleased, *somewhat* reluctant. Words that intensify are sometimes called **intensifiers.**

quotation A **direct quotation** (also called **direct discourse**) is the exact repetition of someone's spoken or written words. An **indirect quotation** is a report of someone's written or spoken words not stated in the exact words of the writer or speaker. See **11d** and chapter **40**.

reflexive pronoun A pronoun that ends in *-self* or *-selves* (*myself* or *themselves*) and refers to a preceding noun or pronoun in the sentence: *He* added a picture of *himself* to his web page. When used to provide emphasis, such a pronoun is called an **intensive pronoun:** The president *herself* awarded the scholarships. See **26a(2)**.

refutation A strategy for addressing opposing points of view by discussing those views and explaining why they are unsatisfactory. See **7e(2)** and **7g(1)**.

relative clause See **adjectival clause.**

relative pronoun A word (*who, whom, that, which,* or *whose*) used to introduce an **adjectival clause**, also called a **relative clause.** An antecedent for the relative pronoun can be found in the main clause. See **22b(2).**

restrictive element See **essential element.**

rhetorical appeal The means of persuasion in argumentative writing, relying on reason, authority, or emotion. See **7f.**

rhetorical audience Specific people whom the author considers capable of being influenced by his or her words and of bringing about the proposed change in action, attitude, understanding, or policy. See **1c.**

rhetorical opportunity A chance for a writer to resolve an issue or problem with the purposeful use of language. See **1a–b.**

Rogerian argument An approach to argumentation that is based on the work of psychologist Carl R. Rogers and that emphasizes the importance of withholding judgment of others' ideas until they are fully understood. See **7g(2).**

secondary source A source that analyzes or interprets firsthand information. See **9a(1).** COMPARE: **primary source.**

sentence modifier A modifier related to a whole sentence, not to a specific word or word group within it: *All things considered,* the committee acted appropriately when it approved the amendment to the bylaws. See **27a(4).**

signal phrase See **attributive tag.**

simple predicate See **predicate.**

simple subject See **subject.**

split infinitive The separation of the two parts of an infinitive form by at least one word: *to completely cover.* See **22a(3).**

squinting modifier A modifier that is unclear because it can refer to words either preceding it or following it: Proofreading *quickly* results in missed spelling errors. See **27d(3).**

Standardized English The usage expected in most academic and business settings. See the **Glossary of Usage.**

subject The general idea addressed in a piece of writing. See **2a.** COMPARE: **topic.** Also, the pronoun, noun, or noun phrase that carries out the action or assumes the state described in the predicate of a sentence. Usually preceding the predicate, the subject includes the main noun or pronoun and all modifiers. A **simple subject** consists of only the main noun or pronoun. See **21b** and **21d.** COMPARE: **predicate.**

subject complement See **complement.**

subjective case See **case.**

subjunctive mood See **mood.**

subordinating conjunction See **conjunction.**

subordination The connection of a grammatical structure to another, usually a dependent clause to an independent clause: *Even though customers were satisfied with the product,* the company wanted to improve it. See chapter **30.**

syllogism Method for deductive reasoning consisting of two premises and a conclusion. See **7h(2).** See also **premise.**

tense The form of a verb that indicates when and for how long an action or state occurs. See **25b** and **25c.**

theme The main idea of a literary work. See **12c(7).**

thesis The central point or main idea of an essay. See **2c.**

tone The writer's attitude toward the subject and the audience, usually conveyed through word choice and sentence structure. See **3a(3).**

topic The specific, narrowed main idea of an essay. See **2b.** COMPARE: **subject.**

topic sentence A statement of the main idea of a paragraph. See **3c(1).**

Toulmin model A system of argumentation developed by philosopher Stephen Toulmin in which a claim and supporting reasons or evidence depend on a shared assumption. See **7g(3).**

transitions Words, phrases, sentences, or paragraphs that relate ideas by linking sentences, paragraphs, or larger segments of writing. See **3d** and **24c(5).**

transitive verb A verb that takes an object. The researchers *reported* their findings. See **21d.** COMPARE: **intransitive verb.**

usability testing The process of soliciting reactions from potential users of a website or other complex electronic document in order to improve the content or design of the document. See **5d(3).**

verb A word denoting action, occurrence, or existence (state of being). See **21a(1)** and chapter **25.**

verb phrase A main verb and any auxiliaries. See **22a(2).**

verbal A verb form functioning as a noun, an adjective, or an adverb. See **22a(3).** See also **gerund, infinitive,** and **participle.**

vocative Set off by commas, the name of or the descriptive term for a person or persons being addressed. See **37b(3).**

voice A property of a verb that indicates the relationship between the verb and its subject. The **active voice** is used to show that the subject performs the action expressed by the verb; the **passive voice** is used to show that the subject receives the action. See **25c.**

warrant According to the Toulmin model, the underlying assumption connecting a claim and data. See **7g(3).**

Answers to Exercises in Part 9

Chapter 46 Determiners, Nouns, and Adjectives
Exercise 1 (p. 794)
1. Absence makes the heart grow fonder.
2. Actions speak louder than words.
3. Bad news travels fast.
4. The best things come in small packages.
5. Blood is thicker than water.
6. Don't cry over spilled milk.

Chapter 47 Verbs and Verb Forms
Exercise 1 (pp. 802–803)
Answers will vary. The following are possibilities.
1. describes: simple present; literary present
   described: simple past; completed past action
   discusses: simple present; literary present
   discussed: simple past; completed past action
2. damaged: simple past; completed past action
   have damaged: present perfect; action originating in the past and continuing
   did damage; emphasizes past action
3. provide: simple present; general truth
   provided: simple past; completed past action

do (not) survive: simple present; general truth
did (not) survive: simple past; negated past action
4. has left: present perfect; action occuring in the past with current relevance
   had left: past perfect; action occurring previous to another past time or action
5. is flourishing: present progressive; ongoing action
   was flourishing: past progressive; ongoing action in the past
   has been flourishing: present perfect progressive; action originating in the past and ongoing
6. study: simple present, habitual action
   will study: simple future, future action

Exercise 2 (p. 804)
Answers will vary. The following are possibilities.
1. We had expected the storm to bypass our town, but it made a direct hit.
2. We would like to have had prior notice; however, even the police officers were taken by surprise.
3. Not knowing much about flooding, the emergency crew was at a disadvantage.
4. Having thrown sandbags all day, the volunteers were exhausted by 5 p.m.
5. They went home, having succeeded in preventing a major disaster.

Exercise 3 (p. 807)

Answers will vary. The following are possibilities.

1. Nations at war should follow the Geneva Conventions. *obligation*
2. Everyone must be treated humanely. *obligation*
3. In various wars, humanitarian groups were able to protect innocent victims. *ability*
4. Without humanitarian groups, many more people might have lost their lives. *conjecture*
5. Critics of past wars state that more aid should have been provided. *criticism*

Exercise 4 (p. 810)

1. Overpopulation has brought about great changes on earth.
2. Deforestation often leads to extinctions.
3. High levels of carbon dioxide result in increased global temperatures.
4. Proposals for curbing emissions should be looked over/at closely.
5. Scientists have taken on/up the challenge of slowing the destruction.

Exercise 5 (p. 811)

1. My uncle is interested in most but not all sports.
2. He was excited by the World Cup matches in South Africa.
3. However, he did not like the annoying sound of the vuvuzelas.
4. Soccer is his favorite sport; baseball he finds boring.
5. He jokes that being a sports fan is a tiring job.

Chapter 48 Word Order

Exercise 1 (p. 813)

1. Sam made an amazing short video.
2. He has never made a better video than this one.
3. He posted it immediately on his blog.
4. He used strange green lighting in all the action scenes.
5. Sam always uses a handheld camera.

Exercise 2 (p. 816)

1. The Human Genome Project, which Francis Collins initiated, turned into an international effort.
2. Prior to 1953, scientists did not know for certain whether the structure of DNA was a double helix.
3. The discovery of the double helix, which James D. Watson and Francis Crick described in 1953, eventually led to the study of human genetics.
4. Without an understanding of gene sequences, scientists would not know how people inherit traits.
5. No one can predict with certainty how people in the future will use this knowledge.

Credits

These pages constitute an extension of the copyright page. We have made every effort to trace the ownership of all copyrighted material and to secure permission from copyright holders. In the event of any question arising as to the use of any material, we will be pleased to make the necessary corrections in future printings.

pp. 9–10, 18: Malala Yousafzai with Christina Lamb, *I Am Malala* (New York: Little, Brown, and Company, 2013), 31, 67, 146–161.

p. 11: Atul Gawande, "Crimson Tide" in *Complications: A Surgeon's Notes on an Imperfect Science* (New York: Picador, 2002), 150.

p. 17: Kathleen Dean Moore, "The Happy Basket" in *Wild Comfort: The Solace of Nature* (Boston: Trumpeter, 2010), 21–22.

pp. 17–18, 46–47: Nina G. Jablonski, *Skin: A Natural History* (Berkeley: University of California Press, 2006), 3.

pp. 24–25, 28, 31, 36: Freewriting, thesis statements, and outline used by permission of Mary LeNoir.

p. 30: Frank McCourt, "Foreword," in *Eats, Shoots & Leaves* by Lynne Truss (New York: Gotham, 2003), xi.

p. 30: Richard Selzer, "Diary of an Infidel: Notes from a Monastery" in *Taking the World in for Repairs* (New York: Morrow, 1986), 13.

pp. 30, 58: Anne Lamott, *Bird by Bird: Some Instructions on Writing and Life* (New York: Anchor Books, 1995), xii, 129–130. Copyright © Anne Lamott. Anchor Books, a division of Random House.

p. 31: Amnesty International, "Abolish the Death Penalty," http://www.amnesty.org/en/death-penalty.

p. 33: Mary Pipher, "Growing Our Souls" in *Writing to Change the World* (New York: Riverhead-Penguin, 2006), 53.

p. 34: Lynn Z. Bloom, *The Seven Deadly Virtues and Other Lively Essays* (Columbia, SC: University of South Carolina Press, 2008), 33. © Lynn Z. Bloom.

p. 34: Charles Seife, *Zero: The Biography of a Dangerous Idea* (New York: Penguin, 2000), 5.

p. 38: Brenda Jo Brueggemann, "American Sign Language and the Academy" in *Deaf Subjects: between Identities and Places* (New York: New York University Press, 2009), 29.

pp. 39, 40–41: Amy Poehler, *Yes Please* (New York: Harper Collins, 2014), 3, 13. Copyright © 2014 by Amy Poehler.

p. 41: Sonia Sotomayor, *My Beloved World* (New York: Alfred A. Knopf, 2013), 68.

pp. 42–43: Sam Swope, "The Case of the Missing Report Cards," in *I Am a Pencil: A Teacher, His Kids, and Their Wonderful World of Stories* (New York: Holt/Owl, 2005), 140.

pp. 43–44: From "Topic of Cancer" by Christopher Hitchens from *Vanity Fair*, September 2010, p. 204. Used by permission of the author.

p. 44: Jordynn Jack, *Autism and Gender: From Refrigerator Mothers to Computer Geeks* (Chicago: University of Illinois Press, 2014), 65. Copyright © 2014 by the Board of Trustees, University of Illinois Press.

pp. 44–45: svgop.com

p. 47: Joel Arem, *Rocks and Minerals* (Totnes, England: Geoscience Press, 1994).

p. 52: Dorothy Allison, *Two or Three Things I Know for Sure* (New York: Penguin/Plume, 1996), 6.

p. 53: Rick Roth, "Snake Charmer," interview by Sara Martel, *Sierra,* January–February 2011, 11.

p. 55: Terry Tempest Williams, "The Clan of One-Breasted Women" in *Refuge* (New York: Random House/Vintage, 1992), 281.

p. 55: Michael Eric Dyson, "Orator in Chief," in *Articulate While Black: Barack Obama, Language, and Race in the U.S.* (New York: Oxford University Press, 2012), ix.

pp. 55–56: Django Paris, *Language across Difference* (Cambridge, England: Cambridge University Press, 2011), 163.

p. 56: Patricia J. Williams, *Open House: Of Family, Friends, Food, Piano Lessons, and the Search for a Room of My Own* (New York: Farrar, 2004), 3.

p. 56: Melissa Gotthardt, "The Miracle Diet," *AARP,* January/February 2007, 26.

p. 56: bell hooks, *Teaching Critical Thinking: Practical Wisdom* (New York: Taylor & Francis/Routledge, 2010), 7–8. © 2010 Taylor & Francis/Routledge.

p. 57: From "Not Seeing the Forest for the Dollar Bills" by Donella Meadows, *Valley News,* June 30, 1990. Reprinted by permission of Sustainability Institute.

p. 57: John Elder, *The Frog Run: Words & Wildness in the Vermont Woods* (Minneapolis, MN: Milkweed Editions, 2001), 95–96.

p. 58: Kathy L. Glass, "'Tending to the Roots': Anna Julia Cooper's Sociopolitical Thought and Activism," *Meridians* 6.1 (2005): 23–55.

pp. 58–59: Howard Rheingold, *Net Smart: How to Thrive Online* (Cambridge, MA: MIT Press, 2014), 1, 32–33. © Howard Rheingold, 2014.

pp. 61, 632: Malcolm Gladwell, *Blink: The Power of Thinking without Thinking* (Boston: Little, Brown, 2005), 13–14.

p. 61: Richard Lederer, "English Is a Crazy Language" in *Crazy English* (New York: Pocket Books, 1989), 3.

p. 62: Charlotte Hogg, *From the Garden Club: Rural Women Writing Community* (Lincoln, NE: University of Nebraska, 2006), 28. © 2006 by the Board of Regents of the University of Nebraska, Lincoln, Nebraska.

p. 65: Rickey Vincent, *Funk: The Music, the People, and the Rhythm of the One* (New York: St. Martin's Press, 1996), 103. Copyright © 1996 by Rickey Vincent.

p. 66: Tal Birdsey, *A Room for Learning: The Making of a School in Vermont* (New York: St. Martin's, 2009), 34.

p. 66: Robert Karen, *The Forgiving Self: The Road from Resentment to Connection* (New York: Anchor/Random House, 2001), 21. Copyright © 2001 by Robert Karen.

p. 67: Mary E. Curtis and John R. Kruidenier, "Teaching Adults to Read: A Summer of Scientifically Based Research Principles" (Jessup, MD: National Institute for Literacy, 2005), 9, accessed October 27, 2010, http://www.eric.ed.gov/PDFS/ED493064.pdf.

p. 67: Ronald D. Siegal, *The Mindfulness Solution* (New York: The Guilford Press, 2010), 89. Copyright © Ronald D. Siegal.

p. 68: Constance Holden, "Identical Twins Reared Apart," *Science*, 207 (March 1980), 1323–25.

pp. 68–69: "Spellings Addresses PTA Convention," *The Achiever* 4.10 (September 2005), n.p., accessed October 27, 2010, http://www2.ed.gov/news/newsletters.achiever.2005/090105.html.

pp. 74, 76–79: Writer's memo and first draft by Mary LeNoir. Used by permission of the author.

pp. 85–94: "How Student-Athletes Really Choose a College" by Mary Lenoir. Used by permission of the author.

p. 158: Cornel West, *Race Matters* (Boston: Beacon Press, 2001), 3.

pp. 161, 163, 164: "The Tucson Shootings: Words and Deeds" by Debra Hughes originally appeared in *Narrative* magazine. Reprinted by permission of *Narrative* magazine and the author.

pp. 167–168: Mary Pipher, *Writing to Change the World* (New York: Riverhead-Penguin, 2006), 223–24.

pp. 181–186: "Friday Night Fright: Banning Kids' Tackle Football" by Billy Lucas. Used by permission of the author.

p. 197: Jeremy Bentham, *The Principals of Morals and Legislation* (Oxford: Clarendon, 1823), 313.

p. 197: Derek Bok, *The Politics of Happiness: What Government Can Learn from the New Research on Well-Being* (Princeton, NJ: Princeton University Press), 4.

p. 212: Natalie Angier, *Woman: An Intimate Geography* (New York: Anchor/Doubleday, 2000), 355.

p. 213: "Cocksure" by Malcolm Gladwell, *New Yorker*, July 27, 2009, 39.

p. 213: "Is Military Incompetence Adaptive?" by Richard Wrangham from *Evolution and Human Behavior*, 20:1 (January 1999).

p. 223: Brian Halweil, "Emperor's New Crops" in *Taking Sides: Clashing Views on Controversial Environmental Issues* (11th ed.), edited by Thomas A. Easton (Dubuque, IA: McGraw, 2005), 256.

p. 224: Andy Rees, *Genetically Modified Food: A Short Guide for the Confused* (Ann Arbor, MI: Pluto, 2006), 8.

p. 228: Jim Cullen, *The American Dream: A Short History of an Idea That Shaped a Nation* (New York: Oxford University Press, 2004), 7.

p. 230: Joel Achenbach, *"Electrical Grid,"* *National Geographic,* July 2010, 137.

p. 231: Carl Zimmer, *Soul Made Flesh: The Discovery of the Brain—and How It Changed the World* (New York: Free Press, 2004), 7.

p. 232: Michael Hanlon, "Climate Apocalypse When?" *New Scientist*, November 17, 2007, 20.

p. 233: Joseph M. Marshall, III, "Tasunke Witko (His Crazy Horse)," *Native Peoples,* January/February 2007, 76–79.

p. 239: Keith Wilcox and Andrew T. Stephen, "Are Close Friends the Enemy? Online Social Networks, Self-Esteem, and Self Control," 90.

p. 250: Susan Kates, "Adoption Story," in *Red Dirt Women: At Home on the Oklahoma Plains* (Norman, OK: University of Oklahoma Press, 2013), 19. Copyright © by the University of Oklahoma Press.

pp. 262–267: "The Role of Storytelling in Fighting Nineteenth-Century Chauvinisim" by Kristin Ford. Used by permission of the author.

p. 263: Silas Weir Mitchell, *Fat and Blood: And How to Make Them* (Philadelphia: Lippincott, 1882).

p. 276: Steven Pinker, *The Sense of Style* (New York: Viking, 2014), 28, 37.

pp. 311–319: "Genetically Modified Foods and Developing Countries" by Marianna Suslin. Used by permission of the author.

p. 325: Excerpt from "Gender Stereotypes and Perceptions of Occupational Status Among University Students" by Danielle Dezell. Used by permission of the author.

p. 329: Excerpt from abstract to Matthew Gervais and David Wilson's article "The Evolution and Functions of Laughter and Humor" from *Quarterly Review of Biology* 80:4 (December 2005), 395.

p. 330: Higher Education Academy Psychology Network (2008). Case study from *Improving Provision for Disabled Psychology Students.* Available from http://www.psychology.heacademy. ac.uk/ipdps.

pp. 332–350: "Gender Stereotypes and Perceptions of Occupational Status Among University Students" by Danielle Dezell. Used by permission of the author.

p. 355: F. J. Sulloway and R. L. Zweigenhaft, "Birth Order and Risk Taking in Athletics: A Meta-Analysis and Study of Major League Baseball," *Personality and Social Psychology Review* 14 (April 30, 2010), 412.

p. 365: Excerpt from "Tricksters and the Marketing of Breakfast Cereals" by Thomas Green from JOURNAL OF POPULAR CULTURE, Vol. 40, No. 1, 2007. Reprinted by permission of Blackwell Publishing Ltd.

pp. 377–78: "The Social Status of an Art: Historical and Current Trends in Tattooing" by Rachel L. Pinter and Sarah M. Cronin. Used by permission of the authors.

pp. 391–392: Daniel C. Dennett, "Some Observations on the Psychology of Thinking about Free Will" in *Are We Free? Psychology and Free Will,* edited by John Baer, James C. Kaufman, and Roy Baumeister (New York: Oxford University Press, 2008), 8. © 2008. Used by permission.

p. 395: Excerpt from reflection paper by Matthew Marusak. Used by permission of the author.

p. 397: Excerpt from position paper by Kaycee Hulet. Used by permission of the author.

pp. 400–402: "Not So *Suddenly Last Summer*" by Matthew Marusak. Used by permission of the author.

pp. 404–407: "Two Annunciations" by Carla Spohn. Used by permission of the author.

pp. 432–437: "Local Politics and National Policy in a Globalized World: South Africa's Ongoing Electricity Dilemma" by Cristian Nuñez. Used by permission of the author.

pp. 440, 450–56: Research question and "Observations and Calculations of Onion Root Tip Cells" by Heather Jensen. Used by permission of the author.

p. 443–444: Excerpt from paper on agate formation by Michelle Tebbe. Used by permission of the author.

pp. 446–448: "Lichen Distribution on Tree Trunks" by Alyssa Jergens. Used by permission of the author.

p. 510: Bill McKibben, "Small World," *Harper's*, December 2003, 46–54.

p. 540: Bill Holm, *Eccentric Islands: Travels Real and Imaginary* (Minneapolis, MN: Milkweed Editions, 2001), 7.

p. 546: Ken Carey, *Flat Rock Journal: A Day in the Ozark Mountains* (San Francisco: Harper, 1995), 1.

p. 619: James Shreeve, "Beyond the Brain," *National Geographic Magazine*, accessed August 9, 2011, http://science-nationalgeographic.com/science/health-and-human-body/human-body/mind-brain/.

pp. 628–29: Paul K. Humiston, "Small World," in *I Thought My Father Was God* by Paul Auster (New York: Holt, 2001), 183.

p. 629: Jame Gorman, "Finding a Wild, Fearsome World beneath Every Fallen Leaf," in *The Best American Science and Nature Writing 2003*, edited by Richard Dawkins (Boston: Houghton, 2003), 67.

p. 630: Annie Dillard, "The Stunt Pilot," in *The Writing Life* (New York: Harper/Perennial, 1990), 93.

p. 632: Malcolm Gladwell, *Blink: The Power of Thinking without Thinking* (Boston: Little, Brown: 2005), 8–9.

pp. 632–33: Antoine Bechara, Hanna Damasio, Daniel Tranel, and Antonio R. Damasio, "Deciding Advantageously before Knowing the Advantageous Strategy," *Science* 275 (February 28, 1997), 1293.

p. 645: Jesse Jackson.

p. 646: Jean Kilbourne, *Deadly Persuasion* (New York: Free Press, 1999).

p. 646: Gretel Ehrlich, "About Men," in *The Solace of Open Places* (New York: Viking/Penguin, 1986), 52–53.

p. 649: Rebecca Solnit, Storming the Gates of Paradise: Landscapes for Politics (Berkeley, CA: University of California Press, 2008), 115.

p. 649: Kenneth Libbrecht, *The Snowflake: Winter's Secret Beauty* (Stillwater, MN: Voyageur Press, 2003), 35.

p. 650: Adam Haslett, "Devotion," in You Are Not a Stranger Here: Stories (New York: Doubleday/Anchor, 2003), 65.

p. 651: Woody Allen, *Side Effects* (New York: Ballantine, 1986), 83.

p. 651: Joan Didion, "On Keeping a Notebook," in *Slouching towards Bethlehem* (New York: Farrar, Straus & Giroux, 2008), 139.

p. 654: Michael Pollan, *The Botany of Desire: A Plant's-Eye View of the World* (New York: Random House, 2002), 18.

p. 659: Rob Sheffield, Talking to Girls about Duran Duran

p. 659: Parker Palmer, *The Courage to Teach: Exploring the Inner Landscape of a Teacher's Life* (San Francisco: Jossey Bass, 2007).

p. 659: Walker Evans, *Unclassified* (Zurich, Switzerland: *Scalo*, 2000).

p. 660: Pico Iyer, "In Praise of the Humble Comma, *Time*, June 13, 1988.

p. 673: Dictionary entry for "cool" from *Newbury House Dictionary*.

p. 677: Louise Erdrich, "The Leap," in *The Red Convertible: Selected and New Stories 1978–2008* (New York: Harper Perennial, 2010), 205.

p. 678: Charles Wohlforth, "Conservation and Eugenics," *Orion*, July/August 2010, 28.

p. 678: Loida Maritza Pérez, *Geographies of Home* (New York: Penguin, 2000).

p. 678: Hisaye Yamamoto, "Las Vegas Charley," in *Seventeen Syllables* (San Diego, CA: Harcourt, 1994).

p. 678: Denise Chavez, *A Taco Testimony: Meditations on Family, Food and Culture* (Tuscon, AZ: Rio Nuevo, 2006).

pp. 678–679: Jane Kramer, "The Reporter's Kitchen, *New Yorker*, August 19, 2002.

p. 679: Gayle Pemberton, "The Zen of Bigger Thomas, in *The Hottest Water in Chicago: Notes of a Native Daughter* (Middletown, CT: Weslyan University Press, 1998), 168.

p. 705: Richard F. Thompson and Stephen A. Madigan, *Memory: The Key to Consciousness* (Washington, DC: Joseph Henry Press, 2005), 83.

p. 721: Martha Graham, "An Athlete of God" in *This I Believe: The Personal Philosophies of Remarkable Men and Women* (New York: Holt, 2007), 84.

p. 722: Anita Erickson

p. 722: Tracy Kidder, *Mountains beyond Mountains: The Quest of Dr. Paul Farmer, a Man Who Would Cure the World* (New York: Random House, 2009), 218.

p. 726: Diane Ackerman, *A Natural History of Love* (New York: Vintage/Random House, 1995), 86.

p. 733: Oliver Sacks, "The Last Hippie" in *An Anthropologist on Mars* (New York: Vintage/Random House, 1995), 59.

pp. 734–735: David Weinberger, *Small Pieces Loosely Joined: A Unified Theory of the Web* (New York: Basic Books, 2003), 10, 170.

p. 736: Patricia Gadsby, "Endangered Chocolate," *Discover*, August 1, 2002.

p. 737: T. S. Eliot, "The Love Song of J. Alfred Prufrock"

p. 738: Wallace Stevens, "The Snow Man," in *The Collected Poems of Wallace Stevens* (New York: Random House/Vintage, 1990), 10.

pp. 760–761: Excerpt by Nadine Gordimer in *For the Love of Books: 115 Celebrated Writers on the Books They Most Love* by Ronald B. Shwartz (New York: Grosset/Putnam, 1999), 102.

p. 760: Excerpt by Ved Mehta in *For the Love of Books: 115 Celebrated Writers on the Books They Most Love* by Ronald B. Shwartz (New York: Grosset/Putnam, 1999), 181.

p. 767: Gary Snyder, *Back on the Fire: Essays* (Berkeley, CA: Counterpoint Press, 2008), 107.

Index

Numbers and letters in color refer to chapters and sections in the handbook; other numbers refer to pages.

(cont.)

(cont.)

(cont.)

REVISION SYMBOLS

ab	41a(10), 43a–d	Abbreviation	**mm**	24c–e	Misplaced modifier
ac	41a(10), 43e	Acronym			
adj	20a(4), 24a–c	Adjective	**n**	43f–g	Numbers
adv	20a(5), 24a–c	Adverb	**^**		Omission
agr		Agreement	**¶**		Paragraph
	25c	pronoun-antecedent	**//**	29	Parallelism
	26f	subject-verb	**( )**	39f	Parentheses
v̇	37	Apostrophe	**.**	39a	Period
arg	1c(3), 8	Argument	**pl**		Plural
awk		Awkward	**pred**	20c	Predication
cap	41	Capital	**pro**	25	Pronoun
coh		Coherence	**?**	39b	Question mark
	24c–d	modifiers	**" "**	38	Quotation marks
	4c	paragraphs	**red**	34a(1)	Redundant
:	39d	Colon	**ref**	25d	Reference
,	35	Comma	**rep**	29b, 30d, 34b	Repetition
cs	23	Comma splice	**rev**	4a–g	Revision
con	34	Conciseness	**;**	36	Semicolon
cst	15a	Consistency	**sg**		Singular
		verb tense	**/**	39i	Slash
		point of view	**sp**	40a–e	Spelling
coor	28b–c	Coordination	**sub**	28a, 28c	Subordination
—	39e	Dash	**[ ]**	39g	Square brackets
⌊		Delete	**t**	26b	Tense
dev		Development	**trans**	3d	Transition
	3g	essays	**∩**		Transpose
	3f	paragraphs	**u**		Unity
. . .	39h	Ellipsis points		4c	paragraph
emp	30	Emphasis		27	sentence
ex	33	Exactness	**ⓧ**		Unnecessary comma
!	39c	Exclamation point			
frag	22	Fragment	**usg**	32, Glossary of Usage	Usage
fs	23	Fused sentence			
hy	40f	Hyphenation	**var**	31	Variety
id	33c	Idiom	**wc**	32c–d, 33a–d	Word choice
ital	42	Italics	**w**	34a–b	Wordiness
log	8h–i	Logic	**ww**		Wrong word
lc		Lowercase			

CONTENTS